The World of
WILLIAM PENN

The World of
WILLIAM PENN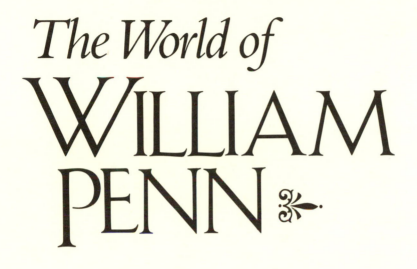

edited by Richard S. Dunn
and Mary Maples Dunn

UNIVERSITY OF PENNSYLVANIA PRESS *Philadelphia* 1986

Preparation and publication of this volume has been assisted by the
Philadelphia Center for Early American Studies

Library of Congress Cataloging-in-Publication Data

The World of William Penn

　　Bibliography: p.
　　Includes index.
　　1. Penn, William, 1644–1718.　2. Pennsylvania—His-
tory—Colonial period, ca. 1600–1775.　3. Quakers—
Pennsylvania—History.　4. Pioneers—Pennsylvania—
Biography.　5. Quakers—Pennsylvania—Biography.
6. Quakers—England—History—17th century.　I. Dunn,
Richard S.　II. Dunn, Mary Maples.
F152.2.W65　1986　　974.8'02'0924 [B]　　86–6970
ISBN 0-8122-8020-2

Designed by Adrianne Onderdonk Dudden

To our fellow editors of
The Papers of William Penn:

Edwin Bronner
David Fraser
Alison Hirsch
Craig Horle
Richard Ryerson
Jean Soderlund
Scott Wilds
Joy Wiltenburg
Marianne Wokeck

Contents

Tables   xi

Maps   xiii

Abbreviations   xv

Introduction   xix

WILLIAM PENN RECONSIDERED

1   *The Personality of William Penn*   3
   MARY MAPLES DUNN

2   *The Young Controversialist*   15
   HUGH BARBOUR

3   *Penny Wise and Pound Foolish: Penn as a Businessman*   37
   RICHARD S. DUNN

4   *A Representative of the Alternative Society of Restoration England?*   55
   J. R. JONES

5   *William Penn, 1689–1702: Eclipse, Frustration, and Achievement*   71
   CAROLINE ROBBINS

PENN'S BRITAIN

6   *Agricultural Conditions in England, circa 1680*   87
    JOAN THIRSK

7   *The World Women Knew: Women Workers in the North of England During the Late Seventeenth Century*   99
    CAROLE SHAMMAS

8   *Out of the Mainstream: Catholic and Quaker Women in the Restoration Northwest*   117
    MICHAEL J. GALGANO

9   *The Irish Background to Penn's Experiment*   139
    NICHOLAS CANNY

10 *Quakerism: Made in America?*   157
    RICHARD T. VANN

PENN'S AMERICA

11 *"The Peaceable Kingdom:" Quaker Pennsylvania in the Stuart Empire*   173
    STEPHEN SAUNDERS WEBB

12 *Brother Miquon: Good Lord!*   195
    FRANCIS JENNINGS

13 *From "Dark Corners" to American Domesticity: The British Social Context of the Welsh and Cheshire Quakers' Familial Revolution in Pennsylvania, 1657–1685*   215
    BARRY LEVY

14 *William Penn's Scottish Counterparts: The Quakers of "North Britain" and the Colonization of East New Jersey*   241
    NED LANDSMAN

15 *Promoters and Passengers: The German Immigrant Trade, 1683–1775*   259
    MARIANNE S. WOKECK

MEETING HOUSE AND COUNTING HOUSE

16 *Puritanism, Spiritualism, and Quakerism: An Historiographical Essay   281*
MELVIN B. ENDY, JR.

17 *The Affirmation Controversy and Religious Liberty   303*
J. WILLIAM FROST

18 *Quaker Discipline and Order, 1680–1720: Philadelphia Yearly Meeting and London Yearly Meeting   323*
EDWIN B. BRONNER

19 *The Early Merchants of Philadelphia: The Formation and Disintegration of a Founding Elite   337*
GARY B. NASH

20 *The Great Quaker Business Families of Eighteenth-Century London: The Rise and Fall of a Sectarian Patriciate   363*
JACOB M. PRICE

Notes on Contributors   401

Index   407

Tables

7.1   *The Women who Transacted Business with the Fell Household by Marital Status, 1673–78.   103*

7.2   *Occupational Group, Sex, and Marital Status of Those Supplying Goods and Services to the Fell Household, 1673–78.   105*

7.3   *Goods and Services Supplied to the Fell Household by Sex of Suppliers, 1673–78.   108–109*

8.1   *"Additions" in the Lancashire Recusancy Registers, 1678–79: Men with Catholic Wives.   123*

9.1   *Depositions by English Settlers in Munster, 1642.   144*

10.1   *Origins of British Friends as Shown in Certificates Received in Philadelphia, 1681–1750.   159*

10.2   *Occupational Distribution of Bristol Men's Monthly Meeting, 1682–1704, and of Male Quaker Emigrants from Bristol.   161*

13.1   *323 Personal Estates of "Middling" Northwest Men, 1660–91.   221*

13.2   *Land and Lease Bequests in 253 Northwest Wills, 1660–91.   223*

13.3   *Children under 18 Years in 15 St. Asaph Parishes, c. 1681–84.   225*

13.4   *Patterns of Bequest in 253 Northwest Wills, 1660–91.   228*

13.5   Hearth Assessments in Selected Merionethshire Parishes, 1664.   232

13.6   Estimated Annual Agricultural Income of 49 Quakers in Pembrokeshire,
        Carmarthenshire, and Merionethshire, based on Tithe Seizures,
        1660–85.   233

19.1   Religious Affiliation of the Philadelphia Merchants.   354

19.2   The Personal Wealth of Philadelphia Merchants at Death.   354

19.3   First-Generation Philadelphia Merchants.   355–358

19.4   Second-Generation Philadelphia Merchants.   359–362

20.1   Characteristics of 14 London Quaker Business Families.   369

Maps

3.1   *John Thornton and John Seller.* A Map of Some of the South and Eastbounds of Pennsylvania in America. *London, 1681.* HSP. *(Detail.)*   44

3.2   *The Geographical Origins of First Purchasers, 1681–1685*   47

9.1   *William Penn's Ireland*   140

12.1   *William Penn's Purchases from the Indians, 1682–1684*   199

14.1   *The Delaware Valley, 1680–1684*   242

Abbreviations

APS
: American Philosophical Society, Philadelphia

BL
: British Library, London

CCRO
: Chester County Record Office, Chester, England

CSPD
: Anne Everett Green, et al, eds., *Calendar of State Papers, Domestic Series, 1603–1704,* 85 vols. (London, 1857-1972).

CUCRO
: Cumbria County Record Office, Carlisle, Cumbria, England

DNB
: Leslie Stephen and Sidney Lee, eds., *Dictionary of National Biography,* 63 vols., plus supplements (New York and London, 1885-1900)

FLL
: Library of the Religious Society of Friends, London

GSP
: Genealogical Society of Pennsylvania, Philadelphia

HCL
: Haverford College Library, Haverford, Pennsylvania

HMC
Historical Manuscripts Commission

HSP
Historical Society of Pennsylvania, Philadelphia

JFHS
Journal of the Friends Historical Society (London)

LCRO
Lancashire County Record Office, Preston, Lancashire, England

Micro.
The Papers of William Penn, Microfilm edition, Historical Society of Pennsylvania (1975), fourteen reels plus guide. References are to reel and frame

Minutes of the Provincial Council
Minutes of the Provincial Council of Pennsylvania (Philadelphia, 1852)

NLW
National Library of Wales, Aberystwyth, Cardiganshire, Wales

NNRO
Norfolk and Norwich Record Office, Norwich, Norfolk, England

PA
Samuel Hazard, et al, eds., *Pennsylvania Archives* (Philadelphia and Harrisburg, 1852–   )

Penn, *Select Works*
William Penn, *Select Works,* 4th ed., 3 vols. (London, 1825; reprint, New York, 1971)

Penn, *Works*
[Joseph Besse, ed.], *A Collection of the Works of William Penn,* 2 vols. (London, 1726; reprint, New York, 1974)

PMHB
Pennsylvania Magazine of History and Biography

PRO
Public Record Office, London

PWP
Mary Maples Dunn and Richard S. Dunn, eds., *The Papers of William Penn* (Philadelphia, 1981–   ); multivolume series in progress

TCD
 Trinity College Library, Dublin

Thirsk, *Agrarian History,* 4
 H. P. R. Finberg, ed., *The Agrarian History of England and Wales,* vol. 4,
 1500-1640, ed. Joan Thirsk (Cambridge, 1967)

Thirsk, *Agrarian History,* 5
 H. P. R. Finberg, ed., *The Agrarian History of England and Wales,* vol. 5,
 pt. I, 1640–1750, ed. Joan Thirsk (Cambridge, 1984); vol. 5, pt. II,
 1640–1750, ed. Joan Thirsk (Cambridge, 1985).

Tolles, *Meeting House*
 Frederick B. Tolles, *Meeting House and Counting House: The Quaker Merchants of Colonial Philadelphia, 1682–1763* (Chapel Hill, N. C., 1948)

Vann, *Development of Quakerism*
 Richard Vann, *The Social Development of English Quakerism, 1655–1755*
 (Cambridge, Mass., 1969)

WCRO
 Westmorland County Record Office, Kendal, Eng.

WMQ
 William and Mary Quarterly

Introduction

William Penn was incontestably one of the seminal figures of the late seventeenth century. He played a crucial role in protecting and sustaining the Quaker movement during its worst period of persecution; he was a major writer of religious, political, and didactic treatises; he championed religious toleration, civil rights, participatory government, interracial brotherhood, and international peace at a time when all of these noble causes were thoroughly unpopular; he participated conspicuously in English public life, parading his heterodox opinions for four decades; and he founded a thriving colony, arguably the most successful colony in America. Yet Penn has never been an easy person to understand or appreciate. Partly this is because he combined so many seemingly contradictory attitributes: he was at one time or another a rebellious son, a doting parent, a persecuted martyr, a deferential courtier, a religious enthusiast, a political lobbyist, a patrician gentleman, a weighty Friend, a polemical disputant, a sententious moralist, a shrewd entrepreneur, an improvident spendthrift, a visionary idealist, and an absentee landlord. Penn's Quakerism has generally mystified or irritated the secular-minded observers of his career. Penn's close association with the autocratic and impolitic James II has sullied his credentials as a political liberal. And Penn's sojourn in debtor's prison has raised embarrassing doubts about his basic competence and practical sense.

There are other obstacles to understanding this man. He was truly a hybrid Anglo-American, the only major actor on the seventeenth-century colonial scene whose achievements in the Old World were approximately equivalent in significance to his achievements in the New World. Penn's counterparts in Massachusetts such as John Winthrop and John Cotton, or in Virginia such as Captain John Smith and Sir William Berkeley, had very peripheral careers in England by comparison. And none of the other lords proprietor who founded colonies in the New World, nor the royal governors who came over to represent the crown, had anything like his personal impact in America. This means that the historian must take a transatlantic view of William Penn and follow his activities on both sides of the ocean, for his successes and failures in England and in America were always closely interrelated.

Furthermore, Penn's milieu was exceptionally wide and variegated, and his circle of acquaintance was very large. He lived simultaneously in a Quaker world and in a non-Quaker world, and he knew personally many hundred people in both worlds. He preferred the country to the city, but spent much of his life in London, Bristol, Dublin, and Philadelphia. He was a south-of-England man, but journeyed a number of times to the "dark corners" of northern Britain, where many Quakers lived. He made four long visits to Ireland and lived nearly a decade there altogether, more than twice the time he spent in Pennsylvania. He made several lengthy trips to France, Holland, and Germany. All of these travels are important in understanding his career, for Penn's experiences in the various regions of the British Isles and in Europe all helped to shape his actions as a colonizer in America. Thus anyone who studies this extraordinarily energetic man needs to recreate the multifaceted seventeenth-century environment in which he lived and worked.

This volume, a collaborative effort by twenty specialists in Anglo-American political, economic, intellectual, religious, and social history, is designed to address most of the interpretive problems described above. The undersigned editors have been working on this book for a number of years. Since 1978 we have been supervising an edition of *The Papers of William Penn* in five volumes, and at an early stage in this project we decided that we wanted to celebrate in a big way the three hundredth anniversary of Penn's royal charter for Pennsylvania in March 1681 — and coincidentally the publication of our first volume of *Papers* — by holding a public conference entitled, "The World of William Penn." A conference committee was formed, funds were raised, twenty-two panelists agreed to present papers, and the conference took place in Philadelphia on 19–22 March 1981. The high individual quality of the papers presented at this meeting, and their unified character when taken as a whole, encouraged us to convert these conference papers into a collection of essays. The University of Pennsylvania Press (which is publishing *The Papers of William Penn*) agreed to produce this book. Nineteen of the twenty-two panelists at the conference are represented in this volume. We regret that the other three panelists — Bernard Bailyn, Daniel Hoffman, and Margaret Spufford — were unable for various good reasons to contribute their papers, but in partial substitution Mary Maples Dunn (who was not a panelist at the conference) has written the opening essay for this collection.

We have arranged the twenty essays into four sections. In the opening section the five essays bear directly on William Penn himself, much more so than in the rest of the book. Here the five authors present a variety of perspectives on Penn's behavior at critical junctures in his life. Mary Maples Dunn frames this discussion with a broadly argued essay on Penn's inner world, in which she discusses his emotional makeup and personality. Drawing upon her editorial work with Penn's personal correspondence, Dunn assesses his relations with his parents, and his two wives (as well as with other women), with fellow Quakers, and with social superiors and social subordinates. The next four essays focus more specifically upon particular stages of Penn's career. Hugh Barbour examines Penn's religious writings in the years 1668–75, immediately after his convincement. Barbour, a specialist in seventeenth-century Quaker apologetics, explores why the young Penn was such a combative writer, discusses the character of his theological debates, and considers their impact upon his future development. Richard S. Dunn then looks at Penn's performance as a businessman in the years 1672–85, when he achieved his greatest entrepreneurial success but also plunged heavily into debt. Drawing upon his editorial work with Penn's business records, Dunn examines Penn's relationship with his steward Philip Ford and traces the connections between Penn's experience as an Anglo-Irish landholder and his selling of Pennsylvania. In an essay that overlaps with Dunn's chronologically, J. R. Jones considers Penn's close association with James II during the years 1673–88. Jones, who is a specialist in English Restoration political history, explores Penn's role at the Stuart court and his views on Catholicism and absolutism in order to account for his "alternative" role in Restoration politics. The final essay in this section by Caroline Robbins explores Penn's writings on moral and didactic themes during the years 1689–1702. Robbins, a specialist in English intellectual history, focuses here on a series of Penn's books and pamphlets remarkably different in nature from the early debate tracts analyzed by Barbour. She argues that Penn achieved high intellectual distinction as a writer during these otherwise frustrating years.

The next group of five essays considers various formative features of Penn's environment in England and Ireland. Joan Thirsk, a specialist in agrarian history, launches this discussion with a broad survey of farming conditions in England at the time Penn was recruiting farmers for Pennsylvania. Thirsk explores the development of agricultural diversification and new specialty crops in the 1670s and 1680s; her emphasis on modernization in English agriculture compares interestingly with Canny's commentary on farming in Ireland, Levy's on Wales, and Landsman's on Scotland. The next two essays discuss the economic and social circumstances of women in northern England, where Quakerism was particularly strong and where

Penn recruited some of his colonists. Carole Shammas, a specialist in An-glo-American economic history, analyzes the household account book of Margaret Fox, the Quaker matriarch, to get a close look at the pattern of female labor and employment in Lancashire during the 1670s. From this evidence Shammas deduces that the great majority of women in this local-ity worked at one time or another during their lives as peddlers or day laborers or live-in servants, and that they were segregated into these infe-rior and low-paying jobs by males who took the more attractive work. Michael J. Galgano, a specialist in Restoration social history, sets up a comparison between two large groups of religious outcasts in northern England: Quaker women and Catholic women. He finds that by every measure the female Quakers challenged the Anglican establishment more combatively and uncompromisingly than their Catholic counterparts and also experienced much harsher persecution. Nicholas Canny, a specialist in early modern Irish history, next surveys the character of English settlement in Munster, where Penn was a large landholder. Canny argues that the English planters of Penn's day had considerably less chance for success in Munster than their predecessors who had initiated English settlement there before 1641, because land, labor, and capital were all getting scarce in Ireland by the Restoration era. Richard T. Vann, a specialist in British Quaker demography, rounds out this section by discussing a central ques-tion: How many of the people who emigrated from England and Ireland with Penn in the 1680s were Quakers? Surveying a large mass of statistical evidence from Quaker registers, Vann contends that "only a minority of the first settlers of Pennsylvania were British Quakers in good standing," but he goes on to argue that many of these emigrants converted to Quak-erism once they reached America.

With the third group of essays the scene shifts to America. Stephen Saunders Webb, a specialist in British imperial history, first examines the circumstances under which Penn obtained his charter for Pennsylvania in 1680-81. Since Webb believes that the thrust of Stuart colonial policy at this time was toward purposeful military centralization, he regards Penn's proprietary grant for a Quaker colony as an anomaly to be explained by his excellent court connections and perfect timing. Webb also stresses that Penn had to accept severe restrictions on his proprietary privileges during the course of the charter negotiations. In the next essay, Francis Jennings, a specialist in Indian history, explores Penn's diplomatic relations with the Delawares, Iroquois, and other tribes. Like Webb, Jennings sees Penn as an anomaly: he was one of very few Englishmen in the seventeenth century who treated the native Americans with elementary justice and decency. But Jennings also stresses that Penn was trying to expand his territorial claims vis-à-vis New York and Maryland through Indian diplomacy, and that he expected to obtain trading profits from his chain of friendship with the Indians. The next three essays are all transatlantic, following particular ethnic groups of settlers from the Old World to the New. Barry Levy, a specialist in American colonial family history, discusses the Quakers from Wales and from the Welsh border county of Cheshire who migrated to Pennsylvania in the 1680s and 1690s. Levy argues that the Quakers who lived in Wales and Cheshire were so handicapped by poverty and mortality that they could neither sustain independent family life nor protect and nurture their children. But by moving to Pennsylvania these people achieved a radical change: autonomy for their households, love and nurture for their families, and independence for their children. In a parallel essay, Ned Landsman, another American colonial social historian, discusses the Quakers from Scotland who migrated to New Jersey in the 1680s. Landsman argues that these Scottish Quakers were more interested in joining up with fellow Scots than with fellow Friends, and so they chose East New Jersey rather than Pennsylvania. Once settled in America, they soon abandoned Quakerism while retaining other peculiarly Scottish social and cultural traditions. Marianne S. Wokeck, a specialist on colonial Pennsylvania, concludes this section by examining one of Penn's most distinctive legacies: the promotion of migration from Germany into Pennsylvania, which began in the 1680s and became a mass movement in the mid-eighteenth century. To explain the dynamics of this migration, Wokeck focuses on the merchants who organized the trade and on the immigrants who came over, and she shows how this business changed character as the volume of German migration rose, peaked, and ebbed.

The final group of essays comments upon the central dualism in Penn's life and in Quaker history—the tension, sometimes creative and sometimes corrupting, between the Friends' inward spiritual faith and their external work ethic. The late Frederick B. Tolles embraced both sides of this subject in his admirable book, *Meeting House and Counting House.* Our authors are more modest. Three of them discuss the meeting house and two the counting house. Melvin B. Endy, a specialist on the history of early Quakerism, initiates the meeting house discussion with doctrinal definitions. He argues that it is a mistake to describe the seventeenth-century Quakers as extremist Puritans. They were a Spirit-oriented group, doctrinally distinct from Puritanism, and linked much more closely to other Spiritualists such as the Familists, Seekers, and Ranters. J. William Frost, another historian of early Quakerism, examines why Penn and his fellow Friends made such a major point of refusing to swear oaths. Frost shows how the oath controversy tended to distance Quakers from all other sects, and how the long struggle to work out an acceptable alternate form of affirmation produced bitter internal quarrels among Friends, during which they lost sight of many of the original issues. Edwin B. Bronner, also a specialist in early Quaker history, takes up the question of institutional organization among Friends and compares the development of yearly meetings and of disciplinary rules in England and America. Bronner minimizes the organizational distinctions between Philadelphia and London Quakers and argues that the two communities kept in close touch through the exchange of books and epistles, and the frequent transatlantic visits of Public Friends. Turning to the counting house, the final two essays offer a broad comparison between the Quaker merchants of Philadelphia and London. Gary B. Nash, a specialist in early American urban history (among other topics), identifies the principal Philadelphia merchants of 1681–1740, and shows that Quaker merchants active during the first generation (1681–1710) failed to perpetuate themselves and were replaced by a new merchant elite (1711–40) of quite different character. Nash argues that these second-generation merchants were more successful businessmen than their predecessors, but were far less active in politics, and were also no longer predominantly Quakers in religious affiliation. Some of these findings are echoed by Jacob M. Price, a specialist in economic history (among other topics), as he traces the fortunes of fourteen great Quaker business families in eighteenth-century London. Since Price focuses on particular families that sustained their business firms over several generations, and that intermarried with the other leading Quaker business families, he naturally finds less discontinuity than Nash. But Price does see significant long-range changes: by 1790 most of his families had shifted from overseas trade into banking and brewing, and as they accumulated great wealth and entrenched themselves in the British upper middle class, they deserted the Society of Friends for the Church of England.

In the course of preparing this volume the editors have had a great deal of help from many people. We wish to thank the Philadelphia Center for Early American Studies, the Institute of Early American History and Culture, the Conference on British Studies, and the Conference of Quaker Historians and Archivists for pooling forces ecumenically to sponsor the conference of March 1981 that launched this book. We thank Stephen B. Baxter, Jacob M. Price, and Thad W. Tate for joining us in devising the conference program, and Richard R. Beeman and Ann F. Stanley for doing such a fine job of managing the conference. We especially thank the National Endowment for the Humanities, the McLean Contributionship, the Philadelphia Yearly Meeting of the Religious Society of Friends, the Public Committee for the Humanities in Pennsylvania, the Shoemaker Fund, and the Society of the College at the University of Pennsylvania for funding the conference and thereby making this book possible. We thank Craig W. Horle for his crucial and expert editorial assistance. Marjorie George, Margaret Yasuda, Marianne Wokeck, and Joy Wiltenburg all helped with word processing, and Scott M. Wilds did the coding. Deborah Stuart was our copy editor, and Adrianne Onderdonk Dudden was our designer. We thank Ingalill Hjelm and her colleagues at the University of Pennsylvania Press for all of their help with this project. And lastly, we know that it is customary in perorations such as this to thank one's spouse most of all — which we can scarcely do — and so instead we offer our gratitude to the eighteen historians who have joined us in this collaborative effort to understand and appreciate the world of William Penn.

RICHARD S. DUNN
MARY MAPLES DUNN

❧·WILLIAM PENN RECONSIDERED

1 ⟡ The Personality of William Penn

It is a commonplace to observe that William Penn regularly inhabited two worlds — the world of power, privilege, and authority, and the peculiar egalitarian, spiritual, and persecuted world of the Friends. Historians are suspicious of applications of psychology to actors so long departed from the scene, and yet one must ask questions about the inner world of William Penn — about his emotional makeup and personality — if we are to understand how he was able to move between these spheres, what tension or conflict existed for him, and what this ambivalence contributed to his development, his ideas, and his public behavior.

It is not easy to understand William Penn's personality — too much of the evidence we have for his life is contained in public papers.[1] Few personal and intimate materials have survived; we have nothing written by him before he was sixteen, and very little before he converted to Quakerism. About twenty-six hundred Penn documents have survived the vicissitudes of three centuries, but only seventy-five of these are private family letters. It is possible, if the person who vandalized the Penn papers in 1870 was a disgruntled, illegitimate, and disinherited member of the family as has been suggested, that family papers were the special target of wanton destruction. It is also possible that the family placed greater value on the public papers. William Penn's son, Thomas Penn (1702–1775), who arranged and filed the family papers, was primarily interested in documents which related to his proprietary claims and revenues. It would not be surprising to learn that he was little interested in his father's family by his first wife; whatever the reason, the only letter from Gulielma Penn to William Penn survives because it was intercepted and preserved in the Public Record Office.[2] Nor would it surprise those engaged in the study of women to discover that he was more interested in his grandfather than his grandmother. Whatever Thomas Penn's central concerns, the fact is that the largest number of personal papers which have been preserved are exchanges between William Penn and his father, and between William Penn and Hannah Penn, the second wife and mother of Thomas. We know that everyone in the family was literate, and we know from references in the extant Penn papers that much family correspondence was exchanged which is now lost.

Pictures may be worth a thousand words, but we have only two portraits of Penn, and they may be misleading. One is of a handsome boy in armor, the other of a complacent fat man. Neither carries any suggestion of the belligerent, activist Quaker. We must therefore look at his social experience and what we know of his behavior in order to arrive at or infer the emotional determinants and habits which are such an important part of personality.

Emotional habits are formed very early. We know about William Penn's early emotional development that as a youth he exhibited a strong mystical streak. By his own account, he had mystical experiences by the time he was twelve or thirteen.[3] There was no pattern for this in his family; he said, pathetically, "I had no Relations that inclined to so solitary & Spirituall a Way; I was as a Child alone."[4] His father was an energetic warrior, and a man who was capable of changing sides in the civil war. If he had dreams, they were dreams of a rather worldly glory, of social and political success for his son. The mysticism of the son may have been an early attempt to escape from the authority of his father, or from his father's dreams. We can be reasonably certain about Penn's relationship with his father because the collection of their correspondence is revealing, large for a set of personal papers (containing eight letters from son to father, and nineteen from father to son), and because their fairly stormy relations have been documented in other ways. We may begin with the inference that they never knew each other particularly well.

William junior could have seen but little of his father when he was a young boy; his mother and his older sister were his chief companions until he was eleven. His father left London in command of the *Fellowship* just days before his birth in October 1644 and was at sea with the Irish squadron until August of 1645. William senior may then have visited London, but he was stationed at Milford Haven until January 1646, when he set sail for Ireland where he stayed until August. He was in England for two months before he was given command of the *Assurance* in which he was at sea for the next year. He was rear admiral of the Irish fleet in 1648 and vice admiral in 1649. In 1650 he was at Deptford, fitting a new ship, the *Fairfax;* in

December he went on cruise in the Azores and Mediterranean, and did not return to England until March 1652. From May 1652 until July 1653 he was pretty consistently in action in the Dutch war; he then spent perhaps a year at home until December 1654 when he sailed for the West Indies, where he remained until August 1655. He retired to his Irish estates in October 1655. He was then with his son a great deal, until the boy went up to Oxford at sixteen.[5] The father certainly missed much of young William's development and was not there to observe and influence the boy as he learned to negotiate his way within the family. The son did not see enough of his father to absorb the father's standards of manliness and success, and he may have viewed his father, on the sailor's occasional visits home, as an interloper who deprived him of his usual measure of his mother's attention.

A Freudian would no doubt be tempted to interpret the mysticism and other later escapes from the standards of the father in powerfully psychoanalytical terms, and it is indeed very difficult to avoid thinking about William junior's early religious life as a rejection of authority. In fact, between the ages of seventeen (when he was expelled from Oxford) and twenty-two (when he converted to Quakerism) we see the double strand of religion and rebellion constantly coming together. At Oxford he joined forces with others of puritan persuasion to object to the prayer book and to ritual which seemed too popish (for example, wearing the surplice). He could not have been very surprised when he was sent down in 1662, although in later years he looked back at himself with pity and referred to his experience as "my persecution at Oxford," a "hellish darkness and debauchery." But he seemed to relish "the bitter usage I underwent when I returned to my Father, whipping, beating, and turning out of Dores."[6] This may suggest feelings of guilt about what he was doing, or even about what he was thinking, and the Oxford conflict was followed by several years in which he tried to be the good son. He went to France to study; he acted enthusiastically as his father's envoy to Charles II; he went to Ireland to manage the family estates, and he even helped put down a mutiny there in 1666; he made friends with rich and worldly men.[7] It is certain, then, that Penn knew the kind of man his father wanted him to be.

Penn became a Quaker in 1667, and his father was, predictably, furious. The son could share with Quakers powerful feelings of possession by the spirit and enjoy a certain freedom to interpret and act on those feelings in an individual way. But he must also have taken a lot of pleasure in the ways in which Quakers flouted social conventions. For example, they used the familiar "thee" with everyone, including duke and king. This may seem merely quaint today, but in the seventeenth century it was very important to know to whom one must use the formal form of the personal pronoun (one's social superiors) and to whom one might use the familiar form (intimates or inferiors). Pronouns were a part of the system by which people identified their places in society. Therefore to use "thee" indiscriminately was a way of defying social authority, structure, and values, and perhaps defying the father.

This overturning of language convention is matched by an attack on the dress code of seventeenth-century England. "Hat honour" was important in Penn's day in the same way that pronouns were. Hats were off in the presence of superiors, and Penn's refusal to doff his hat before judge and king must have given him little frissons of fun. The importance of hat behavior is demonstrated in an amusing legend. According to the story, Penn was once at the court of Charles II, and of course, unlike the other courtiers, he was wearing his hat. The king therefore swept off his own hat, explaining to Penn that "only one person wears a hat here." The story is a nice one because it illustrates the meaning of the hat, Penn's entree at court, his stubborn independence—and Charles's wit.[8] But Penn kept his hat and his head in more serious circumstances, too. In one of his many court appearances, he was fined for contempt of court because he refused to take off his hat. Actually, according to his testimony, his hat was forcibly removed when he came into court and was returned by order of the bench. The judge then asked him to remove it, which Penn declined to do "Because I do not believe that to be any Respect." The upshot was the fine for contempt about which Penn wryly observed, "not we, but the Bench should be fined." We may observe that Penn was willing to use the hat as a means of defiance of authority at a high level.[9]

Quakerism even gave Penn good religious grounds for disobeying his parents. His father was angry when he converted, but he could justify disobedience by insisting that he was compelled to follow the divine light. In an unpublished essay on marriage, he argued that parents' consent to a true marriage (that is, one made by God) should be sought but was not necessary, a position at great variance with the accepted wisdom of the propertied classes. Penn married after his father died, and his bride was an heiress as well as a devout Quaker. Nevertheless, he considered the point an important one to make.[10]

Becoming a Quaker in 1667 was therefore neither socially acceptable nor acceptable in an elder son, and relations between the admiral and his son William were really bad almost all of the time after the expulsion from Oxford until the father's death. And even at the end there was plenty of tension. Admiral Penn was very ill for some months before he died on 16 September 1670. During most of that August and the first week of September, his son was in Newgate prison and at the center of the Penn-Mead trial, which was to prove a benchmark case in the history of religious liberty and trial by jury. William junior wrote to his father frequently. He was at some pains to tell him, among other things, of the judge's public slurs on the reputation of the admiral (surely not pleasant reading for a dying man), and of his own defense of his father; the mayor, he said, would

"see me whipped himself, for all I was Penn's son, that starved the seamen.
. . . I told him I could very well bear his severe expressions to me concerning myself, but was sorry to hear him speak those abuses of my father, that
was not present." On 9 September, as the case wore down and all that
remained was the fine for contempt of court for having refused to take off
his hat in the courtroom, he wrote that however much he wanted to see his
father, whose condition was much worse, he could not agree to paying the
fine in order to be released. It was a matter of principle. But he did very
shortly relent, the fine was paid, and he went home to his dying father. In
a final burst of filial piety, he erected a monument to his father at St. Mary
Redcliffe, Bristol, including all his military panoply and naval pennants. A
display so un-Quakerly in its composition forces the observer to ponder on
the son's inner conflicts.[11]

William Penn was, then, a religious rebel or rebellious religious. In his
early years as a Friend, he was persistently contentious; the rebellious and
religious strains continued to be central in his personal development until
at least 1678. He engaged others of every religious stripe, from conservative churchmen to rather mad sectarians, in religious debate. This took a
number of forms; he wrote a great many tracts for publication, he engaged
in public and private debates, he courted arrest in order to extend the debate
into the civil sphere.[12] In many ways, his language was sharper and more
interesting at this stage of his life than at any other—he clearly relished the
quarrel with authority (or with his father) at every turn. He became powerful in the use of invective, and he was not very polite. Consider this
furious borrowing from the Book of Revelation in a letter to Ludowick
Muggleton, a man who thought he had been chosen by God to say who
would be saved and who damned; and he damned more than a few Quakers.

> Boast not, thou Enemy of God, thou Son of Perdition, and Confed-
> erate with the unclean Croaking Spirits reserved under the Chaines of
> Eternal Darkness; . . . on you I trample in his Everlasting Dominion,
> and to the bottomles Pit are you sentenc'd, . . . where the Endles
> wormes shall gnaw, and tortur your Imaginary Souls to Eternity.[13]

He was only slightly more polite to Richard Baxter, the most noted Presbyterian of the day. Penn accused him of "tedious Harangues," "Envye,
and artifice," and "virulent, and imperious . . . behaviour."[14]

This aggressive, argumentative, and conflicted young man is an attractive character, and those qualities were the source of some of his most
enduring accomplishments. During his first imprisonment in 1669 he began to develop his ideas on the principle of liberty of conscience and the
need for government to balance different religious interests. In a letter
written in 1669 from the Tower of London to Henry Bennett, earl of
Arlington, this part of the inner conflict between his two worlds, and his
solution to it, rings clear: "What if I differ from some religious apprehen-

tions publiquely Impos'd am I therfore Incompatible with the well-being of humain Societys? Shall it not be remembred with what successe Kingdoms & commonwealths have liv'd by the discreet ballanceing of Partys?" His later struggles for liberty of conscience, or at least a toleration, led him to understand the nature of constitutional guarantees of civil rights, which he was able to realize in the creation of a new society or "holy experiment" in America.[15] But his rebelliousness had its darker side, too, particularly as he moved into middle age. It placed real obstacles in the way of developing close relationships with men of his own class; and yet it was never successful enough to allow him to establish true friendships with those who were coreligionists but not gentlemen. He was not even equal in contest; one opponent, Richard Baxter, objected that Penn spoke out against tithes which supported poor but serious ministers "while hee swims himselfe in wealth."[16] The effect was to create a real emotional and social distance between him and others.

Penn used his well-born acquaintances to advantage. This is particularly evident in the acquisition of the charter to Pennsylvania, but a useful example is also found in George Villiers, second duke of Buckingham. Buckingham was notorious for his profligate life but also known for his belief in religious toleration. Penn tried on several occasions to secure Buckingham's support for persecuted Friends, or for Penn's own political campaigns for liberty of conscience. When Buckingham was attacked for writing a pamphlet on religious liberty in 1685, Penn wrote two tracts in his defense. Penn probably realized that his association with this member of the Restoration elite was not quite appropriate for a simple Friend of the truth, since he went out of his way to have his letters to Buckingham destroyed, and suggested that he hoped only to help Buckingham improve his record before the duke died by giving him a chance to be of service to the kingdom.[17]

Buckingham, in his private life, carried to an extreme attitudes and behaviors which made up the social ethos of the Restoration elite. It was hardly a world in which a young Quaker convert could feel at home; if his Quakerism was a barrier between him and his social equals, for companionship he had to look to Quakers. But because of differences in social station, an uncomfortably large number of those early Quaker friendships acquired a patron-client character, and many were eventually destroyed by quarrels. The clients did not take kindly to that role. Consider the break with Thomas Rudyard, who had been a close associate for many years, and a companion on Penn's travels in England, Holland, and Germany. Penn had employed Rudyard as a lawyer, and they worked closely in provoking and prompting cases of conscience. Rudyard developed many of the arguments in the famous Penn-Mead trial when they went into print; he was also Penn's closest collaborator in devising a constitution for Pennsylvania. Indeed, the two men worked as partners in that effort, jointly composing many of the drafts for the constitution. Yet by 1684, when Rudyard had become a landowner in Pennsylvania, Penn complained about his un-Quakerly habits and refused to make him master of the rolls in Pennsylvania. A few months later, they were in sharp disagreement about the assignment of waterfront lots in Philadelphia, and Rudyard signed a remonstrance against Penn.[18] Philip Ford, a faithful steward for many years, is another excellent example of the faults of the patron-client relationship between Friends. Ford, who spent years in service to Penn, also silently built up a case of indebtedness which allowed Ford's heirs to sue Penn for £20,000 and send him to debtor's prison. Ford's wife, Bridget Ford, who was generally present when loans were negotiated, was particularly resentful and angry for what she seemed to think were a rich man's failures to live up to promises, and it is entirely possible that Penn behaved toward Ford with a patrician's lack of understanding for the middle-class creditor.[19]

The fact that Penn had few really intimate friendships is without a doubt a key to his bad judgment about people, or perhaps it is the other way around, and his bad judgment contributed to his failure to find true friends. In any case, he made many inappropriate appointments to office in Pennsylvania; that is, he misjudged both the candidates and the Pennsylvanians they would govern. His judgment rested principally in a form of *noblesse oblige* — he appointed people to office; expected them to do their duty; considered it inappropriate to check up on them; and then broke with them in anger and disappointment when they failed. A case in point is Penn's secretary, Philip Theodore Lehnmann, who worked for Penn from 1672 to 1685. He left behind in Pennsylvania vitally important papers which would have supported Penn's claim to Maryland territory when Penn returned to London from Pennsylvania in 1684. As Penn put it, "I am now here wth my finger in my mouth," and he was so angry that he fired Lehnmann.[20] The appointment of John Blackwell, a puritan Cromwellian who had moved to Massachusetts, as governor of Pennsylvania, 1688-89, was a fascinating case in which Penn seemed to allow full rein to the authoritarian side of his character, but when Blackwell engaged in vigorous dispute with the colonists in order to secure Penn's authority and collect his rents, Penn failed to support Blackwell, dismissed him, and allowed the Provincial Council, as a whole, to act as his deputy governor.[21]

There were exceptions. Penn found in George Fox a substitute father of sorts, who called forth a respect and affection which Penn did not easily hold for men. Letters to "Dear George" have a personal and intimate quality which, despite ritual effusions of Quaker love, does not often appear in Penn's correspondence.[22] Penn was also capable of a special intimacy with women, especially with well-born women who had similar religious beliefs. It has been observed by others that well-born and well-educated women in the seventeenth century were often attracted to radical sects, in which they were more open to religious experience and participation than they could be in the more structured and organized traditional churches which enjoined silence on women. Between these women and Penn there were no barriers of authority or class, and they could establish good rapport. We see this first in respect to his marriages.

Penn married twice, both times probably as much for money as for love. His first wife, Gulielma Springett, was an heiress; her father, Sir William Springett, was a puritan of a rich London family. She was educated, deeply religious, and intelligent. In short, they were equals in family, class, wealth, and religion, and they could talk to each other. Penn's understanding of his passion for Gulielma may be inferred from the unpublished essay on marriage, probably written shortly before they were betrothed. In it he describes a transcendent understanding of love which is the will and pleasure of the Lord, and which in the first instance could only be recognized by the couple themselves, who must refer their case to the "Light" before going to their parents. He was confident that the Lord would not approve or bless an unsuitable match and defined suitability as "station" or class, education, and life style, as well as temperament.[23]

Penn's second marriage was less clearly suitable. His bride, Hannah Callowhill, was the only child of a wealthy merchant, and Penn was accused of marrying her for her money. She was twenty-five to his fifty-one when they married, and she had not been easily convinced that he was the love of her life. Her family wanted them to live in Bristol, and although he said he liked "a citty less then a little house," he agreed to give up his very large house in the country and insisted that he believed "lowness as well as plainness" to be important parts of his character. But his letters to her during the courtship were very loving and tender: "My hand is the messenger of my heart, that most entirely loves thee, . . . And if thou Couldst believe, in how little a house I could live with thee, at least thou wouldst think I placed my happiness more in thee than any outward conveniences." Although she wrote many letters to him, only those of a later period were preserved, and they too speak of an affectionate relationship. They were both Quakers, and used to money and comfort. She was an educated woman who wrote easily, kept careful accounts, and was not unduly deferential to her husband, although she was careful of his interests.[24]

This rapport with women is also observable in 1677, when Penn traveled to Holland and Germany and was frequently entertained by sectarian women. One of the most important was Elizabeth, Princess Palatine; others were Anna Maria, Countess von Hoorn, and Anna Maria von Schurman, the Labadist and daughter of Lord Sommelsdiijk, who had been one of the richest men in the Netherlands.[25] To these women, Penn was able to open his heart and life; with a little prompting he told the princess and her followers the story of his conversion and the troubles and trials which followed in his life, in a session which began at three in the afternoon and went on until eleven at night, with just one break, for supper.[26] One could speculate that he might have had a more emotionally satisfying career had he been able to maintain friendships like these; but in fact, Penn was probably not capable of a continuous relationship.

Penn had another quality which underlines the way he maintained emotional distances from other people. He was a tremendously restless person, constantly traveling. He once called himself "a wayfareing man" and referred to his life as a pilgrimage.[27] This could be seen as the quintessential Anglo-American quality, but one he had in common with his sailor father, too. In any selected year before 1712, when he had a debilitating stroke, he is found on the move. His roving went far beyond what was normal for the Quakers (except for George Fox) who traveled extensively in an informal ministry. It began, perhaps, with the Grand Tour after he was expelled from Oxford; and continued with his trips on family business to Ireland. Throughout his life he made the usual circuit from town for business, back to his house in the country, and so on. His wife and children remained in the country, and like his father, he was an absentee father a good deal of the time. Even the patient Gulielma complained in a low-key way to Margaret Fox, and Hannah once wrote "I cannot with any Satisfaction endure thy absence much Longer."[28] He journeyed frequently in the Quaker ministry—to Germany, Holland, all over England; he traveled to Pennsylvania.

He loved a whirlwind life. His journal of his trip to Holland and Germany is revealing—it was a rough trip of three months. Sometimes he traveled for as long as twenty-four hours in an open cart, or walked for ten or twelve miles. He was forced out of some towns, detained in others. He loved every minute and recorded distances, inns, miles, weather, prayers, with real gusto.[29] If we look at the whole year of 1677 (from March to March) we find him in March in London and in Arundel, Sussex; in May in London; in June in Bristol; in July in Harwich and then on to Holland and Germany where he was constantly on the move until November when he returned; in November he was in Warminghurst and London; in December in London; in January in Buckinghamshire and Bristol; in February in Bristol; but in March back in London again. Twenty years later, in 1698, he was just as active: February found him in London, March in Bristol and London, April in Bristol, May in Dublin, June in Waterford and Cork; he was in Cork in July and in August but in September and October was in Bristol; in November he returned to London.[30] This ceaseless activity extended itself to his political life, too. He went out on the hustings for the Whigs (and especially for Algernon Sidney) in 1678–79; he was equally busy in the task of getting his colonial charter; and when he returned from his first trip to Pennsylvania he hustled for James II. One wonders if there was any calm at the center of the hurricane, or if he had to keep on the move to avoid meeting even himself.

As Penn got older, the distance between him and his Quaker associates widened, and his affinity for the ways of his father became more pronounced. He was always happy to live well. Warminghurst, his house in Sussex, was a grand gentleman's country seat, large enough to entertain meetings of several hundred Friends. Pennsbury, his Pennsylvania estate, was designed to suit proprietary status. He spent liberally to support his station — for example, between 1672 and 1674 he ordered three coaches built; ordered food to set a luxurious table, and clothes and silver fit for a gentleman.[31] After he became proprietor of Pennsylvania he came more and more to enjoy authority. His notes to his secretary, James Logan, were often curt and peremptory, for example, and he was impatient with people who disagreed with him. But his letters were also dipped in self-pity for what he saw as lack of appreciation and misunderstood benevolence. He could refer to himself as the "Old kind abused landlord" without self-consciousness.[32]

It is easy to conclude that he had come full circle, and that in the end, despite all the resistance, he became the man his father wanted him to be. In a way he was successful far beyond even his father's dreams — he held title to a province as large as England and was a landlord on a colossal scale. In short, we could conclude that class allegiance outweighed the hostility to authority which was generated in his youth.[33] But in terms of historical significance, this was not the measure of his success. He had deeply seated emotional responses to the authority of others; this created in him an inner conflict which enabled him to set checks to his own excesses in the handling of power and to make significant contributions to the spiritual and political development of Englishmen and Americans. He conceived of and established a society without military defenses, with freedom of religion, with a criminal code humane beyond anything known to Englishmen, with a written constitution containing guarantees of rights and checks on the power of the proprietor. The vision that made these things possible came from his resistance; the situations in which vision could become reality came from the wealth and status that led to influence and grants of favor. He was a man whose greatness was greater than the sum of his parts.

NOTES

A preliminary version of this essay was presented at a symposium on William Penn held at the American Philosophical Society on 12 November 1982 and was subsequently printed in *Proceedings of the American Philosophical Society,* vol. 127, no. 5, 1983. This expanded version is printed here by permission of the American Philosophical Society.

1. For a discussion of the preservation and character of the Penn Papers, see *PWP,* 1:10-13,
   2. See ibid., 1:157.

3. See ibid., 1:265, 476.

4. In a letter of 22 Nov. 1673, ibid., 1:265.

5. For Sir William Penn's career between 1644 and 1660, see Granville Penn, *Memorials of the Professional Life and Times of Sir William Penn, Knt.*, 2 vols. (London, 1833).

6. *PWP*, 1:476.

7. Ibid., 1:31, 33-35, 41, 48.

8. For the origins of Quaker language and hat usage, see William C. Braithwaite, *The Beginnings of Quakerism* (London, 1912), pp. 139-40, 486-99.

9. The testimony is recorded in *Works*, 1:10.

10. The essay on marriage was probably written in 1671; see *PWP*, 1:231-33. Penn's mother was a witness at his wedding in 1672, ibid., 1:238.

11. The trial is documented and the letters to the dying admiral are printed in ibid., 1:171-80.

12. See the essay by Hugh Barbour in this volume on Penn as a controversialist; his debating style may be studied in *PWP*, 1:57-98; his trials and appeals to Parliament are in ibid., 1:172-79, 205-7, 259.

13. Penn to Muggleton, 11 Feb. 1669, ibid., 1:87.

14. Penn to Baxter, 6 Oct. 1675, ibid., 1:338-39.

15. For the relationship between Penn's Quakerism and his political ideas, see Mary Maples Dunn, *William Penn: Politics and Conscience* (Princeton, 1967). The letter to Arlington is in *PWP*, 1:91.

16. Baxter to Penn, 6 Oct. 1675, *PWP*, 1:342.

17. The best treatment of Penn's use of his friends in acquiring the charter is in Joseph E. Illick, "The Pennsylvania Grant: A Re-evaluation," *PMHB*, 86:375-95. For Penn's relationship with Buckingham, see Dunn, *William Penn: Politics and Conscience*, pp. 41, 122, 145; and *PWP*, 1:71-72n. Buckingham's pamphlet was *A Short Discourse upon the Reasonableness of Men's having a Religion, or Worship of God* (London, 1685); Penn defended it twice, in *A Defence of the Duke of Buckingham's Book* (London, 1685) and *Annimadversions on the Apology of the Clamorous Squire* (London, 1685).

18. On the Penn-Mead trial and Rudyard's authorship, see Dunn, *William Penn: Politics and Conscience*, pp. 13-19; on the constitution, see *PWP*, 2:184-211; and on the break between the two men, *Micro.* 4:913 and *PWP*, 2:569-78.

19. For further discussion of the lawsuit between Penn and Philip Ford, see the essay by Richard Dunn in this volume. The Penn-Ford case of 1705-8 will be covered in vol. 4 of *PWP*. For Bridget Ford's discontent, see *Micro.* 12:362.

20. The incident is documented in Penn to James Harrison, 7 Oct. 1684, *PWP*, 2:601-3. Penn replaced Lehnmann with William Markham; see the commission in *Micro.* 5:148.

21. Dunn, *William Penn: Politics and Conscience*, pp. 157-61, and for Blackwell's dismissal on 25 Sept. 1689, *Micro.* 6:341.

22. See Penn to Fox, 4 Mar. 1676, *PWP*, 1:359-61.

23. Unfortunately, very little correspondence between William and Gulielma Penn survives. The first known letter to her is dated 7 Oct. 1668; they were married on 4 Apr. 1672. *PWP*, 1:68, 231-41.

24. Letters from Penn to Hannah Callowhill will be printed in vol. 3 of *PWP* and are available in the microfilm edition. See particularly 9 Feb. 1695/6, *Micro.* 7:108.

25. See *PWP*, 1:440-46, 485-89 for Penn's meeting with the princess and the countess, and ibid., 1:489-99 for a long letter from Penn to the countess. The meeting with von Schurman is recounted in ibid., 1:474-79.

26. Ibid., 1:443-44.

27. In a letter to John Gratton, 12 Dec. 1695. This letter will appear in vol. 3 of *PWP* and is in *Micro.* 6:003.

28. Gulielma Penn to Margaret Fox, 24 Aug. 1684, *PWP,* 2:597-98, and Hannah Penn to William Penn, 13 Oct. 1703. This letter will appear in vol. 4 of *PWP* and is in *Micro.* 11:085.

29. In "An Account of My Journey into Holland & Germany," 22 July — 12 October 1677, *PWP,* 1:425-500.

30. These travels are deduced from letterheads in *PWP,* vol. 1, and forthcoming vol. 3.

31. See his account with Philip Ford, for example, for the years 1672-74, *PWP,* 1:577-621. Silver sent to his American household is listed in ibid., 2:287-90.

32. Penn to James Logan, 26 Aug. 1700, *Micro.* 8:524; Correspondence of James Logan, HSP, 1:46, 40.

33. Gary B. Nash, in *Quakers and Politics: Pennsylvania 1681-1726* (Princeton, 1968), sees him as an aristocrat more than a Quaker.

2 ⟨ *The Young Controversialist*

A survey of the men, issues, and documents in William Penn's early theo-logical debates casts light on the stages of his growth as a writer and thinker. Penn saw the roots of the prophetic absolutism of the early Quak-ers in universal human religious and moral experience. Out of this perspec-tive on theology grew Penn's pioneering role in sketching out the ideas of Protestant liberalism for Friends.[1] This essay shows that Penn's wrestling with the human limits of "leadings" from God prepared him for his role as "weighty Friend." But also we find that the mood and agenda of a debater kept Penn from producing writings more centered in his own experience, such as he achieved in ethics; and this in the end made his theological books less known and loved than Robert Barclay's.

William Penn returned to England from Ireland just before Christmas of 1667 as a newly convinced Quaker, eager to prove himself against his admiral father and the courtly world. He had already championed Irish Friends in prison with both tongue and pen. Within thirteen months he was a prisoner in the Tower of London for a tract he had written against the Trinity. Penn was twenty-four, and it was his third major Quaker booklet, a defense of Friends and part of a theological debate, as were most of his writings for the next eight years. There were exceptions: in Penn's seven months in the Tower in 1669, though his most traumatic time, he was able also to write the first version of *No Cross, No Crown*. In 1670 came his first tracts on toleration. But mainly, by 1675, some thirty-six titles and forty-five hundred octavo pages later, he had developed from being the young champion of Friends, with "some smattring of learning," to being their "greatest undertaker" of written and spoken debate.[2] His "wordiest" year was 1674. Thereafter his mind turned to new continents and English toleration.

Penn found the issues, the opponents, the format of theological debate and the producing of "debate tracts" already given to him as traditions fixed for Quakers. Their style had been prepared in the 1640s by the Puritan Commonwealth's outburst into print: sermons, doctrinal works, pleas for and against toleration, and posthumous spiritual diaries and memorials (foreshadowing Friends' journals), but also theological treatises and lists of heresies and heretics. Between 1653 and Penn's arrival in 1667, the Quakers' own share in this snowstorm already included 324 works equivalent to some five thousand folio pages.[3]

The debated issues arose out of Friends' claims to have brought a prophetic challenge from God to all human individuals and institutions, a call to self-judgment under the Light of moral truth, which was the Spirit of Christ within each person. The first Quaker "Publishers of Truth," the itinerant preachers such as Edward Burrough and Richard Hubberthorne, alternated between man-on-man tracts of rebuttal and their proclamations of the Day of the Lord, calling all England to repentance. Even the gentleman scholar Isaac Penington, who by choice wrote leisurely discourses at home, came forward twice to rebut the Seventh-Day Baptists. Such verbal and written battles reflected the Quakers' understanding of their movement as "The Lamb's War" being waged by the Spirit of Christ against worldwide evil. Since Friends shared an inward and spiritual version of the radical Puritans' apocalyptic hopes, loyalty demanded that Quakers single out and oppose evil wherever it appeared. Their earliest tracts, such as *False Prophets and False Teachers Described*,[4] simply challenged the Puritan pastors both for their professionalism and for contending that a Christian cannot hope to be made perfect. Prophetic Quakers commonly confronted rectors in their own pulpits, as John Banks challenged "priest" George Larkham of Cockermouth in 1660: "if thou be a minister of Christ, stand to prove thy practice, if it be the same the Apostles was and is."[5] Under such circumstances the Puritan pastors, who were supported by tithes, had to reply, for their jobs and also their personal calling and deepest experience were at stake. Richard Baxter, for instance, had been sick when Friends Thomas Goodaire and Richard Farnworth came to Kidderminster. Presented with a list of queries, Baxter realized that "if I say nothing, they will insult; if I write them [a reply], they will print it" (with Quaker rebuttals, of course). He decided to beat the Friends into print.[6] No Quaker willingly gave the impression that he had been silenced, and even kindly old Francis Howgill could not ignore a title like *Hell Broke Loose, or a History of the Quakers*.[7]

Although lurid stories of Quaker conduct, such as those of the psychotic John Gilpin, galloped through a chain of Puritan tracts,[8] and Quaker conduct was satirized, the Puritans' main counterattack was against every heresy in Quaker doctrines. Their booklets rehearsed not only previous verbal debates but also the legal trials for blasphemy, which the pastors instigated in light of Quakers' claims to be filled and infallibly guided by the same Spirit that was incarnate in Christ. Quakers were not misunderstood. In the first such trial, at Lancaster assizes before "forty priests" in October 1652, George Fox was acquitted, since two of the three judges were Puritans versed in theology and sympathetic to Quakerism. But at Appleby in December 1652 James Nayler was not so lucky (nor was Fox at Carlisle the following summer). Fox's own manuscript survived from these trials, and both the pastors' version and the two Quaker tracts based on the trial confirm their adversaries' accounts reassuringly.[9] Many of the issues were as clearly stated by both sides at Lancaster as in all the elaborations that followed. And though the pattern is as old as the trials of Abelard and Eckhart, such trials may have set the format by which each Quaker and anti-Quaker debating tract felt obliged to rebut sentence by sentence an opponent's writing, in true medieval dialectical style.

Friends appealed to no authoritative code or treatise of Quaker doctrines, for in every situation the direct leading of the Spirit must rule. But Friends needed to protect themselves against charges of heresy and to guarantee the Spirit's prophetic authority within individual Friends who judged the morality of their hearers. Hence a double tendency: all early Friends reaffirmed each challenged doctrine in virtually uniform words; yet they never quoted as authorities Fox or any other Friend. The Spirit had to be assumed to speak consistently but individually in all the Children of Light, even about issues which Quakers had not studied theologically. Friends used Bible texts surprisingly frequently and consistently: this too was rooted in their need to demonstrate the Spirit's consistency in all ages, quite as much as in any *ad hominem* appeals to the Puritans' scriptural guide. The Bible could justify Quakers even in their rude language.[10]

As Penn rushed into the scrimmage, he inherited not only a traditional style of religious word warfare but also his specific opponents. Besides examples that will be explored later, Penn inherited from Edward Burrough and James Nayler, who had died a dozen years earlier, their dispute with Richard Baxter, which led Penn into a public debate with Baxter in 1675, and letters of some heat exchanged between the two men, but nothing in print.[11] Penn's earliest and most crucial debates, however, were those he joined in 1668 in personal support of George Whitehead, the young north-country Friend with whom in the same weeks he went to plead for governmental toleration with the newly dominant duke of Buckingham and with Secretary of State Sir Henry Bennett, earl of Arlington.

Penn's first opponent in debate (in this case only in writing) was Jonathan Clapham, proud to be a graduate of Trinity College, Cambridge.[12] He had been already the parish minister at Wramplingham in Norfolk when George Whitehead and Christopher Atkinson passed through in 1654, as part of the first nationwide mission of the Quaker "Publishers of Truth," spreading out in pairs across England from the moorland northwest.[13] A tract debate began about singing Psalms, but Clapham's third response changed the subject. In *A Full Discovery and Confutation of the Wicked and Damnable Doctrines of the Quakers,* he reopened the whole gallery of Quaker heresies on the Scriptures, Jesus's human body, the Trinity, the Resurrection, Justification, and human perfectibility. But Clapham also prefaced his tract with a fiercely Presbyterian epistle, attacking Oliver Cromwell's policy of toleration.[14] Naturally Clapham's call for persecution led Friends to protest their *Truth and Innocencie.*[15] There the debate rested during the first years of the Restoration, while Quakers crowded the jails, and Clapham, faced with the Act of Uniformity, decided to accept the Anglican prayer book and surplice rather than join the two thousand Puritan pastors who were "ejected" from their parish pulpits. But in 1668, in the interim between the first and second Conventicle Acts, when the "dissenting" clergy had won new respect by their brave ministry during the plague and London fire, Clapham felt the need to justify his conforming and appealed to his Puritan brethren by *A Guide to the True Religion.*[16] He favored national unity, and "condescension towards those that differ in controverted points of lower Nature, even to a degree of complyance . . . with the stream of the times."[17] Clapham wanted a comprehensive national church offering salvation for all, except (since he needed some straw men) the atheists, heathen polytheists, Moslems, Jews, Papists, Socinians, and Quakers.

For young William Penn, loyal also to Whitehead, such a target was too tempting to pass up. Penn's own first tract, *Truth Exalted,* had indeed been written in a tone of prophetic warning (to which he occasionally returned after visits to Ireland or Holland, and again in the Tower version of *No Cross, No Crown*). But Penn's tract against Clapham, *The Guide Mistaken,* was quiet and learned as befitted a humanist.[18] He began his formal rebuttal:

> When I retrospect upon that time I once imploy'd in a conversation with Books, and call to mind the excellent Defence of Origen, and Apology of *Tertullian* on the behalf of those primitive Christians, and also the Learning, Gravity, and Reason of *Du Plessy, Grotius, Amiraldus,* etc. . . . I cannot but acknowledge myself surpriz'd to find a discourse so raw and undigested as Jonathan Clapham's.[19]

But in his preface Penn had mentioned Clapham's "conforming spirit" and his epistle to Cromwell, and at the end of his tract he returned to Clapham's personal career under the kaleidoscopic regimes of the Commonwealth, saying, "the only constancy I can remarque of J. Clapham has been the keeping of his parish through his very great inconstancy in his perswasions."[20] In this tract Penn made some careful points: for instance, the fact that the Light within men is universal does not show that it is natural. But to answer Clapham's arguments Penn had to revive the old assertions of Fox and Hubberthorne that the word *Trinity* is not biblical, and that the Bible does not speak of three persons in God.[21] Even in denying he was a Socinian (Unitarian), Penn praised Socinus's "exemplary life and grave deportment" and "stronger arguments" as "very singular."[22] Although the issue of the Trinity had been incidental for Penn, the trench lines for the next battle had been drawn.

Clapham did not reply; but Penn was at once drawn into another verbal debate alongside George Whitehead, against two dissenting ministers who had accepted ejection but became public heroes again during the plague. Thomas Vincent, though a well-known writer, had not attacked Quakers until two members of his congregation were won away.[23] Thomas Danson, however, had confronted Quakers Whitehead, Hubberthorne, and Samuel Fisher while he held his own parish at Sandwich.[24] Whitehead was well known as a Quaker debater: nineteen of his twenty-eight tracts before the argument with Vincent had been debate tracts, against sixteen non-Quaker opponents, and he clung to that style in later years when most Friends had dropped it. In Whitehead's tracts, the relation of Jesus's human life to Christ's Spirit within men was often mentioned, and in one discussed at length,[25] but in only one tract did the Trinity arise.[26]

Thus Thomas Vincent, trying to hold together his church membership, knew that the Quakers could be challenged on both the Atonement and the Trinity. After two private encounters which he cut short, Vincent met Penn and Whitehead in front of his own congregation in a hall at Spitalfields. He rigged the meeting for maximum dramatic effect. He brought to aid him not only Danson but also two other Puritan ex-pastors, the vituperative William Maddocks and the silent Thomas Doolittle. He began to prepare his hearers before Whitehead and Penn arrived, and when they did, he gave the Friends no chance to expound their prophetic teachings but attacked at once "their opinions which I had asserted were damnable,"[27] beginning not with the well-worn Atonement issues (though he raised them later) but with the Trinity. Vincent used much Nicean theology, Thomistic terms, and school logic. In comparison with Vincent's metaphysics, Whitehead's satirical comparison of three divine persons in one Godhead to a "unity" of the three men Peter, James, and John in one Apostle clearly lacked subtlety. The debate lasted from two o'clock until dark, after which Vincent led a prayer, blew out his candles, and retired. Penn seems to have fared better than Whitehead. Against so renowned an opponent he made no show of higher learning or virtue as he had against Clapham. Penn tried in vain to arrange a rematch with Danson and Vincent,[28] and then took up his pen to present the Quaker arguments.

Under the circumstances, the little, thirty-six-page *Sandy Foundation Shaken* was mild, clear, and compact. Penn's preface briefly described the Spitalfields meeting. He went on to challenge "the vulgar doctrine of Satisfaction being Dependent on the Second Person of the Trinity" by showing that God's forgiveness predated Jesus's death. He rejected "the Justification of impure Persons by imputative Righteousness," since God makes men pure and thus justified. But in his first chapter Penn had attacked the Trinity as three separate persons, the issue over which Vincent and even Clapham had called Penn a Socinian.

Penn's *Sandy Foundation* ignored the label of Socinian. On each point, it began with biblical arguments and then appealed by syllogisms to "right reason."[29] Penn tried to show that each of the three Persons must be either finite or infinite; neither way could they logically be parts of an infinite God. He claimed that three Persons or "subsistences" would imply three essences. Penn also invoked the early church fathers, at this point reflecting translations by the English Socinian John Biddle, and arguments from Biddle's books.[30] Clearly Penn was surprised when his tract put him and his printer John Darby into prison.[31]

Within weeks[32] both Vincent and Danson had spelled out Penn's heresies for the public.[33] Vincent's contribution, *The Foundation of God standeth sure,* stuck to Penn's three points. After telling his own Spitalfields story, he tried to correct Penn's metaphysics.[34] But he also tried to prove that if Penn thought only one person in the Trinity was divine, presumably the Father, then for Penn, Christ was not divine, which opened him to the charge of blasphemous heresy.[35]

But the issue of the divinity of Christ was the opening Penn and Whitehead needed. It is not clear which man saw it first or why neither saw it earlier. Biographers have traditionally held that this was the fruit of a visit to Penn in the Tower by the royal chaplain Edward Stillingfleet, who was in touch with the Privy Council.[36] But the divinity of Christ had already been affirmed by both Friends in earlier books.[37] So their new tracts, Penn's *Innocency with Her open Face* and Whitehead's much longer *Divinity of Christ,* could reaffirm Christ's divinity without retracting anything and could deny indignantly the charges of Socinianism,[38] thus freeing Penn from the Tower. Early Quakers indeed did not make Christ's spirit an inferior being distinct from God the Father. Instead they regarded the Creator-God, the Spirit of Christ, and the Holy Spirit that transformed men, as one and the same. Whitehead noted at once,[39] as Penn did in a later letter to Dr. John Collinges,[40] that the Quaker heresy was not Socinian but Sabellian, an overemphasis on spirit and the unity of God. In milder forms this had been the heresy of Saint Augustine and even of Saint Paul; no one was ever burned for it. The overstress on the unity of God, however, had already made trouble for any Friend who tried to show how the human Jesus was related to the Christ-Spirit, and how that relationship differed from the role of God's Spirit in our own human lives.[41] Fox denied that Jesus had a human soul.[42] Fortunately for Friends, Vincent and Danson did not probe deeply into these Quaker ideas.

When the Friends replied in 1669, George Whitehead dealt with Danson's *Synopsis,* after fifty pages against Vincent.[43] But Penn's *Innocency with Her open Face,* written in the Tower, once again spoke only about Christ's divinity, satisfaction, and justification. Now he admitted that he knew "*no other name* by which *Remission, Attonement and Salvation can be obtained,* but *Jesus Christ.*"[44] The tract ended with "Lines added by a Friend" (perhaps George Fox):

> We are bought with a price, and therefore we are to glorifie God with
> our bodies, souls and spirits, which are his; . . . Christ's blood was
> shed for all men; and by his Blood he redeems from iniquity; not that
> people should live in iniquity, . . . for he came to make an end of sin.[45]

In the later years of his life, Penn would emphasize increasingly all men's need for forgiveness.[46]

Before and after his release from the Tower, Penn was busy with publishing the first, short, ethically intense version of *No Cross, No Crown;* he was also involved with the Penn-Mead trial, two Newgate imprisonments, trips to Ireland and Holland, and the writings all these entailed.[47] At home there came his father's death and his courtship of Gulielma Springett at the Peningtons. The last round of Penn against the Trinity was therefore delayed until 1672. It is misleading to regard these later tracts simply in terms of Socinian doctrines. The link was the people involved. Penn had been a friend of Thomas Firmin and Henry Hedworth, the chief surviving disciples of the Socinian John Biddle in London.[48] It remains unclear how honest Penn had been earlier in claiming not to know that the books he had quoted were Socinian, but even in *Innocency* he did not condemn Socinus:

> I have read of one Socinus, of . . . a noble family in Sene [Sienna] in
> Italy, who about the year 1574, being a young man, voluntarily did
> abandon the glories, pleasures and honours of the great Duke of Tus-
> cany's court, . . . and became a perpetual exile for his conscience, whose
> parts, wisdom and gravity made him the most famous with the Polon-
> ian and Transylvanian Churches. But I was never baptized into his
> name, . . . and if in any thing I acknowledge the verity of his doctrine,
> it is for *the Truth's Sake.*[50]

Penn sensed in Socinus a kindred spirit. Firmin was angry, however, that Penn nonetheless affirmed the divinity of Christ. In 1672 Hedworth wrote the first of two major tracts, to which Penn replied.[50] Hedworth's tracts were anonymous, and the first avoided any clearly Unitarian stand, which led Penn to complain that the tract attacked him by arguments from both sides at once. Penn descended for once into the biblical Billingsgate[51] typical of Quaker tracts of the 1650s, attacking Hedworth's "Owl-light way of stabbing men . . . for the promotion of his Biddlean or Socinian

Cause."[52] Penn showed that his opponent's handling of Bible verses reflected Socinianism, and that he denied the divinity of God's Spirit, that is, the Light.[53]

Penn wrote a basically systematic theological book, however, which he had never done before, even in his *Serious Apology for the Principles and Practices of the Quakers* (1671), which had been a careful statement of Quaker ethics written against two Irish ejected Presbyterians. Penn's *Spirit of Truth Vindicated* ignored Hedworth, except at start and conclusion, and turned to a careful exposition of the key issue, as Penn saw it: the Light of God within men.[54] Using Hedworth's title only as a springboard for his thesis, Penn tried to prove that the Light which showed and overcame sin must be *saving* and hence divine, not "natural" in man, and also *morally* infallible:

> God's Holy and unerring Spirit is or should be the proper Judge of Truth, Rule of Faith and Guide of Life among men. . . . [It is] not from the strength of mans Reason, Memory or utmost Creaturely Ability that his Knowledge of Religious and Heavenly Things comes. . . . God's Children are not without an Infallible Teacher and Leader in the Things that appertain to their Eternal Salvation. . . . Men must not think to see all at once; and . . . God has afforded his People in all Ages such a measure of his Eternal Spirit, as hath been sufficient to *Inform, Rule and Guide* them. (Pp. 16, 17, 21, 72, 34)

Some early passages of *Spirit of Truth* belong among Penn's best writing and led him on the next year to a more diffuse but theologically more original book, *The Christian Quaker.* Penn had also made, in *Spirit of Truth,* one of the early Quakers' best statements to date about the Bible:

> The Scripture is much like the shaddow of the true Rule, which may give us some ground to guess what the Rule it self is, . . . a kind of secondary Rule, carrying with it a Testimonial Confirmation, that what we are led by is the TRUE SPIRIT, because the People of God in old time enjoyed the same, [just] as the Eternal Spirit first of all confirms the Divine Authority of Scriptures to us. (Pp. 38-39)

Penn's method in this book was still to lay down, in each area, first biblical and then rational proofs, but each section was long enough to stand alone. He once again quoted at length from scholarly sources; but whereas he named anti-Trinitarian church fathers from memory in *Sandy Foundation*[55] and may have poured out his topically organized "common place book" into the first *No Cross,*[56] here he seems to have used directly from the Latin the commentaries of Beza, Chrysostom, Drusius, Erasmus, Henry Hammond, Maldonat, and Tollet.[57] One cannot help admiring Penn's disciplined diligence in this year of his marriage, and we may suppose that the books he cited were in the library of Isaac Penington, his new father-in-law (whose Quaker principles rarely let him quote authorities himself).

The tie to Penington may have curious implications, since among the commentaries Penn quoted were those of Crell and Schlichting, which this time he used in Latin and explicitly named as Socinian.[58] From Penington too he may have learned the doctrine that Christ's body was a garment, which Penn now adopted.[59]

Penn paraded his studies in replying to Hedworth, who "looked upon him as a man of some Learning,"[60] but since Penn had turned systematic, their second round of tracts was for once shorter than the first: Hedworth came out with an orderly defense of Socinianism, and Penn finally supplied Hedworth's name as his anonymous opponent. The contest died.

The claim of infallible guidance by the Spirit, however, on which Penn had met the challenges of Hedworth and the Puritan pastors, now became a challenge and problem for Penn himself when he needed to distinguish the Quakers from the followers of Lodowick Muggleton. Muggleton continued to prophesy, after beginning as the mouthpiece to John Reeve (who soon died) in 1647, the same year that Fox first became known. Muggleton represented a reduction to absurdity of the Quaker type of life and message: a working-class prophet, describing direct divine inspiration, he claimed the right in God's name to curse those who rejected him and presented in a seemingly Antinomian form a new ethic, and new interpretations of biblical teachings.[61] Like the debates with Clapham and Vincent, the Quaker fight with Muggleton predated Penn's own involvement by at least four tracts on each side, and Muggleton had issued eight tracts earlier before any Friends took him on.[62] Muggleton and Reeve had called on Cromwell to protect them as the new prophets and dispose of their enemies.[63] In 1662 Friends entered the debate.[64] Soon Fox and Penington also responded, and Muggleton naturally fulminated against each.[65] Muggleton cursed Friends for rejecting God's word. Josiah Coale and Thomas Loe, who had fathered Penn into Quakerism, died within the year. Penn wrote an angry letter to Muggleton for boasting about the death of Coale, and another nearly four years later, in which he repeated the dialogue of a recent visit he and Whitehead had had with Muggleton.[66] Penn's only published tract against Muggleton, *The New Witnesses Proved OLD HERETICKS* (1672), tied up Muggleton's doctrines with the early Christian heresies of Tertullian, the Gnostics, and Manicheans,[67] but Penn mainly used logic and ridicule, especially by lining up contradictions in the Muggletonians' early books. Where he attacked their claim to infallibility, however, Penn was exchanging positions with the attackers of Quakerism.[68] Some of the same issues also had arisen in Penn's dealing with Jean de Labadie,[69] the French prophet or mystic whose commune at Herford in the Rhineland he had visited in 1671, and whose followers would have made good Quakers.

But the key issues of the authority of personal revelation and the apparent fallibility of divine "leading" meanwhile arose closer to home, within the Quaker community itself. The case of James Nayler, whose disciples had felt a prophetic call to bring him into Bristol in 1656 in a reenactment of Jesus's Palm Sunday entry into Jerusalem, had shaken all Quakers into testing and watching the impulses which seemed to be leadings of the Spirit. Some of Nayler's group at Bristol, notably Robert Rich, the "mad merchant," later also supported John Perrot, the sensitive but individualistic Friend who came back from papal prisons in 1660 and polarized Friends by keeping on his hat during Friends' prayers which he did not feel led to join. Perrot, reported an angry opponent,

> is said to have written to Jane Stocks [Stokes] whilst he was a prisoner in Rome, the purport of which is obedience to God in all things, [even] though he should command what once he did to his servant Hosea. Now for the truths sake, which is everlastingly pure, . . . was it ever heard that ever any person unless the Ranters, would put the Question, as if the holy, blessed, pure God might command beastly and unholy actions. . . . At that time was J. Perrot a married man and Jane Stokes was at Rome in the time of J. Perrots imprisonment.[70]

Perrot's case activated all the typical conflicts over Antinomianism: the call to submit to God beyond good and evil (as in the sacrifice of Isaac), claims for private freedom, and sexual overtones. Anne Hutchinson had taken this route out of Massachusetts and its covenants. Before turning to Quakerism, Isaac Penington had explored another variety of Antinomianism, a holy passivity perhaps close to mental breakdown.[71] The hostile report about Perrot cited above came from John Bolton, who had been in Exeter jail while Nayler and his friends were there, and who later as a wealthy Londoner and weighty Friend took responsibility for the Quakers' refusal of a cash gift from Robert Rich, then a moral citizen settled in Barbados, but who had attacked Fox's ostracism of Perrot.[72] Penn found himself aligned with Bolton against Nathaniel Smith, a Rabelaisian character who claimed that in Lancaster Castle dungeon George Fox had tried to teach him that the world was flat. Smith admitted coming to London as a "Student of Physick" in hopes that Friends would provide him with patients, and a wife and house as well. A willing widow was visited, but Smith's drinking and bedroom skirmishes resulted in a quarrel with another Friend. Smith's complaint was thrown out (along with Smith himself) when he tried to bring it before "the Quakers Spiritual Court" (the Quaker men's Two Weeks Meeting presided over by John Bolton). Friends were still angrier when Smith printed his whole tale.[73] William Penn wrote "A Prefatory Observation" in reply, angry, incoherent, and rhetorical, which fortunately was never printed,[74] but the whole episode makes Penn's response in 1672–73 to other troublesome Friends, William Mucklow and the Pennymans, more understandable. Penn was never tempted by Antinomianism, whether saintly or salacious.

John and Mary Pennyman were mistaken by both Friends and non-Friends for characters like Smith. They too had supported Perrot. John

Pennyman had been "disowned" after a confused "leading" to burn the Bible and other books on the floor of the Royal Exchange. When Grace-church Street Meeting therefore refused to oversee his marriage, Penny-man rented the Merchant Tailors' Hall for a memorable feast and staged his wedding around purely personal vows with the widow Mary Boreman.[75] Penn's own letter to Mary was kind and recounts his personal religious pilgrimage.[76] But John and Mary, who had already issued a half-dozen broadsides about their case, were not to be won back and continued for years both to haunt Friends and to write against them.[77]

The tensions aroused by these various kinds of libertinism were brought into focus by William Mucklow's tract *The Spirit of the Hat* in 1673. Refusal to remove his hat when other Friends prayed had been Perrot's badge. Because of this, John Pennyman, who had written bravely at the Restoration against "hat-honour" to judges,[78] had rallied to Perrot's cause. In turn, "the hat" came to be linked with the wider issue of George Fox's authority to set up men's monthly meetings (1667–69) and especially the separate women's monthly meetings for business (1671–72), and the central [Monday] "Morning Meeting" of Quaker "ministers," to oversee printing and itinerant preaching. Penn supported Fox in urging both these steps. Fox expected the consensus of Friends' experience, the "sense of the meeting," to concur. Whether Fox was asserting, or was permanently delegating his own powers as leader has been argued ever since. By 1675 this issue would lead to the Wilkinson-Story separation, creating an open rift among the Quakers that faded only slowly over two decades.

The preface of *The Spirit of the Hat* won no Friends by citing Smith's *Spiritual Court* and attacking Penn for self-contradictions in the Hedworth and Faldo controversies; it was written by an unidentified "C.J." The main tract by Mucklow began more tenderly, by remembering the spontaneity of the earliest Quakerism. Rather than set up rules, said Mucklow, "wait at the Feet of Jesus till God reveals. . . . Witness an unity in Spirit with [one's] Brother, though in a different Exercise."[79] Before he published this pamphlet, in the previous autumn of 1672, Mucklow had written to Penn privately, strongly but without rancor, to ask certain basic questions about Friends' new uniformity, as shown by hats:

1. Whether under the Gospel Administration & in the Gospel Worship there ought to be any Ceremonies or forms practised.
2. Whether pulling off the Hat in time of Prayer be not a Ceremony or form.
3. Whether keeping it on be a sufficient ground for giving Judgment against such, as Sower[s] of Dissension, & out of the unity of the Body, & whether you are not the Men, that is the Quakers (so called) . . . that have so censur'd severall & consequently are not for Liberty of Conscience.[80]

Mucklow and his non-Quaker wife had also been censured by Bolton for asking rights of burial in the Quaker burial ground. When Penn replied to Mucklow to answer his complaints, he sounded unhappy with both sides on this issue.[81]

On the wider issue of uniformity, Penn's letter was firm and kindly, though in a paternal way. It is striking, however, that his arguments were precisely those which Latitudinarian Anglicans were then using to compel dissenters to stay in the national church despite its rituals:

> Though the Gospel Worship is of a more interiour & Spiritual Nature, . . . yet there is somewhat exteriour or bodily, that is relative & adjunctive & bears a part in the Worship that is paid to God. . . . In short, as the Soul Worships, so does the Body. . . . Second, . . . the pulling off the Hatt, little in itself, is of some weight to us, . . . no Anti-Gospel form. . . . Third, . . . the separating & singular practice of the Hat on in prayer, [even] if it had been right, it cost more than it was worth[82]

Friends were furious with Mucklow's attack on Fox.[83] Penn published *The Spirit of Alexander the Coppersmith* (1673), which said it was no time for a Quaker to give aid and comfort to their persecutors: "What greater Demonstration of Implacableness can there be, when so many are against us?"[84] In 1673 Parliament had forced Charles II to withdraw his Declaration of Indulgence; the jails were full again.[85] Individualists like Mucklow, John Wilkinson, and Thomas Story, who felt led to worship alone at odd hours faced no persecution.

Penn's main argument, however, came again perilously close to those of Catholics and Anglicans that Friends had thus far rejected:

> There is either such a Thing as a *Christian Society,* sometimes call'd a *Visible Body,* or *Church,* or there is not. . . . If there be, then this *Church* either has *Power* or not. . . . The Question then is . . . *whether we as a Believing Body have the Holy Spirit or no?* . . . As for his saying, *Every Member is Equal,* it is false: For though it belongs to the same Body, yet not the same Service; some are in that sense more Honourable than others. . . . G. Fox having an Occasion to Speak of *Liberty of Conscience,* said . . . *No Liberty out of the Power,* that is, *The Power of God.* Nor in reality is there: for all Consciences that are defiled, or enslaved by Wicked Works, they are not truly free. . . . What! Liberty to the *Presbyterians, Independents, Baptists, etc.?* NO . . . for then in vain are we become Quakers.[86]

Like Fox and Robert Barclay, Penn never sounded so conservative as in this controversy with the Quaker individualists. Mucklow pointed out the frightening intolerance of Penn's authoritarianism and turned against Penn his own words against the "Traducing Anabaptist" John Morse: "Who thus adventure to persecute [when] without power, Let who will believe they would not do it if they had power."[87]

In another tract against Mucklow, *Judas and the Jews Combined against Christ and his Followers,* Penn opens in even more savage language, denouncing Mucklow as a "Socinian," a "Lyar," and an "Apostate." For defense Penn appealed to the works of very conservative churchmen. But he did go on to tell the story of Perrot and his band of individualists, reminded his readers of the joy and glory that the united Quaker movement had brought to its members in earlier days, and finally discussed the need for discipline within a religious group. Penn asked

> Whether such a Society Body or Church, after due Admonition given to any dissenting or innovating Person, may not Lawfully and Christianly deny their Communion in Testimony against that wrong Spirit such Person or Persons may be acted by?[88]

Penn had tried to handle the perennial religious problem of clashing or divergent claims for inspiration and divine truth and had begun to suggest the ways such experiences must be tested. But it remained for Barclay to spell out the issues more carefully and to suggest the basis of the Quaker methods of consensus that were emerging.[89] But in the furnaces of five years' pressure from within and outside Quakerism, Penn the loyal controversialist had become Penn the "weighty Friend." He now attended the "Morning Meeting" whenever he was in London, drafted the Yearly Meeting's epistle which asked local meetings to regulate marriages, disputes between members, cases of tithe-paying and misconduct, and other epistles asking for the recording of Quaker prisoners and Quaker history.[90] He led in trying to mediate the dispute with the next group of Quaker individualists to protest old-time local leaders led by Wilkinson and Story. But William Mucklow, for his part, returned in later years to the Quaker fellowship he had left and accepted its group guidance.

We come finally to note Penn's other theological writings of 1672 to 1674. In quantity, all previously was prologue. Penn's two books against the Congregationalist pastor John Faldo, *Quakerism a New Nick-name for Old Christiantiy* and *The Invalidity of John Faldo's Vindication,* were almost as long as Penn's total tract output in his first five Quaker years. Penn was in fact annoyed when Faldo replied to his first 254-page challenge in only 96 pages. Topically these two tracts spanned the whole battleline of Quaker and Christian doctrines.[91] The kindly Sussex minister Henry Hallywell, who preached on "the Fulness of God's own Goodness,"[92] forced Penn to match his astonishing knowledge of Quaker writings (on which Penn did well) and those of the Familists with whom Hallywell compared Friends (here Penn was outclassed). Penn's reply, *Wisdom Justified of her Children* (1673) was pithier than ever on the universality of prophetic morality, and the relation of the Light to both divine reason and fallible human reasoning.[93] He sketched out English Reformation history as his own life story and as Puritan sacred history (culminating in the Quakers).[94] He also managed a solitary essay, *Urim and Thummim, or the Doctrines of Light and Perfection* (1674) against Samuel Grevill. But the biggest of all theological debates for Penn and other Friends was started by a *Dialogue between a Christian and a Quaker* (1672) by the Baptist Thomas Hicks, who quoted cleverly from Quaker books.[95] Hicks drew in other Baptists and six Quaker writers besides Penn, reaching a total of twenty books or 226 sheets (1,900 quarto pages) within two years.[96] This exchange led up to the two great day-long debates on 9 and 16 October 1674 at the Baptists' Barbican Hall and the Quakers' Wheeler Street Meeting House. Five Quakers — Penn, Whitehead, George Keith, Stephen Crisp, and Thomas Ellwood — argued against Hicks and four other Baptists before crowds estimated as upwards of three thousand, until the galleries gave way. The Quakers' efforts in these debates were satirized in an amusing broadside, *The Quaker Ballad.* John Bunyan vividly remembered these debates and recited the standard list of Quaker heresies which another Baptist reprinted fifteen years later.[97]

Although the public debates were becoming more spectacular, Penn's writing became less so. In all his tracts against Hallywell, Hicks, and Faldo, his tone was leisurely and careful. Although Penn's tract structure was still often accusation and reply, he could now use attacks on Friends as convenient pegs for a systematic exposition of Quaker beliefs, written more to convince the general reader than to win a debate. This development we noticed as early as 1671 in *Serious Apology* and still more in his 1672 work, *Spirit of Truth.* It was climaxed by Penn's half of *The Christian Quaker* (nominally against Hicks) in 1674.

Fuller discussion of these longer works of 1673 and 1674 must be left for other contexts, and they should be studied in terms of Penn's versions of Quaker doctrines (for which in general Melvin Endy's book remains normative).[98] Penn's part of *The Christian Quaker,* which left Whitehead to tackle Hicks's specific arguments, is a long work mainly on the universality and saving power of the Light of God within all men. (A second edition did not mention Hicks.) Penn's barrage of classical quotations was used this time as examples of the Light, not just as authorities. In this book he tried to show systematically that the Light, which Friends had always claimed was present within all men, had in fact led pagan philosophers such as Socrates and the Stoics *to salvation.* They knew and obeyed God, even though they did not know that the Light which taught them virtue should carry the name of Christ. Penn now spoke of the *logos* as the "Word-God." Although often tedious, *The Christian Quaker* was thus also the work which best undergirded the fundamental affirmation of Penn and all Quaker and Protestant liberals, namely, that all truth is one and is from God, and all humans can recognize it. Already every person knows truth enough to start on the way to salvation, and to obey until fuller Light is received. Penn drew from this approach to truth a new basis for Friends' relationship to non-Quakers, notably those in the English government, and built on it his program of political reform by consensus of sensitive consciences, the model he left for later reformers.

We must ask therefore why Penn, who had become since the Penn-Mead trial the theological and political spokesman for Friends, did not become their theological leader and was not credited with the definitive Quaker doctrinal book. This turned out to be Robert Barclay's *Apology*, first published in 1676 in Latin, with an English edition two years later. Barclay's personal witness, especially to the powerful experience of Quaker worship, has made that book a favorite of Friends in all periods. But Penn's own equivalent experience was in ethics, not worship, as he showed in his best-loved *No Cross, No Crown,* and later in his crisp *Fruits of Solitude* in the tradition of Stoic aphorisms. Penn was proud of his Welsh ancestry. His garrulity made his theological works too long, and in them he had preferred to quote philosophers as authorities, rather than enter with insight into their positions. This may show that it was the debater's viewpoint, even more than the debating style, which was never enough transcended in Penn's theology. For on key Quaker issues, such as the "saving" nature of the Light, its universality, the nature of God, of Christ, and of Jesus, Penn made better statements than Barclay, even if he too could be fuzzy or rationalistic.

In the long works against Hallywell, Faldo, and Hicks, Penn had also said all he could on most topics. His later theological works, lively but not subtle,[99] may show that he had reached his limits as a thinker. At the Barbican debates, moreover, he may also have felt that he had achieved enough laurels as a debater to overcome his frustrations in most of his contests since his early demolition of Clapham. He was ready now for new worlds and new kinds of human interaction.

NOTES

1. See Hugh Barbour, "William Penn, Model of Protestant Liberalism," *Church History,* 48 (1979):169; and more generally Melvin B. Endy, Jr., *William Penn and Early Quakerism* (Princeton, 1973), pp. 274–82.

2. Thomas Vincent, *The Foundation of God Standeth* (1668), p. 5; John Faldo, *Quakerism No Christianity* (1675), "To Reader."

3. Most were in fact unbound octavo pamphlets printed in London by Giles Calvert or Thomas Simmonds. The most complete list is Joseph Smith, *A Descriptive Catalogue of Friends Books* (London, 1867), which calculates by printers' "sheets" (i.e., 1 sheet = 4 folio = 8 quarto = 16 octavo pages). Thus Smith counts 297 sheets published by Penn between *Sandy Foundation* and the end of 1675. For the yearly totals of Quaker writings (based on Donald Wing's *Short-Title Catalogue,* as well as Smith), see Hugh Barbour and Arthur Roberts, *Early Quaker Writings* (1973), app. by David Runyon.

4. By Thomas Aldam and five other Friends imprisoned in York Castle, 1652/53.

5. John Banks, *Journal* (1712), p. 10. Although Banks described a divine "lead-ing," his words echoed those of George Fox against Larkham in *The Great Mistery of the Great Whore* (1659).

6. Richard Baxter, *The Quakers' Catechism* (1655), was answered by [James Nayler], *An Answer to a Book Called the Quakers' Catechism* (1655). Even so, when Baxter's second blast ignored James Nayler's reply to his first, another Quaker, Edward Burrough, took him to task. Baxter's *One Sheet Against the Quakers* (1657) was picked up by Burrough, *Many Strong Reasons Confounded* (1657).

7. This tract by Thomas Underhill (listed as published in 1660), was replied to by Howgill, *Mouth of the Pit Stopped* (1659).

8. John Gilpin (see *The Quakers Shaken,* 1653) was already insane by the time he followed Quaker "leadings"; he was quoted eagerly by Francis Higginson, *Irre-ligion of the Northern Quakers* (1653); Thomas Weld et al., *The Perfect Pharisee* (1654); and Ralph Farmer, *The Great Mysteries of Godlinesse and Ungodlinesse* (1655).

9. For a transcript and facsimile, see George Fox, *Journal,* ed. Norman Penney (Cambridge, 1911), 1:68-70, 413. Fox and James Nayler, *Saul's Errand* (1653), seems to have been published independently of *A Brief Discovery of the Three-Fold Estate of Antichrist* (1653) by Thomas Aldam and his York fellow prisoners. In rebuttal, Francis Higginson, *Irreligion of the Northern Quakers* (1653), expanded the issue to many aspects of Quaker behavior. Each was often requoted.

10. James Nayler (*Answer to Quakers Catechism,* p. 6) rebuked Baxter for calling the Quakers' queries

> nothing but a bundle of filthy railing words [such] as "Serpent," "Liar," "De-ceiver," "Child of the Devil," "cursed Hypocrite," "dumb dog." I say every rational man may well marvel; that these words should be so hastily by thee called filthy railing words, . . . seeing there is not one of these words but by the Spirit of Jesus they have been used, to such . . . to whom they belong, . . . in Scripture.

11. See *PWP,* 1:337-52.

12. Clapham's *Guide to the True Religion* (1668) is ascribed to J[onathan] C[lapham], M. A. of T[rinity] C[ollege], C[ambridge].

13. The two traveling Friends had been given by Clapham a manuscript of six arguments in favor of singing the "Psalms of David" in worship. The Quakers answered in *David's Enemies Discovered* (1655), using the usual Quaker argument that every act of worship must be directly led by God's spirit and express the worship-per's actual "spiritual state." Clapham's *Short and Full Vindication of . . . Singing of Psalmes* (1656) came out that winter, lest "any boast that the reason why I did not answer them was because I could not" (ibid., "To the Reader"). Whitehead single-handedly replied with *Cain's Generation Discovered* (1656).

14. Here Clapham recanted his former willingness to separate church and state and came out in favor of a theocracy like John Cotton's. See Clapham, *A Full Discovery and Confutation of the . . . Quakers,* epistle, p. A3.

15. By Richard Hubberthorne (1657). Even Fox answered Clapham as part of a 410-page reply to all attackers of Quakerism. See his *The Great Mistery of the Great Whore* (1659).

16. Clapham seems to have hoped in this tract to repeat the latitudinarian themes and success of William Chillingworth's *Religion of Protestants a Safe Way to Salvation* (1638).

17. Clapham, *Guide to the True Religion,* p. A-5.

18. Even Hubberthorne (*Truth and Innocencie,* "To the Reader") had hit Cla-pham harder: "You that be called Independents, . . . cast men in prison for tythes;

. . . Wicked Seeds-men, to sow your lyes abroad, . . . say that Quakers deny prayers. Dost thou not think all the Nation will see thee and you to be lyars?"

19. Penn, *Guide Mistaken,* p. 5. Phillippe DuPlessis Mornay, Moyse Amyraut, and Hugo Grotius, although Calvinists, had each spoken for toleration, and Penn had studied for a year at the Saumur Academy Mornay had founded. Penn may be referring specifically to Moyses Amyraldus (= Amyraut), *A Treatise Concerning Religions* (Eng. ed. 1660), Grotius, *de veritate Religionis christianae* (Eng. trans. 1631), and DuPlessis-Mornay, *On the Truth of the Christian Religion* (Eng. trans. from 1576).

20. Penn, *Guide Mistaken,* p. 54.

21. Hubberthorne, *Truth and Innocencie* (see also idem, *A Collection of the Several Books* [1663], pt. 2, p. 29); Fox and Nayler, *Saul's Errand,* p. 12.

22. Penn, *Guide Mistaken,* p. 32. It is clear that Penn at this point had noticed the Socinians' uncompromising ethic and ignored their theology.

23. See *PWP,* 1:72-73; William Penn, *Sandy Foundation Shaken* (1668), preface; Thomas Vincent, *The Foundation of God Standeth Sure* (1668), chap. 2. Vincent had written good pastoral *Words of Advice,* and about the *Wells of Salvation,* both in 1668, and had stirred the ashes of the fire of London by tying them to *Christ's Certain Appearance* (1667; 13 editions by 1681).

24. Danson had reported three debates with them in *The Quakers Folly* (1659) and rebutted Whitehead's reply. These tracts were familiar finger exercises on the Quaker doctrines of the universality of God's light in men and the possibility of perfection, the inadequacy of justification by Christ, substitutionary atonement, and the secondary authority of Scriptures. George Whitehead, *The Voice of Wisdom,* and Thomas Danson, *The Quakers Wisdom* (both 1659) had each over 50 octavo pages. Samuel Fisher did not rehash the debate in writing, but he included Danson's scriptural views along with those of Baxter, Owen, and John Tombes in his 747 folio pages of biblical criticism, *Rusticus ad Academicos.*

25. George Whitehead, *The Seed of Israel's Redemption* (1659), although mainly about the superseded "types" of Old Testament priesthood and ritual, described in detail Jesus' human life, death, and the Resurrection, but said that the saints "share in the death and resurrection of Christ" by suffering the Cross to the self within (p. 46).

26. Here in *Truth Defending Quakers* (1659) Whitehead denied not only that the word Trinity was biblical but that it made any sense to talk of God as three separate persons, three "He's," (even though the Father, Christ, and the Spirit could each be called "He").

27. Vincent, *Foundation of God,* p.12.

28. See *PWP,* 1:73-81.

29. Penn and Whitehead evidently agreed upon this strategy before the Spitalfields debate (*Sandy Foundation,* p. B1). Although Vincent Buranelli, in "William Penn and the Socinians," *PMHB,* 83 (1959):369-81, suggests (p. 370) that Penn got the pattern of alternating Scripture and appeals to reason from the Socinians, I have not found this pattern in any of the writings of Biddle, Knowles, or Hedworth, or of the translated writings of Polish Socinians (Schlichting, Socinus, Crell, Przypkowski, Stegmann) that Penn had read. Biddle's *XXI Arguments drawn out of the Scripture, Wherein the Deity of the Holy Spirit is . . . refuted* (1653; reprint, 1691) states syllogisms first and uses prooftexts to support their premises. Rationalism was then in style at Court and throughout Europe, but Penn may owe his own pattern to Amyraut, who wrote "ut . . . Deus sit, quod natura recta ratio omnes homines pariter doceret" (*Dissert de Myst Trin.,* 1:35). As Danson's *Synopsis of Quakerism* (1668), p. 17, did not fail to remind Penn, Amyraut was orthodox on the Trinity. In his six-volume *La Morale Chretienne* (Saumur, 1652-60), Amyraut tried to separate natural morality from faith (ibid., 3:16).

30. See Barbour, "William Penn, Model of Liberalism," p. 169. At Spital-fields, the "Three Apostles argument" was first used by Whitehead, but he may have learned it from Penn who added Biddle's list of early Church Fathers and other items.

31. See *JFHS*, 46 (1954):54. The technical charge was printing without a license, but this was a law only enforced in special cases. In relation to dissent, England had had a change of heart and of government since the plague and the fire of London, and Sir Roger L'Estrange's powers under the 1662 Licensing Act were now less often enforced against printers.

32. Both books were out before 1668 (old style) ended in March.

33. Danson, *Synopsis of Quakerism,* also picked up Whitehead's earlier tracts and other Quaker heresies. Thus pp. 46ff. dealt with Whitehead's *Voice of Wisdom;* pp. 64ff. added an attack on Samuel Fisher; pp. 68ff. turned on Nayler; pp. 74ff. answered also Robert Turner and George Fox "the Younger" (the London theo-cratic Friend and not the Quaker pioneer).

34. "The Father is infinite, the Son infinite, the Holy Ghost infinite . . . and yet there are not three infinites but one infinite, and the reason is because these and all other essential attributes agree to the persons onely in regard of the Essence from whence they flow" (Vincent, *Foundation,* p. 45). The same argument is used in Danson, *Synopsis,* p. 10.

35. Vincent, *Foundation,* p. 28. The rarely enforced "Draconian Ordinance" of 1648 had made it a capital offense to deny the divinity of any of the three persons of the Trinity.

36. On the Atonement, indeed, both Penn and Whitehead at once used Stil-lingfleet's new book, *Six Sermons Concerning . . . the Sufferings of Christ* (1669). They supported thereby the Quaker doctrine that Christ's death was an act of God's mercy, not a penalty payment. "Most of *Socinus* his arguments," said Stillingfleet (ibid., p. 270), "are levell'd against an opinion, which . . . none need to think themselves obliged to . . . that Christ paid a proper and rigid satisfaction for the sins of men, considered under the notion of debts, and that he paid the very same, which we ought to have done, which in the sense of the Law is never call'd Satis-faction, but strict payment." Yet Stillingfleet did believe in satisfaction and atoning sacrifice as *central* for salvation, in a way Penn and Whitehead never did.

37. Whitehead, *Son of Perdition,* p. 8; Penn, *Guide Mistaken,* p. 28.

38. Whitehead, *The Divinity of Christ and Unity of the Three that bear Record in Heaven,* (1669) p. 38; pt. 2, p. 55; Penn, *Innocency,* p. 23.

39. George Whitehead, *Christ Ascended Above the Clouds* (1669), p. 14 against John Newman's *The Light Within* (1668).

40. *PWP,* 1:270-74.

41. The issue arose at Fox's Lancaster trial, and at the Massachusetts General Court which banished Quakers on pain of death. Isaac Penington (and Whitehead later) distinguished "between that which is called Christ and the bodily garment which he took. The one is flesh, the other Spirit. The body of flesh was but the veil." Isaac Penington, *An Examination of the Grounds or Causes which are said to Induce the Court of Boston, in New-England* (1660), in his *Works* (1761), 1:266; see also White-head, *Christ Ascended,* p. 18; idem, *Son of Perdition,* p. 8; Endy, *William Penn,* pp. 274-82.

42. Fox, *Great Mistery,* in idem, *Works,* 3:180. Like Penn and most Friends he also stressed that Jesus Christ had shared human sufferings, and we share his Cross in every act of self-denial.

43. Whitehead also went on to answer John Owen's *Brief Declaration . . . of the Doctrine of the Trinity,* taking on simultaneously all "the ridged *Presbyters,* that will count a man a *blasphemous Heretick, Socinian, Arian,* and what not, if he can't repeat

his Creed . . . in their invented School-terms" (Whitehead, *Divinity of Christ,* p. 10).

44. Penn, *Innocency,* p. 16.

45. Ibid., pp. 35-39. Since Fox was in the north of England and then in Ireland from Mar. until Aug. 1669, perhaps this appendix and the publication of *Innocency* came after Penn's release from the Tower in July 1669. Stillingfleet's report to the Privy Council would then be based on seeing the manuscript.

46. See William Penn, *A Key Opening* (1692), and his sermons as transcribed from the 1680s.

47. The first *No Cross* was proofread and amended after Penn left the Tower. In 1670 was published *The Great Case of Liberty of Conscience* as well as the actual report of the Penn-Mead trial, *The Peoples Ancient and Just Liberties,* and Penn's defense of it, *Truth Rescued.* The turn of the year also saw Penn's *Seasonable Caveat against Popery* written in Ireland, and a few months later *Een Basuyne Geblaesen,* his equally fiery prophecy against the Dutch. Much damning had gone over the water before Penn returned to theology in his *Serious Apology.*

48. See Buranelli, "William Penn and the Socinians," esp. pp. 372, 378.

49. Penn, *Innocency,* p. 13.

50. *The Spirit of the Quakers Tried;* and Penn's *Spirit of Truth Vindicated* (both 1672). These were followed the next year by Hedworth's *Controversie Ended* and Penn's *Winding-Sheet for Controversie Ended.*

51. Billingsgate (the language of the fishmarket) was their own term: see Whitehead, *Divinty of Christ,* p. 11; Hedworth, *Controversie Ended,* p. 5; Penn, *Winding-Sheet,* p. 8.

52. Penn, *Spirit of Truth,* p. 6.

53. Nominally, however, Hedworth's first tract was aimed at George Fox's careless scriptural quotations from memory in the *Great Mistery* 13 years before, focusing only toward the end on Fox's rejection of oaths and titles and his approval of women preachers, and claims for infallibility. Since Fox himself was at the moment unavailable in the American colonies, Penn cried foul, whereupon Hedworth pleaded ignorance. Penn, *Spirit of Truth,* p. 5; Hedworth, *Controversie Ended,* p. 4.

54. Edward Burrough, Isaac Penington, and Francis Howgill had each earlier tried to write Quaker theology systematically, but their theological works were their least remembered. See Edward Burrough, *A Declaration to All the World of our Faith,* (1657); Francis Howgill, *Some of the Mysteries of God's Kingdom,* (1658); Isaac Penington, *The Way of Life and Death* (1658).

55. The list was from Biddle.

56. In the much larger and rearranged second edition of 1682, Penn grouped many of his quotations from classical and modern European sources, no longer by topic but by nation and period.

57. Penn amassed 15 pages of commentaries and quoted versions in eight languages (plus others Latinized) on the key "Quaker verse," John 1:9: "this was the true Light, that enlightens every man, coming into the world." In *No Cross* and *Christian Quaker* most of Penn's Greek, Latin, and French sources were quoted second-hand, but in *Spirit of Truth,* he translates Erasmus's original Latin and perhaps Chrysostom's Greek (see p. 56) and quotes the others verbatim with comments. See also Herbert G. Wood, "William Penn's *Christian Quaker,*" in Howard H. Brinton, ed., *Children of Light* (1938), pp. 1-24, which I read only after reaching similar conclusions.

58. See Barbour, "William Penn: Model of Liberalism." Penn's own Latin copy of Crellius is in the Library Company of Philadelphia and his Biddle tracts and translations in English were sold from his estate in the nineteenth century.

59. Penn, *Winding Sheet*, p. 6.

60. [Hedworth], *Controversie Ended*, p. 4.

61. Muggleton said not only that God was forever solitary but that in descending for incarnation he had transformed his divine body (already human in form) into a physical one, leaving Elijah on his throne in heaven to "mind the store" while he was away on earth. See John Reeve and Lodowick Muggleton, *A Transcendent Spirituall Treatise* (1652), p. 31; and idem, *A General Epistle from the Holy Spirit* (1653), p. 2. For similarities to George Fox's doctrine of Jesus's "Spiritual body" on earth, see Endy, *William Penn,* p. 278. Muggleton had also picked up the Aristotelian ideas that a "chaos" of raw matter and water existed out of which God created the world, and that the human soul began and ended with the body (Reeve and Muggleton, *Transcendent Spirituall Treatise,* p. 62; idem, *A Divine Looking-Glass* [1656], chaps. 2, 6, 17 passim; and idem, *Joyful News from Heaven* [1658]).

62. Besides the above, Muggleton wrote *A Letter presented unto Alderman Fouke* (1653); *A Remonstrance from the Eternal God . . . unto the Parliament and . . . Lord General Cromwell* (1653); *A True Interpretation of the Eleventh Chapter of the Revelation of St. John* (1662). Muggleton and Reeve repeatedly had described the three experiences by which Reeve was called of God to be one of the "two witnesses" of Rev. 11.

63. Compare *Remonstrance from the Eternal God* with *Transcendent Spiritual Treatise,* p. 46.

64. Richard Farnworth wrote in 1662 the short *Truth Ascended* against the claim by the "Witnesses" to a divine commission, and Muggleton replied to this, and to letters by Farnworth and Edward Bourne, in *Neck of the Quakers Broken* (components are dated 1662; evidently the whole was published by 1667, despite doubts by Wing and the Dunns).

65. George Fox, *Something in Answer to Lodowick Muggletons Book, . . . The Quakers Neck Broken* (1667); Isaac Penington, *Observations on some Passages of Lodowick Muggleton* (1668); Lodowick Muggleton, *An Answer to Isaac Pennington, Esq.* (1669); and *A Looking-Glass for George Fox* (1668).

66. *PWP,* 1:87-88; *Micro.* 1:469.

67. Penn took most of his information from standard fourth-century church histories by Eusebius, Socrates, Scholasticus, Theophilus, and others; see Penn, *New Witnesses,* pp. 12, 16, 19.

68. Muggleton published a long *Answer to William Penn* in 1673, which mainly cursed him and repeated old revelations, and Penn apparently was too busy to reply.

69. See *PWP,* 1:215-19; *Micro.* 1:446.

70. John Bolton, *Judas his Treachery,* pp. 5, 19.

71. See Barbour and Roberts, *Early Quaker Writings,* pp. 225-30; Andrew Brink, "The Quietism of Isaac Penington" in *JFHS,* 51 (1965-67):30-53; Christopher Hill, *The Experience of Defeat* (New York, 1984), pp. 118-28, 138-42. Puritan forms of Calvinism emphasized inward submitting to God's inscrutable will and easily led to Antinomianism, like John Cotton's or Kierkegaard's. Here conscious self-affirmation was not the issue, as it became for Nietzsche and Dostoyevski. Thus Penington's "God beyond good and evil" led him to the Book of Job, not to libertinism.

72. John Bolton, *Judas his Thirty Pieces Not Received* [1667]; Robert Rich, *The Letter sent by Robert Rych, to William Bayly* (1669); and idem, *Second Letters from Barbadoes* (1669), responded to by John Bolton and George Fox, *Judas his Treachery Still continued* (1670). See Kenneth Carroll, *John Perrot, Early Quaker Schismatic* (London, 1971), pp. 106-7. Even Penington was for a while sympathetic to Perrot, keeping him ten days as a house guest.

73. Nathaniel Smith, *The Quakers Spiritual Court Proclaimed* [1668], pp. 11-12. Friends noted that the tract was dedicated to the Rt. Hon. George Lord Delamer of Cheshire, who helped pay for it, and carried a preface by a local priest, Randolph

Yarwood. Among the Quaker tracts in reply were John Bolton and W[illiam] D[ewsbury?], *Justification of the Righteous Judgment of God on Nathaniel Smith* (1669), and *The Innocent Assemblies and Good Order of the People of God* (1669), a series of Testimonies by individuals Smith had accused of mistreating him.

74. See *Micro.* 1:184. "I am . . . constrained to this exposal of my thoughts, least my being mute might give to[o] great a ground for a Conjecture." Penn was not thus far regarded as a "weighty Friend" or a spiritual counselor to other Quakers, though in addition to committee reports, personal letters to Friends, and a testimonial upon the death of Josiah Coale, he had published *A Letter of Love to the Young Convinced* (1669), whose caution against pride reflected wisdom Penn had learned in Vincent's theological ambush that sent him to the Tower and also the shadow of the impending second Conventicle Act. In 1673 he began writing epistles to the Quakers he had visited in Holland and North Germany.

75. See Lesley H. Higgins, "The Apostatized Apostle, John Pennyman," *Quaker History*, 69 (1980):102-18. A street ballad came out about the dancing at "the Quakers' Wedding." Yet the Pennymans were both solid citizens in their forties (it was her second marriage and his third, as Quaker mortality rates were high during the Conventicle Act).

76. *PWP,* 1:262-67.

77. Joseph Smith recorded 23 tracts in Pennyman's last 30 years, mostly directed at Quaker leaders, though he still regarded himself as a Friend.

78. [John Pennyman, Humphrey Woolrich, and Thomas Coveney], *Some Grounds and Reasons for not Putting off the Hat [Before] Magistrates* (1660).

79. Mucklow, *Spirit of the Hat,* p. 11.

80. Quoted in Penn's reply to Mucklow, 11 Oct. 1672, *PWP,* 1:249-59.

81. "If J.B. had wrong'ed thee, thou shouldst not have made so ill an use of it as to have aggravated it against the Body, but either have been satisfied in clearing thy Conscience to him, or have born it" (*PWP,* 1:257).

82. Ibid., 1:251-54.

83. *The Spirit of the Hat* also raised the cases of Mary Pennyman's brother, of John Osgood, and of James Claypoole against John Bolton, and charged that Fox let men kneel before him and covered up the adulteries of Quaker ministers and of a Quaker doctor (was this Smith?) to save "the Body" of Friends from public scandal and keep "Foxonian" unity.

84. Penn, *Spirit of Alexander,* pp. 6-7.

85. Mucklow's chief target, George Fox, was then in his longest imprisonment at Worcester, and Penn (who had had two more imprisonments of his own at Newgate) was working every legal angle to get him freed.

86. Penn, *Spirit of Alexander,* pp. 7-10, 13.

87. Mucklow, *Tyranny & Hypocrisie Detected* (1673), p. 14. This anger of Penn, when crossed, may help to explain why he was never made Yearly Meeting "clerk," for which his political risk-taking with Whigs and Jacobites is often blamed. When Penn replied again (*Judas and the Jews* [1673], p. 6.), he did not hesitate to quote Mucklow's even more telling summation: "How dangerous a thing it is, for a Man to engage himself publickly for the singular Party upon the Account of Religion is greatly manifest in the Leading *Quakers,* and especially in *W. Penn,* for whose Parts and Education one would expect more than ordinary candor and Ingenuity."

88. Penn, *Judas and the Jews,* p. 11.

89. Robert Barclay's *Anarchy of the Ranters* (1674) covered the same issues and made better justifications than Penn had done for Quaker discipline: it showed the shared nature of Quaker religious experience, the role of mutual confirmation, and the place of the experienced and sensitive "weighty Friend" in recognizing the true and common elements in individuals' "leadings."

90. See, for example, *PWP,* 1:328-33, 363-65, 377-79.

91. Penn's *Quakerism a New Nick-Name* stated Quaker teachings on the Light less fully than did *Spirit of Truth,* but went on to the divinity of Christ, his human body, and minor points. *The Invalidity of John Faldo's Vindication* rounded this out with thorough, clear statements of Friends' attitudes to Scripture, the church, preaching, the Sacraments, Justification, the human soul, and after-life; see also *PWP,* vol. 5, items 20A-B, 26.

92. Henry Hallywell, *The Sacred Method of Saving Humane Souls* (1677), p. 12.

93. See Stephen Angell, "Religious Toleration, Truth and Reason in the Thought of William Penn: a Study of *An Address to Protestants upon the Present Conjuncture* (1679)" (M.A. Thesis, Earlham School of Religion, 1982).

94. These themes Penn worked out more fully in the preface to *The Christian Quaker* (1674) and in the long introduction to George Fox's *Journal* (1694) which was soon published separately as *The Rise and Progress of the People Called Quakers;* see the essay by Caroline Robbins in this volume, and *PWP,* vol. 5, items 22A-B, 97, 98A-B.

95. Penn's *Reason against Railing* (1673) responded to Hicks's dialogues and attempted brief imaginary dialogues in reply. But mainly Penn ran through the same list of issues as before. At times he broke new ground: chap. 7 is probably the best statement in early Quaker literature on the idea of the *Seed,* the element within humans that can respond to the Light, and which, once the soil is broken within, can grow into the "new man" in the image of Christ. Penn's *Counterfeit Christian Detected* (1674) first refuted mistakes in Hicks's latest response, *The Quaker Condemned,* and then with a free hand again summarized Quaker doctrines; see also *PWP,* vol. 5, items 23, 28.

96. This whole cluster of tracts has been microfilmed by FLL, and is available from World Microfilm Services, London.

97. In *Grace Abounding* (Oxford, 1962), p. 39.

98. Endy, *William Penn;* see also Barbour, "William Penn, Model of Liberalism."

99. Three of these, the preface to George Fox's *Journal* (1694), *A Key Opening the Way* (1692), and *Primitive Christianity Revived* (1696), became favorites among Friends and were often reprinted (see *PWP,* vol. 5, items 94A-M, 104A-C). Part of their secret was to recapture for a later generation the ethical intensity and joy of early Friends. Like Penn's tracts in response to his friend George Keith, who had turned the title "Christian-Quaker" against him, these works clung closer to the experiences and phrases of Christian orthodoxy. The era of the Toleration Act persuaded Friends to show their respectability. Perhaps his struggles with James II and the unsaintly Pennsylvania colonists had taught Penn the depth of sin, and that all men need forgiveness.

RICHARD S. DUNN

3 ❧ Penny Wise and Pound Foolish:
Penn as a Businessman

One of the major paradoxes in William Penn's career is that he achieved remarkable entrepreneurial success when marketing his new colony in the early 1680s, yet the selling of Pennsylvania plunged him into financial distress and led to his eventual insolvency. Few salesmen in the seventeenth century could match William Penn. He persuaded the cynical and nearly bankrupt Charles II to grant him 45,000 square miles of prime American real estate; he persuaded about six hundred investors to buy shares in this new colony; and he persuaded about four thousand people to join him in emigrating to Pennsylvania. Penn's advertising campaign was the most effective English colonial recruitment drive since the Puritans had founded Massachusetts half a century before. Nearly fifty ships carried immigrants and cargo to Penn's colony in 1682–83; thanks to this massive initial investment, Pennsylvania was an instant success. But the proprietor personally did not profit. Although he sold nearly three-quarters of a million acres of Pennsylvania land, Penn incurred expenses in the early 1680s that far exceeded his income. By 1685 he was £4,000 in debt to his steward Philip Ford, and well on the road toward bankruptcy and debtor's prison. Why did Penn's marketing skill bring him such poor returns? Was he cheated by the colonists? Or by his steward Ford? Or was he personally to blame?

Inspection of Penn's business records suggests some answers to these questions. These business records have not received the attention they deserve. Although many key documents are lost or destroyed,[1] we do have considerable information about Penn's property holdings in England and Ireland in the 1660s and 1670s before he founded Pennsylvania, and an extensive set of Penn's accounts with his steward Ford in the 1670s.[2] Ford's accounts for the 1680s are missing, but there is plenty of data on Penn's land sales in his new colony.[3] Putting this information together, it becomes clear that Penn's business experience as a young man in the 1660s and 1670s heavily influenced his management of Pennsylvania in the 1680s. It is also apparent that the Quaker founder's combination of entrepreneurial resourcefulness, recklessness, and negligence in the 1680s were long-established traits. Since Philip Ford played a key role in the selling of Pennsylvania, it is particularly important to observe his prior dealings with Penn. Ford became Penn's steward in 1669 and handled most of his master's work for a dozen years before the founding of Pennsylvania.

As J. R. Jones reminds us in his contribution to this volume, in becoming a Quaker Penn put himself out of the upper class into which his father had worked his way. But he remained a landed gentleman. Penn told his wife that he would rather have a decent country estate of £100 a year than be a London merchant making £10,000 a year.[4] This was easy for him to say, because in actuality his decent country estate always vastly exceeded £100 a year.

When Admiral Penn died in 1670, he left his son 12,000 acres of Irish farm land in county Cork. Much of this was pasture land in the fertile coastal valleys east of Cork city.[5] Penn never wished to settle in Ireland; he did not maintain a house in county Cork, and he handled his estate as absentee property. But he took close personal interest in these Irish lands. Before he inherited the property he stayed for two extended periods in county Cork: for nearly two years in 1666–67 and again for a year in 1669-70. On the first visit he outmaneuvered his chief rival claimant, Colonel Peter Wallis, and secured his father's title to the Cork property from the Court of Claims in Dublin. On both visits he made leases with his father's twenty-four tenants, who rented on average 500 acres of Penn land apiece. Almost all of them were Englishmen, fairly recent arrivals in Cork, who probably sublet their land to Irish peasant farmers. They were by no means easy people for young Penn to deal with. Wallis and several others were disappointed claimants to his property. Most of them despised his Quakerism. All of them were trying to squeeze their own profit out of Irish agriculture. Knowing that his task would be formidable, Penn hired an impecunious Quaker schoolmaster named Philip Ford to come with him to Ireland in 1669 as his assistant. The daily entries in the pocket diary kept by Penn during this second Irish visit show how he toured his lands and inspected his fields, how he sent Ford on frequent errands, how he negotiated with one tenant after another, and haggled sometimes for weeks over rental terms.[6] In the end he secured total rents of about £1,100 a year, or a little less than 2s. an acre. This was a much lower yield than one could get from English farm rents, but it was not a low return for an Irish landlord.

When he returned to England, Penn appointed William Morris, a Quaker who lived in county Cork, as his rent collector.

In 1672 Penn married a Quaker heiress, Gulielma Springett, and through her acquired title to several thousand acres in Kent and Sussex. No inventory of these properties has survived, but we can tell that Gulielma held parcels of land in at least twelve parishes, mostly in the heavily forested Weald of Kent and Sussex. This Springett land was of relatively low value.[7] The identifiable tenants were non-Quaker small holders who paid low rents — about four shillings an acre, which was double Penn's Irish rent, but far below the going rate for good English farm land. Before her marriage, Gulielma had toured her properties periodically, accompanied by her Quaker tutor Thomas Ellwood.[8] After 1672 William Penn staged a similar tour every six months or sent Philip Ford.[9] There is no evidence that he farmed any of this Springett land directly, but as in Ireland he played the role of conscientious proprietor.

Penn's property in Ireland and England, if his tenants paid their rent as scheduled, should have provided him with an annual income of about £2,000. This was a small figure when set against the landed wealth of such great aristocrats as the earls of Salisbury or Rutland, who could each command an annual return of over £10,000 from their agricultural properties in the Restoration era.[10] But judged against any other standard, William Penn was a large landholder. In 1688 Gregory King surmised that the 16,000 English landed gentry — baronets, knights, esquires, and gentlemen — had an average income of only about £350.[11] However faulty King's estimate may be, modern studies of large landholders in a number of seventeenth-century English counties confirm that a man with Penn's assets was a very substantial squire, at the top end of the gentry scale.[12]

Penn certainly considered himself to be a substantial squire. During his first four years of marriage, he rented a large house in the village of Rickmansworth, northwest of London, and then in 1676 he bought a 350-acre Sussex estate: Warminghurst Place, which had a park, gardens, orchards, and a magnificent hilltop view of the surrounding Downs. The grandiose manor house, surmounted by a long row of tall chimneys, was described by Penn as being "very large, but ugly." There was room at Warminghurst Place for twenty or thirty residents, and the house was large enough so that up to two hundred Quakers regularly met there for worship.[13] These illegal Quaker meetings brought Penn to the attention of two neighboring Sussex J.P.s, who were members of parliament from leading county families. When they prosecuted him, Penn took it as a social insult, protesting that he possessed "as good a stake in the Country as either of them."[14] Penn's affluence was a sore point with his anti-Quaker adversaries. For example, Richard Baxter, the Presbyterian, branded Penn as a noxious hypocrite who pretended to adopt a plain and simple style "while hee swims himselfe in wealth."[15]

Throughout the 1670s Penn employed Philip Ford as his London business manager. Ford paid Penn's bills to tradesmen, paid wages to some of his servants, posted and received his letters, hired porters and messengers, and sent large quantities of household supplies to Rickmansworth in the early 1670s and to Warminghurst in the later 1670s. Whenever Penn visited London, Ford paid his master's coach hire or boat hire and other incidental expenses. He also frequently supplied Penn, his wife, and his mother with pocket money. To cover these expenditures, Ford received cash, bills of exchange, and goods on Penn's account, chiefly from his tenants in Ireland and England. Ford kept meticulously detailed accounts, itemizing each transaction to the halfpenny.[16] For example, he recorded the postage of every letter or bundle of letters, by which means we can discover that Penn sent or received about a thousand letters during a two-year span in 1672–74. Every few months, Ford balanced his books. When Penn was presented with an account, he signed it without making any inspection, for he trusted his Quaker steward completely. From Ford's viewpoint, this finicky and laborious service was well worth while, for he received an annual salary of £40 plus business expenses. More important, throughout the 1670s Ford generally had the continuous use of several hundred pounds in Penn's cash balance. This enabled him to open a dry goods shop in Bow Lane, where he sold ladies' hoods and scarfs, and to marry and raise a family.

Meticulous as Ford's accounts are, they cannot give us a complete picture of Penn's income and expenditures, since Ford handled only the London end of Penn's business. In the early 1670s, when Penn lived nearby at Rickmansworth, Ford did much more work for him than in the late 1670s, when he lived further away at Warminghurst. Ford's accounts suggest that Penn was having trouble collecting rent from his tenants; Ford received about £500 a year in Irish rents and another £500 a year in English rents—about half the total due to Penn. But it may be that Penn channeled only part of his rental income to Ford, just enough to balance his London accounts. What the Ford accounts unmistakably show is that Penn throughout the 1670s was spending considerably more than £2,000 a year and living well beyond his means. During the Rickmansworth years, in order to cover expenses, Penn sold some of his wife's property in Kent and contracted £2,000 in loans, on which he paid 6 percent interest. The move to Warminghurst in 1676 increased his problems. The new estate cost Penn £4,500. We have no figures on Penn's income from his Warminghurst farm land, nor do we know how much Penn's new large house cost to maintain. But we do know that he sold over a thousand acres of Gulielma's land in Sussex for £5,800 in order to pay for Warminghurst and its upkeep. Evidently this was not enough, for Penn also contracted a series of new loans in the late 1670s totaling £8,700 (in modern currency, over $1 million). As of 1680 he had paid back very little of this money. His interest charges alone amounted to more than £500 a year. Thus the evidence indicates that

Penn faced mounting financial pressures, and that he badly needed a fresh source of income when he decided to petition the king for land in America.

Why was Penn failing to make ends meet? There is no surviving evidence that Philip Ford was falsifying his accounts in the 1670s, or that he burdened his master with commissions and hidden charges. There *is* evidence that Penn's tenants were defaulting on their rent; in 1672 and again in 1676 Penn justified his sale of land in England by stating that he could not procure the rents due him in Ireland.[17] On the other hand, Penn himself was probably delinquent in his payment of quitrents to the crown; he owed £113 a year in quitrents on his Irish estate and seems to have paid little if any of this money.[18] And Penn was certainly somewhat extravagant in his living habits. He bought a grand house that he could not afford and maintained a staff of six or eight servants and clerks. He bought expensive household furnishings and clothes in London and kept a good table, judging by the barrels of oysters and scallops sent him by Ford, and the shipments of venison, salmon, sturgeon, partridges, and larks, and such fruits and vegetables as gooseberries, strawberries, cherries, asparagus, and artichokes, with brandy and whiskey to wash it all down.

But Penn was no voluptuary. Much of his income in the 1670s went to Quaker causes. He spent a great deal of time and money traveling around England, Ireland, Holland, and Germany on lengthy and frequent missionary journeys. He also spent a great deal of time and money lobbying for the Quakers at the royal court and at Parliament, or negotiating with local magistrates all over the country to relax their persecution. By 1680 he had written about fifty books, pamphlets, and broadsides in defense of Quakerism, which he published at his own expense.[19] Doubtless he helped to subsidize other Quaker publications and to support many activities of the movement for which we have no financial record.

Penn's solution to his problem was not to retreat, but to expand. In 1680 he asked Charles II to grant him proprietary title to a huge territory in America. He grounded this request on a claim that the crown owed his father a debt "of at least £11,000"—a debt that he calculated had increased with interest to £16,000. Penn's petition to the king has disappeared,[20] and the circumstances surrounding his father's claim are far from clear, but it appears that during the Dutch war of 1665–67 Admiral Penn incurred victualing expenses for which he was never reimbursed. The admiral was also probably owed part of his salary, and he may have loaned the government money during the war which was not repaid. William Penn had tried to recover this money, but with the Stop of the Exchequer in 1672 the government defaulted on its obligations to Admiral Penn.[21] If Charles II had repaid the admiral's money to his son in 1680, William Penn's financial problems would certainly have been solved. But Penn knew that he had a far better chance of obtaining American real estate than English specie. When the king granted him the Pennsylvania charter in March 1681, Penn announced the news to fellow Quakers in the following words: "perhaps, this way of Satisfaction has more of the hand of God in it, then a downright payment."[22] By obtaining the proprietorship to a Quaker colony, he could vastly expand his service to his coreligionists and to the general cause of religious and political liberty — and at the same time greatly enlarge his property holdings. As he observed to Secretary Blathwayt in the Colonial Office, Pennsylvania offered him a chance to serve God, to honor the king, and to make his own profit.[23]

It was, however, by no means obvious in 1681 that Penn would be able to promote his new colony effectively, let alone make a profit. Emigration from Britain to the American colonies had declined sharply in the 1670s. The young people who had flocked to New England, the Chesapeake, and the West Indies from the 1620s through the 1660s because of population pressure, high unemployment, and low wages at home were now staying in England because jobs were increasingly available for them there during the closing decades of the seventeenth century.[24] Even the Quakers, though they suffered extensively from imprisonment and harrassment in the 1670s and 1680s, had their doubts about William Penn's holy experiment. Many Friends believed that the true site of their holy experiment lay not in America but in England, where God's chosen people were being tested through persecution. In this view, Quakers such as Penn who escaped this suffering by emigrating to Pennsylvania were betraying their divine mission.

In meeting this challenge, Penn drew not only upon his experience as an English and Irish landlord but upon five years' experience as a manager of Quaker colonization in New Jersey. Since 1675 he had served as one of three trustees for Edward Byllynge, the bankrupt Quaker proprietor of West New Jersey. Byllynge's trustees decided to organize the colony into a joint stock venture; they divided West Jersey into one hundred shares, which they offered at £350 apiece to Quaker purchasers. Penn and his fellow trustees spread information about West Jersey to Quaker meetings all over Britain, and they recruited groups of purchasers and settlers from such diverse places as London, Dublin, Northamptonshire, and Yorkshire. Yet the results of this promotional effort were only moderately encouraging. In five years the trustees disposed of about fifty shares, but the great majority of these were in payment of Byllynge's debts. It appears that they actually sold only about ten shares by 1680.[25] If the trustees received as much as £3,500 for West Jersey shares, which is doubtful, they probably spent all of this money on administrative costs. Nor did the trustees persuade many people to move to New Jersey. Despite the attractively liberal terms offered to settlers in the West Jersey Concessions of 1676, fewer than a thousand people had emigrated to West Jersey by 1680. Most of those who came were small farmers and tradesmen who either rented modest tracts from the trustees at minimal quitrents or bought small pieces of land from the various shareholders. Few prospective settlers purchased land outright from the trustees because the price per share was too steep. Those shares that were marketed were often split among several purchasers; in this way an investor who could not afford to risk £350 could buy one-seventh of a share for £50. When William Penn reviewed his experience as a New Jersey trustee, it must have occurred to him that he would make very little money from Pennsylvania unless he altered the terms of purchase and settlement.

In the eighteen months between March 1681, when he received the charter, and August 1682, when he left for Pennsylvania, Penn plunged energetically into the business of promoting and selling his colony. He drew heavily upon his expertise as a Quaker apologist, and he used his widespread personal connections within the Quaker movement. To start with, he advertised Pennsylvania more widely than West New Jersey. After consulting with shipmasters, merchants, American colonists, and weighty Friends, he published a ten-page tract, *Some Account of the Province of Pennsylvania in America,* which he then reworked and issued in abridged form as a broadside entitled *A Brief Account of the Province of Pennsylvania.* By 1685 Penn had composed nine promotional pamphlets about his colony, most of which were published in several different editions or versions.[26] He wrote these tracts in a deliberately modest and understated style, quite different from his earlier Quaker apologetics which had been belligerent in tone and provocative in content. As he had done previously with his religious literature, Penn sent copies to the leading Quakers he knew in England, Ireland, Scotland, Wales, and Holland. Friends in Amsterdam and Rotterdam translated a number of these pieces for circulation among Dutch and German readers who knew about Penn from his travels in Holland and the Rhineland in 1671 and 1677.[27] In his promotional writings Penn made no mention of his Quakerism, nor of his plans for a holy experiment. He did not need to, for he was well identified as a Quaker. But Penn was clearly trying to reach a non-Quaker audience as well. His tracts consistently addressed practical questions: What is the location and climate of Pennsylvania? What crops can be grown there? How much does the land sell or rent for? How much must a family pay to travel across the Atlantic? What supplies should an emigrant bring? Without claiming that his colony was a natural paradise, Penn made it sound like an extremely inviting place. Readers who wanted more information were directed to see Philip Ford at his London shop in Bow Lane, or Penn's London printer Benjamin Clark and his London lawyer Thomas Rudyard nearby in Lombard Street.

One of Penn's most effective promotional devices was a large map of Pennsylvania, which was engraved for him by the cartographers John Thornton and John Seller in 1681 and sold to prospective colonists in at least four London shops.[28] According to this map, two broad rivers, the Delaware on the right edge of the map and the Susquehanna in the center

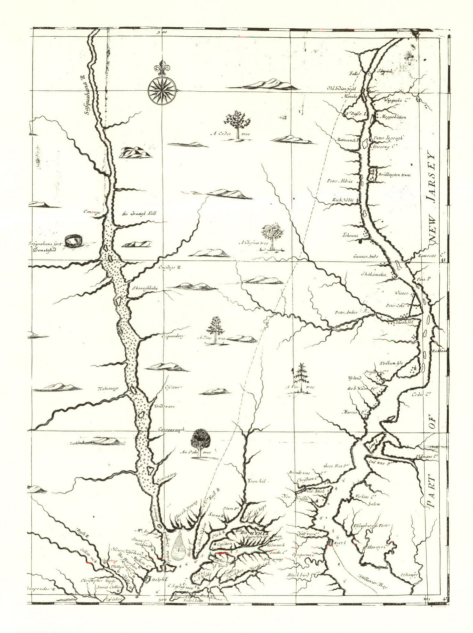

MAP 3.1 *A map of Some of the South and East Bounds of Pennsylvania in America, by John Thornton and John Seller. London, 1681. (Detail.)*

of the map, provided easy access to the colony. A string of homesteads along the west bank of the Delaware River and other settlements at the head of Chesapeake Bay demonstrated that an advanced party of colonists already lived in Pennsylvania, ready to entertain newcomers. There was no indication of Indian habitation, only an abandoned Indian fort high up the Susquehanna. There was a vast reservoir of unoccupied interior land — decorated on the map with small hills and with chestnut, walnut, cedar, and pine trees — which was available for new settlers. The accompanying description claimed that this map corrected the errors of previous cartographers. In fact, Thornton and Seller introduced a number of extremely serious inaccuracies. The two great rivers were drawn as though they flow nearly straight south, whereas in fact the mapped section of the Delaware flows southwest and the mapped section of the Susquehanna flows southeast. According to this map, the Susquehanna rather than the Delaware was the chief avenue into the colony. And most important, the southern boundary of Pennsylvania — stated in the royal charter as the fortieth degree of latitude — was drawn nearly fifty miles too far south. This error encouraged Penn to suppose that all of the planters who inhabited the northern quarter of Maryland on upper Chesapeake Bay lived within his jurisdiction. Acting on this assumption, he sent a letter to the planters of northern Maryland in September 1681, directing them to stop paying taxes to their proprietor, Lord Baltimore.[29] This letter naturally outraged Lord Baltimore and precipitated an acrimonious boundary dispute between the two proprietors which escalated into an outright border war by 1684. The Maryland boundary dispute consumed much of Penn's time and energy during his stay in America, 1682–84, and seriously diverted him from his central objectives in Pennsylvania.

In other respects, Penn's aggressiveness worked much better. He gave away small allotments of Pennsylvania land to George Fox and a few other leading Quaker ministers, which undoubtedly helped to win support for his project within Quaker circles. And he offered his land to prospective buyers at terms that were attractive and competitive with the land market elsewhere in America. Penn's price was 2s. 6d. an acre, scarcely more than the annual rental for his land in Ireland. He advertised his land in large blocs of 5,000 acres at £100 apiece; by offering so much for so little he hoped to persuade affluent investors to buy substantial tracts and send over servants and tenants to develop them. He soon discovered, however, that only a small number of his customers — about 11 percent — were willing to invest as much as £100 in Pennsylvania wilderness land. More than half of the First Purchasers in the 1680s paid him only £5 or £10 in order to buy small parcels of 250 or 500 acres. After consulting with some of his chief prospects, Penn announced in July 1681 that the purchasers of the first 500,000 acres would receive bonus lots in his capital city, the future Philadelphia.[30] These bonus city lots proved to be among Penn's most alluring baits. By April 1682 he had sold his first half million acres. Penn also recognized that he needed future income once the initial boom in Pennsylvania land sales ended, and so he required each purchaser to pay him a small annual quitrent of 1s. per 100 acres. Colonists unable or unwilling to buy land could rent it from the proprietor, again at a bargain rate, for a penny an acre.

Penn appointed land agents in Ireland, Scotland, Wales, Lancashire, Cheshire, Wiltshire, Bristol, and Amsterdam. He himself made several selling trips to the west of England and recruited investors in London, Sussex, Buckinghamshire, and the other home counties. His lawyers drew up the deeds of sale, and Philip Ford collected the money. In July 1681 Penn opened his land office. Philip Ford bought the first 5,000-acre share in the colony for £100.[31]

The net result of all this salesmanship was very substantial. Between July and October 1681, Penn sold 320,000 acres to 259 purchasers. By August 1682, when Penn himself sailed for America, he had sold another 300,000 acres to another 250 buyers. He sold some more land once he reached Pennsylvania, though not very much, and during his absence Ford in England sold close to 100,000 acres to another 69 buyers. Thanks to Ford's detailed accounts, we have variegated information about 589 persons who bought 715,000 acres of Pennsylvania land—equivalent to about half the acreage in Chester, Philadelphia, and Bucks counties — between July 1681 and March 1685.

Who were these First Purchasers? Richard T. Vann, in his contribution to this volume, argues that less than half of them were active Quakers in Britain, though the non-Quakers often joined the Friends once they reached Pennsylvania. Ford's records show that they tended to be town dwellers rather than country folk. In occupational terms, 8 percent of the First Purchasers identified themselves (like Penn) as gentlemen, another 6 percent were members of the professions, 14 percent were merchants or shopkeepers, a very large 48 percent were craftworkers, and only 23 percent were farmers — the chief occupation in the new colony. In geographical terms, as map 3.2 demonstrates, Penn recruited from all regions of the British Isles, Holland, France, Germany, and America. Nonetheless, 88 percent came from England, and 47 percent came from the cities of London and Bristol and the counties of Cheshire and Wiltshire. Penn drew almost no clients from the Puritan counties — Essex, Suffolk, Norfolk, Cambridgeshire, Lincolnshire — that had supplied the bulk of the emigrants to New England fifty years before. More surprisingly, he drew few purchasers from the north of England where Quakerism was especially strong. Ned Landsman shows in his essay in this volume that Scottish Quakers who emigrated in the 1680s preferred East New Jersey to Pennsylvania because other Scots were going there. Likewise, it appears that Quaker emigrants from the north of England were attracted to West Jersey, where

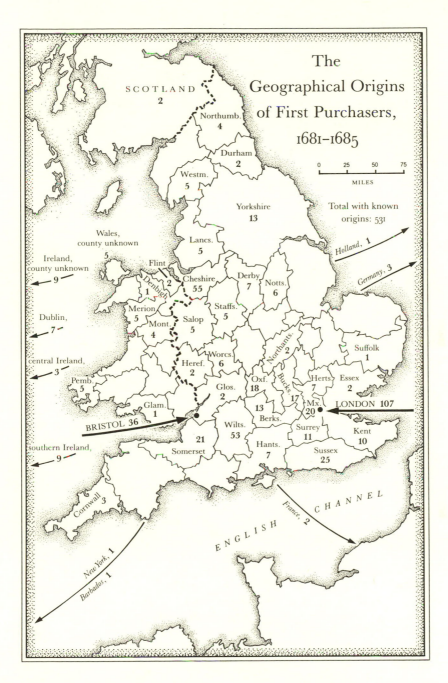

The
Geographical Origins
of First Purchasers,
1681–1685

0   25   50   75

MILES

Total with known
origins: 531

SCOTLAND
2

Northumb.
4

Durham
2

Westm.
5

Yorkshire
13

Wales,
county unknown
5

Lancs.
5

Flint
2

Denbigh
1

Cheshire
55

Derby
7

Notts.
6

Holland, 1

Germany, 3

Ireland,
county unknown
9

Merion
5

Mont.
4

Salop
5

Staffs.
5

Northants.
2

Suffolk
1

Dublin,
7

Worcs.
6

Heref.
2

Bucks.

Herts.
7

Essex
2

central Ireland,
3

Pemb.
5

Glos.
2

Oxf.
18

Berks.
13

17

Mx.
20

LONDON 107

BRISTOL 36

Glam.
1

Wilts.
53

Hants.
7

Surrey
11

Kent
10

southern Ireland,
9

Somerset
21

Sussex
25

Cornwall
3

France, 2

ENGLISH   CHANNEL

New York, 1

Barbados, 1

MAP 3.2

numerous settlers from Yorkshire were already established. In general, Penn recruited most effectively where he had personally spent much time and was well known (Ireland, for example). His local agents were also crucially important. Richard Vickris distributed promotional literature and collected money for him in Bristol; John Harris in Wiltshire; John Simcock and Thomas Brassey in Cheshire; Richard Davies, Lewis David, and Thomas Wynne in Wales.[32]

The First Purchasers who invested in Pennsylvania in 1681–85 supposed that the money they paid to Penn brought him great profit. Modern historians have tended to echo this belief. But in fact the Pennsylvania land sales actually increased Penn's financial problems. As we have seen, he sold his land cheap in order to attract as many buyers as possible. Even so, if the 589 recorded First Purchasers had all paid for their land in full, he would have received £14,300—a sum larger than the crown debt to his father. But some of these "purchasers" were relatives or friends who received their land as gifts. Others were Penn's creditors who settled for real estate in lieu of cash. Others made only partial payments, and at least 30 paid nothing and left their land conveyances in Philip Ford's hands. Penn actually received somewhat over £9,000 from his land sales of 1681–85 — a very considerable sum. But once he embarked on his colonial venture, he incurred heavy new expenses. Unfortunately, we have no account of these expenditures, but the cost of negotiating the charter, of advertising the colony, and of establishing an administrative staff was certainly sizable. We know that Philip Ford shipped goods valued at nearly £3,000 on six vessels bound for Pennsylvania in 1681–82 and charged these shipments to Penn's account. Part of this cargo was the proprietor's personal and household baggage, but most of it was clearly designed for sale in Pennsylvania — such items as 3,000 tobacco pipes, 600 pounds of shoes, 1,600 pairs of woolen hose, and 60 horse collars.[33] When Ford balanced his books, the cost of these supplies, combined with the other payments he had made for his master, greatly exceeded Penn's income from land sales in Pennsylvania.

On 6 July 1682, when Penn was getting ready to leave for Pennsylvania, Philip Ford presented him with an account for the period since October 1680. This document no longer survives, but it can be partly reconstructed. Ford credited Penn with £5,089 in Pennsylvania land sales and debited him with £1,201 in goods shipped to Pennsylvania. This account, which must have included much other English and Irish income as well as a great many English and Pennsylvania expenditures, closed with a balance of £521 in Penn's favor. If Penn supposed that he was now at last living within his income, he was quickly disillusioned. On 23 August 1682, when Penn had boarded the ship *Welcome* and was about to sail for America, Philip Ford visited him on his ship and presented him with a further account for the seven-week period from 6 July to 23 August. In this new account, Ford credited Penn with a further £1,604 in Pennsylvania land sales and debited him with massive colonizing expenses for which the details are lost; among the debits was £1,449 in goods shipped on the *Welcome*. This account closed with a balance of £2,851 in Ford's favor. Penn, preoccupied with his voyage, signed this account without inspecting it — his usual habit. He also signed two other instruments presented by Ford: a mortgage on 300,000 acres of Pennsylvania land, and a bond of £6,000 as security for his repayment of the debt to Ford.[34] At the time Penn does not appear to have been troubled by these transactions, for he no doubt assumed that his debt would be liquidated when Ford sold more land for him. On 25 August he granted Ford's wife and children 5,000 acres of Pennsylvania land; the following day he signed a power of attorney to Ford, authorizing his steward to handle his English affairs while he was in America.[35]

Years later, Penn came to believe that Ford had cheated him in 1682. He claimed that Ford had falsified his bookkeeping, caught him by surprise on the *Welcome* when he had no leisure to study the figures, and thus tricked him into signing over a lien on his colony. Ford may indeed have been guilty of sharp practice. When Penn studied the 1682 account more than twenty years later, he protested that Ford had billed him for £914 in goods which were shipped for other Pennsylvania investors.[36] But if we accept Penn's revised calculation, he still owed Ford nearly £2,000. As for the accusation that Ford caught him by surprise in August 1682, Penn appears to be the more guilty party here, for if Ford had not tracked him down he would have embarked for America without signing for the goods he had ordered Ford to load on the *Welcome*. Ford had reason for concern about Penn's debt in August 1682. He could figure that the boom in Pennsylvania land sales was ending. He might never see Penn again. He had no assurance of repayment. And he had lost the chief advantage of his stewardship, the cash balance in Penn's account which he had been able to draw upon for many years. Ford and his family now held 10,000 acres in Pennsylvania land grants, which was more American real estate than they could easily develop. His mortgage on 300,000 acres was not a mechanism for stealing the colony from Penn, but a device to encourage Penn's settlement of his accounts.

Once Penn had reached an accomodation with Ford, he departed for Pennsylvania to supervise his holy experiment. The years 1682–84 marked the zenith of his career. Penn's strong personal leadership provided much of the momentum for Pennsylvania's initial success. But the proprietor's two-year stay in America was a period of large expense and small income. Many years later, when reminiscing about this visit, he asserted: "I came in person and it Cost mee 10500 in the First 2: y^{rs}."[37] Penn may have been exaggerating, but he did spend heavily on trade goods in order to clear his title to the land along the Delaware River with the local Indians. He maintained a retinue of colony officials and household servants. He started to build a manor house at Pennsbury. Penn's records for almost all of these expenses have disappeared. How much money he made or lost on the hosiery and horse collars shipped over by Philip Ford we also cannot tell, but we do know that Penn bore the full cost of the colony government in 1682–84, because the Assembly levied no taxes. In April 1683, when the Assembly passed a liquor tax to help defray Penn's charges, the proprietor magnanimously (and unwisely) remitted the tax for a year. The following spring, when he tried to start collecting this liquor tax, the Philadelphia merchants protested that such a levy would ruin their business, and they persuaded Penn to accept £500 raised by voluntary subscription—which in fact he never received.[38] The First Purchasers who came over with Penn to stake out their land were quick to complain that their lots in the country and in Philadelphia were poorly sited and inadequately surveyed. They were also predictably reluctant to pay the proprietor any quitrents. Penn had pledged that he would not start collecting rents until 1684, but by November 1683 he was so pressed for cash to buy winter supplies that he sent a collector through his territory to try to gather the rents early.[39] However, even had the colonists paid what they owed him, Penn could only realize about £300 a year in quitrents. And he found few customers for new land purchases in 1682–84, since the acreage already patented satisfied the needs of the early settlers. By the summer of 1684, when the colonists learned that Penn was returning to England in order to protect his colony from Lord Baltimore, they saw him as less of a patriarch and more of a landlord. A group of Philadelphia inhabitants presented him in July 1684 with a "Remonstrance and Addresse" which complained bitterly that he was reneging on his promises, and encroaching on their privileges.[40]

If Penn had any lingering hope that he would make a quick profit from his colony, it was dashed when he returned to England late in 1684. He found that Philip Ford had received £8,000 on his account while he was in Pennsylvania, but much of this was English and Irish rent money, and only £2,300 was in Pennsylvania land sales. Meanwhile, Ford had charged Penn's account with nearly £10,000, so that by March 1685 Penn's stated debt had climbed to £4,293. As before, Penn endorsed this account without inspecting it. Only later did he discover that Ford had billed him for about £1,000 in compound interest on his debt and commissions on each transaction. The two men had now reached an impasse. Penn could not or would not pay Ford's claims, and Ford had no way short of a law suit or a public confrontation — which would have been highly distasteful in the Quaker community — of obtaining any satisfaction. Penn continued to employ Ford, though less than before. Between 1685 and 1699 the two men made a series of contractual agreements, in which Penn kept renewing his obligations to Ford on increasingly stringent terms. He first mortgaged, then leased, then sold Pennsylvania to Ford, although Ford never attempted to exercise any control over the colony.[41] Penn made periodic payments to his steward, but never enough to stop the debt from escalating steadily. By 1687 Ford claimed that Penn owed him £6,000. By 1696 he claimed £10,657. It was at this point that Penn deeded his entire colony to Ford as a form of collateral, and in 1697 he rented it back from him at an annual fee of £630 — which he did pay at least in part.[42] Penn never made a settlement with his steward: he treated his obligation to Ford more cavalierly and recklessly than Charles II had treated his obligation to Admiral Penn. Ford died in 1702, leaving a strong legal claim to the proprietorship of Pennsylvania, which he bequeathed to his widow and children. They in turn could reach no accomodation with Penn and sued him in the courts of Exchequer, Common Pleas, and Chancery to recover debts, damages, and Pennsylvania. In October 1707 a special verdict in Common Pleas awarded the Fords £2,908, which Penn refused to pay, chosing debtor's prison instead. When it appeared that he would also lose in Chancery, Penn finally settled with the Fords in 1708 by paying them £7,600 — a sum which he could only raise by borrowing from a circle of wealthy Quakers. Warminghurst had already been sold in 1707 to pay off other debts.[43]

Most commentators on this curious saga have concluded that Philip Ford was a knave and William Penn was a fool. In my view, the first of these judgments is unjust and the second is inadequate. Ford was certainly not a knave in the early 1680s. He was a principled man who suffered arrest and fines for refusing to do militia duty or pay tithes. He worked very hard for Penn, and for the success of Pennsylvania, and after mid-1682 he received no compensation for these labors. If he then began to doctor his accounts with excessive charges, they were paper charges, for Ford never collected his debt. As for Penn, he was by no means a total fool. He was a first-rate recruiter of colonists. He sold land on attractive and well-calculated terms. If he had charged a higher price per acre, he might have made more money, but he would not have lured so many colonists to Pennsylvania. Approximately half of the First Purchasers actually came over to Pennsylvania in the 1680s and took up land; their collective commitment assured the success of the colony. Had the First Purchasers paid Penn in full for the land they bought, paid him the quitrents they owed, and paid taxes to help defray his costs of the colony government, Penn would have had no crisis with Ford. But the Pennsylvania First Purchasers were like Penn's Irish and English tenants — they had a healthy prejudice against landlords, especially absentee landlords.

William Penn had his own country gentleman's prejudice against London merchants like Ford who grubbed around with columns of figures. Certainly Penn's greatest character defect, before and after the founding of Pennsylvania, was his inability to live within his means. He preached bourgeois thrift, but he practiced noblesse oblige. It is peculiarly ironic that in August 1682, as he was preparing to embark on the *Welcome* and just before he learned of his large debt to Ford, Penn composed a long letter full of

Polonius-like parting instructions to his wife Gulielma, who was staying behind with the children. "Cast up thy income," he advised her, "and see what it daily amounts to by wch thou may'st be sure to have it in thy sight and power to keep within compass, and I beseech thee to live low and sparingly, till my debts are paid."[44] He might have tried to follow some of this advice himself. One is reminded of another famous inmate of debtor's prison — Mr. Micawber — and his sage advice to David Copperfield: "Annual income twenty pounds, annual expenditure nineteen nineteen six, result happiness. Annual income twenty pounds, annual expenditure twenty pounds ought and six, result misery. The blossom is blighted, the leaf is withered, the God of day goes down upon the dreary scene, and—in short you are for ever floored. As I am."[45] Whereupon Mr. Micawber borrowed a shilling from David for porter, and cheered up.

NOTES

1. See the extensive inventory of Penn's missing business records, 1649-99, relating to property in England, Ireland, and New Jersey, in *PWP,* 1:563-69.

2. Penn's accounts with Ford for Apr. 1672-July 1674 and Apr. 1677-Mar. 1680 are printed in ibid., 1:577-645.

3. A list of 589 First Purchasers of Pennsylvania land, 1681-85, compiled from seven manuscript lists kept by Philip Ford and Penn's other agents, is printed in ibid., 2:630-57. This list corrects John E. Pomfret, "The First Purchasers of Pennsylvania, 1681-1700," *PMHB,* 80 (1956):137-63. Pomfret worked from later printed lists of the early purchasers, which are less reliable.

4. William Penn to Gulielma Penn, 4 Aug. 1682, *PWP,* 2:272.

5. See the discussion and list of Penn's lands and tenants in Ireland, 1669-70, in ibid., 1:570-73.

6. See Penn's Irish Journal, 1669-70, in ibid., 1:110-28.

7. See the abstracts of Springett property transactions, 1672-78, in ibid., 1:646-49. For background discussion on the Weald in the seventeenth century, see Thirsk, *Agrarian History,* 4:57-59; C. W. Chalkin, *Seventeenth Century Kent* (London, 1965), chaps. 1, 3-6.

8. G. G. Crump, ed., *The History of the Life of Thomas Ellwood* (New York, 1900), pp. 157-60, 162.

9. For example, Penn took Ford with him on a tour of Gulielma's property, 10-13 July 1672; he sent Ford alone on another tour, 25-29 Nov. 1672. See *PWP,* 1:583, 586, 591, 595.

10. Lawrence Stone, *Family and Fortune* (Oxford, 1973), pp. 155, 161, 206.

11. Peter Laslett, *The World We Have Lost* (New York, 1965), pp. 32-33.

12. H. J. Habakkuk, "English Landownership, 1680-1740," *Economic History Review,* 10 (1939-40):3; Alan Everitt, *The Community of Kent and the Great Rebellion, 1640-1660* (Leicester, 1966), p. 329; J. T. Cliffe, *The Yorkshire Gentry from the Reformation to the Civil War* (London, 1969), pp. 28-29; Gordon Batho, "Landlords in England," in Thirsk, *Agrarian History,* 4:290-301.

13. Penn's house was torn down shortly after he sold it in 1707, and the Warminghurst property is now held by the duke of Norfolk. The house and land is described in *PWP,* 1:648-49; in William Penn to Hannah Callowhill, 9 Feb. 1696 (*Micro.,* 7:108); and in Francis Hill's 1707 map of Warminghurst (*Micro.,* 13:359).

14. William Penn to the earl of Middlesex and Dorset, 17 Nov. 1677, in *PWP*, 1:515.

15. Richard Baxter to William Penn, 6 Oct. 1675, in ibid., 1:342.

16. Twelve accounts between Ford and Penn survive, starting immediately after Penn's marriage. Accounts nos. 1–6 cover the span from Apr. 1672 to July 1674. The next five accounts are missing. Accounts nos. 12–17 cover the span from Apr. 1677 to Mar. 1680; of these, account no. 12 is incomplete. The twelve accounts are printed in *PWP*, 1:577-645.

17. C 54/4342; C 54/4459, PRO, abstracted in *PWP*, 1:647–48.

18. *PWP*, 1:333-34, 571.

19. See the forthcoming *William Penn's Published Writings, 1660-1726: An Interpretive Bibliography*, by Edwin B. Bronner and David Fraser, which will be issued as vol. 5 of *PWP*.

20. Only a mutilated fragment of Penn's petition of c. May 1680 was found by searchers in the 1730s; it is printed in *PWP*, 2:32-33.

21. Elliptical references to Admiral Penn's victualling claim can be found in the Penn Papers, HSP, and in the State and Treasury Papers, PRO. I have searched without success in the Admiralty Papers, PRO, for further evidence of Admiral Penn's claim. See *PWP*, 2:30-31.

22. William Penn to Robert Turner et al., 12 Apr. 1681, ibid., 2:89.

23. William Penn to William Blathwayt and Francis Gwyn, 21 Nov. 1682, ibid., 2:311.

24. E. A. Wrigley and R. S. Schofield, *The Population History of England, 1541-1871: A Reconstruction* (London, 1981), pp. 161–62, 219, 402, 408.

25. The West New Jersey land sale records are lost. John E. Pomfret describes the pre-1680 English and Irish purchasers in his article, "The Proprietors of the Province of West New Jersey, 1674-1702," *PMHB*, 75 (1951):117–146; and in his book, *The Province of West New Jersey, 1609-1702* (Princeton, 1956), pp. 86-92. To colonists already living in New Jersey, shares were offered at the reduced price of £200. See *PWP*, 1:413.

26. *Some Account of the Province of Pennnsylvania* was published in Mar. or early Apr. 1681; *A Brief Account of the Province of Pennsylvania* was issued in at least three versions in 1681-82; *The Frame of Government of the Province of Pennsilvania* and *William Penn's last farewell* were both published in 1682; *A letter from William Penn . . . to the Committee of the Free Society of Traders* was issued in at least four printings in 1683; *Information and Direction to Such Persons as are inclined to . . . Pennsylvania* was issued in 1684; and *A Further Account of the Province of Pennsilvania* was issued in at least two printings in 1685. Two tracts stating Penn's case in the boundary dispute with Maryland were also issued in 1685.

27. Dutch translations include *Een kort Bericht Van de Provintie ofte Landschap Penn-sylvania* (Rotterdam, 1681); *Missive van William Penn* (Amsterdam, 1684); and *Tweede Relaas Van William Penn* (n.p., 1685). German translations include *Eine Nachricht wegen der Land-schaft Pennsilvania* (Amsterdam, 1681); and *Kurze Nachricht Von der Americanischen Landscaft Pennsilvania* (n.p., 1683).

28. *A Map of Some of the South and eastbounds of Pennsylvania in America, being partly Inhabited* (London: John Thornton and John Seller, [1681]). This map is described by Jeannette D. Black, *The Blathwayt Atlas, Vol. II, Commentary* (Providence, R.I., 1975), pp. 102-8. The copy of this map owned by the HSP was given by Penn to his non–Quaker economist friend Sir William Petty. The copy in the John Carter Brown Library was acquired for the Colonial Office by William Blathwayt.

29. William Penn to James Frisby et al., 16 Sept. 1681, *PWP*, 2:111-14.

30. Penn's "Conditions or Concessions" to the First Purchasers, 11 July 1681, is printed in ibid., 2:96-102.

31. Land sale to Philip Ford, 14 July 1681, ibid., 2:102.

32. For fuller discussion of the First Purchasers, see Gary B. Nash, *Quakers and Politics: Pennsylvania, 1681-1726* (Princeton, 1968), chap. 1, and Pomfret, "First Purchasers of Pennsylvania," pp. 137-63.

33. The invoices for Ford's shipments, found in the London port books, are printed in Marion Balderston, "William Penn's Twenty-Three Ships," *Pennsylvania Genealogical Magazine*, 23 (1963):27-67; see also William Penn to the Lord Keeper of the Great Seal, 23 Feb. 1705, Penn MSS, Ford versus Penn, HSP.

34. The mortgage and bond are printed in *PWP*, 2:291-93.

35. The power of attorney is printed in ibid., 2:293-95.

36. For Penn's retrospective comments (some of which are patently inaccurate) on Ford's accounts of 6 July and 23 Aug. 1682, see his statement to the Lord Keeper, 23 Feb. 1705, Penn Papers, Ford versus Penn, HSP.

37. William Penn to Charlwood Lawton, 2 July 1701, *Micro.* 9:309.

38. For the abortive liquor tax, see *PWP*, 2:411-12, 558-59.

39. William Penn to his tenants, 9 Nov. 1683, ibid., 2:500-501.

40. Ibid., 2:569-78; Nash, *Quakers and Politics,* chap. 2.

41. Seventeen of the Penn-Ford contractual agreements for 1685-99 will be abstracted and printed in *PWP*, vol. 3.

42. William Penn to the Pennsylvania Commissioners of Propriety, 23 May 1698, *Micro.* 7:677.

43. For details on the Ford debt, 1685-1702, see the rival statements by Penn and the Fords (both frequently erroneous) in Penn MSS, Ford versus Penn, legal papers, 1682-1708, HSP. The Ford-Penn case is summarized in Catherine Owens Peare, *William Penn* (Philadelphia, 1957), pp. 388-404, and will be documented much more fully in *PWP*, vol. 4.

44. William Penn to Gulielma Penn, 4 Aug. 1682, *PWP*, 2:270.

45. Charles Dickens, *David Copperfield*, ed. Nina Burgis (Oxford, 1981), pp. 142, 150.

J. R. JONES

4 ❧ A Representative of the Alternative Society of Restoration England?

The title of this essay requires explanation, since it may seem to be gimmicky or trendy, more relevant to the history of the 1960s than the 1660s. It is designed to draw attention to the crucial point about William Penn's public career — that by becoming and remaining an active Quaker he excluded himself from the governing class, into which his father had methodically and purposefully worked his way. The movement which Penn joined was legally restricted and persecuted; ministers and magistrates regarded the Quakers as the most radical and dangerous of all dissenting sects. Yet William Penn achieved a unique prominence, exerting considerable (if intermittent) influence. It is the purpose of this essay to examine some of the reasons for his success as an advocate, acting not just for the Quakers but for the wider cause of religious toleration, and to explain the background to his career as policy adviser to James II.

Penn's conversion to unfashionable Quakerism isolated him in two senses. Very few lords, gentlemen, lawyers, and politicians who had supported the parliamentarian cause refused to conform after 1662 to the restored Church of England, and only a handful of the younger generation of the upper class emulated him by subsequently defecting.[1] This social decapitation accentuated tendencies in the dissenting churches to parochialism and introspection. Penn provoked suspicion among his fellow Quakers by his refusal to retreat to the self-contained and retiring pattern of life.[2]

Most dissenters became understandably preoccupied with personal and local struggles to endure persecution and survive savage if intermittent repression. Clerical leaders and spokesmen, like Richard Baxter and Edmund Calamy, continued to testify but failed to develop or adapt themselves to changing circumstances. Their theological and polemical writings and sermons narrowed in their appeal and became stale by sheer repetition, whereas Penn's breadth of vision and imaginative liveliness constantly attracted attention. He was one of the few dissenters who displayed an ability to generalize issues, to develop new and original concepts, and to communicate these in terms that were intelligible to a general audience that did not share the particular experience, principles, and concerns of the separatist dissenters.

Penn's ability to conceptualize, to concern himself with the general as well as the particular, together with sincerity and integrity, also distinguished him from most of the other political intermediaries who operated in Restoration politics. It is a major theme of this essay that an understanding of Penn's public career, and of his success and influence, depends on locating him as a leading example of this type of political intermediary and confidential adviser. Usually such men seem to belong to the fringe of politics. Their activities when dispassionately analyzed rarely live up to contemporary myths, or are essentially disreputable. But political intermediaries like Penn, Sir John Baber, Edward Petre, Robert Brent, Edward Coleman, and Sir Thomas Armstrong played a crucial, if by definition obscure, role in Restoration English politics.[3] Many intermediaries dealt only in the small change of patronage — soliciting and selling favors, appointments, and pardons. But some took astute advantage of the opportunities afforded them by the constant uncertainties and shifting balances of power and influence, and the realignments of individuals, groups, and factions, that characterized the reigns of Charles II and James II.

Charles himself contributed largely and deliberately to these political uncertainties. As a matter of policy he consistently maintained clandestine contacts with private individuals outside the court and the administration. At times of crisis especially he engaged in secret negotiations with opposition factions and politicians. Through intermediaries, who in seventeenth-century terminology lacked a "character," and so could be disowned or sacrificed without compunction or difficulty, he actively discussed alternative lines of policy to those that had been enacted by Parliament and were being enforced by judges and ministers. The characteristic informality of his court helped Charles to conceal his intentions, to deceive friends and servants as well as opponents, and to undertake sudden and unexpected switches of policy. Charles prized himself on his skill in dissimulation, but his deviousness and agility were attributes which he had to develop and practice in order to defend the rights of the crown, and especially to defeat the Whig campaign to oust James from the succession by passing an exclusion bill.

Even at times of apparent quiet and stability Charles had no option but to make use of unorthodox methods, including unofficial agents. The authority of the executive had been circumscribed by Parliament's refusal in 1660–62 even to contemplate restoring the prerogative courts abolished by statute in 1641–42—the Star Chamber, High Commission, and Council of the North.[4] This left the king and his ministers with very limited institutional means of supervising, directing, and controlling subordinate administrative entities, and particularly the commission of the peace which governed the counties. They also lacked independent and disinterested sources of information about events and developments in the localities.[5]

Although far less devious an opportunist than Charles, James had equal need for unofficial contacts and independent informants who were not part of the machinery of local government. His conversion to Catholicism erected a barrier of distrust between himself and most of his subjects. Every move and statement was open to misrepresentation. Knowing that he could not rely on Charles's assurances that his rights of succession would be preserved at all cost, James had to organize his own network of contacts, intermediaries, and informers.[6] He began to use William Penn in 1673, the year when the Test Act forced him to resign his offices. Similarly after Clarendon's fall in 1667 all leading ministers, knowing that under severe pressure they would be abandoned by Charles, insured themselves by establishing links through agents and intermediaries with opposition leaders and factions, foreign states, and prominent individuals at court, in London, and the provinces. Parliament had to be managed. Political activity took place then on two levels. Below the formal and official transaction of affairs a secret and extremely complex political world operated, on very different principles, using a variety of approaches and techniques. Not surprisingly this political underworld overlapped with the criminal segment of society; as an upright and dedicated champion of religious liberty Penn had to work in the same dark area as spies, perjurers, conspirators, and confidence tricksters —several of whom ended on the gallows.

By contemporary standards Penn was himself a most dangerous criminal. Those intermediaries who spoke for the dissenters (and also for the Catholics) operated outside the law; they and those whose cause they pleaded were law-breakers. Magistrates and even more the vigilant bishops led by Gilbert Sheldon watched their efforts with fear, suspicion, and loathing. The bishops, in fact, consistently tried to undermine the dissenters' attempts to influence Charles and James. When Penn began to work as an intermediary in 1670–71, he was following the example of Thomas Manton and Sir John Baber who acted for the Presbyterians. His own periods of closest association with James (1673–76, 1685–88) coincided with the times

at which three conspicuously energetic and overambitious Catholic intermediaries also served James; Edward Coleman, executed for treason in
1678; Robert Brent, the organizer of the campaign to pack Parliament in
1687–88; and Father Edward Petre, the universally hated bogeyman of
1688.[7]

Penn stands out as the exceptionally successful practitioner who achieved
greater influence than any other intermediary in Restoration England. His
principled refusal to conceal his activities provides one main reason. He
proclaimed his mission openly and frankly, saying that he took it for his
"calling and station" to work for his persecuted coreligionists.[8] He behaved
temperately, without obsequiousness, but he refrained from provocative
language. He did not infringe Quaker egalitarian principles, but his social
tact and sense of what was appropriate enabled Penn to use the superior
social standing achieved by his father, and an exceptionally wide circle of
friendships and connections. Many of these were with such prominent men
at court as Sir William Coventry, the second earl of Sunderland, Laurence
Hyde, and Sir William Petty, who would not have responded to brusque
or doctrinaire approaches.
     Penn valued his connection with James above all others. In the years
after 1671 he used James to influence Charles, with whom Penn had friendly
but intermittent and generally inconclusive meetings. These usually produced royal promises, and often pardons for individual Quakers, but Charles
could never be relied upon to maintain a policy, or to carry out policy
changes to which he momentarily agreed.[9] Allowing Penn frequent access
was only a part of his opportunistic maneuvering, which had as its conscious purpose the manufacture of political uncertainty by generating speculation about his own intentions. By seeing Penn and other intermediaries
Charles made his avowedly pro-Anglican ministers (Clarendon and Danby
especially) and the bishops realize that they did not have a monopoly in
tendering advice. James by contrast prided himself on constancy and plain
speaking. He never tried consciously to deceive friends or opponents but
openly expressed his feelings and stated his real intentions. Another private
virtue which worked out to his public disadvantage, in the fluid situations
and cynical climate of his time, was his refusal to believe evil of others, or
to sacrifice servants, principles, and policies for expediency. He relied on
promises and undertakings given him.[10]
     These attributes insured personal friendship and long-term political
association once Penn convinced James of his sincerity and trustworthiness.
The two men had in common, as the crucial development in their lives,
conversion from the established church to faiths that were intensely unpopular and subject to broad legal restraints. Neither man ever contemplated
an expedient return to the Church of England; the desire to establish toleration provided the basis of their working relationship, before and after
James's accession in 1685. However, in the 1670s Penn worked discrimi-

natingly to engage other influential courtiers and politicians. At first he like other dissenters placed his hopes on the duke of Buckingham, who seemed in 1668 likely to become chief minister in place of Clarendon. Buckingham, always something of a dilettante, relied heavily on an entourage of assistants and advisers drawn from a wide political and social spectrum —courtiers, royal mistresses, bureaucrats, peers and MPs committed to the "Country" opposition, scientists, latitudinarian and dissenting clergy, radicals, and former republicans.[11] Buckingham never became chief minister, but as a member of the Cabal ministry he contributed to Charles's public switch to a policy of toleration in the Declaration of Indulgence (1672). After the Cabal broke up and the Declaration had to be withdrawn (1673), Penn maintained his contacts with Buckingham as well as James. This led Penn into closer association with the Country opposition, in which Buckingham took a leading role, and also his father's old collaborator and James's first mentor, Sir William Coventry. At first in seeking toleration James also drifted into association with the Country opposition, but from 1676 he reconciled himself with the Court and Lord Treasurer Danby, despite the latter's enforcement of ostentatiously Anglican policies.[12] However, this did not entail a break with Penn, who maintained contact with some important if still junior Court politicians—including his old friend from their brief time at Oxford University, the earl of Sunderland, and Laurence Hyde, later earl of Rochester and James's lord treasurer.

During Danby's tenure of office (1673–79) Penn could occasionally intervene on behalf of individuals but he could not influence policy. The "standing" Cavalier Parliament, elected originally in 1661, contained a substantial and intransigent Anglican majority; progress toward religious toleration required its dissolution. When this came, in January 1679, it was as a result of the hysterical alarm and suspicion provoked by the so-called Popish Plot. In the ensuing crisis the earl of Shaftesbury mobilized popular support by deliberately fanning the flames of religious intolerance in his Whig campaign to force through a bill excluding James from the succession. Given his personal links with James, and his sincere hatred of religious intolerance in all its forms, it is not surprising that Penn, despite his associations with the Country opposition, never became a Whig adherent of exclusion.

Penn was one of the very few Englishmen of his generation who escaped becoming trapped in a rigid, unchanging, and corrosive antipapist ideology. Of course he rejected Catholic theology, ritual, and especially its sacerdotalism. In 1670 he published *A Seasonable Caveat against Popery,* which, by modern standards, contains much scurrilous material. But by comparison with contemporary antipapist polemics it is restrained and moderate.[13] Penn consistently differed from virtually all Country opposition politicians in that he did not predicate a direct connection between Catholicism and absolutism. This enabled him to include Catholics in his proposed toleration and made him immune to the propaganda case developed by Shaftesbury and the first Whigs to justify the exclusion bill. Paradoxically it was what historians have described as a central Whig concept, that of "interest" as the factor governing men's behavior, which prevented Penn from becoming a Whig exclusionist, and sharing in the Whig defeat of 1681. He dismissed the Catholics as constituting such an inconsiderable interest (1:270 of the population) that they could never hope to destroy the Protestant religion or the constitution.[14]

Although he argued at length (and somewhat casuistically) that it was not in the "true interest" of the Church of England to continue persecution, Penn believed that the politically minded and worldly Anglican bishops calculated otherwise and would continue to do so. Whereas almost all other opposition politicians thought that the threat to religion, liberties, and properties came from the papists and absolutists, personified in James, Penn contended in 1679 – 81 (and again in 1686 – 88) that the real danger came from the bishops, and such political allies as Danby, who would never accept toleration because they wished to use the dissenters as a pretext for their attempts to monopolize office, authority, and power. Penn directed his biting anticlericalism against the Anglican bishops and their actual current behavior not, as did almost everyone else, against apprehended or potential threats from the Pope, Louis XIV, the Jesuits, and the native Catholics.[15] This divergence stemmed from his own experiences. Quakers, almost uniquely among dissenters, had never compromised or become even temporarily quiescent during periods of persecution. Consequently Quakers had often suffered prolonged imprisonment in vile conditions, distraint of their property, and disruption of family and business life. Interestingly, however, Penn's profound distrust of the Anglican hierarchy and his comparative indifference on the subject of popery were shared by another celebrated victim of Anglican intolerance. As the names John Bunyan gave to the characters personifying irreligion and persecution in *Pilgrim's Progress* reveal, he also believed that the Anglican clergy and magistrates were the enemies of religion.[16] He described how Christian safely passed a cave inhabited by the giant Popery, which had formerly been shared with Pagan, who was now dead. They had feasted on pilgrims whose bones, ashes, and bloodstains covered the entrance. But now Popery afforded no danger:

> though he be yet alive, he is by reason of age, and also of the many shrewd brushes that he met with in his younger days, grown so crazy and stiff in his joints, that he can now do little more than sit in his cave's mouth, grinning at pilgrims as they go by, and biting his nails because he cannot come at them.[17]

Ironically, at the moment when *Pilgrim's Progress* first appeared for sale, the informer Titus Oates had just arrived in London to launch his fabricated "discoveries" of the Popish Plot, which convinced virtually everyone and certainly almost all dissenters of the need for emergency action. By ruthless exploitation of the plot, and dynamic leadership, Shaftesbury emerged as leader of the first organized party, the Whigs, and the dismissal of Danby with the dissolution of Parliament transformed the political scene. Penn for a few months emerged as an important but unsuccessful activist, working with old associates from the Country opposition. He lacked the agility and unscrupulousness to succeed in the rough and tumble of electoral competition in 1679, a year with two general elections. Characteristically he acted as electoral agent to an eccentric candidate, Algernon Sidney, an elderly republican who was out of the mainstream, having recently returned after seventeen years of voluntary exile. Penn ludicrously mismanaged attempts to get him elected to Parliament for two winnable constituencies, Guildford and Bramber.[18] But he made a major contribution as a pamphleteer. His *England's Great Interest in the Choice of this new Parliament,* published before the autumn elections of 1679, is written with an economy rare at the time.[19] Its main theme recurs throughout Penn's career — the need for the individual (whether M.P., voter, juryman, or faithful Christian) to exercise and persist in his independent judgment, and to consider the public interest before his own private concerns. The advice it contains can be represented as a translation into political and electoral terms of the qualities that enabled Quakers to endure decades of persecution; Penn urged his readers to speak out against evil and corruption (in this context pensioners of Danby and the court), to resist flattery and favors, to place adherence to principle before the customary obligations of community and neighborliness. He advocated electing bold men, able to resist pressure. Poor men, the ambitious, "prodigal and voluptuous persons," should be shunned. Penn encapsulated characteristic social as well as political values when he recommended voters to have

> an eye on men of industry and improvement. For those that are ingenious and laborious to propagate the growth of the country will be very tender of weakening or impoverishing it. You may trust such.[20]

The effectiveness of this Whiggish-sounding pamphlet can be established by noting the repetition of many of its arguments in later pamphlets, especially those published before the 1681 elections. However, an analysis of Penn's political writings during the exclusion crisis reveals very significant divergences from the style, arguments, and stated objectives of the mass of Whig polemics. Penn avoided personalities; he abstained from character assassination. Remarkably he did not mention James by name and must have been literally the only political writer not to do so. Penn devoted much more attention to the past malpractices of the court under Danby, with comparatively little beyond some very general references to the Popish Plot. He had a purpose in diverging from the main Whig lines of argument. Whig propaganda aimed at mobilizing support for exclusion, at overcoming doubts about its legitimacy and practicability. As always, Penn kept religious toleration as his primary objective. But he now expanded his arguments into a much wider case, in which religious liberty was portrayed as an indispensable element in a new settlement that would bring about constitutional security, social harmony, economic development, and political stability. Implicitly Penn was putting forward a complete and coherent alternative to the Whig panacea of exclusion; his arguments were presented in *One Project for the Good of England: that is, Our Civil Union is our Civil Safety*, published in 1679.[21]

Penn's deployment of positive and general arguments contrasted with the negative character of orthodox Whig polemics, and the special pleading of most of his fellow dissenters. Whig journalists and politicans trapped themselves in a corner by insisting that an exclusion bill alone could give the nation security. Only when it passed could other desirable reforms be taken up; in the Whig view it was dangerous to propose or try to pass them earlier, as they might weaken the case for exclusion. Shaftesbury needed disaffected dissenters for his campaign; contented by any measure of toleration they might lapse into inactivity. Penn also faced up to formidable practical objections against establishing religious toleration. Obviously dissenters would benefit, but others feared that toleration would have further divisive effects, both socially and politically, or even plunge the nation into anarchy and moral confusion. Later, when repeating his arguments in 1686 –88, Penn set out to combat objections that toleration must necessarily lead to a strengthening of royal authority, including an expanded army, in order to enforce order in a nation divided permanently into competing religious sects.

Penn looked forward with confidence in *One Project* to a more united and politically stable nation. No longer suspect as separatists, the dissenters would be united with all their fellow subjects on the basis of their common civil interest, an argument that after 1685 he explicitly developed to include Catholics also.[22] Arguing that religious unity was now and forever an unattainable ideal, Penn substituted what he admitted was a lower, but still entirely valid, principle — "civil interest." Catholics must therefore disavow papal claims to exercise authority in England, but the main and most important prerequisite of civil union was the explicit abandonment by the Anglican hierarchy of all attempts to enforce religious unity and uniformity by coercive means. Penn argued that experience had shown the futility of all such attempts, and that they had actually created unnecessary disaffection. Mixed with these claims was an element of calculation. Whereas the Whig demands would have significantly weakened royal powers and authority (which explains Charles's unexpectedly obstinate resistance to them), Penn's proposal for toleration would weaken the church, not the crown. Consequently it could be revived, with minor modifications, when James clashed with the Tories and Anglicans at the end of 1685, and religious toleration again became a practical possibility.

Penn did not continue to be politically active after the end of 1679. As the Whig party systematically intensified pressure on Charles to abandon James, so Penn faded out of the political scene. This disassociation from the Whigs was of absolutely crucial importance. Otherwise he would not have received his charter for Pennsylvania, and certainly not as early as March 1681 on the eve of the decisive defeat of the Whigs through the dissolution of the week-old Parliament held at Oxford.[23] Penn's success in obtaining the charter stood in sharp contrast to the official treatment of all other dissenters (including Quakers) in the years that followed. Dissenters suffered for their association with the Whigs, but Penn found himself powerless to intervene on their behalf. Charles owed his victory over the Whigs to the support given him by the original Tories, and the bishops and parochial clergy formed the heart and soul of the Tory party. It would be politically impossible for Charles to prevent clergy, grand juries, and magistrates from renewing exceptionally severe enforcement of the penal laws. Nor could Penn count on James, although he maintained contact. The Anglican clergy unanimously rallied to defend James and defeat exclusion, despite their earlier misgivings at his conversion. Largely through the agency of Francis Turner, the Anglican bishops concluded a close alliance with James during Charles's last years.[24] Consequently Penn found that he could achieve nothing in England; only by going to Pennsylvania could he serve the cause of religious liberty.[25] Even when he returned in October 1684 he discovered almost entirely unfavorable conditions and could do no more than re-establish personal contacts with James.[26] The latter became even more dependent on Tory and Anglican assistance in the first months of his reign, in the suppression of Monmouth's rebellion. Although the west-country Quakers wisely remained neutral, the local dissenters flocked into the rebel army, confirming the popular belief that dissent and rebellion were connected, and provoking another period of severe religious persecution.

There followed another of the "revolutions" characteristic of the Restoration period, a sudden major reversal of political alignment and attitudes. In November the Tory majority in the "loyal" parliament offended James by rejecting his strongly expressed demands (which included civil rights as well as toleration for Catholics). His attempts to pressurize individual peers, M.P.s, and office-holders into compliance rapidly proved counterproductive. This rift with the Tories enabled Penn to re-establish himself in the royal confidence. First he obtained the release of all Quaker prisoners, and orders for the cessation of prosecutions against his coreligionists.[27] Then he began to work for the extension of toleration to all dissenters and in a permanent form. This involved becoming an active and open agent of royal policies and, in the public mind, the man primarily responsible for their changed direction. By contrast with his earlier and more private career as an intermediary, Penn became a public figure in 1686-88. His activities attracted a great deal of hostile attention, although less than those of the more shadowy Jesuit intermediary, Edward Petre. Penn's importance can be appreciated by examining the crucial and difficult tasks he undertook for James. He visited the Hague in the summer of 1686 in an unsuccessful attempt to persuade William of Orange to pledge his support for repeal of the Tests as well as the penal laws.[28] After helping to draft the 1687 Declaration of Indulgence Penn took charge of the organization and presentation of addresses of thanks from grateful deputations of dissenters, from whom in return were elicited promises of support at elections for royal candidates. Penn toured the country preaching publicly, praising James for instituting toleration, and urging all Protestants to trust the king's sincerity.[29]

In a series of widely circulated pamphlets Penn elaborated the thesis that not only was toleration now attainable at the hands of the king but it would provide the essential guarantee for the liberties and properties of the nation in a general constitutional settlement.[30] Penn took advantage of a convergence between the political strategy on which James had already embarked, alienating most Tories and Anglicans, and a new realism on the part of the dissenters. He had a relatively easy task in persuading the dissenters that they would never obtain toleration by espousing opposition politics; ambitious demagogues had exploited their support but done nothing for them. He also asserted, but by 1688 less convincingly, that they could never expect the Anglican hierarchy to concede toleration in a permanent form. On the other hand James already agreed with his contention that the bishops would not sincerely accept toleration but were waiting for his death and Mary's accession to reverse all his policies. Penn helped to convince James that by abandoning the alliance with the Tories and Anglicans he was actually strengthening his position. In his *Persuasive to Moderation* (1686) Penn argued that if the dissenters were given toleration they would prove to be far more reliable allies, and he cited the Tory defeats in the elections of 1679 and 1681 as evidence of the party's lack of popular support.[31] But he never confined himself to short-term or opportunistic arguments; the case that Penn advanced in 1686–88 represented a logical development of the thesis he had been presenting for twenty years.

Anglican insistence on continued enforcement of the penal laws was denounced as the principal cause of social and political divisions. By its severity the Church had provoked civil war in 1642 and gone close to doing so again in 1679–81. In *Good Advice to the Church of England, Roman Catholic and Protestant Dissenter* (1687) Penn repeated biting attacks on the ambition and worldliness of the bishops, the pastoral incompetence or indifference of the clergy, and their fears for a future in which they would have to compete on equal terms with dissenters and Catholics. Anglican intransigence left James and the dissenters with no alternative but to trust each other. But Penn promised that toleration would totally transform domestic politics. It would depoliticize religion, which had provided demagogues with grievances to exploit. Instead of being bitterly split by religious differences, local communities would live in harmony. Traders, manufacturers, and artisans would no longer have their business activities disrupted by fines, forfeitures, and imprisonments. Prosperity would follow from toleration.[32] This it could be expected would provide a vivid contrast with the economic depression that had affected France since Louis XIV's revocation of the Edict of Nantes in October 1685, which ended toleration of the Huguenots. Rather unconvincingly, in the light of James's policies in Ireland during 1687 and 1688, Penn believed that this example of depression in France removed any possibility of imitative action anywhere in Britain.

Since Penn continued to believe in the intrinsic malignity and hostility of the Church of England, he realized the need to mobilize the maximum support for James in order to enact toleration in a durable form. He knew that Declarations of Indulgence, based on a suspending power that most politicians and lawyers considered to be unconstitutional, provided no permanent security for religious toleration. Charles had had to withdraw Declarations in 1662 and 1672. Penn himself had ominously failed to persuade James's son-in-law, William, to pledge a continuation of the royal policies. Therefore Penn advanced the idea of a new fundamental statute, that in practice would prove to be irrevocable, which he called a new *Magna Carta* of religious toleration. A propaganda element undoubtedly lay behind this proposal, to reassure those who could never entirely bring themselves to trust a Catholic king, but Penn had made a similar proposal in 1675 when he had urged it on the Country opposition.[33] Such a statute would not only act as a guarantee of religious liberty but it would also commit James to reliance on parliament, and so inspire reciprocal loyalty and cooperation on the part of peers and M.P.s. Penn proposed inserting a clause that would, by requiring all office-holders and M.P.s to take an oath to respect and enforce toleration, make it virtually impossible to repeal the statute. In addition, such an oath (or, for Quakers, a declaration) would either force Anglicans to abandon their objections to toleration, or (like those nonjurors who refused the oaths to William and Mary after 1688) to drop out of official and political life altogether. Local magistrates would have no option but to accept the rights and liberty of dissenters and Catholics.[34]

This general proposal committed Penn to James's campaign to pack a parliament that would repeal the penal laws and tests. This involved widespread changes in all areas of local administration — the corporations, the commission of the peace, and the militia—as well as in central government. The results were disastrous for James. The general reaction was to fear that he was systematically preparing to subvert parliament and establish absolutism by statutory means. Penn's reply to these criticisms, that James was actually "unpacking," that is, enlarging political as well as religious freedom, failed to carry conviction.[35] Virulent attacks and vicious caricatures (the latter usually depicting him as a Jesuit, or at least a Catholic convert) made Penn aware of his increasing isolation. Few dissenters committed themselves wholeheartedly to James's policies, and the king had to rely increasingly on cynical manipulation and legal intimidation rather than on mobilizing genuine support. Despite his ingrained hostility to the Anglican hierarchy Penn, realizing that under royal pressure the clergy were becoming respected and popular as champions of protestantism, recommended discontinuing the prosecutions of the fellows of Magdalen College, Oxford, and the seven bishops. James ignored him. Consequently Penn moved silently away from him, as he had distanced himself from the Whigs in 1679. In the last months before the Revolution he became a helpless observer of James's errors and was replaced as confidential adviser by rasher and less realistic men.[36]

Developments after 1688 relegated Penn to comparative obscurity, as his message lost its relevance. The Convention Parliament judged the new intellectual and political atmosphere correctly when it passed a restrictive Toleration Act in 1689. This grudgingly redeemed in a minimal form the promises that had been made by the Anglican bishops to prevent the dissenters from collaborating with James. The act did not establish religious freedom or give dissenters equal civil rights; it merely exempted them from the penalties of the laws.[37] Toleration was based on expediency, not principle. Politicians agreed that it was in their own interest, and by extension that of the nation, to allow the dissenters to worship separately and quietly on the fringes of life. For Penn religious endeavor was the central purpose of life. He had engaged in politics solely in order to bring about the conditions of freedom in which true religion could flourish. Admittedly he used the concept of interest as an argument for toleration, but it was something worldly and temporal, and therefore subordinate. Penn welcomed James's institution of religious freedom as opening up unlimited opportunities for Christian witness; it would put an end to the spiritual apathy, empty formalism, and prevalent immorality and religious indifference that he blamed on the Church of England. But after the Revolution, material interest outweighed religious principles. At all political levels — for ministers, office-holders, M.P.s, members of public and private corporations, and most voters — interest in a material sense provided the main motive forces. Offices and places, government contracts, commercial privileges, pensions and sinecures, appointments and promotions, and private legislation on enclosures, navigable rivers, canals, and turnpikes became the currency in which the rewards of political success were paid. Those, like Penn and the High Anglican nonjurors, who retained a belief that politics should serve religious purposes, were pushed out to the fringe of political life.

Penn's political career, and the ideals for which he worked, have been generally overlooked or misunderstood because he and they do not fit tidily into the obvious categories of Court against Country, Whig against Tory. Contemporaries naturally thought ill of such an influential political intermediary and associate of James, but his integrity preserved him from succumbing to the temptations of self-advancement, enrichment by corrupt means, and irresponsible intriguing that tainted most of his rivals — Petre, for example. Yet by worldly standards Penn was a failure, and beset by renewed financial anxieties he withdrew into the citadel of his Quaker faith, leaving as his true memorial the city of Philadelphia and the province of Pennsylvania.

NOTES

1. Isaac Pennington, Robert Barclay, George Keith, and Lady Conway of the Ragway circle are the most prominent examples. See Marjorie Hope Nicolson, *The Correspondence of Anne, Viscountess Conway* (New Haven, 1930).

2. Mary Maples Dunn, *William Penn, Politics and Conscience* (Princeton, 1967), p. 74; Thomas Clarkson, *Memoirs of the Private and Public Life of William Penn* (London, 1813), 2:97n.

3. Baber acted as "protector" at court for dissenting ministers; officially he was a physican to Charles. Petre, the Jesuit brother of a peer, was believed to be James's chief private adviser in 1687-88. Brent, a Catholic attorney, organized royal intervention in the constituencies in preparation for elections. Coleman acted as private secretary for both James and Mary of Modena; discovery of his secret correspondence with Louis XIV's advisers led to his execution in 1678. Armstrong, hanged in 1684, served the duke of Monmouth as his political agent.

4. Significantly, only some bishops raised the possibility; for example, see F. J. Routledge, ed., *Calendar of the Clarendon State Papers*, vol. 5, 1660-1726 (Oxford, 1970), p. 248.

5. Penn explicitly noted this: "it is the infelicity of governors to see and hear by the eyes and ears of other men; which is equally unhappy for the people." *The Great Case of Liberty of Conscience* (1671), in *Select Works*, 2:128; see also *PWP*, vol. 5, items 9A-D.

6. Before his accession James maintained a separate household at St. James's palace, but for confidential business he employed personal associates, particularly the Talbots (Richard and Peter), George Legge, John Churchill, and Lord Peterborough.

7. J. R. Jones, *The First Whigs* (London, 1970), pp. 25-26, 51; John Miller, *James II, a Study in Kingship* (Hove, Sus., 1978), pp. 77, 79-80, 88-89; 149-50, 153-54, 171, 174, 180-81, 184, 186, 198, 200; J. R. Jones, *The Revolution of 1688 in England* (London, 1972), pp. 24, 34, 81, 123, 145-48, 172.

8. Clarkson, *Memoirs*, 2:20-21, 23-24.

9. Dunn, *William Penn*, p. 22.

10. The latest and most perceptive study of James is the one by John Miller, cited in n. 7, above.

11. Clarkson, *Memoirs*, 2:57-58. Among other associates were Bishop John Wilkins, the ex-Levellers John Wildman and Roderick Mansell, Sir George Etherege, and Sir Ellis Leighton.

12. Miller, *James II*, pp. 76-81.

13. In *Select Works*, 2:165-92. This tract was published originally in Ireland in 1670, with a second issue printed in London the following year (*PWP*, vol. 5, item 7A). An example of Penn's scurrility is his charge that the Pope maintains profitable brothels in Rome (*Select Works*, 2:187).

14. *Select Works*, 2:525-27, 578; Clarkson, *Memoirs*, 1:254-55; Dunn, *William Penn*, pp. 134-35.

15. See especially *The Great Case of Liberty of Conscience* (1670), in *Select Works*, 2:158-60, 161-64; *A Persuasive to Moderation* (1686), in ibid., 2:533-37; *Good Advice to the Church of England* (1687), in ibid., 2:547-58; *An Address to Protestants* (1679), in ibid, 3:45-47, 93-96, 129-35, 153-62.

16. Bunyan's venom is directed against Judge Hategood, Formalist, Hypocrisy, Mr Two-tongues, Mr Facing-bothways, Mr By-ends, and the compliant jury. John Bunyan, *Pilgrim's Progress*, ed. J. B. Wharey and R. Sharrock (Oxford, 1975), pp. 92-97.

17. Bunyan, *Pilgrim's Progress*, p.65.

18. Clarkson, *Memoirs*, 1:250-52; Robert W. Blencowe, *Diary of the Times of Charles II* (London, 1843), 1:114-16; Alexander C. Ewald, *The Life and Times of Algernon Sydney* (London, 1873), 2:56-62; 138-41.

19. *Select Works*, 3:181-88; *PWP*, vol. 5, item 50.

20. *Select Works*, 3:186.

21. Ibid., 3:189-205; *PWP*, vol. 5, item 51.

22. Clarkson, *Memoirs*, 1:216; *Select Works*, 2:530, 570, 578-83.

23. The last stages of the charter were passed at a time of mounting tension. The charter was approved on 23 Feb., Charles signing the royal bill five days later, against the background of elections that were going disastrously wrong for the court and the Tories. The date of the Charter was 4 Mar.; the Oxford Parliament met on 21 Mar., to be dissolved a week later, amid serious fears of a coup or a new civil war.

24. Robert Beddard, "The Commission for Ecclesiastical Promotions, 1681-84," *Historical Journal*, 10 (1967):25-30.

25. Penn also sought personal security at a time of Tory attacks on dissenters and Whigs, referring in an undated 1681 letter to "when I am gott to my new granted Province in America, where the charge of the Voyage will secure me from the revenge of my enimys." *PWP*, 2:92-93.

26. Dunn, *William Penn*, pp. 108-12, 144.

27. *CSPD, 1685*, p. 357; *1686-1687*, pp. 62, 71, 138, 303, 315, 329.

28. Clarkson, *Memoirs*, 1:475. Gilbert Burnet, *History of His Own Time*, 3d ed. by M. J. Routh (Oxford, 1833), 3:139-40. Burnet said of Penn what many contemporaries said of him, that he was "a talking vain man."

29. Dunn, *William Penn*, p. 117. Clarkson, *Memoirs*, 1:496-97; C. E. Whiting, *Studies in English Puritanism* (London, 1931), p. 184; *HMC*, 10th Report, 4:376; 14th Report, 2:401.

30. *Select Works*, vol. 2, contains (pp. 504-42) *A Persuasive to Moderation* (1686), and (pp. 543-87) *Good Advice to the Church of England, Roman Catholic and Protestant Dissenter* (1687); see also *PWP*, vol. 5, items 72A-D, 82A-G. After John Dryden and Henry Care, Penn was the most important of James's apologists.

31. *Select Works*, 2:534.

32. Ibid., 2:146; 3:194-96.

33. See *England's Present Interest Considered* (1675), in *Select Works*, 2:269-320; *PWP*, vol. 5, items 39A-C; Dunn, *William Penn*, pp. 47-57.

34. Clarkson, *Memoirs*, 1:143-47.

35. Dunn, *William Penn,* pp. 149-50.

36. Father Edward Petre and Robert Brent formed part of the inner group or *camarilla* of advisers; Sir Nicholas Butler and Edward Nosworthy acted as electoral organizers.

37. The 1689 Act followed John Locke, not William Penn, in excluding Catholics (and atheists) from toleration.

5 ❧ *William Penn, 1689–1702:*
Eclipse, Frustration, and Achievement

The name of William Penn immediately recalls the great Quaker founding father of Pennsylvania. Yet the image evoked thereafter may well vary with the particular situation in which his life and work be considered. From December 1688 when James II fled to France until Penn's return late in 1701 from a second and last sojourn in America, frustrated ambition and declining vigor dominate many accounts. After that return, illness became more frequent and financial embarrassments greater. Old age developed quickly, and actual disability extended from about 1712 to 1718.

Any study of Penn in his fifties, our present concern, has often focused on familiar biographical detail, and, as remarked by a friend in 1696 after the death of Springett, the favorite son, Penn's portion was always "to have wormwood mingled with his drink."[1] Suspicions of popery and Jacobitism, sparked by association with the now exiled monarch, led the new government to suspend his authority in the American province. The deaths, not only of Springett and of his beloved wife Gulielma, but also of several close Quaker friends, induced deep sorrow. Penn's secret retirement, brought on by constant harassment in the early nineties, resulted in distinct coolness from other Friends. Such a retreat from persecution was frowned on, even forbidden to Quakers.[2] Querulous criticism and demands for help from the colonists produced no satisfactory result before, during, or after disbarment from the Proprietary.

With authority restored, and distrust diminished, Penn made a fortunate second marriage and resumed activities — controversy, travel, agitation for further Quaker privilege, and preaching. He was one of those who in

1697 informed Peter the Great at Deptford about the Quaker faith. Before the second Atlantic voyage of 1699, he revisited his long-neglected Irish estates without greatly improving their yield, and communed with Friends in that island. The American stay of less than two years was unrewarding. The Charter of Privileges he felt obliged to sign in October 1701 on the eve of departure abandoned or reversed much of his original plan.[3] No wonder that he then began those never completed negotiations for the sale of the colony.

These aspects of Penn's career will be disregarded here. Examination of the extraordinary quality of intellectual achievement during this period of frustration may suggest some illumination of an enigmatic and elusive personality. Complete coverage of works then written will not be given, but a glance at a few pieces on history, on relations between states and between colonies, and some discursive and general reflections may suggest characteristics not always remembered.

Originally published in 1694 as a preface to George Fox's *Journal*, Penn's *Rise and Progress of the People called Quakers*, appearing separately in the same year, immediately developed a life of its own. Brief, it showed a certain freshness. "Great Books . . . grow Burthensome," he averred in an introductory epistle.[4] Six short chapters offered a summary relation of former dispensations of God up to the emergence of the Quakers, whose fundamental principles, discipline, ministry, and organization were outlined. The sixth and final chapter exhorted Friends to maintain integrity and urged those as yet unconvinced to find salvation in this faith.

The fifth chapter concentrated upon the "First Instrument" of God, George Fox, and resembled the "characters" — pen portraits — popular at the time. Penn had already written tributes to deceased associates like Josiah Coale, Thomas Loe, Robert Barclay, and John Burnyeat, the last two of whom died in the same year as Fox, 1690. Writing but a preface he dwelt briefly on biographical detail, mentioning by name a few early Friends as well as persons like Judge John Bradshaw, the regicide, who deflected persecution. Taking up after 1675 when Fox's *Journal* narrative ended, and he was often with Fox, Penn succinctly suggested his continued services to Quakers near and far, as well as to the movement as a whole. For example, Fox helped persuade doubters that regularity and organization were necessary and not in the least like the rules and demands of the established church they had left.

Intimate traits received frank and affectionate commentary. Not "Notional or Speculative," Fox was "no Man's Copy." An original, sometimes even appearing "Uncouth and Unfashionable," he was ignorant of "Sophistical Science." Although Fox spoke at times in abrupt and broken sentences, his prayers and sermons revealed a "profound" understanding which with "an Innocent Life" opened to many, including the unlearned, the true religion. Often as he had been in his company, Penn declared, he had never observed him out of place, nor unequal to any occasion. The *Journal* of this great man "by whom God was pleas'd to gather this People" should be widely studied. Penn concluded by apostrophizing his late friend: "Many sons have done Virtuously in this Day; but, Dear George, Thou excellest them All."[5]

While *The Rise and Progress* had a crispness not often found in other Quaker writings, *An Essay towards the Present and Future Peace of Europe,* published in 1693 and also a product of retirement, was in a very different vein.[6] Twice reprinted before Penn's death, it has always attracted readers. The argument was secular and was offered to an audience of warring states. Penn wrote that he welcomed constructive criticism of remedies put forward to ameliorate the "incomparable miseries" of war-torn Europe, seldom in his lifetime free from hostilities for more than a few months. Conflict, Penn believed, despite the claims of men like Oliver Cromwell, did not bring peace, but only disorder, impoverishment, and devastation.

Peace, eminently desirable, could only be brought about by justice, and justice by government — "chief expedient against confusion." A European or even Imperial assembly, diet, parliament, or estates, composed of representatives of each sovereign state, the number of deputies being proportionate to size, could prevent war. Meetings taking place at intervals could be held in a round room to avoid disputes over precedency. A record to keep all informed of proceedings would be kept in Latin and French, the languages most commonly known. Decision would be reached by ballot, three-quarters of the whole constituting a majority. Liberty and orderliness of debate would be the concern of a presiding officer, chosen by turn from each of the anticipated ten areas — Penn would have welcomed Russia and Turkey but did not expect their immediate cooperation. To the chair all speeches would be addressed; and no absenteeism would be allowed.

Penn expected objections. The stronger powers would never agree; this, he hoped, might be overcome by the united strength of the rest. Disuse of soldiering might be feared as conducive of effeminacy; education could surely remedy this. In a peaceful world younger sons could find ample employment as merchants, husbandmen, or "ingenious naturalists." Loss of sovereignty might be resented but would not be felt in domestic affairs. The enormous benefits of a warless Europe — or even universe — would be discovered in the absence of bloodshed, a greater reputation accorded Christian realms, an economy of money, prevention of destruction, a greater ease and safety for travel and traffic, and a freedom for princes to marry for other than reasons of state. If the Turks did not join, Christendom even so would be more secure against threat. Some interested in the quest for peace have read these reflections thoughtfully; others have termed Penn naive. Yet it may be questioned whether that epithet might not be applied to any designers of international leagues or unions that depend upon the ultimate rationality of man.

The Quaker cited earlier examples — that of the United Provinces recently described by Sir William Temple. Penn had also studied a plan often attributed to Henry IV of France, but probably mainly the work of Maximilien de Béthune, duc de Sully, influenced by *The New Cyneas* of Eméric Crucé. Penn, who credited Henry with its authorship, may have read *The Grand Design,* when it was published in France in the mid-seventeenth century. But the European arrangements proposed by Penn incorporated in them the old Gothic repesentative tradition. A friend and avowed disciple, John Bellers, also moved by the recurrence of war, resumed the elder Quaker's theme in *Some reasons for an European State* (London, 1711), adding some sensible remarks about disarmament as a necessary ingredient of peace. He further presented a plan for a council where ecclesiastics might discuss matters about which they agreed, rather than those about which they differed.[7] The same warring conditions decided Charles St. Pierre to bring out in Paris in 1712 his thoughts about making peace perpetual in Europe. He wanted a treaty of alliance insuring through its signatories — "a confederation of kings" — that withdrawal from the pact would entail loss of power and even territories by the warmongers.[8] Penn was apt to be overoptimistic, but in these reflections upon a desired peaceful world, as in others about political behavior, he often anticipated modern prejudice and thinking.

Penn was, of course, involved in colonial enterprise long before the nineties. One of three trustees for Edward Byllynge's West New Jersey settlement (until he obtained the Pennsylvania Charter in 1681), he acquired holdings there, and after the death of Sir George Carteret in 1680, others in East New Jersey. For Pennsylvania he wrote promotional literature, drafted frames and laws, and described prospects and qualifications for would-be emigrants.[9] Such establishment overseas, he felt compelled to argue, was a benefit to the home country, rather than (as often stated) a drain on population and wealth. Colonies were, he declared, "the seeds of nations," following the thoughts already outlined by Jan de Witt, Josiah Child, Francis Bacon, and others. One of Penn's statements justifying colonization was reprinted in *Select Tracts relating to the Colonies* (London, 1732), probably to promote the currently proposed Georgian colony.[10] Penn continued to be expansionist, issuing a broadside in 1690 advocating development of the Susquehanna area, about whose strategic and cultural value he had remarked during the first American visit.[11]

Penn had surely not anticipated the lack of enthusiasm for the regime he had so carefully outlined on obtaining Pennsylvania. A few months among the colonists seems not to have taught him the arts of management. Yet he observed difficulties outside the realm of domestic politics. By the nineties the increase of piracy in western waters and war in Europe and over the Atlantic area added complications not only in places affected but also in those not actually involved. Penn turned his thoughts about America and Europe to interrelationships. Two plans, one solely of his own devising, the other drawn up in concert with two colonial governors, offered suggestions. He had remained in touch with the colonists and in 1695 received a letter, often referred to, from Peter de la Noy of New York declaring that the American colonies needed reorganization.[12] This was an idea long current and evoking various schemes from 1643 on, but none having lasting effect.[13] De la Noy may have prompted Penn's decision to write.

In December 1696 Penn presented to the newly reactivated Board of Trade *A Brief and Plain Scheme how the English Colonies in the North Parts of America . . . may be made more useful to the Crown and one another's Peace and Safety with a Universal Concurrence.* The Board, interested, asked Penn to bring it back in more formal fashion. This he did in February 1697. In 1698 it was printed in London along with some suggestions by others in Charles Davenant's *Discourses on the Publick Revenues and the Trade of England.*[14] Penn's tract provoked commentary in ensuing years largely from defenders of the rights of their own particular area. Only a brief summary of the seven points of *A Brief and Plain Scheme* is necessary. A meeting of two deputies from each of the ten settlements should be held once a year or, in wartime, more often. This assembly should be presided over by the king's commissioner, specifically named, and should meet in a central location. This was likely to be New York, whose governor could indeed be appointed chair, "after the manner of Scotland," and also, if needed, act as general of the agreed upon forces. Quotas of men and money should be determined in concert. Penn, although head of a Quaker colony, was obliged by the promise required when given back the province, to see the navigation laws enforced and a due measure of assistance afforded the war effort. He was anxious to see this fairly undertaken. His proposal for setting quotas was probably the most important point. Moreover, discussions about treatment of debtors, would-be bigamists fleeing one colony for another, and the convicted trying to escape the sentences of their own courts, were recommended. Commercial injuries could be adjudicated. If the Board of Trade had carried out the policy, very much in the air of the later years of the seventeenth century, of putting all colonies under royal control, it might have implemented some of these ideas, or others similar to them.

In New York in the first week of October 1700 the governors of Virginia and New York, together with Penn, debated schemes very like these, with a common body to adjust border disputes between states, unify coinage, deal with marital and financial defectors, and regulate laws of naturalization and marriage. Also put forward were plans for common encouragement of timber exportation, and a fairer distribution of loot seized from pirates. Neither project aimed at any amalgamation of the several settlements; both were directed to the improvement of relations between them.[15] Penn's vigorous defense of proprietary rights, vowing

that colonies like his cost Westminster less than those where a royal governor ruled, was in vindication of the property rights needed to bring him
revenue.[16] But he hoped for easier contacts of one colony with another,
and by mutual agreement, to obtain fair treatment for Pennsylvania and
lessen tensions between states.

Nothing significant transpired. Neither the Board of Trade nor, it
must appear, the majority of colonists were prompted to further action for
a good many years, and then under different circumstances. But Penn,
frequently insensitive to the wishes of Pennsylvanians about their domestic
government, and often unfortunate in his choice of assistants, nevertheless
revealed real understanding of difficulties present or likely to develop among
the various American units. He offered what might be deemed a federal
method of solving those problems. Desirable concessions should be possible if agreed upon together. In neither European nor American matters did
he think in terms of a force able to impose peace and concord upon the
rest. He was ahead of most contemporaries. Even where a union was being
implemented in Britain, only a few like Andrew Fletcher and Robert Molesworth were far-sighted enough to think of equal cooperation between
all sectors — Ireland, Wales, Scotland, and England — of what was to
become the United Kingdom, ruled in fact only or chiefly from one capital
city.[17] As noted, Penn had read Temple, but otherwise he reveals little or
no attention to ancient or modern federations.

The preface to one of Penn's most popular works, *Some Fruits of Solitude in Reflections and Maxims relating to the Conduct of Human Life* (London,
1693),[18] explained the little book as in part "the Result of serious Reflection," in part "the Flashings of Lucid Intervals." God, Penn declared, had
blessedly given him retirement—time he could never before have called his
own. Before troubles induced retreat, he had been extremely busy. During
this relief he could "turn over the Leaves" of past activities and write for
the "moral instruction of readers." There is nothing of which "we are apt,"
he wrote, "to be so lavish as of Time, and about which we ought to be
more Solicitous . . . .Time is what we want most, but what, alas! we use
worst." Man should keep "a ledger" to what end he employs it. Penn
would have agreed with George Savile, marquis of Halifax, that "Mispend-
ing a man's time is a kind of self-homicide, it is making life to be of no
use."[19]

Though frankly admonitory, the manner and style of both parts of
Fruits of Solitude (hereafter cited as A and B) are different in arrangement
and mode from Penn's other tracts. They were professedly in a style grown
increasingly popular from the days of Michel Montaigne[20] and were fashionable in the latter half of the seventeenth century. In such works as *Moral
Reflections and Maxims* (1665) by François, duc de la Rochefoucauld, *The
Pensées* (c. 1662) by Blaise Pascal, and the *Maxims* of George Savile (written
contemporaneously but not published until 1750) may be found examples

of the manner of *Fruits of Solitude*. Penn had studied Montaigne and may also have read when in France the works of Pascal and de la Rouchefoucauld. Most aphorists used the term *moral* but usually remained cynical or defensive commentators, analysts, and apologists rather than the admonitor that was Penn.

Significantly, Penn began by reflecting upon ignorance. Men are, he thought, more likely to observe the beauties of Windsor Castle and Hampton Court than to study the living, walking tabernacle of their own bodies, and the stately volume of the world in which they live (A, 1-3).[21] Nature, whose "rules are few, plain and most reasonable" is "very legible" and deserves further investigation (A, 9-11). If man be "the index or Epitomy of the World," he has only to scan himself "to be learn'd in it" (A, 17). "God's works," nature, meant a great deal to Penn. To him nature could instruct if read properly, whereas for La Rochefoucauld, "Nature gives merit, and Fortune sets it at work"; indeed, nature "marked out to every man at birth the bounds of his virtues and vices."[22] But for Penn it was the reality declaring God's power and wisdom. The country provides "the Philosopher's *Garden* and *Library*," a sweet retreat where all can learn its easily legible lessons (A, 223). Countrymen, to be sure, often neglect their opportunities and fail to realize that while cities are but man's handiwork, the country is God's provision for food, study, life, and learning. Penn's enjoyment of the beauties as well as the uses of nature is apparent throughout his work but especially in *Fruits of Solitude* and in his description of Pennsylvania to the Free Society of Traders.[23] He not only noted animal and vegetable products likely to be useful to potential settlers but also remarked upon the flowers which could enrich even a London garden.

Keenly aware of the deficiencies of contemporary education, Penn wrote that "the first Thing obvious to Children is what is *sensible*" — that is, what is seen, heard, and felt. Instead, memory is strained with words, grammar, and strange tongues to produce scholars rather than men (A, 4-6). Natural genius in the young for "*Mechanical* and *Physical* or natural Knowledge" is neglected. Languages are useful, but the child would prefer making tools and playthings (A, 6-8). Regrettably, books by naturalists and mechanics were not translated into Latin and adapted to a youthful pace, thus making familiar a foreign vocabulary (A, 15).

In *The Advice of William Penn to his Children,* written about 1699 and published posthumously in 1726 by Jane Sowle,[24] Penn counseled his family to read less and meditate more. But he urged the study of manuals suitable to the offspring of the ruling class likely to serve as justices, sheriffs, and coroners, and such other works generally serviceable on clerkships and wills.[25] As we have seen,[26] he himself had read widely. But as *Fruits of Solitude* suggest, he attached as much importance to solitary, observant inquiry and reflection.

As for recreation, both old and young are limited in Penn's view to conversation with godly friends, and occupation in garden or laboratory (A, 58), although Robert Barclay would have added the reading of history.[27] Possibly Barclay's emphasis on history was reflected in Penn's admiration for the *Memorials* of Sir Bulstrode Whitelocke for which he wrote a preface in 1709 declaring "I take history then, to represent us as in a glass the whole world at one view . . . a sort of pre-existence." England regrettably had produced no Livy or Tacitus to provide such a "glass in which we should see that true understanding and admiration of the wisdom of the Creator" we need.[28]

"Man being made a Reasonable and so a Thinking Creature," there is nothing, Penn wrote, "more worthy of his Being, than the right Direction and Employment of his Thoughts" (B, 63). Pascal in the same vein had thought man only a reed, yet "a thinking reed."[29] But the Quaker's admonitions were perhaps more explicit. "Manage thy Thoughts rightly, and thou will save time. . . . Always remember to bound thy Thoughts to the present Occasion" (B, 68-69). Avoid *"Vulgar Errors"* (A, 155). Remember that though there is truth in rhetoric it may also lead to error (A, 138-39). "Inquiry is *Human;* Blind Obedience, *Brutal"* (A, 156). Reason should prevail: "Tis quite another Thing to be *stiff* than Steady in an Opinion" (B, 155). Without reason man is a beast; the wise man governs himself by the reason of his case. "A reasonable Opinion must ever be in Danger, where Reason is not Judge" (B, 161). Reason is common to all. "It is for want of examining it by the same light and measure that we are not all of the same mind" (B, 169). The inference was to utilize both the Light within and judicious inquiry before making decisions.

Not only must the wise man apply intelligence to his problems, he must also value sense above wit. "A man may be a fool with wit," wrote La Rochefoucauld, "but never with judgment."[30] Or, as Penn phrased it, "Less Judgment than Wit is *more Sail than Ballast"* (A, 171). Wit is "fitter for Diversion than Business" (A, 170). The wise man must take everything into account and be neither officious, captious, nor critical (B, 59-60).

As well as reflecting on education and continuing inquiry, Penn of course emphasized personal virtues: moderation in food, drink, and dress. Excessive avarice should be avoided, but careful management, expenditure never exceeding income, is essential. Penn apparently never followed this admonition himself; as La Rochefoucauld said, "Tis easier to be wise for other people than for ourselves."[31] A marriage for love and companionship is better than a union based on money. A good wife should never be treated as a servant but regarded as an equal partner. Wives and friends should be carefully selected. Men are often, Penn surmised, more concerned about the breed of animals than of posterity, the children of the next generation. Both marriage and friendship should be sought with those of similar tastes with whom intercourse of soul rather than of sense can be enjoyed (A, 79-82). Unprofitable society should be eschewed; only that likely to reward, pursued (A, 128, 133). He cautioned that people can be "Witty, Kind, Cold, Angry, Easy, Stiff, Jealous, Careless, Cautious, Confident, Close, Open," but in the wrong time and place (A, 159). Wisdom never adventured where the probability of advantage did not exceed that of loss (A, 264). Yet society must be had. "Tis a great folly to set up for being wise by oneself."[32]

Fruits of Solitude and the *Advice* reveal the social thinking of Penn as one of the gentry. Children should all be treated alike save the eldest who deserves a double portion.[33] The young should be obedient (A, 174) and grateful (A, 177). A structured society, accepted as a matter of course by Penn and contemporaries, demands servants. They should not be domineered over and must be treated considerately. In turn they should be faithful, hardworking, careful, and trustworthy (A, 192-200). The good servant serves God in serving his master and receives double wages — to wit, both here and hereafter (A, 207). In remarking that Indians were shocked at men being called servants, a term they used only for dogs (B, 268), Penn declared that the Almighty had made all men of the same physical elements but had arranged them in ranks, some subordinate and dependent. This same inequality can be found from king to scavenger and in stars, trees, fishes, birds, and so on. Yet the mighty were not created to serve their own pleasure but to promote the public good (B, 255-66).

Remarking that men love change, Penn declared that this is because they, like the whole world, are composed of changeable elements. All subsist by revolution. Yet they often cannot bear to reflect on the last, greatest, and best alteration (A, 487). Death being the way and condition of life, we cannot really live if we are unable to die. Life never ends, simply changes from time to eternity (A, 503). By contrast Pascal found death easier to accept without thinking about it. Men cannot escape death, reflected La Rochefoucauld, but submit to it out of insensibility and custom rather than of resolution. "The sun and death are two things that cannot be steadily lookt on."[34]

Rather more generally Penn considered public life, religion, and the obligations they entail. "A Private Life is to be preferred," the honor and gain of public office bearing no proportion to the comfort of them (A, 370). Yet the public must be served, and those that do so deserve reward (A, 377). They will also be accountable to God (B, 262). Penn recognized as legitimate many governments. A free government, whatever its form, is that where "the laws rule and the people are a party to those laws."[35] Like clocks, governments are valuable for the motion men give them. Men likewise are esteemed for their proper "going" (A, 254). Pascal on the other hand discovered the power of kings in the folly of the people. He refused to take politics, even that of Plato and Aristotle, seriously.[36] The governor of Pennsylvania was much more concerned, if not with form, then with character. In his preface to the 1682 Frame of Government, Penn had written that government is to secure men from the abuse of power. Liberty without obedience brings confusion, but obedience without liberty, slavery.[37] In *Fruits of Solitude* he distinguished between rex and tyrannus, one ruling by law, the other by absolute power (A, 330-69). Good princes should cultivate wisdom, seeking love rather than fear, and never straining their authority too far. The universal aim is happiness. Perhaps this echoed good Bishop Richard Cumberland; the end of government should be to bring felicity to all (A, 350). The ambition of a people could shake a regime; maladministration, that of a tyrant (A, 331). Let the people think they govern, and they will be governed (A, 337). The prince with the assistance of ministers and councilors carefully selected for their interest and ability should work for the general good (A, 353-62).

Government is ruined by three things: looseness, oppression, and envy (A, 363). When reins are slack, manners are corrupted, effeminacy begotten, and industry destroyed (A, 364). Oppression results in a poor country and a desperate population (A, 365). Envy disturbs society and clogs "the Wheels" (A, 367). Good officials should have clean hands, assiduity, dispatch, impartiality, and capacity. Delay, for example, is often more injurious than injustice (A, 380-95). Justice should be blind, with the same scale for rich and poor (A, 408). Penn differentiated between impartiality, indifferency, and neutrality. Where right or religion calls for decision, a neuter must perforce be either coward or hypocrite (A, 432).

Luxury should be discouraged, if necessary by sumptuary laws (B, 227). Exertion is wholesome for both body and mind, besides supplying the want of parts (A, 57, 233). Only a miserable nation can offer no better employment for the poor than the production of superfluities. Liberality and frugality mixed well together: the very trimmings of the vain world would clothe all the naked (A, 50, 52-54, 73). Superfluities abolished might make possible almshouses, and excess would at the same time disappear (A, 53).

True godliness, Penn believed, does not turn men out of the world but enables them to live more profitably by exciting the endeavors of others in it. Religion is, after all, the fear of God demonstrated in good works. Pure and undefiled religion is to visit the fatherless and widowed in charity and piety. There is neither use nor necessity for endless investigation, as Penn may have felt Pascal's inquiry into truth to be. "Men may tire themselves in a Labyrinth of Search, and talk of God: But if we would know him indeed," wrote the Quaker, "it must be from the Impressions we receive of him" (A, 511). The less form in religion, the better since "God is a Spirit" (A, 507) and value lies not in *"verbal Orthodoxy"* (A, 472).

Pious and devout souls are everywhere of one religion (A, 519). The truly pious loves his particular persuasion for its devotion (A, 519-20).

Public worship may truly be valuable but God who is everywhere at once might be better served "in resisting a Temptation to Evil, than in many formal Prayers" (A, 473, 478). Conformity may be reasonable where conscience is not against it, but a weakness in religion and government "where it is carried to things of an indifferent Nature" (B, 249, 251). Penn condemned censoriousness (A, 41). "They have a Right to censure, that have an Heart to help: The rest is Cruelty not Justice" (A, 46). To have religion solely upon authority, and not from conviction, is "like a *finger watch,* to be set forwards or backwards, as he pleases that has it in keeping" (A, 523). Conscience and charity are all important. Where love prevails, "we shall all be *Lovely,* and in *Love* with *God,* and *one* with *another*" (A, 556).

These achievements of the years of frustration provide glimpses of Penn's character that are not, perhaps, as sharply revealed in the years of greater activity and influence. His writing of Quaker history focuses clearly on essentials. Similarly, *An Essay* and the *Brief and Plain Scheme* deal briskly with the secular alignment of states and colonies, while *Some Proposals for a Second Settlement* pursues the potential for colonial expansion. Not many contemporaries, as noticed, examined methods of federal union. Penn perceived the difficulties and concessions reconciliation would make necessary, though the extent of the task was not fully comprehended. Concordance was urgent if disagreements and war were to be prevented. That implementation did not follow his suggestions in no way renders them less illuminative of his thinking. And if inclined to underestimate a general reluctance to take positive steps, he nonetheless understood the essential role of frequent consultation by some kind of representative assembly.

Wide reading and travel influenced Penn throughout life. One result may be seen in his curiosity about Indians, and another in recognition of the special needs of both earlier settlers and later immigrants lacking the British background of his Quaker purchasers. *Fruits of Solitude* displays acquaintance with other than legal, political, and controversial literature. Penn was very little of a cynic. He was, in spite of his troubles, convinced that men could be talked or cajoled into reasonableness, good government, and charity in religion. Successful in missionary work, he was the reverse in convincing the Pennsylvanians of the virtues of laws and frames proposed. Quite possibly this sprang from a failure to understand human beings as such.

Penn, like Barclay, was not a leveler.[38] Every person had an appointed rank and good relations between social categories were important. Save for his Quaker belief in religious liberty and in greater forebearance toward malefactors, he was very much the conscientious and reflective Englishman, born to service and a share in government. His love of the beauties of the wonderful world in which he lived led to a simple interpretation of natural laws easily discovered and leading to peace among men. In his treasured retreat, Penn contemplated a better life and seldom delved deeply into the matter of obstacles likely to stand in the way of achieving it.

Fox, the "great instrument" of Quakerism, and Barclay, its first philosopher, rightly occupy the highest place in the esteem of the Society of Friends. Penn, although dedicated, was distracted by vicissitudes of fortune different from those caused by persecution shared by all early members. He had charisma and showed fierce energy in argument with unbelievers but was often guilty of hasty judgment about those of whom he disapproved. Farsighted about larger issues, he seemed unable at times to cope with smaller problems. Great complications in social relationships, a continued association with the rich and powerful, his role as proprietor placing him in the ruling class of the day—all these factors help to blur the Quaker image, even when so much of his activity directly concerned the Friends.

Yet in spite of frustrations and disappointments, Penn remains the greatest of colonial founding fathers. His interest in boundaries, in peaceful relations with the natives, in an open-door policy for would-be emigrants, and his perception of certain intercolonial problems, and of the harm wrought by European disunity, all reveal him to be capable, not only of legal argument and religious persuasion, but also of constructive thinking about questions still of universal concern. In the writings of the years of Penn's last major exertions may be traced what the late Frederick Tolles once called a "final distillation" of thought and character.

NOTES

1. Mrs. G. Locker Lampson, ed., *A Quaker Post-Bag* (London, 1910), p. 130.

2. Robert Barclay, *An Apology for the True Christian Religion,* 8th ed. (London, 1780), pp. 507-12.

3. The original Charter of Privileges, adopted 28 Oct. 1701, is located in Miscellaneous Manuscripts Collection, APS. A printed version can be found in *Minutes of the Provincial Council,* 2:56-60.

4. In *Works,* 1:859; *PWP,* vol. 5, item 98.

5. *Works,* 1:878-84.

6. See Frederick B. Tolles and E. Gordon Alderfer, eds., *The Witness of William Penn* (New York, 1957), pp. 140-59; *PWP,* vol. 5, items 95A-B.

7. See A. Ruth Fry, *John Bellers, 1654-1725* (London, 1935).

8. See Sylvester John Hemleben, *Plans for World Peace* (Chicago, 1943), esp. pp. 1-95, which examines the ideas of such men as Sully (1560-1641); Cruce (1590-1648); St. Pierre (1658-1743); and Temple (1648-1699).

9. See, for example, Penn's *Some Account of the Province of Pennsylvania* (1681), in Tolles and Alderfer, *Witness,* pp. 116-22; *PWP,* 2:137-227; see also *PWP,* vol. 5, items 58A-B.

10. Charles M. Andrews (*The Colonial Period of American History* [New Haven, 1934-38], 4:337-38) regards Penn's paragraphs as a separate tract entitled *The Benefit of Plantations or Colonies* (1680), but see *PWP,* vol. 5, item 56. Verner W. Crane, in *Bibliographical Essays, a Tribute to Wilberforce Eames* (Cambridge, Mass., 1924), pp. 281-89, establishes the date of *Select Tracts* and suggests its probable promoters.

11. See *Some Proposals for a Second Settlement in the Province of Pennsylvania* (London, 1690), on *Micro.* 6:410. A facsimile is printed in *PMHB,* 28:between 60 and 61.

12. De la Noy's letter to Penn of 13 June 1695 is on *Micro.* 6:960, and is printed in *Documents Relative to the Colonial History of . . . New-York,* ed. E. B. O'Callaghan (1856-87), 4:221-24.

13. For example, see Frederick D. Stone, "Plans for the union of the British Colonies of North America, 1643-1776," in *History of the Celebration of the one Hundreth Anniversary of the Promulgation of the Constitution of the United States,* ed. Hampton E. Carson (Philadelphia, 1889), 2:439-503.

14. (London, 1698), 2:259-61; see also Tolles and Alderfer, *Witness,* pp. 135-37, who note (p. 135) that there is no evidence that Benjamin Franklin, Joseph Galloway, or other eighteenth-century statesmen interested in union ever read Penn's *A Brief and Plain Scheme.*

15. On 31 Dec. 1700 Penn enclosed "The Heads Discoursed of at New York" in his letter to the Board of Trade. See CO5/1260/85, PRO, on *Micro.* 8:755.

16. Numerous letters by Penn at HSP dwell on the injustice of various plans to take away proprietary rights; see, for example, to Charlewood Lawton, 21 Dec. 1700 (*Micro.* 8:700), 2 July 1701 (*Micro.* 9:309), 18 Aug. 1701 (*Micro.* 9:385); to the earl of Dorset, 27 Aug. 1701 (*Micro.* 9:448); and to Sir Heneage Finch, 27 Aug. 1701 (*Micro.* 9:477).

17. For more on relations between Westminster and the colonies, see Alison Olson, "William Penn, Parliament and Proprietory Government," *WMQ,* 3d ser., 18 (1961):176-95; I. K. Steel, *Politics of Colonial Policy* (Oxford, 1968), chap. 4. For Molesworth, Fletcher, and others, see Caroline Robbins, *The Eighteenth Century Commonwealthman* (New York, 1968), pp. 148-49, 183-84 and passim.

18. A sequel, *More Fruits of Solitude,* although probably written in the 1690s, was not published until 1702. For both of these tracts, I have relied on *Works,* 1:818-58; see also *PWP,* vol. 5, items 96A-D, 125.

19. George Savile, *Complete Works,* ed. J. P. Kenyon (Baltimore, 1969), p. 244.

20. Penn quotes Montaigne in his 1669 tract, *No Cross, No Crown.* See *Works,* 1:420-21. This tract, along with *The Christian Quaker* (London, 1673), and Penn's letter in Oct. 1693 to Sir John Rodes (see Locker Lampson, *The Quaker Post-Bag,* pp. 3-7, which can be found on *Micro.* 6:774) all afford evidence of Penn's extensive reading in a variety of sources.

21. The letters A and B in parentheses refer to *Some Fruits of Solitude* and *More Fruits of Solitude,* respectively, while the numbers which follow each letter refer to particular maxims as listed in *Works,* 1:820-58.

22. La Rochefoucauld, *Moral Reflections and Maxims,* 2d ed. (London, 1726), pp. 153, 189.

23. See *A Letter from William Penn . . . to the . . . Free Society of Traders . . . in London* (London, 1683), a draft of which can be found in *PWP,* 2:442-60.

24. See *Works,* 1:893-911. It was published under the title, *Fruits of a Father's Love.* See *PWP,* vol. 5, items 134A-B.

25. In *Works,* 1:898-900.

26. See n. 20, above.

27. See Barclay, *An Apology,* 8th ed., p. 541.

28. William Penn, preface to Bulstrode Whitelock, *Memorials of English Affairs to the Death of James* (London: 1709), pp. i-vii; see also *PWP,* vol. 5, items 130A-B.

29. *Pensées,* pp. 347-48.

30. La Rochefoucauld, *Reflections and Maxims,* p. 456.

31. Ibid., p. 132.

32. Ibid., p. 231.

33. *Advice to Children,* in *Works,* 1:901.

34. Pascal, *Pensées,* pp. 166–68; La Rochefoucauld, *Reflections and Maxims,* pp. 23, 26.

35. *Preface to the First Frame of Government for Pennsylvania,* in Tolles and Alderfer, *Witness of William Penn,* p. 111.

36. *Pensées,* pp. 330–31.

37. *Preface to the First Frame of Government for Pennsylvania,* in Tolles and Alderfer, *Witness of William Penn,* pp. 110, 112.

38. See, for example, Barclay, *An Apology,* 8th ed., p. 516. Penn's attitude has already been discussed. These views support arguments that Penn was not responsible in any large part for the innovative "Concessions and Agreements" for West New Jersey; see L. Violet Holdsworth, "The Problem of Edward Byllynge," pt. 1, in *Children of Light, Essays in Honor of Rufus M. Jones,* ed. Howard F. Brinton (New York, 1938), pp. 85–108; John L. Nickalls, "The Problem of Edward Byllynge," pt. 2, in ibid., pp. 109–32; John E. Pomfret, *The Province of West New Jersey* (Princeton, 1956), pp. 93–94.

PENN'S BRITAIN

JOAN THIRSK

6 ⟨ Agricultural Conditions in England, circa 1680

Economic circumstances are only one set of factors driving people to emigrate, and in concentrating on these, I would not be thought to rank them above religious and intellectual conviction. William Penn's own background would sober any economic historian's extravagant claims on this score. He was brought up in Essex—in the Wanstead-Chigwell area. This would incline one to guess that he did not see acute agricultural distress around him. He was living in a forest area where livestock keeping and fattening were being greatly encouraged by the nearness of the London market. The inhabitants of forests generally in the seventeenth century had advantages over those living in more arable regions. They had many different resources at their disposal, many alternative ways of earning a living. London had a voracious appetite for meat, and Romford, not six miles from Wanstead, was a notable livestock market, attracting dealers from all over England. Moreover, the wealthier citizens of London were developing sophisticated tastes, which graziers in the counties round about took the trouble to satisfy. A glimpse of the care taken to pander to these fastidious tastes is given in a report dated 1681 on the way young stock were fattened for veal in Essex and its neighboring county of Hertfordshire. At Tring in Hertfordshire, some thirty-two miles from Penn's home, they gave their calves chalk to lick and bled them regularly to make their flesh white before killing them at nine weeks. At Leyton in Essex, only three miles from Penn's childhood home, they fattened their calves quickly by feeding them a mash of rice, malt, flour, a little cream and chalk powder, even adding brandy.[1] It is unlikely that Penn in his childhood was made acutely aware of a depressed agricultural society. He was more likely to come into contact with a peasantry enjoying modest comfort. The fact that Puritanism was strongly entrenched in this part of Essex seems a much more significant influence on his life than the problems of agriculture.

Nevertheless, trends in the agricultural economy undoubtedly colored the lives of Penn's fellow emigrants and played a part in their decisions to leave England. Continuous complaints were voiced at the low prices of agricultural produce throughout the second half of the seventeenth century. Yet the majority of the population remained at home. So we must expect the agricultural scene to have offered grounds for optimism, even though mixed with disappointment and gloom. The reactions of individuals to a challenging set of economic problems could be very different.

The principal problem in agriculture from the farmer's point of view was centered in cereal-growing regions, and was caused by a superabundance of grain, which led to a relentless fall in its price. This state of affairs continued for virtually one hundred years from about 1650 to 1750.[2] One has to appreciate the full effect of this nagging discouragement over a very long period. Grain growers had to learn to accept it as the natural state of affairs and adapt to it. Many of them did so effectively. They sought out new outlets for grain and found ingenious ways of increasing their income from other enterprises. But it was a very different situation from that which men had known for about 150 years, from 1500 to 1650, when the rising population called for more and more grain, and demand generally kept prices high.

Although periodic bad harvests reminded everyone of their precarious dependence on cereal crops, grain supplies began to look fairly secure from the 1570s onwards. And early in the seventeenth century the first signs of the problem of excessive plenty began to appear. At Westminster in 1621 it was freely being said that grain prices were too low for the husbandman to live, that the kingdom had plenty of land for cereals and was more in need of pasture and cattle.[3] As population growth slackened thereafter, supplies of grain plainly began to exceed demand. The effect was masked by war in the 1640s, and by a series of bad harvest years between 1646 and 1651, which were coupled with such excessive rainfall that even the pasture farmers suffered. Much land was flooded, and cattle and sheep fell sick; in the summer of 1648 the hay rotted in the fields.

A graphic picture of these traumatic years emerges from Ralph Josselin's diary, written from Essex. In November 1649 his family was giving up one or two meals a week in order to give some food to the poor. In the northern counties of Cumberland and Westmorland in 1649 the poor were said to be "almost famished and some really so, the number whereof are too many and more than I shall now mention that have died in the highways for want of bread." A certificate from the county committee and J.P.s of Cumberland alleged that thirty thousand families in the county that year had "neither seed nor bread corn nor monies to buy either."[4] Yet six months after the first good season returned, in autumn 1651, men began to take the full measure of national food production under peaceful conditions. The problem of a surplus of foodstuffs was recognized in May 1653 when it was reported from Oxford that a bushel of wheat, which some years before cost 10s., was being sold for 2s. 6d. or 3s. (As a benchmark, it is worth remembering a statement made later in the seventeenth century that farmers could not survive if the price of wheat fell below 4s. a bushel.) Early in 1654 a letter from a Surrey gentleman, William Turnbull, spoke of the cheapness of everything "not only in the northern parts but also throughout this nation," while from Norfolk in 1655 came more news of "the hardness of the times by which grain is so cheap as has not been known in late days."[5]

In 1654 Parliament was moving toward a decision to allow the export of all foodstuffs, but this was in November just when the question of making Cromwell lord protector engaged attention. On the very day when the bill to allow the export of grain was to be reported, members spent all day debating what the lord protector's title should be. Men had to wait until the end of 1656 before a measure was finally agreed on to permit the export of all foodstuffs. For cereals it provided that when wheat prices were as low as 5s. a bushel (and other cereals proportionately) free export was allowed. The urgent need somehow to encourage grain growers to continue growing grain can be gauged from the price indices for wheat in this period. If an index number of 100 is used to represent average wheat prices between 1640 and 1750, the figure stood at somewhere between 140 and 176 in the bad harvest years of the late 1640s but fell to far less than half that figure (57) in 1654.[6]

At the Restoration the policy to encourage grain exports in order to maintain prices for growers was reaffirmed in 1663 and strengthened in 1670 by an act allowing exports when prices were even higher than before. Then in 1673 the policy was put on an entirely new footing when farmers were actually paid bounties for exporting grain. A larger overseas market *had* to be found for England's surplus, and farmers were now to be paid for their success in finding such markets.

Throughout the later seventeenth century it remained public policy to support cereal growers one way or another. Cereals, after all, were the staple food of the population, but cultivating cereals was not an activity that made men rich. As a pamphleteer put it in 1677, "our lands fall [in value] for want of being improved some other way besides planting corn, breeding for wool, etc., which are become so low in price as scarce to turn to account." Or, as Sir John Lowther, owner of a large estate in Cumbria, explained in the 1680s: he grew corn to employ the poor but never made any profit out of it.[7]

Low grain prices were not the only cause of farmers' complaints. The pamphleteer of 1677 also referred to the low price of wool. This had caused anxiety from about 1614 onwards and was due to changing circumstances in continental cloth markets. The competitive textile industries of Europe reduced the demand for English cloth, and since Englishmen thought that the foreigners' success derived in part from their use of English wool, they secured a ban on wool exports in 1614. No arguments by the wool producers subsequently succeeded in persuading the government to change its attitude and adopt the same policy toward them as was adopted toward corn growers, that is, to encourage wool exports. So wool prices continued to fall, and whenever the matter was debated in Parliament, in the 1660s, 1670s, and 1680s, the ban on wool export was reaffirmed.[8]

Two kinds of agricultural region where low corn and wool prices hit farmers hardest were the wolds and downlands of England, where the farming system relied on these two crops in combination (the sheep flock was folded at night on the light arable soils, in order to keep them fertile for grain); and some vale lands on clays and loams where sheep and cereals were combined with other livestock enterprises. These kinds of countryside were extensive in southern, eastern, and central England. Nevertheless, it would be a mistake to look to these regions for a picture of universal misery in the second half of the seventeenth century. Not all wool producers were at a loss to find a market for their wool. Smuggling was rife, and those with easy access to the coast, especially the Channel coast, found many quiet coves and inlets from which to dispatch their wool to France at an eminently satisfactory price.[9]

The corn growers offer even more examples of ingenuity. Men had been criticized in the 1570s and the 1580s for their moral irresponsibility in using grain to make starch.[10] Nevertheless, this proved a useful way of using surplus grain in the seventeenth century. Yet more grain went to feed livestock, and more still went into a whole new range of stronger beers and ales, using larger quantities of barley than before.[11] Grain also went into the distilling of spirits. Whereas brandy, *aqua vitae,* and other spirits had been valued purely as medicines in the early seventeenth century, they came to be regarded as daily refreshment by the end. Exports of beer, spirits, and malt helped further. The Commonwealth first allowed beer exports by its Act of 1656, and although this policy was not found acceptable in 1663, it was again permitted in 1670; some slightly conflicting evidence points to an increase of beer exports to Ireland as a result. Distillers were encouraged first by a prohibition on the import of French brandies and spirits in 1689, and secondly, in 1690, by financial incentives to use English malted corn for spirit making "for the greater consumption of corn and the advancement of tillage." In addition, export was promoted by allowing a "drawback" of threepence a gallon on all spirits made from English malted corn that were sent overseas. Finally, from 1697 onwards malt exports were promoted by allowing a 'drawback' of the excise duty on all quantities sold abroad. As a result the foreign market for English malt expanded apace; its price allowed the Dutch to buy it far cheaper than if they had made their own from barley bought in the Baltic.[12]

Thus the most efficient grain producers had plenty of ways of overcoming low prices. And there were many efficient farmers in the seventeenth century, especially on the light soils of the wolds and downlands, where both the routine of cultivation and the social structure enabled them to farm to best advantage. Cereal growing is most economically managed in large units, and large farms were numerous in this kind of country. Moreover, farmers had taken up the use of clover, sainfoin, and lucerne in their arable rotations, and had introduced the floating of water meadows, so that, as grain prices fell, they could still prosper, partly through better stock management. For small farmers with holdings that were too small to function efficiently, however, and in those arable regions where the conditions were not absolutely ideal for grain, the low prices of cereals and of wool, continuing for generations, wore down the most courageous spirits.

Nevertheless, alternative courses of action were many. A considerable number of special crops had been introduced since the mid-sixteenth century which were of inestimable value in supplementing sagging incomes from conventional agricultural produce. First were vegetables and fruits, innumerable in range and variety, which greatly diversified diet; second were industrial crops such as dye plants (woad, madder, weld, and saffron), teasels, hemp and flax, and coleseed for oil. Third were a miscellaneous group of food and medicinal plants such as hops, tobacco, liquorice, herbs of many kinds, and even canary seed for feeding to caged birds. And finally in the years after 1650 men took increasing interest in growing trees for timber. Many of these crops did not call for fundamental reorganization of the farming routine. They were either, like coleseed, inserted into an existing arable rotation, or they called for a small piece of land to be set aside for one special crop. Thus they involved minor adjustments, which enabled individuals to take advantage of the unusually high prices which these specialities fetched. Not all these alternatives were available to all farmers, but for most there was something. Thus we find hop growing spreading remarkably through southeastern England and the West Midlands, occupying small plots of land of as little as two acres. Coleseed spread from East Anglia throughout the eastern half of England including east Yorkshire. Orchards multiplied in the West Midlands, and cider and perry-making became serious commercial enterprises. The legislation, which allowed the export of beer and spirits, included cider for the first time in 1688 — a sure sign that it was becoming a substantial business.[13]

The success of all these special crops explains why they figure so prominently in the agricultural literature in the second half of the seventeenth century. Some historians have been puzzled at the attention paid to what they have called "marginal activities like fruit growing, bee keeping and so on."[14] They were not frivolities; they were the lifelines in a period of difficult agricultural conditions. The general trend of earnings from traditional products was so discouraging that men had to find alternatives. In the event, their ingenuity was remarkable.

The diversification of agricultural systems in the seventeenth century, implicit in the account above, makes problems for anyone wishing to generalize about the nature of the agricultural depression. The opportunities for adjustment varied much from place to place, and when new crops were known and available locally, they were not taken up by all. Plainly, the opportunity for marketing many special crops was greatest around London and other large towns. John Aubrey in the 1680s, for example, described the vegetable growing in Somerset and Wiltshire which supplied the Bristol market. Cabbages, carrots, and turnips made a living for many gardeners and some farmers. A crop like woad suited different circumstances. It came to the aid of large farmers and also provided much work for agricultural laborers, but it did not suit the circumstances of husbandmen. Some communities found no lifelines, and in some arable regions the disappearance of the small landowner is well documented. Margaret Spufford has shown the process under way well before 1640 in the cereal/sheep country of Chippenham, Cambridgeshire.[16] In other places it can be well documented in the later seventeenth century. Because England was breaking down into many specialized regions, each exploited its unique local circumstances in different ways. This meant unique experiences.[17]

In pasture farming country, new avenues for enterprise opened up which in a general way may be said to have given the rural population still more varied opportunities for making a decent living. Rural industries multiplied in number and spread into more places. Livestock enterprises prospered because the demand for meat did not fall as much as the demand for grain. The Irish Cattle Acts in 1663 and 1667, which were originally devised to help the graziers who fattened animals in the south and east, greatly stimulated livestock rearing in the north and west. A new era of opportunity opened for dairy producers, since larger industrial populations placed more reliance on cheese as a foodstuff which did not have to be cooked. Some highly commercialized dairying regions developed in the West Midlands and around the Newcastle coalfield, and the scale of individual enterprises increased.[18]

Increased market demand in pastoral areas was met by significant improvements to grasslands. They are less conspicuous in our records than changes in arable systems which can be readily identified through new rotations and the introduction of more varied crops. But, in fact, the attention paid to the quality of grassland wrought a virtual revolution in its feeding capacity. Much has been written about the floating of water meadows which enabled farmers to bring on grass in the middle of March and cater for the lean month of April. Farmers could, for example, advance lambing times and get a high price for early lamb at the butcher. But watering was an expensive system, available only to farmers who had a good deal of cash. A very considerable, but cheaper, improvement was wrought by the use of fertilizers, especially lime. And taking the kingdom as a whole, it is probable that lime wrought more widespread improvement in pastoral country in the course of the seventeenth century than water meadows. A modern experiment on acid soils in Hertfordshire has shown that yields of barley and beans can be increased by as much as 10 and 12 percent by liming. The evidence shows this improvement in England from the sixteenth century onwards, and in Scotland from the early seventeenth century.[19]

It was lime which enabled some derelict grassland in Gloucestershire to support tobacco crops year after year, when tobacco was in danger of drawing away manure that should have gone to enhance the yields of cereals. The value of lime is much emphasized in Aubrey's survey of agriculture. Indeed, he claimed in the 1680s that Irchenfield district was the barrenest part of Herefordshire before the liming of land was known. However, Aubrey also underlined the fact that lime was not cheaply available everywhere.[20] The need to improve supplies thus became one of several arguments in favor of river improvement. Not all pasture farmers could benefit equally before 1700. Where lime was available in abundance and the use of more nutritive plants like clover and rye grass was introduced, we may guess that pasture farmers had the opportunity to improve the quality and quantity of their fodder for livestock with benefits to both dairying and meat production. But advances were not evenly distributed.

In examining the gradual spread of agricultural improvements in the sixteenth and seventeenth centuries, I have concluded that the nobility, gentry, and well-to-do merchants were necessarily the pioneers of new crops, systems of cultivation, and management.[21] The distribution of such men with interest, initiative, and the cash to experiment was patchy. Hence the diffusion of improvements was patchy. Gentry favored residence in nucleated villages. Such settlements were characteristic of grain-growing country. But villages were thinly spread in pastoral areas where settlements mostly took the form of scattered farmsteads and hamlets. Hence the pioneering influence of gentry on agricultural improvement hardly penetrated some regions until the end of the seventeenth century.

In the West Midlands, where gentry, especially many younger sons, had moved in to set up estates around 1600, they were extremely effective in pushing new ideas and new practices. Their example was quickly followed by ordinary farmers because the industrial and commercial development of that part of England was going rapidly forward. But their influence was much slower in spreading through Cheshire and Lancashire and slower still in spreading through Westmorland, Cumberland, and, of course, Scotland.

Turning from general developments in the seventeenth century to the more immediate experiences of the farming population around 1680, we see that a spirit of gloom pervaded public pronouncements on the condition of the farming interest. But, of course, landlords spoke loudest and were most influential at Westminster. An inquiry was launched in Parliament in 1669 into "the decay of rents and trade."[22] The decay of rents was related to the difficulties of letting agricultural land because of low farm prices. But in this connection most publicity was given to the low rents of pastures, which had not benefited as expected from the ban on Irish cattle imports, and this disappointment sprang mainly from the Home Counties. Margaret Gay Davies's investigations into landlords' rent rolls in Northamptonshire, north Buckinghamshire, and Warwickshire show persistent complaints of rents "ill paid" or land "flung up by tenants for want of ability to pay." The years 1678-79 were the first in two decades when the Verney family in Buckinghamshire saw some amelioration of their troubles in securing rents. Other estates varied in their fortunes in the later 1670s, some seeing an improvement, others hardly noticing any. But the permanent pastures of the Southern and East Midlands were worst hit by falling rents, and landlords here did not represent the whole community of pasture farmers. Those in the north and northwest, paying low rents and lightly taxed, were much more content with the new state of affairs. The Irish Cattle Acts had benefited them unexpectedly.[23]

Nevertheless, low prices drew gloomy comments from many different quarters in the 1670s. We may gauge the pessimism of men looking to the future in the following comments. In 1676 wool was described as a drug on the market; butter, cheese, and grain prices had fallen. In 1677 grain and wool were described as again low in price, and wheat so low that a farmer could not live. From Derbyshire came a land agent's plea for understanding from his master. He could not raise rents, since tenants could not be found even at the present rent. A Hertfordshire landlord received even gloomier letters from Wales. In June 1679 a letter from his agent told him "that the markets here are so quite down that I am in despair of any rent for you. There was but one drover at the last Newtown fair who bought scarce twenty cattle." In August of the same year the agent wrote again of rent arrears. He had received only £3 after two local fairs, whereas usually he expected to collect £100–150. These complaints came from pastoral areas. In the 1680s attention shifted to the grain-growing regions, hit by a dramatic fall in cereal prices. Fluctuations in price had kept hopes of a long-term improvement alive in the 1670s. But in the 1680s the index of wheat prices, which had stood at 100 in 1680, fell to 66 by 1688. Farmers received a price that was 33 percent below average. In a 1689 letter from Birdsall, East Yorkshire, a land agent advised his master, "in these uncertain times we would do as well to let it [a vacant farm] at almost any rent, as keep it in hand. Have sold 40 quarters of barley, at 13s. 4d., 13s. 6d., and 13s. 8d., but at present our markets are so low, can sell no more." The 1690s were to bring far worse problems, though for a different reason. The barren years were 1692 – 99, when grain rose in price because the harvests failed year after year. Times of plenty did not return till 1700.[24]

The depressed condition of conventional agriculture in the second half of the seventeenth century broke many small farmers, and accounts for the general observation, made long ago by A. H. Johnson, that this was the age marking the disappearance of the small landowner.[25] But the prolonged depression stimulated many alternative activities which flourished and brought salvation to members of all classes of rural society. Rural populations, in pastoral areas especially, benefited from the spread of consumer industries. And for those communities which relied increasingly on bought foodstuffs, low prices were a benefit.

No mention has so far been made of the difficulties for smallholders and cottagers brought about by enclosure. Enclosure proceeded steadily in the second half of the seventeenth century, especially in more northerly counties. But procedure by agreement made it a less bitter experience, and price levels plainly did not encourage a massive movement. As parishes became enclosed, new relationships of interdependence or conflict were likely to develop with neighboring parishes which remained open. In other words, tension could increase if land use changed in enclosed parishes, and unemployed laborers or dispossessed cottagers were obliged to move on into those parishes still lying in common field. As a midland commentator had expressed it bitterly in 1656, "The enclosures get the gain, and have the ease and poor open fields pay the shot and endure all the drudgery."[26] On the other hand, some neighboring parishes contrived new economic relations which gave commonfield farmers a new, positive, and vital role in the changing local economy, supplying grain to their neighbors who now concentrated on a branch of pasture farming.

In short, the specialized farming regions, which are well documented for sixteenth-century England, were all undergoing more varied and more subtle changes of direction in the seventeenth century, partly as a result of industrial expansion (especially in the West Midlands, Yorkshire, and Lancashire), partly as a result of rising standards of living which were associated with a more diversified diet, and partly as a result of expanding opportunities to export food abroad. These agricultural developments might have been perceived in a positive way by those who responded to the challenges. Among traditional farmers, however, who felt they lacked any room to maneuver, the long-term outlook was depressing. Thus in seeking explanations for late seventeenth-century migration from England, we may well learn more from changing local economies and the structure of local societies than from overgeneralized accounts, which portray conditions in terms of extreme contrasts and fail to notice subtle local influences.

NOTES

1. Joan Thirsk and J. P. Cooper, eds., *Seventeenth-Century Economic Documents* (Oxford, 1972), pp. 175–76.

2. A full account is contained in Thirsk, *Agrarian History,* vol. 5, pt. II, chap. 13.

3. W. Notestein, F.H. Relf, and H. Simpson, eds., *Commons Debates, 1621* (New Haven, 1935), 2:178, 453; 5:491, 514; 7:618; Thirsk and Cooper, *Economic Documents,* pp. 1, 122.

4. Thirsk and Cooper, *Economic Documents,* pp. 48–52.

5. Thirsk, *Agrarian History,* vol. 5, pt. II, chap. 16.

6. Ibid., vol. 5, pt. II, chaps. 13, 16.

7. *Proposals for Building in every County a Working-Alms-House* (1677), in *Harleian Miscellany,* 4 (1745):465; A. B. Appleby, *Famine in Tudor and Stuart England* (Liverpool, 1978), p. 160.

8. Thirsk, *Agrarian History,* vol. 5, pt. II, chap. 16.

9. Ibid.

10. Joan Thirsk, *Economic Policy and Projects* (Oxford, 1978), pp. 89–90.

11. I owe this information to Dr. Peter Clark.

12. Thirsk, *Agrarian History,* vol. 5, pt. II, chap. 16.

13. For a full account of these different crops, see ibid., vol. 5, pt. II, chap. 19.

14. K. Tribe, *Land, Labour and Economic Discourse* (London, 1978), p. 64.

15. Thirsk and Cooper, *Economic Documents,* p. 179.

16. Margaret Spufford, "Peasant Inheritance Customs and Land Distribution in Cambridgeshire from the Sixteenth to the Eighteenth Centuries," in *Family and Inheritance,* ed. J. Goody, J. Thirsk, and E. P. Thompson (Cambridge, 1976), pp. 160–61.

17. The more elaborate farming specialization of small localities is well illustrated in the regional chapters in Thirsk, *Agrarian History,* vol. 5, pt. I.

18. Ibid., vol. 5, pt. II, chap. 16; P. R. Edwards, "The Development of Dairy Farming on the North Shropshire Plain in the Seventeenth Century," *Midland History,* 4 (1978):175ff.

19. E. Kerridge, *The Agricultural Revolution* (London, 1967), pp. 251ff.; M. A. Havinden, "Lime as a Means of Agricultural Improvement: The Devon Example," in *Rural Change and Urban Growth, 1500-1800,* ed. C. W. Chalklin and M. A. Havinden (London, 1974), pp. 104ff.; I. Whyte, *Agriculture and Society in Seventeenth-Century Scotland* (Edinburgh, 1979), pp. 198–208; Thirsk and Cooper, *Economic Documents,* pp. 126–27.

20. Thirsk and Cooper, *Economic Documents,* pp. 180–81.

21. Thirsk, *Agrarian History,* vol. 5, pt. II, chap. 19.

22. Thirsk and Cooper (*Economic Documents,* pp. 68–95) print both the minutes of the House of Lords' committee investigating this depression and the views of other observers.

23. Margaret Gay Davies, "Country Gentry and Falling Rents in the 1660s and 1670s," *Midland History,* 4 (1978):86–96; J. V. Beckett, "English Landownership in the Later Seventeenth and Eighteenth Centuries: The Debate and the Problems," *Economic History Review,* 2d ser., 30 (1977):579–80.

24. *CSPD, 1676,* p. 113; *Harleian Miscellany,* 4:467; D1101/F9, Derbyshire Record Office; John Wilson to Sir John Witterwronge, 20 May 1679 and 7 Aug. 1679, D/ELW E60, Hertfordshire Record Office.

25. A. H. Johnson, *The Disappearance of the Small Landowner* (London, 1963), pp. 135-36; Thirsk, *Economic Policy,* pp. 167ff.; M. Rowlands, *Masters and Men in the West Midland Metalware Trades before the Industrial Revolution* (Manchester, 1975), chaps. 2, 3; David Hey, *The Rural Metalworkers of the Sheffield Region* (Occasional Paper, 2d. ser., 5, Dept. of English Local History, Leicester University [Leicester, 1972]).

26. Thirsk and Cooper, *Economic Documents,* p. 150.

7 ◦ The World Women Knew:
Women Workers in the North of England During the Late Seventeenth Century

"Hitherto the historian has paid little attention to the circumstances of women's lives." Sound familiar? Actually, it is the opening sentence of a book published in 1919, *Working Life of Women in the Seventeenth Century*.[1] Alice Clark's classic remains today the best treatment available of the world English women of the era knew, despite the fact that she made no attempt to cover every facet of their existence. To Clark, the vital point to grasp about the lives of seventeenth-century women was their active participation in all sectors of the market economy — agriculture, industry, commerce, and the professions — because it contradicted the conventional wisdom of her own time that women lacked the physical and mental strength to perform well as workers and, therefore, had to confine their limited energies to domestic endeavors. During the succeeding centuries, she argued, capitalism had forced women to abandon one area of gainful employment after another until by the twentieth century it became possible to deny that females possessed the capacity for productive labor. By rediscovering the seventeenth-century world of women's work, one could refute the Victorian precepts about women's place that had so restricted the opportunities of Clark and her female contemporaries.

Over sixty years have passed since the publication of *Working Life* and one feminist movement has given way to another. Reconsideration of the life and times of working women in the seventeenth century is merited for at least two reasons. First, as economic studies of occupational segregation and dual labor markets pile up, Clark's observations concerning women's performance record in the early modern workforce, the reclassification of jobs as male only, and wage inequality take on added significance. Her argument points up the need for further research on women's status in pre-industrial settings, to discover how and why male and female career patterns diverged. How widespread was women's work outside of the home? What kind of work did spinsters, wives, and widows usually perform? To what extent did occupational segregation exist in agricultural communities, and did the benefits of the family economy adequately compensate for whatever wage discrimination took place?

The attacks in recent years by feminist theorists and the "New Home Economists" on the standard practice of defining work to exclude domestic labor suggests a second reason why a reconsideration of women's pre-industrial employment is in order. In *Working Life,* Clark operated within the traditional definition, explaining that she had omitted

> the highest most intense forms to which women's productive energy is directed . . . the spiritual creation of the home and the physical creation of the child [because] though essentially productive, such achievements of creative power transcend the limitations of economics and . . . there would be something almost degrading in any attempt to weight them in the balance with productions that are bought and sold in the market.[2]

Her position here has been criticized,[3] and rightly so, although it becomes more understandable when placed in the context of her times. Clark wanted men to associate women with something more than childbearing, child-rearing, and housework. By accepting the orthodox piety that labor in the home was too sacred for economic analysis, she could concentrate on her principal objective, the demonstration of women's ability to function in the paid workforce, and avoid the problems involved in quantifying mother-hood. Now, however, the inseparability of the roles has become clear. In light of what we currently know about seventeenth-century demography and household division of labor, it is impossible to explain women's position in the marketplace or evaluate their contribution to the economy without taking reproduction and domestic services into account.

Those investigating the participation of women in the preindustrial workforce consistently run into problems with sources. Parish registers, probate records, and muster rolls often furnish specific occupational labels for men but either exclude women workers altogether or only mention the social characteristic that men, traditionally, have found most intriguing about the opposite sex — their marital status. Using standard sources, a recent study of the early modern occupational structure in England tried to estimate the employment status of women as well as men but could only classify 13.8 percent of the female population around 1700 — 12.8 percent as servants and 1 percent in other occupations.[4]

As Alice Clark demonstrated, a more promising source for the discovery of how women earned—or failed to earn—a living exists in household account books. Before the age of the office and the factory, the organizational unit for both market and home production was the household. It functioned as the prime requisitioner of goods and services, and the richer the family firm the more ordering that went on. Account books record these purchases and often the names of the sellers of the labor and commodities. But they, too, can be biased against the economic role of women because they often only include the purchases for farm production or items ordered by the master of the household from shopkeepers. Payments to peddlers and laborers who provided domestic goods and services, a disproportionate number of whom were women, are omitted or lumped together under the sum received by the lady of the household. For example, accounts for the William Penn household, kept by his business manager Philip Ford, contain interesting information about goods bought from London tradespeople and income from family estates, but the goods and services requisitioned from the community around their houses at Rickmansworth and Warminghurst are hidden in the allowances given Penn and his wife.[5]

The ideal account book for my purposes, therefore, would have been kept either by an unmarried estate owner (or his steward who supervised all activities) or by a lady of the house who ran both the family business and the household. An excellent example of the latter type exists for one of the most famous menages in seventeenth-century England, the household of Margaret Askew Fell Fox. Alice Clark used examples from these accounts in her book and wrote an introduction to the printed volume published in 1920. It is this amazing document, covering the years 1673–78, that will provide a base for my own analysis.[6]

The life of the Fell women is a story in itself, and they have been the subject of numerous books and articles.[7] "Typical" would be a poor word to use in describing the family unless one was also prepared to argue that matriarchy was the dominant form of household organization north of the Sands in the Furness district of Lancashire. Margaret Askew was born at Marsh Grange in 1614, the daughter of a Lancashire gentry family with only one other child, also a girl. The absence of male heirs resulted in handsome portions of £3,000 each for the sisters, no small amount in early Stuart Furness. At seventeen Margaret married Judge Thomas Fell of Swarthmoor Hall, a man almost twice her age, and from then until about the age of forty, Margaret had a baby nearly every two years. Eight children survived to adulthood—seven girls and one boy. Despite the seniority of her husband and her large family, Margaret was far more than a handmaiden to greatness. She took a lively interest in religious issues, which in the context of revolutionary England also meant political disputes, before George Fox arrived on the scene. When the Quaker leader did come to the

Swarthmoor area in 1652, it was Margaret, not her husband, who made the Hall the headquarters for the movement. Judge Fell neither joined the Friends nor interfered with his spouse's activities. After Thomas Fell's death in 1658 and even after her marriage to Fox in 1669, Margaret retained control over Swarthmoor and with her daughters managed that estate along with Marsh Grange despite the machinations of her disaffected son, George, and imprisonment by the authorities for her religious activities. All her daughters converted and married Friends. It was a middle child, Sarah, who actually kept the accounts.

Margaret and her daughters fought hard in the 1670s to establish the Swarthmoor Women's Meeting. Its development followed naturally from her pamphleteering against those who attempted to use Saint Paul's admonition against women speaking in churches to deny females full participation in the movement. Throughout this campaign, however, she kept her base among male Quakers not simply by marrying Fox but also by having the Hall serve as a rest and recreation spot for traveling preachers and, generally, knowing what services men expected women to perform.

While the extraordinary Fell women are not the focus of the analysis here, their activities dictated what was bought, sold, and recorded. As leaders in the Swarthmoor Women's Meeting, they entered in the accounts that organization's aid to poor women, which resulted in more females appearing as objects of charity than might otherwise be the case. Presumably the somber Quaker lifestyle affected the family's consumption habits and thus the goods and services they bought, although here the deviation might be less than expected. Margaret Fox refused to accept the Friends' dress code, and critics within the movement complained of the naked necks and fine apparel of the Fell women. Margaret and her daughters energetically ran their own affairs, and consequently those economic activities associated with women, such as dairying, got full attention; the smallest purchases made for domestic purposes found their way into the account books.

Even the force of Margaret Fox's personality, however, could not transform the spare environment or the sluggish economy of the Furness district. North of the Sands in Lancashire may not have been the last place God made — we all have our favorite candidates for that honor — but it must have been near the end of the list. The villagers of Ulverston, the community nearest to Swarthmoor Hall, lived in considerable isolation, with even travel to the nearest provincial centers proving arduous. A hilly road awaited the traveler to Kendal in Westmorland, and traffic to Lancaster could pass over the Sands only when the tide was low. Nor could the area be characterized as being abundant in resources, aside from perhaps peat moss. The Furness district was truly the north of England, resembling its neighboring counties much more than it did the rest of Lancashire.[8] In this commercially underdeveloped region, the labor force depended more

TABLE 7.1   *The Women who Transacted Business with the Fell Household by Marital Status, 1673–78*

Business Transacted	Single	Widowed/ Married	Status Unknown
Selling Goods/Services[a]	87.2%	53.0%	46.0%
Receiving Charity only	2.6	6.0	14.3
Buying only	7.7	41.0	34.9
Lending at Interest only	2.6	0.0	4.8
N =	39	83	63

SOURCE: Norman Penney, ed., *The Household Account Book of Sarah Fell of Swarthmoor Hall* (Cambridge, 1920).

[a]The goods and the services sold by these women are itemized in Table 7.3. Many of them also bought goods from the Fells and a few also received charity.

upon the landed gentry and less upon the shopkeeper and the small industrialist to furnish consumer goods and to supply jobs than in the more southern portions of late seventeenth-century England.

The names of approximately 185 women appear in the Fell account book as transacting business with the household or receiving charity. Alice Clark has already described the large number of jobs performed by seventeenth-century women and has explained how the work differed by marital status and class. The single woman labored usually as a live-in servant while the married woman, according to Clark, centered her efforts on production for home needs. The scarcer the family resources, the more the wife had to seek occasional labor and personally peddle commodities she had produced or bought to resell. What we would like to know is what proportion of women had to seek employment outside of their own homes.

In table 7.1, women who worked for or sold goods to the Fells have been separated from those women who only bought products from them or banked money for interest with the family. Charity recipients went into yet another category. After removing the women paid by the Fells for their labor services and the welfare cases, only one third of the women remain, and clearly many of these women labored for other gentry families such as the Prestons or the Doddings who had estates as large as or larger than Swarthmoor Hall. Indeed, some of those who show up only as buyers in the accounts may have actually been peddling Fell household products to the community. For example, there were women who paid the Fells for cheese that they had taken out on consignment and sold. Other women who bought cheese may also have been peddling it rather than using it for home consumption, but since the records are not clear, these women had to be classified as buyers only. Considering this situation, it is difficult to believe that any more than 10 percent of women in the Furness community escaped having to go out into the world at some time to help the family earn a living.

As might be expected, single women had the highest percentage of sellers of goods or services, at 87.2 percent. Their contribution to the workforce should not be underestimated. In preindustrial English society, the years of working spinsterhood constituted a large portion of the average woman's life. As we all know, a girl did not attend school to age eighteen, work three years, and then retire at age twenty-one to enjoy fifty years of wedded bliss. Rather, she commenced her career by age twelve, probably as a casual laborer in agriculture, and did not marry until her middle or late twenties. Ten to 15 percent of females did not marry at all. During the years of marriage, a woman's mortality rate rose because of increased age and recurring pregnancies. If she survived her husband, the widow past thirty had chances ranging from slim to none for remarriage. Thus the working time spent as an unmarried woman could easily equal or exceed the working time spent as a wife.

It is also no surprise that widows and women of unknown status comprised the greatest proportion of charity recipients. (In table 7.1 I combined the widows with those for whom it was impossible to determine marital status because many of the latter were described as "old" and they had work patterns similar to those whose husbands had died.) The social tracts of early modern Europe are replete with references to the poverty of widows. Presumably, most of the non-Quaker needy in the community received support from the parish or sought other sources of benevolence. Those women for whom the Fells provided commodities that they could peddle have been counted as sellers of goods or services rather than charity cases.

Exactly what kind of work did the women in the Fell account book perform? Table 7.2 divides women of each marital status into occupational groups and contrasts their job distribution with that of the males in the accounts.[9] Looking first at the women, it can be seen that about a quarter of all groups engaged in some form of occasional day labor in the fields and gardens. Single women, as assumed, appeared most often as live-in servants, hired by the year. Judging by the agricultural products sold by the Fells and the consumer goods purchased, these women probably tended the dairy, raised poultry, and brewed beer, in addition to doing general housework and helping out at harvest time. Married women primarily peddled food and manure (the latter counted in table 7.2 under agricultural labor because so many of the manure gatherers also did day work on farms), but also spun and knitted. Widows and those of unknown status spread themselves over the categories more evenly than either of the other two groups.

In a comparison of the occupational distribution of the two sexes, it is not surprising that more men appeared in the managerial and professional

TABLE 7.2   *Occupational Group,[a] Sex, and Marital Status of Those Supplying Goods and Services to the Fell Household, 1673–78.*

Occupational Group		Women			Men
	Single	Married	Widow and Status Unknown	Total	
Managerial and professional[b]	0.0%	0.0%	6.9%	1.9%	9.8%
Craftwork	8.8	15.9	13.8	13.1	27.9
Retailing — dry goods, imports	0.0	2.3	20.7	6.5	7.3
Retailing — food, farm products, supplies	5.9	38.6	13.8	21.5	12.2
Personal service[c]	52.9	4.5	0.0	18.7	14.5
Agricultural day labor[d]	29.4	25.0	24.1	26.2	24.2
Combination of the above	3.0	13.6	20.7	17.1	4.2
N =	34	44	29	107	165

SOURCE: See Table 7.1.

a. Investors in Fell enterprises and depositors of money have not been included here. Thus there is no capitalist category.
b. The 2 women were midwives.
c. Primarily live-in servants, but nurses and mail carriers also fall into this category.
d. Includes those who gathered manure and peats and sold these items to the Fells.

ranks in craftwork, and the retailing of manufactured goods and imports, while women had higher proportions in personal service and retailing of food. About a quarter of the women, as of the men, performed agricultural labor. A recent study of harvest work on a mid-seventeenth-century Yorkshire estate found that women put in 38 percent of the time required to bring in the field crops.[10] Many women not only worked at harvest but also devoted many hours to the cultivation of the garden, flax, and hemp.

Another noteworthy piece of information contained in table 7.2 is that a higher percentage of women than men did work in more than one occupational group. If the selling of manure had not been included with agricultural day labor, this difference would have been even more pronounced. The maid servant automatically became a Jill-of-all-trades, but it appears that specialization was not easy for women after marriage (13.6 percent, combination of categories), and even more difficult for widows (20.7 percent). Also the Fells were not the only customer or employer for these women. Many of them were doing other kinds of jobs for another employer. According to the picture that emerges, men as they matured moved from servant and apprentice to a higher status or more specialized job within their sector, while women remained unspecialized and always in a low-ranking position looking anxiously for where they fit into the workforce. The married woman or the widow lacked even the assurance of a year's employment. Men in preindustrial society might be forced to practice dual occupations, but women had to endure a lifetime of ever-changing miscellaneous tasks.

It is customary to discuss women's work in the context of their household's economy. Clearly the income of the wife, husband, and sometimes the daughter and son went into the household pot, and to survive the family operated as a cooperative unit. At the same time, often in the rural slice of life exposed in the Fell account book the male was either dead or lacked the resources and expertise to structure the paid labor of the females in his household. While marriage and children affected the kind of employment a woman sought, her husband's or her father's job often had litttle to do with her own, nor could he instruct her in those skills she needed to earn a salary, jobs being so identified with one sex or the other. Few women, I suspect, learned from a man how to spin flax, make cheese, or deliver a baby.

To get a sense of the extent to which work was designated as either male or female, it is necessary to go beyond occupational groupings and examine specific tasks. Because Alice Clark wished to demonstrate women's capacity to perform all sorts of employment, she probably underestimated the amount of job segregation that existed in the seventeenth century. Table 7.3 reveals the number of men and women who carried out the various services needed by the Fells. Beginning with professional and managerial services and craftwork, we see that employment in both areas split totally by gender. Men engaged in estate management, legal work, tax collecting, and teaching. Women functioned as midwives. Twenty-six women were artisans, all of them either spinners or knitters. Forty-nine men did craftwork, following the trades of carpenter, smith, plasterer, saddler, weaver, whitener, fuller, dyer, tailor, and so on. None, however, spun or knitted.

Retailing presents more of a mixed picture, but that may be partially illusory. Men owned the shops where the Fells regularly placed their orders for imported goods and the finer fabrics. Women peddled small amounts of ribbons, coarse cloth, and candles, occasionally making sales to the Fells. Most of the selling they engaged in, however, involved food and other agricultural supplies — primarily poultry, butter, and manure. Manure gathering was an activity so near to day labor that, in Table 7.2, it has been included under that category rather than retailing. Married men sometimes peddled geese and butter that I suspect had been raised or made by their wives, but women less frequently sold those things associated with the male world, such as coal and livestock. Mostly wives and widows carried out the peddling and some actually produced the product they sold, but if they did so on a large scale they or a servant sold it at the Thursday market in Ulverston or elsewhere. They usually did not go door to door. In fact, most of the female door-to-door peddlers did not produce what they ped- dled but obtained it from people such as the Fells who, after shipping products to major ports and marketing more in the locality, sold the residue to them to re-sell. Alice Clark resurrected the term "regratresses," used by contemporaries to describe these women and drew attention to their pov- erty-stricken situation in the seventeenth century. Borough authorities fre- quently passed laws forbidding their activities because they competed with provisioners who had shops. In the countryside, where these shops seldom existed, the women apparently could operate without fear of prosecution.[11]

Servants hired by the year appear under the personal service category in table 7.3, although they performed both farm and domestic labor. A significant proportion of single women worked as farm servants during the early modern period. According to household surveys for the south of England, about 33 percent of women aged fifteen to nineteen, 66 percent of those between twenty and twenty-four, and 10-20 percent of those between twenty-five and thirty-four lived in families as servants. There is no reason to believe that the percentages were any lower in the north.[12]

Servants at both Swarthmoor Hall and Marsh Grange appear in the accounts, and it may be that there were other servants paid by someone other than Sarah Fell. At any rate, considering from the accounts only those servants that belonged to Swarthmoor Hall, it appears that Margaret Fox kept two female servants and four to five male servants in the house at one time. The turnover during the five-year period was greater for the women than the men. Seldom did the women stay longer than the year for which they were hired, a pattern that seems quite common all over England at this time.[13] Although the maids' tasks are not specified, occasionally the accounts do give glimpses into their employments. They marketed the dairy goods and the garden vegetables and thus probably also saw to their production, although the most extensive dairying occurred at Marsh Grange. Male tenants and employees outside of the Hall milled the grain and malted the barley, but the maids most likely baked and brewed since the Fells purchased insufficient amounts of bread and drink for everyday use. The household bought soap and some candles but orders for tallow indicate candles also were manufactured in the home. Men servants often received money for their expenses while staying in neighboring towns on errands, but no such references occur for the maids, implying that they stayed close to the Hall and under constant supervision. The errand runners who were women were not servants, and as a rule their errands took them to other

TABLE 7.3   *Goods and Services Supplied to the Fell Household by Sex of Suppliers*

Goods and Services	Women	Men
Professional and Managerial		
a. Legal work	0	5
b. Midwifery	2	0
c. Estate and business services	0	10
d. Teaching	0	2
Craftwork		
a. Woodwork	0	9
b. Metalwork	0	7
c. Plastering	0	6
d. Leatherwork	0	7
e. Rope and basketwork	0	2
f. Clothwork		
1. Spinning	22	0
2. Bucking yarn	0	1
3. Weaving	0	4
4. Whitening	0	1
5. Fulling	0	2
6. Dyeing	0	2
g. Apparel work		
1. Tailoring	0	2
2. Hatmaking	0	3
3. Gloving	0	2
4. Knitting	4	0
5. Hosiery	0	1
Retailing		
a. Shopkeeping	0	9
b. Peddling — dry goods	13	5
c. Selling/peddling — provisions		
1. Victuals — drink and meals	5	2
2. Meat		
a. Red	0	1
b. White	11	5
3. Bread	3	0
4. Butter/cheese	11	2
d. Selling/peddling — farm supplies		
1. Livestock	0	4
2. Hay	2	1
3. Manure	15	8
4. Peats	1	8
5. Coal	0	2
6. Other	9	14

TABLE 7.3   *(continued)*

Goods and Services	Women	Men
Personal Service		
a. General (servants)	18	18
b. Wet-nursing	2	0
c. Errand running	3	3
d. Carting and mail carriers	0	11
e. Chimneysweeping	0	1
Agricultural and Mining		
a. Arable		
1. Harrowing	3	8[a]
2. Manuring	1	3
3. Ploughing	0	2
4. Weeding	0	3
5. Hedging	0	4
6. Haywork	16	5
7. Shearing (reaping)	0	1
8. Mowing	0	4
9. Threshing	0	5
b. Garden		
1. Gardening	0	7
2. Weeding	6	0
c. Flax and hemp ground		
1. Weeding	4	0
2. Pikeing	1	0
3. Pulling hemp	7	0
4. Rippling and setting toppins	0	2
5. Braking	0	3
6. Swingling and hatchelling	5	0
d. Livestock		
1. Salving sheep	0	7
2. Clipping sheep	0	1
3. Veterinary work	0	7
e. Peatwork	6	4
f. Leading ore	0	3
g. Other	2	4
N =	172	225

SOURCE: see Table 7.1.

NOTE: The Account Book lists by name 107 women and 165 men; laborers whose names were omitted in the accounts are not included here. Many people carried out more than one labor service.

[a]At least 5 of these were boys.

households, not to towns. We may assume the maids did some farm work. At least no great distinction was made between house and farm workers, for when one of the maids took a leave because of the death of a parent, one of the girls who did field labor filled in for her.

The breakdown by sex of the tasks involved in agricultural day labor on the Fell estates reveals even greater segregation than might be expected.[14] As far as field work was concerned, Table 7.3 indicates that males and females had only two job descriptions in common: harrowing and, at harvest time, haywork. With harrowing, though, most of the males can be identified as boys, not adults, while the term "haywork" is so vague that we cannot be sure men and women did the same things. Women on the other hand dominated the land set aside for the growing of vegetables, fruit, linen, and hemp. Once again, however, what men do, women do not. In the garden, men do "gardening" and women do "weeding." In the growing and harvesting of flax and hemp, women performed all the tasks from weeding to hackeling except for the rippling (a combing that separated the flax seed from the stalks) and braking. Both of these chores required considerable physical exertion but then so did the pulling of hemp and the swingling of flax, drudgery carried out by women in the Fell household. The rest of the per diem labor was completely segregated except for peatworkers, and again the description makes it unclear whether both sexes performed the same chore. In other regions and other countries, tasks assigned here to males might have been reserved for females and vice versa. What did remain constant, however, was that everywhere jobs were identified as either masculine or feminine.[15]

Where such deep occupational segregation by sex exists, the problem of comparing wages is compounded. Nevertheless, it seems possible to contrast the rewards given to some workers within the same occupational groupings. For example, women who practiced the craft of spinning earned little better than 1d. a day for their efforts while men who toiled as wood-workers (joiners, wrights, coopers) and plasterers received at least 4d. I am not referring here to men who built houses but to laborers who carved out a wooden bowl or patched a garden wall.

The agricultural day labor of a woman seldom merited above 1d. a day, although that of a man almost always brought 3d. Harvest time normally hiked male wages up to 4-7d., but women went no higher than 2d. Only in competition with boys did women ever come out ahead. Women servants hired by the year at Swarthmoor Hall received between £1 and £2 per year, the most common wage being £1 10s. Men earned between £2 10s. and £3 plus clothing that might total 10s. or more. Although they bought dry goods from shopkeepers through the Fells, maids paid for these items out of their salaries. Aside from the young girls who received bed, board, and apparel instead of wages, the terms of hiring for female servants usually did not include more than some coarse cloth for a shift or two.

Thus, counting in livery, male servants cost nearly twice as much as females. These figures correspond to the ratio between the maximum wages allowed female and male servants hired annually in the extant wage assessments for Lancashire.[16] Wage assessments from counties in the south also indicate that women usually received only 50 to 60 percent of the wages their male counterparts earned, although pay was higher there for both sexes than it was in the north.[17]

Many explanations have been offered for the pay differentials that have, historically, existed between the sexes, and a full-fledged industry on wage discrimination now exists in the economics discipline. In preindustrial societies, where so many jobs involved grueling physical labor, it has been argued that the male body with its heavy musculature enabled men to perform certain tasks more efficiently than women, and so they received a more handsome remuneration.[18] This explanation contains an obvious internal contradiction. If we accept the notion that men's larger frame and muscle development made them better suited for certain types of labor, then might we not also assume that the more delicate bodies of women would have predisposed them to other types of jobs — watchmaker, jewelrysmith, or surgeon, for example — that were well rewarded by seventeenth-century English society? The complexity of the early modern economy was such that brute force was not the only attribute in high demand. Yet women, it appears, did not dominate the London Goldsmith Company or the College of Barbers and Surgeons. Clearly other factors were operating.

It is here that the research done in recent years on women's fertility and domestic labor becomes particularly valuable, and the difficulty in confining discussions of work simply to paid employment becomes apparent. Considering the occupational segregation and the wage discrimination in all sectors of the economy, and the fact that, if anything, women's position in the labor market grew more precarious as they matured, while males' position, at least until old age, solidified, it is difficult to reach any other conclusion than that the labor market was essentially set up for men, and women were a subsidiary pool of workers being constantly pressured to shift from one type of employment to another in order to facilitate male adjustment to economic change. Thus Clark found women being squeezed out as weavers and brewers by the guilds. As she discovered and others have subsequently underscored, a class analysis alone cannot explain this situation.[19]

Women occupied a subsidiary or secondary position in the marketplace not because their contribution was so minor but because they had (and have) another job — reproduction of the labor force. In the seventeenth century, childbearing, nursing, and infant care took up large portions of women's time. Later, as fertility declined, childrearing became an even more time-consuming task for females. Other chores connected with maintaining and enhancing the domestic environment have, as we know, tradi-tionally been associated with women also. Indeed, there is some evidence that women, at certain times, chose to build up that domestic role and specialize as much as possible in what might be termed the finishing proc-esses — not only childrearing but cooking, sewing, decorating, and so forth.[20] Thus women cannot be viewed as simply passive objects contin-ually having their world remade by men. At the same time, one has to recognize the very limited number of options from which women could choose in the world of work.

Theoretically, a woman's pay for reproduction and domestic services took the form of support from her husband and, to a lesser extent, espe-cially in England, her children. How one measures that wage in dollars and cents or pounds and pence is a matter of some debate in current economic literature. Even more hotly contested is the allegation that these fictive transfer payments allow women's wages in the labor market to be dis-counted. Interestingly enough, when others received the monetary fruits of women's labor — for example, when masters hired out their slaves — wage differentials shrank. A recent econometric study of nineteenth-cen-tury American slavery shows that, through their teens, women engaged in heavy field work earned more than men for their masters, and during the prime work years from twenty to forty, their net earnings amounted to between 70 and 85 percent of those estimated for males.[21] The free labor market seldom has placed such a high value on women's contribution.

No data exists that permit us to measure how well women got "paid" for their *total* services in the seventeenth century, but there are some indirect ways to ascertain their rewards. It has often been commented upon that females, particularly widows, appear in disproportionate numbers on the poor rolls, but the phenomenon has never been explored in any depth. The recent study of the English occupational structure, mentioned earlier, did include a category for those in the records who had "poor" after their names rather than a job description or marital status. The figures show that of those estimated to be "poor," women comprised 76 percent in 1688; 83 percent in 1700; and 86 percent in 1740. It might be argued that the author-ities more readily gave aid to women labeled "poor"; yet after subtracting pensioners and the relieved poor from the total, nothing changes. Females continue to be as highly overrepresented.[22]

These figures, it seems to me, are the inevitable consequence of a labor market that awarded women between 33 and 60 percent of the wages of men, inheritance laws that bestowed on the widow approximately 33 per-cent of the family resources that a widower would receive, and marriage practices that produced large numbers of spinsters and widows. That En-glish society found this system functional is an interesting comment on its power structure and priorities. If we are to obtain a complete picture of the world of work women knew in the seventeenth century or the early modern period in general it is clearly necessary to study both women's activities in the labor market and their domestic services. Interestingly enough, it is the latter that in recent years has been most closely examined while, to paraphrase Alice Clark, historians have paid little attention to the circumstances of women's participation in the preindustrial workforce. There are excellent reasons why this has been the case. An enormous gap exists in our historical knowledge of what has been viewed as a static private world. Now research on women in the labor market needs to catch up so that we can analyze the two worlds in tandem.

NOTES

I wish to thank Margaret Spufford for the comments and criticisms she made on the original version of this paper.

1. Alice Clark, *Working Life of Women in the Seventeenth Century* (1919; reprint, London, 1982). The new edition has an introduction by Miranda Chaytor and Jane Lewis that pulls together what is known about Alice Clark's life.
2. Ibid., p. 4.
3. Louise A. Tilly and Joan W. Scott, *Women, Work, and Family* (New York, 1978), p. 5; see also Elizabeth Pleck, "Two Worlds in One: Work and Family," *Journal of Social History,* 10 (1976):178-95; Heidi Hartmann, "Capitalism, Patriarchy and Job Segregation by Sex," in *Capitalist Patriarchy and the Case for Socialist Feminism,* ed. Zillah R. Eisenstein (New York, 1979), pp. 207ff.
4. Peter H. Lindert, "English Occupations, 1670-1811," *Journal of Economic History,* 40 (1980):702-4.
5. The Philip Ford Accounts, 1672-80, appear in *PWP,* 1:577-645.
6. Norman Penney, ed., *The Household Account Book of Sarah Fell of Swarthmoor Hall* (Cambridge, 1920). The manuscript was transcribed by Charlotte Fell-Smith.
7. Isabel Ross, *Margaret Fell: Mother of Quakerism* (London, 1949); Helen G. Crosfield, *Margaret Fox of Swarthmoor Hall* (London, 1913); Maria Webb, *The Fells of Swarthmoor Hall,* 2d. ed. (Philadelphia, 1884); see also Milton D. Speizman and Jane C. Kronick, transcribers, "A Seventeenth-Century Quaker Women's Declaration," *Signs,* 1 (1975):231-45.
8. Joan Thirsk groups Furness with Cumberland, Westmorland, and Northumberland in her discussion of the farming regions of England. See Thirsk, *Agrarian History,* 4:16. J. D. Marshall, "Agrarian Wealth and Social Structure in Pre-Industrial Cumbria," *Economic History Review,* 2d ser., 33 (1980):503-21, presents a mixed picture of the area's development. On the one hand, he finds a near doubling of inventoried wealth between 1660 and 1690 and between 1720 and 1750, but he also maintains it was "still fundamentally a subsistence economy."
9. I did not include unnamed sellers of goods and services. Most often Sarah Fell omitted a name when she received a bill for whatever labor or commodity had been bought. Thus male shopkeepers are probably disproportionately excluded by the omission, but this only marginally affected women's percentages.
10. Michael Roberts, "Sickles and Scythes: Women's Work and Men's Work at Harvest Time," *History Workshop,* 7 (1979):3-29.
11. Clark, *Working Life,* pp. 207ff.
12. Ann Kussmaul, *Servants in Husbandry in Early Modern England* (Cambridge, 1981), p. 71.
13. Ibid., pp. 66-69.

14. K. D. M. Snell has recently argued that "there is abundant supportive evidence for a very wide range of female participation in agricultural tasks before 1750 in the south-east, when their work extended to reaping, loading and spreading dung, ploughing, threshing, thatching, following the harrow, sheep shearing, and perhaps even working as shepherdesses. In other regions similar work continued more noticeably into the nineteenth century (particularly in parts of the north, where the 'bondage' system was practised)." See Snell, "Agricultural Seasonal Unemployment, the Standard of Living and Women's Work in the South and East, 1690-1860," *Economic History Review*, 2d ser., 34 (1981):427. The Fell account book suggests that in the Restoration North (1) women were an important part of the agricultural labor force, and (2) field and pasture tasks were sharply divided by gender with women being primarily responsible for haywork and weeding and usually excluded from ploughing, mowing, reaping, threshing, and caring for sheep. In the two wage assessments extant for Lancashire (see n.16, below), female wage rates were given for the hay and corn harvests and for annually hired servants (1595), and later (1725) for haymakers, shearers (i.e., reapers), and for three grades of annually hired servants. Female rates were not given for common servants in husbandry, mowers, ditchers, hedgers, palers, and threshers hired by the day, week, and month.

15. For example, see Judith C. Brown and Jordan Goodman, "Women and Industry in Florence," *Journal of Economic History*, 40 (1980):73-80, a city where women predominated as weavers in the wool and silk industries.

16. Lancashire wage assessments exist for the years 1595 and 1725; see W. E. Minchinton, ed., *Wage Regulation in Pre-Industrial England* (Newton Abbot, England, 1972), pp. 206-34. These assessments set the top limit on what pay employers could offer workers. The annual wages paid servants in the Fell employ follow the 1725 schedule fairly closely. In 1725 the wage assessment provided that the best woman servant who could take charge of the household would be paid a maximum of £2 10s. while the male chief servant in husbandry would be paid a maximum of £5. The chambermaid, dairymaid, and wash maid or other "mean" servant could earn up to £2, whereas a common male servant in husbandry hired annually could receive up to £4 and a man servant of 20 to 24 could be paid no more than £3 10s. There are wage rates for women under 16 (£1 10s., though), and none for men under 16, implying that girls could start their wage earning a year or two earlier than boys. The 1725 assessment is printed in Frederic Morton Eden, *The State of the Poor* (London, 1797), 3:cvi-cvii. For field work paid by the day, the wage assessments only list rates for women during hay and corn harvest. The wages paid to female field workers were similar to the harvest rates with meat and drink in the 1595 assessment (a limit of 2d. for the corn harvest and 1d. for hay harvest), while actual wages paid the males amounted to more than those in the 1595 assessment but a little less than the maximums in that of 1725. The 1595 assessment appears in Paul L. Hughes and James F. Larkin, eds., *Tudor Royal Proclamations* (New Haven, 1969), 3:149-50. Generally, the wage assessments for male and female day labor show smaller differentials than did the pay given each sex in the Fell account book.

17. Roberts, "Sickles and Scythes," p. 19; Kussmaul, *Servants in Husbandry*, pp. 143-44.

18. The argument Roberts makes ("Sickles and Scythes," pp. 19-20) for the existence of wage differences in harvest work and yearly service implies that they were basically due to the physical superiority of males. Much of the same kind of reasoning seems to guide Snell in "Seasonal Unemployment."

19. On this point, see Hartmann, "Capitalism, Patriarchy," p. 211.

20. Carole Shammas, "The Domestic Environment in Early Modern England and America," *Journal of Social History*, 14 (1980):1-24.

21. Robert William Fogel and Stanley L. Engerman, *Time on the Cross: The Economics of American Negro Slavery* (Boston, 1974), 1:74 (fig. 17), 82 (fig. 22); see also Robert L. Ransom and Richard Sutch, *One Kind of Freedom: The Economic Consequences of Emancipation* (Cambridge, 1977), p. 236.

22. Lindert, "English Occupations," p. 703.

MICHAEL J. GALGANO

8 ❧ Out of the Mainstream:
Catholic and Quaker Women in the Restoration Northwest

As Charles Stuart progressed in splendor along the road from Dover to Whitehall in May 1660, Catholic voices joined with Protestant in celebrating the return of monarchy. Ardent supporters of his father throughout the Civil Wars — and his own steadfast guardians during the trying days following Worcester — they had suffered substantially for their loyalty and anticipated fuller personal and religious freedom from the new king. The royal procession drew no such paeans from Quakers. The demise of the restored Rump Parliament marked the nadir of their expectations for toleration, the abolition of tithes, and law reform. When Catholic hopes were later dashed by the narrow Anglicanism of the Cavalier Parliament, most resumed a passive posture seeking to avoid any confrontation with ecclesiastical or secular authorities. They could never subscribe to the heinous oaths; yet they publicly complied with most laws, posed no imminent threat to the known order, and consequently endured only periodic persecution. In contrast, the early Quakers, infused with the fervor of new dissent, affronted English sensibilities, provoked public officials, and refused to compromise with existing customs or traditions. Because of the animosity the sect aroused, Quaker persecution remained intense and regular. Catholics, recusants for nearly a century, returned underground patiently adhering to their ancient beliefs and rituals in private, while Quakers vocally defied all efforts to bring them to conformity.[1]

In the rural Northwest of England, far from the mainstream of Restoration society, both Catholics and Quakers were numerous. Lancashire contained perhaps the largest concentration of papists in England, and the hamlets of Westmorland and Cumberland included sizable numbers of Friends; thus, the region is appropriate for studying these extremes of religious dissent. Examination of the two communities in concert is attractive for several reasons. Representing opposite poles of the spectrum, they shed light on the religious, social, and economic practices of societies beyond the Anglican mainstream. Though Catholics steadfastly tried to avoid the mainstream, national forces, culminating in the disastrous reign of James II, overwhelmed and undermined them. Quakers also actively resisted assimilation; yet after 1688 persecution lessened and they were afforded a modicum of freedom within the established order. But my comparison poses a formidable methodological challenge, since the two groups had radically contrasting attitudes toward the accumulation of records. Country Catholics shunned publicity, retained few incriminating personal documents, and usually attempted to obscure their tracks in every way. Quakers kept meticulous accounts of their sufferings, penned numerous spiritual autobiographies, generated vast quantities of assorted materials, and openly drew attention to themselves. Therefore, to reconstruct the Catholic experience the historian must assemble his evidence from elusive and spotty sources. In contrast, to reconstruct the Quaker experience he must sift through voluminous archives—gathered both by tormentors and by members of the sect.

If Catholics and Quakers remained outside the pale before the Glorious Revolution, so too did the geographical area which spawned them. The severe terrain, harsh climate, and poor roads repelled southerners, who viewed the Northwest as isolated and mysterious. Samuel Pepys recorded that serpents roamed the wastes of Lancashire ready to devour unsuspecting larks, and Daniel Defoe saw Westmorland as the wildest, most rugged territory encountered on his famous tour. Even hearty travelers were reluctant to repeat Celia Fiennes's sidesaddle sojourn into the area, because accomodations, particularly in the Lake shires, were scarce.[2] Those who did, however, found a countryside dotted with small holdings more suited for pasture than the plow, averaging fewer than eight acres even for yeomen, and single-story cruck-framed houses containing slight evidences of wealth. Since the Elizabethan statute against overcrowding and fire hazards — requiring four acres of land for the construction of the meanest cottage — was in force, the small size of the tenements is remarkable. Normally food, shelter, and clothing adequate to family needs could be produced; nevertheless, memories of actual starvation were vivid after 1660, for inclement weather might upset the balance between survival and despair at any time. The union of the crowns of England and Scotland and subsequent pacification of the northern boundary created additional anxieties as tenant-right security gave way to leases with steep entry fines. By 1700 many peasants, reacting to a depressed grain market and to overpopulation relative to available agricultural resources, limited or abandoned their corn crops and became market producers of livestock. While conditions favored the cattle industry, outsiders would continue to observe hardworking families, who seldom tasted meat or wheat bread, slaving together on their tiny plots.

Stark economic realities therefore determined that men and women alike share in the onerous labors of subsistence agriculture. Few northwestern women enjoyed the transfer of field responsiblilities to their spouses that Pehr Kalm witnessed further south, which prompted him to depict England in 1748 as "a paradise for ladies and women."[4] Instead, long after he wrote, in 1794, Lake District women still performed a multitude of strenuous tasks from driving harrows and plows to operating single-horse dung-carts.[5] The household economy retained its vitality in the three counties, and the more than two hundred thousand women dwelling there were essential contributors to its survival.[6]

Many of these women were Catholic or Quaker. Because the church was the largest assembly outside the family in which women participated actively, it is a logical institution to employ as a basis for analysis. Although their roles as wives and mothers in many ways mirrored those of other women, both Catholic and Quaker women, because of the peculiarities of their beliefs, had distinctive characteristics. Religion influenced childrearing practices as well as relations with family, friends, and the established society. Both faiths offered women special opportunities for independent existence beyond marriage and the hearth. Both presented possibilities for greater geographical mobility to women, through apprenticeship networks, education, marriage with fellow believers, and religious service. Who were the women attracted to the two extremes of English ecclesiastical dissent? How were they distributed through the social scale? Of those who wed, how many sought partners outside the church or meeting? What attitudes did they have toward children in general and daughters in particular? What roles did those who remained unmarried assume within the spiritual community? Were Catholic and Quaker women accepted or ostracized in their small hamlets and villages? The area they inhabited, their religion, and their sex excluded them from the English mainstream; however, an examination of these women will enhance our comprehension of an important and neglected segment of feminine society during the Restoration. In this essay, I will discuss first Catholic women and then Quaker. In the final section I will compare the two groups.

I

In the aftermath of the Popish Plot hysteria 5,754 adult Catholics were returned to the quarter sessions for Lancashire.[7] This aggregate included 3,178 women (55.2 percent). Of these, 2,259 were, or had at one time been, married, while 919 remained single. Among the married women,

1,037 married Catholics, 585 married outside the church, and 637 were widows whose deceased husbands' religious preferences cannot be determined. While it would be erroneous to claim precision for any statistics based principally upon seventeenth-century recusancy records, the sums do suggest some general observations. Even if we suppose that every widow named had been married to another papist, still, 25.9 percent of all wives in this Catholic group married Protestants. Assuming that their social backgrounds closely approximated those of their mates, these women came exclusively from the common classes. The high proportion of mixed marriages stood in marked contrast with the early part of the century when such actions signified apostacy.[8] The returns also indicate a larger percentage of single women among Catholics than in the overall population. Marriage was the desired state in preindustrial societies, the key to complete acceptance into the adult world, and nearly 90 percent of all women would wed at some point in their lives. Nevertheless, 28.9 percent of the Catholic women were unmarried. Doubtless some of the female servants returned to the quarter sessions married. Many, however, remained single. Family reconstitutions in seven Northwest parishes between 1660 and 1700 reveal that 24.9 was the average age at first marriage.[9]

For Catholic women, religion was becoming a secondary consideration in selecting a spouse and most mixed marriages were free from serious discord. The quarter sessions petitions for Lancashire from the end of the civil wars to the death of Charles II contain only two instances of conflict that developed out of the marriage of a Catholic to a non-Catholic. In 1647 Thomas Cranage complained that the papist widow of John Proctor had disrupted her Protestant husband's burial service by placing a linen napkin shaped to form a cross on his corpse. When the Brindle clergyman removed the "superstitious" item, an altercation ensued. Over three decades later, in June 1679, another dispute erupted concerning Myles Green, who had married the Protestant daughter of Gilbert Nightengale and resided with his wife's family at Barton for ten continuous years. By 1679 Nightengale wanted the Greens to leave, and the churchwardens threatened to levy a £5 fine if they remained in the parish, whereupon Green petitioned the justices at Ormskirk for permanent settlement.[10] Other disputes were doubtless arbitrated privately, because Catholics shunned the courts except in times of extraordinary emergency.

By the time of the Restoration, interfaith marriages among the humble were becoming commonplace. Since a majority of adult Catholics were female, opportunities for the women were restricted unless they accepted Protestant partners. Catholic women without property did not have to worry about inheritance settlements. But they knew that if they remained unmarried and bore bastards, they would become burdensome to the parish. The Act of Settlement limited mobility, especially for unattached women. Men had much freer movement in search of work and were readily accepted by those anxious to employ them. Of more than eight hundred requests for habitation brought to the Lancashire Quarter Sessions during the reign of Charles II, 66.5 percent came from bachelors and only 27.1 percent from women. The latter group included many widows reduced to poverty.[11]

Options open to women of gentle birth were different. Connubial ties were almost always made inside the Catholic community to guarantee religious solidarity in the household and on the manor. Daughters of the gentry who chose not to marry could leave their homeland to enter the contemplative continental nunneries. Gentry estates offered relatively safe quarters to resident clerics and frequently provided sanctuary to the travel-ing priests who served the poor. The leaders of rural Catholic society risked economic and social ruin to adhere to their beliefs, and marriages were seldom contracted beyond the religious pale. Virtually all of the eighty-four convicted Lancashire papist gentlemen whose names appeared on the recusancy rolls of 1678 and 1679 and whose properties were valued for the Treasury in 1682 had married other Catholics. On the rare occasions when mixed marriages did occur, the non-Catholic party usually converted. For example, William Anderton of Euxton wed Mary, Protestant daughter of William Farrington of Werden, in 1671. She adopted her husband's religion and was listed with him as a popish recusant in 1679. One of the parties to the postnuptial settlement of this marriage was a neighbor, Hugh Diccon-son of Wrightington. Reared a Protestant, he married Agnes, Catholic daughter of Roger Kirkby, in 1652. Dicconson probably converted in 1668, because William Blundell wrote that he had become a "good Christian" in that year.[12]

Priests sometimes acted as matchmakers for gentry families, identify-ing eligible parties, making necessary introductions, and facilitating nego-tiations. Henry Heaton, a Jesuit, helped William Blundell find a wife for his son in 1668 by bringing together the younger Blundell and Mary, the daughter of Rowland Eyre of Derby.[13] The more traditional method of locating desirable spouses was through an informal network of Catholic friends and neighbors. The rural gentry regularly visited one another and sometimes cooperated in educating their progeny. Occasions for feasting, fellowship, and the enjoyment of such pastimes as hunting, fishing, bowls, cards, and musical or juggling performances proved valuable in bringing together the future Catholic leaders of the Northwest. In Lancashire, par-ticularly in the region bounded by Preston, Southport, Liverpool, and Wigan, where there were many recusant gentry families, marriage arrange-ments were often made with close neighbors and, one presumes, childhood acquaintances or friends. Because of the plethora of papists, Catholic daughters from this area were much in demand as brides for gentlemen whose lands stretched from Cumberland to Staffordshire. Many of the same male household heads served as witnesses to the formal settlements, thus acting as unofficial marriage brokers.[14]

At least 45.9 percent of all Catholic women returned in 1678 and 1679 entered into clandestine unions with their coreligionists. Some exchanged vows privately in the presence of Catholic witnesses, then awaited sanctification from an itinerant priest, while others were attended by clerics resident in the hidden chapels of the gentry. Once Catholic rites had been performed, the couple paid a wedding fee to the local Anglican vicar to secure proper registration of their action. The charge in Hawkshead parish was 1s. 8d. This necessary step protected the family from fines under the recusancy statutes and placated the established minister. If a couple neglected to pay the fee, they might be accused of illicit cohabitation before the diocesan correction court. This happened to Thomas Hetherington and Margaret Crawe of Lanercost in January 1664, but they paid the wedding charge and were dismissed.[15] Catholics were harrassed much less frequently than Quakers for marriage offenses, indicating that most acquiesced in the payments.

The recusancy registers provide some index to the social standing of men who married Catholic women. Only 87 of the 1,622 husbands with Catholic wives in the registers of 1678-79 were gentlemen or professionals. There are apparent ambiguities in the "additions" to male surnames. The distinction between yeomen and husbandmen is especially imprecise as both possessed small holdings and, in many instances, limited wealth. Also, the terms were not always used consistently.[16] Nonetheless, if the terms are not applied too stringently, an examination of the "additions" yields some useful conclusions about the status of women (table 8.1).

Two-thirds of the men listed in the table earned their principal livelihood from the land. Another quarter earned their principal livelihood as artisans, tradesmen, or laborers, but many of them also maintained small farms. One Catholic shoemaker, Robert Fletcher of Lytham, leased a messuage and tenement of under three acres for 2s. plus boons and services in 1665. A second, William Bryanson, rented parcels of arable and pasture totaling two acres at an annual rent of 4s. fifteen years later. John Wilson, a carpenter from Furness, leased a messuage, three acres, and two little gardens for 48s. a year.[17] In all, perhaps 90 percent of recusant families were engaged wholly or partly in direct contact with the soil. Most Catholic husbandmen worked tracts, including lands used both for cultivation and grazing, of fewer than ten acres.[18] Family reconstitutions demonstrate that two-thirds of all Catholic marriages joined persons from the same parish. Hence, the typical northwestern Catholic bride had strong agrarian ties — being the daughter of a lesser husbandman or of one who mixed farming and a trade — and was raised in the same neighborhood as her mate.[19]

These Catholic farmers and small-scale handicraft workers led insulated lives. With the notable exceptions of carpentry, some building and

TABLE 8.1   *"Additions" in the Recusancy Registers, 1673–79: Those with Papist Wives*

Occupation or Status	Major Category		Subcategory	
	Number of Men	Percentage	Number of Men	Percentage
Gentry and professions	87	5.4		
Agriculture	1086	67.0		
Yeomen			97	6.0
Husbandmen			874	53.9
Laborers			110	6.8
Farmers, Gardeners			5	0.3
Textiles	142	8.8		
Clothiers			7	0.4
Weavers (includes fustian, inkle, linen, silk, woolen)			135	8.3
Leather work	16	1.0		
Tanners			10	0.6
Saddlers			4	0.2
Skinners			2	0.1
Articles of Dress	78	4.8		
Tailors			43	2.7
Shoemakers			31	1.9
Other (includes glovers, hatters, hosiers)			4	0.2
Wood work	49	3.0		
Carpenters			34	2.1
Coopers			11	0.7
Joiners			4	0.2
Building and construction	24	1.5		
Masons			14	0.9
Other (includes glaziers, nailers, plasterers, slaters, turners)			10	0.6
Food and drink	42	2.6		
Millers			27	1.7
Alehousekeepers			14	0.9
Malsters			1	0.1
Dealing and retail trade	27	1.7		
Butchers			16	1.0
Mercers			6	0.4
Grocers			5	0.3
Other artisans	65	4.0		
Smiths (includes black and white)			35	2.2
Wrights			12	0.7
Goldsmiths			3	0.2
Gunsmith			1	0.1
Apothecaries			1	0.1
Miscellaneous			13	0.8
Colliers	6	0.4		
TOTAL	1622			

NOTE: In setting up this table I used Richard Vann's model for his table on "Additions" on the Gloucestershire muster roll, 1608, in *Development of Quakerism*, p. 53.

construction work, and the merchandising of textiles, most of the skills mentioned in the "additions" could be executed in the privacy of the home. The average seventeenth-century village contained roughly two hundred inhabitants; hence, the circle of daily contacts for artisan families was circumscribed.[20] At market, in which larger numbers were encountered, if the product was of high quality and the price reasonable, the producer's religion was of slight consequence. Most recusant workers did not require significant capital investment, and occupations centered in the household provided Catholic wives with considerable economic opportunity.[21]

Businesses serving the public, like alehouses, also offered women occasions to work with their men. Catholic proprietors sometimes transgressed the bounds of acceptable community behavior and incurred the wrath of public authorities. Such was the plight of John and Anne Heyes of Culcheth, who were brought before the justices at Ormskirk in 1681. According to the charge, they "doe frequently suffer servants and neighbors to stay tipleing in time of divine service and at unseasonable times in the night." Protestants in the Northwest permitted alehouses to remain open on Sundays, though not to compete with the parish church for patrons. Roger Lowe, a Lancashire Puritan apprentice, periodically imbibed on the Sabbath, though never in lieu of services. The constables of Culcheth were instructed to "give notice unto the said John Heyes and Anne his wife to forbear Brewing and selling any Ale or Beere for the space of three years next following."[22]

Catholics rarely flouted conventions so openly and, in most instances, could count on the backing — rather than the condemnation — of parish officials when summoned to the quarter sessions. The correspondence of Alan Bellingham and Daniel Fleming, two Westmorland justices, illustrates the degree of protection from persecution they enjoyed. In 1667 an exasperated Bellingham wrote to his colleague that less than half as many papists had been brought before the quarter sessions as had been presented twenty-six years earlier, even though the Catholic population in the shire had increased. He questioned the fidelity of the churchwardens and constables in making their returns and urged that earlier records be searched. Fleming cautioned against hasty action, arguing that Catholics were honorable subjects and asking that more time be extended to recalcitrant authorities.[23] Even in 1679 and 1680, parish officers and neighbors in Lancashire treated local Catholics sympathetically. Immediately after the allegations of Titus Oates became generally known, Catholics were bound by recognizances to appear quarterly before the justices until they agreed to swear the oaths of allegiance and supremacy. At least 116 Lancashire paupers, including 42 women, begged relief from the stiff expenses brought on by their repeated attendance. Some pleas were endorsed by a broad spectrum of the local populace while, in other cases, Protestants seized the initiative and filed the petitions themselves. It was generally argued that the papists, unless excused, would become dependent upon the parish for maintenance. Certainly the obvious pinch in their purses prodded the Protestants to act; nevertheless, they did publicly defend their Catholic neighbors at a very dangerous time. They understood that the papists posed no danger to internal security and their continued persecution would only prohibit them from providing for their families. The combined entreaties were honored and the poor discharged.[24]

II

Quakers in northwestern England drew no comparable measures of support from neighbors and attracted still less sympathy from authorities. When twenty Lancashire Friends were arrested and detained for attending a conventicle in 1664, the justice stated that he "would haue sett many of the poorest sort at liberty if they would but promis to meet noe more, but none of them would either take any oath, giue security, or promis reformation."[25] Quakers, unlike papist dissenters, steadfastly refused to pay fees to the parish clergy to legitimate their private ceremonies. In addition, the new recusants insisted upon public assemblies to "publish the Truth" for all.[26]

Women were exceedingly vocal in the front ranks of northwestern Quakerism. The fact that their strange behavior negated traditional feminine roles may partially explain the absence of community compassion for the sect. Following the example of George Fox, wayfaring missionaries proselytized in the streets and interrupted more structured church services. Catholic nuns, shrouded in their habits, might seem bizarre, but they meditated properly in foreign monasteries while Dorothy Waugh and her traveling companion, Anne Robinson, were being led through the thoroughfare of Carlisle with iron bridles pressed on their faces to silence preaching. Anne Kenebie was imprisoned and attacked for "speaking a few words" to an assembly in Liverpool, and Rebecca Barnes, returning home from a gathering in Ormskirk, was accosted and beaten to death by a local mob.[27] Although the three incidents antedate the Restoration, they illustrate the hostile passions unleashed against first-generation female Friends, who affected a radically different way of life from that of their contemporaries, journeying the highways to preach the new faith. These patterns of abuse were more than mere manifestations of the underlying violence of the times.[28]

Quakers aroused anger in all social classes. Daniel Fleming paid informants to infiltrate their conventicles in Westmorland and successfully pressed Parliament to entrust enforcement of the statutes against them to the less lenient justices of the peace. He fined and jailed Friends of both sexes and every social and economic condition.[29] Death did not always terminate the attacks against Quaker women by rapacious clerics. In 1664 John Watson of Westmorland had goods distrained because both he and his wife refused the Sacrament. She was dead. When a Quaker woman from Staffordshire died in 1682, her husband attempted to inter the body at the Friends' burial ground. The parish minister intervened, demanded his burial fee, and threatened to arrest the corpse and bury it in a ditch. He then stationed himself with two other officials in a house along the route to the cemetery, where he sat drinking. The bereaved widower was so distraught that he buried his wife in the garden and followed her to the grave six days later. According to the narrator of the event the minister "said in my Hearing, that He had rather see all the Hereticks hang'd, than lose one Sixpence by them."[30]

Official records and Quaker litanies of individual and collective sufferings adequately attest to the fervor of the authorities and the intensity of religious persecution; however, the movement was not entirely devoid of defenders. In the Diocese of Carlisle five midwives were accused of unlicensed practice before the Correction Court during the reign of Charles II. All were Friends, including Isabel Toppin of Hutton in the Forest, who was repeatedly returned during nearly two decades. Hutton parish recorded only two Quakers in 1676, and few were listed in the compilations regularly presented to the bishop, which means that numbers of established Protestant women must have trusted Toppin's abilities and, although the parochial officers were sufficiently annoyed to bring charges, they did not try to halt her service.[31] In a second instance, after goods and chattels — being sold at bargain rates in the Carlisle market — were identified as having been seized from Friends in 1680, the people refused to purchase them.[32]

In contrast to their Catholic sisters, Restoration Quakers made no serious effort to escape persecution. Instead, in the tradition of English Puritanism, they emphasized the necessity of suffering in order to achieve eternal reward.[33] This situation was amply demonstrated when the Quaker nemesis, Daniel Fleming, tried on at least two separate occasions to apply a double standard in punishing men and women. The apparent stubbornness of the women thwarted his efforts. In the summer of 1684 he wrote to the churchwardens of Kendal and Windermere citing persons to be fined for failure to attend divine services. Since Quakers were rarely willing to pay such charges, he ordered goods distrained from all save a designated number of poor women. Objecting to preferential treatment, they persisted in absenting themselves and joined the men on subsequent lists of those from whom goods were taken.[34]

Rigorous persecution and lengthy imprisonment imperilled the traveling ministry and compelled fuller attention to the details of church organization. Disagreement regarding the structure and composition of the movement, culminating in the "Wilkinson-Story" controversy, led to the centralization of Quakerism and the establishment of permanent meetings throughout the country. Among the primary objections of the schismatics had been the creation of special women's meetings charged with determining fitness for marriage.[35] Quaker women, from the inception of the sect, exercised significant powers over the formation of families. Couples wishing to wed were admonished first to seek the advice of parents, relations, and fellow Friends, and then to approach the women's meeting to gain their approbation.[36] The women took this duty seriously. In 1678, when informed that Elizabeth Clarke was keeping company with an unbeliever, "as in relation to marriage, soe itt was seen convenient that Ann Nuby & Izabell Willson should goe & discourse her about it."[37] Repenting her wayward actions at the Crook Women's Meeting, she promised not to speak with the young man again.

Isabel Willson understood the situation, as she had been romantically involved with a non-Quaker. Her description reveals some of the problems raised by the prospect of mixed marriage and the dynamic hold Quakerism had on its adherents.

> About seaven years since I being Loose in my mind, & not minding the feare of God, my understanding came to be darkened, & sufered a Light wind to get upp, & soe claime to keepe company with one of the world, he pretending to be a wellwisher to a freind which he thought I had Love for, & soe I was severall times in his company, not upon any account as to marrige God knowe neither did I understand his intent: — and this continued for some years & then he did prepousd his intention of marrige wch I did uterly denye neither was it ever my intent & purpose ever to have any thing to doe wth him upon that account, Thogh I was some time in his Company, not seeing the harme I did receive therby my spirituall sences being benumed & darkened, Till about 4 yeare since, And then the Lords Power begun to stir among freinds, & a neer inspection begun to be had in such matters, & soe I begun to see my selfe wrong, And soe did denye his Company, & then he began to Rage & said he would drown himselfe & the Like, att wch I was troubled And soe Lett in feare, And he perceiving that did use such things to get my Company. But att Last I was forced to denye his Company, whatever became of him & then I see it not but the deceit of the enemy to Lead my mind out from waiteing upon the Lord.[38]

Isabel Willson obviously enjoyed the moonstruck man's attentions, for she had shared his company for quite a period; yet from the outset she made it clear that a lasting relationship was impossible because he was not a Friend. Common religion to foster mutual piety was the critical factor in determining a suitable partner. Once such a spouse had been found, Fox encouraged women to cease entertaining other men to protect their reputations and to glorify God. Persecution hampered Quaker mobility and constricted the opportunities for marriage within the meeting. Therefore, eligible bachelors needed to remain in circulation.[39] Still, it is likely that a Quaker woman possessed a good deal of freedom in selecting a husband so long as he was a fellow seeker after Truth.

After the approval of both the women's and men's meetings had been secured, the marriage was publicly celebrated before relatives and other Friends. Quakers were willing to record the event with the government but balked at paying fees to the parish vicar.[40] Meetings crossed parochial and shire boundaries and, as Friends were adamant in insisting exclusively upon marriages between members of the sect, the worship service functioned to bring together single persons living some distance from each other. Eighty-one marriages were sanctioned by the Kendal Men's Monthly Meeting from 1670 to 1688: thirty-nine couples belonged to the same meeting and forty-two to different ones.[41] Some traced their roots to Cumberland, others to Lancashire; thus, in spite of intense persecution and the dangers inherent in travel, female Friends seem to have chosen husbands from a larger geographical area than was the norm for the remaining population. The party from another region was required to supply written assurances from trusted Quakers in the home meeting attesting to his or her freedom to marry. These documents demonstrate a meticulous concern for godly matches and distinguish the sect sharply from the free-love proclivities of groups like the Ranters.[42]

Northwestern Quakers drew converts from most social classes and both sexes. The sect contained fewer gentry than the Catholics, probably because the gentry were disinclined to join a movement led by their social inferiors. The open endorsement of female preaching, coupled with the designation of specific realms of female responsibility, attracted large numbers of women to the ranks. Many preachers had previously been employed in domestic service, and Quakers were certainly less concerned with social origins than were other religious movements of the time.[43] Nonetheless, social tensions throughout the Northwest militated against marriages like that between Margaret Fell and George Fox. The latter's unique position in the movement overrode his humble beginnings. The majority of Friends, like their Roman Catholic neighbors, came from small farming backgrounds — either yeomen or husbandmen — or else were craftsmen.[44] Of forty-two Quakers fined for attending a conventicle at Bowness in 1678, twenty-five were yeomen, four were tanners, three were shoemakers, and the rest assorted tradesmen. Other lists included similar proportions although husbandmen were more prominent on certain returns. Interestingly, the term "husbandman" sometimes designated the son of a Quaker yeoman. Reginald Holme and his son, John, of Skelwith Bridge, were presented to the justices in 1683: the father's "addition" read yeoman, the son's husbandman. John and his sister, Dorothy, who was also returned for attending the conventicle, were older than sixteen years; yet presumably because neither was married, they were both referred to as children.[45] If the term "husbandman" was used occasionally to denote the son of a yeoman still living under his father's roof, the historian must be even more cautious in applying it as an indicator of specific social status. Fortunately

for the historian, however, in the poorer Lake Counties, subsistence farming was the rule, and marriage alliances were probably contracted between
the sons and daughters of small holders, whether called yeomen or husbandmen. The records of individual meetings, in particular the records of
the few persons dependent upon regular relief, and the preponderance in
public documents of those having agricultural occupations, strongly suggest fairly homogeneous social origins.[46]

III

Quakers did not marry primarily to procreate; however, children resulted
from their unions as inevitably as from Catholic ones.[47] The "First Publishers" and their followers were unusually silent on the subject of childrearing.
Before a 1688 reference in a Cumbrian Book of Advice, only two tracts,
printed in 1660, addressed the question. Emphasis on the personal conversion experience and the presence of the Inner Light denied the need for
traditional rites of passage comparable to the Catholic sacramental scheme.[48]
In both communities the family assumed primacy in deepening the spiritual
life of the young. Quaker parents were instructed not only to serve as
virtuous examples for their children, employing their powers to nurture
them in modesty, sobriety, and the fear of God, but also to curb the "Extravagant Humour in the Young Ones, when it doth appear, and not to
indulge it and allow of it; for you are set in your Families as Judges for
God."[49] Catholic fathers and mothers were likewise models for their progeny; but, especially after the reforms of the Council of Trent, greater stress
was placed upon a reciprocal relationship instead of a strict interpretation
of the fourth Commandment, which enjoined children to honor parents
without ordaining a reciprocal response.[50]

Mothers had principal, though not exclusive, responsibility for the
initial years of childhood. Friends exposed their offspring to suffering from
infancy. When Alice Bowman of Staffordshire was jailed for interfering
with a sacramental service in 1663, she carried her suckling child with her.
So too did Elizabeth Morland, imprisoned the next year for attending a
conventicle in Westmorland. Quaker women elected to keep their babies
with them, even during adversity, rather than abandoning them to the care
of others. Isolated from the greater community, and perhaps from the
extended family as well, they were reluctant to entrust their children to
anyone.[51] If a woman was unable to suckle her child, friends or family
from the women's meeting secured a wet-nurse. Mary Fell Lower seems
to have experienced such problems; her breasts were treated after two pregnancies with turpentine and aqua vitae and her daughters were nursed at
home.[52] The first daughter, Margaret, was a great favorite of her aunt,
Sarah, who doted over her, feeding her treacle and white bread through her
first months of infancy and buying her a "pewtr suckleinge bottle," a
porringer, a hat, petticoat, and leading strings. Sarah Fell also paid £4 12s.

2d. in various funeral expenses for the little child in May 1675. The next Lower girl, another Margaret, survived infancy and was weaned from her nurse at thirteen months.[53]

Although there is no direct evidence relating to Catholic nursing habits, economic necessity no doubt compelled mothers of all faiths to breast feed. The £2 fee in the region for a wet-nurse was beyond the means of many.[54] An examination of 904 male inventories for the Diocese of Carlisle between 1661 and 1681 shows that 472, or 52.2 percent, were under £30.[55] Inventories record wealth on hand at death and may not necessarily correspond to amounts available in the prime of a working life; nevertheless, they do suggest crude prosperity at a given moment. For roughly half the populace a sum equal to 6 percent of overall resources would have been needed to employ a wet-nurse. Family reconstitutions indicate that the average household included 1.9 children, while figures for Essex noted that £30 was essential to sustain a family of four, assuming both children were younger than five years.[56] Living costs were higher there than in northern England, but families with inventories of £30 or less would probably have viewed nurses as a luxury.

As children grew, both parents became more involved in their training and education. Traditionally scholars have emphasized the monolithic nature of childrearing customs in preindustrial societies, paying special notice to repression and corporal punishment. Recently, Philip Greven has provided a valuable corrective to this model, designating three patterns which reflect distinct family groupings: the evangelical, the moderate, and the affectionate. Love dominated all three categories and the appeal to physical force represented the breakdown of family discipline.[57] The Catholic William Blundell expressed the moderate pattern: he condoned use of the rod on his daughters only if reason and prayer had failed. A Christmas dialogue, written for performance in 1663 — in which Blundell instructed his three daughters in religion, rhetoric, Latin, humor, and deportment — detailed his strategy. He began by chastising the eldest, Mall, for her immaturity, acceptable in a younger child but intolerable in one approaching adulthood. Each action enraged her father and drove him to seek alternative means of correction. Before he could interject the new form of punishment, Mall disarmed him, appealing to their shared sinfulness and common belief in God's limitless pardon. Demonstrably moved by her use of reason — a clear denial of past childish behavior — as well as by her contrition, Blundell absolved her and withdrew. Mall then assumed his role and became the instrument of learning for her younger siblings. She distinguished between the boisterous climbing and somersaulting of boys, characteristic of their own previous games, and the more "civil" music and dancing of young ladies. Raucous play originated in purgatory and, presumably would extend the stay of all perpetrators there; whereas feminine pursuits began in heaven.[58]

Blundell's dialogue explored Catholic doctrine regarding penance on a relatively sophisticated plane and intimated a catechism-level understanding of the cardinal virtues of faith, hope, and charity by the three girls. Mall's logical and thoughtful argument taught her the power of oral persuasion, a tactic employed fruitfully in convincing her sisters to abandon vigorous exercise for more placid dances. The work was filled with puns and slapstick to entertain as well as instruct. Maturation was a gradual process for Roman Catholics. Mall began to cast aside some immature habits, yet others persisted and were acknowledged. William Blundell visualized childhood as lasting until about the seventh year and was generally sympathetic to its deepest concerns. He urged parents to "Praise your children openly, reprehend them secretly," suggesting that even the young were entitled to respect.[59]

In Philip Greven's terminology, Quaker families also pursued a moderate pattern of child rearing. The Quaker young were held incapable of sin until the age of seven or eight when reason began to manifest itself. For Quaker children the meeting functioned as a surrogate family, aiding parents in all areas of spiritual and physical development. The women's meetings taught young wives and mothers how best to rear children, provided help in placing adolescents as apprentices, and represented their interests should a widowed mother remarry. To protect against straying, children were expected to imitate the examples of their parents. In later years formal education would be stressed through Friends' schools; however, the home and meeting were the principal teachers in the initial generations.[60]

Female education was not uniformly directed to marriage and maternal duties for either dissenting community. To differing degrees both Catholics and Quakers made accommodations for single women. Catholics, especially the offspring of the gentry, might journey to convent schools abroad and remain to take the veil. Families burdened with recusancy fines from the Interregnum and saddled with excess daughters saw the monastery as an escape from financial ruin, while others, less cynical, recognized the inherent worth of the contemplative life and encouraged their girls to seek the special peace and security it promised.[61] For the single daughters of the humble, however, to whom European convents were beyond reach, Catholicism offered no special ecclesiastical role. On the other hand, single Quaker women might preach, proselytize, or participate fully in the women's meetings. Though Friends praised the virtues of matrimony, they also provided meaningful activity in the meeting for women of all social backgrounds.

Catholic and Quaker women represent two distinct visions of the English religious experience: the past and the future. Catholics held their hallowed beliefs and transmitted them in the privacy of the household or the secrecy of hidden chapels. Though they established a parallel structure for baptism, marriages, and burials, they still paid fees to a church whose authority they could not acknowledge. The ease with which they were identified in 1678 indicates that they were known to authorities; yet except in times of peril, they were tolerated. For many commoners, faith had become personalized and intermarriage ceased to be taboo. Numerically dominant, Catholic women followed traditional roles and posed no danger to the social order. Their Quaker sisters sought no compromise with the existing structure; instead, their obstreperous behavior attracted heated persecution and their customs drew ridicule. Quakers insisted upon individual rights and, in a sense, sought to create a state within the state. They rejected tithes, denied oaths, avoided the courts, maintained their own system of poor relief, opposed baptism, demanded their own marriage rites, and condemned the "churching" of women. Persistence led ultimately to toleration as their dissent was legitimated after 1688. Women had assumed new positions in household and meeting, accepting a discipline they had helped to form. In so doing they had instituted models for later active women to emulate.

NOTES

Financial assistance for this essay was provided by the National Endowment for the Humanities, Fellowship in Residence for College Teachers, 1978-79, and the Marshall University Faculty Development Fund, 1981.

1. Privy Council Registers, PC 2/59, fols. 206, 564; PC 2/64, fols. 23, 135, PRO; Caroline Robbins, ed., *The Diary of John Milward, Esq., Member of Parliament for Derbyshire, September 1666 to May 1668* (Cambridge, 1938), pp. 4, 32, 49-50, 104-5; Basil Duke Henning, ed., *The Parliamentary Diary of Sir Edward Dering, 1670-1673* (New Haven, 1940), pp. 70, 80-95, 134-36; *The London Gazette,* 9-12 Mar. 1668; Wilbur Cortez Abbot, "The Long Parliament of Charles II: Part II," *English Historical Review,* 31 (1906):256, 259-60; J. A. Williams, "English Catholicism under Charles II: The Legal Position," *Recusant History,* 7 (1963):132; Margaret Blundell, ed., *Cavalier: Letters of William Blundell to His Friends, 1620-1698* (London, 1933), pp. 92-94; Barry Reay, "The Quakers, 1659, and the Restoration of the Monarchy," *History,* 63 (1978), pp. 193-96, 199-200; William C. Braithwaite, *The Second Period of Quakerism* (London, 1921), pp. 9, 13-14; Hugh Barbour, *The Quakers in Puritan England* (New Haven, 1964), p. 29; Sir Daniel Fleming, Public Office, Proceedings against Quakers, 1663-1700, D/Ry Box 31, various papers throughout, WCRO.

2. Robert Latham and William Matthews, eds., *The Diary of Samuel Pepys* (Berkeley and Los Angeles, 1970-83), 3:22-23; Daniel Defoe, *A Tour Through England and Wales,* intro. G. D. H. Cole (London, 1927), 2:270; Christopher Morris, ed., *The Journeys of Celia Fiennes* (London, 1949), pp. 192-207; J. D. Marshall, "Kendal in the Late Seventeenth and Eighteenth Centuries," *Transactions of the Cumberland and Westmorland Antiquarian and Archaeological Society* (hereafter cited as *TCWAAS*), new ser., 75 (1975):194-95. Kendal, for example, had 279 guest beds, and Carlisle 413 in the 1680s.

3. Properties in Lancashire may have been slightly larger, averaging perhaps 15 to 30 acres. Alfred P. Wadsworth and Julia deLacy Mann, *The Cotton Trade and*

Industrial Lancashire, 1600-1780 (Manchester, 1931), pp. 26-27; see also C. M. L. Bouch and G. P. Jones, *A Short Economic and Social History of the Lake Counties, 1500-1830* (Manchester, 1961), pp. 25, 29; Norman Nicholson, *Cumberland and Westmorland, The County Book Series,* ed. Brian Vesey-Fitzgerald (London, 1949), pp. 2, 4, 63; Richard S. Ferguson, *A History of Cumberland* (London, 1890), pp. 262-63; Edward Hughes, ed., *Cumberland County Council Record Series,* vol. 2, *Fleming-Senhouse Papers,* (Carlisle, 1961), pp. 3-4, 34; G. P. Jones, "The Decline of the Yeomanry in the Lake Counties," *TCWAAS,* new ser., 62 (1962):201, 205-6; idem, "The Poverty of Cumberland and Westmorland," ibid., new ser., 55 (1955):199, 201-2, 205; J. B. Marshall, "The Domestic Economy of the Lakeland Yeoman, 1660-1689," ibid., new ser., 73 (1973):191, 196, 201, 214; Andrew Appleby, *Famine in Tudor and Stuart England* (Stanford, 1978), pp. 39, 41, 44-45, 54, 63, 158-59; David H. Flaherty, *Privacy in Colonial New England* (Charlottesville, 1972), p. 29; M. W. Barley, "Rural Housing in England," in Thirsk, *Agrarian History,* 4:757.

4. Pehr Kalm, *Kalm's Account of His Visit to England on His Way to America in 1748,* trans. Joseph Lucas (London, 1892), p. 328. I am grateful to Professor Charles Perry of the University of the South for directing me to this reference.

5. John Bailey and George Culley, *General View of the Agriculture of the County of Cumberland with Observations on the Means of Improvement* (London, 1794), p. 31; Andrew Pringle, *General View of the Agriculture of the County of Westmorland, with Observations on the Means of Its Improvement* (Edinburgh, 1794), pp. 32, 41; Alice Clark, *Working Life of Women in the Seventeenth Century* (1919; reprint, New York, 1968), p. 62.

6. This figure was reached by halving the 1801 census for Lancashire (672, 731), as suggested by D. E. C. Eversley, and adding that sum to Andrew Appleby's estimates for Cumberland (63,000) and Westmorland (28,300). As 100 girls were born for every 105 boys in the period, a proportion was set up which yielded 213,544 women. Since the average life span of women began to exceed that of men in the era, a relatively wide margin of error was allowed; hence the lower figure of 200,000. *Population: Comparative Account of the Population of Great Britain in the Years 1801, 1811, 1821, and 1831; with the Annual Value of Real Property in the Year 1815* (London, 1831), pp. 130-39; Appleby, *Famine in Tudor and Stuart England,* p. 26; D. E. C. Eversley, "Exploitation of Anglican Parish Registers by Aggregative Analysis," in *An Introduction to English Historical Demography from the Sixteenth to the Nineteenth Century,* ed. E. A. Wrigley, Cambridge Group for the History of Population and Social Structure, vol. 1 (London, 1966), p. 55; Richard T. Vann, "Toward a New Lifestyle: Women in Preindustrial Capitalism," in *Becoming Visible: Women in European History,* ed. Renate Bridenthal and Claudia Koonz (Boston, 1977), pp. 195, 201-3; G. P. Jones, "Some Population Problems Relating to Cumberland and Westmorland in the Eighteenth Century," *TCWAAS,* new ser., 58 (1959):124-25; Louise A. Tilly and Joan W. Scott, *Women, Work, and Family* (New York, 1978), pp. 3, 7; Mary Coate, *Social Life in Stuart England* (New York, 1924), pp. 24, 27, 29-30; Clark, *Working Life of Women,* pp. 1-13, 94-124; Alan Macfarlane, *The Family Life of Ralph Josselin* (New York, 1970), p. 109; Norman Penney, ed., *The Household Account Book of Sarah Fell of Swarthmoor Hall* (Cambridge, 1920), passim.

7. Register of Recusants, 1678-1679, QDV/5, fols. 1, 8, 19d, 46, 50d, 86d, 89, 105d, 109, 111, 111d, 126d, 132, LCRO.

8. Hugh Aveling, "The Marriages of Catholic Recusants, 1559-1642," *Journal of Ecclesiastical History,* 14 (1963):69-71.

9. Peter Laslett, *The World We Have Lost,* 2d ed. (New York, 1971), pp. 98, 104, 108; G. Ohlin, "Mortality, Marriage and Growth in Pre-Industrial Populations," *Population Studies,* 14 (1961):194; Vann, "Toward a New Lifestyle," p. 196. The families were reconstituted from the printed parish registers of Hawkshead,

Lancs.; Newbiggin and Warcop, Westm.; and Bridekirk, Crosthwaite, Dacre, and Greystoke, Cumb. These parishes varied in size; one was small (Newbiggin), while the rest were either large (Hawkshead, Crosthwaite) or middling (Warcop, Bridekirk, Dacre, and Greystoke). H. S. Cowper, ed., *The Oldest Register Book of the Parish of Hawkshead in Lancashire, 1568-1704* (London, 1897); *The Registers of Newbiggin (Westmorland), 1571-1812* (Penrith, 1927); *The Registers of Warcop, Westmorland, 1597-1744* (Kendal, 1914); *The Registers of Bridekirk, 1584-1812* (Penrith, 1927); *The Registers of Crosthwaite, 1562-1812,* 4 vols. (Penrith, 1928-31); Henry Brierly, ed., *The Registers of the Parish Church of Dacre, Cumberland, 1559-1716* (Kendal, 1912); Allan M. Maclean, ed., *The Registers of the Parish of Greystoke in the County of Cumberland, 1559-1757* (Kendal, 1911); see also Quarter Sessions Petitions, QSP/18, Ormskirk, 1 June 1679, LCRO.

10. Quarter Sessions Recognizances, QSB/1/296/38, Wigan, Michaelmas 1647; QSP/502/5, Ormskirk, 2 June 1679, LCRO.

11. This information is based upon a study of 9,613 petitions presented to the quarter sessions for Lancashire, 1660-85, QSP/191-613, LCRO; see also Max Beloff, *Public Order and Popular Disturbances, 1660-1714* (London, 1963), pp. 13-18.

12. Anderton Papers, bundle 28, fol. 138, Wigan Public Library; QDV/5, fol. 89, LCRO; Kenyon Papers, List of Papist Estates, 1682, DDKe 7/21, LCRO; Dicconson Papers, DX/363, LCRO; T. E. Gibson, "Lancashire Mortuary Letters, 1666-1672, from the Crosby Records," *Historic Society of Lancashire and Cheshire,* 36 (1884):46-47; Lawrence Stone, *The Crisis of the Aristocracy, 1558-1641* (Oxford, 1965), p. 731. For a discussion of recusant gentry marriages, see Galgano, "Restoration Recusancy in the Northwest of England: A Social History, 1658-1673" (Ph.D. diss., Vanderbilt University, 1971), pp. 89-108. Lawrence Stone has observed that 60% of the Lancashire squirearchy earlier in the century wed within the county. Papists were no exception. See Stone, *The Family, Sex and Marriage in England, 1500-1800* (New York, 1977), p. 61.

13. T. E. Gibson, ed., *Crosby Records: A Cavalier's Notebook, Being Notes, Anecdotes & Observations of William Blundell of Crosby, Lancashire, Esquire* (London, 1880), pp. 66-67.

14. Blundell, *Cavalier: Blundell Letters,* pp. 84-89, 120-33; Galgano, "Restoration Recusancy," pp. 95-108.

15. Aveling, "Marriages of Recusants," pp. 77-81; Blundell, *Cavalier: Blundell Letters,* pp. 132-33; Cowper, *Hawkshead Register,* p. lvi; Diocese of Carlisle, Correction Court Book, DRC/5/1, fol. 9r, 26 Jan. 1663/4, CCRO.

16. For a discussion of the limits of statistics relating to status or occupation in the age, see Vann. *Development of Quakerism,* pp. 53, 61.

17. Galgano, "Restoration Recusancy," pp. 108-23, 214-86; Clifton of Lytham Papers, DDCl/1754, LCRO; Blundell of Little Crosby Papers, DDBl/44/20, LCRO; Cavendish of Holker Papers, DDCa/48, LCRO.

18. This information is based upon a survey of leases with husbandmen on the estates of Anderton of Euxton, Anderton of Lostock, Blundell of Crosby, Blundell of Ince, Clifton of Lytham, Culcheth of Culcheth, Gerard of Bryn, Ireland of Lydiate, Molyneux of Sefton, Scarisbrick of Scarisbrick, Towneley of Towneley, Tyldesley of Myerscough. See Galgano, "Restoration Recusancy," pp. 214-86.

19. Stone, *Family, Sex and Marriage,* p. 62. Family reconstitutions indicate that 494 out of 1,532 married someone beyond the parish.

20. Laslett, *World We Have Lost,* pp. 7, 11, 56.

21. Clark, *Working Life of Women,* p. 194.

22. Ormskirk, Michaelmas 1681, QSP/542/13, LCRO; William L. Sachse, ed., *The Diary of Roger Lowe of Ashton-in-Makerfield, Lancashire, 1663-1674* (New Haven, 1938), entries for 3 Jan. 1663, 5 July 1663, 9 Aug. 1663, 19 Sept. 1663 (pp. 13, 23, 26, 34).

23. Letters and Papers, no. 828, D/Ry, WCRO. An abstract of Bellingham's letter, but not Fleming's response, is printed in *HMC,* Twelfth Report (London, 1890), app., pt. vii, p. 44.

24. Whalley and Blackburn, November 1678, QSP/490/6, LCRO; Lancaster, Whalley, and Manchester, Jan. and Feb. 1678-79, QSP/495/1, LCRO; Ormskirk, Easter 1679, QSP/498/10, 12, 13, 15-17, LCRO; Ormskirk, June 1679, QSP/502/7, LCRO; Wigan, Michaelmas 1679, QSP/509/9-10, 30-37, LCRO; Ormskirk, Easter 1680, QSP/517/21, LCRO; Manchester, Easter 1680, QSP/523/9, 13-14, LCRO. Beloff (*Popular Disturbances,* p. 37) notes rioting in 1680 through 1682 against attempts to enforce recusancy statutes.

25. Norman Penney, ed., *Extracts from State Papers Relating to Friends, 1654-1672* (London, 1911), p. 185.

26. Joseph Besse, *A Collection of the Sufferings of the People Called Quakers for the Testimony of a Good Conscience, 1650-1689* (London, 1753), 1:2.

27. William C. Braithwaite, *The Beginnings of Quakerism,* 2d ed., rev. Henry J. Cadbury (Cambridge, 1955), p. 125; Norman Penney, ed., *The First Publishers of Truth* (London, 1907); Besse, *Sufferings,* 1:128, 303-4.

28. Beloff, *Popular Disturbances,* pp. 24, 27.

29. Penney, *Extracts from State Papers,* pp. 177, 185, 188, 213; D/Ry Box 31, WCRO, contains many reports of meetings and the materials filed by informants. The informant received one-third of the fine under the terms of the Conventicle Act of 1670. See Braithwaite, *Second Period of Quakerism,* pp. 21, 40-41, 52, 67.

30. Besse, *Sufferings,* 1:653; 2:14.

31. DRC/5/1, fols. 29, 111r, 120, 124r; DRC/5/3, fols. 14, 107; DRC/5/4, 10 Oct. 1682, 22 Jan. 1683, CUCRO; F. G. James, "The Population of the Diocese of Carlisle in 1676," *TCWAAS,* new ser., 51 (1952):138.

32. Besse, *Sufferings,* 1:133.

33. Penney, *Extracts from State Papers,* p. 185; Vann, *Development of Quakerism,* pp. 26-46.

34. D/Ry box 31, letters dated 5 July, 26 Aug., 1 Nov. 1684, WCRO.

35. Vann, *Development of Quakerism,* pp. 96, 102-3; Braithwaite, *Second Period of Quakerism,* pp. 251-57; Arnold Lloyd, *Quaker Social History* (London, 1950), p. 110.

36. DFCF/1/38, Book of Advices, formerly belonging to the Cockermouth Meeting, fols. 169-71, CUCRO; Vann, *Development of Quakerism,* pp. 183-87.

37. Crook Women's Meeting minutes, 1677-1771, QM3, unpaginated, Friends Meeting House, Kendal.

38. Ibid.

39. Ibid., transcript of a letter on marriage from George Fox to the men's and women's meetings; see also Vann, *Development of Quakerism,* p. 159; J. William Frost, *The Quaker Family in Colonial America* (New York, 1973), pp. 150-51.

40. Many examples of persecution are extant. See Besse, *Sufferings,* passim; DRC series, passim, CUCRO; Archdeaconry of Richmond Correction Court, ARR ser., passim, LCRO; Lloyd, *Quaker Social History,* pp. 103-4, cites a 1729 case before King's Bench in which a Quaker who rejected "churching" refused to pay a fee. The court held that since the vicar of Wakefield had done nothing, he was entitled to no fee.

41. Kendal Men's Monthly Meeting minutes, 1670-1726, QM12, Friends Meeting House, Kendal.

42. Ibid., fols. 29r, 30, 33, for example; see also Frost, *Quaker Family in America,* p. 151.

43. Vann, *Development of Quakerism,* pp. 73, 76-79, 85-86; Barbour, *Quakers in England,* pp. 79, 92; K. V. Thomas, "Women and the Civil War Sects," *Past and Present,* no. 13 (1958), pp. 44-45; B.G. Blackwood, "The Lancashire Cavaliers and Their Tenants," *Transactions of the Historic Society of Lancashire and Cheshire,* 118 (1965):27.

44. Barbour, *Quakers in England,* p. 91; Vann, *Development of Quakerism,* pp. 79-81; D/Ry Box 31, WCRO, letter regarding Friends at Bowness, 16 Sept. 1678, indicates that most Quakers were yeomen.

45. D/Ry Box 31, 16 Sept. 1678, 27 Dec. 1683, WCRO.

46. Crook Women's Meeting minutes, 1677-1771, QM3; Windermere Women's Preparative Meeting minutes, MS Book by E. Willson, 1677-1729, QM9A; Kendal Men's Monthly Meeting minutes, 1670-1726, QM12; Account, Memoranda, and Minute Book of Westmorland Quarterly Meeting and Kendal Monthly Meeting, etc., 1658-1699, Kendal and Meetings Near, minutes and records, 1656-1699, QM93, Friends Meeting House, Kendal; D/Ry Box 31, WCRO; Vann, *Development of Quakerism,* pp. 47-87.

47. For a discussion of purposes of marriage, see Lloyd, *Quaker Social History,* pp. 52, 54-58; Frost, *Quaker Family in America,* pp. 150-71.

48. Vann, *Development of Quakerism,* p. 167; Book of Advices, formerly belonging to the Cockermouth meeting, DFCF/1/38, fol. 43, CUCRO.

49. Ibid.

50. Jean-Louis Flandrin, *Families in Former Times,* trans. Richard Southern (Cambridge, 1979), pp. 137-38.

51. Besse, *Sufferings,* 1:653; 2:17; Isabel Ross, *Margaret Fell: Mother of Quakerism* (London, 1949), p. 335; Philip Greven, *The Protestant Temperament: Patterns of Child-Rearing, Religious Experience, and the Self in Early America* (New York, 1977), pp. 21-61 passim; Frost, *Quaker Family in America,* pp. 64-79.

52. Penney, *Household Account Book,* pp. 23, 259; Lloyd, *Quaker Social History,* p. 110.

53. Penney, *Household Account Book,* pp. 25, 27, 33, 37, 39, 59, 65, 135, 141, 177, 215.

54. Quarter Sessions Indictment Book, Kendal, 1655-1691, WQ/I/3, fol. 70, 10 Oct. 1663, WCRO; Penney, *Household Account Book,* pp. 23, 259.

55. This information was gleaned from a survey of probate records, wills, and inventories from the diocese of Carlisle, using intervals of five years, i.e., 1661, 1666, 1671, 1676, 1681; see also Carole Shammas, "Constructing a Wealth Distribution from Probate Records," *Journal of Interdisciplinary History,* 9 (1978):297, for a discussion of the problem of using any probate record to estimate wealth distribution. She estimates that half the population failed to leave wills or inventories, though Alan Macfarlane has suggested that some northern shires have a higher ratio of wills surviving to population than other parts of the country. See Macfarlane, Sarah Harrison, and Charles Jardine, *Reconstructing Historical Communities* (Cambridge, 1977), p. 69.

56. Macfarlane, *Family Life of Josselin,* pp. 45ff.

57. Greven, *Protestant Temperament,* pp. 22-23, 25-28, 32, 35, 45, 50, 151-53, 165, 179, 192, 265-68. Evangelical children were taught to love and fear both God and parent. Moderate parents taught their children love and duty, emphasizing persuasion rather than force. Affectionate children were taught love and reverence; see also Ivy Pinchbeck and Margaret Hewitt, *Children in English Society from Tudor Times to the Eighteenth Century* (London, 1969), p. 263; Thomas Heywood, ed., *The Diary of the Rev. Henry Newcome, from September 30, 1661 to September 29, 1663,* Chetham Society vol. 18 (Manchester, 1849):59-60. Newcome found it necessary to correct his son for irreverent speech; he tried to reason with him, not beat him. He spoke of waking from a nightmare in which he had struck a child in anger. Ashamed of his action, he was thankful it was only a dream. H. Ian Hogbin ("A New Guinea Childhood: From Weaning till the Eighth Year in Wogeo," in *From Child to Adult: Studies in the Anthropology of Education,* ed. John Middleton [Austin, 1970], p. 144) suggests that whipping was employed in that society only to instruct.

58. Blundell, *Cavalier: Blundell Letters,* app. 6, pp. 304-12.

59. Gibson, *Crosby Records,* p. 274. For a similar perception of childhood, see Hogbin, "New Guinea Childhood," pp. 134-35.

60. Lloyd, *Quaker Social History,* pp. 52, 59, 110; Braithwaite, *Second Period of Quakerism,* pp. 257, 567; Frost, *Quaker Family in America,* pp. 64-92.

61. Galgano, "Restoration Recusancy," pp. 193-212; idem, "Negotiations for a Nun's Dowry: Restoration Letters of Mary Caryll, O.S.B. and Ann Clifton, O.S.B.," *American Benedictine Review,* 24 (1973):278-98.

9 ⟨ The Irish Background to Penn's Experiment

The route followed in late 1669 by William Penn on his journey from Dublin to his Irish estates was one that had been in use for centuries by the inhabitants of the province of Munster to maintain contact with the capital. But the haste with which he conducted his journey (30 November – 5 December) suggests that he, no less than the Munster proprietors of earlier years, found the passage through the territories of the Butlers of Ormond an uninviting one. Once he had reached the town of Clonmel and even more so once he had crossed the river Blackwater at Cappoquin, William Penn slackened his pace and took time both to observe his surroundings and to become acquainted with some of his neighbors. This sudden alteration in speed is explained by the fact that as he approached Lismore, "the earl of Cork's great seat," Penn had reached the point from which English settlement in the province of Munster fanned outward in southeasterly, southerly, and westerly directions, and the presence of English settlers as well as the "improved" character of the countryside induced in him a more relaxed attitude.[1]

The Munster settlement that confronted Penn in 1669 was principally an achievement of the first half of the seventeenth century. During these years English planters had been given the opportunity to occupy and develop the confiscated estates of those Old English and Gaelic lords who had resisted the consolidation of governmental authority in the province during the closing decades of the sixteenth century. Not all indigenous proprietors had then been dispossessed, and an uneasy coexistence prevailed

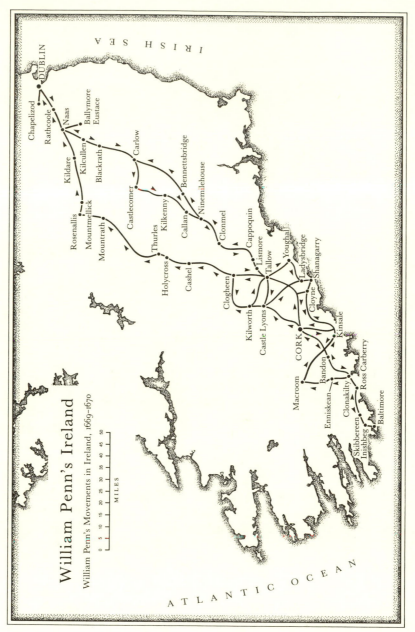

William Penn's Ireland

William Penn's Movements in Ireland, 1669–1670

MAP 9.1

for several decades between the English Protestant planters and the native-born landowners who were generally Catholic. Religious differences contributed to the tension between the two groups, most especially when a continental-trained Counter-Reformation clergy had succeeded in promoting a zealous attachment to the Catholic faith among the native-born elite. The fact that certified membership in the established Protestant church was required of all officeholders in Ireland exacerbated an already tense situation because this effectively excluded the traditional political leaders of the province from positions of trust under the crown. Differing attitudes toward the ownership of land also obtained among the two opposing groups of proprietors, and there is clear evidence that the Catholic landowners, who were becoming increasingly impoverished as a result of their attempts to uphold a traditional dynastic culture, resented the conspicuous wealth acquired by the new English planters and their tenants from their efficient use of the country's resources.

Similar tensions developed in the other provinces of Ireland, and the outbreak of an insurrection in Ulster during the autumn of 1641 triggered spontaneous rebellions in all quarters of the country. English Protestant settlers in Munster were subjected to repeated onslaught by their Catholic neighbors, but they succeeded better than their counterparts in the other provinces in defending their position.[2]

This success of the English settlers in Munster explains why William Penn in 1669 could still witness manifestations of this early settlement. While the Protestant interest in Ireland had initially been weakened by the 1641 rebellion, the long-term consequence of the revolt was to strengthen the Protestant position at the expense of those who had perpetrated the revolt. Oliver Cromwell and his government in England resolved to revenge themselves upon the rebellious Papists in Ireland, and to so reduce them that they would never again be in a position to defy the authority of the government. The war that followed upon Cromwell's intervention in Ireland in 1649 was a campaign of retribution, and the conquest that followed upon the military campaign was designed to dispossess all Catholic landowners who were not able to display their "constant good affection" to the government during the turbulent years following 1641. Much of the confiscated land went to Protestants who were already settled in Ireland, but the greater proportion was allocated to those, such as Admiral William Penn, who had assisted in the Cromwellian attempt to bring the country to subjection. Some few Catholic proprietors who had remained loyal to King Charles II during his years of exile regained portions of their former estates in Ireland following the Restoration of 1660, but the Restoration Settlement in Ireland did little to interfere with the general character of the arrangement that had been implemented during the Commonwealth period.[3]

This explains why grantees such as the Penns still retained an Irish involvement in 1669, but it must be recalled that grantees such as they had

had little opportunity to develop their estates. The picture of English settlement in Munster that confronted William Penn in 1669 cannot have been
essentially different from what it had been in 1641, when depositions were
taken from Protestant settlers in Munster following the 1641 rebellion.
These depositions convey a fairly accurate impression of how the English
planters had been distributed throughout the province at the height of their
success. The most striking sociological feature of these depositions is the
clustering of the settler population in particular regions, leaving a number
of enclaves within the province generally free from English settlement.
These enclaves occurred where the native Catholic proprietors had retained
their property down to 1641, and it was to these areas that fresh Protestant
planters were assigned by those who designed the Cromwellian confiscation.[4] This explains why the bulk of Sir William Penn's Irish estate should
be situated in the Barony of Imokilly: an area that had previously remained
largely in Irish Catholic hands despite being surrounded by baronies which
were densely settled with English Protestant families.[5]

There was a great difference between acquiring and developing land in
Ireland, and even long-established settlers derived little benefit from their
Irish estates during the middle decades of the seventeenth century. Those
estates for which a regular series of rentals survive[6] indicate that virtually
no rent was collected by planters in Ireland during the years 1642–55, and
while attempts were made to collect rent from about 1655, the initial returns were derisory compared with the incomes that Irish planters had
enjoyed during the first half of the seventeenth century. The return on the
estates of newly established landowners was even less satisfactory because
they were frequently burdened with the cost of defending their titles against
rival claimants or against the claims of recently dispossessed Irish proprietors. Thus Sir William Penn was not alone in complaining, as he did in
1667, of the "vast expenses" he had "always been at" because of his Irish
lands. To make matters worse, suitable tenants were difficult to come by in
Restoration Ireland, and rather than have his son enter into contracts with
tenants who did not have the capacity to improve the land, Sir William
Penn instructed his son in 1667 to improvise with whatever tenants were
available provided the leases he granted were for no longer than one year.
This arrangement might have proved satisfactory had Sir William or his
son been permanently resident in Ireland, but it was totally unsuited to
proprietors who chose to remain in England. This may explain why the
father relented his earlier decision and dispatched his son on yet another
visit to Ireland in 1669–70, this time to negotiate leases that would guarantee him some regular income from his Irish estates.[7]

Nevertheless, Cromwellian settlers such as the Penns had reasons for
believing that their Irish, and more especially Munster, lands would eventually produce a profit. In the first instance Munster land was generally of
good quality. The nature of the soil in that part of Imokilly where Sir

William Penn acquired most of his property was characteristic of that in the more prosperous part of the province, and it was described by the surveyor, Sir William Petty, as being well suited to mixed farming with "arable and good pasture and some small quantities of unprofitable bog."[8] Second, the previous settlement of Englishmen in large numbers provided some guarantee of security, especially in the aftermath of Cromwell's military success which had silenced the political opposition to the Protestant interest in Ireland. A more tangible inducement may have been the clear evidence of material success achieved by English settlers in Ireland, and particularly in Munster, during the first half of the seventeenth century. Many visitors to Munster, including Oliver Cromwell,[9] were immediately struck, as was William Penn in December 1669, by the improved and Anglicized appearance of Munster, compared with the generally bleak Irish countryside. For those who had not been to Ireland there was ample evidence in *Ireland's Natural History,* a book composed by the highly respected Dutch scientists Arnold and Gerard Boate, that the new science had been given practical application by particular settlers in Ireland during the earlier part of the seventeenth century and that its application had produced the handsome results that were described in detail by the Boate brothers. Furthermore, the Boates advocated further plantation in Ireland, arguing that the stable conditions introduced there by the Lord Protector provided almost limitless opportunity for those endowed with vision, enterprise, and an understanding of advanced agricultural and manufacturing processes.[10] Thus, apart altogether from the sense of civil and religious duty that might have motivated those who engaged in the Cromwellian plantation of Ireland,[11] there were also plausible economic inducements behind the decision of individuals such as the Penns to establish title to land in Ireland.

What the Boates had to say of the achievements of some English planters in Ireland during the first half of the seventeenth century was unquestionably true, and we get a clear idea of the economic targets that the Penns might have had in mind from the economic performance of those who had settled in Munster before 1641. Evidence on the achievements of English settlers in Ireland derives from literary sources, from estate records, and especially from the depositions made by Protestant settlers after their overthrow in 1641. The primary purpose behind the collection of these depositions was to identify those persons who had engaged in rebellion, but most deponents stated their social position, authenticated their evidence by either signature or mark, and provided an estimate of the goods and chattles that had been lost, probably with a view to future compensation. The literal acceptance of such evidence in particular instances is clearly not permissible unless corroboration can be found from an independent source, but it seems appropriate to divide the deponents into social categories with a view to obtaining a rough impression of the level of economic achievement attained by the various social groups among English settlers in Ireland

TABLE 9.1 *Depositions by English Settlers in Munster, 1642*

	Total Number	Signature	Mark	Proxy	Neither Signature Nor Mark
Knights and esquires	43	29		12	2
Gentlemen	204	166	11	18	9
Merchants and traders	57	36	13	4	4
Clerks	77	68		6	3
Yeomen	307	105	176	11	15
Husbandmen	124	22	86	5	11
Craftsmen	222	65	125	17	15
Widows and Wives	144	18	107	5	14
Servants	1	1			
Status unknown	167	66	74	5	22
Irish Protestants	35	16	15	2	2
TOTAL	1381	592	607	85	97

before 1641. The occasional inventories of goods lost and the more plentiful accounts of the works of improvement that had been destroyed by the rebels provide valuable insights into the agricultural and manufacturing practices that obtained among English settlers in Ireland. The depositions also provide evidence on literacy and enable us to relate ability to sign to the social position of the deponents.

But the limitations of this evidence as a source for economic and social history must also be stressed. The depositions can in no way be employed as a measure of the size of the settler population in Ireland, because only heads of households and especially householders of some wealth or social prominence within the planter community made depositions. We find hardly any statements coming from English Protestant servants, cottiers, or laborers engaged in timber work or iron smelting, who we know to have been present in large numbers. Apart from this social bias, however, there is no reason to believe that what we have is other than a random sample of English settlers from the social categories of husbandman and above, which justifies the employment of the depositions to convey an impression of the geographical distribution of settlers in the province of Munster before the mid-century disturbances. A total of 1,381 individuals, whose residence had been in the province of Munster (excluding County Clare) made depositions in 1642. The social categories into which the deponents were divided and their literacy levels are shown in table 9.1.

It is unfortunate that no depositions made by the Protestant nobility of Munster have survived, but these were few in number. More important is the general absence of Protestant deponents from the lower ranks of society. One is also struck by the low literacy levels among those who described themselves as yeomen and husbandmen. Fifty-seven percent of the yeomen and 70 percent of the husbandmen who deposed acknowledged complete illiteracy by making a mark. Some of these people seem to have been craftworkers who had advanced themselves socially as a result of economic success in Ireland. For example, several yeomen itemized the loss of such items as tan-yards in their depositions.[12] Equally well one finds among the gentlemen many who had originally been merchants or traders,[13] something that is not revealed by the literacy figures because merchants tended to be literate. What developed in Munster was therefore a planter society which experienced rapid upward mobility — a mobility which was carried to its ultimate limit by the earl of Cork[14] — where social position was determined almost entirely by wealth. Exceptions to this generalization are those householders who aspired to the description "Esquire" either by virtue of military rank or by being brothers or sons of knights.[15] These belong more properly with the gentlemen, and when they are so assigned one finds that the losses in goods and chattles claimed by knights and esquires ranged in value from about £2,000 to over £7,000;[16] the losses sustained by gentlemen ranged from about £200 to £1,600 with most in the middle hundreds;[17] and the losses of yeomen ranged from £20 to slightly over £100 (although a few described as yeomen claimed losses up to £600).[18] Husbandmen's losses were not significantly different from those claimed by yeomen,[19] and the losses claimed by craftsmen were in the same range.[20] The wealthiest merchants claimed losses as great as the wealthiest gentry, but much of what they claimed was expressed in terms of debts which had become desperate because of the rebellion.[21]

Those in the knightly class usually had title to land in several counties and baronies, some of it by freehold either from the crown or the principal patentees of planted land in Munster, and more of it by long-term lease from either planter or native proprietors. Most of those who revealed their annual income in rent from their freehold land declared it to have been in the range of £1,000 to £2,000 a year.[22] The principal losses enumerated by the knightly deponents included the burning of residences with their contents; the destruction of orchards and deer-parks; the theft of livestock and grain; the demolition of stone houses that had been erected for principal tenants; the loss of profits from the lands which they rented; and the loss of the value of their investment in making quick-sets, drains, and other improvements.[23] More exceptionally one finds a claim for the destruction of a fishing palace such as that owned by Sir William Hull on the island of Scull;[24] more frequent claims were made for the loss of urban property in Munster towns;[25] and most deponents in this category claimed the loss of money in debts owed to them.

It will be clear from this account that members of the knightly class in Munster were simultaneously middlemen and proprietors in their own right, and that they also farmed a substantial portion of their lands.[26] Claims were made for the loss of livestock and grain, but in almost every case the estimated value of livestock far exceeded that placed on grain.[27] This indicates that the raising of livestock was a commercial venture, while the cultivation of grain tended to be primarily for domestic consumption and the local market. This is not to suggest, however, that the tillage pursued by these proprietors was in any way backward. On the contrary, we learn from the depositions that English yoke oxen were in general use for ploughing;[28] the references to liming and marling are sufficiently frequent to suggest that it was widely practiced,[29] and we can be certain that cultivation on these home farms was pursued on enclosed well-drained fields. The full range of cereals was grown and almost every deponent distinguished between corn in the barn and corn in the ground. This evidence that winter wheat was generally being cultivated establishes that a three-course rotation was in use, and hints of an even more sophisticated rotation system come from the occasional references to large-scale production of peas and beans.[30] We learn from the very detailed inventory of Sir Hardress Waller that his agricultural implements were of English manufacture,[31] and while drays are sometimes mentioned in the depositions, these references are far outnumbered by mention of iron-bound wheeled carts drawn by oxen or wagon horses as the mode of agricultural conveyance.[32]

This evidence is testimony to a level of cultivation which bears comparison with the most advanced tillage in contemporaneous Europe, but we must still bear in mind that livestock was the principal commercial commodity and that the agricultural revolution brought by the planters to Ireland was essentially in the realm of animal husbandry. The Irish economy had always been primarily pastoral and the true scale of the revolution which occurred can only be appreciated when account is taken of the poor quality of the native breeds of cattle and sheep which were valued more for their hides, fleeces, and tallow than for their meat.[33] These animals continued to exist (and in this context it is relevant to mention that tanners were the single largest group among the deposing craftsmen), but the English proprietors favored cattle and sheep of English stock, and it was their successful breeding of these which made possible the trade in live cattle (and subsequently in barreled meat) which became an increasingly important element in Irish exports during the seventeenth century.[34] The existence of enclosures on the planters' land prevented the promiscuous mixture of the imported stock with native breeds, and there is clear evidence that the planters were keenly aware of the advantages of selective breeding. Most planters at the highest social level took pride in their stud farms,[35] and there are several suggestions in the depositions that cattle and sheep were also bred on a systematic basis. First, a distinction was drawn between livestock of English and Irish breeds; second, attention was paid to castrating animals; and finally we find specific references to selective breeding, as (in Hardress Waller's inventory) to "780 choice breeding ewes, and 50 choice riding rams."[36]

Turning from the knights to the gentlemen of Munster, we find deponents who held most of their land by lease from the large proprietors and in turn sublet a substantial part of their property to yeomen and husbandmen. The gentlemen were thus in almost every case middlemen, but the chief landlords were not totally dependent on them because they frequently leased part of their property directly to yeomen and husbandmen, as also to merchants and traders. Whoever the tenant, it was normal, whenever he was granted a long-term lease, that the tenant contracted to build upon and improve the property that had been rented to him. That these conditions were observed and that the advanced agriculture exemplified by the proprietors was imitated by the tenants emerges clearly from the statements made by all categories of deponents. It is also clear that mixed farming obtained at all social levels; frequent references were made by the less affluent deponents to the loss of such items as beehives and garden fruits.[37] Nor was the value of these negligible: one Giles Bennett, a glover, bewailed "the loss of an orchard that he had planted wherein he had one hundred trees which he valueth £7 per annum."[38] There are also several references to root crops being cultivated, and while it is likely that these were for domestic consumption, the testimony of a County Kerry deponent that a man was attacked by the rebels when digging potatoes in his garden[39] suggests production for fodder. Even the poorest of the deponents were well above subsistence level and consequently did not see fit to itemize the contents of their houses, or to mention such mundane items as dunghill fowl. Neither is there much information on housing. All that can be stated is that the wealthier the tenant the better the chance of his having had a stone and slated house.

What can be gleaned from the depositions indicates that the Boate brothers were more than justified in their observation that wherever the English settled in Ireland it "was filled with as goodly beasts, both cows and sheep as any in England, Holland, or other the best countries of Europe."[40] Agriculture in the province of Munster, a province which had not been visited by either Gerard or Arnold Boate, was probably more advanced than what they had witnessed, and it seems beyond question that this was the wealthiest English planter community that had developed in Ireland—or for that matter anywhere beyond the confines of England[41]— during the first half of the seventeenth century. This community was hemmed in by areas that had few English settlers, and the English in Munster tended to view their pockets of settlement as a geographical extension of the English west country.[42] It is likely that most deponents below the rank of knight had come from that part of England, and the trade of the Munster port towns tended to be focused on Bristol and the smaller towns on either side of the Severn.[43] But trade was not by any means confined to England

and everything suggests that this community was as outward looking as it was enterprising. The export of pipe-staves, which was a thriving business in the early decades of the century when forests were systematically being felled by the planters, ranged from the Canaries to the Netherlands. Munster towns seem to have maintained regular trading contacts with the Netherlands,[44] and one man, Henry Turner, a burgess and clothier of Bandonbridge, claimed a loss of £400 a year which he had previously earned by dealing with "Mr. John Quarles of Amsterdam, a Dutch merchant but an Englishman who was bound in a thousand pound bond to take and receive of him in one year and half six hundred broad clothes and to receive the money upon the delivery."[45]

Efforts had been made from the beginning to establish trading contacts with England's infant transatlantic colonies, and tobacco ships from Virginia continued to call intermittently at Kinsale. A market for tobacco developed rapidly in Munster, and we learn from Gaelic as well as English sources that tobacco smoking was widely practiced at all social levels and in both communities.[46] A West Indies contact was also maintained as is evident from three depositions made by wives who declared their husbands to have been absent in various islands there.[47] Nor did Jonas Clone, a merchant of Youghal, think it unusual that his bills and papers should be in the "custody of a friend of his in James town."[48]

When account is taken of this flourishing planter economy in Munster one can understand why, after the reassertion of English authority in the province, individuals like the Penns should be attracted to Munster and why propagandists like the Boates should recommend settlement in Ireland to such as they. But what the Boates, and for that matter the Penns, did not allow for was that the development of this economy had depended in the first instance on the availability of land, labor, and capital, and that all of these variables were less readily available in the Restoration period than they had been before.

Of the three, land was the commodity most freely available to English Protestant settlers throughout the seventeenth century. However, some of the choice land acquired during the Cromwellian confiscation, in which the Penns had acquired their grant, was almost immediately recalled to satisfy those in Ireland who had remained loyal to the royalist cause. The Irish land policy of the government of Charles II explains why the Penns had to abandon their initial allocation in the vicinity of Macroom (restored to the earl of Clancarty) in exchange for land in Imokilly and in west County Cork.[49] Having accepted this exchange the Penns were still well provided for, in terms of acreage, but undeveloped property was of little value in itself, and if the new proprietors were to emulate the settlers of the early seventeenth century (who were just then restructuring their estates) they required large amounts of cash and large numbers of tenants skilled in advanced agricultural techniques.

The easiest way to obtain money for investment in the Irish economy was to have it transferred from England, but shrewd observers had consistently advised against this course,[50] and proprietors and their tenants had usually to make do with whatever cash could be found within Ireland itself. During the first half of the century successful proprietors frequently had resort to the use or misuse of office either to obtain land or to expand upon crown grants, or to squeeze money from neighboring Catholic landowners under threat of exposing weakness in their titles. Such stratagems — which have been graphically described by Terence Ranger[51] — provided penniless proprietors with cash, or at least placed them in a position to acquire money through the sale of portions of their lands. Having thus obtained sufficient money to cover the cost of building or renovating an appropriate residence and to stock a home farm, the proprietor usually accepted native tenants on short-term leases, but later displaced these in favor of more skilled English tenants on long-term improving leases. These new tenants, like the landowners themselves, enjoyed an income from rent, and both groups acquired a further injection of cash through the direct exploitation of the natural resources of the country. Meat, grain, hides, and tallow were the more profitable commodities, but the steady income that accrued from these was supplemented by the windfall which derived from the destruction of forests and the development of coastal fisheries. Lumber and fish played the part in the development of the planter economy in Munster that staple cash crops do in most colonial situations, and it was the exploitation of these commodities through the first decades of the seventeenth century that enabled landowners and tenants alike to develop their land to its full potential.

But the success of the early seventeenth-century planters in Ireland meant that little opportunity existed for the fresh wave of settlers who arrived at mid-century. By this time there were few surviving Catholic landowners whose precarious position might be exploited for personal advantage, and the comprehensive settlement and resettlement of Irish land during the Cromwellian and Restoration periods greatly reduced the opportunity for profit through the discovery of concealments and defective title. By this time, also, most of the natural forests which lay close to the profitable land in Munster had been cleared, and the only new settlers who even attempted to profit through iron-smelting or the sale of pipe-staves were those, like Sir William Petty, who would contemplate settling on poorer agricultural land.[52] Claim had also been established to the better fishing grounds during the earlier part of the century, and to make matters worse the pilchards, which had been the most plentiful fish, seem to have deserted Irish waters by the late seventeenth century. This combination of circumstances meant, therefore, that new planters in Ireland were at a distinct disadvantage, as compared with those who had preceded them, when it came to raising cash to develop their estates, and many settled for a one-time profit by selling their recently acquired estates to the established proprietors at a low price.[53]

As if this were not a sufficient disincentive to planters, those who sought to develop estates in Ireland after mid-century also encountered difficulty in attracting suitable tenants from England. Demographic and economic trends in England were largely responsible for this,[54] but the exaggerated reports of the massacre of Protestants during the 1641 rebellion, which were propagated throughout all parts of England, did nothing to improve the situation.[55] Furthermore, many tenants who had previously settled in Ireland fled the country following the rebellion in 1641, and it is likely that large numbers of these were absorbed into the expanding English economy of the Restoration period and never returned to Ireland. It is thus possible that there were fewer rather than more English settlers in Ireland during the Restoration period, and when another major influx to Ireland from Britain occurred at the very end of the seventeenth century it was from Scotland rather than England that the migrants came. These people settled principally in Ulster. Since they had come from Scotland, where agricultural practice was backward, and since they were fleeing from starvation conditions, they were not the type of tenants likely to promote a revolution in agriculture.[56]

Thus all new planters in Ireland, and more especially those in Munster, encountered difficulty in attracting suitable tenants to their estates, and those who did not sell their property to long-established settlers were frequently obliged to lease farms to these at low rents, or to concede leases to the native proprietors whom they had just dispossessed. The list of tenants who were eventually established by William Penn on his father's property shows that he had to resort to precisely these expedients, and this explains why the returns to the Penns as head landlords remained at an extraordinarily low level.[57] From what has already been said of William Penn's two visits to the estates which his father had acquired in Ireland it is evident that he encountered problems that were general to all new planters in the country. His inspection of the trenches erected by Colonel Peter Wallis "in the great bog where he had made a double ditch two miles quicksetted and many great ditches across," as well as his two visits to John Hull's island[58] indicate that Penn was interested in improvement. However, the absence of any mention of his promoting improvements on his own lands suggests that he found the cost insuperable. The Penns never resolved the problem of finding suitable tenants, and the solution that William Penn hinted at in 1667 of inviting Quakers from England to occupy his estate did not meet with the approval of official authority in Munster. By virtue of his social position William Penn was himself generally exempt from molestation because of his religious beliefs, but he was greatly aggrieved by the persecution in Munster of Quakers from humble backgrounds, and he petitioned the earl of Orrery to exert his influence to prevent "so malicious and injurious a practice to innocent Englishmen" which, he believed, was "contrary to the practice elsewhere and a bad argument to invite English hither."[59] The predictable curt rejection that his petition received from Orrery demonstrated, what had previously been made manifest in the pre-1641 period, that utopian groups would not be tolerated by official authority in Ireland.

This realization, added to the unpromising economic circumstances that confronted him, may explain why William Penn chose to attempt the establishment of a new colony in America in preference to developing what his father had already acquired in Ireland. But in advancing this as a plausible explanation of William Penn's choice one must emphasize that there is no hard evidence to support this proposition, and one must recall that Penn was by no means the first planter to transfer his interest from Ireland to America. Some who had settled in Ireland even during the boom years abandoned their efforts there to pursue a less predictable future in America. Emanuel Downing, the Calverts, Captain Newce, and Daniel Gookin are the most notable of those who made the transfer during the pre-1641 period, and the action of none of these amounted to what would today be described as economic sense.[60] Nevertheless, the experience which these men and William Penn had obtained in Ireland must have impressed upon them that colonization could be a source of profit to the enterprising, and that the principal benefits went to those who were first on the ground.

NOTES

This essay is intended as a preliminary and, it might be emphasized, a tentative statement of the conclusions I am deriving from extensive research toward a book to be entitled *Ireland in the English Colonial System, 1580-1650*. I conducted my research while I was a member of the Institute for Advanced Study, Princeton. I am grateful to Dr. Thomas Bartlett, Dr. David Dickson, and Professor Jim Donnelly for their criticism of this essay.

1. William Penn, "My Irish Journal," in *PWP*, 1:99-143, esp. 109-10 (entry for 4 Dec. 1669). For a map of Penn's journey, see p. 140 in this volume.

2. On this general background, see T. W. Moody et al., eds., *A New History of Ireland*, vol. 3, *Early Modern Ireland, 1534-1691*, ed. T. W. Moody (Oxford, 1976), esp. pp. 187-287; D. B. Quinn, "The Munster Plantation: Problems and Opportunities, " *Cork Historical Society Journal*, 71 (1966):19-40; Nicholas Canny, *The Upstart Earl: A Study of the Social and Mental World of Richard Boyle, the First Earl of Cork, 1566-1643* (Cambridge, 1982); idem, "The Formation of the Irish Mind: Religion, Politics and Gaelic Irish Literature, 1580-1750," *Past and Present*, no. 95 (1982), pp. 90-116. The first comprehensive study of British settlement in seventeenth-century Munster will become available with the publication of Michael Mac Carthy Morrogh, *The Munster Plantation, 1580-1641*, (Oxford, forthcoming), and a fresh appraisal of general developments in early-modern Ireland is presented in Nicholas Canny, *From Reformation to Restoration: Ireland, 1534-1660* (Dublin, forthcoming).

3. T. C. Barnard, *Cromwellian Ireland: English Government and Reform in Ireland, 1649-60* (Oxford, 1975); idem, "Planters and Policies in Cromwellian Ireland," *Past*

and Present, no. 61 (1973), pp. 31-69; Karl Bottigheimer, *English Money and Irish Land: The "Adventurers" in the Cromwellian Settlement of Ireland* (Oxford, 1971); idem, "The Restoration Land Settlement in Ireland: A Structural View," *Irish Historical Studies,* 18 (1972):1-21; Moody, *New History of Ireland,* 5:289-385 and 420-51.

4. Depositions for Co. Waterford, MS. 820, TCD; depositions for Co. Tipperary, MS. 821, TCD; depositions for Co. Cork, MSS. 822-25, TCD; depositions for Co. Kerry, MS. 828, TCD; depositions for Co. Limerick, MS. 829, TCD. Further depositions were collected in the early 1650s, but these shed little light on social and economic conditions before 1641 and have generally been disregarded. It was widely believed that the close proximity of Catholics to the English settlers had been responsible for the initial success of the rebellion; see, for example, Richard Lawrence, *The Interest of England in the Irish Transplantation, stated* (Dublin, 1655). Lawrence was writing principally of Ulster, where he deplored the way in which the planters were dispersed indiscriminately among the native population. Penn must have been familiar with the views of Lawrence since he went to see him in Dublin; see *PWP,* 1:106.

5. Book of Survey and Distribution for County Cork, PRO, Dublin. A study of this book reveals that Penn received a total of 6,774 Irish acres, of which 3,955 were situated in the barony of Imokilly; 2,620 acres in the barony of Barriroe; and 198 acres in the parish of Lislee, barony of Ibawne. Those in Imokilly who forfeited the land which was granted to Penn were Edmund Power of Inchy, Garret Curtin, Edmund Fitzgerald, Redmond Condon, Edmund Power of Shangarry, James Fitzgerald of Milsane, Thomas Fitzgerald of Ballylawrence, Morris Fitzgerald, William Power of Shangarry, Nicholas Meagh, Gerald Fitzjames, Anthony Dowle, and William Cotter. Those in Barriroe who forfeited were O'Heas, O'Harts, McCarthys, O'Donovans, Dermot O'Mahony, and Thomas Kallanane. In Ibawne those who forfeited to Penn were Dominic Roche, Dermot O'Shaghnus, and John Oge O'Hea. For maps and further details of Penn's Irish lands see *PWP,* 1:570-73.

6. The estate records with which I have greatest familiarity are, for Munster, the Lismore estate records (for which rentals are available at Chatsworth House and the National Library of Ireland) and the Perceval estate records (Add. MSS., 47,036ff, BL); and, for Ulster, the Davies estate records (Hastings MS., box 76), and the Rawdon estate records (Hastings MS., box 75), Huntington Library, San Marino, Calif.

7. The general problems faced by new planters in Ireland are discussed in Barnard, "Planters and Policies." The quotations are from Sir William Penn to William Penn, 9 Apr. 1667, and 21 May 1667, in *PWP,* 1:44-47.

8. This was the description offered by William Petty in his parish maps for this vicinity of the barony of Imokilly (the parish maps are available in the National Library of Ireland).

9. Cromwell's reaction was reported by Roger Boyle, Lord Broghill, who accompanied the lord protector to the province. See Thomas Birch, ed., *The Life of the Honourable Robert Boyle* (London, 1774), 1:xii.

10. Gerard Boate, *Ireland's Naturall History,* with a preface by Arnold Boate (London, 1652), esp. pp. 97-98, 124-30, 135-37; see also *Present State of Ireland together with some remarks upon the ancient state thereof* (London, 1673), esp. pp. 70-74. I wish to thank Dr. David Dickson for drawing my attention to this second item.

11. This theme is the subject of Barnard, *Cromwellian Ireland.*

12. Of the 26 yeomen who deposed from the barony of Cosmore and Cosbride, Co. Waterford, Thomas Carter and John Rosbick claimed compensation for items associated with tanning, and a third, Edward Rushell, claimed the benefit of the iron works of Lisfinny, as well as agricultural losses (MS. 820, fols. 270, 112, 101, TCD).

13. An interesting case is that of Thomas Carter the younger, who made claims to gentility and signed his deposition, whereas his illiterate and poorer father went by the description of yeoman (MS. 820, fols. 270-71, TCD). George Sakly, gent. (MS. 822, fol. 106, TCD), revealed his original position by claiming a £58 loss in "household stuff and shopwares," and at least two gentlemen deponents, Humfrey Hunt and Robert Horne, revealed that they had originally been malsters (MS. 823, fols. 49, 114, TCD).

14. On Cork, see Canny, *The Upstart Earl.*

15. Those whose exalted title was justified by military rank but whose wealth did not match the title were Lt. William Cade, who claimed loss of goods and chattles worth £446.11s; Capt. James Finch, whose losses were estimated as worth £815; Cheney Polden, ensign to Capt. Peregrine Banister, whose losses were estimated as a mere £192; and John Strange, the serjeant of arms for Munster, who claimed a loss of £400 (MS. 824, fol. 90; MS. 822, fols. 58, 268; MS. 825, fol. 253, TCD). The depositions for Sir Percy Smyth, Thomas Dant, and Sir Thomas Meredith (MS. 820, fol. 116; MS. 823, fol. 137; and MS. 821 fol. 78, TCD) are clearly incomplete, which leaves William Thomas, two Thomas Nevells, Walter Bird, and William Mead (MS. 822, fols. 152, 179, 35; MS. 824, fols. 27, 216, TCD), each with losses ranging from £300 to £600, as clear misfits in the upper category. Abell Morgan, Richard Osborne, and Josias Farlow (MS. 820, fols. 210, 214; MS. 822, fol. 185, TCD), with losses respectively of £1,410, £1,163, and £1,304 seem also to be somewhat out of place in the upper category.

16. The documents on which this estimate is based are as follows: MS. 820, fols. 54, 138-39, 221, 306-7; MS. 821, fols. 44-45, 130; MS. 822 fol. 170; MS. 823, fols. 19, 41-42, 153, 187; MS. 824, fols. 23-24; 112, 144, 166, 207, 252-59, 261-64; MS. 825, fols. 51, 153, 170, 261; MS. 828, fol. 255; MS. 829, fols. 246, 250, 269, 284-90, 310-11, 335, TCD.

17. On the basis of gentlemen deponents from the barony of Cosmore and Cosbride, all but four are in the range of £133 to £740. Of the remaining four, one is incomplete, and the others claimed losses of £1,681, £1,344, and £51. The relevant documents for this barony are MS. 820, fols. 73, 94, 100, 107, 134, 146, 148, 162, 175, 179, 184, 195, 216, 234, 271, 283; MS. 823, fol. 90, TCD.

18. This generalization is again based on evidence from the barony of Cosmore and Cosbride. Of these, all but five fit the description given. Among the remaining five, the claimed losses were £623, £333, £259, £177, and £7. The relevant documents are MS. 820, fols. 20, 62, 68, 71, 72, 78, 101-2, 112, 120, 142-43, 154, 160, 173, 180, 196, 201-2, 203, 205, 238, 256, 270, 279, 296, TCD.

19. In the barony of Cosmore and Cosbride, husbandmen's claims ranged between £12 and £172. The relevant documents are MS. 820, fols. 40, 147, 151, 182, 212, 252, TCD.

20. Of the craftsmen from Cosmore and Cosbride, all but five claimed within the range £20 to £93. The remaining five claimed respectively £11, £127, £140, £201, and £439. The relevant documents are MS. 820, fols. 38, 83-84, 119, 122, 129, 136, 159, 166, 170, 190, 208, 247, 281, 304, 310, 311, TCD.

21. Among the wealthy merchants of Munster, Tristan Whitcombe of Kinsale (MS. 822, fols. 26-27, TCD) claimed a loss of £5,565, but of this amount, £3,986 was accounted for in debts; Edward Crockford of Cappoquin (MS. 820, fol. 92, TCD) claimed a loss of £3,691 of which £1,679 was accounted for in debts; Robert Fennell of Cork City (MS. 824, fol. 234, TCD), claimed a loss of £2,960 of which £1,350 was accounted for in debts; and Christopher Croker of Lismore (MS. 820, fol. 39, TCD), who claimed a loss of £2,200, accounted for £2,000 of this in debts.

22. Sir Richard Osborne of Whitechurch, Co. Waterford, claimed annual losses of £1,000 from his freehold, and £200 from the office of clerk of the crown

and peace for Cos. Tipperary and Limerick, and the city of Limerick (MS. 820, fol. 221, TCD). A claim for an annual rent of £1,400 was made for Capt. William Jephson of Mallow (MS. 823, fol. 19, TCD). A claim for an annual rent of £2,587 was made on behalf of Sir Philip Perceval (MS. 824, fol. 166, TCD), and a claim for £1,006 a year was made on behalf of Sir William St. Leger of Doneraile (MS. 824, fol. 112, TCD). William Fitton of Anye, Co. Limerick, averred an annual income of "at least £800" from his freehold estate (MS. 829, fols. 310-11, TCD). Nicholas Osborne of Whitechurch, Co. Waterford (MS. 820, fol. 214, TCD), claimed a loss of £126 annual rent from his freehold estate, and William Mead of Ballymartell, Co. Cork (MS. 824, fol. 216, TCD) claimed a loss of an annual rent of £296 from his freehold estate. Sir Percy Smyth of Killenatra, Co. Waterford (MS. 820, fol. 116, TCD), mentioned a loss of £200 annual rent from freehold land in Adare, Co. Limerick, but the incomplete document does not cover his Waterford holdings. Sir William Hull (MS. 824, fols. 252-59) claimed a loss of annual income of £183 from freehold land as opposed to a yearly profit of £1,065 from land held by long lease or mortgage. Finally Sir Hardress Waller (MS. 829, fols. 284-90) placed an annual rental of £1,300 on his freehold land.

23. See the depositions cited in n. 16, above. The most explicit statement on land-improvement is to be found in MS. 824, fol. 256, TCD, where Sir William Hull claimed to have invested £180 "in breaking of rocks at Lymton, stoning the land five times all over to make it good arable land and seperated it into many fields of 8, 10, 15 & 20 acres in a field which before a plough could not work in it, also in drawing the bogs & making gullys underground whereby the bogs became good meadow land, and for ditching and hedging the said land (besides sandings)." To give further authority to these claims, mention should be made of the existence in Waterford of "Mr. Williames who professes himself to be a drainer of bogs and an engineer" (MS. 820, fol. 246, TCD).

24. MS. 824, fols. 254-56, TCD. The other claimants for fishing palaces were merchants such as Tristram Whitcombe (MS. 822, fols. 26-27, TCD), and gentlemen of mercantile background, such as Otto Redish of Youghal, who was partner "in the trade of fishing" with Frances Gibbins and Elizabeth Lewis, both widows and gentlewomen of Youghal (MS. 822, fol. 194, TCD).

25. See, for example, the deposition of Hugh Croker, Esq., who held the town and castle of Cappoquin from the earl of Cork (MS. 820, fol. 54, TCD), or that for Capt. William Jephson of Mallow, who owned houses near the castle of Mallow (MS. 823, fol. 19, TCD).

26. See almost any of the depositions cited in n. 16, above. On "Middlemen" in Irish history, see David Dickson, "Middlemen," in *Penal Era and Golden Age: Essays in Irish History, 1690-1800,* ed. Thomas Bartlett and D. W. Hayton (Belfast, 1979), pp. 162-85.

27. James Wallis of Stradbally, Co. Waterford, for example, cited a loss of £1,134 worth of livestock as opposed to £610 for harvested grain and hay and £150 for corn in the ground (MS. 820, fols. 306-7, TCD). This was a typical claim from the wealthier element among the gentry, while that made by Agmondesham Muschamp of Carrigaline is representative of the more modest gentry. He cited losses of £317 in livestock, £140 for harvested hay and corn, and £50 for corn in the ground (MS. 823, fol. 187, TCD).

28. The overwhelming majority of the gentry deponents cited in n. 16, above, make specific reference to oxen among their livestock and some, like Abell Morgan of Whitechurch (MS. 820, fol. 210, TCD), made specific mention of iron chains for a plough team.

29. References to lime and lime-kilns are very frequent among the depositions cited in n. 16, above, but to dispel any suspicion that lime was being used exclu-

sively for building, it is worth citing from the deposition of Lt. William Cade of the barony of Imokilly, who claimed £35 for the investment on "so much fallow which he manured with a kiln of lime and marl for the seed which afterwards he durst not to sow" (MS. 824, fol. 90, TCD).

30. Sir Hardress Waller claimed to have had six barrels of beans and six barrels of white peas in his store, and to have had six English acres of peas in the ground (MS. 829, fol. 285v, TCD).

31. Ibid.

32. Ibid., and the deposition of Capt. James Finch (MS. 822, fol. 58, TCD).

33. Even so avid a defender of Ireland as Richard Stanyhurst admitted that Irish cattle were of small breed; see Stanyhurst, "Description of Ireland," in Raphael Holinshed, *The . . . Chronicles of England, Scotlande, and Irelande* (1577; reprint, London, 1808), 6:20. The Boates (*Ireland's Natural History,* pp. 89-90) also spoke of the small size of native Irish cattle.

34. Donald Woodward, "The Anglo-Irish Livestock Trade in the Seventeenth Century," *Irish Historical Studies,* 18 (1973):489-523.

35. There are innumerable references to horse breeding in the papers of Richard Boyle, for which see Canny, *The Upstart Earl.* Practically all the gentlemen deponents for Munster listed horses among their losses but some, such as Gamaliell Warter of Cullin, made specific reference to studs (MS. 829, fol. 246, TCD).

36. MS. 829, fol. 284, TCD; see also the deposition of Nicholas Philpot (MS. 824, fols. 261-64, TCD) where, in listing his cattle, he distinguished between working oxen, fattening oxen, steers, milch cows, young steers, heifers, calves, and yearling bulls. A similar concern with stock raising is evident from the estate papers of the period. See, for example, the census of "his flocks" taken on behalf of Sir Philip Perceval in 1635 and 1639 (Add. MSS. 46,920B, fols. 11-12; and 46,923, fol. 64, BL).

37. See, for example, the deposition of a cordier, Richard Prudderagh of Whitechurch (MS. 820, fol. 177, TCD), who mentions the loss of "potato roots and other garden fruits" valued at £6. Richard Belshire, a yeoman of Lismore, listed the loss of two stocks of bees valued at 12s. (MS. 820, fol. 20, TCD).

38. MS. 820, fol. 119, TCD.

39. MS. 828, fol. 222, TCD.

40. Boate, *Ireland's Natural History,* p. 89.

41. On this point, see Nicholas Canny, "The Anglo-American Colonial Experience," *The Historical Journal,* 24 (1981):485-503; idem, "Migration and Opportunity: Britain, Ireland and the New World," *Irish Economic and Social History,* vol. 12 (1985):7-32.

42. This point is developed in Canny, *The Upstart Earl,* chap. 6, but merchants were generally an exception, since they developed trading networks throughout Ireland.

43. See David J. Dickson, "An Economic History of the Cork Region in the Eighteenth Century" (Ph.D. thesis, University of Dublin, 1977), pp. 32-33, 41.

44. Ibid., pp. 546-47; Violet Barbour, *Capitalism and Amsterdam in the Seventeenth Century* (Ann Arbor, 1966), pp. 31n, 121-22.

45. MS. 824, fols. 118-19, TCD.

46. Some traders, like Steven Clove, chapman, itemized their stock. He claimed a loss of "six hundred weight of tobacco, linen yarn, linen cloth, freize, wool and 1 pack of feathers," all of which he valued at £102 (MS. 823, fol. 58, TCD). Jonas Clone, a merchant of Youghal, claimed a loss of 400 weight of tobacco, which he valued at £30 (MS. 824, fol. 251, TCD), and some tradesmen claimed a loss of tobacco in such quantities that they must have been itinerant traders. A case in point is Simon Lightfoot, a blacksmith of Kinsale, who claimed £12 for the loss of "a

horse, laden with tobacco and one pair of scales and weights" (MS. 823, fol. 24, TCD). The most graphic description of such trading in tobacco is to be found in the Gaelic text *Pairlement Chloinne Tomais,* the relevant section of which is printed in Alan Bliss, *Spoken English in Ireland, 1600-1740* (Dublin, 1979), pp. 109-10. The anonymous author of the *Present State of Ireland* contended (p. 151) that among the Gaelic Irish "both men and women of all sorts were extremely addicted to take tobacco in a most abundant manner."

47. MS. 821, fol. 76; MS. 820, fol. 140; MS. 829, fol. 183, TCD.

48. MS. 822, fol. 131, TCD.

49. See *PWP,* 1:40n.

50. See, for example, Goring to Cork, 16 Nov. 1630, Cork Letter Book, 1:683, Chatsworth, where Lord Goring advised Cork to cease investing in Ireland "for me thinks all in an Irish bottom with such pilots as have been and may be again, when we are dead and gone, I cannot allow of."

51. T. O. Ranger, "Richard Boyle and the Making of an Irish Fortune," *Irish Historical Studies,* 10 (1957):257-59; see also T. M. Healy, *Stolen Waters: A Page in the Conquest of Ulster* (London, 1913); Brian MacCuarta, "Newcomers in the Irish Midlands, 1540-1641" (Master's thesis, University College, Galway, 1980).

52. T. C. Barnard, "Sir William Petty, Irish Landowner," in *History and Imagination: Essays in Honour of H. R. Trevor-Roper,* ed. Hugh Lloyd-Jones, Valerie Pearl, and Blair Worden (London, 1981); idem, "Sir William Petty as Kerry Ironmaster," in *Proceedings of the Royal Irish Academy,* 82 (1982):1-32.

53. Barnard, "Planters and Policies."

54. See D. C. Coleman, *The Economy of England, 1450-1750* (Oxford, 1977) pp. 91-172; E. A. Wrigley and R. S. Schofield, *The Population History of England, 1541-1871: A Reconstruction* (London, 1981), pp. 438-43. The author of *Present State of Ireland* admitted the difficulty in attracting English tenants to Restoration Ireland when he mentioned (p. 71) that "the whole country became in a few years indifferently well planted, though not with a sufficient number of people to inhabit the same, which are still wanting and will be so for many years to come."

55. Keith Lindley, "The Impact of the 1641 Rebellion on England and Wales, 1641-5," *Irish Historical Studies,* 18 (1972):143-76.

56. Ian Whyte, *Agriculture and Society in Seventeenth Century Scotland* (Edinburgh, 1979); see also the essay by Ned Landsman in this volume.

57. *PWP,* 1:570-73.

58. Ibid., 1:112, 118. From what has been said it is likely that John Hull's island of Inishbeg was a location for catching and curing fish.

59. Penn to Orrery, c. 4 Nov. 1667 (*PWP,* 1:51-52); and Orrery's reply of 5 Nov. 1667 (ibid., 1:53). The hopelessness of Penn's quest in looking to Orrery, or any other member of the Boyle family, for assistance in gaining toleration for Quakers will be evident from reading Canny, *The Upstart Earl,* and J. R. Jacob, *Robert Boyle and the English Revolution* (Ithaca, N.Y., 1979).

60. The cases of Newce and the Calverts are well known, and Downing's career in Ireland will be the subject of a forthcoming book by Rolf Loeber, entitled *Downing's and Winthrop's Plantation in Ireland: The Preamble to the New England Migration.* I am grateful to Rolf Loeber for permitting me to see a manuscript chapter of this work. The career of Gookin has been traced in Fredrick W. Gookin, *Daniel Gookin, 1612-87, Assistant and Major-General of the Massachusetts Bay Colony* (Chicago, 1912). Those relatives of Winthrop who remained in Ireland have had their situation and connections studied in detail in Mac Carthy Morrogh, *The Munster Plantation.*

RICHARD T. VANN

10 ⟨ Quakerism: Made In America?

The English (and Irish) career of William Penn has been thoroughly explored, but the same cannot be said of the thousands who came with him or followed him from the British Isles to Pennsylvania. This essay is a statistical treatment of some of those relatively anonymous thousands. It focuses on those who were Quakers, and asks, in particular, what was their sociological background and their relationship to British Friends. Since much of the argument rests on an interlocking series of statistical estimates, its conclusions must be regarded more as hypotheses than as established historical facts; but if these hypotheses should turn out to be near the truth, the implications for the character of Quakerism as it developed in North America are considerable.

Before we can answer these questions, we face the task — and it is a considerable one — of identifying the British Quakers. Since there were no membership lists, there is no way to tell exactly who were Friends. However there are a number of sources susceptible to quantitative treatment which can give us a reasonable idea. Of these, the most important are Friends' registers of births, marriages, and burials, which began to be kept systematically as early as 1655, and the records of Quaker sufferings, especially the monumental compilation by Joseph Besse.[1]

The most substantial sources used in this essay were compiled for quite another purpose: a study of the demography of British and Irish Quakers from 1655 to 1840.[2] From that point of view, it is a nuisance that any Quakers left Britain at all, since it is usually impossible to follow their reproductive histories once they arrived in America. Sometimes, however, and particularly in the family lists which the Irish Quakers maintained, there was direct information about members of the family who had emigrated to America; and so it was occasionally possible to track families which passed out of observation in Ireland but emerged again in Pennsylvania. I have used four sources in trying to identify the British and Irish Quaker emigrants to America and place them within the occupational structure of Great Britain. First, there are the Irish family lists which survive for most Irish Quaker families and which constitute ready-made family histories, without the possibilities of error which afflict most attempts to construct such family records. Unfortunately there are few such lists for the English Quakers, and these are difficult to exploit. The second and chief source for England, therefore, is some 6,500 "family reconstitution forms" extracted from the Quaker registers of births, marriages, and burials and from genealogies compiled by Quaker families. These forms reconstruct the history of each family by recording at what ages the parents married, how many children they had and at what intervals, and the ages at death of all members of the family. (Of course it is rare for all this information to be available for a family; more often one has to make do with some dates and not others.)[3] Family-reconstitution forms were compiled for the great majority of the Irish Quakers, and for from 15 to 20 percent of the English (and Welsh) ones. The parts of England covered in the family-reconstitution study were Westmorland, Yorkshire, the Western Quarterly Meeting (Herefordshire and Worcestershire, as well as Wales); Cheshire and Staffordshire; London and Middlesex; and Sussex and Surrey (all by 10 to 15 percent samples) and Bristol, Norwich and Norfolk, Cambridgeshire, Huntingdonshire, Bedfordshire, Hertfordshire, Buckinghamshire, Berkshire, and Oxfordshire (the complete Quaker populations in these counties, so far as they were reflected in the registers). Thus we have a nominal file of almost all the Irish Quakers and from 15 to 20 percent of the English ones.[4]

To strengthen the evidence for this particular study I also read about 15 percent of the English monthly meeting minute books and compiled a partial list of English Friends who had received certificates of good behavior and clearness of engagements of marriage from their English monthly meetings as part of their preparation for emigration.[5] (Particularly in the early years, these were often asked for after the English person or family had already arrived in Pennsylvania, but later it became customary for Friends in good standing to take their certificates with them.)

These certificates, and the occasional mentions in the Irish family lists, are direct evidence of emigration to America. To supplement these sources I have attempted nominal linkage between the English and Irish Quaker forms and the American Quaker registers as digested and published by Hinshaw.[6] When the same surnames appear with a tolerable fit in ages, we may be reasonably certain that we have traced the family across the Atlan-

TABLE 10.1   *Origins of British Friends as Shown in Certificates Received in Philadelphia, 1681–1750*

Period	Wales	Ireland	England	London	Home Counties	East Anglia	South Coast	West Country	Mid-lands	North
1681–1690	6	5	75[a]	12	5		7	29	9	5
1691–1700	5	1	66	20	2		5	17	6	16
1701–1710	1	15	40	16		3	2	3	5	11
1711–1720	5	14	76	25	1	1	2	17	7	23
1721–1730	1	18	35	9		2	3	5	2	14
1731–1740		14	28	11				7	3	7
1741–1750	1	11	21	8	3	1			1	8
TOTAL	19	78	341	101	11	7	19	78	33	84

NOTE: Certificates were entered by their dates, not the date of registration in Philadelphia.

[a] Includes eight from England who could not be allocated geographically.

SOURCE: Albert Cook Myers, *Quaker Arrivals at Philadelphia, 1682-1750* (Philadelphia, 1902).

tic. I have also matched the names of those known to have been involved in the settlement of Pennsylvania against the indexes in Besse's *Sufferings*. A list has been compiled of First Purchasers of land from William Penn, but only a little over half of these actually took up residence in Pennsylvania.[7] Fortunately there is another list from which we can make a start; it is the record of certificates from Britain received by Philadelphia Yearly Meeting, which represent about one-third of all those received by the nineteen monthly meetings in Pennsylvania.[8] Since our English sample is regionally skewed, it is useful to look first at the regional distribution of these certificates presented to Philadelphia Yearly Meeting, as is done in table 10.1.

The first striking fact to emerge is the predominance of the cities in supplying emigrants from England. About 30 percent of the English Friends presented certificates from London — a share which remained surprisingly stable after the first decade, when it was only a bit over 15 percent. Bristol here has not been separately tabulated, but, as we shall see, it provided a substantial part of the West Country Friends, who altogether amounted to almost a quarter of the whole. These two cities, then, supplied something like 40 percent of the certificates which English Friends brought with them or sent back for. In Ireland, on the other hand, Dublin was not more heavily represented among the certificates than its Quaker population would have warranted, and the same is true of Cork, although it was a frequent port of embarkation.

This geographic distribution already gives us a hint about the social background of the Quaker emigrants; and this hint is what we must content ourselves with for the Irish Quakers, since the great defect in their otherwise splendid records is absence of occupational designations. We estimate that we can discover only about two hundred occupations out of about two thousand Irish families whose demographic history has been reconstructed. It is significant, however, that the pattern of settling in a large city (even if for only a short time) before emigrating does not seem to have existed to anything like the same extent in Ireland. This suggests that many of the Irish Quaker emigrants had been engaged in agriculture, which as far as we can tell was the occupation of many Irish Friends. As table 10.1 makes plain, one of the distinctive features of Irish Quaker emigration is that it was heavier in the eighteenth century than in the last two decades of the seventeenth. By that time a good many Friends in Ireland had set up as traders of some sort, and it is known that Irish Quaker emigration was quite sensitive to fluctuations in the business cycle, dead times of trade being followed often by an appreciable exodus of ruined tradesmen.[9]

Occupational information from the English Quaker marriage and burial registers is, in contrast, plentiful in some areas even in the period which most concerns us, the 1680s. Occupational information is particularly rich for London, but unfortunately London Friends, who tended to be more elaborate and systematic in their record-keeping, sometimes kept separate books or boxes in which certificates to go to America were entered and kept. These have not always been preserved; a cross-check of certificates presented to Philadelphia Friends from Southwark Monthly Meeting shows no mention of them in the voluminous minutes of Southwark.

For Bristol, however, it is possible to make some comparison of the social structure of Bristol meeting as a whole and that of the emigrants from it. This is done in table 10.2. As with any table, there are complexities of interpretation. Since we know the occupations of only fourteen emigrants, comparisons can only be suggestive rather than conclusive. We are also dependent on the occupational terminology of the time, which sometimes conceals as much as it reveals. It is particularly confusing that workers in a trade and substantial entrepreneurs in that trade might be called by the same name. For example, it took a considerable amount of capital to set up as a soap-boiler, but the man with that capital and one of his ordinary employees might both be described in a marriage register as "soap-boilers." The distinction between wholesale and retail trade is also hard to draw, and since production was only beginning to be capitalistically organized, it was still common for artisans to keep a shop in which they sold what they had made directly to the public. It is thus quite probable that some of the Bristol Friends have been misclassified in table 10.2; but unless all these errors went in the same direction, the basic pattern is fairly clear. Few of the more substantial Friends in Bristol — and there were a good many of these — emigrated; on the contrary, emigration was almost entirely confined to the artisans, retail shopkeeepers, and workers in the textile industry.

TABLE 10.2   *Occupational Distribution of Bristol Men's Monthly Meeting, 1682–1704, and of Male Quaker Emigrants from Bristol*

Occupation	All Bristol Friends		Emigrants From Bristol	
	No.	%	No.	%
Gentry, professional, and official 9 schoolmasters, 2 surgeons, 2 physicians, 5 others	18	5.5	1	7.1
Wholesalers 30 merchants, 24 soap-boilers, 11 grocers, 8 mercers, 5 linendrapers, 4 glovers, 4 distillers, 3 malsters, 3 brewers, 2 mealmen, 7 others	101	30.6	2	14.3
Retailers 9 bakers, 4 victuallers, 4 hosiers, 3 tobacconists, 2 butchers, 3 others	25	7.6		
Textile workers 17 tailors, 16 silkweavers, 13 weavers, 4 sergemakers, 2 merchant tailors, 2 woolcombers, 2 silkmen	56	17.0	5	35.7
Artisans, servants, and laborers 24 shoemakers, 13 coopers, 11 carpenters, 9 mariners, 9 pewterers, 5 laborers, 5 shipwrights, 4 blacksmiths, 4 saddlers, 4 curriers, 4 masons, 3 corkcutters, 3 tilers, 3 wire-drawers, 3 felt-makers, 2 carriers, 2 nailers, 2 rope-makers, 2 tobaccocutters, 15 others	127	38.5	6	42.9
Agricultural workers 3 gardeners	3	0.9		
TOTAL	330		14	

SOURCE: Russell Mortimer, ed., *Minute Book of the Men's Meeting of the Society of Friends in Bristol, 1667-1686*, Bristol Record Society Publications, vol. 26 (Bristol, 1971), pp. 245-48; idem, ed., *Minute Book of the Men's Meeting of the Society of Friends in Bristol, 1686-1704*, Bristol Record Society Publications, vol. 30 (Bristol, 1977), pp. 294-97.

NOTE: Index references to persons who were not Friends or who did not live in Bristol during this period have been eliminated.

We have identified more Quaker emigrants from Bristol than from all of the rest of the country outside London, and occupational data from the rest of the country in the 1680s are somewhat sparse. What we have compiled fits the same general pattern found in Bristol. In particular, even in the rural areas, artisans — rather than yeomen or husbandmen — predominated among the emigrants. In this respect, as one would guess, there is an appreciable difference between the occupational distribution of the First Purchasers and the first settlers, even though a majority of First Purchasers did take up residence. Among the First Purchasers, 8 percent called themselves gentlemen; 6 percent were members of the professions, 14 percent merchants or shopkeepers, and 23 percent were listed as having agricultural occupations, leaving almost half in the broadly defined category of craftworkers.[10]

Just as we can more readily keep track of emigrants from some parts of England than others, so those who show up in the family-reconstitution files in the 1680s are likely to have been already married and to have started their families before emigrating. Most of the earliest emigrants had already been born before the Quaker system of record-keeping became very comprehensive, and young unmarried men — who always constitute a substantial part of emigrating populations — are unlikely to be detected. Later, however, it is occasionally possible to trace the births of emigrants in the Quaker records. The scattered evidence that we have suggests that most of these later emigrants were in their twenties or thirties; entire families, although sometimes found, are definitely the exception. Those who emigrated in the 1680s, so far as we can tell, were almost all younger sons — perhaps because so many of the early Friends were younger sons[11] — but later there do not seem to have been more younger sons than one would expect in a random distribution, given what we know about the average size of Quaker families. One reason for this may be that testamentary patterns among Friends tended to be more egalitarian, with less tendency to single out the oldest son as the chief heir than was found in English inheritance patterns generally.

None of this is very surprising, except possibly the relative absence of yeomen and husbandmen among the English Quaker emigrants. In our sample, London and Bristol were heavily represented, which of course would minimize the number of farmers; but even among the First Purchasers fewer than a quarter seem to have come from the agricultural sector. For all the benign character of the Pennsylvania climate — at least until winter set in — many must have attempted to farm in strange conditions with scant stock of farming lore to draw on.

Our findings suggest that Penn's marketing strategy in promoting his new settlement was well focused. The promotional literature addressed itself chiefly to "Industrious Husbandmen and Day-Labourers" and then to craftsmen. He also made a particular appeal to younger sons and to all

those who were "much clogg'd and oppress'd about a Livelyhood."[12] But
how many of these, after all, were Quakers? How does it happen that after
reading 15 percent of the minute books and reconstituting up to 20 percent
of the English Quaker families, with almost complete coverage for Ireland
as well, we were able to identify so few emigrants? It is to this difficulty
that we must now turn.

It was surprising that I could not find more British and Irish Quakers
who had emigrated to Pennsylvania, since most historical works about the
founding of Pennsylvania give the impression that it, like New Jersey
before it, was settled fairly massively by British and Irish Quakers as part
of a concern widespread among them that there be a colony in the New
World in which Quakerism could be transplanted to soil which would be
much more favorable for its unhindered growth. The emphasis which earlier historians put on escape from persecution as a principal motive was
effectively challenged by Frederick Tolles, who correctly pointed out that
Friends' approved strategy for confronting persecution was civil disobedience, and those who did not engage in this were suspected of "shunning
the cross."[13] Joseph Illick, however, has ingeniously reformulated the idea
that the founding of Pennsylvania was a matter of great moment to the
Quaker community by arguing that colonization was a vital part of the
Quaker impulse almost from the beginning, and that the settlement of
Pennsylvania was a corporate effort befitting the new sense of discipline
and coherence that had been created by persecution and by Friends' response to it.[14] He even speaks of the Quakers' "monolithic" response to
Penn's invitation to emigrate and estimates that some eight thousand people, almost all of them English, Welsh, and Irish Quakers, had already
removed to Pennsylvania by 1685.[15] Other historians have been less ven-
turesome in committing themselves to specific figures but generally leave
the impression of a mass Quaker migration. Isaac Sharpless, for example,
suggests that two thousand people arrived in 1682 alone, and that all the
prominent ones among these, at least, were Friends. Contingents came
from Yorkshire and the Midlands, London, and Bristol, and a "small army"
from Wales.[16]

If there really was an exodus of British Friends on this scale, why did
it leave such relatively modest traces in most of the English and Irish
records? Part of the answer, at least, lies in the gaps in the documentary
record. The preservation of Welsh records, in particular, seems to have
been spotty. The most comprehensive source is the Irish family lists, which
do show the substantial Irish emigration of the eighteenth century but are
much less revealing about whatever emigration may have gone on in the
seventeenth. As I have already observed, even if the registration of births,
marriages, and burials had been complete, it only began around 1655, and
so could only inform us about those already married or those who reached
adulthood from about 1675 onwards. (We have not been able to make a

systematic search of parish registers which might have entries of the births of people subsequently converted to Quakerism, but the probability of finding many such entries is small, given the inadequacies of parish-register keeping during the Civil War and Interregnum.) Accidents of recording or preservation of certificates may lead us to underestimate badly the number of them that were issued, though there is a possibility of cross-checking records of Pennsylvania against those of England and Ireland to see how extensive this source of error might be. Also, it is possible that a great many Friends never bothered to get a certificate in the first place. If they failed to do so, however, they were acting against the good order of Truth, since the very first meeting of Friends in Philadelphia minuted that "friends of this Meeting do bring in their Certificates from the respective meetings of friends they belong'd to in other Countries."[17] Since the main purpose of such certificates, at least in the beginning, was to attest to general good character and, in particular, freedom from engagements of marriage elsewhere, those people already married must have had less incentive to apply for one. This means that the certificates are the best source for the unmarried, while those already married should appear in the registers of marriages or (as parents) in the registers of births.

It would be rash to argue that no British Quaker emigrated without leaving some trace in the records, whether it be a certificate of clearness from engagements of marriage, a record of sufferings, monthly meeting minute book references, or nominal linkage through family reconstitution of the registers of vital events. Nobody who has worked with the seventeenth-century British Quaker records, splendid as they are in comparison to those of the Established Church or other Nonconformists, would accord them this degree of confidence. But I think it is equally rash to claim that the vast majority of British Friends who emigrated did so without leaving any such trace. And yet in wide tracts of Eastern and Southern England — Norfolk, Huntingdonshire, Bedfordshire, North Oxfordshire, South Lincolnshire, Hampshire — one can read very extensively in Quaker sources without encountering more than the most widely scattered references to any English people going to America at all. Furthermore, although our family-reconstitution work is unable to give any precise aggregative figures for the size of the British Quaker population at any given time, it does give us a general sense of what was happening to the size of the population as a whole. The estimate of eight thousand Quaker emigrants would have been something like 15 percent of the entire English, Irish, and Welsh Quaker population, and no doubt concentrated among young adults. If so many had emigrated between 1681 and 1685, there should have been a pronounced fall in the number of marriages recorded in the next few years; but no such fall can be distinguished.

Let us hazard a different guess at the number of English and Welsh Quaker emigrants in good touch with their meetings and conforming more or less faithfully to Friends' testimonies who emigrated to Pennsylvania before 1700. For this purpose let us assume that Philadelphia preserved only one-quarter of all the certificates for Pennsylvania, and that only one-third of the early English and Welsh emigrants ever had a certificate. We shall also assume, to compensate for the regional skew of our sample, that our nominal coverage is only one-tenth of the entire population, and that half of the emigrating Quakers were at an age when they would not have shown up even if the registration of vital events had been complete. Even with these assumptions — every one of which is on the low side, I believe — the number of English and Welsh Quaker emigrants in good touch with their meetings and conforming more or less faithfully to Friends' testimonies could not have been much greater than one thousand in the 1680s and another thousand in the 1690s. This means that only a minority of the first settlers of Pennsylvania were British Quakers in good standing.

The estimate doubtless sounds rather low for the first years; but if an estimate like that of eight thousand Quaker emigrants before 1685 were to hold up, we would have to assume that all our allowances for underregistration need to be multiplied at least tenfold. No work yet done with English Quaker materials justifies inflation of numbers on such a heroic scale.

The chief problem with an estimate as low as the one I have presented is that it suggests that Quakers in good touch with their meetings and conforming more or less to Friends' testimonies may even have been as few as ten percent of all emigrants into Pennsylvania before 1700. Although this may seem unlikely, before we dismiss this possibility out of hand we should examine the evidence. As we all know, William Penn had no intention of founding a purely Quaker colony, and he made vigorous efforts to recruit people of other persuasions. The relative success of this effort can be seen in an analysis of the group of First Purchasers from Penn himself. There were 589 persons who bought or were granted land, and of these only 198 can be established to have been Quakers through entries in the registers and indexes of suffering. Another twenty-eight might have been Friends, though exact identification is impossible, and thirty-seven lived outside England and Wales. The vast majority of these were Irish, but there were also grants to people living in France, Germany, the Netherlands, Barbados, and New York. The majority of purchasers, however, cannot be identified as English or Welsh Quakers; and these 326 people bought over 45 percent of the land, whereas those certainly or possibly English and Welsh Quakers bought less than 40 percent of it.

This analysis does not include all early Pennsylvania landholders. It leaves out the Swedish, Dutch, and English settlers who came to the Delaware Valley before 1680, the colonists who settled in the Lower Counties, and all those who bought from someone other than Penn. Furthermore, many of the purchasers did not themselves emigrate. Nevertheless, the list of First Purchasers from Penn suggests not a great corporate enterprise of the Society of Friends, but Penn's own (and necessarily idiosyncratic) network, extending from the famous (Sir William Petty, John Aubrey) down to the humble, and spreading well beyond the boundaries of Quakerism.[18]

What sort of people were drawn into this network? I suspect that many of the early emigrants fell into a category somewhere between a whole-hearted adherence to Quakerism and total indifference or hostility to it. Let us consider, for example, John Fenwick, who is well-known for his share in the Quaker purchase of land in New Jersey. Fenwick is usually described as a Quaker yeoman who lived in Buckinghamshire, but I know of no reference to him in any Quaker records from that county; nor does he figure much in the records of Berkshire. Although he is recorded as a sufferer by Besse,[19] he was in no sense prominent among Friends, and his ties to Quakerism may even have been somewhat tenuous. The same might be said of John Archdale, who lived in High Wycombe, Buckinghamshire, as well as in North Carolina, but who played only a negligible part in Quaker affairs in his English county. When we descend to the level of the ordinary emigrant, we probably enter that penumbra of attenders and sympathizers with early Friends which may have been as numerous, or even more numerous, than the indisputable Quakers. This penumbra, I suspect, contributed more emigrants than the clearly identifiable Friends. They could have been close enough to the colonization project to join in it without having the standing to enter the births of children in the registers, and without the obligation to apply for a certificate from their monthly meeting.

If the magnitude of emigration of British and Irish Quakers in full membership has been considerably exaggerated, as I am suggesting, there are obvious further implications for the history of Pennsylvanian, and indeed of American, Quakerism. I can only draw out here the most rudimentary of those implications: that from a relatively early period, the majority of American Friends had either come to adulthood in America or had been converted to Quakerism after they came to America. To show that this is so, we need to indulge in one more estimate: the number of Quakers in Pennsylvania during the first two decades of settlement. For this, fortunately, there is one piece of good evidence: a census of Chester Monthly Meeting in 1688 which showed seventy families and seventy-two male adults.[20] There were more than seven persons to an average family. Jack Marietta, to whom I am indebted for drawing this material to my attention, estimates that the Philadelphia Monthly Meeting was about twice the size of Chester, which would give it some 1,100 members. If we assume that the ratio between city and country Friends in 1688 was the same as that estimated by James Logan in 1702 — namely, twice as many in the country as in the city — this would give a total Quaker population in 1688 of some 3,300.[21]

Of these 3,300, I estimate that not more than about a third were British Quaker emigrants in good standing, as I have defined them; and if this was the proportion around 1688, it must have declined steadily in the decades which followed. Even though the immigration of the English Quakers continued, and that of the Irish even increased, the demography of the American Quakers was such that their children would soon come to predominate, at least numerically, even if there had been no further conversions of other people who lived in Pennsylvania.[22] Furthermore, there is no reason to think that conversions entirely ceased, and in the first two decades of settlement there must have been substantial additions to Quakerism among the new emigrants to Pennsylvania, just as there had been earlier in New England, New York, Maryland, Virginia, and the Carolinas.[23] Here, indeed, the situation was ideal for widespread convincement. There were no other churches already established and jealous to guard their version of the Christian commonwealth from the inroads of Quakerism. The civil magistrates were, for once, supportive, so no one need suffer for joining with Friends; Quakerism levied no tithes or onerous financial burdens on the people and there were frequent visits from English ministering Friends who could in public meetings proclaim Friends' principles. Under such circumstances, it would have been unusual if Quakerism had remained only an affair of those who were already staunch Quakers before they left England.

For a long time the leadership in Pennsylvania Quakerism was exercised almost entirely by those who were born in England and were Quakers before they arrived in Pennsylvania. The Quaker movement was also knit together by the visiting of English Friends in America and American Friends in England.[24] Nevertheless, from a very early period the bulk of Pennsylvania Quakers had no adult experience of British Quakerism, and a good many of them probably were, or were the children of, people who were at most attenders. Under these circumstances, it should not be surprising that even from the beginning, British and Irish Friends were sometimes taken aback at what was passing for Quakerism in the American colonies. (I suspect, for example, that many English Friends would have shared George Keith's repugnance to the doctrinal *laisser-croire* of American Friends, had he not expressed it with such arrogance.)

Our statistical exercise, then (if I am anywhere near right in the numbers), suggests that it would be useful to supplement the view that Pennsylvania Quakerism was a more or less straightforward transplant of British Quakerism. I doubt that Pennsylvania was of much moment to British Friends, outside of Penn and his immediate circle; at the height of the Caroline persecution, they had more urgent things to think about. Its founding, if not quite an early illustration of that absent-mindedness in which the British Empire was supposedly founded, at least was a bit remote from their central concerns. This in turn gave American Quakerism a chance to develop its own distinctive character very early. If one seeks an historical analogy, Irish Quakerism would be a better one than English Quakerism. Almost as many Englishmen emigrated to Ireland in the seventeenth century as came to North America, and Quakerism spread quickly among the English who had gone there. (It also did not spread *beyond* the English settlers.) Most Irish Friends were not English Friends who had emigrated, but English people who were converted to Quakerism after they had arrived in Ireland. (Let us not forget that Penn himself was converted in Ireland.)

These circumstances gave Irish Quakerism its own especial flavor, as well. It was rigorous, whereas American Quakerism always tended to be more flexible and fissiparous. The distinctive Irish touch can still be seen in colonial Pennsylvania, where the areas of heavy Irish settlement produced the monthly meetings which tended to be toughest in the enforcement of the discipline.[25] Irish Quakerism could not have produced the enormous range of personalities which are the glory, and occasionally the scandal, of American Quakerism. But neither, in all likelihood, could English Quakerism have thrown off so many vigorous, if curious shoots. In some ways John Woolman was probably just as much an exotic to the English Quakers of his time as — if I may cite a descendant of both Irish and American Quakers — Richard Nixon was in ours.

NOTES

1. *The Sufferings of the People of God Called Quakers, for the Testimony of a Good Conscience,* 2 vols. (London, 1753).

2. David Eversley and Richard T. Vann, *Friends in Life and Death: The Demography of the British and Irish Quakers* (forthcoming).

3. The best description of family reconstitution in English remains the chapter by E. A. Wrigley in *An Introduction to English Historical Demography,* ed. E. A. Wrigley (London, 1966), pp. 96-159.

4. Historical accident accounts for the fact that some counties are sampled and others completely reconstituted. Work on the counties sampled, carried out by volunteers under the direction of David Eversley, had begun before I started on the other counties, where it seemed advisable to have contiguous counties in order to maximize the chance of keeping in observation families which moved about. A sample which would maximize the chances of finding people who went to America would have been drawn quite differently, as Table 10.1 shows: we would have had more from the North and West of England, and less from the Home Counties and East Anglia. We wanted to concentrate on areas where the most numerous Quaker communities were located; and except for Bristol, the West of England and Wales had comparatively few (for an estimate of the density of Quaker population in the first decade of the eighteenth century, see Michael R. Watts, *The Dissenters,* vol. 1 [Oxford, 1978]). It is of course possible that the paucity of Quakers in the West of England and Wales around 1700 (and the relatively poor preservation of Welsh records) is the result of large-scale emigration from those areas. A claim that this was so would amount to an argument from silence; and while in the nature of things such arguments cannot be refuted, our use of several different kinds of evidence makes this one somewhat less plausible.

5. Minute books read in manuscript were from the following men's monthly meetings: (St.) Alban's, Herts.; Biddlesden, Bucks.; Markyate, Beds.; North Somerset; Stotfold and Clifton, Beds.; Upperside, Bucks.; Lammas, Lynn, Norwich, Tivetshall, Wells, and Wymondham (all in Norfolk); Huntingdon; Banbury, Oxon.; Reading, Berks.; Westminster (London); and Southwark, Sur. Printed minute books, in addition to the ones cited in table 10.2 from Bristol, were Harold W. Brace, ed., *The First Minute Book of the Gainsborough Monthly Meeting of the Society of Friends 1669-1719*, Lincoln Record Society, vols. 38 (1948); 40 (1949); and 44 (1951); Jean and Russell Mortimer, eds., *Leeds Friends' Minute Book, 1692-1712*, Yorkshire Archaeological Society Record Series, vol. 139 (York, 1977). As far as I know, certificates of Friends going to America are entered only in monthly meeting minutes.

6. William Wade Hinshaw, *Encyclopedia of American Quaker Genealogy* (Ann Arbor, 1936-50), vol. 2.

7. This list was compiled and printed in *PWP*, 2:630-64.

8. To 1751 there were 302 certificates for Irish Quaker emigrants; 78 of these were received by Phila. Monthly Meeting. According to the well-known estimate by James Logan in 1702, there were twice as many Friends in the country as in Philadelphia (see Rufus Jones, *The Quakers in the American Colonies* [New York, 1911], p. 522). It is not clear to what extent new immigrants would distribute themselves the same way as the existing population, but it seems reasonable to suppose that some would stay briefly in Philadelphia and then move to other parts of the colony.

9. For the largest collection of information on Irish Quaker occupations, see Irish Historical Manuscripts Commission, *Quaker Records, Dublin, Abstract of Wills*, ed. P. B. Eustace and Olive Goodbody (Dublin, 1957); Olive Goodbody, *Guide to Irish Quaker Records*, "List of Documents Held at Eustace Street." For the connection between the business cycle and the emigration of tradesmen, see Isabel Grubb, "Social Conditions in Ireland in the Seventeenth and Eighteenth Centuries as Illustrated by Early Quaker Records" (Master's thesis, University of London, 1916), p. 28.

10. *PWP*, 2:632.

11. See Vann, *Development of Quakerism*, p. 85.

12. William Penn, *Some Account of the Province of Pennsilvania* (London, 1681), quoted in Edwin B. Bronner, *William Penn's "Holy Experiment"* (Philadelphia, 1962), pp. 25-26.

13. Tolles, *Meeting House*, pp. 34-37.

14. Joseph Illick, *Colonial Pennsylvania: A History* (New York, 1976), pp. 11, 21.

15. Ibid., pp. 21, 42. The estimate of 8,000 emigrants seems to rest on William Penn's *Further Account of Pennsylvania and Its Improvements* (London, 1685).

16. Jones, *Quakers in the American Colonies*, p. 422.

17. Quoted in Albert Cook Myers, *Quaker Arrivals in Philadelphia, 1682-1750* (Philadelphia, 1902), p. iv.

18. *PWP*, 2:631.

19. I wish to thank Edwin Bronner for pointing this out for me, and for stimulating my quantitative work on Besse as a source.

20. This was turned up by Barry John Levy in "The Light in the Valley: The Chester and Welsh Tract Quaker Communities and the Delaware Valley, 1681-1750" (Ph.D. diss., University of Pennsylvania, 1976), pp. 89-92.

21. Another way of calculating is to take Logan's ratio and work from the estimated population of Philadelphia, since Logan thought that one-third of these would be Friends. Since there was no contemporary census of Philadelphia, we have to choose from a considerable range of estimates, but since it works against

my case, I shall first calculate on the basis of the estimate by Gary Nash and Billy G. Smith that the population of Philadelphia in 1693 was 2,100, which would make the number of Friends in Pennsylvania also 2,100. See Nash and Smith, "The Population of Eighteenth-Century Philadelphia," *PMHB*, 99 (1975):362-68. The estimate of John K. Alexander ("The Numbers Game: An Analysis of Philadelphia's Eighteenth-Century Population," *PMHB*, 98 [1974]:314-24), is 4,389 for 1700, which would make the figure of 3,300 in 1688 (and thus 3,300 Quakers in Pennsylvania then) seem plausible.

22. For eighteenth-century American Quaker demography, see Robert V. Wells, "Family Size and Fertility Control," *Population Studies*, 25 (1971):73-82; and idem, "Quaker Marriage Patterns in a Colonial Perspective," *WMQ*, 29 (1972):415-42.

23. Bronner, *Holy Experiment*, p. 17.

24. The classic treatment of this is Frederick Tolles, *Quakers and the Atlantic Culture* (New York, 1960).

25. I owe this information to Jack Marietta who kindly permitted me to see his manuscript on church discipline among American Friends, since published as *The Reformation of American Quakerism* (Philadelphia, 1984).

PENN'S AMERICA

11 ❧ "The Peaceable Kingdom:"
Quaker Pennsylvania in the Stuart Empire

Pennsylvania's place in England's empire was assured in November 1680. It was the first month in five years and the last month forever in which so large a grant of land and authority could have been conceded by the crown. The concessionary, of course, was William Penn. He got his grant because his politics were piebald and his timing was perfect.

In February 1679 Penn's friend Robert Spencer, second earl of Sunderland, became a secretary of state. In March the great proponent of imperial centralization, the earl of Danby, resigned the treasury. He was replaced at the head of imperial affairs by the new president of the privy council, the champion of oligarchical self-government in both England and America, the earl of Shaftesbury. Spurred by Shaftesbury, Penn wrote powerful propaganda for a whig parliament and for the further prosecution of the Popish Plot. In April the Commons resolved that the plot took its sustenance from the duke of York's religion and, in May, they added that therefore the duke, the king's brother and heir, should be excluded from the succession to "the imperial crown." King Charles thereupon prorogued the parliament (and he dissolved it in August). Both sides prepared for civil war. It broke out in Scotland in June, only to be repressed by royal troops and loyal militia. Scotland was then given over to the none too tender mercies of the duke of York. That the tide had turned in favor of the crown was clear to some when, in October 1679, Shaftesbury was dismissed from the council. Abandoning Shaftesburean politics in December, Penn told a key crown functionary "that he saw plainly so much extremity intended on this syde, as well as on that . . . that he resolved to withdraw himself from all manner of meddling, since things to him appeared violent and irreconcilable."[1]

Barred from plotting by his own fears of civil war and by the orders of his Quaker colleagues, Penn petitioned the king for an American proprietary in April 1680. In May the earl of Sunderland moved up to the southern department of state, with its presumed preeminence in colonial affairs. On 1 June Sunderland secured the king's order to the privy council's plantations committee to consider Penn's request favorably. Well might William Penn label Sunderland "one of the first in the business of my American Colony." Penn's petition was for land, in part payment "of debts due to him or to his father from the Crown." Some of the proposed province had been conquered from England's Dutch rivals in 1664, and governed since, by officers of the duke of York. All of it might be construed to be the duke's. On 23 June 1680 the duke's secretary, Sir John Werden, warned the privy councilors that they could not grant land which his royal highness claimed by conquest. On 25 June, therefore, the plantations committee ordered Penn to consult the duke "for adjusting their respective Pretensions."[2]

There was ample political reason for the duke to agree to such an adjustment. Elections were going forward for another parliament which was expected to demand his exclusion from the succession. During July 1680 Shaftesbury and company tried to have the duke indicted and his property confiscated on the ground that he was a Roman Catholic. The political support of others, who, like himself, dissented from the Church of England was now and remained always a prime concern for James Stuart. As the leading Quaker politician, Penn was worth purchasing. Once bought, his loyalty might be further assumed from that of his father, Sir William Penn. Having been a Cromwellian general at sea, Sir William had altered his politics (just as his son was doing) and become the duke of York's captain of the fleet in the greatest English naval victory of the seventeenth century. The duke had promised the dying admiral that he would favor his son. Having already helped William Penn in English religious matters, the duke extended his assistance to Penn in America. The duke accepted arbitration which denied his right to collect quitrents in Quaker West Jersey, of which Penn was a trustee and for which he had asked the duke's indulgence. Then, on 6 August 1680 the duke granted property deeds to the proprietors of both East and West New Jersey. When the court returned to London from Windsor on 9 September 1680, William Penn called on the duke at St. James's palace to explain his expanded American ambitions. On 16 October 1680, four days before the duke left London for his Scots exile, and five days before parliament began its first session, the duke's secretary wrote to his "honoured friend," William Blathwayt, secretary to the plantations committee,

> that His Rll. Highns. Commands Me to Lett you know (in order to your Informing Theire Lordsps. of it) That He is very willing Mr. Pen's Request may meete with Successe: That is, That He may have a Grant of that Tract of Land which lyes on the North of Newcastle Colony (part of Delaware) & on the West Side of Delaware River, beginning about the Latitude of 40 degrees & extending Northwards & Westwards as far as His Majesty Pleaseth; under such Regulations as their Lordsps. shall think fit.[3]

Since 1675 their lordships had been regulating provincial autonomy in the interest of the crown, most notably in Ireland, Jamaica, and Virginia. The councilors of the crown had added to the militarized executive of garrison governments a "new model" of legislation. Under it, provincial parliaments were to be reduced to accepting laws written in England by the crown. All the provincial legislatures protested against the new model, encouraged to do so by attacks on the imperial executive at the time of the Popish Plot. The royal governors–general also objected to the metropolitanism of the new model, for it reduced their discretionary authority in the provinces. Several of the governors-general sought royal confirmation of the compromises they struck between imperial orders and provincial objections. They were also alarmed at the prospect of being out of England "if the cards came to shuffling" in the struggle between court and country. They sailed home in the spring and summer of 1680.[4]

The most prominent of these executives, the earl of Carlisle, governor-general of Jamaica, had arrested his chief opponent on the island, Samuel Long, and sent him to England. Sometime Cromwellian captain and speaker of the Jamaica assembly, recently the island's chief justice, Long was indicted by Carlisle before the plantations committee of the privy council for his treasonable opposition to the new model of imperial government. Yet the meeting of the Exclusion Parliament combined with the pleas of the moderates, led by the earl of Halifax, secured Long's release on 18 September 1680.

Then the Jamaican whigs and their London merchant allies counterattacked. On 28 October they demanded that the crown extend the protection of English law to its provincial subjects. Charles II had never conceded this. The Anglo-Jamaican opposition asked that judicial appeals from the colony go to English judges, not to the King-in-Council. They insisted that the king limit the military authority of his colonial captain-general, the governor, and that he order the governor-general to share chancery, church, and admiralty jurisdictions with his councilors, representatives of the Anglo-Jamaican elite. Finally, to insure these crown concessions, the dissident colonists and their London correspondents asked the crown for permission to publicly finance and officially instruct a permanent London lobby. The lobby was designed to sustain their assembly's association with the English parliament, an association which, as they saw it, had just coerced the crown.

In the wake of Long's enlargement and Anglo-Jamaican demands, it seemed that hopes for colonial enfranchisement stood fair. On 1 November 1680, William Penn pleaded before the privy council's plantations committee for consideration of his proposed proprietary patent and, at the same time, the committee recommended that the king trade a "deliberative voice" to the Jamaica assembly in return for its grant of taxes to the crown. To this King Charles agreed on 3 November. He restored the authority of the Jamaica assembly, ostensibly on the basis of a new commission for Barbados but in fact on the basis of a compromise created by Lord Culpeper, governor-general of Virginia. By this, certain bills previously presented as parts of the new model were now to be passed into law by the provincial parliaments, together with revenues for royal administration. All other pending imperial issues were referred by the King-in-Council to the royal law officers and judges.[5]

Accordingly, on 8 November 1680, the attorney general (who had just given the plantations committee a preliminary report on the territorial bounds of Penn's patent), was ordered to review the draft charter for the province's government which Penn had put forward. That Penn's patent would receive favorable consideration seemed sure for, on 11 November, the Commons passed a bill to exclude the duke of York from the succession. At this crucial juncture, Penn's political price was high and his patent was further considered on 14 November. The crown's champion in the Lords' exclusion debate of 15 November was the earl of Halifax, potent alike in the parliament and on the plantations committee. Exclusion failed before Halifax's eloquence and, as Penn afterward wrote to the earl, "the country I enjoy by the King's goodness and bounty, came not into my hands without the marks and prints of thy singular favor."[6]

The very dimensions of that country, however, were still to be determined in mid-November 1680. Both of the determiners were deeply involved in the exclusion crisis. First, there was the duke himself, whose lands were to be granted. Once the Lords had defeated the bill to exclude the duke from the succession, the frustrated Commons attacked lesser minions of monarchy. On 24 November 1680 the Commons impeached Sir Francis North, lord chief justice of the Common Pleas, to whom the king had referred the definition of Penn's grant. It was Lord North (the progenitor of another prerogative man much involved with America) whom King Charles personally ordered, in the plantations committee, to resolve the most debated issues in what became the imperial settlement of 1680-81.[7]

In each colonial case, lesser legal officers and Council functionaries defined the issues which North determined. Following Penn's plea of 1

November, the attorney general had listed the debatable parts of Penn's proposed boundaries: prior New England claims to the region; the unknown extent of "the Indian Countries" which were to bound Penn's patent to the north and west; and the claims of the existing Dutch and Swedish settlements on the Delaware, most of which were now governed by the duke of York, but some of which had been absorbed into Lord Baltimore's Maryland government.[8]

On 18 November, the privy council clerk for the plantations committee referred these issues to the duke's secretary, Sir John Werden. Werden's response was instructive. While legal counsel must be taken by the plantations committee, he wrote, there were inescapable limitations to the grant: (1) because no certain lines of latitude and longitude had been taken and the relevant rivers had not been explored, there could be no precise description of the proposed patent; (2) Penn would have to rely on the duke's general intent to make him a grant similar to those of the Jerseys (which he had just confirmed), and rest assured that "all the benefits are intended to this Pattentee that others enjoy"; (3) the duke had determined that Penn's patent would be bounded by the Delaware to the east and by the duke's Newcastle colony to the south, and he would make no more precise definition. "I confess," wrote the duke's American secretary, very much pestered by Penn, "I doe not understand why 'tis precisely necessary to insist on Just such a number of Miles more or lesse in a Country of which we know soe little."[9]

On or about 23 November 1680, within the ambit circumscribed by the attorney general's questions and the duke of York's determinations, Lord North finally defined a colony. Penn's proprietary was to extend north three degrees from latitude forty degrees north, and to reach five degrees west from the Delaware River at the boundary with Newcastle. Out of the exclusion crisis a colony had come. This territorial resolution was supposed to be ratified by the plantations committee on 18 December, but the meeting was devoted to denying the republican requests of the Jamaicans, a clear indication of the changing political climate. Penn had received his province at the last possible moment for, on 10 January 1681, the Exclusion Parliament was prorogued. On 15 January the "Boundaries of Mr. Penn's Patent as settled by Chief Justice North, with Sir J. Werden's alterations [were] read and approved" by the plantations committee.[10]

The crown had committed itself to the physical boundaries of Penn's patent, but its proprietary and political dimensions had not been defined. Lord North, now freed from parliamentary impeachment and sure of the king's support, decided that "all the benefits . . . that others enjoy" would not be permitted to William Penn, proprietor. Penn would be expected to serve the imperial purposes of the English crown even more than his predecessors had been. From the outset of English colonization, however, proprietary grants had been the mechanism by which a state still operating on medieval principles of personality associated with itself the military services, financial capital, and quasi-feudal manpower of noble entrepeneurs. Even since the restoration of Charles II, all of England's imperial expansion had been achieved under the aegis of proprietary grants by the king to men who, like William Penn, were English courtiers, Irish colonizers, and Atlantic cosmopolitans.

Introduced to court in his teens by his father, the Cromwellian general and royal admiral, educated at Oxford (in American colonization, among other things), sent to tour the continent with the young nobles who afterward helped him secure his charter, administrator of his father's share of the Irish plantations won by Cromwellian conquest, a suppressor of the Carrickfergus garrison's mutiny and consequently an applicant for commissions as company captain and as town and fort governor in Ireland, naval aide to his father with the fleet in 1665, and afterward a determined defender of his father's reputation "as a General and as a Seaman," William Penn was a young gentleman educated to rule and adept in garrison government. His first portrait was painted in armor. His early letters speak of colonization, occupation, and war.[11]

From the last of these, Penn was carried by Quakerism (until made to raise military funds by the crown as the price of reacquiring his colony). The needs of persecuted Quakers, however, urged Penn to reintroduce himself to James, duke of York. And it was Penn's involvement in Quaker colonization of the duke's New Jersey grants which prepared him to write that "Colonies are the Seeds of Nations." Penn, like his ducal friend, tried to emulate the Romans who "not only reduc'd, but moralized the Manners of the Nations they subjected; so that they may have been rather said to conquer their Barbarity than them."[12]

To extend England's cultural and territoral empire had been the goal of the duke's father, Charles I, and of William Penn's exemplar, Caecilius Calvert. That their charter for Maryland was what Penn proposed for his own proprietary appears in extensive identities of language, sequence of clauses, and in the comments of the crown's lawyers. Both patents were premised upon the propagation of "the Christian religion" and on the extension of "the territories of our empire." Both were rewards to heirs for their father's services to the crown. After associating paternal merit with monarchy (in an appropriately Filmerian fashion) both charters next described the territories granted and "erected them into a Province" of England. The lands, waters, and resources of the provinces were conveyed to the proprietors in identical legal language. In both patents there followed delegations of royal political power to the proprietors, saving, however, their allegiance to the king, requiring elected local legislative assemblies, and confining both proprietarial rule and provincial law to English models. Provincial appointive power was granted to both proprietors, together with authority to constitute ordinances in emergencies, a very contentious authority in the royal governments of the 1680s. Also the subject of continuing debate was the power given the proprietors to transport colonists and capital to the province and to return colonial produce to England, thus establishing a trade the proprietors could tax from seaports they were authorized to establish.[13]

The capacity to carry on Atlantic commerce was an essence of colonies, and it would receive repeated attention from many hands as the patenting process went forward, but the privy council's plantation committee gave its most serious consideration to eliminating from Penn's patent Calvert's most puissant power, that of a captain-general. The inescapable circumstances of colonization by conquest of native territories, in competition with European rivals and outlaws, had turned all major provincial executives into generals, despite the crown's desire to restrict military authority to regular officers. "*Because in so remote a Countrey and situate near so many barbarous nations the Incursions as well of the Savages themselves as of other Enemys pirates and robbers may probably be feared,*" both the Maryland and the Pennsylvania proprietors were granted the powers of a captain general to levy men, train them, and make war.[14]

Given the subsequent limitations that the crown would place on Penn's proprietorial war and trade, however, the patentee's greatest power was to grant land, to whomever he chose, on any terms. Like Calvert, Penn added to this authority to convey in fee the capacity to create manors and manorial courts (Lord North, himself enamoured of and enriched by manorial courts, did not object to this proprietorial profit). The crown ordered its officers to assist the proprietors in the exercise of these privileges and added the traditional injunction to the royal judges to interpret patent provisions in the proprietor's favor. How little this might mean, however, was anticipated in a clause new to Penn's patent by which the king "Provided always that no Interpretation be admitted thereof by which the Allegiance due unto us our heirs & successors may suffer any prejudice or diminution." A later Lord North could be proud of his ancestor's prescience.[15]

It was the measure of imperial centralization that, although nineteen of the twenty-three paragraphs of the Calvert charter were at least partly repeated in Penn's patent, so many of the proprietary powers granted Lord Baltimore in 1632 seemed to royal officials to be too extensive in 1680/81, and that they placed so many limitations, novel to proprietary patents, on the grant to William Penn. The proximate causes of the prerogative's assertion were the Jamaica settlement and three London lawyers.[16]

Two days after Penn asked the plantations committee to consider his patent, the King-in-Council restored the Jamaica assembly's deliberative faculty. But the Council also emphasized the military and political prerogatives of the governors-general and, on 9 November 1680, added that the concession of legislative authority was contingent upon the passage of royal revenue bills. On 11 November the exclusion bill cleared the Commons. Himself a "timidous" man, and under attack in the Commons, it is not surprising that the attorney general, Sir Cresswell Levinz, submitted nothing in writing about the Penn patent when, on that very day, he reported on it to the plantations committee meeting. The notes of that session, however, remarkably reflect the emerging imperial settlement, that new balance of executive and legislature, of discretion and due process, which was the upshot of the previous five years' struggle between the prerogative, the provinces, and the parliaments. In that contest, the attorney general had shown himself to be expert in taking positions which favored the crown but which did not actually expose him to the country. He had refused to draft the royal proclamation against petitions for the Exclusion Parliament, but he had issued what the lord chief justice wrote. Then, on 27 October Levinz exposed North's authorship to the Commons, gaining their praise for himself and setting up the chief justice's impeachment. Levinz, the attorney general, thus stood midway between Penn's whig lawyer, Sir William Jones, and Lord Chief Justice North, in that trio of legal luminaries who shaped the fundamental law of William Penn's province.[17]

It was in keeping with Levinz's "wonderfully cautelous" character that he once again, as with Penn's boundaries, defined without determining the difficulties that Penn's proposals posed to the crown's prerogatives and the country's law. Levinz evaded the royalist rewriting of Penn's patent (and left it to the lord chief justice) when he resigned as attorney general and ascended the bench early in February 1681. His identification of Penn's requested powers "wch are not agreable to Law here but are in the Lord Baltimores Patent" had called the crown's attention to proprietary legislation, appointment of judges, punishment of crimes, proclamation of ordinances, and acts of incorporation. All of these, Levinz had told the lords of plantations, were beyond the competence of English corporations. Some even exceeded royal jurisdiction, in England at least.[18]

During November 1680 the plantations committee amended Penn's proposals in most of these respects. In legislative matters, Penn and his assembly were not only to conform to the example of English law (American proprietors had been ordered to do this since 1584) but also were required to observe the emerging legal standard of "reason." Penn's own ordinances were bound by "reason" and, also unlike Lord Baltimore's proclamations of law, were controlled by English precedents in cases of property, felony, and inheritance. So, too, were all such laws of Penn's province.[19]

Besides asking provocative questions about the legal and legislative clauses proposed by Penn, the attorney general had observed that such economic privileges as shipping provincial produce into England and Ireland, constituting ports, granting land, and permitting freedom from royal taxation all were more than subjects in England could claim. The attorney general's observations on the economic autarchy of the Calvert-Penn draft were obvious and inescapable, for the economic autonomy of England's colonies had been under attack even longer than had their legal freedoms. Therefore, the plantations committee found it a simple matter to add to Penn's draft patent the distinctions and discriminations which had coalesced into an imperial economic policy over the half century since the king granted Calvert's charter. Not only were the royal customs reserved on colonial goods imported into England — that had been done in the Maryland grant — but Penn's people were also bound to "observe the Acts of Navigation and other Laws in that behalfe made."[20]

To the plantations committee's notes of the attorney general's analysis had been added, in another hand, the caution that Penn, unlike his predecessors, should have "noe power to Settle Churches." The first result of this determination to deny ecclesiastical power to the dissenting proprietor was the omission of the bishop of Durham clause from Penn's patent. Much has been made of this excision, largely because the Durham clause, as it appeared in Calvert's charter and was copied by Penn into his proposed patent, has been said to have conferred full royal authority on the grantee. Apparently, however, the Durham clause in American charters was intended only to give the proprietor physical control of churches and church property and did not convey the bishop's palatine power. The Calvert charter thus contained provisions regarding feudal rights, courts, and incidents, military command, and powers of probate and pardon, none of which would have been required if the proprietor was a palatine prince, benefiting from the dictum that "what the king has without, the bishop has within." This point had been clarified in the Carolina charter (1663), which extended ecclesiastical authority to the proprietors without naming the bishop of Durham or describing any part of his jurisdiction. Penn's patent, probate and pardon aside, had neither the Durham clause nor any of the various ecclesiastical powers granted previous proprietors.[21]

After they made these ecclesiastical, economic, and legal amendments and excisions, the plantations committee put Penn's patent aside until after the king dissolved the Exclusion Parliament on 18 January 1681. Four days later, the lords of the committee had the amended document read to them. Thereupon they decided to move from mere tampering with the text Penn had placed before them to the addition of imperialist clauses. They instructed their leading member, the lord chief justice, newly freed from the burdens of managing the House of Lords and from the menace of the Commons' impeachment,

> to take the said Patent into his Consideration and to provide, by fit clauses therein, that all Acts of Sovereignty as to Peace and Warr, be reserved unto the King, and that all Acts of Parliament concerning Trade and Navigation and his Maties Customs be duly observed and in general that the Patent bee so drawn that it may consist with the King's interest and service, and to give sufficient Encouragement to Planters to settle under it.

To complete the chief justice's imperial mandate, the bishop of London added that Penn ought to be compelled to admit Church of England clergy to the colony.[22]

The chief justice's subsequent recommendations for Penn's patent were extensively anticipated by his resolution of the Jamaica case, settled on 18 December 1680. This decision had admitted local property rights and allowed provincial courts to protect them. These legal concessions, together with the reconstitution of the assembly, subject to royal review of its enactments, were all the local liberty the crown would concede. North made it clear that the colonies would not be allowed the laws of England. Nor might they appeal to the English judges. Instead, the appellate jurisdiction of the privy council was reaffirmed. The assembly could dispatch agents to England, but only if they reported to the crown. The martial authority of the king's captain general and the maritime jurisdiction of the duke's vice admiral both were confirmed despite provincial protests.

Such decisions were appropriate to North's belief that "a man could not be a good lawyer and honest but he must be a prerogative man" and they were in keeping with his private counsel to King Charles: limit parliament's sessions; suppress the Scots rebels; discipline England's provinces overseas in Ireland and America. The imperial politics of the period were reactions to North's central principle "that a conquered nation should receive laws at the pleasure of the king alone." Like the English state itself, like the kingdoms of Scotland and Ireland, the American provinces were the political consequences of conquest from European rivals or native inhabitants. A "peaceable kingdom" was a contradiction in imperial terms, but Penn, inheriting earlier English conquests in America, won law as well as land from the political efforts of provincial pioneers. Thus Lord North admitted that the king had conceded some legislative liberties to the provinces which could not now be recalled. Taxation in particular had usually to depend upon representation. North also conceded that the further a province was from the throne of England the more legislative and administrative flexibility its executive must be allowed.[23]

Beyond conquest, North believed that the church was the greatest support of royal rule in both kingdom and empire. The Barbados case, resolved in October 1680, had just sketched the structure of an ecclesiastical program for the colonies. The bishop of London's imperial authority was now to be extended to America by the bishop's colonial commissaries, and by his licensed clergy and missionaries, operating in reorganized parishes, all supported by freshly instructed governors-general. Almost all of this structure of church authority was to be visited on Penn presently in his patent or on his province after 1700.[24]

The agency by which the overseas conquests of church and crown were to be administered, North insisted, was the privy council and its plantation committee. One of the shibboleths of Restoration politics was that privy council administration had produced the national awakening and Atlantic achievements of the Elizabethan era. Only extremists — Shaftesbury (and his Council of Trade and Plantations) before 1675, and York (working through the cabinet) after that year — had publicly rejected this doctrine. The creation of the standing committees of the Council for Trade and for Plantations in 1675 made the conciliar doctrine manifest in imperial administration. Charles II himself had felt bound to bow to it by reconstituting his Council in 1679. He promised that all important policies would be set by it. To rationalize this responsible Council, members ex officio were added. One of these was the lord chief justice of Common Pleas. Given North's conciliar convictions, it is ironic that he immediately undermined the authority of his peers by becoming one of "those few great officers and courtiers whom the king relied on . . . and [who] had the direction of most transactions in the government, foreign and domestic." Certainly the king gave special emphasis and authority to North's positions within the plantations committee. This was the only Council structure that preserved the intent of the previous year's reform, and the chief justice intended to make Penn's patent the vehicle by which the overseas authority of the Council and its committees was written into the imperial constitution of 1681.[25]

Imperially instructed by the plantations committee, by the recent political resolutions for all the most important royal provinces, and by his own devotion to crown, church, and council, Lord North revised William Penn's patent in several stages. The first stage was an analysis and modification of existing proprietarial authority. In legal affairs, the chief justice strengthened the perennial proviso that provincial peace keeping and the administration of justice must conform to English practice. He added that the proprietor's pardoning power did not extend to treason against the king. He implied that Penn's Council, like Baltimore's, should be the primary agency of administration. North made it clear that the assent of an elected assembly (but not its initiative, debate, or amendment) was required to make laws and raise taxes. He insisted that these laws must be subject to the recently developed review of the privy council. In his demands that imperial discipline depended on the enforcement by the privy council of English legal precedent and practice, North acted on his belief that the law he personified would uphold the crown he served: "for the court of England was now so steadily determined to act in all things according to law, that the faction could find no way to annoy them but by corrupting the law itself." And Lord North did his best to prevent William Penn and his dissenting colonists from corrupting English law in Pennsylvania.[26]

To extend English regulations to the proprietary province, North insisted that "A Strict Provision" must be inserted in Penn's draft charter to command provincial obedience to the Acts of Trade and Navigation and to insure the free functioning of the king's customs officers in the province. The chief justice did not share the country view (which William Penn himself had once propounded but had now also to combat) that "all foreign trade was loss and ruinous to the Nation." Instead, the minister of the crown applauded what its enemies decried. In their eyes, "the mortal evil of foreign trade was the good supply it brought to the crown, by which it could be supported without being continually at the mercy of parliament for supplies." To protect the king's customs, as well as to preserve the crown's military and diplomatic prerogatives, Lord North recommended that restrictions be added to Penn's patent forbidding him or his colonists to trade with any state at war with the king or to war with any state at peace with the king. The Indians were excepted. With them, the chief justice wrote, Penn's provincials might deal "as they shall think fit."[27]

There followed North's substitution for the bishop of Durham clause. This provided that whenever twenty colonists applied to the bishop of London for a cleric, his nominee should act in the province "without any denial or molestation whatsoever." This establishment of the Church of England was the only denominational authorization in the charter. It attested to the rising imperial importance of Bishop Compton and ultimately, as William Penn put it, it made the Quakers "dissenters in our own Countrey." The royal rationale that so restricted Penn's plans was simply put by the king: "I have the law and reason and all right-thinking men on my side; I have the Church and nothing will ever separate us." So Charles II warned Shaftesbury and the exclusionists at Oxford on 21 March 1681, the sixth and penultimate day of the last parliament of his reign. Lord North, the chief justifier of this parliament's dissolution, had already seen to it that "law and reason" were at work for the crown in Penn's draft patent. Now he had provided for the church as the king's cause required. North, Compton, and the Council acted to subvert Penn's fundamental purpose for his province: "it was to be free of the church's power and out of her reach," Penn protested, "that we went so far, and not to make colonies for her but from her, for ourselves."[28]

After he amended and restricted Penn's proposed patent in legal, economic, and ecclesiastical areas, the chief justice made five additions to his own proposals. First, he further limited Penn's pardoning power: it was not to extend to murder or beyond the provincial borders. Second, to the paragraph which mandated the review of provincial legislation by the privy council (now standardized in royal commissions and newly added to Penn's patent), North added clauses which declared that the two-year review period was to begin on receipt of the laws by the privy council or its plantations committee, but which echoed the Jamaica case by permitting the provincial legislature to repeal laws not confirmed by the crown.

Naturally the chief justice was fully informed of the pending, ponderous, *quo warranto* proceedings against the charters of Massachusetts and

Bermuda for evasions of the Acts of Trade and Navigation. Therefore, third, he now added to his injunction that Penn compel his people to obey the acts a warning that failure to do so would cause the crown to lay a writ of *scire facias* against Penn's patent (this was the efficient instrument which, as it did not require service on or appearance by the defendant, would be used to annul the charter of Puritan Massachusetts).[29]

North was also aware of the recent disastrous mistreatment of the Indians in the Leeward Islands, Virginia, and Massachusetts. On re-reading his grant to Penn's colonists of a free hand with the natives, the chief justice made a fourth amendment. It reserved the royal right to regulate both military and economic relations with the Indians.[30]

North's fifth amendment treated two especially important issues: the imperial authority of the privy council and its plantations committee; and the distinction between public authority, which was ultimately reserved to the crown in every proprietary province, and private property, which the crown secured by patent both to the proprietor and to his grantees, the denizens of his province. Speaking for King Charles, the lord chief justice provided that all provincial power, whether ecclesiastical, civil, or military, "shall be subordinate and Subject to the Power and regulation of the Lords of the privy council of US Our Heires and Successors or of our or their Com. for the affaires relating to Forrein Plantations." On the other hand, everything concerning "the Propretry of the Province . . . or any owner-ship" of lands or leases, goods or chattels "therin was left to the said Wm Pen his Heires or Assigns."[31]

Having proposed that this balance between imperial prerogative and private property be held by the privy council and its plantations committee, North returned Penn's patent to that committee. There, during February 1681, Sir John Werden (the duke of York's secretary), Sir William Jones (William Penn's attorney), and William Blathwayt (secretary to the planta-tions committee, privy council clerk, and imperial auditor general) all of-fered additions and amendments on behalf of their principals.

Werden's relation to Penn's patent had hitherto been confined to def-initions of the duke's generous territorial grants. But a principle of the imperial settlement of 1681, of which Penn's grant was becoming a part, was that the crown would not be generous with grants of political power. Such a power, at once commercial, legal, military, and maritime, was the duke of York's authority as lord high admiral. This had been preserved in the dominions despite the Catholic duke's refusal to conform to the Angli-can Test Act (which applied only to offices within England). The duke's power as admiral in America had just been reasserted in the face of the attacks upon it by the whiggish Jamaica assembly. It was presently con-firmed and confined to all the governors-general as the duke's vice admi-rals, and to his own lieutenant in New York. It would not now be granted to a private person, not even to Admiral Penn's son. Lord North's casual note, which had tossed admiralty authority into a clause conferring on Penn the power of probate and of administering wills, soon had entered against it the decisive declaration that "Admirall Jurisdiction belongs to the Duke of York and cannot be granted [by] the King. Nor is it proper to be granted. Shall be Exunt." And so it was.[32]

Besides executing the directives of Lord North and his colleagues in the plantations committee, William Blathwayt made numerous changes of his own in the draft of Penn's patent. Since the imperial reorganization of 1675-76, Blathwayt had arranged all the privy council's plantations business and he also audited all the royal revenues produced in the colonies. As supervisor of the various colonial spokesmen in London, and of his own deputy auditors in America, Blathwayt, more than any other bureaucrat, understood the imperial value of agents. His familiar scrawl now added a draft clause to Penn's patent whereby the king required the proprietor to "appoint an attorney or agent" in London, who was to register with "the Clerks of Our Privy Councill for the time being or one of them" and who was to be authorized, unlike the agents of recalcitrant Massachusetts, "to appear in any of our Courts at Westminster" to answer for provincial trespasses against the Navigation Acts and to pay fines, on pain of royal resumption of the provincial government.[33]

The force of this, and many other centralizing clauses in Penn's patent, was weakened by Sir William Jones's clever changes in the wording of the penultimate draft. In addition to monetary motives, Jones had ideological incentives to protect Penn's rights of private property and to assert his political power as proprietor against that of the Stuart monarchy. Even before Jones resigned as attorney general (in February 1679, amidst the Popish Plot prosecutions) and went into opposition, he had put himself on record in favor of colonial claims against the crown. Jones's opinion that the concessions of Charles II to the Jamaicans in 1662 could not now, in 1679, be revoked, was the primary legal premise on which deliberative powers were restored to American assemblies in 1680 and 1681. During the summer of 1680, it was Jones's arbitration that secured freedom from the duke of York's taxes for the proprietary New Jersey provinces. His next opinion won the duke's entire cession of the Jersey grants to the proprietors. William Penn was one of Jones's principals for the New Jersey cases and he subsequently retained him to secure his own proprietary patent. Jones was reputed to be "the greatest lawyer in England" when he entered parliament in November 1680. He immediately undertook the Commons' prosecution of Lord Stafford. Then he managed the exclusion bill. And Jones was speaking for the Commons' right to impeach non-nobles before the Lords when Charles II dismissed the Exclusion Parliament. After the Oxford Parliament was dissolved, Jones composed the influential pamphlet which defended parliamentary power and its use to exclude the duke from the throne, a reply to Lord Chief Justice North's defense of the king's dissolution of parliament to protect the succession to the crown. Jones was otherwise free by February 1681 to apply his Harringtonian principles to the defense of William Penn's patent.[34]

Penn recalled, twenty-one years after the fact, that Jones "was of Opinion that power followed property in these cases," that is, that political authority was necessarily conceded by the crown together with proprietary grants. Even though "Bull-faced Jonas, who could statutes draw / To mean rebellion and make treason Law" had come late to Penn's patenting process, it was likely he who suggested influential changes in the surviving portions of the Penn-Calvert draft and to North's revisions and Blathwayt's amendments. These included an explicit right for the proprietor to rule through "deputies and lieutenants." This prevented the residential requirements recently placed on royal governors-general from being extended to Penn. An expansion of Penn's legislative power was secured by adding "peace and safety" to the purposes of provincial law. North's regulation of provincial property law and the definition of felony by English models was annulled by an additional phrase: "untill the said laws shall be altered by the said William Penn . . . and by the Freemen of the said Province." Penn himself boasted of the substitution by Jones of "five years" for "six months" as the term within which provincial laws had to be dispatched for imperial review, and of "six months" for "two years" as the time which the crown was allowed for its considerations.[35]

What even so masterful a legal author as Sir William Jones could do nothing about, however, was the ongoing process of excision of vital powers from Penn's draft patent. Military authorities joined ecclesiastical jurisdictions on the list of powers now denied to Penn but which had been granted previous proprietors, Calvert in particular. "Peace and safety" was at best a less explicit authority than that given Lord Baltimore "to build and fortify castles, forts and other places of strength," albeit the omissions were in keeping both with Penn's purported pacifism and with the restored monarchy's campaign against corporate fortifications. The elimination of the martial law clause, one in a series of revisions by William Blathwayt, was also significant. Given the recent use of martial law in imposing the imperial executive on both the crown's British kingdoms and on its American provinces, the elimination of this clause reduced proprietary power in Pennsylvania and forecast imperial intervention in Penn's province.[36]

The crown's military units were still in place in Virginia, and the royal bill of oblivion for acts committed in Bacon's Revolution was being considered by the privy council, even as Penn's patent was on the table. The councilors also, and none more than North, were concerned with the aftermath of the recent rebellion in Scotland. That outbreak was seen as the preface to renewed English civil war, a war which was almost ignited at the Oxford Parliament in March 1681. The role of the army in pacifying "tumult and sedition" was thus much on the minds of the ministers, and both the omission of the martial law clause from Penn's patent and the wholesale pardon to the Virginia revolutionaries suited the chief justice's argument to Charles II. North told his king that, while "his majesty's defensive weapons were his guards . . . his offensive weapons [were] the laws: and that enemies were to be resisted by opposing force to force but to be punished only by law." That is, Lord North agreed that the crown must crush resistance and rebellion by military means but the chief justice insisted that beaten rebels must then be judged by civil law, not at martial discretion. Resort to martial law, once order had been restored, only exacerbated the martial inclinations of the imperial executive. "Great men and governors," the chief justice said to his sovereign, "are very propense to err in the notion of power and, out of impatience of opposition and desire of revenge, resort to force which, early or late, turns the evil upon themselves." This position, manifest in empowering Penn to resist invasion or insurrection as a captain general but denying him authority to exercise martial law in peacetime, accorded with North's moderation in the forceful and impassioned world of Anglo-American politics. During the exclusion crisis, working between oligarchy and absolutism, North neither bent "one way, by undermining the guards and the militia (which was the drift of the faction) nor the other way by setting up the militia against property (which was calumniated)."[37]

However moderate North might be in the struggle between overmighty subjects and their vengeful sovereign, he was opposed in principle to frittering away the prerogative in the provinces. Instead, and nowhere more than in Penn's patent, the chief justice "laboured as much as he could to set up the just prerogatives of the crown which were well known in the law and to the lawyers." Likewise, North sought to eliminate the provincial privileges which had been granted by the crown to proprietors such as the Calverts in the imperial nonage of the earlier Stuarts.[38]

From either a whig or a Quaker viewpoint, the most serious of the crown's contractions of privilege was the omission from Penn's patent of the Calvert charter's tenth paragraph. It had conferred on Maryland's colonists the status of "natives and liege men . . . of our Kingdom of England and Ireland." It had extended to these subjects "all privileges, franchises and liberties of this our kingdom of England." By the excision of paragraph ten, Penn's people lost their clearest claim to the rights of Englishmen, many of which were now also denied to the crown's colonists by the imperial settlement of 1681.[39]

As we have seen, one of the most active agents of that settlement was William Blathwayt. Since May 1676 Blathwayt had been the "Secretary to the Committee of Foreign Plantations" of the privy council. In July 1678 he became a clerk of the Council, and in May 1680 he was named auditor general of the crown's American revenues. In each of his capacities, Blath-

wayt now further amended Penn's patent, incorporating in it changes incidental and mechanical, altering significant words, substituting or excising
whole clauses of the greatest importance to the future of William Penn's
province.[40]

The sum of Blathwayt's alterations showed him to be a man typical of
his time and station. Like most of his contemporaries, the colonial secretary
made even radical changes by recurrence to precedent, avoiding the dread
appearance of novelty while serving the political needs of the moment. For
example, he had eliminated the much controverted and jealously guarded
power of martial law from the Penn patent by reinserting a clause from the
Calvert charter. As a royalist and a bureaucrat, Blathwayt obeyed his orders
"to do all that may honestly and justly tend to the King's advantage and
profit and to the augmentation of the Rights and Prerogatives of His
Crown." In revising Penn's patent, Blathwayt affected clauses political,
fiscal, and religious, as well as military. He perpetuated the political obligations of Pennsylvanians to the crown, enhanced royal incomes from
provincial sources, and strengthened the provincial jurisdiction of the king's
courts, while he eliminated Pennsylvania's diplomatic competence and denied it international military authority, these being both the chief strengths
of the royal prerogative and those most crucial to the colonies. Blathwayt's
little interlineations also protected the imperial jurisdiction of the king,
lords, and commons, that is, the English regulation of Pennsylvania's trade,
commerce, and navigation.[41]

Of William Blathwayt's large-scale alterations, perhaps the most striking was his excision from the Pennsylvania patent of the clause which
promised religious freedom to Penn's people. This extraordinary declaration of the liberty of conscience was taken, as the editors of *The Papers of
William Penn* tell us, presumably by William Penn himself, "nearly verbatim
from the Rhode Island Charter of 1663." This clause was first amended
and then struck from Penn's patent by Blathwayt. The colonial secretary
thus left Pennsylvanians subject to the imperial Church of England. Both
English law and the specific provisions of an Anglican chaplaincy (suggested by Bishop Compton, written by Chief Justice North, and now
strengthened in the Pennsylvania patent by Secretary Blathwayt) meant
that, as William Penn so bitterly exclaimed, the Holy Experiment had
failed before it began.[42]

At last, on 24 February 1681 the plantations committee of the privy
council made its final revisions in Penn's patent and presented to Charles II
"the Draught of a Charter constituting William Penn Esq. Absolute Proprietary of a Tract of Land in America." Penn's application and expectation
had been based on the Calvert charter of 1632, but the document now
offered to the king instead reflected the intensification of English empire in
America since the civil wars.[43]

Even the premises of colonization had been reordered toward empire. Whereas Charles I had rewarded the Calverts' "laudable and pious zeal for extending the Christian religion, and also the territories of our empire," Charles II first commended William Penn's "desire to enlarge our English Empire and promote such usefull Commoditys as may be of benefit to us and our Dominions as also to reduce the Savage Natives by gentle and just manners to the Love of Civill Society and Christian Religion." In half a century of revolution and reaction, religion had fallen from first place to last in England's American priorities, and its primary function had changed from Christianization to civilization. Messianic mission had been displaced by political indoctrination. The bishop of London had reentered the imperial scene to extend the state religion to the colonists, not to convert the natives. Further, the bishop was prepared to resort to the remains of the "new model" of imperial legislation to achieve the Anglicanization of Penn's province. At the conclusion of the debate on Penn's draft, the bishop was permitted by the plantations committee to write a bill to be imposed upon and enacted by the provincial legislature, "for the settling of the Protestant religion in this country."[44]

Not only had imperial expansion replaced religious mission as the primary purpose of provinces, but the extension of empire was now seconded in plantation planning by colonial commodity production. This was valued as much because it enhanced the crown's customs as because it promoted English prosperity. Therefore, efforts unprecedented in earlier proprietary patents were made in Penn's patent to secure provincial observation of the customs, commercial, and shipping acts of the English Parliament and to have them enforced in Penn's proprietary by the king's officers. Acts and officers alike were the products of a generation of English attention to empire.

Much has been written about William Penn's claims on the crown for a share of that empire. Certainly Stuart monetary, political, and personal debts were paid by this, the penultimate proprietary patent. The only debt recognized in the charter itself, however, was that of the royal brothers to Sir William Penn for his military services under their command, at Lowestoft in particular. There the old admiral, acting as the duke of York's fleet captain, had directed England's fleet in its most signal victory of the seventeenth century. Sir William had sunk the opposing admiral's ship and, as his son boasted, had seen to it that *"24 ships were taken, burnt, and sunk; 2500 prisoners (said to be) brought home, besides what were slain and wounded of the Hollanders; at the expense of but one old Dutch prize (that for want of sail fell into their body) and about 300 Englishmen slain."* The credit for all of this sinking and slaying had been loyally and wisely left by Sir William Penn to his superior, the lord high admiral, James, duke of York and Albany. So much were Sir William's services on the minds of those who granted the new province that the patent, as it was copied into the plantation office records by a royal clerk, was given to Sir William Penn, not to his son. In this symbolic and significant scribal error, the king wrote that, "having regard to the memory and merits of his late father in divers Services and particularly to his conduct courage and discretion under our Dearest Brother James Duke of York in that signall Battle and Victory . . . [we] do give and grant unto the said Sir William Penn his heirs and assignes all that Tract or part of Land . . . and do call it Pensilvania," a name, the distraught William Penn explained, "the king would have given . . . in honor of my father." The son never escaped Sir William's shadow, for it extended all across the English empire of Cromwell and Charles II, from the conquest of Jamaica to the patenting of Pennsylvania.[45]

Indebted to his sire for the province, William Penn was more subordinate to his sovereign than were any of his proprietary predecessors. And even they had been given their territories by the king, as Penn was, "Saving always to us our heirs and successors the Faith and Allegiance of the said William Penn, his heirs and assigns and of all other the Proprietarys, Tennants and Inhabitants . . . and saving also unto us our heirs and successors the Sovereignty of the aforesaid Countrey." The crown had never liberated colonial proprietors from England's empire, but unprecedented limits were placed on Penn by the restriction of many proprietary powers, by the royal review of the provincial government's acts, by the immediate imposition of the crown's officers on the province, and by the pending presence of the state church's clergy, the dictation of an imperial agency, the elimination of ecclesiastical and diplomatic authority, and the reduction of military power in Penn's patent.[46]

Beyond present imperial supervision and regulation, Pennsylvania was threatened by a much-noted revision of the king's traditional pledge to proprietors that he would not tax property within their boundaries. The new patent provided that in Pennsylvania the king might tax "by consent of the Proprietary or Chief Governor or Assembly or by Act of Parliament in England." This portentous provision peered forward, past many false starts and abortive proposals, to the aggressions of the King-in-Parliament, united by Lord North's heir and namesake, against the privileges of all the American provinces. English authority was both present and potential in the patent for Pennsylvania. It passed the seals on 28 February 1681, part of that constitutional definition of empire, the imperial settlement of 1681, which not only dictated the place of Quaker Pennsylvania in the Stuart empire but which also defined Anglo-American government for a century to come.[47]

NOTES

1. Quoted in Mary Maples Dunn, *William Penn: Politics and Conscience* (Princeton, 1967), p. 74, which source also explains Quaker quietist pressures on Penn.

For an example of Penn's partisan propaganda, see *England's Great Interest In The Choice Of This New Parliament* (1679), in *Select Works*, 3:181-88; see also David Ogg, *England in the Reign of Charles II* (Oxford 1955-56), 2:586. It is remarkable that so little of Penn's partisan stress on the rule of legislative law and censorship of the executive appears in the patent for his province or the Frame he composed for its government. Note Penn's appreciation for an authoritarian administrator in Stephen Saunders Webb, *1676: The End of American Independence* (New York, 1984), pp. 303-4, 403.

2. For these developments and the extant fragment of the petition, see *PWP*, 2:30-39. Werden admonished the Lords to "Tye up the Governement of such New Colony, as neere as may be, to the Lawes of England" (ibid., 2:38). The agents of Lord Baltimore were concerned that Penn's southern boundary be the Susquehannah Fort and that no arms be sold the Indians by Penn's people. See ibid., 2:36-37; *PA*, 2d ser., 16:347-49.

3. *CSPC, 1677-1680*, pp. 587, 597; Joseph E. Illick, "The Pennsylvania Grant: A Re-evaluation," *PMHB*, 86 (1962):376-77; idem, *William Penn the Politician: His Relations with the English Government* (Ithaca, 1965), pp. 18-19; William Penn, *A Persuasive To Moderation* (1686), in *Select Works*, 2:504-42 (see also *PWP*, vol. 5, items 72A-D); Werden to Blathwayt, 16 Oct. 1680 (CO 1/46, fol. 58, PRO, printed in *PWP*, 2:44).

4. Stephen Saunders Webb, *The Governors-General, The English Army and the Definition of the Empire, 1569-1681* (Chapel Hill, N.C., 1979), pp. 176-326, 373-403.

5. Ibid., pp. 299-310; *CSPC, 1677-1680*, pp. 623-25; *PA*, 2d ser., 16:350.

6. Penn to Halifax, 24 July 1683 (*Micro.* 4:311), quoted in Illick, "Pennsylvania Grant," p. 392. For the order to the attorney general, see CO 1/46, fol. 83, PRO. Penn does not cite specific occasions of Halifax's favor. The gracious, and prudent, contemporary convention called for acknowledgments to all presumed patrons. Reasons for Penn's presumptions are given in Webb, *Governors-General*, pp. 301, 303, 324, 461.

7. Webb, *Governors-General*, pp. 303-4; CO 1/46, fols. 62, 75, PRO; *CSPC, 1677-1680*, pp. 613, 615-17, 621-22.

8. CO 1/46, fols. 73, 83, PRO (the former printed in *PWP*, 2:43-44); *CSPC, 1677-1680*, pp. 623, 625-26, 628.; *PA*, 2d ser., 16:350.

9. Werden to Blathwayt, St. James, 20 Nov. 1680 (CO 1/46, fol. 110, PRO, printed in *PWP*, 2:47-48); see also same to same, 23 Nov. 1680 (CO 1/46, fol. 118, printed in *PWP*, 2:49); CO 1/46, fols. 105-6; *CSPC, 1677-1680*, pp. 633-35.

10. CO 1/46, fol. 124, PRO; *CSPC, 1677-1680*, pp. 635, 638-40; *1681-1685*, p. 3.

11. See Granville Penn, *Memorials of the Professional Life and Times of Sir William Penn, Knt.* (London, 1833), 2:19-20, 138, 167-68 passim; W. Penn, *A Persuasive to Moderation*, in *Select Works*, 2:522-42.

12. W. Penn, *The Benefit of Plantations, or Colonies* (1680), in *Select Tracts Relating to Colonies* (London, [1700?]), p. 26. There is some question about whether this tract was written by Penn; see *PWP*, vol. 5, item 58, n. 3.

13. For the charters of Maryland (1632) and Pennsylvania (1681), see David C. Douglas, ed., *English Historical Documents*, vol. 9, *American Colonial Documents to 1776*, ed. Merrill Jensen (New York, 1955), pp. 84-93. William Robert Shepherd (*History of Proprietary Government in Pennsylvania* [New York, 1896], p. 10) states that the Pennsylvania charter "was orginally drafted by Penn himself from that of Maryland as framed for Lord Baltimore in 1632." See also CO 1/46, fols. 101, 212-28, PRO; *PWP*, 2:45-46.

14. Charter provision italicized in CO 1/46, fol. 224, PRO.

15. CO 1/46, fol. 228, PRO.

16. Of the four omissions, two were imperially important: par. 10, which conferred English citizenship on Calvert's colonists; and par. 12, which granted martial law powers to Maryland's captain-general. They are discussed below. Par. 14 of the Calvert charter authorized the award of local titles of honor to reward good behavior "both in peace and war." The clipped currency of Carolina Cassiques and Baronets of Nova Scotia had never been high, but Penn, despite his presumed Quaker principles against titles, is said to have sought the power to create a provincial nobility (Shepherd, *Proprietary Government*, p. 10). Par. 21, which separated Maryland from Virginia, seemed irrelevant, even invidious, in a Pennsylvania patent, now that Virginia's northern claims were erased.

17. See CO 1/46, fol. 90, PRO; *CSPC, 1677-1680*, p. 629; *DNB*, s.v. "Jones, Sir William," "Levinz, Sir Cresswell," "North, Francis"; Roger North, *The Lives of the Norths*, ed. Augustus Jessop (London, 1890), 1:119, 230.

18. CO 1/46, fol. 90, PRO, printed in *PWP*, 2:46-47.

19. CO 1/46, fol. 218, PRO.

20. Ibid., fols. 90, 222.

21. Ibid., fol. 90, printed in *PWP*, 2:46-47, where the added clause is said (n. 10) to be in Blathwayt's hand. Shepherd (*Proprietary Government*, pp. 5-6) is especially clear on counties palatine, and further states that "in one of the rough drafts of the charter [Darnall's?] . . . was the provision that Penn should be given the powers of a bishop of Durham as amply as they had been bestowed on Baltimore," which Shepherd thinks was amply indeed. See John Darnall's draft charter for Pennsylvania, in *PWP*, 2:40-43; see also Charles M. Andrews, *The Colonial Period of American History* (New Haven, 1936-38), 2:282; Hampton L. Carson, "The Genesis of the Charter of Pennsylvania," *PHMB*, 43 (1919):319. At the World of William Penn Conference, Philadelphia, 1981, David W. Jordan expressed doubts about this interpretation of the limits of the Durham clause in American charters. These doubts may be strengthened by Darnall's inclusion of that clause in his suggestions to Penn. I preserve the argument here in hopes of provoking further attention to this subject.

22. *PA*, 2d ser., 16:355; *CSPC, 1681-1685*, p. 34, printed in *PWP*, 2:57-58.

23. North, *Lives*, 1:239; Samuel Weldon Singer, ed., *The Correspondence of Henry Hyde, Earl of Clarendon, and of his brother Lawrence Hyde, Earl of Rochester* (London, 1828), 1:183-87.

24. *CSPC, 1677-1680*, pp. 590, 622.

25. Godfrey Davies, "Council and Cabinet 1679-88," *English Historical Review*, 37 (1922):47-66. Penn's *A Persuasive to Moderation* was submitted to "the king and his Great Council" and defines monarchy as this duo (*Select Works*, 2:504, 531); see also North, *Lives*, 1:243, 328; *DNB*, s.v., "North, Francis." Webb (*1676*, pp. 169-99) reviews the development of the privy council's imperial role.

26. See CO 1/46, fol. 101, PRO, printed in *PWP*, 2:58-60; North, *Lives*, 1:231.

27. CO 1/46, fol. 101, PRO; Penn, *Benefit of Plantations*, in *Select Tracts*, pp. 26-28, 30; North, *Lives*, 1:194. For Penn's countrified criticism of foreign trade see his petition to parliament (1678?) in *PWP*, 2:49-56.

28. William Penn to Charlewood Lawton, 10 Dec. 1700, RG 21, Pennsylvania Historical and Museum Commission, Division of Archives and Manuscripts, Harrisburg, Pa. (*Micro.* 8:662), which also notes that Compton's further efforts "to gett savings for that Ch . . . was opposed by the E. of Radnor, then President." The number of "twenty" colonists was supplied, presumably by Compton, on 28 Feb. 1681, at which time clerical freedom was reiterated by the addition of "any denial" and "whatsoever" to "molestation" (compare CO 1/46, fol. 101V with ibid., fol. 228, PRO). Winfred Trexler Root (*The Relations of Pennsylvania with the British Government, 1696-1765* [New York, 1912], p. 222), quotes Penn on flight from the church (from *HMC, Duke of Portland MSS*, 4:80).

29. Philip S. Haffenden, "The Crown and the Colonial Charters, 1675-1688: Part I," *WMQ*, 3d ser., 15 (1958):297-311. Note, however, that, at this stage of the proceedings, corporate, not proprietary, charters were under attack. Some of Haffenden's arguments have been challenged by Richard S. Dunn, "The Downfall of the Bermuda Company: A Restoration Farce," ibid., 3d ser., 20 (1963):487-512. According to Secretary Blathwayt, Chancellor Finch suggested an even more arbitrary method for the revocation of the Pennsylvania patent: at the will of the king or of six privy councilors, i.e., the plantations committee. See *PWP*, 2:63.

30. See Add. MSS 30, 372, BL, where the governor of Pennsylvania is grouped with royal appointees.

31. CO 1/46, fol. 101v, PRO.

32. Ibid. For a different reading of this text, see *PWP*, 2:59; see also North, *Lives,* 1:253, n. 1.

33. Stephen Saunders Webb, "William Blathwayt, Imperial Fixer: From Popish Plot to Glorious Revolution," *WMQ*, 3d ser., 25 (1968):3-21; CO 1/46, fol. 102, PRO.

34. *DNB*, s.v. "Jones, Sir William"; Robert C. Ritchie, *The Duke's Province: A Study of New York Politics and Society* (Chapel Hill, N. C., 1977), pp. 166-67; Penn to Sir Heneage Finch, 27 Aug. 1701, William Penn Letterbook, Penn Papers, p. 132, HSP.

35. Penn to Finch, 27 Aug. 1701; John Dryden, "Absalom and Achitophel," in *Poems of Affairs of State,* ed. Elias F. Mengel, Jr., vol. 2 (New Haven, 1965), p. 477; CO 1/46, fols. 214, 218, PRO; Illick, "Pennsylvania Grant," p. 390. Blathwayt rewrote North's paragraph. It was this which gave Jones his opportunity. See *PWP*, 2:61-63, 74, n. 25.

36. *PWP*, 2:76, n. 62; par. 9, Maryland Charter, in *American Colonial Documents,* ed. Jensen, p. 88.

37. CO 1/46 fol. 156-58, PRO; North, *Lives,* 1:315-16.

38. North, *Lives,* p. 316.

39. *American Colonial Documents,* ed. Jensen, p. 88.

40. Webb, "William Blathwayt, Imperial Fixer," pp. 3-21.

41. Treasury Group, 64/89/1ff, PRO.

42. *PWP*, 2:61-77, esp. pp. 62, 71, 76 (n. 63).

43. CO 1/46, fol. 212, PRO; *PWP*, 2:40-43.

44. *American Colonial Documents,* ed. Jensen, 1:85; CO 1/46, fol. 212, PRO; *CSPC, 1681-1685,* pp. 13-14.

45. G. Penn, *Memorials of Sir William Penn,* 2:292-96, 318-20, 322-33, 337, 349-51, 358-60, 492; CO 1/46, fol. 212-14, PRO; Andrews, *Colonial Period,* 3:281. For the wording of this passage in the royal charter which passed the Great Seal, see Jean Soderlund, *William Penn and the Founding of Pennsylvania,* p. 41. Shepherd (*Proprietary Government,* p. 9), asserts that the admiral "had sought in extinguishment of this [£16,000] debt to obtain a grant of land in America, but failing in this, at his death suggested the plan to his son." That the son justified even his religious nonconformity, as well as his devotion to James Stuart, by his father's example is hinted at in *A Persuasive to Moderation,* in *Select Works,* 2:524.

46. Compare the quotation in CO 1/46, fol. 214, PRO. with par. 5 of the Maryland charter (*American Colonial Documents,* ed. Jensen, p. 86), and the patent of 1584 to Walter Raleigh, in *New American World,* ed. D. B. Quinn (New York, 1979), 3:269.

47. CO 1/46, fol. 228, PRO.

12 ⟨ *Brother Miquon: Good Lord!*

I must begin with a confession of strong bias: I *like* William Penn. His faith was strict but tolerant, and he lived up to it. He was decent, earnest, and kind. But he has been ill served by the hagiographers who elevated him to sainthood and thus diminished his humanity. Penn was a man of his time and a lord over great domains. If he rejected a title of nobility as vain show, he insisted on the substance of lordship as True and Absolute Proprietary of Pennsylvania, a title that many an English nobleman would have been glad to take in exchange for shabby baronies.[1] He struggled to maintain the powers accompanying that title. He played an active and surprisingly effective role in the royal court. What distinguished him from most of the peers of Stuart England was his preservation of an ideal from the Middle Ages. Clinging to the prerogatives of lordship, he tried to be a *good* lord.[2]

Penn's status put him into many sorts of official relationships simultaneously. He had to deal with the crown and its bureaucracy, the investors whose finances were necessary to found his colony, the settlers whose bodies and skills were even more necessary, the neighboring colonies of New York, West New Jersey, and Maryland (not to speak of the three lower counties of Delaware), the Quaker community that acknowledged him as a leader, his many employees and servants, and his difficult family. And, finally, he had to deal with Indians — not just generic, homogenized Indians, but many different tribes and bands of Indians with different particular interests and objectives. It was not enough for Penn to have good intentions toward all Indians. He had to negotiate with particular sets of them in situations that required favoring one group against another. The issues of morality were simple compared to the issues of practice.

Dealings with Indians could not be neatly separated from relationships with other colonies, nor from Penn's entanglements with his own colony's litigious settlers. Far from being a terrible menace, Indians of friendly tribes were a source of profit and wealth through trade of English manufactured goods for the Indians' skins and furs; and Penn counted on that trade for an income to defray the expenses of his government. But he was Johnny-come-lately in the trade. Swedes and Dutchmen had engaged in it along the Delaware and Susquehanna Rivers for half a century before Pennsylvania was founded. The merchants of Albany strove to monopolize the trade of the Iroquois Five Nations who might otherwise have come down the Susquehanna to do business. Among Penn's own colonists the wealth-producing potential of the Indian trade was appreciated and exploited. Soon after the colony's founding, a busy center of trade sprang up on the Schuylkill River near present-day Phoenixville, only thirty miles up the river from Philadelphia; but it was run by a refugee Huguenot family and Canadian *coureurs de bois,* and it wholesaled its peltry through an English company in New Jersey.³ When Penn suggested in 1703 that the Pennsylvania Assembly should grant him a fur trade monopoly in lieu of taxes, his provincial secretary James Logan refused even to offer such a proposal to the Assembly. "The merchants will never bear it," he responded. "Contrivance and management may give thee a share with the rest, but more is not to be depended upon."⁴

The Indians of Penn's province had been through much turmoil before his new colonists arrived on the scene, and yet more was in store. The Indians on the Susquehanna River had been caught up in the violent politics of Bacon's Rebellion in Virginia; they were attacked and dispersed by combined forces from Virginia and Maryland, and they fled to the woods. Offered protection by New York Governor Edmund Andros in 1676, they found sanctuary among Indians within his jurisdiction which then included all of what was later to become Pennsylvania. Most of the Susquehannocks chose to join the Iroquois Five Nations in New York's Finger Lakes region. Some, however, settled with hosts in the Delaware Valley. The separation created enduring problems of Indian right to land ownership in the Susquehanna Valley homeland of those refugees. Which Indians had rightful title? Which of them could cede it validly to an English purchaser? The problem was very much alive at Pennsylvania's founding, and it was to give Penn much trouble, as will be shown further on.⁵

Andros's disposition of the Susquehannocks was part of another of his arrangements, called the Covenant Chain, which gave Penn additional concern in Indian affairs. This Covenant Chain was a loosely knit set of treaty-made alliances by means of which Andros had formally ended hostilities between Indians and colonials in New England and along the Susquehanna River and Chesapeake Bay. Taken together, these alliances constituted a confederation embracing all the Indians of Andros's New

York, including those refugee Susquehannocks and the Delawares as well as the Iroquois and others. A special inner alliance of the New York government with the Iroquois Mohawks acted as a sort of steering committee for the whole Chain confederation, and the Mohawks, together with their brother Iroquois, assumed a status elevated above the other tribes. This status came into question when Pennsylvania's founding disrupted the Covenant Chain by truncating New York's jurisdiction in 1681. Penn took the process a step further by creating his own Chain of Friendship with "his" Indians, separate from the Covenant Chain and in some respects competitive with it, especially in trade.[6]

According to the rules of European law, Penn's action should have settled the issue of tribal ranking, but the Iroquois went by their own rules. They continued to pretend to authority, and they continued to regard the Pennsylvania tribes as part of the Covenant Chain. New Yorkers saw opportunity in the situation to lay their own claim, by means of the Covenant Chain, to prerogative in the affairs of Pennsylvania's Indians; but they were repeatedly rebuffed by the Indians themselves who successfully appealed for protection by the Pennsylvanians.[7] During William Penn's time, the tension prevailing in Penn's backwoods was not a simple matter of race, religion, or nationality; one English colony competed with another, and various Indian tribes contended for superiority, in intricate combinations. The issues were muted during Penn's lifetime: the contending parties remained formally at peace with each other, and their competition rarely surfaced in formal records, but the tensions were perpetual.

From the moment he received his charter, Penn became involved in Indian affairs. As the bishop of London gratuitously informed him, the Indians had a native right of land ownership and should be compensated for it.[8] The bishop neglected to help out by identifying which Indians had right to which lands. Penn's charter right derived from the crown's claim to sovereignty which was based on conquest of the resident Dutch who had previously conquered the earlier resident Swedes. But no one had conquered the earliest residents of all, and no one was very eager to make the attempt, so Penn's charter had what he called an "incumbrance" upon it. This was in sharp contrast to the situation in Penn's Irish estates where no legal incumbrance existed because the Irish had been beaten down by Cromwell. Penn seems not to have felt any moral obligation to pay off Irishmen. However much he might have sympathized with Indians, his obligation to them was legal, and precedent existed for it.[9]

What Indian right meant in practice was that Penn had to guarantee removal of the incumbrance before he could persuade investors to put up the money he needed for capital. Without a guarantee of clear title, who would buy land? In his prospectus, therefore, and in all his "Original Rights" sold to speculators in England for unsurveyed land, Penn guaranteed title against that Indian incumbrance.[10] There was no issue, therefore, of whether he would buy Indian rights. The questions narrowed to which Indians, which tracts, when to buy, and how much he would pay. This said, one must add in justice that Penn accepted his responsibility without quibble, and instructed his agents in the colony to make purchases before he came over personally.[11]

Unfortunately it was not possible to negotiate a universal quitclaim from generalized Indians to match the extent of Penn's charter claims. Every valley and every segment of a stream had to be acquired from the particular Delaware Indians whose rights were recognized by neighboring Indians. The process was long and expensive, and it must be said to Penn's credit that he paid fair prices that did indeed "satisfy" the sellers. By 1685 he calculated that he had laid out £1,200 in presents and purchase money for tracts that amounted to a small region of southeastern Pennsylvania.[12] Had the rest been bought at the same rates, the total Indian purchase price would have added up to much more than the debt that King Charles II had discharged by his grant, even if the bribes be added that Penn had had to pay to grease his charter through the crown's officialdom.

It is necessary to stress that Penn's early purchases were from the Delawares. A long cherished myth has it that the Delawares had been conquered by the Iroquois and thus had lost their native rights of possession to the conquerors. Penn knew better, and so should we. The conquest myth arose partly because of Delaware acceptance of the role of intermediaries between the Iroquois and other tribes; this peacemaking role was assigned to women within a tribe and so, by extension, the Delawares became the "women" of intertribal affairs.[13] In Europe, however, women were subject to men's orders, so colonials misread the Indian custom. The intercultural misunderstanding was helped along by the chicanery in later years of William Penn's sons who connived with the Iroquois to suppress the Delawares when the latters' land prices rose irritatingly high. More of that later.

The Iroquois call Penn "Onas" in their language, and that name has become prominent because of Pennsylvania's mid-eighteenth-century policy of alliance with the Iroquois; but William Penn held the Iroquois Five Nations at arm's length. "His" Indians were, in the first place, Delawares, and their name for him was "Miquon." Both Onas and Miquon meant *feather,* and since goose quills were used for writing, they punned on Penn.

No document has survived for a Great Treaty between Penn and the Delawares though the tradition of such a treaty being held under an old elm tree is strong. Supposedly this took place at the Indian village of Schackamaxon, now the Kensington neighborhood of Philadelphia. Benjamin West painted a huge, anachronistic picture commemorating it, and Voltaire quipped that it was the only treaty never sworn to and never broken. Voltaire was half right. There is ample evidence, to my mind, that Penn himself kept his pledged word but that his successors violated the

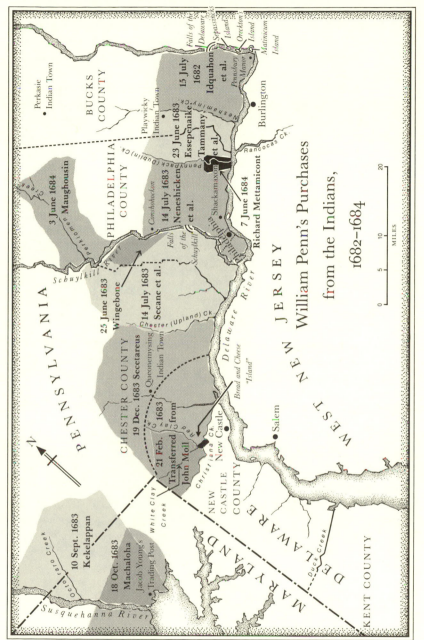

MAP 12.1

William Penn's Purchases from the Indians, 1682–1684

Delaware treaty and destroyed the document that would have exposed their breach of faith. The best evidence that the treaty took place is the fact of Penn's purchases of Delaware lands. Such transactions could not have been made without prior political agreements, whatever those agreements may have been.

But there are also other documents that testify directly to the treaty's having been held. In 1728, at a conference with Delaware chiefs, Governor Patrick Gordon referred to "the Links of the Chain made between William Penn and you" and went on to recite "the nine Articles or Links of the Chain, as in the Treaty held at Conestogoe." In 1731 the same governor narrated a historical review:

> When W. Penn first arriv'd here with his people He immediately called together the Chiefs of the [Delaware] Indians, and told them he was come over to them with leave of the great King of England and had brought a great number of good people to live amongst them who should furnish them with what they wanted, that they should be his brothers and his people and the Indians should be the Same. They exceedingly rejoyced at this, they bid him and his people welcome. He made a Strong Chain of Friendship with them which has been kept bright to this day.[14]

In the terminology used in Indian diplomacy a chain of friendship was a political bond that could only be created by treaty. As for the reference to this chain being like the one held at Conestoga, it is a clear indication that the substance of the Delaware treaty was the same as that in Penn's later treaty with the Susquehannocks which will be noted farther on.

Penn did not buy Indian rights ignorantly, and the Indians did not cheat him by making him pay again and again for the same tract. Neither of these long-accepted notions is true. At the outset, Penn had the advice of Swedish and Dutch colonials who had lived along the Delaware nearly fifty years before Pennsylvania's founding. These veterans traded with the Indians, knew the Delaware language, and had previously dealt in land transactions under earlier regimes.[15] They knew precisely each Indian chief's rights and where his boundaries extended. As to multiple purchases, Penn understood why that might sometimes occur quite properly. In 1683 he explained it to Captain Markham:

> It hath been the Practice of America, as well as the Reason of the thing itself, even among Indians and Christians, to account not taking up, marking and (in some degree) planting a Reversion of Right; for the Indians do make People buy over again that Land [which] the People have not seated in some years after purchased, which is the Practice also of all these [colonial] Governments towards the People inhabiting under them.[16]

He was accurate about the colonial governments, and if he could have foreseen the future he would have been just as accurate about the government of the United States which, in successive Homestead Acts, has required homes to be built on allotted tracts within specified times to avoid forfeiture of right. Indians sold land not only as owners of real estate but also as governors over territory.[17] Penn bought in the same dual capacity. I have come to believe that, by the time Penn negotiated, both sides know what they were doing, however much their customs may have differed fifty years earlier.[18] If Penn had to buy what had previously been purchased by Dutchmen or Swedes, it was because no homesteads had been set up on the tracts in question or because the earlier so-called purchases had been made fraudulently. As to the fact of fraudulent purchase there is considerable evidence.[19]

The Indians had learned that their marks on a quitclaim deed gave up all rights permanently when Europeans did move in, unless residual hunting and fishing rights were specified. Penn never paid twice for his own purchases because he organized a mass migration of Englishmen, Welshmen, and Germans to occupy what he bought. What sometimes appears like a second payment to the same Indian, as in the case of Chief Tamenend, is really the purchase of diverse rights owned by the same person — as nowadays a man might have one kind of property right in a house, another in shares of a corporation, a third in a condominium, and so on. Indian rights were not as savagely simple as they have been assumed. As a sachem, Tamenend had a chiefly right that might be compared very roughly with that of eminent domain. As head of a family he had a right to specific hunting territories. As a person he might also have a right to occupy and cultivate a tract within his village. And, through kinship, he could share in more general rights enjoyed by relatives. These rights were not coextensive. They had to be discharged separately and specifically according to the particular persons involved in each one.[20]

Penn's determination to be fair was soon recognized by the Delawares. Because their population had declined precipitously from epidemic diseases they made no difficulty about selling real estate (simultaneously ceding territorial jurisdiction) so long as Penn would agree to their terms. There was plenty of room upstream in the back country for the Delawares who were left. Penn and his agents were able to get quitclaims along the Delaware River's west bank upstream as far as a point in lower Bucks County near Wrightstown, but negotiations for land beyond that point ran into a snag. Penn arranged purchase of a tract by Indian measure of a day-and-a-half's walk, but the direction of the walk came into sharp dispute, and chief Nutimus, who owned the land upstream beyond a tributary called Tohickon Creek, denied flatly that his land was part of the transaction. There was some hot argument, but Penn had to hurry back to England to meet a political crisis, so the issue remained unresolved. Meantime Penn acknowledged his failure to consummate purchase. He did sell grants of land within Nutimus's territory, but it was only to nonsettling speculators in England, and he carefully omitted from his grant deeds his usual guarantee against an Indian "incumbrance" on the title. And when he returned to Pennsylvania for his final visit in 1699–1701, he made no claim of purchase.[21]

We must distinguish carefully between Penn's goals and motivations. He sincerely intended justice to the Indians, but he also understood well that purchase of Indian tenure rights could confer advantage in boundary disputes with neighboring colonies, and he had grand dreams of magnificence for his own province. He conceived that his chartered northern boundary included the southern tier of counties of what is now New York, including most of the territory of the Iroquois tribes. And he supposed that his southern boundary, at the fortieth degree of latitude, included the head of Chesapeake Bay where he planned to found a second seaport at the entrance of the Susquehanna River to match Philadelphia on the Delaware. When he arrived in America, however, he discovered to his great chagrin that the fortieth degree ran many miles north of the Chesapeake. Indeed it runs slightly north of Philadelphia as laid out by Penn in 1682, and it bisects the modern city's sprawl. If Lord Baltimore had ever won his maximum claim under Maryland's charter, which placed Maryland's northern boundary "under" the fortieth degree, most of modern Philadelphia would lie in Maryland. Baltimore's problem was to make the crown believe that "under" the fortieth degree meant the same as "up to" the fortieth degree.[22]

Penn's altruism did not include giving away the best part of his colony. He promptly worked up an argument about the location of the fortieth degree that was just as casuistical as Baltimore's argument about the meaning of "under." Their contention, in and out of court, lasted some eighty years. To strengthen his case, Penn made a strategic Indian purchase. Baltimore's agents had previously been ceded both shores of the Chesapeake Bay up to its head from the Susquehannock tribe but had overlooked that critical spot at the head of the bay. Penn bought it, and founded a claim upon the purchase.[23] Pacifist that he was, when that Quaker lord committed himself to his own kind of battle, he was formidable. When Chancery finally dictated the boundary line to be surveyed by Mason and Dixon, it split the difference, and the Penn family gained half a degree of latitude. Maryland saved the Chesapeake, but Penn's Indian purchase had gained time that enabled the Penns to save Philadelphia.

Penn's northern boundary led to conflict also, and again he resorted to an attempted Indian purchase to cinch his claim. Under one construction of his charter, Pennsylvania's northern boundary at the forty-third degree of latitude would have included the Mohawk Valley and the modern city of Buffalo. Penn aimed at New York by commissioning agents to purchase the Susquehanna Valley from the Iroquois Five Nations.[24] In this instance, physical geography foreshadowed political boundaries. Though the main trunk of the Susquehanna River lies entirely within present-day Pennsylvania and Maryland, its tributary branches reach up in treetop fashion almost to the Finger Lakes. If Penn had succeeded in his Susquehanna purchase he would have gotten a firm claim on southern New York west of the Hudson Valley. He would also have established treaty relationships with the Five Nations that might later be parlayed into supporting his charter claim all the way up to the forty-third parallel. Not all of this seems to have been evident to New Yorkers at the time, and perhaps not entirely to Penn either though he showed every sign of pressing his territorial claims as far as they would go. But the Indian connection was clear.

Albany's reason for existence was trade with the Indians. When Penn's commissioners approached Albany's officials to arrange a purchase treaty with the Iroquois, the Albanians became alarmed. They quizzed an Indian about the Susquehanna's topography and were aghast at his responses. The trading center that Penn proposed to set up at Conestoga on the Susquehanna would be easier for most Iroquois to trade in than Albany. It would be instant ruin. Pennsylvania was a worse threat than New France.[25]

The merchants took steps. The records become a bit murky at this point, so we must guess at the means they employed. The results are clear enough. The Iroquois frustrated Penn totally by deciding to "give" the Susquehanna in trust to New York's Governor Thomas Dongan to preserve for them against encroachers.[26] Dongan cannily worded the Iroquois deed to make it grant the Susquehanna to his person rather than to his office, and he made it an unrestricted grant rather than a deed of trust. The Iroquois, in their unlettered state, became the victims of his confidence game, and so did Penn.

The Iroquois understanding of their Susquehanna deed was reported by Onondaga Chief Canasatego in 1744 at the treaty of Lancaster. Dongan, said Canasatego, "pretending to be our good Friend, . . . advised us, in order to prevent Onas's [Penn's], or any other Person's imposing upon us, and that we might always have our Land when we should want it, to put it into his Hands; and told us, he would keep it for our Use . . . and not part with any of it, but at our Request."[27] Dongan had other intentions. After he returned to his native Ireland to become the earl of Limerick, he blackmailed Penn out of £100 for the deed. I think that Penn smelled an odor of something unsanctified about the whole affair, or he would have paid a much larger price. Instead, he bought the deed to eliminate a nuisance.[28]

While Dongan remained as governor of New York the nuisance was real and costly. Penn's people could not get into the Susquehanna Valley safely, so his colony remained very much more restricted than its charter made it out. In fact, the colony consisted of settlements on the west side of the Delaware River from Chester up to Tohickon Creek and over to the watershed that divides the Delaware basin from the Susquehanna. Beyond those lines lay Indian territory. Penn stretched his scruples far enough to sell some lands for speculation in that territory, but he did not warrant them against the Indian incumbrance, and he did not authorize settlement.[29] His clear intention was to buy the Indian claim later, when the formalities could be fulfilled. His problems were a shortage of ready cash and an accumulation of debt.

His plans had been laid well enough, but his timing was off, and he had underestimated the capacity of opponents. Land sales and quitrents eventually produced great wealth for his descendants, but for the time being Albany barred him from the Susquehanna and squatters settled without paying anything in the territory disputed with Maryland. The Indian trade was engrossed by a whole host of merchants in Delaware, West New Jersey, Albany, and in Pennsylvania itself, and it was a no-holds-barred business. In 1686 Thomas Dongan went so far as to demand of the Iroquois that they plunder the traders based on Pennsylvania's Schuylkill River, but that was too extreme even for the Iroquois. They refused with the curt observation that it "would get us in a new trouble."[30]

The Susquehanna Valley held promise for reviving Penn's depleted finances. As soon as he could get uncontroverted possession, he could sell its fertile lands to new immigrants for ready cash and a steady quitrent income. More income could be realized from the trade that had concentrated on the Susquehanna River since the days of New Sweden. The river's branches, navigable by canoe, extended southward to the Chesapeake Bay and the Potomac Valley, northward to Iroquoia, and westward to within a few miles of easy portaging to the Allegheny River; and from the Allegheny a trader had access via the Ohio River to the vast Mississippi Valley and its multitude of hunting Indians.[31] By a combination of oddly assorted circumstances, Penn managed by 1700 to gain access to the Susquehanna. He paid off Dongan. Crushing defeats of the Iroquois by New France and its Indian allies eliminated possible obstruction from that quarter. The remnants of the original Susquehannock inhabitants of the valley fled from the French wars to re-establish residence at their old homeland Conestoga. And when Penn approached them in 1701 to buy the Indian right to the valley, they were eager to exchange it for his protection and some badly needed goods.

The treaty by which that purchase was effected is the first one made by Penn for which the text has been preserved in full.[32] It is also the last treaty negotiated by William Penn personally rather than by agents. And according to Governor Patrick Gordon, its terms repeated those of Penn's Great Treaty with the Delawares. It is therefore worth analysis. It consists of a preamble and ten articles. Besides the pledges of reciprocal good will and assistance, the articles are distinctive in certain specific respects. Though the Indians living near "Christian" inhabitants are required to conform to colonial laws, they are also to have the privileges and immunities of those laws like any other inhabitants. One may take that with a grain of salt;

whatever Penn may have intended, Indians did not sit on Pennsylvania juries.[33]

The treaty was highly practical in other respects: it conveyed to Penn the Susquehanna Valley east of the river, thus opening up large tracts of territory for sale to colonials. It prescribed controls over the Indians' trade; they were to do business only with traders licensed by Penn or his agents, and they were to trade only with Pennsylvanians. Thus the treaty was a heavy blow at Albany. The Susquehannock Indians agreed also to prevent all "strange" Indians from settling along the river until Pennsylvania's government approved. This issue arose from the desire of Indians from the Potomac Valley to get away from Maryland's mistreatment. Penn accepted them, but required the Susquehannocks to be responsible for their good behavior.

The treaty took the Indians of the Susquehanna Valley into Penn's Chain of Friendship. It conveyed land, controlled trade, and arranged juridical relationships, all at the expense of New York and New York's partners, the Iroquois Five Nations. Onondaga Chief Ahookasoongh subscribed his name to the treaty; but, although he is described as "brother to the emperor" of the Iroquois, his name appears tenth among twelve Indian signers.[34] He certainly did not dictate terms. This treaty set back the Iroquois in all their pretensions: it denied their ownership of the Susquehanna territory; it diverted trade from the path through Iroquoia to Albany; and it made the Susquehannocks rather than the Iroquois responsible for the Potomac newcomers. Penn's friendship with "the" Indians was definitely weighted in favor of his own client tribes. His religion required him to deal fairly with all. His lordship demanded distinctions. He saw no contradiction.

He seems to have had some unrecorded conversations with Ahookasoongh, looking toward establishment of treaty relations with the Iroquois. Later in the year he entrusted a wampum belt and message to Delaware chief Scollitchy to take up to the Grand Council of the Iroquois, but the Delawares were in no hurry to promote rapprochement between Pennsylvania and the overweening Five Nations. They stalled. After Penn returned to England, the Delawares simply ignored his charge until changing circumstances reminded them to fulfill it. That they were far from being under Iroquois domination at the time is shown by the length of time they held Penn's belt without delivery — it was eleven full years.[35] We still do not know, and probably never will know, what Penn told them to say in his behalf, or whether they reported it accurately when they got around to it. In the early years of the eighteenth century the Delawares were as jealous of their special partnership with Pennsylvania as the Mohawks were of Albany's alliance. In those years the Delawares carried themselves in proud independence. The myth of their subordination to the Iroquois was not concocted until 1742, long after most Delawares had migrated to the

Ohio country and those remaining in the east had lost their former power and prestige.[36]

William Penn's labors created the conditions for his colony's growth, but he was never to reap the harvest of his own sowing. Preoccupied with affairs in England and the calamitous financial setbacks in his Irish estates, he lost control of Pennsylvania to people on the scene whose interests differed from his own. Dominant among those persons was his ubiquitous secretary James Logan, a master of intrigue and manipulation. Logan served as the Penn family's steward in America, and like many another steward served himself in the process. William Penn had hardly embarked on his final return in 1701 to England when Logan conspired with equally unscrupulous friends to encroach upon the reservation that Penn had set aside for the Delawares along Brandywine Creek; and Logan kept whittling away at that reservation until it disappeared completely.[37]

The Indian trade on the Susquehanna for which Penn had striven so hard became Logan's trade. After Penn had a stroke in 1712 that disabled him from any sort of supervision, Logan set up his own trading post at Conestoga, manned it with his own traders, and trundled his Conestoga wagon back and forth between the post and Philadelphia. He acquired immense influence over the development of the lower Susquehanna Valley, exercising great power over Indians and European immigrants alike, and enriching himself by means that he often chose to keep secret, with good reason. It was over Logan's ferry that German and Irish colonizers made their way to settle in the Shenandoah Valley and along the mountain coves leading to Ohio.[38]

Logan's prosperity had been made possible by Penn's policy of hospitality for Indians at the Susquehanna. Besides the Susquehannock/Conestogas, some Senecas sought refuge there from the French wars. Shawnees trekked there all the way from La Salle's fort on the Mississippi. Piscataway/Conoys fled there from brutal treatment by Marylanders. In 1710 Tuscaroras negotiated sanctuary in the valley from belligerent Carolinians. For a time the Susquehanna's population of refugee Indians grew almost as fast as its community of refugees from Europe, and all those Indians made their livings primarily by hunting and trading. They provided the profits that became capital for Pennsylvania's western expansion.[39]

During the early eighteenth century the Iroquois Five Nations slowly rebuilt their strength to gain a position of ascendancy — not command — over those broken and fragmented tribes. So long as William Penn had held effective control, he had protected the refugees by his own Chain of Friendship, a significantly separate alliance from the Covenant Chain that bound the Iroquois to New York. But Penn's successors found advantage in cultivating closer ties with the Iroquois. By successive treaties in 1710, 1722, 1732, and 1736, they loosened New York's monopoly on trade and aid from all the Iroquois except the Mohawks until finally they brought Pennsylvania into the Iroquois Covenant Chain alliance system.[40] In 1736

James Logan offered to recognize only the Iroquois as spokesmen for all the Indians formerly protected by Pennsylvania if the Iroquois would police those reduced and broken tribes who were becoming restive under the exploitation of Logan's policies and henchmen.[41]

But all that came later, and William Penn's policies and methods are not to be confused with those of Logan and Penn's sons. The Founder was not only a lord, but a good lord. As missionary John Heckewelder reported in 1817, "Never will the Delawares forget their elder brother Miquon, as they affectionately and respectfully call him." During Miquon's time, "Pennsylvania was a last, delightful asylum" for the Indians.[42]

Yet the Indians left Pennsylvania, and in 1755, at the onset of the Seven Years' War in America, many of them returned as avenging furies to kill, burn, and destroy. The Quakers of that era were dumfounded, as many a student has been since, for if William Penn's kindness to the Indians had been acknowledged and appreciated by the Indians themselves, surely they should not have turned murderously against Penn's own people. The interpretation of this puzzle most frequently given in subsequent histories rests heavily upon a conception of Indians as savages lacking the natural capacity for gratitude inherent in persons fully human. The Quakers, however, could not believe that, for such a notion violated their deepest religious beliefs about the brotherhood of man. In 1756 they organized *The Friendly Association for Regaining and Preserving Peace with the Indians by Pacific Measures* and subscribed thousands of pounds to finance its work, part of which involved interrogating friendly Indians and unearthing old documents.[43]

The Quakers discovered a dual solution to the puzzle of Indian ingratitude. In the first place, they learned that Penn's special people, the Quakers, had not been attacked though they lived across the length and breadth of the province. The Quakers' Yearly Meeting in 1758 recorded their "Thankfulness for the peculiar favour extended and continued to our Friends and Brethren in profession, none of whom have as we have yet heard been Slain nor carried into Captivity."[44] In the second place, they learned that Pennsylvania's allegedly kind treatment of the Indians had changed since the 1680s. The researching Quakers found that they had to distinguish between William Penn's policies and those of his successors.

Pennsylvania's Indians did not "retire before the advance of civilization" as the old bromide has it; they were pushed westward by a series of harsh processes initiated and supervised by provincial officials. In summary, the several regional groups of Indians who inhabited Pennsylvania were treated as follows:

1. The Brandywine Delawares.

At the founding of Pennsylvania, there were perhaps five hundred Delaware Indians living on the Brandywine Creek in Chester County, whose attachment to what is even yet a marvelously beautiful country is not hard to understand. They ceded a region to William Penn in 1683 (see the purchase from Secetarius on map 12.1), but accepted his word that Indians and colonists should live together in a community of brotherhood. The Indians did not try to amalgamate with the English. Rather they wished to live nearby while preserving their own village society and customs. Today we might call it an effort at cultural pluralism. The Brandywines requested and received a reconveyance of a portion of their lands to be reserved for them forever. As they understood it, their reservation included the entire Brandywine Creek from its mouth to its headwaters on its west branch, together with a strip of land one mile wide on both sides of the creek.

Encroachment on the reservation began almost immediately after William Penn's final departure from his province in 1701, and between 1702 and 1726 the whole reservation was consumed by colonials with the full knowledge and approbation of the provincial commissioners of property dominated by Secretary James Logan. Along the way, Logan acknowledged the Indians' right to the land and offered grudging compensation, but when he discovered that their copy of Penn's reservation grant had been destroyed in a cabin fire, he brushed them off and punished the colonials who had supported their claims. Made landless, the Brandywines migrated westward, some of them stopping off at the Susquehanna River, others continuing to the "Ohio country" (which included the Allegheny Valley).[45] As late as 1751 an emigrant named Nemacolin told the story to Virginia's agent Christopher Gist.[46]

2. The Tulpehocken Delawares.

After William Penn bought lands of the Delawares headed by famous Chief Tamenend, or Tammany, the Indians vacated this part of their territory and migrated to the remainder in the Tulpehocken Valley. Today this segment of the Great Valley of the Appalachians is known as Lebanon Valley after the town subsequently built there, but in the early eighteenth century it was "the land of the turtles" whose creek joined the Schuylkill River where Reading now stands. Like the valley of the Brandywine, the Tulpehocken was good, fertile land as "Pennsylvania Dutch" farmers have since demonstrated.

In 1722, Governor Sir William Keith directed a flow of Palatine German immigrants into the Tulpehocken Valley, probably after being bribed.[47] For once, James Logan told the Indian side of the ensuing troubles, being moved to it by enmity toward Governor Keith. The Indians, wrote Logan to John Penn (William's son), were much abused by having their Corn (which they never use to fence) destroy'd by the Cattle of these new-comers whom they knew not. And at length they were oblig'd entirely to remove, which being directly contrary to all Stipulations with them, tis certain they have the same reason for this as all those other Indians on this Continent have had for the foundation of their Wars that in some place they have carried on so terribly to the destruction of the European Inhabitants.[48]

But the Tulpehockens remained at peace. Most of them migrated to the Ohio Country where they set up new villages on the Allegheny River. Their chief, Sassoonan, remained behind, living as a guest in the Iroquois village of Shamokin at the confluence of the west and north branches of the Susquehanna River. In 1732 he signed a formal cession of the lands already lost, receiving partial compensation and a promise of more; but when he appeared at James Logan's house in 1733 to collect the rest, Logan gave him "a righter notion of the bargain," and the embittered chief departed with the conviction of having been cheated. Having lost his people and his lands, he took to the bottle and died an alcoholic.[49]

3. The Minisinks and "Jersey" Delawares.

The region above Tohickon Creek's junction with the Delaware River was inhabited by a number of Indian bands. Just north of the creek was the land of Delaware Chief Nutimus whose people moved cyclically back and forth across the Delaware in the seasonal rhythm of transhumance. These were so-called Jersey Indians. Higher up the Delaware were the Minisinks and a village of Shawnees whose mingled peoples have since become the Munsies. Their lands were seized without compensation by the notorious Walking Purchase organized in 1737 by Thomas Penn and James Logan.[50]

When Nutimus and his followers protested, Logan and Governor George Thomas summoned the Iroquois to suppress them. In return for substantial considerations, the Iroquois obligingly menaced the protesters and ordered them out of their own lands. As rationalization, Onondaga Chief Canasatego invented a "conquest" supposedly made by the Iroquois at a conveniently unspecified time, which has ruined histories ever since. The conquest was in fact under way at that moment by the combined strength of the Iroquois and the province, but it reached only the eastern Delawares.[51] Those in the Ohio Country, who by this time constituted the bulk of the tribe, heard of the proceedings without acquiring any new love for Pennsylvania or Penn's sons.

4. The mixed tribes of the lower Susquehanna.

The trunk line of the Susquehanna, below the junction of the west and north branches, was inhabited during the early eighteenth century by Conestogas, Shawnees, Conoys, and fragments of other broken tribes. Traders moved in with them, whom they were glad to have, but after 1710 immigrant bands of colonial settlers came from Switzerland, Germany, and Northern Ireland. These were less welcome. In a familiar pattern, they drove out game at the same time as their domesticated livestock foraged in the Indians' cornfields. James Logan conspired with the Taylor family of surveyors to allot lands to the newcomers despite Indian protests, and when the protests became annoying Logan turned these Indians over to the Iroquois as he was simultaneously disposing of the Delawares. Here, too, there was flight from the invasion, and here, too, it left a residue of strong ill will toward Pennsylvania.[52]

Some details of these proceedings could not be uncovered until the private papers of the actors became available for research long afterward, but members of the Friendly Association and the Pennsylvania Assembly unearthed enough from 1756 to 1758 to perceive the substance of what had happened and to realize that the Indians had lifted the hatchet against the province because of genuine tragic grievances. The Friends discovered also the shameful fact that many of their own immediate forebears had been involved in dispossessing those Indians, and they resolved to make restitution by reviving the policies of revered William Penn.

To do this, they had to set themselves directly in opposition to the authorities who had forsaken those policies. Friends' subsequent struggle against Thomas Penn and his governors, and the crown's superintendent of Indian affairs Sir William Johnson, is outside the scope of this essay. What can be said relevantly, however, is that their efforts resulted in the holding of a great treaty at Easton in 1758, the outcome of which was a promise from the crown's agents that Indian territory as it then stood would be held inviolate. In response, the warring Delawares and Shawnees made peace.[53] The crown's promise was repeated as an edict in the Royal Proclamation of 1763, and it became law by Parliament's Quebec Act in 1774. It was not Friends' fault that the law and the government that enacted it were overthrown.

NOTES

1. For William Penn's ideas on nobility, see *No Cross, No Crown*, 2d ed. (London, 1682), chap. 11.

2. See T. H. Breen, *The Character of the Good Ruler: A Study of Puritan Political Ideas in New England, 1630-1730* (New Haven, 1970), pp. 7-14.

3. For New Sweden, still standard, though unacceptably ethnocentric, is Amandus Johnson, *The Swedish Settlements on the Delaware: Their History and Relation*

to the Indians, Dutch and English, 1638-1664 (Philadelphia, 1911); for New Netherlands, see C. A. Weslager, in collaboration with A. R. Dunlap, *Dutch Explorers, Traders and Settlers in the Delaware Valley, 1609-1664* (Philadelphia, 1961); for the Schuylkill traders, see Albright G. Zimmerman, "Daniel Coxe and the New Mediterranean Sea Company," *PMHB,* 76 (1952):86-96; Daniel Coxe, "Account of New Jersey," ibid., 7 (1883):331; Coxe's memorial is in Clarence W. Alvord and Lee Bidgood, eds., *The First Explorations of the Trans-Allegheny Region by the Virginians, 1560-1674* (Cleveland, 1912), pp. 231-49. But note that Coxe and his traders were not Virginians.

4. Penn to Logan, 20, 24 Feb. 1703 (but compare these dates with *Micro.* 10:735), in *Correspondence Between William Penn and James Logan, and Others,* ed. Deborah Logan, Memoirs of the Historical Society of Pennsylvania, vols. 9-10 (Philadelphia, 1870-72), 1:163-64, 170; Logan to Penn, 9 July 1703, ibid., 1:202; see also *Micro.* 10:1031.

5. Francis Jennings, "Glory, Death, and Transfiguration: The Susquehannock Indians in the Seventeenth Century," *Proceedings of the American Philosophical Society,* 112 (1968):15-50. Note: because the present essay summarizes much intricate detail from scattered sources, it is impossible to argue and document every point *de novo.* Reference will therefore be made as necessary to my previous studies for full supporting evidence.

6. Francis Jennings, "The Constitutional Evolution of the Covenant Chain," *Proceedings of the American Philosophical Society,* 15 (1971):88-96; minutes of Penn's treaty with the Susquehannocks, 3 Apr. 1701, Penn Papers, Indian Affairs, 1:45, HSP, printed in *Minutes of the Provincial Council,* 2:14-18.

7. Jennings, "Constitutional Evolution," pp. 91-93.

8. William Penn to Lords of Trade, 6 Aug. 1683, *CSPC, 1681-1685,* p. 470.

9. See Francis Jennings, "Virgin Land and Savage People," *American Quarterly,* 23 (1971):519-41; idem, *The Invasion of America: Indians, Colonialism, and the Cant of Conquest* (Chapel Hill, N.C., 1975), chap. 8.

10. William Penn, *Some Account of the Province of Pennsilvania* (1681), in *Narratives of Early Pennsylvania, West New Jersey and Delaware, 1630-1707,* ed. Albert Cook Myers (New York, 1912), p. 208; see also *PWP,* vol. 5, items 58A-B. Examples of Penn's guarantee of freedom from Indian claims are the "Lloyd Rights" original indentures, 6 and 7 Feb. 1681, Gratz Collection, Papers of the Governors, case 2, box 33-a, HSP. For a contrasting deed to lands sold in unpurchased Indian territory which does not contain the guarantee, see confirmation by William Penn of a grant to John Streper, 24 June 1705, Streper Papers, Bucks County, pp. 187-89, HSP; see also Penn's statement that "the land shall be clear of all Indian claims," in Concessions to Subscribers, 28 Oct. 1701, in Frank H. Eshleman, "The Birth of Lancaster County," *Publications of the Lancaster County Historical Society,* 12 (1908):11-12.

11. Penn's instructions, 30 Sept. 1681; William Penn to the kings of the Indians, 18 Oct. 1681, and his additional instructions to William Markham, 28 Oct. 1681, in *PWP,* 2:120, 127-30.

12. William Penn, *A Further Account of the Province of Pennsylvania,* 12 Dec. 1685, in *Narratives,* ed. Myers, p. 276.

13. Anthony F. C. Wallace, "Woman, Land, and Society: Three Aspects of Aboriginal Delaware Life," *Pennsylvania Archaeologist,* 17 (1947):1-35; John Heckewelder, *An Account of the History, Manners, and Customs of the Indian Nations Who once Inhabited Pennsylvania and the Neighbouring States* (1819), rev. ed. William C. Reichel, Memoirs of the Historical Society of Pennsylvania, vol. 12 (Philadelphia, 1876), pp. 56-67. A fuller analysis of the "woman question" appears in Francis Jennings, *Ambiguous Iroquois Empire* (New York, 1984), pp. 161-62.

14. *Minutes of the Provincial Council,* 3:336 (11 Oct. 1728); Indian treaty held at Philadelphia, 17 and 18 Aug. 1731, in James Steel's Letter Book (1730-1741), 2:274, HSP.

15. The most prominent among the Swedes was the interpreter Lasse Cock. An instruction to him is in *Minutes of the Provincial Council,* 1:334-35 (24 Apr. 1690); see also Harry Emerson Wildes, *William Penn* (New York, 1974), p. 143.

16. William Penn to William Markham, c. 1 Sept. 1683, in *PWP,* 2:474.

17. Discussed in the works cited in n. 9, above.

18. The probable circumstances of precontact land tenure are discussed most persuasively in Wallace, "Woman, Land, and Society."

19. See Jennings, "Glory, Death, and Transfiguration," pp. 50-53.

20. Compare Wallace, "Woman, Land, and Society," p. 2, with Frank G. Speck, "The Wapanachki Delawares and the English: Their Past as Viewed by an Ethnologist," *PMHB,* 67 (1943):341.

21. See n. 10, above, and Francis Jennings, "The Scandalous Indian Policy of William Penn's Sons: Deeds and Documents of the Walking Purchase," *Pennsylvania History,* 37 (1970):19-39. The issue is discussed more fully in Jennings, *Ambiguous Iroquois Empire,* chaps. 12, 17.

22. Penn's charter is in *Minutes of the Provincial Council,* 1:17-26. Penn had requested three degrees of latitude for his grant, on the understanding that it would begin at Maryland's northern boundary. The actual language of the charter sets Pennsylvania's southern line "from twelve miles distance, Northwards of New Castle Towne unto the three and fortieth degree of Northern latitude." Sources for the charter negotiations are in *PWP,* 2:30-78.

23. Deed, 18 Oct. 1683, in *PWP,* 2:492. For the controversy over this purchase, see Jennings, "Glory, Death, and Transfiguration," pp. 46-48.

24. Commission and instructions, 2 Aug. 1683, *PWP,* 2:423-24.

25. Sources are printed in E. B. O'Callaghan, ed., *Documentary History of the State of New York* (Albany, 1849-51), 1:394 (hereafter cited as *Doc. Hist. N.Y.*); and in *PWP,* 2:479-80, 481-82, 487-89; see also the "draught" of the Susquehanna Valley, with comment in Lawrence H. Leder, ed., *Livingston Indian Records,* (Gettysburg, 1956), pp. 69-70, and interleaved between pp. 70-71.

26. Details in Gary B. Nash, "The Quest for the Susquehanna Valley: New York, Pennsylvania, and the Seventeenth-Century Fur Trade," *New York History,* 48 (1967):3-27.

27. Treaty minutes, *Minutes of the Provincial Council,* 4:706-9 (26 June 1744).

28. Deed, Dongan to Penn, 12 Jan. 1696, Gratz Collection, Governors of Pennsylvania, case 2, box 33-a, HSP; Earl of Limerick (Dongan) to Penn, 25 Jan. 1708, Penn-Forbes Collection, 2:67, HSP.

29. The telltale phrase in Penn's patents for land is "free of incumbrance." When that is omitted, it means that the land lies in unceded tribal territory. For specific cases, see Francis Jennings, "Miquon's Passing: Indian-European Relations in Colonial Pennsylvania, 1674 to 1755" (Ph.D. diss., University of Pennsylvania, 1965), pp. 318-32.

30. Dongan twice urged the Iroquois to raid the Schuylkill trading center. His first effort is recorded in the treaty of 30 Aug. and 1 Sept. 1686 which I have reconstituted from two incomplete texts: New York Council minutes, 5:163-69 (mutilated by fire) and *Doc. Hist. N.Y.,* 1:403-5 (extracts made before the fire). Dongan's second effort is recorded as of 25 Apr. 1687 in Leder, *Livingston Indian Records,* pp. 112-13. Copies of the reconstituted treaty are deposited in the New York State Archives, Albany, and the Newberry Library Iroquois treaty archive, Chicago.

31. Cadwallader Colden, "Observations on the Situation, Soil, Climate, Water Communications, Boundaries &c. of the Province of New York," 14 Feb. 1738, in *Doc. Hist. N.Y,* 4:173-74.

32. Articles of Agreement, 23 Apr. 1701, *PA,* 1st ser., 1:144-47.

33. A remark of Penn's has been interpreted to mean that he intended Indians to sit on juries; to wit, that in cases of differences between colonials and Indians, "Six of each side shall end the matter." This reflected Penn's historical scholarship rather than his intentions about courts. When, early in the tenth century, England and Wales faced each other across a line between jurisdictions and judicial systems, their Marcher lords had arbitrated some differences with boards of six men from each side. See William Penn, *Letter to the Society of Traders* (1683), in *Narratives,* ed. Myers, pp. 235-36 (see also *PWP,* vol. 5, items 67A-C); Doris Stenton, *English Justice Between the Norman Conquest and the Great Charter, 1066-1215,* (Philadelphia, 1964), p. 7.

34. *PA,* 1st ser., 1:146.

35. *Minutes of the Provincial Council,* 2:546-49 (19 May 1712). The manuscript draft has chief Scollitchy calling the Delawares "friends of the 5 Nations," and carrying "presents" to the Iroquois. These remarks were altered by insertion and substitution to "friends and Subjects of the 5 Nations" carrying "tribute." Cf. photostat of the manuscript in Society Collections, HSP, with the formal manuscript record at the Pennsylvania Historical and Museum Commission, Harrisburg.

36. Francis Jennings, "The Delaware Interregnum," *PMHB,* 89 (1965):174-98.

37. See n. 45, below.

38. Francis Jennings, "The Indian Trade of the Susquehanna Valley," *Proceedings of the American Philosophical Society,* 110 (1966):406-24.

39. Paul A. W. Wallace, *Indians in Pennsylvania* (Harrisburg, 1961).

40. Treaty minutes, Conestoga, 31 July 1710, Penn Papers, Indian Affairs, 1:34, HSP; treaty minutes, 17 Aug.-10 Sept. 1722, in *Documents Relative to the Colonial History of the State of New York,* ed. E. B. O'Callaghan and Berthold Fernow (Albany, 1856-87), 5:657-81; *Minutes of the Provincial Council,* 3:435-52 (23 Aug.-2 Sept. 1722); ibid., 4:79-84, 90-95 (27 Sept.-14 Oct. 1736).

41. James Logan to Conrad Weiser, 18 Aug. 1736, Logan Papers, 10:64; Weiser to Logan, 17 Oct. 1736, ibid., 10:65, HSP.

42. Heckewelder, *Account of the Indian Nations,* p. 78. Heckewelder's recounting of the Delaware and Mahican traditions has been confirmed in all essentials by this writer's researches; his *Account* deserves a very respectful reading. Though denounced by Francis Parkman, Heckewelder wrote honestly, which is more than can be said for Parkman, whose Social Darwinian propaganda dominated all his publications. See Francis Jennings, "A Vanishing Indian: Francis Parkman Versus His Sources," *PMHB,* 87 (1963):306-23; idem, "Francis Parkman: A Brahmin among Untouchables," *WMQ,* 3d. ser., 42 (1985):305-28.

43. The best accounts have been written by Theodore Thayer, in *Israel Pemberton, King of the Quakers* (Philadelphia, 1943); and idem, *Pennsylvania Politics and the Growth of Democracy, 1740-1776* (Harrisburg, 1953). Thayer has the unfortunately rare distinction of having consulted the Quaker sources.

44. Minutes of the Yearly Meeting Held at Burlington for New Jersey and Pennsylvania, 1758, Bk. A3, p. 121, Quaker collection, HCL.

45. C. A. Weslager, *Red Men on the Brandywine* (Wilmington, Del., 1953), supplemented in Jennings, "Miquon's Passing," pp. 107-14, 235-45, 290-91.

46. Christopher Gist's Second Journal, 7 Dec. 1751, in *George Mercer Papers Relating to the Ohio Company of Virginia,* ed. Lois Mulkearn (Pittsburgh, 1954), p. 34.

47. Minutes of conference with the Indians, 4-5 June 1728, Penn-Physick MSS., 6:25, HSP, esp. the appended deposition of Godfrey Fidler.

48. James Logan to John Penn, 2 Aug. 1731, Penn Papers, Official Correspondence, 2:181, HSP.

49. Logan to Thomas Penn, 16 Aug. 1733, *PA*, 2d ser., 7:145; see also Francis Jennings, "Incident at Tulpehocken," *Pennsylvania History*, 35:335-55.

50. Anthony F. C. Wallace, *King of the Delawares: Teedyuscung, 1700-1763* (Philadelphia, 1949), chap. 2; Jennings, "Scandalous Indian Policy."

51. Canasatego's speech, *Minutes of the Provincial Council*, 4:578-80 (12 July 1742).

52. Jennings, "Indian Trade of the Susquehanna Valley."

53. Easton Treaty minutes, *Minutes of the Provincial Council*, 8:174-223 (7-26 Oct. 1758).

13 ❧ From "Dark Corners" to American Domesticity:

The British Social Context of the Welsh and Cheshire Quakers' Familial Revolution in Pennsylvania, 1657–1685

The Quaker farmers of early Pennsylvania were familial radicals, particularly in light of their native roots. From 1681 to 1720, Cheshire and Welsh
Quaker settlers made a society in southeastern Pennsylvania that successfully inverted the ideals and purposes of their old regions' family system.
In contrast to their former marriage alliances which had been arranged or
haphazard affairs, they avowed before the whole community a spontaneously loving and holy attachment to their freely chosen mates. In contrast
to their former sociability and dependence, the couples then worked to
accumulate enough land and cash to protect their children from ever being
dependent economically on spiritually killing men and women of the "world."
And in contrast to their previous society's emphasis on honor and shame,
when the children began to arrive, the reborn couples gratefully accepted
the advice and rules of the experienced local men's and women's monthly
meetings for the purpose of uncovering and nurturing the Light in their
children. Pennsylvania became an arena for realizing familial ideals seemingly undreamed of in England.

　　The literary and historiographical record says little about the familial
and social radicalism of the Delaware Valley's late seventeenth-century inhabitants. Advocates of humility and silence, these Quaker settlers rarely

boasted loudly about their accomplishments. The somewhat confused and worried Anglican missionaries on the scene, like the Reverend George Ross, failed to elaborate their reports that the "fatal weed of Quakerism" was being cultivated in the Delaware Valley "with the utmost skill and tenderness."[1] Perhaps only Voltaire, exiled in England from 1726 to 1728, detected and publicized the broad significance of these upland livestock farmers' bold activities. In his *Letters Concerning the English Nation,* Voltaire wrote four letters, more than for any other topic, on the Quakers. After speaking to them, reading their literature, and attending some of their meetings for worship, he concluded that they fanatically tried to replace the prevailing European ethic of honor and power with one of love. In their Pennsylvania refuge, he wrote, they had "established the power of the Quakers in America," and had created an alternative society: "A new sort of spectacle: a sovereign whom everyone *thee'd* and *thou'd,* and spoke to with one's hat on; a government without priests; a people without weapons; citizens all of them equals — except magistrates — and neighbors free from jealousy." Voltaire judged Pennsylvania the most effective radical effort of his times. "William Penn could boast," wrote Voltaire, "of having brought forth on this earth the Golden Age that everyone talks so much about, and that probably never was except in Pennsylvania."[2] A cavil might be raised, however, that Voltaire never saw the Quakers in their Pennsylvania habitat.

Sophisticated early American historians have ignored this familial and social revolution less because of the lack of contemporary description than because of their own assumptions. James Lemon and James Henretta, while arguing about the *mentalité* of Pennsylvania farmers and artisans, have agreed to ignore the possibility that the Quakers in Pennsylvania redesigned the English family according to their radical religious thought. Following the current wisdom, they describe the Quaker settlers socially as carriers of traditional "middling" habits of thought, and, although they disagree about what that tradition was in every detail, both believe that it necessarily limited the social impact of the settlers' radical religious faith in the Delaware Valley.[3]

It is widely assumed that the seventeenth-century "middling" family was grounded on economic necessity. This family was above all "a 'business' — an absolutely central agency of economic production and exchange," as John Demos has written. "Each household was more or less self-sufficient; and its various members were inextricably united in the work of providing for their fundamental material wants."[4] Religion is supposed to have been subordinated in the daily life of the household to the tasks of survival. Streamlined for production and consumption, the household was usually nuclear, composed of a husband, wife, and children — with perhaps a servant or two. Familial relations were orderly, authoritarian, and unaffectionate, byproducts of economic function, befitting a home that was a factory and a "little commonwealth." Their economic center-piece was land. The "middling" household insured its survival by passing on its land or lease to one male child, while other children, in return for childhood work and obedience, received comparable money and goods to reach an equal, sex-appropriate level of independence and dignity. Most historians have agreed that continuity and autonomy, not merely maximizing profit, was the aim of the family's economics; so households were proto-bourgeois—"middling," not "middle class." In order to thrive, however, such households required self-denying, laborious children and parents. Appreciating such hard work, one historian described American settlers, the Quaker farmers included, as "England's middling people — the most valuable cargo that any captain carried on his westbound voyage."[5]

This cluster of assumptions unluckily obscures most early Pennsylvania settlers' previous family experience and thereby reduces their imagination, achievement, and humanity. Historians have too rarely asked whether "middling" households (those of yeomen, husbandmen, artisans, retailers, and merchants) were truly self-sufficient "little commonwealths" or whether nonresident people played vital economic roles in such households.[6] They have too rarely asked how such households' economic structure varied in the widely differing social and economic regions of seventeenth-century Britain. Answering such questions may not change the present interpretation of family life in colonial New England. Massachusetts' early settlers came generally from wealthy southeastern England where real "little commonwealths" with childrearing traditions emphasizing independence may indeed have been established.[7] Without ambiguity, however, a majority of Pennsylvania's early settlers came from British regions too poor to support yeomen, husbandmen, and artisans with familial traditions emphasizing household autonomy.

Pennsylvania social historians must find their own relevant evidence to construct household models, especially as the issue of household autonomy has important psychological and social implications. Cross-cultural research by anthropologists has established that parents rarely teach their children to be stupidly independent, if they themselves have long relied on relationships outside the household. Such parents teach their children to be wisely dependent.[8] And if the "middling households" in Britain from which the Pennsylvania immigrants came had never been "little commonwealths," but were actually long beholden on outsiders for survival and the completion of essential tasks, they would not customarily teach or show their children the ways of independence or privacy. Only a major spiritual cataclysm would move them in that uncharted direction.

Redefinition can begin with study of the British social context of 1,500 people from Cheshire and Wales who settled in southeastern Pennsylvania between 1681 and 1695. Their social and geographic environments in northwest Britain were similar to those of the great majority of other

Pennsylvania settlers. Indeed, Thomas Holme's famous survey map of Pennsylvania (1687) depicts three counties filled with dispersed, contiguous farmsteads, an English highland settlement pattern, complete with highland place names: "Radnor," "Haverford," "Darby," "Marple," "Edgemount," "Ridley," and "Chester." Far fewer place names told of lowland, fertile English origins: "Chichester" after a town in Sussex, or "Kennet" after a town in Wiltshire. An examination of nearly six hundred First Purchasers of Pennsylvania land confirms that more of them (47) came from Cheshire in the northwest than from any other county, and that well over 60% came from the poorest highland areas of Britain. Virtually no one came from richly developed East Anglia. In any case, the Welsh and Cheshire settlers developed almost 20% of the settled land in Holme's map (the Welsh Tract and eastern Chester County). During the first four decades, they also accumulated considerable economic and political power, promoting such early leaders as Griffith Owen, the counselor; John Simcock, president of the Free Society of Traders; David Lloyd, the speaker of the Assembly and chief justice; and Thomas Lloyd, the deputy governor. Early Pennsylvania political history prominently features these men, though their social origins remain obscure.[9]

Certainly seventeenth-century southern Englishmen recognized, and even exaggerated, the pecularities of life in northwest Britain. Southeastern Puritans thought Cheshire and Welsh people were unusually ignorant spiritually, residents of "the dark corners of the realm," areas cursed by poverty and thereby inadequate clerical incomes, excessively large parishes, and evil traditions.[10] Post-Restoration southerners condemned northwesterners for their poverty. Daniel Defoe, a native Londoner, toured England in 1705 seeking evidence that it had emerged as an economic power. He hated the sight of Welsh mountains, poor farmers, black cattle, and tiny towns. He described Wales as "a country looking so full of horror, that we thought to have given over the enterprise and have left Wales out of our circuit."[11] E. B.'s *A Trip to North Wales* (London, 1701) was even meaner in spirit. Describing Wales was an aesthetic challenge, he wrote, "because a Titian, a Michael Angelo, and a Vandike equally display their art in portraying a loathsome dunghill, as in describing a magnificient palace."[12] Welsh houses were one-room hovels teeming with people and animals, "and who can say which are the greater brutes." "Should a man have a chimney on top of his thatch'd mansion," wrote E. B., "he would stand in danger of being picked for high sheriff."[13] Both southerners expressed alarm when they discovered that many northwesterners liked their region. Defoe noted that Welsh gentlemen were so silly as to "believe their country to be the pleasantest and most agreeable in the world." E. B. depicted one of them "pointing to a house . . . that the sun shown through in about five and forty places: 'Got knows (says my old gentleman) our family has flourished here these eleven hundred years."[14]

Southern Englishmen were poor ethnographers. But even Defoe and E.B. rightly understood that northwesterners wrestled with a stingy and difficult environment. Most of the Welsh settlers who came to Pennsylvania had lived in Merionethshire, Montgomeryshire, and Radnorshire, where more than 58% of the land was well over five hundred feet above sea level; where winds buffeted the mountains; and where the growing season was cool and short.[15] Just east of the northern mountains, the Cheshire plain broke flat and pleasant. But excepting the coastlands of the Irish Sea, the Wirral peninsula and the Dee-Gowy lowlands, deep clay soil made arable farming arduous and expensive.[16] Most seventeenth-century Cheshire farmers kept the land in grass, raised cattle and cows, and lived on dispersed farmsteads. North Welsh farmers raised sheep and black cattle, ate dairy products and oat bread, and lived on dispersed farms on tiny patches of fertile land. North Wales and Cheshire lacked people, money, and markets. Northwest farmers therefore lost much of the value of their modest commodities to middlemen, who trekked Welsh cottons (a cheap coarse woollen cloth) and black cattle along bad turnpikes to reach their final markets, over two weeks away in southern England. Cheshire cheese was shipped south. Waterers, keepers, and fatteners also took their share.

Northwesterners had few economic opportunities locally. There were few craftsmen among Welsh livestock farmers and weavers. "I need not describe Llanberis parish [Merionethshire] unto you," wrote a Welsh traveller in 1690, "in which neither miller, nor fuller, and any other tradesman but one tailor lives."[17] Cheshire's economy was only slightly more diverse. The hides of milk cows and cattle, supplemented by water and oak bark, supplied significant leather-working in northern and central Cheshire. Chester also had a small shipbuilding and linen industry, Nantwich a salt-making works, and Macclesfield a button-making industry.[18] The city of Chester looked impressive, "the largest city in all this side of England that is so remote from London," as Defoe described it, a walled, cathedral town, with a population of some 7,500 people.[19] Chester flourished, not as an industrial powerhouse, but as an oasis of sophisticated services for the region, being the center of county government, regional courts, the county market, the local gentry's social life, and the ecclesiastical establishment. According to the 1664 hearth tax returns, only the gentry and ecclesiastics owned lavish houses — the bishop's palace had 17 hearths, Lady Calveley had 16 hearths, Lady Kilmorey had 16 hearths, and Sir Geoffrey Shakerley had 12 hearths, whereas the largest houses of Chester's leather masters and merchants had 7 hearths.[20]

Though they had titles of well-earned dignity, northwest "middling" people — yeoman, husbandmen, and artisans — were generally poor and powerless. Symptomatically, few householders were identified as laborers. Livestock required only a few laborers, preferably live-ins, to handle the animals' needs and often untimely emergencies. In any case, farmers of relatively unprofitable northwestern land could not pay many laborers. An inspection of 348 inventories between 1660 and 1681 in Cheshire, Radnorshire, Brecknockshire, and Merionethshire uncovered only five men who called themselves, or were called by the assessors, "laborer." Myddle, in Shropshire contained, throughout the seventeenth century, only three or four laborers' households, some 4% of the total.[21] At least the region supported many tenant farmers; the gentry had ample marginal land to let. Many men called themselves "husbandman," "tradesman," and even "yeoman," who rented acres of mountainside for their small herd of cows, cattle, and sheep. Their similarly situated neighbors would so honor them. But such men had much less wealth than "middling" people in southeastern England.

Southeastern yeomen and husbandmen usually farmed large farms, grew crops which they marketed nearby, heavily capitalized their farms, and kept a large labor force of out-living farm laborers. Symptomatically, laborers' households were common. In Clayworth, Devon, 32.4% of the householders in 1688 were laborers. In Terling, Essex, 56.2% of the householders in the late seventeenth century were laborers.[22] As the Welsh historian David W. Howell noted, most Welsh farmers, "when compared with the substantial tenants of the large farms of the southeast and southern midlands of England . . . belonged to the laboring class."[23] Of course, Welsh and Cheshire farmers were not wage-earners and had little, if any, class consciousness. This assertion is helpful, however, for northwestern farmers and farmer-artisans lived a subsistence existence and were unable to provide economic independence for themselves or their children. Their efforts therefore supported the wealth and power of the provincial gentry, or a larger kin group, rather than the autonomy of their own households.

Self-sustaining "little commonwealths" were reserved in the northwest for the few who were rich and privileged. Between 1660 and 1691, a great majority of Welsh and Cheshire yeomen, husbandmen, and artisans had paltry land resources and tiny personal estates. In a sample of 323 probate inventories of artisans, husbandmen, and yeomen in Cheshire, Merionethshire, and Radnorshire, only in Cheshire did the yeomanry have personal estates equivalent to that rank in some richer areas of England. Margaret Spufford has found that the inventories of fifty-eight yeomen in Cambridgeshire in 1660 had a median personal estate of £180 with a range from £12 to £1132.[24] By comparison, fourteen yeomen in Cheshire in 1660 had a median personal estate of £150 5s. with a range from £65 to £595. The hillside yeomanry of Radnorshire and Merionthshire were much poorer: they had median personal estates of £36 10s. and £27 respectively, only slightly larger than most laborers' households in southern England. And by any standard, husbandmen in all these counties were poor (see table 13.1). Reflecting the relative articulation of Cheshire society by 1660, Cheshire husbandmen were much poorer than Cheshire yeomen: a median

TABLE 13.1   *323 Personal Estates of "Middling" Northwest Men, 1660–91*

	Yeomen		Husbandmen		Artisans		All	
Personal Estate (£)	No.	%	No.	%	No.	%	No.	%
Cheshire 1660, 1681 (104)								
200 +	13	37	4	9	2	8	19	18
160–199	5	14	1	2			6	6
120–159	5	14	3	9	7	29	15	14
80–119	4	11	10	22	3	13	17	16
40– 79	4	11	15	33	1	4	20	19
0– 39	4	11	12	27	11	46	27	26
TOTAL	35		45		24		104	
Median Income (£)	171		70		81.5			
Merionethshire 1670–1691 (89)								
200 +	1	4	1	2			2	2
160–199	3	11	1	2			4	4
120–159	2	7	2	4			4	4
80–119	1	4	5	9	1	17	7	8
40– 79	4	14	10	18	1	17	15	17
0– 39	17	61	36	65	4	66	57	64
TOTAL	28		55		6		89	
Median Income (£)	36.5		33		81.5			
Radnorshire 1675, 1685 (130)								
200 +	1	2	1	1			2	2
160–199								
120–159	2	5	1	1			3	2
80–119	2	5	2	2			4	3
40– 79	4	10	15	18			19	15
0– 39	30	77	64	77	8	100	102	78
TOTAL	39		83		8		130	
Median Income (£)	27		25		10			

SOURCES: Cheshire County Probate Records, 1660, 1681, CCRO; Merionethshire Probate Records, 1670-91, NLW; Radnorshire and Brecknockshire Probate Records, 1675, 1685, NLW.

of £70 compared to a median of £171. Yeomen and husbandmen had similarly paltry personal estates in Radnorshire and Merionethshire (see table 13.1). Finally, well over half the Cheshire yeomen, husbandmen, and artisans had estates of less than £101, or too little capital to run "little commonwealths."

Most northwest "middling" households avoided the high costs of autonomy. With limited resources, survival was expensive enough. Charles

II's statistician, Gregory King, estimated that the expense for food annually per capita in a husbandman's household in 1688 was £3 5s.[25] A small family would have needed £19 a year to eat decently. The historian Peter Bowden estimated that in 1650 a livestock farmer blessed with five hundred acres would have spent £15 in overhead costs for every ten acres.[26] Running a small Cheshire or Welsh livestock farm was far less expensive per acre, but overhead did exist. While such costs were plausibly met, the costs of autonomy were wisely avoided. On the autonomous household model, the cost of parenthood additionally required placing all children into lucrative positions promising independence. Daughters needed portions large enough to attract independent men; sons needed a lease and livestock or a good trade. Apprenticeship, the least expensive route to a livelihood, was a costly route to independence. The overseers of Audlem parish, Cheshire, paid in 1701 only £5 to apprentice a poor boy, Joseph Austin, for seven years to a shoemaker; but nobody expected him to rise above being a journeyman.[27] To make an independent tradesman, however, William Stout's parents in nearby Lancashire paid £30 in 1679 to apprentice him to an ironmonger and paid £129 more in 1687 to stock his first modest shop in Lancaster.[28] Having an average of some five cows, four steers, and thirty sheep, most Merionethshire and Cheshire husbandmen dodged defeat by allowing, if not encouraging, their childrens' movement into dependent positions as mere tenants, journeymen, servants. According to the seventeenth-century yeoman, Richard Gough, over 70% of the households in Myddle, Shropshire had nearly always boosted their sons to become tenants, servants, or minor, dependent tradesmen. A Myddle butcher happily sent his son, Francis Jones, in the early seventeenth century "to be a servant at Stanwandine Hall when he was but young; he continued there a menial servant about thirty years."[29] Other Myddle sons also became grooms, cooks, and bailiffs with their parents' hearty approval. Nobody thought such dependency disgraceful or unusual. Among ninety-six "middling" daughters in Myddle, 3% married cottagers, 17% small renting tradesmen — tailors, blacksmiths — and 80% tenant farmers.[30]

Most late seventeenth-century northwest British farmers used their lease-land to survive, not to erect emotionally and economically stocked familial fortresses against society. Most farmers and small artisans had leases of at least two or three lives to give their children and kin, but few thought it worthwhile. Even among the most privileged rural group in this region, the Cheshire farmers, only a small majority in a sample of 253 wills between 1669 and 1681 passed land or a lease to even one son or relative (see table 13.2). Among all the Welsh yeomen and husbandmen who left a will or who had estates of between £100 and £199 between 1670 and 1691, only 32% bothered to bequeath their land or lease to children, spouse, or kin. Few yeomen in Radnorshire or Merionethshire, and few husbandmen in

TABLE 13.2   *Land and Lease Bequests in 253 Northwest Wills, 1660–91*

Personal Estate (£)	Cheshire, 1660–81				Three Welsh Counties,[a] 1670–1691			
	Gives Land or Lease		Gives No Land or Lease		Gives Land or Lease		Gives No Land or Lease	
	No.	%	No.	%	No.	%	No.	%
200+	17	61	11	39	8	62	5	38
100–199	16	53	14	47	6	32	13	68
0– 99	23	59	13	41	30	24	97	76

[a] Merion, Radnor, Brecon

SOURCES: Cheshire County Probate Records, 1660, 1681, CCRO; Merionethshire Probate Records, 1670-91, NLW; Radnorshire and Brecknockshire Probate Records, 1675, 1685, NLW.

any of these counties controlled valuable land or expressed a durable familial interest in a piece of cattle or sheep pasture.

Northwest households were only temporary residences for children. And they gave little economic support to children after childhood. In this total region, the dairy-farmed Cheshire plain promised most to support a large number of autonomous "middling" households. Yet the demographic returns of forty-seven rural artisan Cheshire households belie such a hope. These forty-seven households, formed by marriages between 1656 and 1681, were in seven different parishes, the majority rural.[32] In order to gain complete demographic data for analysis, a biasing criterion for selection was that either the husband's or wife's death, or a note of remarriage, be recorded in the parish register. Such selection means that these people, remaining so long in one parish, were probably more stable and prosperous than the average. But even such statistically privileged Cheshire "middling" households failed to control the social place or lives of their children autonomously.

Perhaps because of the bias of the sample, each of the forty-seven marriages lasted an average of twenty-two years, durable even by modern standards. In every other way, however, these households were for transients. They were less fertile and less healthy than similar southeastern English families in Terling, Essex. The Cheshire families produced 176 children or 3.75 live births per household; Terling families (1550–1724) had 3.86 live births per household. Fewer Cheshire children survived childhood diseases. The Cheshire families produced an average of 2.34 surviving children; Terling families produced an average of 2.7 surviving children. Though living with relatively few children, the Cheshire parents saw most of their offspring drift away from home permanently. Among the 110 surviving children, 59 (54%) neither died nor married in their parents' parishes. They had probably left home and the parish between the ages of eight and sixteen for service and never returned. Giving a clue to why so many left, the children who survived to live in their home parishes rarely gained independence or opportunity to establish an autonomous household. For example, among the women who stayed or returned, nine or 41% never married, dying at an average age of forty-six. Among the men who stayed or returned, ten or 34% never married, dying at an average age of fifty-three. Those who did marry in their home parishes tended to do so late in life. The Cheshire women married at an average age of twenty-six and the men at an average age of thirty-two. With better parental support, people in southeastern England were able to marry younger. From 1700 to 1746, a period coeval to these Cheshire marriages, the average age of Terling women at first marriage was 24.4, and that for men was 24.7 — more than seven years younger than their northern counterparts.[33]

These Cheshire "middling" households clearly failed to raise their children into independence. Of the 176 children born in these 47 households, 66 or 37.5% died young, 69 or 33.5% left home at most likely early ages and never returned, and 19 of those who did stay—or 11% of all surviving children—apparently could not be provided with marriage portions. Only 32 children, a mere 18% of those born, married in their parents' parishes, usually late in life; these people were visibly influenced by their parents' lives and work. Such dispersion of children defined a permanent agricultural "proletariat," not a set of autonomous "middling" families rising or falling in status and self-control.

In North Wales the households of husbandmen and yeomen were also extremely porous. The most revealing demographic source for late seventeenth-century Wales are the St. Asaph *notitiae,* which describe most parishes in Montgomeryshire. In 1681, the same year that many Montgomeryshire Quakers prepared to leave for Pennsylvania, the bishop of St. Asaph, William Lloyd, asked his ministers to provide him with the names of the heads of households in each parish, the number of people in each household, and the number and ages of all people, including servants, who were under eighteen years of age. The ministers returned the *notitiae* between 1681 and 1687. An analysis of a sample, 16 of the 108 parishes, including 1,979 households, 8,937 people, and 3,048 children, shows remarkable family dispersion.[34]

The mountain farms of late seventeenth-century Montgomeryshire housed astonishingly few children. The percentage of the population that was under eighteen years of age was significantly smaller than in almost any other area of Britain. Gregory King, the statistician, estimated that in the 1680s over 45% of the English population was aged eighteen or under. He calculated that children and youth composed 33% of London's population, 40% of other urban areas, and 47% of the agricultural villages. The historian Peter Laslett's findings for Lichfield, Staffordshire (1695), and

TABLE 13.3   *Children Under 18 Years in 15 St. Asaph Parishes, c. 1681–84*

Parish	Population	Households	People per Household	Children	Children per Household	Percentage of Children
Aberhafesp	289	51	5.66	95	1.86	32.9
Berriew	1059	243	4.35	340	1.39	32.1
Betts Cedewain	460	109	4.22	150	1.37	32.6
Castle Caerinion	471	111	4.24	188	1.69	39.9
Cemmes	517	96	5.38	173	1.80	33.5
Darowen	313	65	4.82	114	1.75	36.4
Guildsfield	1905	409	4.66	627	1.53	32.9
Hirnant	86	26	3.30	21	.8	24.4
Landrinio	491	125	3.93	163	1.30	33.2
Landysilio	510	116	4.40	199	1.72	39
Llandyssil	383	86	4.45	115	1.34	30
Llan Elian	310	75	4.13	105	1.4	33.9
Llanwoddyn	393	76	5.2	155	2	39.4
Llanyvill	414	92	4.5	153	1.66	36.9
Meifod	1336	298	4.5	450	1.5	33.7
TOTAL	8937	1978	4.5	3048	1.54	34.1

SOURCE: Parochial Notitiae for the Diocese of St. Asaph, 1681-1687, SA/Misc/1300-1491, NLW.

Stoke-on-Trent, Staffordshire (1701), suggest the near accuracy of King's general calculations. In Lichfield, 47.5% of the population was aged nineteen or younger, and in Stoke-on-Trent 48.5% of the population was eighteen or younger.[35] But in the sixteen rural parishes of the St. Asaph *notitiae*, only 34% of the population (3,048 of 8,837) was under eighteen years of age. And 32.4% of the households in Montgomeryshire contained no children or servants under eighteen years of age. On the other hand, only 17% of the households in Clayworth, Devon, in 1688 failed to contain children, and this figure would have doubtless been even smaller if servants had been counted, as they were in the St. Asaph *notitiae*[36] (see table 13.3).

Economic backwardness, to be sure, was not invariably the cause for a low percentage of children in English localities. Gregory King figured that London had relatively few children because it was an unhealthy place, where deaths consistently outnumbered births each year, and a booming place, where annually at least 6,000 young adults from all areas of England flocked to seek both amusement and their fortunes. Promise and death made children a relatively small part of the great city's population. But Montgomeryshire was healthier than London and much less magnetic to young adults, who usually preferred city life to mountains and sheep. Thanks only to natural increase, as Leonard Owen has shown, the Welsh population rose during the seventeenth-century.[37] For example, in Meifod, Montgomeryshire (the home of Thomas Lloyd of Pennsylvania fame), 482 baptisms were registered against only 443 burials between 1667 and 1680. In 1693, an unhealthy year, 40 Meifod babies were baptized and 46 people buried: 21 adults and 25 children. Even in this bad year, Meifod gained 15 children.[38] In Meifod's *notitiae,* however, only 33.7% of the population was under eighteen years (see table 13.3) and over 27% of the households had neither servants nor children under eighteen years.

Many Montgomeryshire children vanished from the county in search of a livelihood. The *notitiae* make clear that adult servants in Montgomeryshire often crowded out youth from their usual laboring roles. Without better economic alternatives, people stayed on endlessly as servants. This is why the Welsh gentry failed to provide many places for native children. Among the 1,978 households in these sixteen parishes, there were 36 titled households, having a mean household size of 9.92 people compared to the overall mean household size of 4.5 people. Of the total population dwelling in these privileged homes, however, only 24% were seventeen years or younger, a lower percentage than that of the total population. Six gentry households, averaging 5.8 people, contained no children whatsoever. Even the largest household staffs had few children. Mathew Morgan, Esquire, maintained nineteen hungry people in his grand thirteen-hearth estate in Aberhafesp, but only one in this crew was under eighteen years of age.[39]

Local Anglican ministers understood Welsh children's unemployment and underemployment but could do little about it. "The town of Doglelley is the chief town in Merionethshire in the center of the county," wrote George Lewis in the early eighteenth century, "and hath in it many poor boys and girls, who for want of some charitable provision are forced to stroll and beg their living."[40] Dr. Joseph Jones, dean of Bangor, also sympathized with the beggar children in his parish: "they must go forever and anon to beg for victuals, their being no poor rate settled in these parts, it is the constant method to relieve the poor at their doors and the houses of the several parishes being scattered about at a considerable distance from each other increases the difficulty poor children labor under."[41] The Welsh gentry and the few wealthy yeomen, as this minister noted, often failed to finance a parish apprenticeship system to relieve hungry children. At least their neglect was not gratuitous. With few crafts, pastoral agriculture, and the retention of old servants, nobody could find parish apprenticeships economical. The beggars were not just orphans and bastards but the sons and daughters of small yeomen and husbandmen. Speaking of the newly opened charity schools, the Reverend Humphry Jones, of Glassbury, Radnorshire, noted in 1701 that many parents "would be glad to have their children taught but they are not able to find them victuals or clothes, except they stay home and do some work or go out to beg."[42] Many Welsh husbandmen sent their children south with their Welsh cottons and cattle, because they could only keep their children near home by working them on their profitless farms or as day-beggars on the mountainsides.

No economic collapse in the late seventeenth-century northwest is needed to explain this bad situation. Northwestern people did not fall by sin or economic depression from a former state of "middling" household adequacy. They had always been poor. A detailed analysis of the lay subsidy rolls of 1524 and 1585 has shown that the northwestern counties, when they were not exempted for poverty or border defense, returned only one to nine shillings an acre, compared to fifty shillings an acre for such southeastern counties as Kent, Essex, and Sussex.[43] Such deficits in productivity continued almost unchanged into the middle seventeenth century. According to a correlation of the Ship Money evaluations of 1636 with acreage in each county, Cheshire earned an evaluation of one pound for every 400 acres, the north Welsh counties earned an evaluation of one pound for every 451.8 acres, and the southeastern counties of East Anglia earned much higher evaluations: one pound for every 52 to 200 acres.[44] By the late seventeenth century, economic trends were generally helping the northwesterners. Population growth in north Wales certainly caused "middling" households severe problems in relation to child support and promotion, but lower prices for arable crops after 1660 (though a worry to southern farmers) benefited northwest livestock farmers by lowering feed and food costs. The harvests were better than average at the time of the heaviest Quaker migrations to Pennsylvania. According to W. G. Hoskins, there were seven good harvests from 1665 to 1672, only four good harvests in the 1670s, and a string of good harvests between 1680 and 1685, the major years of emigration.[45] Whether the economy improved or slumped, however, the idea of establishing a "little commonwealth" society in the northwest remained a dream.

Northwestern yeomen and husbandmen learned to live in a different style, as is demonstrated by the wills they wrote. Of course, many poor northwesterners left no wills. In a sample of 422 people between 1660 and 1688 in Cheshire, Radnorshire, and Merionethshire, only 43% of those with personal estates under £100 left wills. Yet in Merionethshire and Cheshire — the counties supplying most early Pennsylvania emigrants — 53% of such poor people did leave wills. Northwesterners defined the effective, economic family as larger than the household residence. Realizing that the household individually lacked means to feed itself and place its children, they often made intimate alliances with other households along kinship or tenant-landlord ties. Indeed, their favored bequest pattern was not nuclear, as defined in table 13.4. Only the richest families in Wales, and the richest and poorest in Cheshire gave most often exclusively to spouse, children, and grandchildren. And when poor people divided their tiny estates exclusively among nuclear family members, few had illusions about the impact of their slight help. They gave their children a few shillings, a cow, and

TABLE 13.4   *Patterns of Bequests in 253 Northwest Wills, 1660–91*

	Cheshire, 1660–81 (94)								Welsh Counties, 1670–91 (158)							
Personal Estate (£)	Nuclear		Nuclear Qualified		Extended		Single		Nuclear		Nuclear Qualified		Extended		Single	
	No.	%	No.	%	No.	%	No.	%	No.	%	No.	%	No.	%	No.	%
200+	18	64	1	4	7	25	2	7	11	85					2	15
100–199	16	53	3	10	6	20	5	17	9	47	1	5	7	37	2	11
0–99	24	67	1	3	7	19	4	11	59	46	7	6	23	18	38	30
TOTAL	58	62	5	5	20	21	11	12	79	50	8	5	30	19	42	26

SOURCES: Cheshire County Probate Records, 1660, 1681, CCRO; Merionethshire Probate Records, 1670–91, NLW; Radnorshire and Brecknockshire Probate Records, 1675, 1685, NLW.

NOTES: "Nuclear" is defined as bequeathing 95% or more of the estate to immediate family (spouse, children, grandchildren); "nuclear qualified" is 94–90% of the estate to immediate family; "extended" is less than 90% to immediate family. These bequests are made by married men and women with children or grandchildren; or widowed men and women with children or grandchildren; or married men and women without children. Singles, including bachelors, spinsters, childless widows, and widowers are placed in a separate category because defining a "nuclear" pattern for them was impossible.

some sheep, so they could make a decent deal with landlords or employers, whose needs and kindness the children would soon consult for their livelihoods.[46] Many poor men and women also involved more distant kin in their bequest plans and thereby in their real economic families. Such an extended (economic, not residential) family echoed tribal traditions, especially in Wales, and wisely kept a modicum of economic power among the shared holdings of kin and friends.

Privileged households could ignore kin, though many politically remembered poor relations and loyal tenants and servants. Robert Viscount Cholmoldely, the owner of a great fifty-eight-hearth seat in south Cheshire, gave little to the church, kin, servants, or tenants in his will. Sumptuously private, he simply gave £300 annually to his wife; £6,000 to his second son; £8,000 to his unmarried daughter; and the endless lands to his eldest son.[47] However, a quarter of the wealthiest men and women in Cheshire (those with estates above £200) gave over 10% of their estates to kin; and sometimes even more. In 1660 William Higginson, yeoman of Allostock, gave his wife and son two farms, and his grandchildren £40. He also gave a favorite nephew, Robert Higginson, two farms in fee simple, made him an executor, and entrusted him with the responsibility of paying the legacies.[48]

Among the north Welsh gentry, deep networks of local dependency were clearly visible. These people seldom shared with kin, but gave consistently small bequests, usually amounting to less than 5% of the estate, to their loyal servants and tenants. In Towyn, a riverport in Merionethshire, William Vaughan, Esquire, gave £2 to the Bangor Cathedral and £2 to repair the parish church building. He desired "my wife and son Jenkin heir-at-law to be good and charitable to and to take care of Catherine David my nurse; Rees Jones my servant; Lewis William Evan, John Thomas, John Ellis, my old servants and decayed tenants." Vaughan also "forgot" the debts of two tenants, remitted to "tenant Lewis ap Rees 5 shillings a year from the year he became my tenant," gave one servant £2, another 10 shillings, his main servant Rees Jones "the messuage where he dwelleth for natural life," a local lunatic woman maintenance for life; and his dear nurse Catherine David £2 annually. Mr. Vaughan was clearly involved in many of his people's households.[49]

For families closer to poverty, those with estates from £101 to £199, sharing with kin was a wise and frequent strategy. Thomas Boult, a butcher in Sandbach, Cheshire, with a personal estate of £138, left a wife and young son. Having a worrisome labor problem in his household, he gave his older nephew and apprentice, John Boult, all the tools, the shop, and a chamber in his house for four years. During this time, John Boult was the breadwinner and head of household. The butcher's ties to his siblings were also deep; he gave £2 to his sister and £1 to his brother.[50] The inclusion of capital, as well as labor, also explained the frequent sharing of "commonwealths." Joseph Whisham, a Cheshire yeoman in Allostock with a profitable dairy farm, owed much of his prosperity to the financial help of his mother-in-law. He had a wife, two young sons, and three daughters. He made his eldest son heir of his fee simple farm and gave his children a total of £100. He split the farm during their lives, and the livestock, evenly between his wife, Marie, and his "dear" mother-in-law, Alice Meesham. The old woman was clearly being repaid.[51]

Involvement of kin in the household was flaunted by the Welsh. Prudently wide definitions of the household economy articulated ancient tribal loyalties and dignities. Dying in 1681 with a pregnant wife and a young daughter to survive him, Morgan David, a Merionethshire yeoman, gave almost a third of his estate to his siblings and their children. The estate was divided, he proudly said, "one half to pay legacies and funeral expenses, one fourth to children, and one fourth to the wife, according to the ancient and ordinance custom of North Wales." From a personal estate of £107 he gave money, livestock, and weaving equipment worth at least £26 to his sister, two brothers, a nephew, and two nieces. The remainder went to his wife and daughter. Indeed, if his pregnant wife's unborn child survived, he or she was to get "£10 deducted from my daughter Elizabeth's share." The percentage designated for Morgan David's more extended kin network was clearly inviolable.[52]

Trying to generate more economic power than their poor households individually could muster, a large number of poorer "middling" people also involved kin in their household economies. While William Penn was reading his Pennsylvania charter, a farmer named Joseph Buckeley died in 1681 in Haughton, Cheshire with a lease for three lives, a personal estate of just £23, a wife, two young sons, and a young daughter. Deciding not to allow his nuclear family to consume his estate quickly, he included neighbors and kin in his economic family. He gave £3 to his kinsmen, John Wilson and Edward Masse, and provided an endowment of over £1 a year to his sister and, after she died, to his niece. This amounted to a remarkable share of his tiny estate.[53] In some cases the extended family erased all signs of nuclear family exclusivity. In the summer of 1678, the widower Phillip John Phillip of Landack, Merionethshire, spread his miniscule estate equally among his child, nephews, and nieces. The nephews got between 10s. and £1 apiece, the nieces got £1 apiece, and Phillip's legitimate son, Morris, got 10s. Phillip also made a nephew, rather than his son, sole executor of the estate.[54]

Married but childless men (thirty-five cases) usually favored the children of siblings above their own wives. In 87.5% of these cases the wife received only half or less of the estate, the other share going to sisters, brothers, and mostly to nieces and nephews. Childless men typically made a nephew or niece, not the wife, the heir of the lease or freehold. John Denison of Wereneter, Cheshire, gave his wife only half his tenement and half his personal estate of £107. The rest went largely to the children of his brother.[55] Also involved in the economy of the households in the northwest were the fifty-three single people who left wills (21% of the total). Controlling significant wealth, they spread their money among the children of siblings and friends. Owen Evan of Llanvair, Merionethshire, divided his £12 among a brother, sister, nephew, and six friends: the largest bequest was £2 and the smallest 2s.[56] Singles usually gave most to children. While giving a ewe to an adult male cousin, a heifer to another, and £2 to his girlfriend, William ap Arthur, husbandman, gave £2 and a calf from his £37 estate to a young nephew and £10 to another young nephew.[57]

Many poor men and women recognized that landlords, who had more wealth and power than they did, were naturally involved in their household economies and possibly in their children's futures. Many poor tenants tried to engage these landlords emotionally and financially on their children's side by paying honor and homage to them. Mary Dutton of Overton lived on land belonging to Mr. James Gerrard, so she made him an overseer of her granddaughter and named Mrs. James Gerrard an executrix of her estate.[58] James Whitelegge, a Cheshire husbandman, gave his landlady three sheep, £2, and his whip.[59] James Hease of Preston-on-the-Hill, a poor family man, offered in 1660 a five-shilling piece of gold to his master and mistress to "drink for my sake," hoping perhaps that his long service would be momentarily remembered and so would his children .[60] Indeed, gifts, needs, honor, affection, and children crossed social ranks and households easily. The nominally "middling" householders of the northwest muddled through by sharing wealth and by sharing children.

An educated Shropshire yeoman, Richard Gough, wrote a loving description of the shared family life in his Shropshire village. Gough's *History of Myddle* (1701) details the promiscuous movement of children and wealth among families. And later, as the historian Michael Anderson has recently shown, the northwesterners' tradition of economic reliance and sharing with kin helped laboring households in Lancashire adjust in the nineteenth century to the dislocations of industrialization.[61] Most northwesterners were well-served by their nonprivatized, extended family system. But in the middle of the seventeenth century, the newly arisen Quakers became disillusioned with this system. Experimenting with a new, purified sense of self, they sought to protect their greatly appreciated children from bad moral examples. Rejecting the authority of Anglican traditions and even the sole authority of the Bible, and therefore the teaching ministry and sermons, the Quakers believed that God's Word was born into every man and woman because of Christ's Resurrection and could be experienced in communal silent meetings for worship and in tender relations between Quakers, the "Light" answering the "Light." The essential features of their new, scattered communities in the northwest were Quaker meetings for worship, idiosyncratic language customs, human relations based almost solely on love and tenderness, and the holy nurture of Quaker children. Dividing human communication into a redemptive language of "the Light" (best experienced in the best Quakers) and a destructive, carnal language of the "world" (the evil ensnaring society around them), they especially hated seeing their children joining the promiscuous English labor force. John Bevan of Glamorganshire wrote that he emigrated to Pennsylvania in 1682 at his wife's demand to stop the "corruption" of his children "here by the loose behavior of youthes and the bad examples of too many of riper years."[62] Most northwesterners felt insulted and threatened by the Quakers' exclusivity. Richard Gough praised Myddle's Cromwellian pastor, Joshua Richardson, for trying with sermon and Bible to make his parishioners deeper Christians within the normal social networks. But Gough could not tolerate the Quakers' shunning of Myddle's interlocking networks of family and church life. "That phanatical, self-conceited sort of people," he huffily described the few Quakers in his parish.[63]

Unluckily, most Quakers in the northwest lacked the means to overpower the ecological limitations of the local economy and to exercise much prolonged control over their children. They were chiefly poor farmers. Among the 266 Cheshire families recorded in the Quaker registers between 1660 and 1681, only 29 (11%) lived in the five largest Cheshire towns, and only 30 (19%) lived in the fourteen market towns. There were 12 Quaker families in the city of Chester and even fewer in the other cities. Most (81%) lived in rural villages. The two largest Quaker strongholds in 1662

TABLE 13.5   *Hearth Assessments in Selected Merionethshire Parishes, 1664*

	All Households		Quaker Households	
Hearths	*No.*	*%*	*No.*	*%*
6+	10	1.1	0	0
3–5	30	3.3	3	13
2	101	11.3	4	18
1	750	84.2	15	68
TOTAL	891		22	

SOURCES: Charles Browning, *Welsh Settlement of Pennsylvania* (Philadelphia, 1912); Thomas Allen Glenn, *Merion in the Welsh Tract* (1896; reprint, Baltimore, 1970); Leonard Owen, ed., Merioneth Taxpayers of the Tudor and Stuart Periods, NLWMS, 18962d, NLW.

NOTES: The following parishes were included, as spelled by the chief assessor: Tregoray, Tregannon, Tremorva, Llangussil, Trepadgaden, Kistalgarth, Penmaine, Treredkin, Pennarth, Dolgetly, Nanney, Straelin, Lanvachreth, Keven Arrowen, Diffridon, Dolgelder, Garthgunnoth, Trebrithtyr, Tranne. Householders exempted from the tax because of poverty were not reported.

—Pownal Fee and Mobberley, which each had 21 Quaker households—sat in the rural plain of north-central Cheshire.[64] There were no real cities in Radnorshire, Merionethshire, and Montgomeryshire. Of a sample of 522 Welsh emigrants to Pennsylvania, only 3% came from even small market towns.[65]

In the "middling" northwest style, most Quaker families were poor. Barry Reay has exhaustively examined the social position of early Cheshire Quakers between 1657 and 1684. Among the men who became Quakers during these years, he found that 3% were gentry, 15% retailers, 8% artisans, 60% yeomen and husbandmen, and 4.5% laborers. From the hearth tax returns, he found that the average Cheshire household contained 1.4 hearths and the average Quaker household 1.6 hearths. Over 60% of the Quakers lived in houses with one hearth.[66] In Wales, the hearth taxes show that the overwhelming majority of Merionethshire and Montgomeryshire Quakers lived in rural parishes in one-hearth houses and cottages. Tithe seizures of forty-four Quakers between 1662 and 1681 show that their average holding in livestock and crops was a paltry £18 (see tables 13.5 and 13.6). Aside from a few wealthy families, the Quakers were small pastoral tenant farmers and craftsmen, typical powerless residents of the northwest.

The organizing of monthly meetings in the 1670s helped poor Quakers to place their children in other Quaker households in the region. Nevertheless, Quakers in the northwest were being defeated by the scarcity which had done so much to create the interlocking household system they found morally uncontrollable. Persecution, including untimely jailings and heavy fines, worsened the situation. Seeking customers and offering religious survival, the Quaker William Penn promoted his new colony of Pennsyl-

TABLE 13.6   *Estimated Annual Agricultural Income of 49 Quakers in Pembrokeshire, Carmarthenshire, and Merionethshire, based on Tithe Seizures, 1660–85*

Income (£)	No.	%
60+	2	4
50–59	3	6
40–49	2	4
30–39	6	12
20–29	5	10
10–19	14	29
0–9	17	35

SOURCES: "An Account of Particulars of the Sufferings of the People of God Called Quakers on Account of Tithes," film 239, box 172, FLL; MS Great Book of Sufferings, FLL.

NOTES: The tithe report figure has been multiplied by ten to get estimate of income. In 21 cases, estimate was based on average of 2 or more tithe seizures.

vania as the place to save Quaker familialism. He promised that Pennsylvanians could form townships of 5,000 acres, with each farmer having ample, contiguous holdings from 100 to 500 acres apiece. He advertized that cheap land would permit a "more convenient bringing up of youth" and would end English parents' addiction "to put their children into Gentlemen's service or send them to towns and learn trades."[67] Native northwestern Quakers endorsed this plan.

After seeing the Pennsylvania land in 1683, Thomas Ellis, a Quaker leader in Montgomeryshire, broke into a "Song of Rejoicing." He proclaimed the reality of a new society of retentive, fond-fostering households, newly supplied by the seemingly endless acreage. "Pennsylvania a habitation with certain, sure, and clear foundation," wrote Ellis in the first verse, "where the dawning of the day expels the thick, dark night away." Ellis had accepted old Puritan criticism about the spiritual health of his homeland. But he also gave explicit expression to Pennsylvania as a society planned to correct the religious, social, and familial abuses of "the dark corners." Being a Welshman, Ellis well understood the implications of wealth and poverty. "Lord give us here a place to feed," he wrote in the second verse, "and pass my life among thy seed, that in our bounds true love and peace from age to age may never cease." "Feed" and "seed" referred figuratively to spiritual nurture and the graced offspring of God's Word, and literally to human, animal nourishment and the natural hunger of Quakers' children. Uniting the divine and the natural, Ellis noted that the Quaker families had to be able to feed and retain their children themselves in order to promote and sustain a community of the Light. Ellis's final verse was an unembarrassed vision of parallel spiritual and economic growth: "Then shall trees and fields increase, heaven and earth proclaim thy peace that we and they — forever Lord — show forth thy praise with one accord."[68] In 1685 Ellis returned to England briefly and found some Quakers criticizing the emigrants' spiritual courage. Angered by their ignorance, Ellis wrote testily to George Fox, stressing the relationship between children and wealth:

> I wish those that have estates of their own and to leave fullness in their posterity may not be offended at the Lord's opening a door of mercy to thousands in England especially in Wales who have no estates either for themselves or children . . . nor any visible ground of hope for a better condition for children or children's children when they have gone hence.[69]

Ellis had learned that economic power and Quaker faith were intimately connected.

In the Delaware Valley between 1681 and 1720, the Welsh Quaker and Cheshire Quaker settlers developed households purposefully cleansed of the dependency and sharing they had known in Welsh and Cheshire households. As I have documented elsewhere, a sample of fifty-three Quaker settlers in Chester and in the Welsh Tract bought by the end of their lives an enormous average of 701 acres. Seventy percent of these people bought 400 acres or more. The original settlers farmed only a small percentage of this land, saving the rest for their children's marriages. This land-rich family system was designed to help parents retain and protect their children noncoercively, for in addition to this economic transformation the Quakers had already suppressed the ethic of honor, a mainstay in the northwest. Instead of honor and shame, their methods of discipline, both in the house and in the meeting, developed love through the social recognition and reproduction of motherhood, and guilt through love withdrawal. Believing that every child was born with the Light as well as Adam's sin, that children needed parental guidance and a network of good influence to develop the Light, and that the conjugal family could best perform those tasks, the Welsh Tract and Chester Monthly Meetings held parents responsible for constructing voluntary love marriages, maintaining economically viable nuclear families, and nurturing their children into love and faith.[70]

Change was not total; nor was a "golden age" quite established. Important northwestern cultural peculiarities were incorporated into the Pennsylvania Quaker familial system. The most obvious was the dispersed settlement pattern of the Welsh Tract and Chester County, direct transferrals of the dispersed settlement pattern of Wales and Cheshire. The well-known tribalistic tendencies of the Quakers' marriage code had deep, if hidden, roots in the traditional northwest reliance on kin and patronage for fostering life. In 1705 the Reverend George Ross described the Quakers around Chester with some justice as that "haughty tribe."[71] Indeed, no Quaker settler imagined that their blueprint for household economic autonomy in Pennsylvania would negate communal dependencies and larger familial loyalties. William Penn wanted Pennsylvanians to settle in townships to help achieve natural, collective childrearing. Thomas Ellis called his vision of loving, intimate, solvent households unambiguously "A Song of Rejoicing," unaware of how such households can eat away at public loyalties and meanings and can even create self-centered and self-satisfied individuals. Indeed, the new problems of such self-consciously created "little commonwealths," not the old problems of dependency, would plague Pennsylvania Quaker communities in the eighteenth century. Yet since he had only experienced shared commonwealths and household dependencies, and since he was spiritually saddened by their problems, Ellis may be forgiven for overestimating the benefits of household economic autonomy and for applauding the prolonged and deepened parent-child relations he helped to establish in Pennsylvania.

NOTES

Research and preparation of this article were made possible by grants from the Charles Rieley Armington Research Program on Values in Children, Case Western Reserve University, and by a summer grant in 1979 from the National Endowment for the Humanities.

1. George Ross to Mr. Chamberlayne, Chester, Pa., 22 Jan. 1711, in *Historical Collections Relating to the American Colonial Church,* ed. William Stevens Perry (1871; reprint, Hartford, 1969), 2:68.

2. Voltaire, *Letters on England,* trans. Leonard Tancock (London, 1960), p. 34.

3. See James Lemon, *The Best Poor Man's Country: A Geographical Study of Early Southeastern Pennsylvania* (Baltimore, 1972); James Henretta, "Families and Farms: Mentalité in Pre-Industrial America," *WMQ,* 3d ser., 35 (1978):3–32; James Lemon, "Comment on James Henretta's 'Families and Farms: Mentalité in Pre-Industrial America,'" with a "Reply" by James A. Henretta, Ibid., 3d ser., 37 (1980):688–700.

4. John Demos, *A Little Commonwealth: Family Life in Plymouth Colony* (New York, 1970), p. 183. For other influential books, usually on seventeenth-century New England, which also use this model explicitly or implicitly, see Philip J. Greven, *Four Generations: Population, Land, and Family in Colonial Andover, Massachusetts* (Ithaca, N.Y., 1970); Kenneth A. Lockridge, *A New England Town: The First Hundred Years* (New York, 1970); T. H. Breen, *Puritans and Adventurers: Change and Persistence in Early America* (New York, 1980); David Grayson Allen, *In English Ways: The Movement of Societies and the Transferal of English Local Law and Custom to Massachusetts Bay in the Seventeenth Century* (Chapel Hill, N.C., 1981).

5. Mildred Campbell, "Social Origins of some Early Americans," in *Seventeenth-Century America: Essays in Colonial History,* ed. James Morton Smith (Chapel Hill, N.C., 1959), p. 89. Note that Campbell's interesting statistics in this article must be revaluated in light of the low percentage of laboring households in the regions she studied, and the actual and traditional economic power of households she calls "middling."

6. Even those historians who have criticized the static quality of Peter Laslett's model of the pre-industrial English nuclear family have rarely attacked the economic inaccuracy of that model. See Lutz K. Berkner, "The Stem Family and the Development Cycle of the Peasant Household: An Eighteenth Century Austrian Example," *American Historical Review,* 77 (1972):398–418; idem, "The Use and Mis-

use of Census Data for the Historical Analysis of Family Structure: A Review of *Household and Family in Past Time," Journal of Interdisciplinary History,* 7 (1974):322-29; Tamara Harevan, "Cycles, Course, and Cohorts: Reflections on the Theoretical and Methodological Approaches to the Historical Study of Family Development," *Journal of Social History,* 12 (1978-79):97-109; idem, "The Family as Process: The Historical Study of the Family Cycle," *Journal of Social History* 7 (1973-74):322-29.

7. See, for example, Keith Wrightson and David Levin, *Poverty and Piety in an English Village: Terling, 1525-1700* (London, 1979); A. MacFarlane, *The Family Life of Ralph Josselin, A Seventeenth-Century Clergyman* (Cambridge, 1970). More research is clearly needed.

8. John U. Ogbu, "Origins of Human Competence: A Cultural-Ecological Perspective," *Child Development* 52 (1981):413-29; M. Cole et al., *The Cultural Context of Learning and Thinking: An Exploration in Experimental Anthropology* (New York, 1971); R. W. LeVine, *Dreams and Deeds: Achievement Motivation in Nigeria* (Chicago, 1967); A. Inkeles, "Social Structure and the Socialization of Competence," in *Socialization and Schools,* ed. Harvard Education Review (Cambridge, Mass., 1966); idem, "Society, Social Structure, and Child Socialization," in *Socialization and Society,* ed. John A. Clausen (Boston, 1968); J. W. Berry, *Human Ecology and Cognitive Style: Comparative Studies in Cultural and Psychological Adaptations* (New York, 1977).

9. For the geographical origins of seventeenth-century Massachusetts settlers, see Charles E. Banks, *Topographical Dictionary of 2885 English Emigrants to New England* (Philadelphia, 1937). A copy of the Holme map can be found in James T. Lemon, *The Best Poor Man's Country,* pp. 52-53. For an annotated list of the First Purchasers of land in Pennsylvania, see *PWP,* 2:630-64.

10. See Christopher Hill, "Puritans and 'the Dark Corners of the Land,'" in *Change and Continuity in Seventeenth-Century England,* ed. Christopher Hill (Cambridge, Mass., 1975), pp. 7-75.

11. Daniel Defoe, *A Tour Through the Whole Island of Great Britain* (London, 1724-26), p. 377.

12. E. B., "A Trip to North Wales," in *Five Travel Scripts Commonly Attributed to Edward Ward, Reproduced from the Earliest Editions Extant,* ed. Howard William Troyer (New York: Columbia University Press for the Facsimile Text Society, 1933), p. 15.

13. Ibid., p. 17.

14. Ibid.; Defoe, *A Tour,* p. 391.

15. Frank Emery, "The Farming Regions of Wales," in Thirsk, *Agrarian History,* 4:113-60; B. E. Howells, "Pembrokeshire Farming circa 1580-1620," *National Library of Wales Journal,* 9 (1955-56):239-81, 313-37, 413-39; Frank Emery, "West Glamorganshire Farming circa 1580-1620," ibid., 9:392-400; 10 (1957-58):17-32.

16. Joan Thirsk, "The Farming Regions of England," in Thirsk, *Agrarian History,* 4:80-89; J. Howard Hodson, *Cheshire, 1660-1780: Restoration to Industrial Revolution* (Chester, Eng., 1978), pp. 70-77; C. Stella Davies, *The Agricultural History of Cheshire, 1750-1850* (Manchester, Eng., 1960), passim.

17. John Lloyd of Ruthin to Edward Lloyd at Oxford, Aug. 1683, quoted in Frank Emery, "The Farming Regions of Wales," pp. 116-17.

18. D. M. Woodward, "The Chester Leather Industry, 1558-1625," *Transactions of the Historical Society of Lancashire and Cheshire,* 119 (1967):65-111; idem, "The Overseas Trade of Chester, 1600-1650," ibid., 120 (1968):23-34; J. Howard Hodson, *Cheshire, 1600-1650,* pp. 137-55; Robert Craig, "Shipping and Shipbuilding in the Port of Chester in the Eighteenth and Early Nineteenth Centuries," *Trans. Hist. Soc. Lancs. and Ches.,* 71 (1961):21-60.

19. Defoe, *A Tour,* p. 394; Peter Clark and Paul Slack, *English Towns in Transition 1500-1700* (Oxford, 1976), pp. 46-61.

20. F. C. Beazley, ed., "Hearth Tax Returns for the City of Chester, 1664-1665," *Publications of the Lancashire and Cheshire Record Society,* n. s., vol. 36 (1946); Hodson, *Cheshire, 1660-1780,* p. 97.

21. David Hey, *An English Rural Community: Myddle Under the Tudors and Stuarts* (Leicester, 1974), passim; Richard Gough, *The History of Myddle,* ed. David Hey (London, 1981), passim; D. C. Coleman, "Labour in the English Economy of the Seventeenth-Century," *Economic History Review,* 2d ser., 8 (1956):280-95.

22. Peter Laslett, "Clayworth and Cogenhoe," in *Family Life and Illicit Love in Earlier Generations: Essays in Historical Sociology* (Cambridge, 1977), pp. 50-101; Keith Wrightson and David Levine, *Poverty and Piety in an English Village: Terling, 1500-1700* (London, 1979), p. 23.

23. David W. Howell, *Land and People in Nineteenth-century Wales* (London, 1977), introd.

24. Margaret Spufford, *Contrasting Communities: English Villagers in the Sixteenth and Seventeenth Centuries* (Cambridge, 1974), pp. 25-50.

25. King's estimates are available conveniently in Peter Laslett, *The World We Have Lost* (New York, 1971), pp. 36-40.

26. Peter Bowden, "Agricultural Prices, Farm Profits, and Rents," in Thirsk, *Agrarian History,* 4:663-74.

27. Contract between John Astle and William Gamville, churchwardens, and Joseph Austin alias Longworth and Thomas Salmon, Sr., shoemaker, 19 Aug. 1701, Audlem Parish Records 1669-1809, P113/28, CCRO.

28. J. D. Marshall, ed., *The Autobiography of William Stout of Lancaster, 1665-1752* (Manchester, Eng., 1967), passim.

29. Gough, *History of Myddle,* pp. 238-39.

30. Ibid., passim.

31. Ebenezer Worchester, ed., *Frodsham Parish Church Register, 1555-1812* (Chester, Eng., 1913); Eccleston Parish Registers, 1593-1899, CCRO; M. L. Farrall, ed., *Parish Registers of the Holy and Undivided Trinity in The City of Chester, 1532-1837* (Chester, Eng., 1896); Rev. G. B. Sanford, ed., *Registers of the Parish of Church Minshull, 1561-1851* (Chester, Eng., 1850); Rev. G. E. Warburton, ed., *Warburton Parish Registers, 1611-1752* (Chester, Eng., 1896); Robert Dickinson, ed., *The Registers of the Parish Church of Gawsworth in the County of Chester* (London, 1955); Ferguson Irvine, ed., *The Register of Bruera Church, Formerly in the Parish of St. Oswald, Chester County, 1662-1812* (London, 1910). The distribution of the sample is 5, Church Minshull; 15, Gawsworth; 4, Bruera; 10, Frodsham; 4, Eccleston; 13, Chester; and 4, Warburton.

32. Wrightson and Levine, *Poverty and Piety in an English Village,* pp. 60-61.

33. Ibid., p. 47; R. M. Smith, "Population and Its Geography in England 1500-1730," in *An Historical Geography of England and Wales,* ed. R. A. Dodson and R. A. Butlin (New York, 1978), p. 217.

34. Parochial Notitiae for the Diocese of St. Asaph, 1681-1687, SA/Misc/1300-1491, NLW. Some of these have been published and edited by Milwyn Griffith in *Montgomeryshire Collections,* vols. 59 (1965), 60 (1966), 63 (1971), 66 (1977-78).

35. Laslett, *World We Have Lost,* p. 108.

36. Laslett, "Clayworth and Cogenhoe," pp. 50-101.

37. Leonard Owen, "The Population of Wales in the Sixteenth and Seventeenth Centuries," *Transactions of the Honorable Society Cymmrodorian* (1959), pp. 99-113.

38. Registers of Meiford Parish Church, Montgomeryshire, 1660-1700, St. Asaph collections, NLW.

39. Notitiae for Myvod, 1686, SA/Misc/1453, NLW; Notitiae for Aberhafesp, c. 1684, SA/Misc/1300-1302, NLW.

40. George Lewis of Dogelley to the Secretary, 14 July 1716 (document 4863) in *The Correspondence and Minutes of the S.P.C.K. Relating to Wales, 1699-1740,* ed. Mary Clements (Cardiff, 1952), p. 87.

41. Dr. Joseph Jones of Bangor to the Secretary, 20 June 1716 (document 4840), in ibid., p. 86.

42. Humphrey Jones of Glassbury, Brecknockshire to the Secretary, 23 Mar. 1701 (document 4325), in ibid., p. 76.

43. John Sheail, "The Distribution of Taxable Population and Welsh in England During the early Sixteenth-Century," *Institute of British Geographers Transactions,* no. 55 (Mar., 1972):123.

44. Charles Wilson, *England's Apprenticeship 1603-1763* (London, 1971), p. 363.

45. W. G. Hoskins, "Harvest Fluctuations and English Economic History, 1620-1759," *Agricultural History Review* 16 (1968):15-31.

46. For example, Howell Williams, husbandman of Lanegrin, Merionethshire, gave all his estate to his wife and young children. But his daughter got a marriage portion of 10s.; another daughter got £1, and his only son got only £10. Will of Howell Williams, Lanegrin, 5 Feb. 1683, Merionethshire Probate records, NLW.

47. Will of Robert Lord Viscount Chomordeley, Kells in Ireland, 23 Oct. 1681, Cheshire Probate Records, CCRO.

48. Will of William Higginson, Allostock, 18 Jan. 1660, ibid.

49. Will of William Vaughan, Esquire, Towin, 18 Sept. 1677, Merionethshire Probate Records, NLW.

50. Will of Thomas Boult, Sanbach, butcher, 12 Feb. 1660, Cheshire Probate Records, CCRO.

51. Will of Joseph Whisham, Allostock, 25 July 1681, ibid.

52. Will of Morgan David, Towin, 1 Apr. 1687, Merionethshire Probate Records, NLW.

53. Will of Joseph Buckeley, Houghton, 17 May 1681, Cheshire Probate Records, CCRO.

54. Will of Phillip John Phillip, Llandanock, 5 July 1678, Merionethshire Probate Records, NLW.

55. Will of John Denison, Wereneter, 14 May 1681, Cheshire Probate Records, CCRO.

56. Will of Owen Evan, Llanvaire, 22 Jan. 1675, Merionethshire Probate Records, NLW.

57. Will of William ap Arthur, Llandegrin, 16 Oct. 1678, ibid.

58. Will of Mary Dutton, widow, Overton, 13 Dec. 1660, Cheshire Probate Records, CCRO.

59. Will of James Whitelegge, Sharston, Northenden, 14 May 1681, ibid.

60. Will of James Hease, Preston-on-the-Hill, 6 Apr. 1660, ibid.

61. Michael Anderson, *Family Structure in Nineteenth-Century Lancashire* (Cambridge, 1971).

62. James Levick, ed., "Jon Bevan's Narrative," *PMHB,* 17 (1893):235-45.

63. Gough, *History of Myddle,* 42:172.

64. Cheshire QM Digest of births, marriages, deaths, FLL.

65. Charles Browning, *Welsh Settlement of Pennsylvania* (Philadelphia, 1912); Thomas Allen Glenn, *Merion in the Welsh Tract* (1896; reprint, Baltimore, 1970).

66. Barry Reay, "The Social Origins of Early Quakerism," *Journal of Interdisciplinary History,* 11 (1980-81):55-72.

67. William Penn, "Some Account of the Province of Pennsylvania," in *Narratives of Early Pennsylvania, West New Jersey, and Delaware 1630-1707,* ed. Albert Cook Myers (Trenton, 1967), pp. 98-99.

68. Thomas Ellis, "A Song of Rejoicing," quoted in George Smith, *History of Delaware County* (Philadelphia, 1862), p. 492. The poem was written in Welsh and soon after translated into English by Ellis's neighbor, John Humphry.

69. Thomas Ellis to George Fox, 12 June 1685, Dublin, *JFHS*, 6 (1909):173-74.

70. For the social development of the Welsh Tract and Chester Quaker communities between 1681 and 1730, see Barry Levy, "Tender Plants: Quaker Farmers and their Children in the Delaware Valley, Pennsylvania, 1681-1735," *Journal of Family History* 3 (1978):116-35. For evidence that religious ideology and community institutions, not just real estate, was crucial to the Quaker Family system in the Delaware Valley, see Barry Levy, "The Birth of the 'Modern Family' in Early America: Quaker and Anglican Families in the Delaware Valley, Pennsylvania, 1681-1750," in *Friends and Neighbors: Group Life in America's First Plural Society,* ed. Michael Zuckerman (Philadelphia, 1982), pp. 26-64.

71. George Ross to the Secretary, Chester, 30 Dec. 1712, in *Historical Collections,* ed. Perry, p. 69.

14 ❧ *William Penn's Scottish Counterparts:*

The Quakers of "North Britain" and the Colonization of East New Jersey

The World of William Penn was a Quaker world and an Anglo-American world. We know Penn today principally for his role in the establishment of the Pennsylvania colony, but his interests as a colonizer were far more wide-ranging than that. Within the British Isles of his day, Penn had substantial Irish properties, and he had close connections also among Quaker gentlemen in Wales and Scotland, or "North Britain," as the latter was often called by Anglophilic Scotsmen. Penn, in short, had ties with much of what were then the outlying areas of Britain, and with parts of the Continent as well. Even Penn's New World interests were broader than is often recognized; he was involved in the settlement not only of Pennsylvania but also of the neighboring colonies of East and West New Jersey, which were planned to stand alongside of Pennsylvania as major outposts of the Quaker world. Penn, in fact, played an important early role in bringing settlers from the outlying areas (Scotland, Ireland, and Wales) into the Middle Colonies.[1]

In all of those places, Penn's primary connections were with members of the Quaker movement. East and West Jersey both began largely as Quaker colonies, and it was Penn's goal to establish a Friends' dominion over the whole of the Mid-Atlantic region, including Pennsylvania, both Jerseys, and Delaware. That area, and especially Pennsylvania, was in-

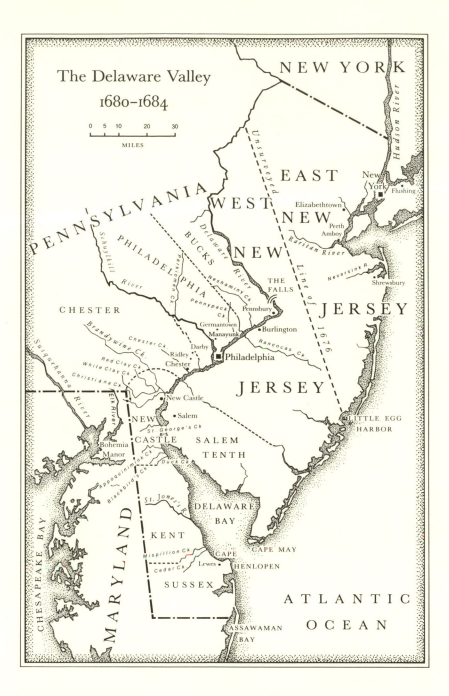

The Delaware Valley
1680–1684

0 5 10   20   30
MILES

NEW YORK

PENNSYLVANIA

Hudson River

Schuylkill River

PHILADELPHIA

Perkiomen Ck

BUCKS

Delaware River

Unsurveyed

EAST

WEST

NEW

NEW

New York

Flushing

Elizabethtown

Perth
Amboy

Raritan River

Neversink R.

Shrewsbury

CHESTER

Brandywine Ck.

Chester Ck.

Neshaminy Ck.

Pennypack Ck.

THE
FALLS

Line of 1676

JERSEY

Pennsbury

Germantown

Manayunk

Darby

Ridley

Red Clay Ck.

White Clay Ck.

Christiana Ck.

Chester

Burlington

Rancocas Ck.

Philadelphia

JERSEY

Susquehanna River

Elk River

New Castle

Salem

NEW

LITTLE EGG
HARBOR

Bohemia
Manor

CASTLE

St. George's Ck

SALEM

TENTH

Appoquinimink Ck

Duck Ck.

Blackbird's Ck

St. Jones's R.

DELAWARE

BAY

CHESAPEAKE BAY

MARYLAND

KENT

Mispillion Ck.

Cedar Ck.

Lewes

CAPE

HENLOPEN

CAPE MAY

SUSSEX

ATLANTIC

OCEAN

ASSAWAMAN
BAY

MAP 14.1

tended to serve as an international Quaker homeland, attracting Friends from England, Wales, Scotland, Ireland, and elsewhere in Europe.[2]

To achieve that goal, Penn created a wide recruiting network employing agents in places as far removed as Bristol, Lancashire, Dublin, and Amsterdam, and he sought to establish others in Scotland, Ulster, and Europe. In so doing, Penn sowed the seeds of his own failures. For if Penn's Quaker contacts in those areas shared his loyalty to Quakerism, they did not necessarily share his goal of Friends' hegemony within English colonies. They worked instead to promote the settlement and the interests of their own countrymen in the area. The settlers from those places blended inharmoniously into Penn's colonies, if indeed they blended at all.

This essay will examine the role of one of the outlying areas — Scotland — in the early settlement of the Middle Colonies. Although that country later would be renowned for its role in the American colonization and settlers of Scottish descent would abound throughout the colonies, the peoples of Scotland were relative latecomers to colonization. It was largely through the efforts of William Penn that Scotsmen first were induced to settle in the colonies.[3]

Penn's goal was to recruit Scottish Friends for Pennsylvania. His Scottish contacts, from the beginning, had other plans. Rather than submerging their efforts under the banner of a common Quaker cause, the Scots developed a general Scottish, rather than a Quaker, colonizing effort. Indeed, much to Penn's disappointment, they abandoned Pennsylvania entirely, in favor of a new Scottish colony 'in East New Jersey. Their actions reflect a substantial misunderstanding by Penn of the degree of unity that existed within the British and Quaker worlds.

When William Penn began organizing his Pennsylvania venture in 1679, one of the men to whom he turned for assistance was Scotsman Robert Barclay, sometimes called "Barclay the Apologist" for his authorship of the well-known *Apology for the True Christian Divinity as held by the People Called Quakers*. Barclay was the owner or "laird" of the estate of Urie in Kincardineshire, located along Scotland's northeastern coast about a dozen miles south of Aberdeen. Some of Barclay's relatives were exceptionally prominent: his grandfather was Sir Robert Gordon of the powerful house of Gordonstoun. Two cousins — James, the earl of Perth and his brother, Viscount Melfort, both of whom were to join Barclay as East Jersey proprietors — were among Scotland's leading Restoration politicians.[4]

In the annals of British Quakerism, Barclay is a well-known figure, standing right alongside such other prominent Friends of the day as George Fox and William Penn; Penn and Barclay, in fact, were regular correspondents. What should not be forgotten in considering Barclay's life is the remoteness of his origins. In the last quarter of the seventeenth century, Scotland constituted, by almost any definition, one of Britain's outlying areas. Just how far Scotland was removed from the center of English society requires an act of historical imagination to comprehend. Few Englishmen visited Scotland, and those who did venture north brought back reports more reminiscent in style of the ethnographer than the traveler. This applied even to visitors who journeyed only as far as the Lowlands, the more Anglicized and only English-speaking area of Scotland. Everything from the unusual manners of the commonfolk to their clothing to their habitats were objects of curiosity and not a little scorn on the part of the visitors. No less a reporter than Daniel Defoe would report back from his first stop in Scotland that

> The first Town we come to is as perfectly *Scots* as if you were 100 miles North of Edinburgh; nor is there the least appearance of anything English, either in Customs, Habits, Usages of the People, or in their Way of Living, Eating, Dress or Behaviour, any more than if they had never heard of an English Nation.[5]

Other visitors were less favorable in their characterizations. It was not difficult to tell when one had arrived in Scotland, John Loveday recorded: "We pass'd over the Esk-Water, and so came into Scotland, as the houses would easily have convinced us, being — some of 'em — mud cots cover'd with Turf."[6]

Scotland was remote from England not only in its appearance but in its whole social system as well. The Scottish social order was unusually stratified and hierarchical and was based upon Roman law. At the top of the social scale, Scotland had a far smaller percentage of landowners than did England, with an average of only about five per parish in most areas. The vast majority of the rural population worked as tenants or servants, and there were almost no Scottish freeholders anywhere but in a small area of the southwest. Scotland's landowners were unusually powerful also; there were no common rights in Scotland, and no equivalents to the English systems of copyholding or customary tenancy. Landowners had almost unrestricted authority over the habitation of their lands, and by all indications, they used that authority to keep close control over the movements of tenants onto and off of their estates.[7]

The Scottish society that the visitors observed was not wholly unique. Some of the same reporters who denigrated Scotland's curiosities conceded that the customs of the people of northern England were little better. As John Loveday wrote, "Tis amusing to hear the English Borderers . . . damn their neighbor Scots in *their own* Language."[8] In this respect at least Scotland was an outlying region not in relation to England as a whole, but only to its cultural center in London and the southeast. In several particulars, Scotland very much resembled some of Britain's other outlying areas.

One very noticeable element that Scotland shared with some of the other outlying areas was its settlement pattern. Scotland's countryside was not settled in villages, as was the English Midlands, nor was it divided into the enclosed farming units of England's southeast. Instead, the countryside was dotted with small hamlets or "farmtouns" as they were called in Scotland, just as were the countrysides of northern and western England, Wales, and Ireland. A farmtoun was much smaller than a village; where a typical village might contain 50, 100, or even 150 households, farmtouns contained from 2 to perhaps 10, with 6 to 8 as the most common size. Many farmtouns were operated by joint tenants, and often involved a substantial amount of cooperative effort.[9]

What distinguished Scotland from the north of England was not so much its social landscape as its cultural traditions. Before the Union of Parliaments of 1707, there had been many centuries of antagonism between the two countries, and the national boundary itself had moved north and south several times over the years during recurrent border wars. Border clans from both sides regularly staged raids across the frontier and returned with impunity, outside the realm of the law. It was in the border regions, in fact, that the legacy of national conflicts traditionally found its most extreme expressions: in Scotland's border ballads, for example, the greatest number of which tell tales of national conflicts and border wars.[10]

Scotland's place within the British World did not go unchanged during the seventeenth century. Despite its isolation, Scotland gradually was being drawn into England's cultural orbit by political and economic changes, starting with the Union of Crowns in 1603. A particular impetus to that movement was the civil war of mid-century, during which Scottish troops fought first on the side of the parliamentarians and later against Cromwell's army. In the course of that war, Scotsmen traveled to England, and Englishmen in turn were stationed north of the border. The Civil War and Interregnum marked the first exposure of Scots to the radical sectarians in the New Model Army—the Quakers, for example—a point to which we will return later.[11]

After the Restoration, national contacts continued less through political than economic means. There was a substantial growth in Scottish trade in the last third of the seventeenth century, most of it with England. Virtually all of that linked the eastern coast of Scotland—principally Edinburgh and Aberdeen—with London and England's eastern ports. The west of Scotland, which was to be so important in the tobacco trade of the eighteenth century, remained relatively uninvolved in Scotland's mercantile activities.[12]

Increasing contact between Scottish and English groups began to affect cultural life in Scotland in the second half of the seventeenth century, particularly in religious affairs, as a variety of English sects gained footholds in Scotland. Not surprisingly those sects, together with the Church of England, made their greatest headway in areas where (and among groups for whom) contacts with the English were the greatest: Edinburgh and the capital region, and especially the northeastern Lowlands around Aberdeen.

Among the Quakers, for example, three of the five monthly meetings in Scotland were located in the northeast (the others were in Edinburgh and Glasgow), as were the majority of local meetings.[13]

No group in Scotland was more affected by English contacts than those who were to join the Friends. Quakerism took root in Scotland principally through the influence of the two most Anglicized groups: the merchants and the landed gentlemen, the only groups who had the means to travel and confront English ways. All of the Quaker meetings were located either within commercial centers or on gentlemen's estates. From the descriptions of English travelers, it is quite apparent that the elite of the northeast — where Quakerism was strongest — was in fact the most Anglicized group in Scotland. John Macky, for example, wrote that the inhabitants of that region were "more courteous, familiar, and affable, than in the Southern parts of *Scotland,* and seem to be another People," while Daniel Defoe reported that northeastern gentlemen had "the politest and brightest Education and Genius of any People so far North, perhaps in the World, being always bred in travel Abroad and in the Universities at Home." Robert Barclay was a good example of such a person: he received a continental education and visited England on many occasions.[14]

To be a Scottish Quaker in the seventeenth century was to maintain a somewhat ambiguous identity. The Friends were among Scotland's most Anglicized groups, and Quakerism itself was a religion brought into Scotland through English influences. To be a Quaker was to adopt an English religion in a society that did not take kindly to all things English. Indeed, Presbyterianism, the national Church of Scotland, had as its major claim to success that it was the only major Scottish religion that was not English in origin. Presbyterian ministers frequently employed anti-English rhetoric, and the religion received widespread support in most of the Lowlands, especially in the border regions.[15]

The identity of the Scottish Friends was ambiguous in another respect also. While Quakerism took root among Scotland's most Anglicized groups, the areas in which it thrived were those that least resembled England in social structure. If the most distinctive features of the Scottish social order were the unusual prerogatives of the landed class and the absence of a class of small landowners, then the northeastern social order was Scottish to an extreme. In that region, the estates of the landowners were the largest, the holdings of the tenants the smallest, and the position of the lower orders the most precarious of any lowland region. Indeed, the position of the lower orders was so tenuous that for common persons, the "disappearance rate" approached 90 percent per decade in many parishes.[16]

The conduct of affairs on Robert Barclay's Urie estate was representative of these seemingly conflicting trends in northeastern society. By any standard, Barclay was among Scotland's most Anglicized gentlemen, yet there was nothing English about the operation of Urie. Barclay kept at least as close control of the habitation of his lands as did his non-Quaker peers, and Barclay's tenants were removed regularly from his lands. Sometimes the removals were forcible, according to the records of the Urie barony court, for such offenses as "illegal shearing" or "laboring a piece of controverted ground." Almost no tenants remained at Urie for any great length of time, the principal exceptions being a small group of Quaker tenants who moved to Urie specifically to join the meeting that Barclay sponsored. (Friends were persecuted in places where no Quaker patron resided.)[17]

The ambiguous identity of the Scottish Friends was evident in Barclay's activities as soon as William Penn approached the Scotsman about supporting the Pennsylvania colony. Barclay discussed the matter with his Scottish colleagues and reported back that several of his countrymen would consider investing, including Quakers and non-Quakers. From that point Barclay's correspondence with his fellow Quaker became a quest for better terms for the Scots. Barclay first insisted that Penn reserve First Purchaser rights for his colleagues, even though they had not yet definitely decided to invest. He then began to bargain for other advantages, playing off Pennsylvania against the Jersey colonies, all the while insisting that the Scots were reluctant to invest only because they were "so ignorant" in matters of colonization. Barclay was well-informed when it came to colonial land values, however: "thou has land enough so need not be a churle iff thou intend to advan[c]e thy plant[at]ion," he chastized Penn in the midst of the negotiations.[18]

More than the high price of Pennsylvania lands concerned Barclay and his colleagues. In December 1681 the Scotsman wrote to Penn that his countrymen would join the enterprise only if they were permitted to maintain direct trade connections with Scotland using Scottish ships. Later he asked that the Scottish lands be granted in a single tract of thirty thousand acres. Already there were hints that the colonization efforts of the Scottish Friends were turning out to be more Scottish than Quaker.[19]

The following year Barclay and his colleagues decided to forego investing in Pennsylvania and obtain instead a more substantial Scottish share of the Quaker colony at East New Jersey. The East Jersey proprietors offered Barclay a free propriety, or one-twenty-fourth share of the colony, on the condition that he recruit four additional proprietors. Barclay's decision effectively ended the involvement of Scottish Friends in Penn's colony; among 589 First Purchasers in Pennsylvania only 2 were "Scotsmen" — George Keith and Arent Sonmans — and even Sonmans was not a native of Scotland.[20]

Once Barclay and his associates opted for East Jersey, they did their best to turn it into a Scottish enterprise. The laird of Urie devoted much time and effort to East Jersey and recruited five other Scots as proprietors. Under Barclay's direction, the Scots systematically sold off fractions of their shares to other Scots, so that by 1684 a full twelve proprieties, one-half of the colony, were in the hands of more than fifty Scottish investors. Barclay established his own network of agents throughout the Scottish world, from Galloway to Belfast, so that more than ninety Scottish merchants and gentlemen were involved in the colonizing effort.[21]

In recruiting those proprietors, agents, and "fractioners" (as the lesser shareholders came to be called), Barclay directed his efforts to creating a Scottish interest, but not necessarily a Quaker interest, in the colony. Three of the original six proprietors were Quakers; the others were Episcopalians with close court connections. Only about a third of the fractioners were Friends (no more than eighteen of fifty-three), while Episcopalians formed a majority of the remainder. (Quakerism and Episcopalianism were the two principal communions among the northeastern gentry.) For Barclay, local ties evidently were at least as important as religious connections: almost half (twenty-five) were members of the northeastern elite, with gentlemen represented more heavily than merchants. Only about half of that group belonged to the Quakers.[22]

In the recruitment of settlers also the Scottish proprietors sought to attract persons who were Scottish rather than simply Quaker. The Scots collectively published six pieces of promotional literature to attract people to their colony, all of which were addressed to an audience of Scots in general, whatever their particular backgrounds. In two publications, the Scots specifically sought to allay the fears of their non-Quaker countrymen by addressing (and then refuting) the question of the possible disadvantages the colony might fall under by having a Quaker governor (Barclay). They stressed instead the advantages of having a governor who was also a Scotsman.[23]

From those early efforts, the Scottish proprietors recruited more than six hundred of their countrymen to emigrate to East Jersey during the 1680s, about half of whom went as indentured servants. These settlers came from a variety of religious backgrounds, with Quaker settlers a clear minority among the Scots. The bulk of the colonists derived from the east and northeast, the homes of most of the proprietors, and some had close connections to members of the proprietary group. Several of Barclay's Urie tenants ventured to East Jersey, for example, as did the tenants of other proprietors and fractioners, both Quaker and non-Quaker. Some of the servants were recruited through Quaker meetings, but overall local connections played a far greater role than did particular religious ties, and the composition of the settlers reflected more of a regional (eastern and northeastern) than a religious character.[24]

That Barclay and his colleagues were willing to abandon almost all religious ties in the colonization effort is evident by their actions in the year 1685. At that time, Scotland's jails were filled with religious prisoners, almost all Presbyterians who were opposed to the government put in place by the Stuarts. They had refused to take the "Test Oath," which renounced Scotland's national covenants. To Barclay, those prisoners provided an opportunity to increase Scottish settlement, and he petitioned the Privy Council for an allocation of prisoners for East Jersey. More than one hundred such prisoners were sent to the colony, and they formed the core of what would be a growing Presbyterian influence within the Scottish settlement.[25]

Under Barclay's direction, the Scottish proprietors—Quaker and non-Quaker—banded together in an effort to keep their interests in the colony distinct from those of the other Quaker proprietors. Even before Barclay officially had recruited any other proprietors, he had drawn up a plan to have one-fourth of the colony's lands separated from the rest and reserved as "Scots lots." When the Scots obtained half of the proprietorships, they issued a new directive, ordering that half of all of the colony's lands be designated Scots lots. And instead of relying on the colony's English surveyor to divide those properties, Barclay hired his own countryman, John Reid, to subdivide the Scottish lands. The Scots then embarked upon an ambitious settlement scheme and in the year 1683 sent a shipload of servants to the colony upon their joint account.[24]

At the time the Scots first became interested in East Jersey, the colony's English proprietors already had drawn up settlement plans for the colony. The Scots acting together countermanded those orders and issued new directives for the Scottish lands. Where the English proprietors had allowed for the selling either of farms or of fractions of proprieties in the colony, the Scots forbade the selling of farms and allowed only fractions to be sold out of their interest. By that plan, each landowner would receive at least five hundred acres. And where the English proprietors had authorized their agents to sell off the quitrents to their lands for fees equal to twelve years' rent, the Scots forbade the selling of quitrents, and instructed that any such rents that had already been sold were to be deducted from the English proprietors' interests in the colony.[27]

The society the Scots envisioned was to be based upon the hierarchical society of Scotland's northeast. It was to be dominated by landed estates farmed by tenants and servants, not unlike the "manors" William Penn planned for Pennsylvania. Where the Scots' plan differed from Penn's was in the inclusiveness of the estates; there were to be no small farms in East Jersey's Scottish lands, according to the proprietary plan, just as there were none in the northeast. Individual estates in East Jersey were to be grouped into clusters, or "neighborhoods" of estates, and deputy governor Gawen Lawrie recommended that each proprietor send thirty or forty servants immediately and more later on.[28]

Everything about the Scottish settlement resembled Britain's outlying areas, including the shape of the landscape. Within a few years, proprietors and fractioners had established several clusters of landed estates located on the colony's "Scots' lots" in the Blew Hills and along the Cedar Brook and the north and south branches of the Raritan River. The Cedar Brook settlement became so popular that by 1685 six Scottish fractioners had settled a total of fifty servants — both Quaker and non-Quaker — at that locale. In a letter to Scotland from that neighborhood, fractioner James Johnstone requested a Presbyterian minister for the new settlement.[29]

Not all of the land in the Scottish sections of the colony was divided into estates or large farms. Especially after 1687, when the indentures of the first servants began to expire, some of the ordinary Scottish settlers began to take up farms in smaller units. Even then, their settlements remained quite different in form from those established by English settlers. Rather than creating individual farms of fifty or a hundred acres, most of the Scottish servants obtained lands together with other servants grouped in clusters that resembled farmtouns. Many petitioned jointly for their lands. Within the small clusters they created, there is some evidence that settlers pooled tools and plows in the early years.[30]

The Scots showed considerable fidelity to Old World settlement patterns. In 1687 a group of seventeen servants petitioned the proprietors for lands located at the Blew Hills, near the proprietary estates. According to the norms of Scottish society, this was far too large for a single settlement, and only six remained at the Blew Hills, while the others dispersed. Five of the others then took up adjoining lands along the Taponemus River in Monmouth County, in what was to become Freehold. This settlement too began to grow, and a few years later a group of six settlers broke away from Taponemus and established a new settlement nearby.[31]

Within a very few years, the Scots had turned the landscape of their portion of the colony into something that resembled an outlying area, composed of estates and small hamlets. The distribution of the population on the Scottish lands visibly contrasted with that on the neighboring English settlements, which were created primarily by migrants from New England and were established either as villages or independent farmsteads. This contrast was heightened by a tradition of substantially separate settlement on the part of the Scottish colonists; both Quaker and non-Quaker settlers clustered within distinctive Scottish areas. The Scots moved frequently within the colony, but the movement almost always took them from one Scottish settlement to another. And there is every indication that the primary interactions even of Scottish Friends were with other Scottish settlers much more than they were with other Quakers.[32]

Ultimately, many Scottish Quakers not only limited their interactions with other Friends; they ceased to be Friends entirely. After arriving in East Jersey and settling among English Quakers, many of the Scots decided not to remain Quakers. Some joined the Episcopal church, the predominant church of the northeastern gentry. Others joined the Presbyterian church, the national church of Scotland, which gradually became their predominant communion. Still others remained Friends, but even they ceased to join with or attend the English meetings.[33]

The pivotal figure in the Quaker schism was George Keith, born in the shire of Aberdeen, who came to the colonies in 1685 to serve as East Jersey's surveyor. Keith was a close associate of Barclay and Penn and a First Purchaser in Pennsylvania. Initially the Scotsman settled in Freehold along with several associates, and there he joined the Taponemus meeting. In 1689 Keith left for Pennsylvania, and soon thereafter he began quarreling with that colony's Quaker leadership over such issues as ministerial authority and what Keith perceived to be a lack of doctrinal emphasis among the Pennsylvania Friends.[34]

Although historians have analyzed the Keithian schism from many perspectives, few have considered the ethnic component of the schism. Within East Jersey, at least, it was of major importance. When Keith split away from the Pennsylvania Friends, he brought most of East Jersey's Scottish Quakers with him. In 1692 the Scottish Taponemus meeting separated from the monthly meeting for what were described as the "gross errors" of the English Friends. Local Quakers clearly recognized the ethnic component of the Keithian movement; in 1706, for example, when a young Scottish woman appeared before the Shrewsbury meeting to announce her intention to marry, the meeting, in an unusual move, first required her acknowledgment that she "never did join with George Keith nor his company."[35] Apparently it was assumed that a Scottish settler was likely to have joined her countrymen as a Keithian.

The long-term trend among Scottish Keithians was away from Quakerism and into their national church. For many, Episcopalianism served as a halfway house. By the second quarter of the eighteenth century, only proprietary families retained a substantial degree of Episcopal membership (as did much of the gentry in Scotland), and the churches they joined were staffed by ministers of the Scottish Episcopal church. Almost all of the rest became Presbyterians.[36]

What happened to the Scottish Quakers can be illuminated by turning our attention to the individual transatlantic lives of a few of Robert Barclay's comrades. For Barclay, no members of the proprietary group would have held more significance than his younger brothers, David and John. In Scotland, landed estates were governed by the laws of primogeniture. Since Robert, as the eldest son, inherited the whole of the Urie property, his brothers had to seek other means of support; mercantile activities in particular seem to have been common for younger sons within the Barclay family. In 1683 the elder Barclay gave brother David an East Jersey propriety and instructed him to take charge of the family's New World interests. When David died at sea, that task, as well as the propriety, passed to brother John.

John Barclay moved to East Jersey in 1684 and settled in Perth Town, the new capital city located at Ambo Point, where he joined the local Quaker meeting. He also took up a landed estate at Cedar Brook with other Scotsmen, where he sent his servants. Apparently John was a much less imposing figure than his eldest brother, and he never attained substantial influence either within the town's growing elite or within the colony as a whole; instead he held a series of minor positions in the colony. In later years his descendants became rather ordinary farmers in the surrounding countryside. Barclay himself joined Keith in leaving Quakerism for the Episcopal church; the bulk of his family ended up within the Presbyterian communion.[37]

In running their estates, gentlemen such as Robert Barclay always could find use for a variety of agents. One man who was employed by two of Barclay's proprietary colleagues was John Reid, a gardener in Scotland. In 1683 Reid completed a long book entitled *The Scots Gardener for the Climate of Scotland* (a book, incidentally, that advocated the adoption of many English farming practices in Scotland). That same year Reid went to East Jersey to supervise that colony's Scottish indentured servants. Apparently Reid was an aggressive individual, and he was able to use his position to obtain a large farm in Freehold for himself, much to the displeasure of several of the proprietors. Reid became a wealthy farmer, and his descendants lived on his estate for generations. During the 1680s, Reid was an important member of the local monthly meeting, but he too followed Keith into the Episcopal church. Unlike the downwardly mobile Barclay family, most of the Reids were successful and remained within that elite communion.[38]

Quaker gentlemen in Scotland often had Quaker tenants, who moved to their estates to attend the meetings that the patrons sponsored. One such tenant was William Redford, who lived in the Border county of Roxburgh under the patronage of Barclay's close friend Arent Sonmans. In 1683 Redford contracted with Sonmans to go to East Jersey as a tenant for ten years. Upon completing his tenancy in 1693, Redford moved to Taponemus, where the local meeting recently had joined Keith in separating from the English Friends, and Redford presumably joined them. Redford remained a small farmer, and, as is often the case with such individuals, the story of his later years remains obscure. Both Redford and his wife were buried in the Presbyterian churchyard.[39]

Ultimately the entrance of the Scots into the East Jersey colonization proved disruptive not only of Quaker meetings but also of the politics of what was originally a Quaker colony and the whole Quaker experiment there. Until 1683 colonial affairs were controlled by English proprietors meeting in London. After that date the Scots, meeting in Aberdeen, formed a countervailing force, overturning many of the English proprietors' plans. By 1685 real power in the colony shifted from both British groups to a new group, the resident board of proprietors, composed of proprietors and fractioners living in the colony who took control of land policy. That group was dominated by Scots (six of seven members) and non-Quakers.[40]

Quite quickly, the proprietary board fell into conflict with the colony's English settlers over the issue of land titles. At the time the proprietors took over the rights to East Jersey, there were already six townships located in the northern section of the colony, some inhabited by English Quakers, each of which claimed the ownership of lands located well beyond the settled bounds of the towns. Some of this land was claimed by Scottish proprietors. To uphold their claim to these lands, the proprietors began granting lands to Scottish indentured servants within what they described as the "pretended bounds" of Elizabethtown, a situation that put ordinary Scottish settlers directly into conflict with their English neighbors.[41]

Another source of controversy arose in 1696, when the Company of Scotland, or "Darien Company," attempted to create an overseas trading colony in Central America. This was a nationalistic venture and was opposed by the English government, which forbade any of the colonists from aiding the Scottish company. Evidently some of the East Jersey Scots were sympathetic to Darien, including some Quakers. The Scottish company directed the venturers to contact one James Dundas of Perth Amboy, who had "suffered much by the English" there. Several other Scots were called before local courts and compelled to post bonds for their good behavior, meaning that they would not aid the expedition. For several years thereafter, the dominant political issue in the colony was whether or not East Jersey could legally employ a Scottish governor.[42]

The culmination of those disputes occurred in 1700, with the outbreak of a series of antiproprietary riots in the colony. The largest disturbance, in the town of Freehold, involved an attack by English residents upon Scottish supporters of the proprietary government, including a few who were or had been Quakers. In the aftermath of those events, the Scots almost to a man became supporters of the proprietors' political positions, and ethnic issues and allegations repeatedly were introduced into local political campaigns. This support transcended all religious bounds. Describing the political situation in the Jerseys to the Lords of Trade in 1703, Colonel Robert Quarry wrote:

> The Contests of West Jersey have always been betwixt the Quakers and her majestys subjects that are no Quakers. . . . The contest in East Jersey is of a different nature, whether the country shall be a Scotch settlement or an English settlement.[43]

When William Penn first solicited Robery Barclay's participation in the American colonization, his goal was to increase support for the Quaker effort and to expand the dimensions of the transatlantic Quaker world. But in recruiting Friends from north of the border, Penn incorporated into his colonies a group with substantially different social and cultural traditions. In Britain, Quakers were a minority almost everywhere, and those differences were not always apparent. In the New World, many dissimilarities were brought to light, and in important respects, the Scottish Quakers turned out to be more Scots than Quaker. To join Barclay's venture — unlike that of Penn — one needed to be a Scotsman rather than a Friend. The Scots developed a separate interest in the colony, separate areas of settlement, a distinctive landscape and settlement pattern, and — after the arrival of Keith — a separate religion as well. Such developments proved to be extremely disruptive of the Quaker experiment and took East Jersey out of the orbit of the other Friends' colonies.

The East Jersey episode can serve as a prelude to what happened to the Quaker experiment elsewhere in the Middle Colonies. In Pennsylvania, Quaker authority would be disrupted largely by a group of Ulster Scots who were, in origin and in religion, even further removed from English Friends than Barclay's group. Historians have often attributed the influx of Ulstermen and other groups into Pennsylvania to the tolerance of the Quakers, but more than tolerance was involved; Penn actively encouraged the participation of Friends from Europe and the outlying areas in his colony, and they in turn often brought in their non-Quaker countrymen. The most important of those Friends was James Logan, an Ulsterman and Penn's personal secretary, who was instrumental in initiating the first settlement of his predominantly Presbyterian countrymen in Pennsylvania. Included among those settlers was Logan's cousin, William Tennent, the founder of the most influential Presbyterian family in the Middle Colonies. Together with the descendants of Barclay's settlers, those colonists from Ulster formed a powerful Presbyterian interest in the Delaware Valley and an important counter to Quaker authority in the region.[44]

NOTES

1. On the Jersey colonies, see John E. Pomfret, *The Province of West New Jersey, 1609-1702* (Princeton, 1950); idem, *The Province of East New Jersey, 1609-1702* (Princeton, 1962); see also Barry J. Levy, "The Light in the Valley: The Chester and Welsh Tract Quaker Community and the Delaware Valley, 1681-1750" (Ph.D. diss., University of Pennsylvania, 1976); and the essay by Nicholas Canny in this volume.

2. Penn's plans for his colony can be traced in *PWP*, vol. 2.

3. The best account of Scottish colonization in East Jersey is George Pratt Insh, *Scottish Colonial Schemes, 1620-1686* (Glasgow, 1922), chaps. 5-6; chapter 6 discusses the almost simultaneous Scottish colonization effort in Carolina. Useful discussions of Scottish colonization generally can be found in Ian Graham, *Colonists from Scotland: Emigration to North America, 1707-1783* (Ithaca, N. Y., 1956); and Malcolm Gray, "Scottish Emigration: The Social Impact of Agrarian Change in the Rural Lowlands, 1775-1875," *Perspectives in American History,* 7 (1973):95-174.

4. D. Elton Trueblood, *Robert Barclay* (New York, 1967); John E. Pomfret, "The Proprietors of the Province of East New Jersey," *PMHB,* 76 (1952):251-93.

5. Defoe, *A Tour Through the Whole Ireland of Great Britain* (London, 1724-27), 3:6; see also P. Hume Brown, *Early Travellers in Scotland* (Edinburgh, 1891); Sir Arthur Mitchell, *A List of Travels and Tours in Scotland* (Edinburgh, 1902); and idem, *Supplementary List of Travels in Scotland* (Edinburgh, 1905). Many of Barclay's letters to Penn are published in *PWP*, vols. 1-2 passim.

6. Loveday, *Diary of a Tour in 1702 Through Parts of England, Wales, Ireland, and Scotland* (Edinburgh, 1890), p. 110.

7. Lord Normand, ed., *An Introduction to Scottish Legal History* (Edinburgh, 1958), pp. 13-16; T.C. Smout, *A History of the Scottish People 1560-1830* (New York, 1969), chaps. 5-6; Ned C. Landsman, *Scotland and Its First American Colony, 1683-1765* (Princeton, 1985), chap. 1.

8. Loveday, *Diary of a Tour*, p. 165.

9. Walton G. Whittrington, "Scottish Field Systems," in *Studies in the Field Systems of the British Isles*, ed. A. R. Baker and R. Butlin (Cambridge, 1973), chap. 12; Gray, "Scottish Emigration"; Kenneth Walton, "The Distribution of Population in Aberdeenshire, 1696," *Scottish Geographical Magazine*, 66 (1950):17-26. On Western England and Wales, see *Studies in Field Systems*, ed. Baker and Butlin; and Thirsk, *Agrarian History*, vol. 4, chap. 1.

10. See William Ferguson, *Scotland's Relations with England: A Survey to 1707* (Edinburgh, 1977); D. L. W. Tough, *Last Years of a Frontier: A History of the Borders During the Reign of Elizabeth* (Oxford, 1928); James Tait, *Two Centuries of Border Church Life* (Kelso, 1889); John Veitch, *The History and Poetry of the Scottish Borders* (Edinburgh, 1893), esp. vol. 2, chap. 4.

11. George Burnet, *The Story of Quakerism in Scotland, 1650-1850* (London, 1952), chap. 1 passim.

12. T. C. Smout, *Scottish Trade on the Eve of the Union, 1660-1707* (Edinburgh, 1963), pp. 2-14; see also Jacob M. Price, "The Rise of Glasgow in the Chesapeake Tobacco Trade," *WMQ*, 3d ser., 11 (1954):179-99.

13. Digest of the Records of Births, Marriages and Deaths in Scotland, typescript in Society of Friends MSS., Scottish Record Office, Edinburgh; see also Burnet, *Story of Quakerism*, chap. 9. On religious divisions in Lowland Scotland, see Gordon Donaldson, "Scotland's Conservative North in the Sixteenth and Seventeenth Centuries," *Transactions of the Royal Historical Society*, 5th ser., 16 (1956):65-80; and G. D. Henderson, *Religious Life in Seventeenth Century Scotland* (Cambridge, 1937).

14. John Macky, *A Journey Through Scotland, in Familial Letters From a Gentlemen Here to his Friend Abroad* (London, 1723), p. 7; Defoe, *Tour Through Britain*, 3:188; Trueblood, *Barclay*, passim.

15. Henderson, *Religious Life*, chap. 8; Ferguson, *Scotland's Relations With England*, chaps. 8-9.

16. Landsman, *Scotland and Its First American Colony*, chap. 1. An illuminating picture of northeastern Scottish society is presented in *List of Pollable Persons in the Shire of Aberdeen, 1696*, 2 vols. (Aberdeen, 1844).

17. The Rev. Douglas Gordon Barron, ed., *The Court Book of the Barony of Urie in Kincardineshire, 1604-1747* (Edinburgh, 1892), pp. 86-89, 100-102 passim.

18. Barclay to Penn, 19 Aug. 1681; 23 Sept. 1681; 8 Oct. 1681; 19 Nov. 1681, in *PWP*, 2:104-5, 115-17, 123-24, 132-33.

19. Barclay to Penn, 23 Sept. 1681; 17 Dec. 1681, in ibid., 2:115-17, 133-34.

20. Pomfret, "Proprietors of East Jersey"; *PWP*, 2:630-64.

21. Pomfret, "Proprietors of East Jersey." Barclay's network of agents can be traced in the advertisements for the East Jersey colony; see *A Brief Account of East New Jersey in America*, and George Scot, *The Model of the Government of East New Jersey*, both in William A. Whitehead, *East Jersey under the Proprietary Government*, 2d

ed. (Newark, 1875), pp. 323-29, 367-475; *An Advertisement Concerning the Province of East Jersey in America* (Edinburgh, 1685); *An Advertisement to All Tradesmen, Husbandmen, Servants and others who are Willing to Transport themselves unto the Province of New East Jersey in America,* printed in *The Bannatyne Miscellany* (Edinburgh, 1858), 3:385-88; George Lockhart, *A further Account of East New Jersey* (Edinburgh, 1685); and *A Brief Advertisement Concerning East New Jersey, in America* (Edinburgh, 1685).

22. Pomfret, "Proprietors of East Jersey"; Digest of Births, Marriages and Deaths in Scotland.

23. *Brief Account of East New Jersey,* pp. 323-29; Scot, *Model of Government,* pp. 427-29.

24. Pomfret, *East New Jersey,* pp. 186ff. For lists of Scottish indentured servants, see *Archives of the State of New Jersey* (hereafter *NJA*), vol. 21, *A Calendar of Records in the Office of the Secretary of State, 1664-1703* (Newark, 1880), pp. 61-76 passim; Digest of Births, Marriages and Deaths in Scotland.

25. *Register of the Privy Council of Scotland,* 3d ser. (Edinburgh, 1908-), 9:208; 10:19-20; 11:157-59ff.

26. "Propositions of Gawen Lawrie," *Proceedings of the New Jersey Historical Society* (hereafter *PNJHS*), n. s., 6 (1921):229-33; Robert Gordon to Gawen Lawrie, "Some Unpublished Scots Proprietors' Letters 1683-84," *PNJHS,* n. s., 7 (1922):10-12; "The Proprietors to Deputy Governor Lawrie and Council," ibid., 1 (1880):446-55; "Account of a Shipment to East Jersey in April, 1683," *NJA,* 1:463-69.

27. "The Proprietors to Deputy Governor Lawrie," *NJA,* 1:448-49; "Instructions to Deputy Governor Lawrie," *NJA,* 1:459-63; "Instructions Relating to the Setting Out of Land in East Jersey," *NJA,* 1:470-74.

28. "Propositions of Gawen Lawrie," p. 232.

29. Letters describing the Cedar Brook settlement are printed in Scot, *Model of Government,* pp. 433-35, 440-42, 444, 459-68.

30. George J. Miller, ed., *Minutes of the Board of General Proprietors of the Eastern Division of New Jersey* (Perth Amboy, 1949-60), 1:156-57ff; Scot, *Model of Government,* p. 467; Will of William Naughty (1703), in Unrecorded Wills, New Jersey State Library, Trenton.

31. Miller, *Minutes of the Proprietors,* 1:156-57ff; *Calendar of Records,* pp. 120, 135-36 passim.

32. Landsman, *Scotland and Its First American Colony,* chap. 5; Peter Wacker, *Land and People: A Cultural Geography of Preindustrial New Jersey: Origins and Settlement Patterns* (New Brunswick, 1975). There are, of course, many ways of measuring the interactions of Scottish settlers. One method is to look at witnesses to wills. Thirty-eight first-generation Scottish settlers left wills before 1720. Seventy percent of the witnesses to those wills were natives of Scotland (74 of 106). Most of those were non-Quakers, even in the wills of Scottish Friends.

33. The most important sources for analyzing the religious affiliations of East Jersey's Scots are Records of the Woodbridge Monthly Meeting, 1686-1728, MS. copy in GSP; "Record Book of the Episcopal Church in Monmouth County, New Jersey. From 1733," printed in John Stillwell, *Historical and Genealogical Miscellany* (New York, 1903-32), 1:157-208; Records of the Old Tennent Church, 2 MS. vols. in Monmouth County Historical Society, Freehold, N.J.; Frank R. Symmes, *History of the Old Tennent Church* 2d ed. (Cranbury, N.J., 1904).

34. Ethny W. Kirby, *George Keith 1638-1716* (New York, 1942); Jon Butler, "'The Gospel Order Improved': The Keithian Schism and the Exercise of Quaker Ministerial Authority in Pennsylvania," *WMQ,* 3d ser., 31 (1974):431-52; J. William Frost, "Unlikely Controversialists: Caleb Pusey and George Keith," *Quaker History,* 64 (1976):16-36; Gary B. Nash, *Quakers and Politics: Pennsylvania, 1681-1726* (Princeton, 1968), pp. 146-61.

35. An Abstract of the Marriages and a Copy of the Records of Births and Deaths of Members of the Shrewsbury Monthly Meeting, 1641-1876, MS. copy in GSP, pp. 168-69; Edgar L. Pennington, ed., "Journal of George Keith," *Historical Magazine Protestant Episcopal Church*, 15 (1951):408.

36. Pennington, "Journal of George Keith," pp. 408-10; Records of the Old Tennent Church, vol. 1 passim.

37. Milton Rubincam, "John Barclay," *PNJHS*, n. s., 18 (1940):202-15, 254-66; Records of the Old Tennent Church, vol. 1 passim.

38. Edith Mather, "John Reid of Hortencia," *PNJHS*, n. s., 15 (1937):1-20; Symmes, *Old Tennent Church*, pp. 134ff.

39. *Calendar of Records,* pp. 59 passim; Digest of Births, Marriages and Deaths in Scotland; Symmes, *Old Tennent Church*, pp. 134-35.

40. Miller, *Minutes of the Proprietors*, vol. 1 passim.

41. Ibid., pp. 55ff; see also Gary Horowitz, "New Jersey Land Riots, 1745-55" (Ph.D. diss., Ohio State University, 1966).

42. Minutes of Monmouth County, 1688-1721, in Monmouth County Courthouse, Freehold, N.J., pp. 153-54; see also George Pratt Insh, *The Company of Scotland, Trading to Africa and the Indies* (London, 1932); idem, ed., *Darien Shipping Papers* (Edinburgh, 1929), pp. 65-66; Pomfret, *East New Jersey,* pp. 300ff.

43. *NJA,* 2 (1881):124-29, 322-27, 544; see also Minutes of Monmouth County, pp. 199-200; *NJA,* 4 (1882):18-20; Pomfret, *East New Jersey,* pp. 300ff.

44. See James C. Leyburn, *The Scotch-Irish: A Social History* (Chapel Hill, N.C., 1962), pp. 191-93; T. C. Pears, Jr., and G. S. Klett, "Documentary History of William Tennent, Sr. and the Log College," *Journal of the Presbyterian Historical Society,* 28 (1950):38-62; Leonard Trinterud, *Forming an American Tradition: A Reexamination of Colonial Presbyterianism* (Philadelphia, 1949), esp. pp. 35-36, 212ff.

MARIANNE S. WOKECK

15 ❧ Promoters and Passengers:
The German Immigrant Trade, 1683–1775

When William Penn traveled the Rhine lands in 1677 as a missionary, his contacts with fellow Quakers and other "seekers" proved important in his colonizing scheme for Pennsylvania a few years later.[1] However, the extensive promotional campaign Penn mounted in Holland and Germany in the early 1680s to attract settlers for his province came to real fruition half a century later than expected and in a fashion largely unforeseen by the founder of the "holy experiment."[2] The magnetism that Pennsylvania exerted for the majority of German immigrants in the colonial period was primarily as the "best poor man's country" rather than as a haven for persecuted seekers of the truth. This shift away from Penn's ideal is to be explained by the favorable overall development of the Delaware Valley region and a variety of adverse circumstances besetting southwestern Germany which combined intricately to shape the influx of German newcomers to Philadelphia before the Revolution.[3] Penn was instrumental in creating conditions that helped to set this transatlantic flow of continental Protestants in motion. His influence was twofold: On the one hand, he planned a colony that consciously included settlers drawn from outside the dominions of the English king, and on the other hand, his personal connections and beliefs were crucial in attracting the first pathfinding and trend-setting group of colonists from Germany to Pennsylvania.[4]

It is hardly possible to exaggerate the significance of this pioneering group—Quakers from Krefeld and Kriegsheim and some members of the Frankfort Company, who founded and settled Germantown in 1683—as the forerunners of about one hundred thousand German-speaking immigrants to the American colonies. Three characteristics of this early migration were especially important as they combined to generate further immigration from the Rhine lands. First of all, this vanguard of settlers and investors in Penn's colony came from a region along the Rhine in which many of the residents had only recently established their homes and among whom the tradition to migrate in response to political upheaval, economic instability, and religious persecution was strong.[5] Second, the Germantown pioneers were people of exemplary but dissenting religious convictions in an intolerant environment, and they had sufficient economic independence to finance the move to the New World. Scholars of other transatlantic migrations have found that both features were typical of early settlers whose success was likely to induce others to follow in their footsteps.[6] The network of ties that connected coreligionists, their families, friends, and former neighbors was essential to lure more immigrants later, after trusted reports about religious toleration, good government, and economic opportunity had singled out Pennsylvania as the preferred overseas destination for Germans willing or pressed to leave their homelands.[7] In the case of the Germantown settlers, there were links between the immigrants and prominent Friends and Mennonites in Rotterdam and Amsterdam. These points of mediation between settlers in Pennsylvania and German Pietists subjected to much religious intolerance were of far-reaching consequence. In particular, the dual role of Benjamin Furly, Penn's continental agent, as leader of the Rotterdam Quaker community and as influential merchant with wide-ranging commercial connections led to the emergence of Rotterdam as the principal port of embarkation for German immigrants to the American colonies.[8] It is this third, commercial aspect of the pioneering migration from Germany that resulted in the development of a transatlantic transportation system for emigrants as a regular business — a characteristic that contributed significantly to broadening the base from which German immigrants to colonial Pennsylvania were recruited. What had begun as an occasional service mostly for coreligionists grew into a highly specialized trading activity conducted by a relatively small number of English merchants in Rotterdam whose interest in profit-making superseded considerations rooted in shared religious beliefs.[9]

The evolution of the German immigrant trade is the focus here. The following account of the transatlantic transportation system views the subject from two different angles. The emphasis is first on the promoters of the trade, namely, the merchants who owned and operated the ships that carried German immigrants from Rotterdam to Philadelphia. The perspective then shifts to the passengers and what they could expect on the long journey from Germany to America.

Regardless of whether the focus is primarily on the passengers or on the promoters, it is important to bear in mind the main outline of the German immigration to colonial Pennsylvania — the first large-scale, voluntary flow of non-British aliens to America. After the initial settlement of the Germantown pioneers in 1683, only a few ships occasionally landed groups of German immigrants in Philadelphia before 1727. After this date, with emigration from the Rhine lands to the colonies established, large numbers began to come regularly. Thereafter the German immigration continued to swell more or less gradually until an immense wave of migrants — about 37,000 — reached Philadelphia during the years 1749–54. Though transatlantic relocation resumed in 1763 after the Seven Years War, the renewed stream of arrivals from continental Europe was now but a retreating ebb (about 12,000) in the twelve years before the Revolution after the high tide mark had passed.[10]

I

Relatively few merchants, together with their correspondents and agents, managed the provision of transatlantic transportation for the large numbers of German immigrants to Philadelphia. They were located in three different centers of shipping and commerce: London, Rotterdam, and Philadelphia. The roles and interests of each of these three particular merchant communities were distinct, and the relative weight of each partner in this "triangular" trade changed over time. Yet continuing successful business relationships between these merchant groups furnished German emigrants with a reasonably reliable system of transatlantic transportation.

At first glance, London may seem unlikely as a significant center in a trade between Rotterdam and Philadelphia. However, the constraints of the Navigation Acts, which stipulated that only British owned and operated vessels engage in the trade between England and her colonies, insured London's importance as the foremost provider and broker of ships engaged in the German immigrant trade. The English merchants in Rotterdam chartered ships to transport German passengers from London ship owners and merchants interested in filling their vessels with profitable freight for the outward route on which cargo space was often, if not regularly, underutilized.[11]

Information about the flow of emigrants, including how many people, what kinds of people, and when they wanted to go, enabled the Rotterdam merchants to manipulate the supply of shipping from England effectively and profitably so long as competition among them was limited.

The gradual increase in the demand for immigrant transportation to the American colonies before 1749 allowed two merchant firms — Isaac & Zachary Hope and John Stedman—to dominate this business.[12] The Hopes set the tone in the immigrant trade and together with Stedman provided the bulk of immigrant shipments to Philadelphia; but during the peak period of 1749–50, other English merchants competed effectively for some share in the trade.[13] After 1763 an almost completely new group of merchants from that of the previous decade supplied transatlantic transportation for German passengers. Yet at all times, London shippers and German emigrants had a rather limited choice among English firms in Rotterdam regularly involved in this trading activity.[14]

The services the Rotterdam merchants provided fell into two categories. One was the securing of freights for the ship's run and the other was the outfitting and provisioning of the vessel.[15] Furnishing provisions and other articles for the use of the passengers on board required management skills in the wholesale market, while supplying emigrant freights depended largely on closely monitoring the emigration flow (a phenomenon over which the merchant had no active control) and channeling it into directions most profitable to the merchant.[16]

In their quest to recruit emigrants more efficiently, the merchants in Holland mainly adopted two strategies. One of them was to attempt to direct emigrants onto their vessels by arranging with the Rhine boatmen—with whom they already maintained a proven network of business contacts — to provide river transportation to Rotterdam on special terms.[17] The other approach was to engage recruiting agents to solicit emigrants for particular merchants. Specific recruiting efforts often combined both methods.[18]

The Rotterdam merchants knew that a successful immigrant returning to his old place of residence to fetch remaining family or friends, to settle his family's inheritance, or simply to visit, was the most persuasive recruiting agent. They therefore offered free return passage to those "newlanders" to recruit or at least to encourage their relatives and former neighbors to take passage on one of their ships.[19] In an effort to recruit on a larger regional or national scale, the Rotterdam merchants also engaged professional agents, but only for a few years around mid-century at the height of the immigrant traffic. These recruiting agents were hired specifically to establish a regionwide network with the help of subagents, and then to organize and oversee the transport of emigrants to Rotterdam.[20]

Regardless of whether the Rotterdam merchants only monitored the German emigration flow or whether they tried to channel it actively, their main function in the emigrant trade was to provide transatlantic transportation on vessels dispatched from London and destined for the most part to Philadelphia. Their profits depended on their role as middlemen in the manipulation of the supply of shipping according to the demand for transatlantic passage. The size of their profit margins was closely linked to the ratio of passengers per ship: the larger the number of emigrant freights on a ship, the more profitable the return. The scope of the emigration flow — and to a lesser extent the degree of competition among the merchants involved in the trade—determined when profits increased.

Philadelphia's role in the "triangular" relationship was shaped by its function as the receiving port. As the trade developed, the Philadelphia merchants evolved from passive to active participants. At present Philadelphia's part in the German immigrant trade is relatively better known than the role of either the English or Dutch points in the "triangle," because from 1727 onward the Pennsylvania authorities registered incoming aliens. Lists of the vast majority of foreign-born men arriving in Philadelphia have survived as a result; these "ship lists" allow us to reconstruct some important aspects of this trade.[21]

Who were the Philadelphia merchants involved in the German immigrant trade? What was their special mode of participation and how did it change over time? A total number of forty-two Philadelphia merchants or firms can be identified as in some way involved in the immigrant trade; at first view, this seems large.[22] A closer look at the distribution through the different phases of German movement to America in the eighteenth century, however, puts the number in quite a different perspective. During the early years of regular immigration and the peak period (1727–55), twenty-two different merchants dealt in some significant way with German immigrant vessels. During the twelve years preceding the Revolution (1763–75), twenty-four merchants participated. Except for four firms, however, there was no overlap between the two periods. More than half of all merchants involved engaged only once in the German immigrant trade. During 1727–55, seven merchants emerged repeatedly as consignees or owners of immigrant ships. Up to 1755, the two firms Charles & Alexander Stedman and Benjamin & Samuel Shoemaker were the recipients of the majority of vessels arriving with German immigrants whose consignees are known. This largely reflects the dominant market shares captured by John Stedman and the Hopes in the departure port of Rotterdam. After 1763, more merchants — eleven of them — participated with some regularity in the lessening immigrant trade. Yet in this period also, four merchants outperformed the rest by considerable margins, with Willing & Morris being responsible for almost one-third of the German immigrants to Philadelphia on the eve of the Revolution.

The growth of the Philadelphia merchant participation in transporting Germans to the Delaware was more dramatic than this broadening of local reponsibility after the era of the Stedmans and Shoemakers indicates, because as the century progressed the Philadelphia merchants *owned* more and more ships that carried immigrants.[23] Until 1748 just seven immigrant ships were registered in Philadelphia and only two of those were at least partially owned by a Philadelphian while four of them clearly belonged to Londoners. By the peak period of 1749–54, the percentage of immigrant ships built and registered in Philadelphia had doubled, and the balance between owners in London and owners in Philadelphia had shifted, so that eight out of eleven ownerships now included at least one merchant who resided in Philadelphia. After 1763 half of all the ships arriving with German immigrants were registered in Philadelphia and only three had no Philadelphia owners. The majority of the merchants (seven out of eleven) who engaged more than once in the German immigrant trade in this later period after the peak transatlantic flow had passed now owned at least part of a ship transporting German immigrants. Another measure of increasingly active participation by local merchants is the fact that Philadelphians owned a rising percentage of the ships that carried German immigrants to Philadelphia more than once.[24] The degree to which transatlantic passage was provided by ships already experienced in the trade increased significantly over time. After the 1750s merchants on the Delaware both managed and owned a larger share of the business to be had in transporting aliens to Pennsylvania.[25]

The change from being simply consignees of German immigrant shipments to becoming actual owners of the ships made it necessary for those Philadelphia merchants who were regularly involved in the German immigrant trade to alter how they managed ships and cargo. In the earlier years of the trade, the majority of the German immigrants arrived with at least part of their fare paid in advance. Any monies that passengers owed were either paid in cash upon arrival — by the immigrant himself, his relatives or friends, or his employer — or pledged (upon sufficient security) by note or bond for later payment at a specified time. Squaring these accounts turned out to be a complicated and rather tedious business for the merchant in Philadelphia, especially after the practice of purchasing transatlantic passage "on credit" in Europe had become widely accepted.[26]

Given the distinct character of the divers functions assumed by London, Rotterdam, and Philadelphia merchants in the German immigrant trade over time, it is important to understand their changing relationship in sharing the profits and risks, and to compare the development of this particular trading activity with what is known of the general features of British overseas trade. London's centrality was derived from her domineering role in England's trade with all the American colonies, including the provision of ancillary functions such as insurance and ship brokerage services. Merchants in London were in the best position to take advantage of a frequent underutilization of cargo space on ships normally sailing with dry goods from England to the American mainland colonies. This problem of cargo for America-bound shipping made the transtlantic transportation of German immigrants especially attractive for merchants involved in overseas trade. In the early years, London merchants with interests in Philadelphia utilized unfilled cargo space on London-owned vessels to transport immigrants — supplied through the services of English merchants in Rotterdam — to Philadelphia. During the peak years of German emigration, providing transatlantic passage became a profitable end in itself, not simply a subsidiary activity for filling vessels. Then after 1763, as the number of Germans wanting to go to Philadelphia subsided, this trade became a supplement to other transactions except that now the immigrant ships were owned and operated out of Philadelphia. Consequently, London's particu-

lar role in the immigrant trade largely shifted from direct supplier of shipping with vested interest in the vessels to that of ship-broker for Philadelphia
business partners who wanted to use their tonnage more fully.

The progressive phases of the German immigrant trade through distinct periods of rise, peak, and decline are most evident and revealing in
Rotterdam's relations with London and Philadelphia. During the early years
of regular and increasing emigration from Germany, the English merchants
in Rotterdam applied their special expertise as middlemen to coordinate the
demand for transatlantic emigrant transportation from continental Europe
with the supply of shipping from England, mostly from London. They
mediated crucially between participants in different and not otherwise directly linked spheres of trade. This coordinating function intensified dramatically when German emigration peaked around mid-century. The boom
in passenger traffic not only brought about an increase in the demand for
the regular services of the Rotterdam merchants — at a price largely set by
them — but also led to their heightened interest in how Philadelphia merchants managed the American end of the voyage.

Two different developments contributed to Rotterdam's closer dependence on Philadelphia. Initially, many of the German emigrants seeking
passage had paid at least half of their fare in advance and the remainder
upon arrival. In other words, the Rotterdam merchants received a substantial amount of remuneration for their services promptly in advance payments from the emigrants. This kept credit lines short — an attractive aspect
in overseas trade where much of the risk was the extension of long-term
credit. The Rotterdam merchants could therefore count on *recouping* their
outlays for procuring, outfitting, and loading immigrant vessels. As the
transportation of a growing number of emigrants required more ships, the
Rotterdam merchants had increasing difficulties in meeting the various
costs involved in the charter and provisioning of ships directly out of the
funds collected from the emigrants. Advance payments now covered a
smaller proportion of the expenses necessary to provide immigrant transportation, because a larger absolute, if not relative, number of German
emigrants chose to "charge" all of their fare at least until arrival in Philadelphia. On the one hand, the widely exploited opportunity of postponing
payment for passage substantially helped to increase the number of emigrants and was therefore largely welcomed because of the potential for
continued high profits. On the other hand, this practice also led to complicated and prolonged lines of credit among the participants in the trade.

Philadelphia merchants assumed many of the additional responsibilities that arose from a wider use of deferred payment for passage. Consequently, they became more intimately and intensely involved in the German
immigrant trade. In addition to their increased investment in shipping, they
developed special services in the credit chain connecting the "triangular"
partners and a growing expertise in gauging the market for German settlers

and servants in America. By mid-century, Philadelphia merchants began to acquire the leading role in the German immigrant trade — mostly at the expense of London merchants who showed less interest in investing in the shipping of this specialized trade. However, at the height of the immigrant trade (1749–54), when large profits were to be made, the most effective concerted effort demanded very close ties between all three ports if the returns from the "triangular" venture were to be brought to fruition: Rotterdam, which provided the German emigrants and provisioned and outfitted immigrant vessels; London, which supplied the additional shipping to meet the extraordinary demand for transatlantic passage; and Philadelphia, which received the human cargo and guaranteed the payment of its transportation. After 1763, as the German emigration flow subsided, English merchants in Rotterdam returned to their role of middlemen in simply coordinating the emigrants' demand for passage with shipping available in London. This meant now in most cases that ships owned by Philadelphians and operated out of their port would make an additional stopover in Rotterdam on their return voyages from England to pick up passengers.

Providing passage for immigrants was at all times firmly embedded in the prevailing structure of ties between business partners on both sides of the Atlantic. Participants in the trade took advantage of that structure for their own use by shifting the weight and readjusting the balance among partners to capitalize on current opportunities for carrying passengers. At the beginning of regular German immigration to Philadelphia, when London provided the bulk of all shipping to the American mainland colonies, German emigrants took passage to Pennsylvania on London-owned and operated ships, which then proceded on their way from Philadelphia to the southern colonies and the West Indies, or both, and from there back to England.[27] At the height of the German immigration wave most of the immigrant vessels still followed this itinerary, but now the number of ships owned in and operated out of Philadelphia had increased. After the disruption of the Seven Years War, as the trend toward greater colonial ownership continued, more of the ships carrying immigrants, after debarking their passengers, went straight back across the Atlantic, reflecting Philadelphia's new direct links with Great Britain and southern Europe.

II

Merchants involved in the transatlantic transportation of emigrants were of course businessmen in quest of profit. They viewed the shipment of Germans as just another overseas cargo, albeit one with a few idiosyncracies that required some special handling. The migrants, however, were unaware of the overall structure and the particular business aspects of the trade. They were therefore surprised and felt exploited when they realized that their well-being during the voyage depended largely on considerations that taxed their worth as cargo. Reacting to difficulties along the way and abusive practices in the trade, most immigrants directed their anger and blame against the newlanders and captains, whom they thought primarily responsible for all ills in connection with the overseas passage, rather than the merchants.

A sizable record of individual experiences by passengers, detailing the long journey from Germany to Philadelphia, has survived. But like the tales of travelers in our age of mass tourism, they tend to comment on the extraordinary. Thus accounts of memorable incidents during the voyage overshadow reports about the more normal, uneventful passages. This trait makes it difficult to assess the experience of the vast majority of migrants for whom no personal records exist. The following discussion attempts to outline typical journeys, focusing on the options available to the emigrants along the way under different circumstances and at different times. The intent is to exhibit the wide spectrum of opportunities and individual experiences and to get at the various forces or circumstances which could make the trip to the New World easy or difficult.

Whatever the causes, reasons, and motives that prompted individuals to leave their homeland, the majority of all emigrants began their journey in the spring. The actual date of departure from home depended on the beginning of the most favorable travel season and on the length of time necessary for the completion of the bureaucratic procedures required for permission to remove legally from the territory of formal residency.[28] The choice of transportation to the port of embarkation — usually Rotterdam — depended on many factors. The prospective emigrant's financial situation was the most important and fixed much of his choice in subsequent strategies for the journey as well. Emigrants with adequate funds for the whole trip generally traveled with chests containing bedding, clothing, provisions, and a variety of other belongings.[29] This made river transportation desirable because it minimized costly overland hauling. Singly or in small groups, those emigrants of more comfortable circumstances could travel down the Rhine according to opportunity.

Emigrants with restricted travel funds had to be more selective in their choice of Rhine passage. The number of people in a given party often determined the actual cost per person. For a large group of people the most economical way was to hire and outfit their own boat rather than chartering one from Rhine shippers already established in the trade.[30] Emigrants unable or unwilling to arrange their own Rhine passage had to engage the services of an agent, often a newlander or boatman working for a Rotterdam merchant, who could offer terms agreeable to the migrant, such as "charging" the expenses of the trip to the passenger's account for later payment.[31] These services, however, invariably raised the cost and curtailed the flexibility for the emigrant in arranging the rest of his long journey. It was therefore advisable to avoid reliance on such agents under any circumstances but especially during the emigration peak (1749–54) when the term *newlander* came to be equated with exploitative and fraudulent practices in the trade.[32]

The duration of the Rhine trip from any of the major collecting points varied according to weather and traffic conditions, and according to the skills of those in charge of expediting arrangements at the many toll stations (there were thirty-six between Strassburg and Rotterdam). To deal effectively with customs officials and other government authorities at the frequent territorial border checkpoints required planning, experience, and money.[33] And once the German emigrants reached the United Provinces of the Netherlands, the Dutch authorities required security as an assurance that impoverished Germans stranded on their way to the American colonies would not become a burden for the Provinces.[34] Evidence of contract with any of the Rotterdam merchants sufficed as security for those otherwise lacking sufficient travel funds to continue their journey. According to the resolution of the States General the merchants were then forced to ship out every emigrant thus signed up at the Dutch border; but this requirement enabled the Rotterdam shippers also to monitor the emigration flow closely and channel people onto *their* ships.

When the Germans arrived in Rotterdam, they made agreements with merchants and captains, either for the first time or by completing contracts which they had signed earlier as subscribers. The terms of these contracts determined much of the quality of life at sea, and without a valid contract, recourse was impossible for the immigrant after arriving in Philadelphia.[35] Whether traveling alone or in a group, emigrants who arrived at the port of embarkation with sufficient funds and independent of ties to a newlander had the best options. Their horizons were especially open and flexible if they arrived early, between April and June, to avoid the crowded conditions that prevailed toward the end of the season during years of heavy emigration.[36] At any one time, there was little difference in the basic price charged for the passage; but the kinds of services included in a contract could result in an economical fare while, conversely, their exclusion could lead to many extra costs adding up to a very expensive deal.[37]

After weighing the relative costs, assessing the soundness and experience of the merchants offering passage, and checking the ships and their masters, the wise emigrant took special note of the following key services: (1) Good drinking water, carried in sufficient quantities in casks designed for that use and that use only, was absolutely vital for the health of the passengers.[38] (2) Good provisions such as "bread, butter, cheese, flour, peas, rice, and the like as well as a third part in lightly salted meat and bacon" were almost as important for the well-being of the passengers on board.[39] (3) Transportation of the emigrants' chests and baggage in an accessible place on the same vessel was critical because these contained vital supplementary provisions such as dried meat and fruit, spices, vinegar, medicine, wine, and brandy, besides bedding, cooking utensils, and change of clothes, all of which were indispensable for a healthy and comfortable voyage.[40]

In Rotterdam, poor emigrants and those under previously contracted agreements with newlanders were often faced with a situation more precarious than that of their wealthier and more circumspect fellow passengers. For emigrants who had purchased their fare "on credit" and could offer little security, it was essential to select a reputable merchant who offered a contractual passage devoid of loopholes designed to add unnecessary charges to the account, and who did not attach unreasonable terms to the deferred payment option.[41] Although a number of emigrants had second thoughts about the wisdom of their migration plan and decided to return, many followed the lead of an agent and accepted his choice of merchant, contract, vessel, and captain without questioning or checking. Such people could only find out later, during the voyage or when settling accounts in Philadelphia, whether their dealings had been with a responsible newlander who had put his previous travel experience to good use for their sake, or whether they must pay dearly for their blind and naive trust.[42]

Most of the vessels engaged in the German immigrant trade to colonial Philadelphia were two- or three-masted ocean-going merchantmen. Most of them registered less than 150 tons, ranging on the average from about 110 registered tons in the 1720s to 138 tons just before the Revolution.[43] Many of them carried one to two dozen cannons for defense against pirates and privateers. The ship *Mary,* built in Philadelphia for a London merchant and registered to carry a 100-ton burden, was one of the smallest ships arriving with German immigrants in Philadelphia.[44] She was 58' long, had a hold 10'6" deep, and the distance between decks varied from 4' to 4'6", scarcely adequate headroom for crew or passengers. The *Crown,* chartered by John Hunt of London and James Pemberton of Philadelphia to carry German immigrants across the Atlantic, was a strong Thames-River-built ship, a prime sailor, and, being appreciably larger in her dimensions, more suited for the trade. She was 25'6" wide and 103' long between decks, with 4'10" height between decks fore and aft, cabin and steerage 50' long and 5'10" high, and a quarterdeck of 50'. It was calculated that the *Crown* could carry above four hundred freights easily, which puts her among twenty-two ships known to have arrived in Philadelphia with more than four hundred German passengers aboard.[45]

The arrangement of accomodations for passengers was the basis for all calculations concerning the vessel's capacity for human cargo. The bunk space for each full freight was commonly specified to be six feet in length and one foot, six inches in width.[46] A ship of the *Crown's* dimensions would yield a maximum of a little over two hundred such spaces between decks. The cabin and steerage could provide room for about another one hundred comparable spaces. Additional berth space, finally, could be obtained by constructing an upper tier of bunks in the cabin and other areas of the ship which offered sufficient headroom and also on deck.[47] The lodgings on some ships were fitted out to accommodate two passengers in an apartment or cabin with hammocks for beds. Others offered sleeping places on makeshift platforms by constructing loose lattices of removable board and putting four freights or more in a compartment.[48] The actual number of persons sharing such a cabin depended on the composition of the freights: families with children were usually most cramped in their quarters since children under five years of age had to share a parent's bunk, and children between five and fourteen were entitled to only half a bedspace each.[49] Unfortunately, nothing is known about the rationale or the actual procedure governing the allocation of cabin space. From the arrangements of passengers' financial accounts by cabin, it appears that groups of families and friends stayed together. Some cabins were shared by single, seemingly unrelated men, some solely by women—with or without children—and many others accommodated an undeterminable mix of passengers.[50] Among immigrants sharing the same general quarters between decks, in the cabin, or steerage, there was apparently no systematic segregation by sex or age.

Crowded conditions were the norm on all ships that profitably carried a mixed load of passengers, their luggage, and provisions. However, crowding was more than just an inconvenience for about half of the total number of Germans who chose to come to Philadelphia before 1776. During the peak immigration years (1749–54) and to a lesser extent also in the single big years of 1738, 1764, and 1773, tight packing was practiced by all merchants in the trade.[51] The average number of passengers per ship followed the now familiar division between three distinct periods of German migration. The ratio of registered tonnage to the number of passengers indicates that during the peak years the managers of this trade handled the increased volume of business by stuffing more immigrants into each ship.

Observers, promoters, and passengers alike were aware that excessive crowding was dangerous to the immigrants' health and threatened their survival. A number of strategies helped immigrants to prevent or at least curb the devastating consequences of overcrowding, and starting in 1763 Pennsylvania effectively regulated the trade in the twelve years of declining flow before the Revolution.[52] Passengers could avoid the most crowded conditions by traveling early in the season (April to June) and better still by eschewing Rotterdam as port of embarkation. Since merchants were usually guided by their most immediate vested interest, some of the Rotterdam merchants seemed little moved by high rates of sickness or mortality on voyages that they arranged as long as payment of all passages contracted upon embarkation was insured.[53] Other merchants, especially those operating in Philadelphia, realized that a combination of some restraint in the practice of crowding with increased attention to maintaining healthy conditions on board ship would better serve their interests.[54] Providing medicines for sick passengers, engaging a physician for the ship's run, insisting on rules for basic cleanliness on board, and installing ventilation pipes were measures designed to reduce the risk of disease and death among passengers.

Given the cramped conditions on many immigrant ships, the daily activities and routines during the voyage were very important. The captains of the immigrant ships determined the rules and procedures on shipboard, which put them in a peculiar position that taxed their cargo management capabilities in a very special way. As a group, captains were professionals in a tough and demanding business. Most of them probably tried to avoid difficulties with their passengers under most circumstances.[55] Adverse situations, however, often made the ships' masters seem to be the unbending opponents of their passengers, even though the captains themselves were never responsible for bad weather, and rarely for the insufficient provisions, lack of good water, or disease on board. Yet they had to deal with these annoying and dangerous events in mostly unpopular fashion: rationing, enforcing strict rules of cleanliness, and insisting relentlessly on the observance of safety guidelines by everybody.

The best arrangement for a bearable life on board was a regular and regulated organization of daily activities. The most important of these was the preparation and distribution of provisions. The daily allowance of meat with peas and the like, as well as the weekly rations of bread, butter, and cheese were furnished to the passengers in messes, composed of five to twelve people. The food was prepared either by crew members, or by passengers who had been engaged for that task, or responsibility was left completely to those sharing in a mess. All passengers agreed that the freedom to make fires on deck to cook additional provisions and to warm children and the sick was indispensable.[56]

Next to the routines implemented to furnish the passengers with their food and drink, certain rules governing rudimentary hygiene and cleanliness contributed significantly to the general well-being of immigrants and crew alike. Mice, rats, and other pests could only be held in check if food was stored and refuse discarded in appropriate places. The most effective practice was a regular and thorough cleaning of all passengers' quarters. Fumigation and twice-weekly washings with vinegar may not seem very effective by modern standards, but generally they resulted in more "sweet smelling" accommodations and above all assured a certain measure of tidiness.[57] Personal cleanliness was equally important, to control for lice, but difficult to achieve under the circumstances. Experienced captains ordered rainwater collected for drink and washing and designated one day of the week as wash day — weather permitting. The picture of a maze of clotheslines on deck may seem quaint; but drying and airing was essential, especially with rain and sea water leaking in everywhere.

Passengers have so often been portrayed solely as victims that it is necessary to point out that the immigrants themselves could significantly compound the trials of life at sea. Merchants, captains, and accompanying newlanders can be held responsible for many of the problems that occurred. They can hardly be blamed, however, for tension and general lack of co-operation and compassion among passengers. The hardships of the voyage seem frequently to have resulted in unabashed selfishness, except possibly among emigrants of deeply religious belief whose basic trust and convictions remained unshaken by the experience.[58] It is also worth remembering, however, that man was always only partially responsible for the outcome of a transatlantic crossing. Eighteenth-century vessels were extremely fragile and vulnerable compared to the forces of wind and sea they braced. The promoters and passengers who braved ocean and weather to carry out such a massive exodus from Europe to America accomplished much in light of all the adversities.

III

The transatlantic transportation of German immigrants to colonial Pennsylvania was shaped by two principal dynamics. On the one hand, the promoters, merchants involved in British overseas trade, tried to take advantage of profits to be made from carrying passengers as one part of their diversified operations. On the other hand, the flow, then ebb, in the number of Germans wanting transportation to Pennsylvania made that commercial opportunity larger at some times than at others and helped to determine who carried passengers and in what manner through the three successive phases of the history of the German migration from the 1680s to the Revolution. Throughout, providing regular overseas passage depended on the successful cooperation of a relatively small number of merchants in three different ports. The "triangular" relationship between London, Rotterdam, and Philadelphia changed over time, however, in response to the relative strength of the interest of each merchant community in the transportation of German immigrants to Pennsylvania. At the beginning of appreciable demand for overseas passage in the 1720s, London dominated the trade because of her almost exclusive investment in suitable shipping. By mid-century, Philadelphia's growing financial and managerial interest in vessels employed on transatlantic routes tipped the balance in favor of the colonial merchants. On the eve of the Revolution Germans came to Pennsylvania mostly on ships built and registered in Philadelphia.

In the early years of migration, Rotterdam merchants played a crucial middlemen's role in coordinating the supply of otherwise underutilized London-owned shipping with the demand for transatlantic passage of people who had come from the lands along the Rhine. By the early 1750s, however, when the demand for overseas transportation to Pennsylvania peaked (over half of the total number of colonial German immigrants to Philadelphia arrived in the years 1749–54), the business of shipping immigrants became an end in itself. It is in this brief period that one can truly speak of an "immigrant trade." During these boom years, when Rotterdam's role in capturing a big share of the would-be travelers was important, Philadelphia's relative weight in the "triangle" grew decisively. Her merchants not only gained importance as owners and operators of ships used for the transportation of German migrants but also asserted their role in the "triangular" commercial process as an indispensable link in the credit chain. And in the years just before the Revolution, when the immigrant trade ebbed, Rotterdam still coordinated the demand for overseas passage with the supply of shipping available in London, but now, however, the vessels that stopped in Rotterdam to take on German emigrants were mostly owned and operated by Philadelphia merchants.

The division of German immigration to colonial Pennsylvania into three distinctive phases of rise, peak, and decline is also crucial to our understanding of the experience of German passengers who crossed the Atlantic. Most of the practices primarily designed to maximize profits at the cost of the well-being of the passengers occurred primarily during the boom period of the trade (1749–54). During these years of peak demand for passage it was most difficult to achieve independence from scheming promoters and flexibility in choosing terms of travel. At the beginning and end of the German immigration, passengers were fewer in number, and there was less incentive to practice profit-maximizing abuses — techniques of exploitation on the trip down the Rhine, and overcrowding and marginal provisioning during the ocean voyage.

Philadelphia's emerging role as the weightiest point in the "triangular" immigrant trade is consonant with what students of Philadelphia's commercial community have found about the growing investment of Philadelphia merchants in shipping. But the Philadelphia merchants' increasing assumption of responsibilities in the "triangular" credit chain needs to be more fully explored, for the way in which Philadelphia merchants dealt financially with migrants had a major effect on what kinds of emigrants could plan a new beginning in America and how successfully these new immigrants would settle into the life of the New World.

NOTES

1. William Penn's account of his journey to Holland and Germany is published in *PWP*, 1:425-508.
2. On the advertising of Pennsylvania on the continent, see William I. Hull, *William Penn and the Dutch Quaker Migration to Pennsylvania* (Swarthmore, 1935), pp. 329-35.
3. The majority of German immigrants to the American colonies originated from the southwestern region of present-day Germany, as well as the Protestant, German-speaking cantons of Switzerland, and Alsace-Lorraine.
4. William Penn in his letter to James Harrison, 25 Aug. 1681 (*PWP*, 2:107-9), anticipates that foreign Protestants will settle in his colony. The ties between the Germantown pioneers, Penn, and the continental Quaker communities are detailed in Hull, *Dutch Quaker Migration*, pp. 178-300, app. B.

5. For details on southwestern Germany as an area of in- and out-migration, see Marianne S. Wokeck, "A Tide of Alien Tongues: The Flow and Ebb of German Immigration to Pennsylvania, 1683-1776" (Ph.D. diss., Temple University, 1982), chap. 2.

6. See, for example, David Grayson Allen, *In English Ways: The Movement of Societies and the Transferal of English Local Law and Custom to Massachusetts Bay in the Seventeenth Century* (Chapel Hill, N.C., 1981), pp. 163-204; Harald Runblom and Hans Norman. eds., *From Sweden to America: A History of the Migration: A Collective Work of the Uppsala Migration Research Project* (Minneapolis, 1976), pp. 116-18.

7. A fine example of a very detailed and influential report home is the letter of Francis Daniel Pastorius to his friends, 7 Mar. 1684, published in part in *William Penn and the Founding of Pennsylvania, 1680-1684: A Documentary History,* ed. Jean R. Soderlund (Philadelphia, 1983), pp. 352-60.

8. At a time of high credit-risk in overseas trade, the advantages of dealing with fellow Quakers who shared the commitment to sound business practices are convincingly demonstrated in Jacob M. Price's essay in this volume.

9. By this time German immigration to colonial Pennsylvania became regular in the late 1720s, Quakerism had declined in Rotterdam. William I. Hull, *Benjamin Furly and Quakerism in Rotterdam* (Swarthmore, Pa., 1941), pp. 247-52, 285-92.

10. For details, see Marianne S. Wokeck, "The Flow and the Composition of German Immigration to Philadelphia, 1727-1775," *PMHB,* 105 (1981):249-78.

11. Many of the goods carried from London to Philadelphia were dry goods of considerable value but of relatively little bulk (see Thomas M. Doerflinger, "Enterprise on the Delaware: Merchants and Economic Development in Philadelphia, 1750-1791" [Ph.D. diss., Harvard University, 1980], p. 94; John Hunt to John Pemberton, 27 Feb. 1748/9, Hunt & Greenleafe letter book, 1747-1749, HSP). The charter practice itself was apparently fairly common, as is evident from the procurement of additional tonnage for the use of the royal navy. See David Syrett, *Shipping and the American War, 1775-83: A Study of British Transport Organization* (London, 1970), chap. 4.

12. For a description of the Hope family and firm, their Scottish, Dutch, English, and American connections, see Marten G. Buist, *At Spes Non Fracta: Hope & Co., 1770-1815, Merchant Bankers and Diplomats* (The Hague, 1974), pp. 3-13; for their ties to the Quaker business elite centered in London, see Jacob Price's essay in this volume. As for John Stedmen, he started out as a captain in the 1730s. By 1750 he had become the owner of several German immigrant vessels, which he managed successfully together with his brothers Charles and Alexander, who settled as merchants in Philadelphia. For information on the German immigrant vessels and their owners, see Ralph B. Strassburger, *Pennsylvania German Pioneers: A Publication of the Original Lists of Arrivals in the Port of Philadelphia from 1727-1808,* ed. William J. Hinke (1934; reprint, Baltimore, 1966); and John J. McCusker, "Ships Registered at the Port of Philadelphia before 1776: A Computerized Listing" (typescript, 1970, HSP).

13. For instance, John Hunt of London together with James and John Pemberton in Philadelphia were eager to profit from the boom in the German immigrant trade in the late 1740s and early 1750s—a time when the Pennsylvania market was glutted with dry goods. John Hunt to John Pemberton, 27 Feb. 1748/9, Hunt & Greenleafe letter book, HSP; James Pemberton to John Pemberton, 5 June 1749, Pemberton Papers, 5:102, HSP.

14. Daniel Harvard & Co., Deuling & Konig, Nicolas & Jan Van Stabhorst, and John Dick, for example, were among newcomers to the trade in the early 1750s; Messrs. Michael Meyer, Hofman, and Crawford were active in the late 1760s. A systematic search in the notarial archives (ONA) in the Gemeentelijke Archiefdienst Rotterdam would establish the number of English merchants in-

volved in the German immigrant trade, and the degree and length of time during which they participated in this business, more precisely than the occasional references in immigrants' letters home and Philadelphia merchants' correspondence and accounts that form the basis of this outline.

15. These are the two standard features typically included in "charterparties," or contracts made between the English merchants in Rotterdam and the captains of immigrant vessels before one of the Rotterdam notaries public. These contracts were collected in notarial archives (the Rotterdam ONA); indices to the ONA are by the names of the charterparties and by name of vessel.

16. More research is necessary in order to establish how the shipping of German immigrants fitted into other merchant activities, such as the rice, tobacco, or provision trade.

17. See, for example, the statements of the Rhine shippers Christiaan Dortsbach and Matthias Zolicoffer on behalf of the merchant Levinius Clarkson, (9 July 1737, Notarial Archives 10305/317, Gemeente Archief Amsterdam) concerning the transportation and delivery of German emigrants.

18. Johann Philip Buch, for instance, was a boatman of Wertheim and also an emigrant agent. In 1754 he recruited passengers for the Hopes who paid him almost 5s. per head. Don Yoder, ed., *Pennsylvania German Immigrants, 1709-1786: Lists Consolidated from Yearbooks of The Pennsylvania German Folklore Society* (Baltimore, 1980), pp. 168-70.

19. John Hunt asked Joseph Crell (28 Feb. 1748/9) to recommend his ship to friends in Germany interested in moving to Philadelphia (Hunt & Greenleafe letter book, HSP). Daniel Harvard offered Johan Christian Schmitt free return passage as an incentive to become a recruiting agent (Adolf Gerber, *Die Nassau-Dillenburger Auswanderung nach Amerika im 18. Jahrhundert* [Flensburg, 1930], p. 22). In the listing of financial accounts of passengers on the ship *Nancy* (which arrived in Philadelphia late in Aug. 1750) newlanders appear with no fare charge next to their names. See "Redemptioners, Philadelphia, 1750-1830," Society Miscellaneous Collection, box 7a, folder 7, HSP.

20. One such large-scale recruiting effort, on behalf of the merchant and New England land speculator Samuel Waldo, is detailed in H. A. Ratterman, "Geschichte des deutschen Elements im Staate Maine," *Der deutsche Pionier: Erinnerungen aus dem Pionier-Leben der Deutschen in Amerika,* vols. 14-16 (1882-84).

21. See Strassburger/Hinke, *Pennsylvania German Pioneers.*

22. For details, see Wokeck, "A Tide of Alien Tongues," esp. table 2.

23. Philadelphia merchants involved in the German immigrant trade can be identified systematically only for the years after 1750. By this date the headings of the ship lists (Strassburger/Hinke, *Pennsylvania German Pioneers*) included the name of the merchant to whom the immigrants were consigned. McCusker ("Ships Registered at the Port of Philadelphia") has information about the ownership of immigrant vessels. Furthermore, the "Tonnage Duty Book" (1764-75), 3 vols., Cadwalader Collection, Thomas Cadwalader Section, HSP, lists the consignees and/or owners of ships entering Philadelphia.

24. The headings of the ship lists (Strassburger/Hinke, *Pennylvania German Pioneers*) provide the information necessary to determine whether a vessel carried German immigrants to colonial Philadelphia more than once.

25. A general trend toward more regular and less circuitous sailing patterns is evident in other trades conducted by Philadelphians during the second half of the eighteenth century. See Doerflinger, "Enterprise on the Delaware."

26. For details, see Wokeck, "A Tide of Alien Tongues," chap. 4.

27. The custom house notices published in the *Pennsylvania Gazette* provide information on the sailing routes of vessels that landed German immigrants in Philadelphia.

28. For details on the procedure necessary to gain manumission from feudal bondage and to receive passports, see Wokeck, "A Tide of Alien Tongues," chap. 2.

29. Germans emigrating to the American colonies usually lost their rights as citizens in the territories where they had lived in Germany. In the vast majority of cases, therefore, the decision to relocate across the Atlantic was final. The fare from Rotterdam to Philadelphia included the transportation of baggage and household goods. Trade goods, however, were subject to customs duties and were not free of charge.

30. Report by Johann Ludwig Runckel to the [Mennonite] Committee of Foreign Needs in Amsterdam, 13 Mar. 1711, "European Mennonites, Amsterdam Archives" (AA), microfilm at the Lancaster Mennonite Historical Society, AA #1321.

31. Some of the passengers' accounts of the ship Nancy (arrived in Philadelphia in late Aug. 1750) and the ship Britannia (arrived in Philadelphia in mid-Sept. 1773) detail expenses incurred prior to embarkation. See "Redemptioners, Philadelphia, 1750-1830," HSP; "Munster [sic] Book" of the ship Britannia, HSP.

32. Gottlieb Mittelberger, Journey to Pennsylvania, ed. and trans. Oscar Handlin and John Clive (Cambridge, Mass., 1960), and Christopher Sauer in the German language newspaper Pennsylvanische Berichte, esp. 16 Oct. 1749, both comment negatively on the practices of "newlanders" at the height of the German immigration to colonial Pennsylvania.

33. Report of Runckel to Committee of Foreign Needs, 13 Mar. 1711, Lancaster Mennonite Historical Society, AA #1321. Alfred Engels (Die Zollgrenze in der Eiffel: Eine wirtschaftsgeschichtliche Untersuchung fur die Zeit 1740 bis 1834 [Cologne, 1959]) details the complicated procedure of passage through just one of the many German territories bordering the Rhine.

34. Rotterdam merchants applied to both the state and federal authorities for permission to conduct German emigrants on their way to the American colonies through the Netherlands. See Resolutien von den Heeren Staaten van Holland en Westfriesland and Resolutien von de H[oogh] M[ogende] H[eeren] Staaten General der Vereeinigte de Nederlandsche Provincien, published annually with the names of the petitioners indexed.

35. L[eonard] M[elchior] emphasized the importance of a transportation contract in his "Advice to German Emigrants, 1749," ed. Hannah B. Roach, Pennsylvania Genealogical Magazine, 22 (1965):226-37, 232; but few of the emigrants seem to have made such agreements before a notary public in Rotterdam. Some of the exceptions are ONA 2098/232, 233 (9 June 1723); ONA 1529/53 (20 June 1725).

36. German emigrants awaiting embarkation to the American colonies had to camp under the sky in Kralingen, a village just outside of Rotterdam. C. Te Lintum, "Emigratie over Rotterdam in de 18e eeuw," de Gids, 11 (1908):6-7.

37. For a discussion of fare prices, see Wokeck, "A Tide of Alien Tongues," chap. 5.

38. The importance of good and sufficient drinking water was emphasized by virtually every immigrant who commented on the voyage. The logistics — the availability of enough water casks for such a large number of passengers for about two months — were formidable: barrels formerly used for wine, beer, etc., were often taken as substitutes, a practice which resulted in many complaints about contaminated water.

39. Most Germans seem to have despised the regular provisions on board. Allegedly, merchants cut provisioning costs by furnishing migrants with food of inferior quality. "The case of the Palatine Protestants who are ship'd from Rotterdam to Philadelphia and Carolina in America in the Months of June and July [1750]," Pennsylvania Miscellaneous Papers, Penn and Baltimore, fol. 115, HSP.

40. Melchior, "Advice to German Emigrants, 1749," pp. 233-34; *Pennsylvanische Berichte,* 16 Nov. 1749. At the height of the immigrant trade, some merchants achieved very high passenger/ship ratios by shipping the passengers' luggage on another vessel, sent at the end of the season when the latecomers did not fill a whole ship. This practice caused deprivation for the passengers who traveled without their chests and led also to substantial loss of property since theft was rampant during the storage period. Without a proper bill of lading which itemized the contents of a chest — a precautionary measure which few emigrants demanded — many immigrants could not even prove, let alone recoup, the loss of goods from a pilfered or stolen chest.

41. Melchior, "Advice to German Emigrants, 1749," p. 232. For instance, the transportation contract of Dunlop & Co. in 1752 offered emigrants who "charged" their fares until arrival no choice of destination in the American colonies. See Ratterman, "Deutsches Element in Maine," 14:354-57.

42. In letters to relatives and friends back home, immigrants did recommend, or warn, against particular newlanders. One such letter by Hans Wyss (4 Dec. 1749) is cited in Andreas Blocher, *Die Eigenart der Zürcher Auswanderer, 1734-1744* (Zurich, 1976), pp. 176-77.

43. McCusker, "Ships Registered at the Port of Philadelphia" and the "Tonnage Duty Book" were the sources for the tonnage of German immigrant vessels. Ships that appeared in both listings show a ratio of .91 *registered* tons to *measured* tons. On the difficulties of standardizing and converting eighteenth-century tonnage measurements, see John J. McCusker, "The Tonnage of Ships Engaged in British Colonial Trade During the Eighteenth Century," *Research in Economic History,* 6 (1981):73-105; see also Doerflinger, "Enterprise on the Delaware," p. 525.

44. See L. F. Middlebrook, "The Ship *Mary* of Philadelphia, 1740," *PMHB,* 58 (1934):127-31, 149-51.

45. The ship *Crown* probably registered around 220 tons (John Hunt to John Stedman, 24 Jan., 14 and 24 Feb. 1748/9, Hunt & Greenleafe letter book, HSP). Freights equalled the number of *full fares.* The number of *passengers* was usually higher than that of the freights, because children between 5 and 14 years of age paid only half fare and children under 4 traveled free of charge.

46. In 1765 legislation against abuses in the immigrant trade specified the height of a bunk as 3'9" (2'9" in the steerage). James T. Mitchell and Henry Flanders, comps., *The Statutes at Large of Pennsylvania from 1681 to 1801* (Harrisburg, Pa., 1896-1915), 6:432-40, sect. 3.

47. Most charterparty contracts allowed the merchant to rearrange the regular structures on deck according to the requirements of the immigrant trade, provided that "the bulkheads of the cabin will be put up again" at the end of the ship's run, at the cost of the chartering merchant. ONA 2344/63 (30 May 1749).

48. Charles W. Baird, *History of the Huguenot Emigration to America* (New York, 1885), 1:186-87; "The Case of the Palatine Protestants [1750]," HSP.

49. Allowing for some individual variation, this general fare scale was standard in all charterparty contracts.

50. The musterbook of the ship *Britannia,* HSP, provides a good example.

51. See Wokeck, "A Tide of Alien Tongues," fig. 8.

52. *Statutes at Large,* 5:94-97; 6:432-40.

53. For all accounting purposes between charterparties, freights were counted upon embarkation in Europe, not upon debarkation in the American colonies.

54. In particular, sick passengers who still owed their fare on arrival would not easily sell as indentured servants — a popular strategy to defray passage debts.

55. For example, Capt. George Wax was "unwilling to expose himself to mutiny on the high seas," which he feared as a consequence if the passengers should

have to starve. "Report on the Petition of Theobald Kieffer and Others, 9 Sept. 1737," SP 42/138, PRO, published in part by Elisabeth C. Kieffer, "The Cheese Was Good," *Pennsylvania Folklife*, 12, no. 3 (1970), pp. 28-29. I wish to thank Elisabeth Kieffer for the use of her photostats.

56. For examples illustrating the different ways in which provisions were distributed, see the report by Francis Daniel Pastorius (1684/5), quoted in *Pennsylvania German Society, Proceedings and Addresses*, 9 (1899):131, 133-37; letter of Hans Wyss (4 Dec. 1749), cited in Blocher, *Die Eigenart der Zürcher Auswanderer*, p. 175; William J. Hinke, ed., "Report of the Journey of Francis Louis Michel from Bern, Switzerland, to Virginia, October 2, 1701-December 1, 1702," *Virginia Magazine of History and Biography*, 24 (1926):10; Mittelberger, *Journey to Pennsylvania*, pp. 15-16.

57. How important contemporaries considered the implementation of such a routine is evident from its incorporation into the law that regulated the German immigrant trade. *Statutes at Large*, 6:432-40, sect. 2.

58. In the accounts that have survived of immigrant voyages, there are strikingly few instances of cooperative and compassionate behavior among passengers. Even emigrants who interpreted the hardships of the journey as a test of their faith in God were more likely to turn inward than to reach out to help their equally unfortunate fellow passengers who lacked the consolation of strong spiritual support.

❧·MEETING HOUSE
and COUNTING HOUSE

MELVIN B. ENDY, JR.

16 ⟨ Puritanism, Spiritualism, and Quakerism:

An Historiographical Essay

The problems posed by the attempt to define Puritanism have driven some scholars to substituting description for definition and others to the use of the term as an umbrella for the religious experience shared by groups as disparate as mildly dissatisfied Anglicans, on the one hand, and the Ranters and other enthusiasts of the Interregnum on the other. I confess that at times the issue has left me less confused than disinterested—namely, when I have remembered that the definition of an historical entity such as Puritanism is in part, at least, dependent upon the focus and aims of the historian. To the extent that this is the case, the debate about the most adequate definition is beside the point. At the same time, I have become increasingly uneasy with what appears to be a developing consensus among a weighty body of interpreters that has opted for what John T. McNeill has called "a recklessly extensive application of the word 'Puritan'" to groups whose religious thought differs in decisive ways from that of English Presbyterians, Congregationalists, and Baptists on the basis of a presumed "continuity of experience" and similar origins.[1] Of particular interest to me is the application of the label to Quakerism, which is increasingly seen as an expression of Puritanism even by scholars reluctant to apply the term to other Interregnum enthusiasts.

Although the major figures in the revival of Puritan studies in the 1930s, Perry Miller and William Haller, referred to Puritanism in broad terms as, respectively, a "point of view," a "philosophy of life," a "code of values," and a "spiritual outlook, way of life, and mode of expression," both scholars were sufficiently concerned with Puritanism as a body of ideas and with what Miller called the "equilibrium of forces, emotional and intellectual, within the Puritan creed," that they applied the term primarily to the movement centering on Haller's "spiritual brotherhood" of preachers and then to the Presbyterian, Congregationalist, and Baptist groups that came into being in England and America.[2] For Miller especially, enthusiasts of any sort were beyond the pale. In the last thirty years, however, students of Interregnum England and colonial America have made us well aware of the similarities between Puritanism and the various kinds of enthusiasts — often called "Seekers," "Familists," and "Ranters" by their contemporaries — that appeared in the heady times of the English Civil War, with the mantle of Puritanism descending especially on that most sober and significant body of religious radicals, the Quakers.

The tendency to emphasize the affinities and minimize the differences between Puritanism and Quakerism has been the dominant note in the most prominent studies of both movements in the last generation. Developing hints dropped by Miller and Haller, among others, concerning the Puritan drive toward unmediated experience of God through the Holy Spirit, many scholars have concluded, in the words of Alan Simpson on Puritanism's relation to Quakerism, that "an enterprise which began in the sixteenth century by exhorting men to prepare themselves for a miracle of grace and ended by asserting the presence of the Holy Spirit in every individual is one movement."[3] The same judgment is found in the most monumental and influential chronicle of American religion by another Puritan scholar, Sydney Ahlstrom, *A Religious History of the American People.*[4] Probably the most influential exponent of the continuity between Puritanism and the Interregnum religious groups is Geoffrey Nuttall, whose study, *The Holy Spirit in Puritan Faith and Experience,* set the tone for a whole generation of students of "left-wing" Puritanism and Quakerism.[5]

Working in the opposite direction to reach the same conclusion, historians of Quakerism of the last generation have seen fit to play down what the Quaker scholar Rufus Jones called the "mystical" element in early Quakerism and to stress its prophetic Puritan spirit. Frederick Tolles sounded the representative note when he wrote that "Quakerism as it arose in the middle of the seventeenth century cannot be understood unless it is seen as one of the variant expressions of the dominant and all-pervading Puritanism of the age."[6] The standard and most influential study of early Quakerism, Hugh Barbour's *The Quakers in Puritan England,* is based on the assumption that "both groups actually stemmed from the same traditions, and most of their crucial doctrines were the same."[7]

My purpose in this essay is to sort out the various themes and emphases in the recent literature stressing the affinities between Puritans and Quakers and to analyze them in the light of a new look at the way in which Puritanism was related in Interregnum England to the rise of what I shall call "Spiritualist" religious groups, including, among others, what were at the time called Familists, Seekers, and Ranters as well as Quakers. My thesis is that although many of the insights of recent scholarship are important correctives to earlier work on both Puritans and Quakers, it is essential to recognize that Puritan roots do not necessarily produce Puritan fruits.[8] A concern for terminological clarity in the definition of Puritanism as well as a full understanding of the place of Quakerism in its contemporary setting and its significance in the history of religious thought require that we distinguish between the Puritans and the Spiritualists of seventeenth-century England and link the Quakers more closely with the latter.

Those who extend the definition of Puritanism to encompass the Quakers and other Spiritualists correctly point out that the narrower definition associated with Miller and Haller was the fruit of an approach to Puritanism that dealt primarily with the history of ideas. This perspective viewed the movement somewhat as a static philosophy or body of ideas and failed to appreciate fully what David Hall has termed its "dynamic and expansive" qualities or its "restlessness."[9] It gave inadequate attention to the experiential and emotional side of Puritanism and, in the words of Richard Schlatter, "left out of account the circumstances, the concrete times and places and social networks in which the thinkers lived."[10]

The spokesmen for the continuity between Puritanism and the Spiritualists usually allow that even the relatively sober Friends differed in some respects from other Puritans and sometimes list the many heresies that orthodox or Reformed Puritans found among the Quakers and other Spiritualists.[11] Although many recent Quaker scholars believe that the doctrinal differences were overshadowed by similarities on the more momentous matters, others, such as Geoffrey Nuttall, are at times ambivalent on whether even the Friends should be called Puritans and admit that there was something in Quakerism "which was genuinely contrary to the Puritans', even the radical Puritans', beliefs and which excited their keenest antipathy."[12] But even Nuttall, the most careful of the students of left wing Puritanism, while noting that the Quakers may not be Puritans "in the exclusive sense," nevertheless finds that they "repeat, extend, and foresee so much of what is held by the radical, Separatist party within Puritanism that they cannot be denied the name or excluded the consideration."[13] Moreover, the revisionists coalesce in their belief that Quakerism and Puritanism are best understood when the Quakers' Spiritualist emphases are seen as the "logical terminus" of the Puritan movement because they indicate "the *direction* of the Puritan movement as a whole."[14]

The *differentium* of the Puritan movement or that which pushed it constantly in the direction of Spiritualism and Quakerism was its tendency toward direct communion with God through his Holy Spirit in independence of all mediatorial means. More specifically,

> In Puritanism what religiously and theologically springs from concentration on the doctrine and experience of the Holy Spirit may be seen more philosophically or psychologically as a concern with immediacy, as an insistence on the non-necessity of a vehiculum or medium. Historically this arose in reaction against, indeed in horror at, a religion throughout which, in priesthood, in sacrament, in invocation of saints, mediation was dominant. It is possible for the reaction to lead, as von Hügel fairly remarks, to dispensing with the Mediator. Originally, it is equally fair to remark, it was the outcome of joy and liberation in a new, direct, personal faith in Christ and a new, direct, personal experience of His Spirit.[15]

As a result of this drive toward immediate spiritual experience one can see in Puritanism, according to Nuttall, the constant thrust toward, and occasional surfacing of, several tendencies which the Quakers and other Spiritualists would carry openly to completion: the belief that the Spirit might operate apart from Scripture; the association of the Spirit's operation not with reason or conscience but with a special spiritual sense; the experience of spiritual leadings that provided infallible certainty of full sanctification and that at times provided "objective" divine knowledge and directives; a tendency toward immediate reliance on spiritual leadings for all worship, including prayer and preaching; disuse of the sacraments and suspicion that the Spirit was hindered by such physical mediating agents; a dispensational view of salvation-history looking toward a third age of the Spirit that would follow upon and improve the dispensation of the gospel as it had improved on the dispensation of the Law; and a mystical tendency — "a sense of being carried out beyond the things of time and space into unity with the infinite and eternal."[16]

The strength of the school of thought that places the Quakers and other Spiritualists in their Puritan environment and on the left wing of the movement lies in its insight into the dynamic nature of Puritanism and in its realization that such terms as Puritanism tend to become abstractions unless defined by reference to individuals and particular groups, historical connections, and patterns and directions of influence. The conditions brought on by the Civil War in England, not primarily continental "mystical" influences, were responsible not only for the splintering of Puritanism into a group of orthodox "denominations" but for the rise of the "fanatics" or enthusiasts to the left of them. Moreover, most of the leaders of the Quakers, Ranters, Familists, and Seekers can be seen to have arrived at their destination after traversing much of the Puritan spectrum. In the course of that trek they found themselves relying less on trained intellectual leaders and more on their own overwhelming experiences of spiritual rebirth.

Nevertheless, terms such as Puritanism, Quakerism, and Spiritualism become confusing and misleading if the concern for patterns of continuity and historical influence is not tempered by an insistence on observing the lines of debate and major points of divergence, as well as the doctrinal differences that produced these divergences. Although historians have clearly benefited from the broadened approach to Puritanism, with its recognition of the Puritan prehistory of the various enthusiasts who arose in the 1640s and 1650s, its appreciation of the "turmoil of feeling" and emotional intensity that lay at the heart of Puritan experience, and its emphasis on the spiritualizing thrust of the movement, the "stretched passion" was not, it seems to me, as elastic as it has been made out to be.[17] Stretched beyond the breaking point, the definition of Puritanism masks an important discontinuity that must be recognized if seventeenth-century English and American religious life and thought are to be adequately understood.

As David Hall has written, "An adequate definition of the Puritan movement must . . . seek to unite the experiential dimension with the formal structure of the Puritan intellect."[18] What seems to have happened in Puritan and Quaker studies is that the Miller-Haller history-of-ideas emphasis on the Puritan intellect has not been united with an experiential thrust so much as replaced by it. Mountains of dispute over religious experience, means of grace, the nature of worship, and doctrine, in which protagonists — as in the case of Quakers and Puritans — see themselves often engaged against mortal enemies denying the central tenets of their faith, are seen as involving simply "feuding, rather than kissing, cousins."[19] In the course of stressing the historical connection among religious groups and the experiential side of Puritanism, many historians seem to have given inadequate attention to the fact that the Presbyterians, Congregationalists, Baptists, Seekers, Familists, Ranters, and Quakers, although not, in most cases, juridically organized denominations, were religious groups that had to state their raison d'etre and define themselves either positively or negatively in doctrinal terms. Even those groups that relied more on the Spirit than on trained intellects and who shied away from doctrinal standards defended their denials and their peculiar beliefs in oral and written theological and historical debates. The content of these debates must be taken seriously by anyone who would understand the seventeenth century in its own terms, and when that is done, there emerges a fundamental dividing line that cannot be ignored. As George Sabine has observed, in the study of seventeenth-century English religious history—and I would add American as well—"no reasonable clarity can be attained unless a line is observed at least between mystics like Winstanley and the Quakers, and those who, like all Calvinists and nearly all Baptists, thought it essential to maintain a creed, a church discipline, and the outlines of rational theology."[20]

Robert Middlekauf has discussed the way in which the Puritans generated and controlled emotion through ideas or intellect, suggesting that the Puritans were no longer Puritans when they let their concern for immediate experience of the Spirit go to extremes and break the controlling casing provided by Scripture, doctrine, and reason.[21] Although, as David Hall has argued, Miller may have overemphasized the "hidden rationalism" of the Puritans to a certain extent, we nevertheless can return some clarity and order to Puritan studies by attending to Miller's conception of Puritanism as an "equilibrium of forces" in which emotion is guided and restrained by intellect, remembering that, for the Puritan, "while the soul does indeed have an access to God, it receives from the spirit no [independent] verdict upon any question, only a dutiful disposition to accept the verdict confirmed by Scripture, by authority, and by logic."[22] The verdict is confirmed by Scripture, according to Miller, because the Puritan knew that in this world man will always "see through a glass, darkly" despite his intensive spiritual experience and that regeneration will always come "through the impact of a sensible species or phantasm, that it is always attached to some spoken word or to some physical experience." It is confirmed by authority because the counterpart to the Puritan sense of inward communication was

> an ideal of social conformity, of law and order, of regulation and control. At the core of the theology there was an indestructible element which was mystical, and a feeling for the universe which was almost pantheistic; but there was also a social code demanding obedience to external law, a code to which good people voluntarily conformed and to which bad people should be made to conform.

It is confirmed by logic because "Puritan theorists sought to unite in one harmonious system both science and religion, reason and faith, . . . to reconcile revelation with natural learning and so to combine in one systematic belief both piety and the inherited body of knowledge."[23]

What seems to me most fruitful in Miller's approach to Puritanism is its recognition that at the heart of the movement certain ideas were in tension and that a Puritan was one who formed a more or less stable equilibrium out of a balancing of polar parts, including not only intellect and affection or mind and heart, but also a Platonic mystical and an Aristotelian sense epistemology, ecclesiastical authority and individual experience, free will and predestination, justification and sanctification, and separatism (in the cause of purification) and transformationism. This seems to be not only a more accurate approach to the mind of the Puritan movement but one that allows the historian to describe how events determined the directions taken by different Puritans in the New World in the seventeenth and especially the eighteenth centuries and how the splintering of the movement took place in Interregnum England. One problematic aspect of the recent emphasis on the "continuity of experience" from right to left on the Puritan spectrum through at least the Quakers is its implicit idealistic assumption that Puritanism, based as it was on a powerful conception of spiritual experience, spewed forth ever more spiritualistic exponents by a kind of inner logic until it reached its terminus in the Interregnum enthusiasts. Although this approach is predicated on a reaction against what is perceived as an overly intellectualistic interpretation of the movement and claims to take seriously the "circumstances, the concrete times and places and social networks" of the Puritans, ironically it seems to explain the direction of the movement by recourse to an inner "thrust" rather than to events such as the Civil War and its turmoil and makes it difficult to account for the complexity and animosity of the splintering process that took place. Certainly the analyses of Nuttall and Simpson and the similar emphases of other recent exponents of the spiritual thrust of Puritanism are based on a keen appreciation of the psychological or inward nature of Puritan thought, but the belief that Quakerism was the logical outcome of the movement makes it difficult to understand how under the press of events the Puritan focus on the process of regeneration could go to a "logical" extreme in more than one direction, whereas the equilibrium image has precisely that virtue.

Probably the clearest illustrations of the loss of balance and the splitting of polar parts were the successive confrontations in that laboratory of Puritanism, Massachusetts Bay, between the colonial pillars, on the one side, and Roger Williams, Ann Hutchinson, and radical New Lights a century later on the other — confrontations that can be seen as resulting from the splitting apart of the poles of the movement under the press of social, political, and economic as well as religious developments. A similar process took place in England in the Interregnum, although here the splinters flew in more directions. In the heady times of the Revolution those caught up in the exhilarating victories of the Roundhead army and insistent on justifying the ecclesiastical and religious freedom they were experiencing found it easy enough to be seized by the self-authenticating raptures of the Spirit, to join the mystics who no longer needed to "see through a glass, darkly," and to move toward a new heaven and a new earth either as chiliasts or as spiritual millennialists. On the other hand, under the influence of the Scots and parliamentary pressure, the sense of responsibility engendered by the duties assigned them at Westminster, and their own dour perceptions of a social and religious scene increasingly plagued by chaos and disunity, the men of a conservative bent inevitably pulled back from the radical implications others saw in Puritan thought. Developing the conservative possibilities in covenant thought, they said that conversion was to be viewed as a process fitting certain prescribed rules and requiring the guidance of trained interpreters of Scripture and spiritual psychology. Their judgment was that this could be done better in churches in which trained clerics, rather than congregations of laity, selected and ordained new ministers, and in which a hierarchy of judicatory bodies could insure uniformity by providing rules for the church and working out the patterns by which the rules could be enforced in church and state. These men could find ample roots in Puritanism for their insistence on hierarchical control by saintly intellects, on the wisdom of adhering to reason in religion, and on the necessity of guided disciplined steps and a dependence on the law both before and after conversion. John Bastwick, the authoritarian Dortian Calvinist; Richard Baxter, the ecumenical rationalist and virtual Arminian; John Goodwin, the moral rationalist; and William Dell, the Antinomian Spiritualist, can all be easily shown to be logical developers of Puritanism.[24]

The understanding of Puritanism as an equilibrium of forces, rather than an outworking of the spiritualistic thrust, also prepares the historian to understand more elements of the long-range consequences of the Puritan movement, since it enables him to see the role that Puritanism played in producing not only enthusiasts and revivalists but also the Unitarians and other liberals of the eighteenth century.

A second problematic aspect of the recent emphasis on the continuity between Spirit-oriented religious groups is a concomitant reluctance to deal with the problem of discontinuity. There seems to be inadequate concern with setting criteria for discerning the points at which Puritanism shaded off into other movements and a corresponding tendency to link in a misleading way religious groups that differed at central points and that perceived themselves as so differing. It is true that there is a certain sense in which the groups loosely called Seekers, Ranters, and Familists — or, to one writer, "locusts out of the bottomlesse pit" — were drawing out the implications of a certain Puritan attitude toward the relationship between God and man in general and their doctrine of the Spirit in particular.[25] But it makes no more sense to argue that Spiritualism was the logical outcome of Puritanism than it would to hold, should the United States see the rise of a significant Communist movement in the near future, that this was the logical outcome of the liberal Democratic program of the 1930s through the 1960s. Communism may incorporate in an extreme form some of the egalitarian concerns of the liberal Democrats, but it also represents a contradiction of some of their central beliefs about man and society. Gerrard Winstanley and George Fox, among other Spiritualists, carried through admirably on the Puritan concern for a Spirit-mediated encounter between God and man, but they did so at the expense of central beliefs shared by the Presbyterians, Congregationalists, and most Baptists. The Puritans' agreement with the Continental Reformed movement on essential points of doctrine and ecclesiology is seldom spotlighted, since these were shared with most religiously literate Anglicans before the Restoration. The historian's need to stress that which distinguishes Puritanism from the Continental Reformed and Anglican churches should not, however, lead to any ambiguity about the Reformed theology of the movement. Puritans believed that in this world man, poor worm that he was, not only was a gross sinner but had no direct access to the divine presence. For this reason God had brought about the salvation of the elect by sending his Son to live and die as a man in history and then to return to heaven to await the final judgment. The Bible was the record of his deeds and the proclamation of his salvation, and through the power of the Holy Spirit this primary Word of God to man could lead one to regeneration and perseverance when read and proclaimed by studious men as a guide for worship and all of life. The focal point of the Bible and of Puritan religion was the belief that man could be justified by the grace of God with no merit of his own as a result of the crucifixion of Jesus.

The upheavals of the Interregnum found many men experiencing hopes and even visions that convinced them that very shortly or even now man no longer was to be restricted to an ambiguous and indirect, if powerful, sense of the divine presence. In the new age of the Spirit that was dawning, Christ within was to replace the outward Christ; no man need be dependent on other men for his religious knowledge, be they apostolic writers or contemporary ministers; and what was important was not a historical story about a divine-human agent floating down or up or a tale about a future coming judgment but the present experience of the eternal Christ lifting one above the fallen state of man. Many of those on the path to this Spiritualist perspective, such as William Dell, John Webster, Richard Coppin, and John Saltmarsh, traveled only part of the way; others, such as the Ranters in the narrow or proper sense, including Jacob Bauthumley, Laurence Clarkson, and Abiezer Coppe, spiritualized organized religion out of existence and ended up with a complete antinomianism and pantheism; and others, such as the Quakers, traveled far down the path but after the Interregnum turned around and tried to work out a compromise between the old faith and the new. There had already developed intraparty disagreement among Puritans on such matters as justification, religious liberty, and even election and its relation to human will, although all but the General Baptists, who were somewhat anomalous in any case, still called themselves Calvinists or Dortians. There could be no similar leeway in such doctrinal areas as the historic drama of Redemption, the significance of the historical Christ, and the revelatory sufficiency of the Bible. Anyone who suggested that the biblical drama was significant primarily as an allegory of God's dealing with each soul, that the historical Christ be replaced as the focus of faith by the Christ within, and that the Bible be replaced by the Spirit as the norm and guide of the Christian, was beyond the Puritan pale. As the polemical works of men as different as the Presbyterian Richard Baxter, the Congregationalist John Owen, and the Baptist John Bunyan make clear, there could be no compromise on these issues.[26]

The Puritans, then, were those representatives of Continental Reformed theology in England who were distinguished from Continental

Reformed religious movements primarily by the way in which they combined a rather extreme — for Reformed thinkers — emphasis on a powerful
experience of God's regenerating grace as a mark of election with an insistence on exteriorizing their regenerate Christian life through a pattern of
self-examination and self-denial leading to saintly behavior, by participation in a visible church patterned after that explicitly ordained in the New
Testament, and, in most cases, by an interest in religious, social, and political reform centered on the hope of turning England into a model Christian
social order. Operating more or less loosely within the Anglican church
before 1640 or gathering separatist congregations apart from it, they formed
after that date until at least 1688 a spectrum of religious bodies including
the Presbyterians, Congregationalists, and Particular Baptists.[27]

The Spiritualists were those Englishmen who, influenced in most cases
by the Puritan emphasis on the interior religious experience, came to believe in the days of the Revolution — and in some cases before — that the
dispensation of the Holy Spirit prophecied in the *Book of Joel* had arrived
or was about to arrive. The Spirit was operating in a uniquely powerful
fashion to produce a new — most often seen as the third — dispensation in
which, as William Dell said, men could climb above "all visible and sensible
things, even as high as God himself," through an experience of a totally
overpowering spiritual death and rebirth.[28] This experience prepared them
to participate in a religious life based wholly on immediate spiritual leadings
and caused them to scoff at the "gross, carnall, visible evidences and mater-
iall beams" that had been appropriate for the previous salvation-history
dispensation.[29] Although Dell and Saltmarsh, as well as several other men
often called Spiritual Puritans or Antinomians, hovered around the edges
of Puritanism, what clearly separated Seekers such as Gerrard Winstanley,
members of the English followers of Henry Nicholas's Family of Love,
Ranters such as Laurence Clarkson, Abiezer Coppe, and Jacob Bauthumley, and the Quakers, among others, from Puritans was not only an extremist reliance on spiritual experience that clashed with the Puritan tendency
to balance polar elements — including external authority and inner experience — but a tendency to carry their spiritual emphasis to the point of
denying central Reformed doctrines and practices including, at least, election, justification by imputation, and Scripture as the key to doctrine and
practice; and ecclesiastical practices, including a set liturgy and the use of
the sacraments.[30]

At virtually every point the new doctrinal and ecclesiastical emphases,
contemporary Puritans believed, could be traced to the Spiritualists' views
of the person and work of Christ, and, more specifically, as Henry More
said in reference to the Quakers, to their "excluding the external Christ
from the business of Religion, and only admitting the internal Christ."[31]
More's charge was an exaggeration, especially as applied to the Quakers,
but despite a good deal of both intentional and unintended ambiguity in

their writings, the Spiritualists shared in varying degrees of conviction the belief that the lynchpin of true religion and universal salvation was not the act of Atonement by which the historical Christ provided, said Puritans, the possibility for the salvation of individuals (the Elect) and the renewal of the Covenant, but rather, the experience of the "eternal" or "inward" Christ who had mediated true knowledge and saving grace to all men in all eras. The Spiritualists were involved, to varying degrees, in a spirit-body dualism, according to which true religious knowledge dealt with noncorporeal realities and was mediated by means of direct intellection or intuition not involving the senses. For this reason they had difficulty believing that true knowledge and grace could be mediated by "sensible," "visible," "corruptible," "outward," and "carnal" means such as a truly human, incarnate Jesus of Nazareth or the Scriptures.[32]

The Quakers do not fit quite so neatly as some of the more radical enthusiasts into the Spiritualist mold, and there are many contemporary Quaker scholars who, while admitting the need for a fundamental differentiation between Puritans and Spiritualists, object to linking Quakers with the latter. Seizing on the tendency of Puritan scholars to stretch the definition of Puritanism, they insist that the Friends were extreme Puritans. According to this approach, Fox and the First Publishers of Truth simply "somewhat impatiently restated the essentials of the Christian [i.e., Puritan] flame that fired up England in their day of spiritual visitation." "The breakthough for Quakerism did not come from the newness of Fox's doctrines. It came when Fox turned north . . . into the largely untouched hill country of Yorkshire, Westmorland, and Cumberland."[33] It is difficult to ignore the mountain of doctrinal controversy between Puritans and Quakers that began to grow from the beginning of the Quaker movement, but under the influence of the Puritan mystique some scholars have been led to conclude, with Frederick Tolles, that Friends were sound on the "traditonal Protestant doctrines of the Trinity, the Deity of Christ, the Vicarious Atonement, and the plenary inspiration and authority of the Scriptures."[34] Others make smaller claims, simply listing Fox's letter to the governor of Barbados as a representative and basically orthodox statement of Quaker doctrinal essentials, or remaining content to point out that, despite doctrinal aberrations on Scripture, the Church, the sacraments, and other matters, the earliest Friends retained the keystone of orthodoxy, a belief in Christ as the watershed and Lord of history, and a reliance on his historical act of Atonement as well as his contemporary indwelling.[35] Whatever their aberrations, they lacked the peculiar dehistoricizing and anti-sense knowledge thrust of the true Spiritualists. In their more careful moments some recent Quaker scholars have been willing to list the Quakers' departures from Reformed theology and their special difficulties in dealing with the person and work of the historical Christ, only to conclude that these differences

292 MELVIN B. ENDY, JR.

in doctrine were somehow overshadowed by the "prophetic" thrust of the movement and that the similarities far outweighed the differences.[36]

The view of Quakerism as a Puritan sect can be explained in part as a result of the mutually reinforcing historiographical situations that have prevailed in Puritan and Quaker scholarship in the last generation. As Puritan scholars have uncovered their subjects' doctrine of the Holy Spirit, Quaker scholars of an evangelical cast have been emboldened to stress the Calvinist-Puritan and orthodox Christian elements in Quakerism by the rise to prominence of Calvinism in the form of Protestant neo-orthodoxy, a desire for inclusion within the ecumenical movement, and the inevitable reaction against the somewhat simplistic liberal or "mystical" interpretation of Quakerism by Rufus Jones that had gained wide acceptance by 1930.[37] But the difficulty of pinning down the Quakers stems from the sources as well as from historiographical developments. Like the other Spiritualists, the Friends were clearly influenced by the spirit-body dualism that led to a denigration of the historical Christ, Scripture, and liturgical ordinances. From George Fox and James Nayler, the closest Quakerism came to having founders, through the former Puritan Isaac Penington and former General Baptist Samuel Fisher, and through more theologically sophisticated writers such as Robert Barclay and George Whitehead, there runs a strong tendency to insist that the spiritual man cannot rely on — indeed, runs a danger in relying on — anything "visible," "corruptible," or "outward." In the words of Fox, the Spirit "draws off and weans you from all things, that are created and external, (which fade and pass away,) up to God, the fountain of life, and head of all things." Therefore, the "new covenant is not according to the old; for the one was of natural things, and the other of inward and spiritual."[38] It followed that the focus of Quaker thought was not the incarnate Christ who died at Jerusalem but rather the "eternal" or "inward" Christ.

At the same time, many of the Quaker writers were conservative by instinct and reluctant to attack openly the central Christological and soteriological structure of Christianity. In the earliest stages of the movement, genuinely confused about the proper means of relating the historical Christ to the inward or eternal Christ to whom they attributed the rebirth of true religion, they tended to avoid the issue. For example, Edward Burrough, in *A Description of the State and Condition of all Mankind* (1656) and *A Standard lifted up* (1657), described man's fallen state and its remedy and in the latter treatise gave an orderly statement of essential Quaker beliefs, and in neither was the incarnate Christ, as opposed to the eternal Christ, mentioned. When pressed by opponents about his failure to mention the historical Christ, Burrough admitted that the Christ he had been referring to was the same as the one who had died at Jerusalem and risen again, making it clear that he took the Gospels literally, but his admission did not imply that Christ's incarnate deeds were essential to salvation.[39]

Burrough was typical in his handling of the issue. Rather than denying the significance of the historical Christ, the Quakers preferred to stress the continuity or essential sameness — at least for the purposes of salvation — between Christ's pre-incarnate, incarnate, and post-incarnate states. But if this studied ambiguity often prevented open heresy on the central Christian doctrines of the person and work of Christ, the Quakers were, in the debates of the day, drawn into explanations that revealed the radical Spiritualist implications of their position. To emphasize the continuity in Christ's states several Quakers referred to the heavenly flesh by which he operated throughout history as a mediatorial principle and referred to his incarnate state in such a manner as either to dissociate the true Christ from his fleshly garment or to make that flesh "incorruptible" and hence not truly human.[40] Moreover, it followed, as Penington said, that it was more appropriate to attribute whatever good resulted from the historical Christ's work to his active divine part rather than the body he assumed, and since the incorruptible, unchangeable divine part could not suffer and die, what the divine incarnate Christ accomplished soteriologically could be done as easily in his pre- and post-incarnate states.[41]

Unlike most of the other Spiritualists, however, the Quakers survived into the Restoration and beyond, were given the time to reflect on their views, and were subjected to the pressure to escape persecution — especially after 1688. Some Quaker leaders, including Fox and Nayler, had from the beginning been less consistent than others in carrying out their spiritualizing to the point of utterly ignoring or denying Christ's Atonement as the watershed of history, and Barclay's *Apology for the True Christian Divinity* made the more conservative or orthodox position central by combining a clear spirit-body epistemology with the position that somehow Christ's atoning act was a causal factor in the salvation even of those who knew only the inner or eternal Christ.[42] Barclay's view of the person and work of Christ hardly satisfied Puritans and Anglicans, and he was even less orthodox in his positions on Scripture and other entailments of his spirit-sense dualism, but he provided the compromise on this central issue that had enabled Quakerism ever since to house both liberals carrying to conclusion the original Spiritualist thrust of the movement and more orthodox, even evangelical, Christians. When to the stick of persecution was added the carrot of the Toleration Act, with its promise of peace for orthodox Christians who could affirm the Trinity and traditional views of the person and work of Christ, even Quaker writers of a less orthodox bent, including William Penn and George Whitehead, tempered their doctrinal statements to win acceptance for Friends. The price of that peace has been the warfare among historians of later generations who have found ample evidence in Quakerism's conflicting signals for their own apologetic or historiographical purposes.

294 MELVIN B. ENDY, JR.

However mixed their signals were by 1690, the Quakers are more appropriately linked with the Spiritualists than with the Puritans.[43] Although many Friends were convinced of their own utter uniqueness, in reporting on their contemporaries many Quaker writers made clear their belief that the Spiritualists had carried the reformation of religion farther than the Puritans to the right of them and in general spoke in more tender terms of the former than the latter.[44] The Quakers' perception of their links to the Spiritualists was shared by their enemies, who invariably perceived them as part of what Henry More called "that smutt of familism" — even if, in time, they came to see them as the least offensive element of what they viewed as the lunatic fringe. In addition, with most of the Spiritualists they rejected the Puritans' Reformed views of election, revelation (and hence Scripture), justification by imputation, original sin, and worship as consisting of the Word expounded from Scripture and the sacraments.[45] When doctrinal differences on these points are viewed as of secondary significance, an interpretative perspective is being brought to bear that does injustice to seventeenth-century religious priorities, as well as to the historic boundary of orthodox Christianity.

Admittedly, however, the key difference between Puritans and Spiritualists was their view of the person and work of Christ. Here the earliest Quakers' central concern with the eternal Christ to the neglect of the historical Christ was enough to place them in the Spiritualist milieu. Clearly, just as it is important to recognize that Puritan roots do not necessarily produce Puritan fruits, it is equally important to realize that the Spiritualist milieu of the earliest Friends is not necessarily a broad enough frame of reference for understanding the religious/theological position of Friends in the wake of Barclay and the pressures of the Toleration Act. However, the fact that the Friends tempered their spiritualizing view of the person and work of Christ, among other doctrines, to fit — if awkwardly — the confines of the Toleration Act does not make even the later Quakers Puritans. It simply places them closer to conservative and hesitating Spiritualists such as the men I have called Spiritual Puritans or possibly places them beyond the pale of earlier classifications. In addition, it leaves us with a chronological complexity and a uniqueness that historical abstractions can rarely accommodate.

I have suggested that debates over definitions of historical terms such as Puritanism at times reflect less a genuine difference in interpretation than a divergence in intention and perspective. It has also been my contention that broad definitions of Puritanism that encompass many Spiritualists have their uses and even provide a needed corrective to other approaches. At the same time, my central argument has been that some definitions are more useful than others for understanding and classifying seventeenth-century English religious groups and that a definition of Quakerism as a religious movement that locates it among the Puritans is decidedly misleading. Some closing remarks about the definitional perspectives and tasks of students of religious movements and their implications for understanding the groups under consideration may make more explicit what is at issue in this controversy.

Students of religious movements have found useful three kinds of definitions, namely, the functional, essential, and formal or elemental (sometimes called the phenomenological). Puritanism has been analyzed from all three perspectives. Scholars such as Christopher Hill, Michael Walzer, and Larzer Ziff, among others, have focused primarily on the ways in which the religious movement performed certain psychological, social, economic, and political functions for its adherents and have defined it primarily as a response on the part of a class or group with distinct personal and social needs. Such an approach sees Puritanism as, for example, a rationalization of the activities of a new middle class or, in the words of Ziff, "a way of coping with the threatening conditions of masterlessness and landlessness."[46]

A second definitional approach, the essential, looks for the *sine qua non* or essential characteristic that marks the movement as a religious or sacred phenomenon and that links a variety of such groups and individuals. What is the characteristic experience of the sacred or perspective on the sacred that is distinctive about this movement and gives it its motivating power? A very common such definition is that found in Francis Bremer's claim that "the earliest and most constant characteristic of Puritanism [is] the belief that the Church of England had not been sufficiently purged of the theology and worship of Roman Catholicism."[47] More common in the literature I have discussed is Sydney Ahlstrom's definition of Puritanism as a spirituality that centered on "an unprecedented emphasis on the need for an inner experience of God's regenerating grace" and "a concern for drawing out man's duties in the church and the world."[48]

The third definitional approach views Puritanism as a complex form of religious expression which, like all significant religious groupings, includes certain forms or elements. This "formal" definition calls Puritans those bodies and individuals who share a common approach to beliefs (myths and doctrines), practices (rituals and ethics), and institutional life or what has been called creed, cult and code, and community. Those interpeters, such as Norman Pettit and Darrett Rutman, who focus on the religious and ecclesiastical thought and practices of William Haller's "spiritual brotherhood" and their successors best exemplify this approach.[49]

A comprehensive view of any developed religion or religious movement requires that we include all three definitions within our purview. The functional definition provides insight into the motivational power and social location of the movement and into its inter-relationships with the other orders of society. The essential definition points to that which unites individuals and subgroups that for a variety of reasons — including social, cultural, and personality differences — express their religious impulse in a variety of ways. It thereby alerts us to patterns of influence and to social and religious dynamics. The formal or elemental definition shows us the full-orbed religious life of a movement and lets us see the relationship among its parts, their relative importance, and the logic of its religious life. Although each of the three can become dominant for certain scholarly purposes, they work best when each modifies the other. An example is the balancing of the functionalist or social historian's emphasis on the repressive and coercive aspects of Puritanism with the emphasis on liberty and voluntarism of those historians focusing on the Puritan views of conversion and church and its historic results or dynamic.

The major problem in much of the scholarship discussed in this essay stems from a lack of sophistication about definitional approaches and especially a lack of clarity concerning which definition is most appropriate for the task at hand. The apologetic concern among Quaker scholars to stress the relative orthodoxy of the earliest Quakers cannot be minimized, but this tendency among historians of Quakerism has been encouraged by the broad definitions of Puritan scholars without this apologetic purpose. The most prominent definition to be found in this scholarship is the essential one. Scholars have sought the one characteristic or perspective or experience that unites rather varied groups and individuals and have stressed the "continuity of experience" among them. But since this has been done with little definitional self-awareness, there has been inadequate recognition of the need to supplement it with other angles or of the bias that is introduced when the essential definition is used almost exclusively to describe a concrete religious body. Having established the identity of Quakers and possibly other Spiritualists as Puritans, the scholars involved, when describing the beliefs, practices, and communities of Quakers, have, on occasion, slipped unwittingly into the assumption that the formal characteristics of the various groups are more similar than is the case.

As my own reference to "Spiritual Puritans" indicates, I have no difficulty with the idea that the thrust of the "Puritan" insistence on a patterned spiritual experience was from right to left or from the somewhat dissatisfied Anglicans of the sixteenth century through the groups that crystallized as the Presbyterians, Independents, Particular Baptists, and General Baptists to the various Spiritualists of the Interregnum. But the existence of that horizontal line or pattern of continuity does not preclude the necessity for drawing vertical lines at certain significant junctures. As Edmund Morgan has written, "the most hotly contested religious differences have often been differences of degree: the shift from orthodoxy to heresy may be no more than a shift of emphasis."[50] Although Morgan was referring to the differences between the Massachusetts Bay Congregationalists and the Baptist Roger Williams, thereby reminding us of the intensity of struggle among Anglicans, Presbyterians, Independents, and Baptists, it cost members of these various groups some time and agony to decide that their differences were great enough to prevent brotherhood. They had no such difficulty deciding that the Quakers and other Spiritualists were of a decidedly different spirit.[51]

However loudly the Puritans and Spiritualists contended within their own ranks, it was not difficult for them to draw the vertical lines separating the two clusters, and it should be even easier for us if we remember to let the task at hand determine our definitional priorities. Since the formal or elemental approach provides the most comprehensive view of religious movements and of their internal coherence and priorities, the historian of religions whose main task is to describe and classify a religious movement in relation to contemporary and to temporally and spatially distant forms of religious expression will usually subordinate functional and essential considerations to formal ones. When such a spotlight is trained on the spectrum of religious expression in seventeenth-century England and America, it becomes immediately apparent that the creed, cult and code, and community of Puritans, on the one hand, and Quakers and Spiritualists on the other, were markedly different. In this line-up the Calvinist creedalist and literalist faces the non-creedal universalist; a formal liturgy of Word and sacrament stands over against inspired silence and spiritual utterance; crusader squares off against pacifist; and a clerical world of coercive authority is pitted against anti-clerical Antinomians. Remembering the horizontal line linking the various "purifying" or "spiritualizing" bodies, we can, to be sure, make some sense of the idea that the Puritans, on the one hand, and the Quakers and Spiritualists on the other, were hissing, if not kissing, cousins. The reasoning or justification is the same as that which makes me a distant relative of the apes. But if the Quakers and Spiritualists were Puritans in the proper sense, then I'm a monkey's uncle.

NOTES

1. McNeill, *Modern Christian Movements* (Philadelphia, 1954), p. 19. The phrase "continuity of experience" is that of Alan Simpson; see *Puritanism in Old and New England* (Chicago, 1955), p. 2.

2. Miller and Thomas Johnston, eds., *The Puritans* (New York, 1938), p. 1; Haller, *The Rise of Puritanism* (New York, 1938), p. 9. The second quotation from Miller is in *The New England Mind: The Seventeenth Century* (1939; reprint, Boston, 1961), p. 77.

3. Simpson, *Puritanism*, p. 1.

4. (New Haven, 1972), pp. 130, 134, 177-78, 208-9.

5. Oxford, 1946. Important articles by influential scholars include Jerald C. Brauer, "Reflections on the Nature of English Puritanism," *Church History*, 23 (1954):99-108; James F. Maclear, "The Heart of New England Rent: The Mystical Element in Early Puritan History," *Mississippi Valley Historical Review*, 42 (1956):621-52; and David D. Hall, "Understanding the Puritans," in *The State of American History*, ed. Herbert J. Bass (Chicago, 1970).

6. Tolles, *Meeting House,* p. 52; see also ibid., pp. 9, 205; idem, *Quakers and the Atlantic Culture* (New York, 1960), pp. 10-11, 59-60, 74-75; and the introduction by Tolles to William C. Braithwaite, *The Second Period of Quakerism,* 2d ed., rev. Henry J. Cadbury (Cambridge, 1961), p. xxvii.

7. (New Haven, 1964), p. 2; see also Barbour and Arthur O. Roberts, *Early Quaker Writings 1650-1700* (Grand Rapids, 1973), pp. 15-16, 21-22, 155; J. William Frost, *The Quaker Family in Colonial America* (New York, 1973), chap. 1; James L. Ash, Jr., " 'Oh No, It is Not the Scriptures!': The Bible and the Spirit in George, Fox," *Quaker History* 63 (1974):94-107; and the essays of T. Canby Jones, Wilmer Cooper, Maurice Creasey, and Christine Downing in the journal, *Quaker Religious Thought.* For the effects of this scholarship, see the influential book by Peter Brock, *Pacifism in Europe to 1914* (Princeton, 1972), esp. p. 255, where he assumes that it has been shown "conclusively" that Quakerism "must be placed squarely within the framework of English Puritanism" and that a realization of the Puritanism of Quakerism is essential to an understanding of the Quaker peace testimony.

8. The metaphor is Richard Vann's in *Development of Quakerism,* p. 31.

9. Hall, "Understanding the Puritans," pp. 331-32.

10. "The Puritan Strain," in *Puritanism and the American Experience* ed. Michael McGiffert (Reading, Mass., 1969), p. 18.

11. See, for example, Barbour, *Quakers in Puritan England,* chap. 5; Frost, *Quaker Family,* chap. 1.

12. Nuttall, *Holy Spirit,* p. 151. Nuttall says elsewhere (*Visible Saints: The Congregational Way 1640-1660* [Oxford, 1957], p. 125), regarding the Anglicans, Presbyterians, Congregationalists, and Baptists who should be classified as Puritans, that Quakerism "was impossible for the churches to include in the differences of judgment which might be tolerated; ministry, ordinances, Scripture itself, all seemed to be denied."

13. Nuttall, *Holy Spirit,* p. 13.

14. Simpson, *Puritanism,* p. 1; Nuttall, *Holy Spirit,* p. viii. On the move away from set liturgies and prayer to spontaneous and Spirit-guided worship, Nuttall writes (ibid., p. 70): "It is not to be supposed that the development represents Puritanism as a whole, although Puritanism as a whole can be understood best when seen in relation to such a development."

15. Nuttall, *The Puritan Spirit: Essays and Addresses* (London, 1967), pp. 102-3; see also Maclear, "Heart of New England Rent," p. 623, and Jerald C. Brauer, "Puritanism, Mysticism, and the Development of Liberalism," *Church History,* 19 (1950):153.

16. Nuttall, *Holy Spirit,* pp. 22-24, 42, 52-60, 63-86, 91-101, 104-12, 146.

17. The quoted phrases are from Simpson, *Puritanism,* p. 21.

18. Hall, "Understanding the Puritans," p. 332.

19. Frost, *Quaker Family,* p. 11.

20. Sabine, ed., *The Works of Gerrard Winstanley* (Ithaca, 1941), Introduction, p. 35.

21. Middlekauf, "Piety and Intellect in Puritanism," *WMQ,* 3d ser., 22 (1965):457-70.

22. Miller, *Errand into the Wilderness* (1956; reprint, Cambridge, Mass., 1964), p. 190. For Hall's remark, see "The Puritans versus John Calvin: A Critique of Perry Miller's *The New England Mind,*" paper read to AHA conference, Toronto, 30 Dec. 1967, cited by Michael McGiffert, "American Puritan Studies in the 1960's," *WMQ,* 3d ser., 27 (1970):49.

23. The first and last quotations are in Miller, *New England Mind,* pp. 281, 77; the second quotation is in idem, *Errand into the Wilderness,* p. 24.

24. For a more extensive discussion of the splintering process of the 1640s, and how it led to Quakerism, see Endy, *William Penn and Early Quakerism* (Princeton, 1973), pp. 21-53.

25. The unattributed quotation is given in Norman Cohn, *Pursuit of the Millennium* (1957, reprint, New York, 1961), pp. 322-23.

26. Especially relevant sources here include: Baxter's transcription of a debate with William Penn, 5 Oct. 1675, Dr. William's Library, London; Owen, *Pneumatologia, or a Discourse Concerning the Holy Spirit* (London, 1674); idem, *Vindiciae Evangelicae; or the Mystery of the Gospel Vindicated and Socinianism Examined* (London, 1655); idem, *Of the Divine Original Self-Evidencing Light, and Power of the Scriptures* (London, 1659); Bunyan, *Some Gospel Truths Opened . . . or, The Divine and Human Nature of Christ Jesus* (London, 1656).

27. The General Baptists, beginning with the congregation formed by John Smyth in Holland in 1609 that returned to England with Thomas Helwys and John Murton in 1612, were too influenced by Mennonite and Spiritualist views to be called Puritans. See John Smyth's final confessions of faith in Robert Barclay, *The Inner Life of the Religious Societies of the Commonwealth*, 3d ed. (London, 1879), app. to chap. 6; Rufus Jones, *Studies in Mystical Religion* (London, 1909), chap. 17; Lonnie D. Kliever, "General Baptist Origins: The Question of Anabaptist Influences," *Mennonite Quarterly Review*, 36 (1962):291-321. On the smaller Continental influences on Particular Baptists, see Donald F. Durnbaugh, "Baptists and Quakers — Left Wing Puritans?" *Quaker History*, 62 (1973):72-75.

28. Dell, *The Building, Beauty, Teaching, and Embellishment of the Truly Christian and Spiritual Church* (1651), in *The Works of William Dell* (New York, 1816), p. 100.

29. John Saltmarsh, *Smoke in the Temple* (London, 1646), p. 14.

30. Other Spiritual Puritans or halfway Spiritualists might include John Webster, Richard Coppin, William Erbury, Joshua Sprigge, Thomas Collier, and possibly Samuel Gorton, Hugh Peters, William Sedgwick, Walter Cradock, Richard Symonds, Henry Denne, Sir Harry Vane, and Morgan Llwyd. For lists and suggestions about Spiritual Puritans, see George A. Johnson, "From Seeker to Finder: A Study in Seventeenth Century English Spiritualism Before the Quakers," *Church History*, 17 (1948):301; Leo F. Solt, *Saints in Arms* (Stanford, 1959), p. 9; Nuttall, *Holy Spirit*, p. 13.

31. *Divine Dialogues*, 2d ed. (London, 1713), p. 565.

32. Representative treatises expressing central Spiritualist ideas include, for Spiritual Puritans: William Dell, *The Building, Beauty, Teaching, and Embellishment, of the Truly Christian and Spiritual Church* (1651); idem, *The Way of True Peace* (1649); idem, *The Crucified and Quickened Christian* (1652); John Saltmarsh, *Smoke in the Temple* (1646); idem, *Sparkles of Glory, or Some Beams of the Morning-Star* (1648); Richard Coppin, *Michael Opposing the Dragon* (1659). For Seekers: Gerrard Winstanley, *Truth Lifting up its Head Above Scandals* (1649); idem, *The New Law of Righteousness* (1649). For Familists: The Familists did not publish separate treatises in the Interregnum, although works of Henry Nicholas began to appear in English after 1646 (see Jones, *Mystical Religion*, chap. 18; idem, *Mysticism and Democracy in the English Commonwealth* [Cambridge, Mass., 1932], pp. 123-30; C. E. Whiting, *Studies in English Puritanism* [London, 1931], pp. 283-88). For the Ranters: Jacob Bauthumley, *The Light and Dark Sides of God* (1650); Laurence Clarkson, *The lost sheep found: or, The Prodigal Returned to his Fathers house* (1660); Abiezer Coppe, *A Fiery Roll: A Word from the Lord to all the Great Ones of the Earth* (1649). On the Quakers, see references below. For a more detailed description of the Spiritualists, see Endy, *William Penn*, pp. 35-53.

33. Barbour and Roberts, *Early Quaker Writings*, pp. 247, 21-22.

34. Tolles, *Atlantic Culture*, p. 109.

35. See Barbour and Roberts, *Early Quaker Writings*, pp. 26, 245, 250; Ahlstrom, *Religious History*, p. 209.

36. Barbour, *Quakers in Puritan England*, p. 2 and chap. 5; Frost, *Quaker Family*, chap. 1; Maurice Creasey, "Early Quaker Christology with Special Reference to the Teaching and Significance of Isaac Penington, 1616-1679" (Ph.D. diss., University of Leeds, 1956). My reservations about the tendency to highlight the connections between Puritans and Quakers to the neglect of important distinctions is by no means unique. The two late elder statesmen of contemporary Quaker scholarship, Henry J. Cadbury and Howard H. Brinton, did not join the Puritan interpretation. See especially Brinton, *Friends for Three Hundred Years* (New York, 1952); and idem, *Quaker Journals: Varieties of Religious Experience Among Friends* (Wallingford, Pa., 1972); see also Lewis Benson, *Catholic Quakerism* (Gloucester, Eng., 1966). Moreover, the lively theological discussions of historical and contemporary issues in *Quaker Religious Thought*, while showing the massive influence of Protestant neoorthodoxy and Quaker ecumenical contacts on many contemporary Friends, also reveal some continuing awareness of Quakerism as a movement radically distinct in ways from historical Protestantism. The works of Brinton and Benson, however, as well as the *Quaker Religious Thought* articles, tend to circulate primarily within the Quaker community and have been overshadowed among historians of England and America by the works referred to above.

37. Vann, *Development of Quakerism*, p. 56, makes the same point; see also Durnbaugh, "Baptists and Quakers," p. 71. Jones's interpretation is seen in many of his works, including *Spiritual Reformers of the Sixteenth and Seventeenth Centuries* (New York, 1914), *Mystical Religion*, and *Mysticism and Democracy*.

38. Epistle 18, in Fox, *Works* (Philadelphia, 1831), 7:26; Fox, *A Clear Distinction between the Old Covenant or Old Testament and the New Covenant or New Testament*, (n.d.), in ibid., 6:59.

39. Burrough, *Memorable Works of a Son of Thunder and Consolation* (London, 1672), pp. 117-20, 243-53, 440.

40. Isaac Penington, *An Invitation to Professors seriously to consider, Whether they or we fail, in the true acknowledgment and owning of the Christ which died at Jerusalem* (n.d.), in idem, *Works* (London, 1681), 2:19; Fox, *A Testimony of What We Believe of Christ* (1677), in Fox, *Works*, 5:152-54.

41. Penington, *Works*, 2:12-13, 18.

42. For Fox, see Epistle 388, in idem, *Works*, 8:236; idem, *The Second Covenant* (1657), in ibid., 4:149-50; idem, *The Pearl Found in England* (1658), in ibid., 4:164. For Nayler, see *Love to the Lost* (1656), in idem, *A Collection of Sundry Books, Epistles and Papers* (London, 1716), pp. 345-54. For Barclay, see *Apology*, proposition VI.

43. In addition to those cited above, other treatises that reveal the Spiritualist affinities of Friends rather clearly include: George Fox, *To all People in Christendom Concerning perfect Love;* idem, *And concerning Christ's flesh which was offered* (1663); idem, *The Great Mistery of the Great Whore Unfolded* (1659); Isaac Penington, *Concerning the Sum or Substance of our Religion, Who, are called Quakers* (1660); idem, *The Holy Truth and People Defended* (1672); Josiah Coale, *A Vindication of the Light Within* (n.d.); George Whitehead, *The Divinity of Christ* (1669); Samuel Fisher, *Rusticus ad Academicos in Exercitationibus Expostulatoriis, or, the Rustick's Alarm to the Rabbies* (1660); George Keith, *Immediate Revelation, or Jesus Christ the Eternall Son of God, Revealed in Man and Revealing the Knowledge of God* (1668); idem, *The Way Caste Up* (1676); Robert Barclay, *The Possibility and Necessity of the Inward and Immediate Revelation of the Spirit of God* (1676). For a more detailed identification and description of the Spiritualism of the early Quakers and its implications for their view of Christ, see Endy, *William Penn*, pp. 60-84, 182-94, 262-69, 274-81, 292-96.

44. See, for example, Edward Burrough, *A Trumpet of the Lord* (1656), in idem, *Memorable Works,* pp. 106-9; see also Geoffrey Nuttall, *Studies in Christian Enthusiasm* (Wallingford, Pa., 1948), pp. 82-83.

45. Despite their denial of the Real Presence in the Lord's Supper and their view of baptism as a seal of the covenant, the Puritans gave the two Protestant sacraments a much more prominent place in their religious views than most Puritan scholars have recognized. A review of the theological tracts of Puritans in colonial America, for example, reveals that debates on the two sacraments were probably more prominent than any other theological subject. The beginning of a corrective is made in E. Brooks Holifield, *The Covenant Sealed: The Development of Puritan Sacramental Theology in Old and New England, 1570-1720* (New Haven, 1974).

46. Ziff, *Puritanism in America: New Culture in a New World* (New York, 1973), p. x.

47. Bremer, *The Puritan Experiment* (New York, 1976), p. 4.

48. Ahlstrom, *Theology in America: The Major Protestant Voices From Puritanism to Neo-Orthodoxy* (New York, 1967), p. 27.

49. Pettit, *The Heart Prepared: Grace and Conversion in Puritan Spiritual Life* (New Haven and London, 1966), esp. chap. 3; Rutman, *American Puritanism: Faith and Practice* (Philadelphia, New York, Toronto, 1970), esp. chap. 1. Haller's clearest exposition of Puritanism is in *The Rise of Puritanism* (New York, 1938).

50. *Roger Williams: The Church and the State* (New York, 1967), p. 11, quoted in J. Sears McGee, *The Godly Man in Stuart England* (New Haven and London, 1976), p. 5.

51. Leonard Trinterud has reminded us that in the Restoration era those Baptists who had become radical sectarians shared as much with the Quakers as they did with those groups that still lived in what he calls the "clerical world" of Puritanism. See "A.D. 1689: The End of the Clerical World," in Winthrop Hudson and Leonard Trinterud, *Theology in Sixteenth and Seventeenth Century England* (Los Angeles, 1971). His perspective reminds us of the need to attend to chronology in discussing terms such as Puritanism and Spiritualism.

J. WILLIAM FROST

17 ‹ *The Affirmation Controversy and Religious Liberty*

When commencing research on the affirmation controversies in England and America, I assumed that by no stretch of the imagination could I relate work on such an esoteric subject to contemporary existence. After all, in spite of a few references in secondary sources, no one had ever bothered to write an article on the subject in any Quaker or non-Quaker historical journal. Either because scholars working on most any topic catch a "disease" which enables them to discourse knowingly on the relevance of their material to any conversational subject or because swearing oaths really is important, the relevance of the topic soon became apparent.[1] To cite three examples:

In the movie *Oh, God,* George Burns, supposedly God, is called to the witness stand to take an oath. To whom does God take any oath and why? The movie made the issue a joke, but the exact same subject occasioned a vivid debate in the seventeenth century.

A second example occurred when a Philadelphia lawyer, a member of a large legal firm, was asked by a fellow member of the bar, in his office, a question about the four horsemen of the Apocalypse. The place to check was the Bible, of which the firm kept several copies for the express purpose of swearing witnesses. The Bibles were used for no other purpose. The seventeenth-century debate over oaths had to do with the superstitious use of oaths divorced from true religious feelings.

A third instance happened when a thirteen-year-old child of a fellow faculty member asked his father whether an atheist who took an oath on the Bible in court was committing perjury. Or, since his oath would presumably be invalid, was it already impossible for him to commit perjury? The seventeenth-century debaters asked the same question in a slightly different way: What function does an oath serve? Does it make a liar tell the truth? Does it add any credibility to an honest man's testimony?

When early Quakers refused to take oaths, they were following a long tradition of religious dissent. In 1577 the Dutch Stadholder announced an exemption from oaths for Mennonites; Rhode Island passed the first law in an English colony allowing an affirmation in 1647.[2] The fear of taking oaths, of violating the express command of Scripture, was widespread among seventeenth-century English sectaries.

In *The Beginnings of Quakerism* William C. Braithwaite argued that the testimony against oaths was one of the elements of radical Protestantism that early Friends adopted with no debate or controversy.[3] George Fox's *Journal* lists the paraphrase of James (let your yea be yea, and your nay, nay) as one of the first testimonies; his early epistles contain only passing references to oath taking and no scriptural citations beyond the references to the Sermon on the Mount and James.[4] Richard Farnworth engaged in a short debate with a magistrate who attempted to tender him an oath.[5] Farnworth refused and was imprisoned, but three days later he was released without swearing and without paying the jailor's fees. A Royalist insurrection in 1655 prompted magistrates to tender suspected papists an oath of abjuration and resulted in the imprisonment of a few Friends.[6]

Quakerism arose after the main fighting of the civil war and after the attempts of both sides to consolidate position by giving individuals oaths of allegiance. Oliver Cromwell was in power and he desired as broad a religious toleration as possible, even conniving at the private worship by Anglicans and Roman Catholics and considering the readmission of Jews to England.[7] Cromwell seems not to have thought that his power rested upon the imposition of oaths and he made little effort to enforce that kind of symbolical form of allegiance. Quakers had more difficulty with outraged local magistrates who were often later overruled by the central government. Before 1660 the main political issues Quakers and Puritans debated were tithes and the necessity of an established form of worship, an educated clergy, and, on these subjects, the Quaker position differed little from other sectarian groups. With seeming widespread misgivings about swearing, and a reasonably mild government, there was little reason for Quakers to think out the implications of their form of scriptural literalism.

If Quakers did not welcome, they at least acquiesced in the restoration of Charles II and proclaimed that the overthrow of the Commonwealth came because of religious persecution. Charles's Declaration of Breda promised "liberty to tender consciences" but the newly elected, strongly pro-Anglican Parliament saw in sectarianism the seeds of sedition and was determined to enforce loyalty to the reformed alliance between the monarchy and the Anglican church. An abortive revolt by the Fifth Monarchy Men in January 1661 occasioned a proclamation against them and Quakers; evidently magistrates had difficulty in distinguishing various shades of so-called "fanatical" opinion.[8] Justices were ordered to give all suspected persons the oath of allegiance. Parliament enacted laws forbidding public sectarian worship, which Friends promptly defied. Convictions under these statutes were not always easy to obtain, but justices had a convenient solution. Anyone suspected of disloyalty could be tendered oaths, and the penalties varied with the type of oaths used. One form of oath was drawn up in the reign of James I after the Gunpowder Plot, and the penalty for the first offense was a fine or, if not paid, imprisonment. A more serious penalty resulted from refusal to take the oaths of allegiance and supremacy initially promulgated in the reign of Elizabeth. Failure to comply left the offender liable to a medieval punishment termed *praemunire,* which involved outlawry, forfeiture of goods, deprivation of income from real property, and imprisonment for life or at the king's pleasure.[9] The prevailing hostility to Friends, which the king did little to check, allowed local magistrates considerable discretion. Since Friends openly defied the laws on paying tithes, meeting for worship, and traveling to preach, there were various offenses which resulted in Quakers being called into court. Friends soon proved adept at finding flaws in indictments (for example, could a peaceful gathering in which no one had spoken be termed a seditious conventicle?), and juries as in the Penn-Mead trial were not predictable; so tendering the oaths proved an easy way to rid the land of troublemakers. Even if not convicted of crimes, prominent leaders could be isolated in prison.[10] A 1662 tract noted 1,013 imprisoned Quakers in England; a broadside the following year listed 400 Quakers in prison, of whom 73 had refused the oaths and had been *praemunired.*[11]

What the peace testimony became in our century, oaths became in the seventeenth century: a major symbol of defiance of government and witness to the principles of Quakerism. Anglicans and Independents wrote pamphlets and treatises upon the necessity for oaths. For the first time Quakers encountered a full range of arguments developed by the "orthodox" over centuries which had received an added impetus from the Anabaptist movement in the Reformation. Clergymen attempted to prove the Quaker position was unscriptural, unnatural, and immoral—destructive of peace and common sense.

The main Anglican argument was that Quakers distorted the meaning of the Bible.[12] Abraham, Jacob, David, and the prophets swore, Deuteronomy contained commandments to swear, and God himself swore on several occasions, including promises to both Noah and Abraham. If God could swear, and certainly God would not do an action that was morally wrong, was it likely he would contradict himself in the New Testament, particularly since Christ had come not to abrogate but to fulfill the Law?

The New Testament was also full of swearing. Paul wrote, "God is my witness"; "Behold, before God I lye not"; and "I charge thee before God and the Lord Jesus Christ." In the book of Revelation, the angel swore by him that liveth forever. Even Jesus swore, since his "Verily, Verily" and "Amens" were a form of swearing. When in the trial before the Sanhedrin, the high priest abjured him "by the living God, that thou tell us whether thou be the Christ, the Son of God. Jesus saith unto him, Thou hast said."

With these examples of swearing in both Old and New Testament, said conservatives, one should consider carefully the two texts cited by Friends:

> (Matt. 5:33–34) Again, ye have heard that it hath been said by them of old time, Thou shalt not forswear thyself, but shalt perform unto the Lord thine oaths: But I say unto you, Swear not at all; neither by heaven; for it is God's throne: Nor by the earth; for it is His footstool; neither by Jerusalem; . . . But let your communication be, Yea, Yea; Nay, nay; for whatsoever is more than these cometh of evil.

> (James 5) But above all things, my brethren, swear not, neither by heaven, neither by the earth, neither by any other oath: but let your yea be yea; and your nay, nay; lest ye fall into condemnation.

What was condemned in these passages, said Anglicans, was not a solemn oath in court or of loyalty but false and too frequent swearing. Since Jews did not like to say the name of God lightly, they were accustomed to swearing by heaven or Moses or Jerusalem. Such swearing was idolatry, and Christ was enforcing Old Testament strictures against swearing by Ba'al or swearing with no intention of keeping one's word.[13] After all, in the same Sermon on the Mount was a command to give away one cloak and to go the second mile. Quakers did not take these commands literally; nor did they pluck out their eyes with any frequency. Jesus often spoke symbolically, as in his words, "This is my body," and a false literalism, used by Roman Catholics, led to abuses.

A second approach favored by conservatives was to link oaths to the moral law. While the ceremonial law of the Jews had been abrogated by the New Testament, the moral law had not. The purpose of the moral law was to create a society in which men could live at peace and worship God. As Heb. 6:6 indicated, the function of oaths was to end strife between men. Since strife between peoples had not ended, the necessity of oaths continued. God decreed in the Ten Commandments that his name was not to be taken in vain, but a solemn oath was just the opposite. God was a reasonable and moral being who would not insist on behavior that would be destructive to society.[14] The moral law was found not just in the Old Testament, but Greeks, Romans, Reformed, Catholics, in fact, all civilized people, had required oaths of some form. Any practice sanctified by universal custom was clearly permissible. Friends were hopelessly utopian, assuming that strife was ended, that men were become trustworthy, and that a simple yea or nay could bind people to loyalty to a government. The excesses of the recent civil war should have brought more common sense.

The Quaker response to the Anglican attack was complex and evolved over time. Suffering on behalf of the "Truth," whether by being committed to prison or by having one's property distrained, stood as an authentication of a Quaker's zeal and, at the same time, burned the testimony deeper into the group's consciousness.[15] The other response, a vigorous pamphlet war, required Friends to deal with their opponents' biblical references and reasoning and risked some degree of dialogue. Just as those who attacked the Quaker position came from different perspectives, so did the Quaker response. Uniformity or consistency was not a characteristic of either side. Eventually, however, many prominent Friends would write against swearing: William Smith, Francis Howgill, Isaac Penington, Robert Barclay, George Fox, Samuel Fisher, George Whitehead, and William Penn.

At first the Quakers combined opposition to oaths with a strongly critical perspective on society. John Crook enclosed in his 1660 tract a devastating attack upon inequities in the system of justice: the difficulties for the poor in obtaining their due, the ridiculousness of a system which required witnesses to swear and then allowed the rich to hire overpriced lawyers paid to lie on their behalf, the falsity in evidence, the lack of punishment for those who lied under oath in chancery suits, the sloppily drawn writs naming fictitious persons like John Doe, and the persecution of the innocent. The purpose of oaths was to end strife, but the English court system, which required opposing witnesses to swear, created animosity.[16]

Morgan Watkins, who composed his 1660 tract in St. Albans jail, continued the strong eschatological awareness of early Friends. An oath requires a promise of future activity, but a true Christian cannot know what God will require of him. To swear "so help me God" is to tempt the Lord. When a witness has violated God's express commandment not to swear, how can he possibly assume that God will help him do any activity?[17] Watkins's position was what terrified the authorities. If, for Quakers, God was immediately present and unbounded, then he might require a religious assassination or revolt. No matter how peaceful Quakers might claim to be, the threat of obedience to an inner voice prompted fears of another Münster.

All Quaker pamphleteers asserted the binding nature and literal truth of the prohibitions in Matthew and James. All denied that the commands could be understood as a figurative prohibition of unnecessary or false swearing. If Jesus had intended this, he would not have needed to say anything and certainly would not have used the "you have heard it of old, but I say unto you" formula. Total prohibitions were not unusual for Jesus, and even the Anglican church upheld the passages next to the swearing text which forbade adultery and divorce.[18]

In dealing with the examples of swearing in the Old Testament, the Quaker position rested upon a disjunction between the Old and New Covenant. This type of argument was familiar, for the Quaker testimony against tithes and for a new spiritual dispensation of the gospel rested upon the same theological foundation.[19] The commands and precepts of the Old Testament were fulfilled and superceded by Jesus. Abraham could swear, under the Law, but Christ abolished the Law. In addition, all Old Testament oaths were voluntary, were not used to compel allegiance, and did not apply to courtroom proceedings.[20] Friends saw nothing unusual in God's doing acts which were not now allowable to Christians. After all, he commanded Abraham to kill his son. God's oaths in the Old Testament were an adaptation to the hardness of heart and shortsightedness of the Jews.

Most important, when God swore a covenant or promise to Abraham, the content of that oath was the promise of Jesus Christ.[21] An oath was a type or figure of Christ, and Christ's coming fulfilled and superceded the promise to Abraham. The New Testament dispensation brought Christ to end sin and strife. A true Christian, who had experienced the inward Light, was liberated from fleshly concerns and had no need to swear.

Just as Christ was a type of an oath, so the Christian's type of an oath was witnessing.[22] Both Old and New Testament advocated establishing truth in any dispute by witnessing. The proclamation of the gospel was a form of witnessing. When Paul was supposedly swearing, he was not kissing a book or raising his right hand. Instead, he was witnessing that he stood within the presence and power of God. Quakers found the Anglican assertion of Christ's swearing a questionable exegesis. Samuel Fisher was quite willing to agree that the high priest swore, but Jesus' answer was no oath. Fisher announced that if Anglicans believed that it was sufficient for the Quaker to stand silently while the judge recited an oath, and then answered questions with a simple declaration, then there would be no dispute. English law, unfortunately, required a response from the person and that answer was different from giving testimony or witnessing in a court.[23]

Whether oaths belonged to Jewish ceremonial and ritual or moral law made no difference, because Christ's commandment was worth more than either. Most Friends assumed that the Ten Commandments summed up the moral law (though there was some equivocation even here), but no commandment mentioned swearing. Oaths had come in after the Fall, but Christ had removed the Fall and restored men to a higher plane. Whether or not swearing was reasonable, God certainly was above reason and his commands were or could be above it. After all, God had commanded sacrifices, forbidden eating of the tree of knowledge, and ordered all males circumcised.[24] It was hard to make these postulates of reason. (A Freudian might be interested in analyzing the frequency with which Quakers discussed circumcision or used it as a metaphor; see, for example, John Lamb, *Friendly Advice: or, A Circumcising Knife to cut off that Superfluous Branch, the Affirmation* [London, 1714].)

The moral law might be universally observed, but was oath-taking prevalent everywhere? At first Friends contented themselves with a few citations from early Christian martyrs, Eusebius, and Fox's *Book of Martyrs.*[25] In time the evidence grew more complex (similar to what was happening with the thee/thou protest against you) and a book issued with the imprimatur of a committee of twelve and probably written by William Penn and Richard Richardson devoted 138 of its 166 pages to citing 207 authorities from pagan, Jewish, early Christian, and modern sources (but only one Anabaptist) on the reasons for not swearing.[26] While some of the citations are suspect, or at least do not prove what Quakers thought they did, sufficient testimony was gathered to show that Christians had from the beginning voiced scruples against the custom.

As for whether Reformed, Catholic, Anglican, and pagan countries required swearing, this could be true and still not be a sufficient precedent. The kingdoms of earth had shown on numerous occasions whether they were under the power of God or of Satan. Since evil prevailed in most societies, it was only natural that the devil had stirred up first the Roman Catholics and then others to insist on oaths.[27] But even in England, the law granted exceptions. The nobility were not required to swear, because their honor as gentlemen was assumed to be sufficient to guarantee truth. Military officers presiding at a court martial were exempted from swearing because of their honor.[28] If the position of a knight or military officer was a sufficient badge of character, why did the laws of England not permit a return to the practice of the early church and allow it as sufficient to say, "*Christianus sum*"?[29] The honor of a Christian, for whom Jesus had come to end all strife, was greater than any earthly title.

A fundamental difficulty in the debate was that there was no strict definition of an oath. Two seventeenth-century compilations, both entitled *Book of Oaths* (1649 and 1689), have hundreds of pages of "oaths" used on various occasions. In the bewildering variety of forms what becomes clear is that, depending upon the history of the office, a person could sometimes qualify by taking an oath that did not invoke the name of God, the Bible, or the words "oath" or "swear." Kings of England had to say "I will"; the 1643 Solemn League and Covenant taken by members of Parliament refers to itself as an oath, yet did not mention God or swearing. Some qualifications for churchmen followed the same format; others required the words "I swear" or "so help me God."[30] The books of oaths show how important and yet how ill-defined oaths were, since the forms were to be employed by magistrates for everybody who taught school, worked as a midwife, accepted any government office, or served on a jury. Most of the declarations required of humble citizens, like Friends, demanded the naming of the deity, the words "I swear," and the invocation "so help me God." But the essential form finally accepted by Quakers in 1695 and 1722 would not have seemed unusual or out of place in either the 1649 or the 1689 *Book of Oaths*.

In the 1660s the Quakers' position was complicated by their inability to decide exactly why God had forbidden oaths or just what an oath actually was. All agreed that using the words "to swear by" made an oath; involving God in some sort of activity such as saying "so help me God" or calling God to curse was an oath.[31] (The phrase "so help me God" did not mean for God to help me tell the truth. Rather, it meant that as I told the truth, so God would deal with me. Damnation was assumed to be the punishment for lying. This kind of oath was termed an imprecation or curse.) Promising to do something and mentioning God was avoided because it could become a lie. Implicit in the Quaker attitude was a belief that the mere mention of the name of God did not constitute an oath. When opponents insisted that it did, Quakers asked why neither civil nor ecclesiastical courts would accept the declaration "in the presence of God" as an oath.[32]

Making a solemn affirmation "in the presence of God" early became a Quaker way of special emphasis. The promises made in a marriage ceremony, adopted from the forms commonly used in Cromwellian England, had the service take place "in the presence of God." In 1673, when attempting to convince Parliament that Quakers were not papists, Quakers offered to promise to all the requirements in the oaths of abjuration and loyalty. The form drawn up by the Meeting for Sufferings and signed by Ellis Hookes "in the name and behalf of the people called Quakers" began, "I A. B. do in the Presence of Almighty God solemnly profess, and in good Conscience declare, it is my real Judgment."[33] When William Penn gave evidence before a parliamentary committee proving that he was not a Roman Catholic, he accented his remarks with a declaration that he stood "in the presence of God."[34] Similar quotations can be found in Burrough, Fox, and Barclay.[35]

Affirming that God was present or witnessed was not an oath, but a theological declaration to which all Christians could agree. After all, God was omnipresent and so he witnessed all actions. No feeling of presence was required, if the person still believed the statement true. If such a position seemed a retreat from the "yea, yea" demanded by Matthew and James, it preserved the reputation of the Apostle Paul, who had strengthened the veracity of his statements in similar language. The only difference was that Saint Paul had voluntarily made the declaration. If Quakers made the declaration in the marriage ceremony, they could also claim to be speaking freely. But what London Yearly Meeting offered to Parliament in 1673 was to agree to a forced form of words.

The offer to use the terminology "in the presence of God" did not appear in all pamphlets. John Crook and Samuel Fisher mentioned it in 1660; Gervase Benson made it prominent in 1669 and 1675.[36] Most of the literature did not specifically address the question, but this negative evidence must be used carefully. Neither Fox nor Penn mentioned this distinction in their tracts on oaths, but both used the form. The disagreement among radical Protestants on the permissibility of offering "in the presence of God" or "witnessing before God" was not even indigenous to Friends. In the 1550s a split developed among Mennonites because certain Anabaptists followed Saint Paul while others insisted on taking literally the words of Christ.[37] When in the 1690s Parliament granted Quakers the right of affirmation, the form used approximated that advocated by the Yearly Meeting in 1673. What is clear is that Quaker acceptance of the parliamentary position should not be seen as a symptom of decline or falling away from the principles of the founders.

Quaker literature on the affirmation does show marked change after the mid-1670s. Early Quaker apologetic literature was not asking for concessions or a favor so much as insisting upon a right. The government learned that the seat of religion was conscience, and conscience could not be coerced. Friends appeared not so much supplicants as asserters of right. They insisted that their position was grounded upon Scripture and should be universally adopted. The evolution in tactics can be illustrated by a consideration of three pamphlets: one by George Fox in 1675, one by William Penn and Richard Richardson in 1675, probably issued through the Meeting for Sufferings, and a third by Theodore Eccleston in 1694, which claimed the approbation of Friends.

Fox's treatise was a purely theological disquisition based solely upon Scripture and containing an exegesis of disputed passages.[38] Political and economic concerns, whether of Quakers or others, occupied no role. God's demand was clear and no compromise was in order. Only those surrendering to sin could be blind to the Truth, and the tract ended with an exhortation to convert to the inward Light of Christ.

The pamphlet by Penn and Richardson was divided into two sections: one contained the precedents for the affirmation and the other a twenty-eight-page introduction defending the Quaker position. The introduction contained neither the radicalism of Crook or Watkins nor the scriptural emphasis of Fox. The traditional theological arguments underlay Penn's work, but the reasons stressed for non-swearing were based upon utility and common sense. Penn's God, unlike Fisher's, would not issue a commandment for which no reason could be given. Swearing was not evil "it self" but was superfluous to "evangelical sincerity." In primitive times oaths had conveyed a sense of awe or dread, but in the 1670s, through overuse, oaths became "a great share of the A la mode Conversation" and were used without fear or wit. Lying under oath does not bring God's immediate judgment, because God moves when he desires and not when a court or witness uses his name. Oaths do not bring credibility to testimony, because they do not establish good reputation. The character of Friends as a peaceful law-abiding group should be sufficient security to the government. Penn pleaded not for an abstract right but "to take this Tenderness of ours into Christian Consideration."[39]

When Theodore Eccleston wrote in 1694, Friends had already been exempted from the worst of their sufferings. The Toleration Act had suspended, but not repealed, the tendering of oaths of loyalty and supremacy.[40] The main difficulty remaining was that Quakers could not appear either to defend themselves or as witnesses in courts. Eccleston's tract was expressly directed to Parliament and designed to aid the passage of an affirmation bill. The tract had only a slight use for theology, scriptural citations, abstract declarations of natural rights, and liberty of conscience. Instead of martyrs or suffering Apostles, Friends are "Merchants, Farmers, Manufactors, Improvers of Lands and Stock" whose hard work and diligence helps themselves and "advances the National Stock." Quakers are represented as peaceful law-abiding citizens who pay their taxes. Unfortunately, in suits in Chancery and Exchequer they cannot recover debts or appear to help their neighbors in lawsuits or give testimony to a grand jury for a felony or death. Even the "gown-men" of Westminster, who previously had made almost nothing from Friends, would find it to their "interest" to grant Quakers relief. If the wool trade suffers, Parliament becomes involved and passes an act. Now Parliament should become involved and pass an act to benefit the Quaker interest.[41]

The emphasis in the tract—that a right of conscience is similar to the rights of interest groups—points toward the commercialization of subjectivity. After all, if conscience need be free, then interest should be free. Freedom, because of the overriding providence of God, works for the benefit of the entire realm. Adam Smith had only to draw out the implications.

Quaker literature advocating an affirmation law in the early eighteenth century reads more like Eccleston than Crook or Fox, and the nuances involving Scripture, theology, and natural rights found in Penn's writings almost completely disappear.[42] What had occurred between 1660 and 1690 to occasion such a change of emphasis? First, Friends had a different definition of success. Success in 1660 still meant conquering the world for Truth, and Quakers relished their position as leading the battle for godliness against the forces of evil. Success in 1690 meant enduring and being allowed to practice peculiar customs in peace. Quakers still thought they alone had the true position on the issue, but no longer did they anticipate persuading other people. Second, the attitude of the authorities to Quakers had shifted.

In 1660 sectarians were a danger to the realm who had grown dangerously large and kept England in turmoil. Sectaries had come out of Cromwell's army and Cromwell was closely associated with a policy of religious toleration. By the 1670s sectarianism did not appear as dangerous as Roman Catholicism.[43] Charles II flirted with Louis XIV, favored Catholics, and worked to insure the succession to the throne of the Catholic duke of York. Anglicans wanted all Englishmen, including dissenters, united against France and Roman Catholicism. Third, after years of bitter theological debate which had seemingly settled nothing, many wanted to avoid theological hair-splitting and insure peace. Cambridge Platonists, Latitudinarian divines, and rationalists could all appreciate a spiritual and inward religion founded in dictates of conscience.[44] Parts of Quakerism seemed similar. Finally, in the 1670s Quakers began to realize that their security could not come only from the monarchy. Effective relief which would be long lasting needed a parliamentary sanction.[45] Whatever the nation at large thought about theology, parliamentary debates were couched in terms of interest and security, not biblical truth. Penn and other members of the London Meeting for Sufferings knew the political system and what would appeal to the members of Parliament. They appealed to Parliament in secular terms and, by so doing, became more secularized themselves.

After the Revolution of 1688, Friends immediately sought relief from oaths through Parliament. Members of the Meeting for Sufferings followed sessions closely and lobbied with influential members of both Houses.[46] On two occasions an affirmation bill passed the Lords only to die in the Commons. Not until after the Whigs came to power and William III added his support did a bill pass the Commons in 1695. According to George Whitehead, whose account of the activities of Friends has to be accepted with reservations, Friends drew up a wording of the bill requiring the statement, "I, A. B., do declare in the Presence of Almighty God." The bishops in the House of Lords balked at this wording as insufficient security and had the votes to defeat the measure. A compromise was worked out, agreed to reluctantly by leading Friends, inserting, after "Almighty God," the phrase "the Witness of the Truth of what I say."[47] Whitehead's account has a defensive tone, because the law was controversial among Friends. Leading Friends had as early as 1690 agreed to a wording of the bill which had contained both phrases.[48] Since Paul had employed both wordings, London Friends could with clear conscience proclaim a major victory for Quakers and toleration.

During the Restoration Quakers had never reached consensus on just what an oath was or why one should refrain from swearing. Now that lack of agreement came back to plague them. The Affirmation Act seemed to some virtually, if not actually, an oath. True, there was no swearing required, but if a Friend had "to declare in the Presence of Almighty God, the Witness of the Truth of what I say," was this any different from an oath? Was it only a bare theological assertion which all might make, or did it stipulate activity by God? Did it require taking the name of God in vain? Certainly, it was beyond a simple "yea, yea, and nay, nay."[49]

The controversy divided London Friends for a quarter of a century, becoming particularly acrimonious whenever the law had to be renewed. Thirty years earlier the disagreement would have caused a schism. Now the infighting took place within the organization established by Fox, which proved unable to end the dispute but adequate to contain the disagreement.

London Yearly Meeting announced an official position on the affirmation issue after a long debate in 1696. The Meeting for Sufferings was commended for its efforts to obtain liberty to use an affirmation and instructed to work for a modification of the formula when the time seemed propitious. Meanwhile, those satisfied with the present form were free to use it and those dissatisfied were not to be compelled to employ it and neither side would reflect upon the other.[50] Complications came because the initial law was for seven years, and the body responsible for renewal, the Meeting for Sufferings, was composed of satisfied Friends who showed neither sympathy nor tolerance of the opposition. The few dissatisfied Friends in the Meeting for Sufferings in 1702 could not stop the majority from proceeding, with only token efforts for revision, to renew the 1696 affirmation for ten years.

In 1712 the dissatisfied Friends would not be so easily cast aside. The Meeting for Sufferings attempted to stifle internal opposition by passing a rule that a member who had spoken once on an issue could not speak again without general consent.[51] Dissatisfied Friends talked about voting and improper procedures. When the Meeting for Sufferings tried to solicit the opinions of Friends in an epistle clearly slanted in favor of the satisfied Friends, their opponents struck off their names from the epistle and circulated a counter letter.[52] Still, the effort to solicit the opinion of every monthly and quarterly meeting continued with both sides organizing their adherents.

At the same time both Quaker groups lobbied with members of Parliament for a new affirmation law. Parliament was at this time dominated by high Tories who passed, over the objections of Quakers and other dissenters, the Schism and Occasional Conformity Acts. Even had Quakers been united, times were not favorable for any sympathetic consideration of Friends, and the divided lobbying resulted in defeat for both sides.

Dissatisfied Friends, opponents of the form granted by Parliament, insisted that the crucial words in Matthew, chapter 5, were "whatsoever is more than these cometh of evil." Jesus' command was not to tell the truth — that had long been a part of Judaism — but to add no form of words to a simple declaration. Any unnecessary attestation, like saying "in the presence of God," was evil and should be avoided. In particular, the invoking of God's name in a court case, and so risking the soul over material goods, was sin. The parliamentary affirmation was so close to an oath as to be indistinguishable; otherwise, it would not be accepted in court.[53]

The examples of Paul's declarations in the New Testament were not sufficient precedent for two reasons. First, Paul's statements had been in matters of faith. Forms which on certain occasions could make an oath did not constitute swearing if spontaneously uttered in prayer, in a sermon, or as a confession of faith. Second, Paul lived in a time of a mixed dispensation in which some customs, like dietary laws and circumcision, were still practiced in the early church. Therefore, Paul's example was not as binding as Christ's command.[54]

The dissatisfied Friends looked at the variety of biblical references to swearing and concluded that an oath could be established by a simple attestation (naming God or saying the Lord liveth) or by a curse, "so help me God." When God swore, for example, he certainly did not put a curse upon himself if he should fail to keep his word. Oliver Cromwell when accepting the Protectorate took an oath (even Coke defined it this way) which had not mentioned swearing and included the phrase "in the presence of God."[55] Those who thought that such a formula was only a theological statement were wrong. True confession had to be inspired directly by God and one had to feel at the very time that God was present and witness to truth. No form upon which London Friends and Parliament agreed could guarantee an individual's continual sense of the presence of God. Quakers opposed what they termed "notional" religion, and the affirmation was just another example of formality.

The "satisfied" Friends, those content with the wording of the law, first responded to opposition by circulating epistles that reprinted declarations of early Friends using the formulas "in the presence of God" and "the witness to the truth of what I say."[56] These epistles, issued under the authority of the Meeting for Sufferings, announced categorically that the affirmation was not an oath without, however, defining what an oath was. In the debate that followed, the dissatisfied used many quotations of principles of early Friends against unnecessary formulas, but the satisfied found many examples of affirmations in religious as well as secular affairs. With both sides invoking the authority of Scriptures and early Friends, no agreement could be reached.

The satisfied Friends did not embark upon a systematic defense of their position until 1713. Their major response came in a tract of 175 pages written by Richard Claridge, a prominent London minister. In addition to its defense of affirmations, the tract is significant for showing the gradual penetration of Enlightenment Christianity upon Quaker apologetics. Claridge insisted upon the reasonableness of Christ's demands and embraced the use of logical methods, like syllogisms, to determine the truth of theological assertations.[57] Earlier Friends had defended the use of reason in temporal concerns but argued that it should not be used in matters of the

Spirit. Showing a self-consciousness in terminology lacking in earlier Quaker theologians like Penn, Claridge defined the term "conscience" and showed the multiplicity in meanings of the word.[58] In his patronizing tone, in his insinuation that the Quakers who opposed him were ignorant (particularly in languages), and in his concern for reasonableness, Claridge relied in his tract on the methods used by Anglican opponents in the 1660s.

For the first time, Friends defined precisely what an oath was. For Claridge, an oath required a curse, made either explicitly like "so help me God," or implicitly.[59] Using the name of God was not sufficient to establish an oath. The essence of Christ's command was to tell the truth and the crucial words in Matthew, chapter 5, "more than these," referred to embellishments of truth. Christ was concerned not with forms of words but with conduct. To Claridge the declarations in the Affirmation Act had no penalty or curse implied and therefore could not make an oath. Statements of truth, including the simple yea and nay, required the implicit assumption of the presence of God. The affirmation form required by Parliament merely verbalized this assumption. Most of Claridge's treatise was devoted to an analysis of Scripture and to writings of early Friends in order to prove their agreement with his definition of an oath. Claridge clearly spoke for the majority of Friends, but, although his treatise went to a second edition, an attempt to gain the endorsement of the London Yearly Meeting failed.

After reading the treatises by both sides, John Lamb formulated a far-reaching denunciation which in tone belonged more to the 1650s than 1713. Lamb said simply: a plague on both your houses. The controversy over affirmations had done nothing but divide Friends and cause acrimony. Both sides wanted a parliamentary law and the only issue was what form was permissible. Although Lamb decided shortly before publication that the dissatisfied position was correct, this was not the main thesis of his pamphlet.

Lamb wanted Friends to return to fundamentals. All the parliamentary maneuverings by Friends were attempts to get a law to avoid sufferings. Yet early Friends had welcomed sufferings as a way to testify to their faith. This was what Friends were now called upon to do, not to bribe legislators to gain a law to protect property.[60] Where the tracts of Skidmore[61] and Claridge were well-organized exegeses of each others' positions, Lamb's work was a series of disjointed witnessing or openings. The power of his position came through its insistence that the essence of a Christian life was radical obedience, not compromises with worldly power.

The Meeting for Sufferings attempted to suppress Lamb's work. Members first met with Lamb to persuade him to withdraw the pamphlet, then dealt with the scribe who copied it, and tried to buy up all copies or cause Lamb to have them destroyed.[62] They even sent an epistle to Lamb's monthly meeting testifying to their disunity with his tract. The speed with which the Meeting for Sufferings operated and the thoroughness of their campaign, something not done with any of the other dissatisfied Friends' works, was testimony that Lamb had struck a sensitive point and one which London Friends did not wish to consider.

The 1714 Yearly Meeting was the high point of discord. The reports of the quarterly meetings showed that twenty counties were in favor of renewing the present affirmation, ten had a predominance of sentiment for renewal, six were against it, four had a preponderance against it, and two were hopelessly deadlocked. Significantly, the pattern of division was geographic. Friends in commercial areas like London, Bristol, and the midlands were overwhelmingly in favor of the present affirmation. But Quakers in the north—in Yorkshire, Westmorland, Cumberland, and Lancashire— were opposed, as were Friends in Ireland and Scotland.[63] No unity could be obtained, but a schism was avoided. After four days of discussion, London Yearly Meeting instructed the Meeting for Sufferings to try for a revised affirmation, but if unsuccessful, to seek renewal. There was to be only one campaign or approach to Parliament and that was to be under the direction of the Meeting for Sufferings.

In 1714 the Meeting for Sufferings contacted many influential members of Parliament in an attempt to get a form which did not mention the name of God. The bill as first proposed in Commons was for renewal, but immediately an amendment for a revised formula was offered. The amendment was overwhelmingly rejected and an attempt to send the bill to committee turned down. The eventual bill made the affirmation perpetual, though extending the restrictions on use to Pennsylvania occasioned major problems there.

The Yearly Meeting accepted the renewal but suggested that the Meeting for Sufferings seek a modification as soon as success was likely. For four years the Meeting for Sufferings did nothing. Then Yearly Meeting pressed the matter again. For another year the Meeting for Sufferings took no action; the Yearly Meeting instructed them again. This time the campaign was initiated in spite of the adverse recommendations of weighty Friends.[64]

Only after Robert Walpole became prime minister could a language more favorable to Friends be obtained. With his support, a bill permitting an affirmation and not requiring the name of God passed the Commons in 1722 without a division. In the Lords the debate was vitriolic, as the opposition tried to use the measure to weaken Walpole.[65] The debate showed that a significant number of influential persons still distrusted not just dissenters but particularly Quakers, and were uncertain whether Friends were Christians or should be tolerated.[66] Walpole did prevail in the Lords, however, and Friends finally gained the right to use an affirmation not mentioning God in civil suits. Not until the nineteenth century could an affirmation be used in jury cases involving the death penalty or as a qualification for office.

The precedent did hold, however, and eventually the Affirmation Act was extended to other denominations. In America a similar struggle over oaths and affirmations took place. Though Walpole's government allowed the affirmation to be used on all occasions in Pennsylvania, political opponents attempted several times to require an oath in an effort to bar Quakers from government. The eventual result was that during the Revolution, most of the new state constitutions enshrined the right of affirmation. In 1787 the Federal Constitution, in the same article forbidding religious tests for office, allowed affirmations. The affirmation phrase effectively forbade discrimination against any person because of religious beliefs. The government would accommodate itself to the religious testimony, not vice versa.

Thus the Quaker campaign for affirmations in England and America made a positive contribution toward guaranteeing the rights of conscience. Unfortunately, in obtaining a legal victory, the Friends forgot the religious and moral issues often mentioned in the literature before 1680. Those issues were:

1. Should a Christian violate a commandment of the New Testament?
2. Does the use of oaths tend to religion or superstition?
3. Does an oath add anything to testimony?
4. Does extending oaths to opposing witnesses require perjury?
5. Are oaths compatible with an adversary system of justice?

There are also modern issues not mentioned by seventeenth-century Friends. For example, in many recent trials both the prosecution and the defense have employed professional witnesses, psychiatrists, and psychologists, to testify either for or against the defendant. These psychiatrists have taken an oath or affirmation to "tell the truth, the whole truth, and nothing but the truth." In an adversary relationship and considering the uncertainties required of professional disciplines, can anyone believe that these witnesses actually tell, or even think they are telling, the "whole truth?" Can anyone's testimony contain "nothing but the truth"?

NOTES

1. James Tyler, *Oaths* (London, 1835) has a thorough discussion of the history of oaths in many cultures. *Encyclopedia Britannica,* 11th ed. (New York, 1914), pp. 939-43, has a good introduction; the most recent edition omits the topic. An excellent treatment of loyalty oaths in England is Caroline Robbins, "Selden's Pills: State Oaths in England, 1558-1714," *Huntington Library Quarterly,* 35 (1972):303-21. In America most controversy involves loyalty oaths administered to selected occupation groups, like secondary and college teachers.

2. William Penn and Richard Richardson, *A Treatise on Oaths* (London, 1675), p. 163; John R. Bartlett, ed., *Records of the Colony of Rhode Island and Providence Plantations* (Providence, 1856-65), 1:111, 150, 282, 396, 441; 2:111-12, 142; *Mennonite Encyclopedia* (Scottdale, Pa. 1955), 4:2-8.

3. William C. Braithwaite, *Beginnings of Quakerism,* 2d ed., rev. Henry J. Cadbury (Cambridge, 1961), 1:139, 195.

4. George Fox, *Journal*, ed. Thomas Ellwood, 8th ed. (London, 1891), p. 39; *Works of George Fox* (Philadelphia, 1831), 7:100, 134, 139.

5. *The Saints Testimony Finished Through Sufferings* (London, 1655), pp. 24-26. Humphrey Smith was imprisoned at Evesham in 1655 after refusing to take the oath of abjuration. He must have been freed shortly thereafter, for in 1656 he was imprisoned again (see *A Representation of the . . . Borough of Evesham . . . from many of the Inhabitants thereof: Directed unto the Protector*). The earliest epistle concerned only with swearing was written by James Parnell probably between 1654 and 1656. It was not published until its inclusion in *A Collection of the Several Writings Given Forth from the Spirit of the Lord, through . . . James Parnell* (1675), pp. 470-76.

6. William C. Braithwaite, "The Penal Laws Affecting Early Friends in England," in *The First Publishers of Truth*, ed. Norman Penney (London, 1907), p. 346.

7. W. K. Jordan, *The Development of Religious Toleration in England: From the Convention of the Long Parliament to the Restoration* (Cambridge, 1938), pp. 144-218.

8. *A Proclamation Prohibiting all Unlawful and Seditious Meetings and Conventicles under the Pretense of Religious Worship*, 10 Jan. 1660[/1], Broadside.

9. *PWP*, 1:291; *First Publishers of Truth*, ed. Penney, pp. 354-55.

10. George Whitehead, *The Christian Progress* (London, 1725), p. 251.

11. *A Brief Relation of the Persecutions and Cruelties that have been Acted upon the . . . Quakers in and about the City of London* (London, 1662), pp. 19, 21; *To the King and Both Houses of Parliament, Now Sitting at Westminster* (London, 1663).

12. Jeremiah Ives, *The Great Case of Conscience Opened . . . about the Lawfullness or Unlawfullness of Swearing* (London, 1660); John Gauden, *A Discourse Concerning Public Oaths and the Lawfulness of Swearing in Judicial Proceedings* (London, 1662); Misorcus, *The Anti-Quaker: or, A Compendious Answer to a tedious Pamphlet, Entitled, A Treatise of Oaths* (London, 1676); Allan Smallwood, *A Reply to a Pamphlet called, Oaths no Gospel Ordinance* (York, 1667). Not all of the literature in favor of oaths was produced by Anglicans. Quakers also had to answer a tract by the Baptist Henry Denne, *An Epistle Recommended to all the Prisons in this City and Nation* (London, 1660).

13. Gauden, *Discourse*, pp. 27-31; Ives, *Great Case*, pp. 12-13.

14. Gauden, *Discourse*, pp. 20-21, 35-37; Smallwood, *A Reply*, pp. 16, 165, 303.

15. William Wayne Spurrier, "Persecution of the Quakers in England 1650-1714" (Ph.D. diss., University of North Carolina, 1976), chap. 1.

16. John Crook, *The Case of Swearing (At All) Discussed* (London, 1663), pp. 6-7, 9, 11.

17. Morgan Watkins, *Swearing Denied in the New Covenant, And its Pretended Foundation raised* (London, 1660), pp. 4-5.

18. James Picton, *A Just Plea Against Swearing, and Against the National Worship of England* (London, 1663), p. 2.

19. Isaac Penington, *The Great Question Concerning the Lawfulnes or Unlawfulnes of Swearing Under the Gospel* (London, 1661), pp. 4-12; Anthony Pearson, *The Great Case of Tithes* (London, 1657).

20. Samuel Fisher, *The Bishop Busied Beside the Businesse* (1662), pp. 8-9. Friends may have learned several of their arguments from other sufferers under the 1660 oaths. An extremely eloquent protest was written by a Baptist; see Samuel Hodgkin, *A Caution to the Sons of Zion: Being an Answer to Jeremiah Ives his Book* (London, 1660).

21. George Fox, *A Small Treatise Concerning Swearing* (London, 1675), pp. 10, 13. Fox is here using a method of exegesis common in the seventeenth century: the interpretation of the Old Testament through the Christ-event. For example, Christians interpreted Job's declaration "I know that my Redeemer liveth," and Isaiah's vision of the suffering servant as meaning that Job and Isaiah had received insight into Jesus Christ's redemption of humankind.

22. Ibid., pp. 19-20.

23. Samuel Fisher, *One Antidote more, Against that Provoking Sin of Swearing* (London, 1660?), pp. 14-15.

24. Gervase Benson, *A True Testimony Concerning Oaths and Swearing* (London, 1669) pp. 28-29.

25. Examples are found in *To the King in Parliament* (1663), and in tracts by Crook and Fisher.

26. Penn and Richardson, *A Treatise on Oaths* (1675).

27. Fisher, *One Antidote*, pp. 36-37.

28. Crook, *Case of Swearing*, pp. 17-18.

29. Fisher, *Bishop Busied*, p. 11.

30. *Book of Oaths* (London 1649), pp. 138, 62-67; *Book of Oaths* (London, 1689), pp. 223-26, 230.

31. Watkins, *Swearing Denied*, pp. 4-5; Crook, *Case of Swearing*, pp. 6, 13-14; Hodgkin, *A Caution to the Sons*, pp. 4, 10-12, where he distinguishes between voluntary and involuntary promissary and assertive oaths. There was also confusion about the distinction between an oath and a vow.

32. Crook, *Case of Swearing*, pp. 13-14; Benson, *A True Testimony*, pp. 300-331; Fisher, *One Antidote*, p. 17.

33. *Truth Seeks No Corners, Being a vindication of the People called Quakers From Any Design of Concealing Papists* (London, 1679).

34. *PWP*, 1:535.

35. George Fox to William Penn, 11 Jan. 1675, *PWP*, 1:299; *A Letter From a Satisfied to a Dissatisfied Friend, Concerning The Solemn Affirmation* (London, 1713), pp. 4-13.

36. Gervase Benson, *A True Testimony* (1669), p. 30; *A Second Testimony Concerning Oaths and Swearing* (1675).

37. *Mennonite Encyclopedia*, 4:7-8.

38. George Fox, *A Small Treatise*.

39. Penn and Richardson, *A Treatise*, pp. 13-15.

40. *A Collection of Acts of Parliament . . . Relative to . . . Quakers* (London, 1777), pp. 1-28.

41. Theodor Eccleston, *A Brief Representation of the Quakers Case of Not-Swearing* (London, 1694), pp. 2-6.

42. *Case of the People Commonly Called Quakers, Relating to Oaths* (c. 1696); *Case of the People Called Quakers, Humbly presented to the Parliament of Ireland* (c. 1724); *Reasons Humbly offered to the Legislature by the People Called Quakers Against the Bill now depending in Parliament intitled An Act to Prevent the Growth of Schism* (c. 1714); *Case of People Called Quakers in Ireland, Concerning Oaths* (n.d.).

43. Raymond C. Mensing, Jr., *Toleration and Parliament 1660-1719* (Washington, D.C., 1979), pp. 34-36, 74, 79.

44. Ibid.; Geoffrey F. Nuttall and Owen Chadwick, eds. *From Uniformity to Unity 1662-1962* (London, 1962).

45. The debate over oaths was part of a much more wide-ranging discussion of liberty of conscience and the necessity of toleration. Some time after 1660 Quakers began adding reasonable and utilitarian considerations to earlier demands based upon natural law, rights of Englishmen, and the spiritual and inward authority of religion. All of Penn's writings on religious freedom utilize various types of evidence. I agree with Ethyn W. Kirby ("The Quakers' Efforts to Secure Civil and Religious Liberty 1660-1690," *Journal of Modern History*, 7 [1935]:407) that the crucial changes came during the 1670s. Unfortunately, Penn's petitions and letters to Parliament during this period, some printed for the first time in *PWP*, vol. 1, are undated. Hugh Barbour, in "Model of Protestant Liberalism," *Church History*, 48

(1979):164-67, also sees major changes both in Penn's thought and in the Quaker movement during this decade.

46. N. C. Hunt, *Two Early Political Associations* (Oxford, 1961), pp. 32-42.

47. When in 1696 the House of Lords added the phrase "the Witness of the Truth of what I say," the minutes of the Meeting for Sufferings (9:203, FLL) referred to "the Small Addition of Some Words Somewhat: Immaterial"; see also Whitehead, *Christian Progress,* pp. 648-55.

48. In negotiations with Parliament in 1690, the following form was proposed to Friends: "I A.B. Do Sincerely and Solemnly Declare in the presence of God that I will true Answer make to all such Questions as shall be asked me And that I will speak the Truth the whole Truth and nothing but the Truth and I call God to Witness and appeal to him as Judge of the Truth of what I shall say." Friends rejected this wording and submitted as a substitute: "I A.B. do Sincerely and Solemnly declare in the presence of God that I will true answer make to all such Questions as shall be askt me in the Case now depending and that I will speak the Truth, the whole Truth and nothing but the Truth and God is my Witness of the Truth of what I shall say." Meeting for Sufferings minutes, 7:190-91, FLL.

49. *Case of Some Thousands of the People called Quakers, in Great Britain, who Conscientiously Scruple the Present Affirmation* (c. 1721); William Penn and Richard Richardson, *A Short Abstract of the Treatise of Oaths,* 4th ed. (Dublin, 1713), pp. 11-15; see also *PWP,* vol. 5, item 38E.

50. London Yearly Meeting minutes, 1691, FLL.

51. Meeting for Sufferings minutes, 21:45, FLL.

52. Ibid., 21:38, 40, 105.

53. Joseph Skidmore, *An Essay upon the Vth of Matthew* (London, 1713), pp. 35, 42-43. Pamphlets of the dissatisfied included John Fisher, *A Position and Testimony Against all Swearing under the Gospel* (London, 1692); *The Case of the People, call'd Quakers, as it concerns an Affirmation* (c. 1707); *The Case of the People called Quakers, With Respect to Many of their Friends in . . . Britain, who conscienciously scruple the Taking of the present Affirmation* (c. 1720); Joseph Skidmore, *Primitive Simplicity Demonstrated: In a Defense of the Essay on the Vth of Matthew* (London, 1714); John Lamb, *Friendly Advice; or, A Circumcising Knife to cut off that Superfluous Branch, the Affirmation* (London, 1714).

54. John Fisher, *A Position,* pp. 5-6, 17.

55. Joseph Skidmore, *Primitive Simplicity,* pp. 54-55.

56. Pamphlets in favor of accepting the 1696 affirmation included *An Epistle From the Meeting for Sufferings by their Order the 17th of the Second Month and 1st of the Third Month, 1696; An Epistle From the Meeting for Sufferings in London, The 16th of the Second Month, 1714; A Letter from a Satisfied to a Dissatisfied Friend, Concerning the Solemn Affirmation* (London, 1713); *The Affirmation Vindicated in a Letter to a Friend* (London, 1713); Richard Claridge, *The Novelty and Nullity of Dissatisfaction: or The Solemn Affirmation Defended* (London, 1715).

57. Claridge, *The Novelty and Nullity,* pp. 68-70. Claridge evidently felt defensive about his use of logic, for he cited examples from Penn, Barclay, and Fisher to show their use of it. Also Skidmore, whom Claridge was attempting to refute, had used a rather unsystematic logic.

58. Ibid., pp. 196-98.

59. Ibid., pp. 11, 13.

60. Lamb, *Friendly Advice,* pp. 6-12.

61. See n. 53, above.

62. Meeting for Sufferings minutes, 21:268, 272, 279-80, 285, 288, FLL; John Lamb, *An Appeal to the Friends, that Attend the Meeting for Sufferings, the Third of the Tenth Month,* 1714.

63. London Yearly Meeting minutes, 5:17-21, FLL. The opposition from the northern meetings to practices of London Friends extended beyond the affirmation

to policies on tithes, etc. Nicholas Morgan is completing a doctoral thesis at the University of Lancaster on Quakerism in Lancashire and its relation to the state which will provide a much needed analysis of the political and cultural divisions among Friends in this period; for some preliminary findings, see Morgan, "Lancashire Quakers and the Oath, 1660-1722," *JFHS*, 54 (1980):235-54.

64. Meeting for Sufferings minutes, 22:55, 72-73, 128, 168, 173, FLL.

65. Charles Realey, *Early Opposition to Sir Robert Walpole, 1720-1727* (Philadelphia, 1931), p. 79; John Plumb, *Robert Walpole* (London, 1960), 2:97-98.

66. William Cobbett, *The Parliamentary History of England . . . to the Year 1803* (London, 1806-20), 7:942-48.

EDWIN B. BRONNER

18 ⟨ Quaker Discipline and Order, 1680–1720:

Philadelphia Yearly Meeting and London Yearly Meeting

In the early days of Quakerism there was little concern for organization. George Fox believed he had a message to share, he felt that the truths which had been revealed to him must be proclaimed to people everywhere, and he moved from place to place preaching the Word of God. The men and women who were convinced by his preaching, and by the Light within, felt this same compulsion to proclaim Truth to others, and, like the disciples of old, they laid aside their everyday work and took to the road to preach. This was a movement in the real meaning of the word, for those who joined felt impelled to move among their fellow human beings to share the Good News which had been revealed to them. There was a sense of immediacy in both the message and the impulse to share it, which militated against stability and organization. The Kendal Fund was one of the few formal creations of the early years, and it existed to collect money and disperse it to traveling Friends.[1]

During the second decade of the movement, the 1660s, thousands of Friends were jailed by the authorities under the statutes enacted against dissenters by the Restoration government. Virtually all of the Quaker leaders were in prison for long terms, and a number died as the result of the hardships they suffered. When Fox came out of Scarborough Castle in September 1666, he began to travel among Friends to give encouragement, provide inspiration, and assess the situation of his followers. He found that Friends had been shattered by their experiences, and he also discovered signs of quarrels and dissension in some meetings for worship.

Early in 1667 Fox felt "moved of the Lord God to set up and establish five Monthly Meetings of men and women in the city of London," as well as quarterly meetings for both men and women.[2] He added, "And the Lord opened to me . . . how I must order and establish Men's and Women's Monthly and Quarterly Meetings in all the nation, and write to other nations, where I came not, to do the same." True to his word, Fox spent the next months traveling from county to county to assist Friends in creating monthly and quarterly meetings for business.[3] In 1668 he participated in the formation of London Yearly Meeting, and the following year shared in establishing Dublin Yearly Meeting. His visit to America from 1671 to 1673 was in large measure for the same purpose, and a number of meetings date from his visit, including New England Yearly Meeting.[4]

By the year 1680 patterns of order and discipline were evolving among Friends, and despite local variations they were similar on the two sides of the Atlantic. Most Quakers in the colonies looked to London Yearly Meeting for guidance. They were visited frequently by traveling ministers from the British Isles, they received books and tracts written by persons such as Robert Barclay, William Penn, and George Fox, and they were also sent pastoral letters by Fox and others.[5] Meetings for business gathered at the local level each month to examine the condition of the members, to provide aid to those in need, to raise questions about persons who were not faithful to good order, and to maintain a simple pattern of life for Friends, including the regulation of marriages and the oversight of burials.

Friends believed that all persons who joined them had undergone a profound religious experience, that they had been reborn in the Spirit, and that they would live blameless lives following that conversion. There were relatively few queries raised as to one's theological beliefs, but it was taken for granted that a new member of the community would live by the strict puritanical code of the day.[6] The monthly meetings were prepared to issue written statements denying that a person was a member of the fellowship if he or she failed to maintain the standards expected of a Friend.

While most of the persons in the American yearly meetings created in the 1670s were colonists who were convinced to join Friends by traveling ministers, a different condition prevailed in the meetings established in the Delaware Valley. Thousands of Quakers migrated to West New Jersey and Pennsylvania from places where there were established meetings, and many of the leading Friends in the new yearly meeting had been prominent in London Yearly Meeting. Such persons were familiar with the practices of older, established meetings and began to follow these procedures in the new settings.

The Quakers who accompanied John Fenwick to southwest New Jersey, where they founded the town of Salem in 1675, organized a monthly meeting the following year, and the Friends who came up the Delaware in the autumn of 1677 to present-day Burlington, formed a monthly meeting shortly after they arrived.[7] While other meetings sprang up around these two original groups, congregations also gathered on the west bank of the Delaware near the falls north of Burlington, and much further south, toward New Castle, in a community called Upland where Upland (Chester) Monthly Meeting was created in 1681.[8] In March of that year William Penn received his charter from Charles II for the province of Pennsylvania, and two months later Friends in the Delaware Valley decided to come together in the autumn for a time of worship and fellowship in sessions called a General Meeting.

The organization which is today called Philadelphia Yearly Meeting likes to use 1681 as the date of its founding. The first printed *Book of Discipline,* on the title page, speaks of "The Yearly Meeting of Friends for Pennsylvania and New Jersey, First Held at Burlington in the year 1681."[9]

Burlington Monthly Meeting, at sessions on 2 May 1681, approved a minute proposing that a "Generall meeting be Yearly Held in Burlington," the first one to meet late in August of the same year.[10] When this sentence was copied into the minute book of the yearly meeting some years later, the wording was changed to read that "a General or Yearly Meeting" be held in Burlington. The monthly meeting records go on to mention that a general meeting was held in Salem early in April 1682, and a second general meeting convened at Burlington in September of that year. The minute book of the yearly meeting described these sessions as a yearly meeting, but the epistle sent out to monthly meetings referred to "Advice from the General Meeting" that had met.

At the sessions in 1683, it was proposed that a general yearly meeting of all Quakers on the North American continent be formed, the first session to be held at Burlington in September 1684. William Penn and others were named to follow up on this proposal, which sounds as if it originated in the mind of Penn.[11] This committee was to correspond with the other groups of Friends and to acquaint London with the suggestion. Clearly a proposal for an intercolonial gathering, rather than for a yearly meeting in the Delaware Valley, it produced little response. While there are no minutes extant from sessions in 1684, a copy of an epistle directed to Friends in London, dated Philadelphia, 24 September 1684, reported, "We have had lately two precious, heavenly and blessed Yearly Meetings; one at Burlington, the other at Philadelphia."[12] These were presumably annual gatherings for worship, rather than sessions for business.

When Friends met in Philadelphia on 15 September 1685, it was noted that there were "Many Friends also from West Jersey [which] shewed their Unity in having One Yearly Meeting." This was the point at which the yearly meeting was created. "It was therefore Unanimously Agreed & Concluded by this Meeting, that there be but One Yearly & General Meeting in this Province and West Jersey, One Year at Burlington, and another at Philadelphia." The 1686 sessions were scheduled for Burlington, and it was proposed that the first three days be used for worship, with the fourth day given over to separate business sessions for men and women. Ministering Friends were asked to gather prior to the yearly meeting session.

In 1685 there were fourteen monthly meetings in six quarterly meetings stretching from New Ark in Delaware to Shrewsbury in East New Jersey. Several smaller meetings clustered around each of the monthly meetings, and there were as many as fifty groups worshipping in homes or even primitive meeting houses by this date. The two largest quarterly meetings were Philadelphia and Chester, and each contained four monthly meetings, if New Ark is counted as part of Chester. The Friends in the Welsh Tract west of the Schuylkill formed one monthly meeting, and there were two north of Philadephia in addition to the one in the center of town. The monthly meetings in Chester Quarter were all in the eastern end of the county except for New Ark which was just over the boundary near present-day Claymont. Falls and Neshaminy were the two monthly meetings in Bucks County. Burlington plus Chesterfield (Crosswicks) were the two organized bodies in the quarterly meeting of that name, while Salem and Shrewsbury Quarterly Meetings contained single monthly meetings in 1685. By the turn of the century only two new monthly meetings had been recognized, and in 1702 two combined, but five more were organized by 1720 as farmers moved beyond the boundaries of the original settlements. Thus there were twenty monthly meetings in the six quarterly meetings in 1720, and some sixty-five preparative meetings.[13]

In order to complete the description of organization, two additional yearly meetings should be mentioned, the Women's Yearly Meeting and the Yearly Meeting of Ministers, later Ministers and Elders. The minute book for the Women's Yearly Meeting begins with a 1681 entry, but it is blank for the next decade. There are references to such a body during these years in epistles and minutes, and in 1784 a statement was made that followers of George Keith carried off the first ten years of records at the time of the schism.[14] London Yearly Meeting did not have a women's yearly meeting, although it had such organizations for business at the quarterly and monthly meeting level. Women gathered at yearly meeting time in London, but not for business. On the other hand, Dublin Yearly Meeting for Women was formed in 1679, and this body must have been the example that Friends followed in Burlington.[15]

The yearly meeting heard reports from the quarterly meetings, it received traveling minutes from "Public" Friends, and it sent epistles to the women in Britain and to the women's yearly meetings in other areas to send greetings and encouragement. In 1705 the women decided to raise a fund for themselves in order to finance any activity they might wish to undertake. The women's body exchanged messages and visitors with the men, and in 1714 wrote an epistle of advice to young Friends. Quaker women gained experience in record keeping, in presiding at meetings, and in keeping financial accounts in this meeting, and in subordinate meetings, which their contemporaries outside the Society were denied. Women sat as equals with men in the Yearly Meeting of Ministers.[16]

The Yearly Meeting of Ministers dates from 1685 and its minutes begin the following year. This body met the day before the start of the larger gathering, in part to decide which Public Friends would assume responsibility for each meeting for worship during the annual session. It also convened at other times during yearly meeting week to hear reports from the local meetings. In 1712 a General Spring Meeting for Worship was initiated in Philadelphia, similar to the general meetings in outlying regions. The ministers, and later ministers and elders, were asked to meet in advance of these sessions for the same purpose.

Two years later a recommendation came up to the yearly meeting from Chester Quarterly Meeting that elders be named in each monthly meeting to meet with Public Friends, especially younger ones.[17] A new generation of ministers was rising, and this proposal seemed an acceptable way in which to provide both encouragement, and, when necessary, some regulation. The concept of solid, responsible persons who might advise Public Friends was first mentioned in the 1670s in England, but no official steps were taken until the eighteenth century. London Yearly Meeting did not officially call for the appointment of such persons until 1727. Elders were added to the Meeting of Ministers in Philadelphia in 1720, but this step was not taken on the other side of the Atlantic until 1758.[18]

While Friends apparently did not keep membership lists in their meetings, they had a very clear understanding of who was part of the fellowship of believers and who was not. A group knew who shared in the spiritual unity of the meeting and also identified those who were lukewarm or turned indifferent, even hostile. They wrote of those who "walked" with them and denounced those they called "disorderly walkers." The 1704 "Discipline" referred to those who "belonged" to the meeting, and the 1719 "Discipline" described "members in full Unity."[19] When a Friend moved from the neighborhood of one meeting to another, he or she was expected to ask his old meeting to provide a certificate which vouched for his "good life and Conversation," and testified that the meeting was in unity with the transfer. Meetings kept these Certificates of Removal, as they were called, or copied them into a record book. They also kept a record of births, marriages, and deaths, and the practice was the same on both sides of the Atlantic.[20] Public Friends were also expected to obtain certificates from their own meetings, and to produce them during travel in the ministry as proof that their service was undertaken with approval at home.

In the 1690s Friends in both Philadelphia Yearly Meeting and London Yearly Meeting were badly shaken by the Keithian Schism. George Keith (1638–1716), a leading Scottish Quaker, had come to East New Jersey as an official of the government under Robert Barclay but soon moved to Philadelphia where he was in charge of the Friends' school. Appalled by a lack of rigorous thinking about religious matters, concerned by emphasis upon the Christ within at the expense of the historical Christ, and dismayed by the ignorance of the Scriptures he saw around him, Keith began to express strong criticism of the Quaker leadership. He soon moved on to denounce the political activities of Friends, rejected slavery, and attacked a number of individual Quakers by name.[21] When the yearly meeting tried to discipline him, he organized a separate faction called Christian Quakers, and after he was disowned, these persons formed a separate church. Keith returned to England to gain approbation from London Yearly Meeting, but even though many had sympathy with his position, he soon antagonized Friends in Britain and was disowned by them as well. He then joined the Anglican church, which ordained him as a priest and sent him back to America under the auspices of the Society for the Propagation of the Gospel in Foreign Parts to convert Quakers to the Church of England.

Many of the persons who left Friends to follow Keith returned eventually to the Society, and Quakers did not suffer any permanent ill effects from the Schism, even though it had stirred great controversy at the time. In the aftermath of the Schism the discipline was tightened on both sides of the Atlantic, and it should be added, doctrinal statements about Christ were also strengthened.[22] Keith had proposed naming special influential persons to oversee the membership in each meeting in order to support the faithful and discipline those who were "disorderly walkers." From this suggestion came the practice of naming overseers in the local meetings. The epistles that were composed at yearly meeting time frequently listed a series of responsibilities that Friends should undertake and also warned members against a number of practices that violated good order.

Friends in the Delaware Valley decided in 1703 to prepare a systematic compilation of such advice and named a committee to gather former documents and minutes relating to discipline. The compilation "relating to good ORDER & DISCIPLINE" was presented to the yearly meeting in Burlington in 1704 and approved after some additions and amendments. This was the first "Book of Discipline" to be drawn up by Friends anywhere; it was copied by hand for the quarterly and monthly meetings, and pertinent sections were also copied for preparative meetings. Reynier Jensen, who operated the press for the yearly meeting, might have printed the document, as some epistles were printed, but Friends chose not to take that action. The statement was not designed for wide distribution; rather it was to be used by each meeting for business. Outsiders would have seized upon a printed statement and started disputations which would only have been harmful. Furthermore, it was not regarded as a permanent statement, for it would be subject to frequent revisions by the yearly meeting.

After an introduction in which New Testament origins of good order were outlined, the committee went on to describe the steps taken in preparing the 1704 document so that "Wee may all walk by the same Rule and mind the same thing." The provisions fell into several categories and they were not as well organized as in later compilations. A description of the meetings for business, and the way in which Friends were to conduct quarterly, monthly, and preparative meetings was provided for the guidance of clerks and others. Detailed instructions to use in supervising marriages, in settling differences between members, and in dealing with persons who violated the good order of Friends were laid down for handy reference. Advice on training children and servants, and on the discipline of young Friends was given, and there were detailed lists of prohibitions to be observed by members and to be enforced by the overseers. The paper ended with these words:

> And now Dear fr[ien]ds Wee shall Conclude with this Caution That as it's necesary for the good Governmt of a Nation to have good Laws and yet to little Purpose without putting them as occasion offers in Execution, So will Rules of Discipline as necesary in the Church be also to little purpose if due Care be not taken to Put them in Practice.

Faithful Friends were urged to take this to heart, that God might be praised, that "Truth [be] kept clear of Scandall," and that all might receive the reward of "Well done Good & faithfull Servant."

To follow up the circulation of the "Discipline," in 1706 the yearly meeting began to ask quarterly meeting representatives about the "Affairs of Truth" in each region. That same year an epistle was sent out to Friends requesting the overseers in each monthly meeting to provide a report on the "state of the Society." The monthly meetings were to give an account to quarterly meetings to serve as the basis for the reports to yearly meeting. Three years later it was decided that the annual summaries from the quarterly meetings should be in writing, and time was put aside to consider these reports and to propose ways to strengthen good order in the Society.

In 1718 a small committee was named to prepare a revised "Book of Discipline," and it brought back a document the following year.[23] Although limited once more to handwritten copies, this version circulated more widely than the 1704 edition. The manuscript was better organized than the previous one, and less wordy, likely a reflection of the fact that David Lloyd (1656–1731) served on the committee. An introduction, written to justify church order, said, "This is called our Discipline . . . in the exercise whereof Perswasion & gentle dealing is & ought to be our practice." It added, however, that when anyone "thro perverseness & Stubborness" could not be reclaimed, he should be subject to "Censure or Disowning" in order to protect "the good Reputation of the whole Body."[24]

After summarizing the provisions for meetings for business, concluding with the duties of overseers, the manuscript turned to rules for personal behavior. This list, which included positive responsibilities as well as things to refrain from doing, varies little from other lists of this sort. A long discussion of settling personal disputes followed. Next was a section on dealing with offenders, including the steps leading to disownment, as well as provisions for appeals against a monthly meeting decision. Regulations regarding marriage took up considerable space and included a sample form for a marriage certificate. "Several other Cautions Advices and matters might have been here added," the manuscript concluded, "but this being intended more particularly as advice in the Order of Discipline & manner of dealing" was not meant to be definitive. Friends were urged to be faithful in their personal lives, and in performing their duties, "That God through all may have Praise, Worship & Honour."[25]

Additional changes were incorporated into the "Book of Discipline" in 1747, and a complete revision took place in 1762. In 1797 the "Discipline" was revised once more and published under the title, *Rules of Discipline and Christian Advices*. This 1797 edition preserved much of the contents from previous versions, for example, the discussion on settling personal disputes from the 1719 "Book of Discipline."[26]

It was in the preparation of an organized "Discipline" that Philadelphia Yearly Meeting deviated most from the practice of London Yearly Meeting, which did not compile a similar manuscript book until 1738.[27] The colonists who settled in North America were much more likely to prepare a written document than those who stayed in Britain. Even before the English Civil War the Pilgrim fathers had prepared the Mayflower Compact. Among Quakers the Concessions and Agreements of West New Jersey were followed by the Charter of Liberties on the Pennsylvania side of the Delaware. In 1701 the colonists not only drew up the Charter of Privileges but a Charter of Property as well, which Penn refused to ratify. It must have seemed a logical step to prepare a written "Discipline" which could be referred to in each monthly meeting.

British Friends, on the other hand, were content to allow precedents and customs to accumulate slowly over a period of time. Material had been issued piecemeal, first by George Fox in his epistles, and later in the annual epistles of the yearly meeting. Rufus M. Jones wrote that the "Discipline" prepared in London "was a thing of slow and almost unconscious growth. Nobody wrote it outright. No individual or even committee 'made' it. It was the creation of the whole group working together."[28] In fact, the rules of good order evolved in much the same way on both sides of the Atlantic and were very similar in tone and form, except for the fact that the Americans wished to have it all collected in written form, and the British did not.[29] New England followed the example of Philadelphia in 1708 when a compilation labeled "Ancient epistles, minutes, advices or discipline" was made, but New England Yearly Meeting did not revise this document on a regular basis as Philadelphia did. The other American yearly meetings did not prepare such books, but New York probably used the 1719 Philadelphia "Discipline" for a time.[30]

The organization of London Yearly Meeting was visible at all times, while Philadelphia Yearly Meeting was nonexistent except for the annual meeting. Since before 1660 London had employed an administrative officer called the Recording Clerk. In addition, the Second Day Morning Meeting met each Monday, and the Meeting for Sufferings also convened once a week at Devonshire House, Bishopsgate, in offices provided by the yearly meeting.[31] Philadelphia Yearly Meeting had no office, no employed staff, and no committees which met regularly between the annual sessions except for the ministers who gathered at the time of the General Spring Meeting.

On the other hand, London Yearly Meeting was able to support itself with voluntary contributions, while Philadelphia Yearly Meeting allocated a portion of the stock, as the treasury was called, to each quarterly meeting. Currency was in very short supply in the colonies, and after voluntary contributions had been tried for a time, the decision was made in 1699 to assess a specific amount. Friends agreed to raise £100 at a time, of which Philadelphia Quarterly Meeting provided £40, and the balance was divided among the others according to numbers in the quarter.[32] The sum was requested every three or four years as needed, not on an annual basis. A separate account was kept in New Jersey beginning in 1706 because of the difference in value of the currency in the two provinces. In both yearly meetings the stock or treasury of the body was examined regularly by a special committee appointed for the purpose.

Participation in the yearly meeting sessions by representatives of the quarterly meetings was roughly the same on the two sides of the Atlantic. In Philadelphia Yearly Meeting each quarter named four or five persons, with the larger naming more than the smaller. The official representatives at London Yearly Meeting included two or four from each quarter except for Yorkshire with eight and London with twelve.[33] Many more Friends shared in the worship sessions at yearly meeting time, but official decisions were made by approximately fifty persons. By 1720 Friends had accepted an hierarchical system of authority that ran counter to the "equal fellowship" that had prevailed in the early years. The 1719 "Discipline" in Philadelphia said that if a superior meeting questioned the decisions of a subordinate one, such a meeting "ought with readiness & Meekness to render a Satisfactory account accordingly."[34] It was also true, however, that the authority of yearly meeting ascended upward from the monthly and quarterly meetings through the appointed representatives.

Jon Butler has made the point that most of the chosen delegates were either Public Friends, or "Weighty Friends" who gave a great deal of time to the Society, and that these men had gathered the power and authority into their own hands. He found evidence that there was some unhappiness with this condition and that many who joined the Keithians were motivated by resentment of those in authority rather than a concern for theological or social issues. Believing that this feeling of frustration continued after the yearly meeting had recovered from the Keithian troubles, he quoted a petition drawn up by Pentecost Teague, a Philadelphia businessman, dated 1699.[35] It is difficult to determine whether Friends accepted or resented the fact that a small number of persons carried on the essential work of the Society. Widespread dissatisfaction might very well have been reflected in the manner in which Friends responded to the discipline, but it has not been possible to identify any correlation. The same conditions prevailed in Britain, but there is no indication of reaction against those in authority in the studies made of this period. We do know that there was some strain between New Jersey Friends and those in Pennsylvania, as well as between rural and urban Quakers. Similar feelings existed in London Yearly Meeting, especially between country and city Friends.[36]

In summary, it seems clear that similarities in good order and discipline between the two yearly meetings were far greater than the differences. The principal differences were that Philadelphia had a written "Discipline," and that London had a paid Recording Clerk on duty to conduct the day-to-day business of the yearly meeting. While the effectiveness of the American yearly meeting was weakened by the lack of a day-to-day staff person, it managed without one, and continued to do so for nearly two centuries. London might have been strengthened by a complete collection of its disciplinary guidelines, but it used the annual epistles to remind Friends of their responsibility. There was a Women's Yearly Meeting in the Delaware Valley, while London did not make provision for a national women's meeting for business until much later. Women gained experience in conducting business affairs in the subordinate bodies on either side of the Atlantic, and they shared fully in the ministry as Public Friends. Overseers and elders were named first on the American side, but British Quakers soon adopted the practice.

Friends on the two sides of the Atlantic kept in close touch with one another and learned from the experience and practice of the other. In 1690 Philadelphia wrote to London asking that six copies of each publication by that body be sent over so that Public Friends could decide whether to buy quantities of such publications. As many as 200 copies of some books were purchased to distribute in the Delaware Valley region. London sent a similar request to Philadelphia in 1703.[37] On an annual basis, the two yearly meetings exchanged epistles which contained a summary of conditions as well as fraternal greetings.[38]

More than fifty-five men and women came to America as Public Friends in these forty years, and a significant number went from Philadelphia Yearly Meeting to the British Isles in the same period. These ministers not only visited the large annual gatherings but usually took a year or more to travel from one local meeting to another to preach, to visit in the homes, to listen, and to give advice and counsel. Undoubtedly these persons did more than either books or epistles to hold the trans-Atlantic Quaker community together. Both Frederick B. Tolles and Thomas E. Drake delivered presidential addresses to the Friends Historical Society in England about the existence of the trans-Atlantic community.[39] Rufus Jones wrote in a similar vein in 1911. "By the opening of the eighteenth century the Friends were *one* people throughout the world, though there was absolutely no *bond* but love and fellowship; . . . instead of being an aggregation of separate units the Society was in an extraordinary measure a *living group*."[40]

Despite the differences which have been noted in this essay, the strong sense of unity was so powerful that it overcame the points of difference. Friends continued to migrate across the Atlantic, not only from Britain to the New World, but in the opposite direction as well, and they were able to settle into the new yearly meeting with a minimum of adjustment.

NOTES

I am indebted to Edward H. Milligan, retired Librarian of the Library of the Society of Friends in London, for reading the manuscript and making several suggestions.

1. William C. Braithwaite, *The Beginnings of Quakerism,* 2d ed., rev. Henry J. Cadbury (Cambridge, 1955), pp. 135-37, 183-85 passim.

2. George Fox, *Journal,* ed. John L. Nickalls (Cambridge, 1952), p. 511; see also Braithwaite, *The Second Period of Quakerism,* 2d ed., rev. Henry J. Cadbury (Cambridge, 1961), chap. 9. Michael J. Sheeran in *Beyond Majority Rule, Voteless Decisions in the Religious Society of Friends* (Philadelphia, 1983), pp. 10-12, cites evidence which indicates that monthly business meetings of some sort were held in the 1650s.

3. Friends came together once each month to conduct the business affairs of the meeting. The monthly meetings of a region, usually the county in England, met together four times a year, hence quarterly meetings.

4. New England Friends have suggested that their yearly meeting was founded a decade earlier in 1661. Arthur J. Worrall (*Quakers in the Colonial Northeast* [Hanover, N.H., 1980], pp. 63-64), indicates that the general meetings before 1672 were not business meetings for matters of discipline.

5. Ibid., pp. 64-68. Worrall found that local converts to Quakerism were not always willing to accept advice and instruction from London, although the dominant element made an effort to follow that example.

6. Vann, *Development of Quakerism,* pp. 128-43.

7. "Inventory of Church Archives of New Jersey, The Religious Society of Friends," typescript prepared by the New Jersey Historical Records Survey Project (Newark, N.J., 1941); see also Samuel Smith, *The History of the Colony of Nova-Caesaria, or New Jersey,* rev. ed (1890; reprint, 1966).

8. *Inventory of Church Archives, Society of Friends in Pennsylvania* (Philadelphia, 1941).

9. Philadelphia, 1797.

10. Burlington Monthly Meeting minutes, Quaker Collection, HCL.

11. The other persons named were: Christopher Taylor, Samuel Jennings, James Harrison, Thomas Olive, and Mahlon Stacey, all leading figures in either West Jersey or Pennsylvania.

12. Phila. Yearly Meeting minutes, Quaker Coll., HCL.

13. Shrewsbury Quarterly Meeting: Shrewsbury, 1670; Woodbridge, 1689; Salem Quarterly Meeting: Salem, 1676; Haddonfield, 1695; Burlington Quarterly Meeting: Burlington, 1678; Chesterfield (Crosswicks), 1684; Little Egg Harbor, 1715; Phila. Quarterly Meeting: Philadelphia, 1682; Abington, 1683; Tacony, 1683 (merged with Abington in 1702); Radnor, 1684; Gwynedd, 1714; Bucks Quarterly Meeting: Falls, 1783; Neshaminy (Middletown), 1683; Buckingham, 1720; Chester Quarterly Meeting: Upland (Chester), 168l; New Ark, Del., 1682; Chichester (Concord), 1684; Darby, 1684; Duck Creek, Del., 1705; New Garden, 1718.

14. Margaret H. Bacon, "A Widening Path: Women in Philadelphia Yearly Meeting Move Toward Equality, 1681-1929," in *Friends in the Delaware Valley: Philadelphia Yearly Meeting, 1681-1981*, ed. John M. Moore (Haverford, 1981), pp. 173-99.

15. Isabel Grubb, *Quakers in Ireland, 1654-1900* (London, 1927), p. 35; Olive C. Goodbody, *Guide to Irish Quaker Records* (Dublin, 1967), pp. 3-4, 28, 43-44.

16. See Bacon, "Widening Path."

17. 18-22 Sept. 1714, Phila. Yearly Meeting minutes, Quaker Coll., HCL; Arnold Lloyd, *Quaker Social History, 1669-1738* (London, 1950), p. 128; *London Yearly Meeting During 250 Years* (London, 1919), p. 33; Jon Butler, *Power, Authority, and the Origins of American Denominational Order . . . 1680-1730* (Philadelphia, 1978), p. 41.

18. New England Yearly Meeting added elders to the ministers in 1701, and New York Yearly Meeting did so in 1704. However, they were not very active in either yearly meeting. Worrall, *Quakers in Northeast*, p. 71.

19. These compilations were only kept in manuscript, and each copy is different from others. The 1704 "Discipline" used was the one combined with the "General Testimony to Youth," and the 1719 "Discipline" was Thomas Lewis's copy. Quaker Coll., HCL. Photocopies of these two disciplines are also available in FLL.

20. Vann (*Development of Quakerism*, chap. 4), effectively refutes the older belief that the concept of membership was formed in the 1730s.

21. Ethyn W. Kirby, *George Keith (1638-1716)* (New York, 1942); Butler, *Power, Authority, and Origins*; J. William Frost, "Unlikely Controversialists: Caleb Pusey and George Keith," *Quaker History*, 64 (1975), pp. 16-36; idem, *The Keithian Controversy in Early Pennsylvania* (Norwood, Pa., 1979).

22. The Yearly Meeting on Ministry issued a paper in 1695 entitled: "Our Ancient Testimony Renewed Concerning our Lord and Saviour Jesus Christ, the Holy Scriptures, and the Ressurection"; see James Bowden, *The History of the Society of Friends in America* (London, 1850-54), 2:28-33.

23. Burlington, 20-24 Sept., 1718; Philadelphia, 19-24 Sept., 1719, Phila. Yearly Meeting minutes, Quaker Coll., HCL.

24. Thomas Lewis copy, pp. 4-5, Quaker Coll., HCL.

25. Ibid., pp. 52-53.

26. In the printed 1797 edition of the *Discipline*, the editors indicated the year of origin for a great many of the provisions. More than 30 citations are for the period before 1711, half of them before the 1704 "Discipline" and the other half after. In no instance is the year 1704 cited, although many paragraphs are credited to the first major revision in 1719.

27. L. Hugh Doncaster, *Quaker Organization and Business Meetings* (London, 1958), p. 24.

28. Jones, *Later Periods of Quakerism* (London, 1921), 1:142.

29. This conclusion is based upon a comparison of the annual epistles sent to the local meetings by London Yearly Meeting with the two "Disciplines" compiled in Philadelphia and Burlington.

30. Worrall, *Quakers in Northeast*, p. 70; letter from Thyra Jane Foster of the Archives Committee, 17 Nov. 1965; letter from Gerald D. McDonald, New York Yearly Meeting Archives Committee, 17 Nov. 1965. Irish Friends did not compile a collected "Discipline" until early in the nineteenth century; instead they leaned heavily on what London Yearly Meeting prepared.

31. *London Yearly Meeting During 250 Years,* pp. 10-11, 138.

32. The allocations were as follows: Chester, £20; Bucks, £10; Burlington, £17; Salem and Gloucester, £10; and Shrewsbury, £3. See Phila. Yearly Meeting minutes, 1699, Quaker Coll., HCL; see also Lloyd, *Quaker Social History,* chap. 12.

33. Phila. Yearly Meeting minutes, Quaker Coll., HCL; Lloyd, *Quaker Social History,* p. 134.

34. Thomas Lewis copy, pp. 9-10, Quaker Coll., HCL.

35. Butler, *Power, Authority, and Origins,*, pp. 32-38, 40-43.

36. Lloyd, *Quaker Social History,* p. 143.

37. 10 Sept. 1690, Phila. Yearly Meeting minutes, Quaker Coll., HCL; 3 Feb. 1703, "Answers to Forreign and Domestick Epistles," vol. 1, FLL.

38. While London Yearly Meeting tended to think of itself as the parent body, there is less evidence of a superior attitude in regard to good discipline and order than in some other relationships; see Edwin B. Bronner, "Intercolonial Relations Among Quakers Before 1750," *Quaker History,* 56 (1967):3-17.

39. Tolles, *The Atlantic Community of the Early Friends* (London, 1952); Drake, *Patterns of Influence in Anglo-American Quakerism* (London, 1958).

40. *The Quakers in the American Colonies* (London, 1911), pp. 314-15. J. William Frost in "The Transatlantic Community Reconsidered," read at the Philadelphia Center for Early American Studies seminar in February, 1984, suggests that the transatlantic community spirit diminished as the eighteenth century progressed.

GARY B. NASH

19 ⬧ *The Early Merchants of Philadelphia:*
The Formation and Disintegration of a Founding Elite

When William Penn organized the Quaker migration to Pennsylvania in 1681 and drafted plans for the founding of its capital city, he demonstrated a keen eye for the realities of colony building and the unromantic work of making a government function. No colony could prosper without a port city facing the Atlantic, and no maritime center could function without a merchant elite. Furthermore, that elite, coordinating the economic life of the colony, would necessarily play a pivotal role in government. Hence, it is not surprising that Penn, who claimed to abhor cities and dislike mercantile pursuits, took pains to recruit a nucleus of merchants to the shores of the Delaware and gave them heavy responsibilities in matters of government.[1]

This essay is concerned with the gathering of this founding mercantile elite in Philadelphia in the years between 1681 and 1710, the failure of these merchants to perpetuate themselves into the second generation, and the emergence in the years from 1711 to 1740 of a quite different merchant community, for the most part not descended from the initial merchant families. Because this pattern bears resemblance to what Bernard Bailyn and David Jordan have described in early Virginia and Maryland and what Richard Dunn has revealed about early Barbados, we may suspect that, while the circumstances differed from colony to colony, founding elites in colonial America were fragile and short-lived — and nowhere more so than in the cities.

In any study of this kind there are many methodological barriers to surmount. Merely to identify who was a merchant in early Philadelphia is a knotty problem. I began with the sixty-seven merchants in the first period who left wills and inventories of estate and the seventy-nine who did so in the second period, but I quickly discovered that the names of many traders left no trace in the probate records. The crumbling deed books in the Philadelphia City Archives provided the best supplement to the initial list, for grantor and grantee are almost always identified by occupation. Still, many merchants never entered the real estate market. Hence, it was necessary to comb the advertisements in the *Pennsylvania Gazette* and *American Weekly Mercury,* the ship registration lists that begin in 1726, and the admissions to freemanship in the records of the Corporation of Philadelphia.[2] No doubt some merchants have still escaped my net, but by recovering 102 traders in the first group and 143 in the second, I presume to have identified a large majority of those who put roots down in the city before 1740.

A second problem is defining the chronological boundaries for the two groups. Generational or cohort analysis is a tricky business; rather than enter this thicket I decided simply to place in the first era all those merchants who came to Philadelphia and established themselves between 1681 and 1710. This is a rather extended founding period but one that coincides with Penn's active involvement in his colony and with the flow of emigration to Pennsylvania, which was sharply curbed after 1700 by Queen Anne's War. The second period commences near the end of Penn's active oversight of his colony and at the beginning of a second wave of immigration; it ends with the advent of an extended period of war in 1740 and covers an era when Philadelphia entered a period of remarkable expansion and economic development.[3]

The publicity surrounding Penn's grant in 1681 and the proprietor's skillful promotional work drew merchants from all over the English-speaking world to the "Holy Experiment." Between 1682 and 1689 at least fifty-six merchants took up residence in Philadelphia. Many were old friends and Quaker colleagues of Penn, men such as James Claypoole, an established West Indian trader living in London; Robert Turner, a Dublin cloth merchant; and Griffith Jones, who had entered the counting house by marrying the widow of a London merchant. The largest number in this first wave came from England, but others flocked in from the West Indies, Ireland, New York, and New Jersey. Many of them were First Purchasers of Pennsylvania land, especially those from England, Ireland, and Wales, and hence were entitled to large city lots in the capital city. Befitting their occupation (and consistent with the sizeable investment they were making in his colony), Penn allocated to them the Delaware River waterfront lots from Dock Creek north to Pegg's Run. Here they built their wharves, warehouses, and crude early dwellings.[4]

Even if we take the absence of the names of five of these founding merchants from the early records of the Philadelphia Monthly Meeting to indicate no affiliation with the Society of Friends, only eight of these fifty-six early traders (14 percent) were not Quaker. They had come to Philadelphia because economic opportunity beckoned and Penn's policy of religious toleration promised freedom for all to compete for advantages in the new colony.

Many merchants in England and elsewhere, including a number of First Purchasers of land, cautiously waited before making the decision to uproot themselves and journey to the Delaware. Not all was peace and prosperity in the early years, and the outbreak of war in 1689 provided a test of whether a pacifist government could function in the militaristic world of the late seventeenth century. But at least twelve merchants did cast their lot with Penn's colony between 1690 and 1695. The most notable were Quakers Isaac Norris of Port Royal, Jamaica; Joseph Pidgeon and Charles Saunders from Bristol; Edward Shippen and Nathan Stansbury from Boston; and Pentacost Teague from Cornwall. A somewhat greater reinforcement of the merchant community occurred when Penn returned in 1699 for a second sojourn in his colony. Of the seventeen merchants who are known to have arrived in Phildelphia between 1696 and 1700, about half came with Penn or as a result of his announced intention to return to Pennsylvania to put an end to political squabbling and usher in a period of maturation and growth. They included a group of men upon whom Penn conferred important offices and upon whom he relied after his return to England in 1701: James Logan and Samuel Finney from Ireland, James Steel from Sussex, John Cadwalader from Wales, William Fishbourne and Richard Hill from Maryland, and Richard Clymer from Bristol.

This turn-of-the-century influx of merchants did not much enlarge the counting house circle; instead, the newcomers replaced traders in the founding group who had succumbed to difficult conditions in the early years and then an epidemical fever that swept through Philadelphia in 1699.[5] No fewer than twenty-three of the fifty-six merchants who arrived between 1682 and 1689 were dead by the turn of the century, including some of Penn's principal officeholders — William Frampton, Christopher Taylor, James Claypoole, John Delaval, George Hutcheson, Thomas Budd, Arthur Cooke, and Robert Turner. The merchant community, though augmented by seventeen arrivals between 1696 and 1700, had seen an almost equal number of its members buried in those five years alone.

About seventeen merchants arrived in Philadelphia between 1701 and 1710, two of them sons of Edward Shippen, who had migrated from Boston in 1694. During the same decade another fifteen merchants died. Thus, from about 1690 to 1710 the merchant community was nearly static in number. But during these same twenty years, as shown in table 19.1, the religious composition of Philadelphia's merchants changed dramatically. In the founding period, from 1682 to 1689, about six of every seven arriving merchants were Quaker; in the two decades beginning in 1690 Quaker merchant arrivals represented exactly half of the merchants establishing themselves in the city.

One further characteristic of this early group should be noted. Nearly one-fourth of them had entered the mercantile ranks from artisan status merely by emigrating to Pennsylvania. Samuel Richardson from Jamaica is the classic example. A Quaker bricklayer who had abandoned England for the Caribbean in the 1670s, he arrived in Philadelphia in 1683 and by the beginning of the eighteenth century was reputed to be the second wealthiest merchant in Philadelphia.[6] Many others duplicated this kind of shipboard mobility in the early years. Among important merchants in the founding period, Humphrey Morrey had been a distiller, Philip James a wine cooper, Griffith Jones a glover, Benjamin Chambers a turner, John Day and Thomas Masters carpenters, Anthony Morris, Gabriel Wilkinson, and Francis Rawle bakers, Thomas Budd a cooper, and William Hudson a bricklayer.[7] Arriving early and purchasing land at a time when £20 would buy a thousand acres of fertile farmland plus a bonus of capacious lots in the budding commercial center of the capital city, these men rose into the economic elite at a dizzying pace probably unparalleled anywhere else in the Atlantic world at this time.

Despite their success in establishing Pennsylvania's trade connections with other mainland colonies, the West Indies, England, and Ireland, Philadelphia's founding merchant elite was not very successful in passing on the mantle of commercial leadership to their sons. Of 143 merchants identified in the period from 1711 to 1740, only 31, or about 20 percent, were the sons of men in the founding merchant group. Some of these sons became important merchant leaders in Philadelphia in the age of Franklin — men such as William Allen, son of a merchant from Ireland who had married the daughter of another first-generation merchant, Thomas Budd; Samuel Coates, son of the prominent early merchant Thomas Coates; William Logan, son of James Logan, Penn's main factotum after 1700; Thomas Masters, Jr.; Isaac Norris, Jr. (as well as two of his brothers); Edward Shippen II and his cousin Joseph; Samuel Carpenter, Jr., and Joseph Wharton, son of First Purchaser Thomas Wharton. But only twenty-four first-generation merchant families produced sons who succeeded their fathers along the Delaware River wharves. Mercantile activity within all of the other seventy-eight families of first-generation merchants ended with the deaths of their founders. During the second generation of the city's history, when Philadelphia experienced rapid growth and economic development, these families played no role in the arena of commerce.

The failure of sons to succeed fathers left vacant a large number of positions in the period after 1710. By that year, in fact, at least 43 of the founding group of 102 were dead and another 28 succumbed in the following decade. To fill their places, and to add to them in a period of growth, came new men whose names cannot be found in the early records of the city. Some of them founded trading houses that would be known throughout the Atlantic world in the decades that followed. In fact, tracing backward from the American Revolution, one finds many more important merchant families that were launched in the second period than in the first. Among them were the Biddles, Bringhursts, Griffits, Inglises, Lawrences, Levys, McCalls, Merediths, Reynells, Stampers, Strettels, Willings, and Wistars—all of whom emigrated to Philadelphia after 1710 and replenished the circle of merchants so depleted by the failure of the first-generation male heirs to succeed their fathers.

Of the 111 merchants in the second generation who were not related by birth to the founding merchant elite, the origins of 71 have been traced. Two-thirds of them (46) were new immigrants to the seaport capital. Several came from Ireland, when trade connections made in the early period facilitated emigration. They included Jonathan Bennett, Thomas Griffits (who came by way of Jamaica and achieved immediate success by marrying the daughter of Isaac Norris), Benjamin Mayne, Richard Nixon, and Robert Strettel. A few came from Scotland, such as George Chalmers and George McCall. But many more arrived from Bristol and London, Philadelphia's important trading partners. They included William Dowell, Thomas Flexney, Peter and Thomas Lloyd, Abraham Taylor, John White, and Charles Willing. As in the early period, New York furnished a few new merchants, notably the founders of the city's Jewish merchant group, Isaac and Nathan Levy and David Franks, who arrived in the late 1730s.[8] The West Indies, especially Barbados and Jamaica, continued to supply Philadelphia with merchants, with at least eight arriving from the islands in this period.[9]

A second group of merchants who established themselves in Philadelphia after 1710 were sons of First Purchasers or others who had come to Pennsylvania in the early years, had taken up land in or near Philadelphia, and had prospered sufficiently to give their heirs a secure base from which to launch a mercantile career. Eleven of the second-generation merchants were sons of yeoman farmers. Peter Baynton, the founder of a famous merchant house, for example, was the son of Benjamin Baynton, a First Purchaser who had settled in Chester County about 1686. Robert Ellis, one of Philadelphia's largest slave traders by the 1730s, was the son of the Welshman Thomas Ellis, an early register general of Pennsylvania and a member of the Welsh community in Merion. Quakers John and George Mifflin were fathered by an early yeoman settler in the Northern Liberties, and an even more famous eighteenth-century Quaker merchant, Israel Pemberton, grew up on his father's rolling acres in Bucks County.

Successful artisans of the founding generation also contributed eleven sons to Philadelphia's second generation of merchants. John Warder, a Quaker hatter and feltmaker, trained his son Jeremiah in his trade in Philadelphia, but the son later became a considerable merchant. One of the sons of malster Thomas Paschall, himself the son of a pewterer and First Purchaser who arrived in 1683, had become an important Philadelphia merchant by the 1730s, as had the sons of carpenter Samuel Powel (Samuel Powel, Jr.), bricklayer John Redman (Joseph and Thomas Redman), and Germantown turner Isaac Shoemaker (Benjamin Shoemaker). However, in light of the rapid turnover in the merchant community in the eighteenth century, it is surprising to find that of the 102 merchants whose origins are known, only 11 were drawn from the artisan class.[10] Although the commercial elite of the city disintegrated rapidly, it was mainly horizontal movement from the outside world that replenished the mercantile ranks rather than internal vertical movement from below.

The failure of most pioneer artisans to propel their sons upward into mercantile circles cannot be satisfactorily accounted for by an absence of opportunity since so many positions were filled from outside. Nor does it seem possible that the low incidence of artisan-to-merchant mobility was caused by pinched inheritance. A large number of Philadelphia's early artisans, in fact, acquired substantial property in the city, which by the time they passed it on to their sons, had multiplied in value. Instead, it appears that most sons of successful first-generation artisans eschewed the commercial life, preferring to follow their father's footsteps as carpenters, silversmiths, bakers, and shipbuilders, while continuing to invest in Philadelphia property. The Emlens, Elfreths, Duffields, and Penroses are only a few of the prominent examples of founding-generation artisans who accumulated considerable wealth, much of it in land, and raised sons who preferred the craftsman's existence to a life in the counting house. A pride of craft seems to have been operating here; it resulted in a tradition of passing on artisan skills to those who might, if they had wished, have entered mercantile pursuits. The numerous examples of unsuccessful merchants in Philadelphia — or successful merchants who had been badly battered during periodic downturns in commerce such as in the 1720s — may also have convinced the sons of successful artisans that the merchant's life was not the best of all worlds.

While it is clear that the mercantile elite was reconstituted in the decades after 1710, the process by which the new group assumed power remains to be analyzed. Other studies of fragile founding elites speak in terms of new men shouldering aside the older group or climbing over their backs on the way to the top. This might be inferred for Philadelphia from the fact that so many new faces appeared while old ones faded. But only by examining the sons of the founding merchant elite — by inquiring into what they did if they did *not* follow their fathers into the counting house — can we know with certainty the causes of elite disintegration.

Of the 102 merchants in the founding group, only 24 produced sons who followed in their fathers' footsteps.[11] Seventy-eight merchants sired no sons who succeeded them. In just over half of these cases (forty) this is explained by the fact that the families either had no sons or lost their sons before they reached adulthood. Far more than we have realized, early Philadelphians did not marry, were sterile, or saw one-third, one-half, or even all of their children die in infancy. A few examples make the point. Four of Philadelphia's most prominent founding merchants — William Frampton, Richard Hill, Samuel Preston, and Robert Turner—produced among them not a single son who lived to maturity. Frampton had no children. Hill's wife bore five, all of whom died in infancy; when she died, he married again without issue. Preston, who married the daughter of Thomas Lloyd, had one son, who died in infancy, and three daughters, one of whom died early. Turner saw his only two sons die as infants. William Hudson's wife, one of those fabled "fruitful vines," presented him with fourteen children, six sons and eight daughters. But of the sons, four died in infancy, one at twenty-six, and the other at twenty-nine.

Among merchants who did produce merchant sons this fearful mortality rate also prevailed. Clement Plumstead had five sons, one of whom succeeded him as a Philadelphia merchant. But the other four died in infancy. Samuel Carpenter produced one merchant son and another who became a minister. His other two sons were buried as babies. Abraham Bickley, who had come first to East Jersey in 1681 and then moved to West Jersey in the 1690s, wore out two wives and spent his life calling for the gravedigger. Elizabeth Gardiner Bickley bore him three children in the five years they spent together before she died; of these two died in infancy. Within a year of his wife's death, Abraham married again, this time to Elizabeth Richardson in Philadelphia. She presented him with nine children, four of whom failed to survive childhood. She died seven days after giving birth to her ninth child in twelve years, and that baby followed her to the grave at two months of age. Only one son by Bickley's second marriage reached adulthood. Of William Fishbourne's four sons, one died at nine months, one at ten years, one at eighteen. Thomas Coates had six sons; four died before adolescence, one died a wastrel at twenty-three, and one, Samuel, became a successful merchant. Edward Shippen had midwives coming to his door all his adult life. He sired eleven children by three wives, celebrating fatherhood for the last time when he was sixty-nine years old. Only four of the eleven children lived to maturity; three were sons of whom one died at twenty-three. The examples could be multiplied but the point is clear: the merchants who arrived in Philadelphia after 1710 did not have to push aside the sons of established merchants but had merely to fill places vacated by the plentiful deaths of founding merchants who themselves had buried scores of sons before they reached adulthood.[12]

Among another group of first-generation merchant families it was not reproductive failure but economic achievement that accounts for the absence of merchant sons. At least a dozen of the seventy-eight merchants whose sons did not succeed them in business were successful enough in acquiring land that their male offspring retired to a gentleman farmer's life on country plantations. Some of the successful early Quaker merchants had themselves withdrawn to the countryside. Samuel Carpenter, one of the most active traders on the Delaware after arriving from Barbados in 1683, quit the city for his Bucks County plantation by 1704. The building of Fairhill and Stenton, the country mansions of Isaac Norris and James Logan, were even grander attempts, shortly after the end of Queen Anne's War, to imitate the life of the rural English gentry. For many sons of the founding commercial elite the preference for country life and the size of their inheritance apparently led to decisions to forego the trials of city merchants. Samuel Finney's sons are good examples. An Irishman, Finney had emigrated in the 1670s to Barbados where he established himself as a merchant. He returned to England in 1681 and fought for the prince of Orange at the end of that decade. Penn induced him to come to Philadelphia in 1699 as part of a corps of officeholders whom he hoped would restore leadership and stability to the colony. A purchaser of large tracts of land from Penn, Finney became captain of the Philadelphia militia, a justice of the peace, and a judge of the provincial court. He pursued mercantile affairs after marrying the widow of another founding merchant, Henry Tregany. But his sons preferred the country life: Joseph took up his father's estate at Tacony, and Charles inherited a plantation in Frankford.

Other examples abound. Joseph Jones, the only known son of Griffith Jones, an important early merchant, officeholder, and First Purchaser of five thousand acres, lived at ease as a Northern Liberties gentleman on his father's inheritance. So did the sons of Christopher Taylor, like Jones a founding merchant officeholder and First Purchaser. One son, a doctor, inherited Tinicum Island and retired early. The other sons took up life in Chester County, where Taylor had located most of his land. Richard Morrey, the son of Humphrey Morrey, lived off his landed inheritance as a Cheltenham gentleman rather than continue the family business. Joseph Richardson, the son of the bricklayer from Jamaica, took up life as a gentleman in Limerick Township north of Philadelphia.[13]

This avoidance of mercantile careers by so many of the sons of the first-generation merchants — perhaps as much as a fourth of the entire cohort — was made possible not so much by their fathers' amassing of personal wealth as by their acquisition of large tracts of land outside Philadelphia and extensive property within the city, which they gained as First Purchasers in England in 1681–82 or thereafter by purchase after arriving in Philadelphia. Land was very cheap in the early years. With £100 an early settler could buy five thousand acres of land outside Philadelphia and, by the terms of the Conditions and Concessions of July 1681, each such purchaser received a bonus of property in the capital city amounting to 2 percent of the country purchase. These terms proved too liberal, but under

Penn's revised plan of December 1682 each First Purchaser received twenty feet of Delaware River frontage for every thousand acres of land purchased in the country and, in addition, a High Street lot twenty-six feet wide and half a block deep.[14] As little as £20 laid out in 1682 was therefore sufficient to guarantee the sons of a first-generation merchant an income for life. Favored by the chronology of their arrival, the merchants of the first generation were supremely situated to make country gentlemen of their sons, if those sons so desired. Years later, Samuel Fothergill, the English Quaker leader, wrote of the sons of the founders: "Their fathers came into the country, and bought large tracts of land for a trifle; their sons found large estates come into their possession, and . . . they settled in ease and affluence."[15]

A corollary of this phenomenon was that second-generation merchants arriving after 1710 found it far more difficult to become large property-holders. A simple comparison makes the point. Laying out £100, London merchant James Claypoole acquired 5,000 acres of country land in Pennsylvania and the Lower Counties, 100 acres in the Northern Liberties, 102 feet of Delaware River frontage in the heart of what became the commercial center of Philadelphia, and a lot, 132 feet broad and 306 feet deep, on High Street, the east-west axis of the town. Samuel Hassell, arriving from Barbados in 1716 with £100 to invest in property, would not have been able to purchase a single Front Street lot, no matter how small, at that price and would have had no country acreage to go with it. To purchase what Claypoole acquired for £100 in 1682, a merchant of the second generation would have laid out a minor fortune.[16]

While early death claimed the sons of many first-generation merchants and country life lured others from the city, a few chose artisan careers. In most of the eight cases I have found this was not forced downward mobility but a preference expressed by the sons. Two of the sons of James Claypoole, president of the Free Society of Traders and one of Penn's closest merchant friends, became artisans. Nathaniel followed the cooper's trade and moved to Maryland sometime after his father's death in 1687. Joseph became a joiner in Philadelphia. Both inherited land, Nathaniel receiving five hundred acres in Philadelphia County and Joseph a plantation on Lewes Creek in Sussex County, Delaware. Thomas Wharton's son followed his father's original trade, that of saddler. The sons of Gabriel Wilkinson, a small trader who had started as a baker, became a carver and a shipwright.[17] Three sons of brothers Christian and John Sprogel, German immigrants at the turn of the century, became a blacksmith, a saddler, and an Indian trader, respectively. But these were unusual cases. The number of fathers in the founding generation who had risen to merchant status from artisan backgrounds greatly exceeded the number of merchant sons who entered the crafts.

The remarkable discontinuity in the merchant community during the first and second generations resulted from fearsome mortality in the early decades of the city's history, which carried away scores of sons who might have perpetuated their father's names along the Philadelphia waterfront, and the unusual opportunity for sons who did survive to live off land inherited from a founding group that literally got in on the ground floor. To add emphasis to this analysis we can examine the wealthiest merchants on the tax lists of 1693 and 1709, those assessed for estates of at least £250.[18] Among this commercial elite of thirty-two founders, seven sired no children at all and only eight reared sons who became merchants. Sixty-four sons were born to the group as a whole. Sixteen died before reaching adulthood, fifteen became merchants, eleven became gentleman landowners, five pursued artisan careers, one became a minister, three remained in the West Indies where they had been born, and thirteen followed unknown careers. Thus were the ranks of Philadelphia's commercial elite open to newcomers of the second generaton.

What were the economic and political experiences of merchants in the first and second periods of Philadelphia's history, and what do they tell us about the nature of early Pennsylvania society?

In entrepreneurial performance, the second generation seems to have outdone the first. The inventories of estate inscribed after the deaths of individual merchants reveal a sharp increase in accumulated personal wealth by the second-generation merchants. Among fifty-one merchant decedents in the first group for whom inventories have survived, the mean personal wealth was £1,267. Among sixty-five second-generation merchants whose inventories are extant, personal wealth averaged £2,646, more than twice as much. This may indicate primarily the growing mercantile opportunities in the period after 1729, when the business slump of that decade receded and an extended period of commercial prosperity began. Only one of every ten merchants with inventories in the first generation left personal wealth in excess of £2,500, and four of these five importers were long-lived men who survived until 1725 or later.[19] In the second generation, more than one of every four merchants accumulated personal wealth in excess of £2,500. As table 19.2 demonstrates, large fortunes were uncommon among first-generation merchants. The largest was accumulated by Richard Clymer, who had emigrated to Philadelphia from Bristol in 1699 and died in 1734 with a personal estate of £9,428. Six second-generation merchants surpassed this performance. They included Caspar Wistar, a German immigrant who arrived poor in 1717 at twenty years of age and died thirty-five years later with a personal estate of £26,667, and William Branson, son of a shoemaker in Berkshire, England, who arrived in 1708 and favored his heirs when he died in 1760 with personal property valued at £36,485.

The economic performance of the first generation may be disguised by the fact that the inventories of estate only occasionally list real property, where the assets of the founding elite were probably concentrated. This propensity for investing in land can be explained by its cheapness in the early decades, but it may also owe a good deal to the uncertainties of trade during the wartime era of 1689–1713. The wars fought during the reigns of William and Anne spanned most of the years during which the founding merchants were active. Wartime commercial disruption, along with piratical activity, which was at its height in this period, undoubtedly dampened the spirits of many for risk taking on the Atlantic sea lanes.

Second-generation merchants, by contrast, operated during a period of uninterrupted peace from the signing of the Peace of Utrecht in 1713 to the outbreak of the Anglo-Spanish War in 1739. To be sure, these later merchants had to endure a protracted dampening of trade in the mid-1720s, but their appetite for entrepreneurial activity must have been whetted by the return of peace in Europe and the colonies, the crackdown on piracy after 1715, the heavy immigration of Scots-Irish and Germans after 1714, the expanding agricultural surpluses that Pennsylvania farmers were producing, and the growing demands of a West Indian market swelled by a rapid increase in the number of slaves involved in sugar production.

Religious values also affected the economic careers of the two generations of merchants. Among the founding group, mostly Quakers before 1700, the commitment to developing the inner life reverberated powerfully. This curbed the appetite for continuous risk-taking, at least among the Quaker merchants, and may have pushed many of their sons toward different career choices. In the second generation, when circumstances encouraged entrepreneurial activity and the price of land soared, the Quaker domination of the merchant community had been broken. A more ambitious business ethic, influenced by changes in religious orientation, energized the Delaware waterfront. Three of every five merchants were Anglicans, Presbyterians, or Jews, men whose religious ethic provided no brake on economic ambition. Even among the Quaker merchants by this time the earlier spirit of equalitarianism, meekness, and self-denying attachment to following the Inward Light had atrophied. The advancing bourgeois ethic also manifested itself among Quaker merchants arriving in the colony. "Birthright" Friends such as Thomas Griffits, Peter and Thomas Lloyd, John Reynell, and Robert Strettel, men who had been reared in a far less visionary milieu than "convinced" Quakers of the founding period, proved to be more aggressive and outward looking than their predecessors in the Quaker capital. Combined with the greater opportunities that came with expansion and an era of peace, this cognitive reorientation among merchants in the second group led to many notable business successes.

In politics we can also note some sharp differences in the experience of the two groups. The failure of most of the founding merchants to rear sons to the mercantile life was paralleled by their inability to transfer political power to their male heirs. This can be seen most directly in analysing the membership of the Council and Assembly.

The first-generation merchants were intensely involved in politics. Seventeen of them served in council between 1682 and 1700, and twelve others received councilorships after the turn of the century. Thirty-one founding merchants served in the Assembly, nineteen of whom also occupied Council seats at some time during their careers (see Table 19.3). In all, two of every five early merchants (42 of 102) served at the highest level of provincial politics. Merchants were not the only political leaders in early Pennsylvania, but they were instrumental in governing the colony during Penn's lifetime.

Despite their crucial governing role in the early years, the merchant founders were not very successful in passing political leadership on to their progeny. The entire founding cohort produced only three sons who served in Council and not more than twelve who were elected to the Assembly. Furthermore, not a single one of the sixty early merchants who had not served in Council or Assembly reared a son who did so.[20]

As a group, the second generation of merchants proved far less active in politics than the first. Twenty-nine of the founding merchants served in Council at some point in their careers and thirty-one sat in the Assembly. But in the second group, which was 40 percent larger than the first, only seven merchants served in Council and eleven in the Assembly, a rate of participation about one-third of that among founding merchants. Partly this may be explained by the fact that a number of early merchants died within a dozen years of reaching Philadelphia, which increased the turnover rate in high political offices. Partly it is explained by the longevity of a handful of early merchants, men such as James Logan, Clement Plumstead, William Fishbourne, and George Roche, who sat in Council for many years and thereby insured that new places were not often available to merchants arriving after 1710. Second-generation voters tended to return the same man to the Assembly year after year, whereas in the early decades continuity of service was apparently much less prized by the electors. Whatever the combination of reasons, political leadership in Philadelphia after 1710 was exercised more by men who were not merchants, such as Andrew Hamilton, Evan Morgan, John Kearsley, and John Kinsey. Commercially more distinguished, the second generation of merchants was politically undistinguished. Many of the leading business figures of the second quarter of the eighteenth century — men such as Samuel Coates, Peter Baynton, John and George Mifflin, John Bringhurst, George McCall, John Stamper, Caspar Wistar, John Reynell, and Charles Willing — played virtually no role in politics at the provincial level.

The failure of a lineally descended political elite to emerge during the first half-century of Philadelphia's history might be considered grist for E. Digby Baltzell's mill — proof that Friends were temperamentally and ideologically incapable of exerting their "class authority" and passing a tradition of leadership on to their sons.[21] Or it might be suggested that this largely self-terminating, first-generation merchant elite contributed to the political instability in Philadelphia during the first quarter of the eighteenth century through their failure to perpetuate their political leverage.[22] Upon close examination, however, neither of these formulations holds much explanatory power.

As regards the Baltzell thesis, it is apparent that the failure of politically active first-generation merchants to furnish sons for the eighteenth-century political elite was partly due to the high mortality rate that left about one-quarter of the early merchants without any sons who survived infancy. Yet it is true that a sizeable number of first-generation merchant political leaders whose sons did survive — men such as Samuel Richardson, James Claypoole, Humphrey Morrey, and Francis Rawle—did not instill in their sons the sense of mission and passion for governing that is said to have characterized the Massachusetts elite in the early years. However, it was not Quaker egalitarianism and defiance of authority that led to such discontinuous leadership, as Baltzell would have it. In fact, such discontinuity seems to have been typical of almost all the American colonies in the first few generations, especially when a high immigration rate kept enlarging the pool of able political aspirants. In Maryland, for example, the fifty-six men who occupied councilorships between 1632 and 1689 produced only two sons who acquired a Council appointment.[23] In Virginia, the record, though it has not been quantified, appears to have been much the same.[24] In New Jersey, the Assembly was not "derived principally from native-born men," let alone sons of early political leaders, until the 1730s.[25]

Political dynasties seem to have been particularly difficult to form in the commercial centers of eighteenth-century America. Alan Tully, in his study of Pennsylvania politics from 1726 to 1755, speaks of "Pennsylvania's tradition of political professionalism" and of a widely acknowledged "obligation to perpetuate the family reputation in provincial affairs."[26] But every one of the twenty-one politically active families he cites came from rural areas outside the city. In Puritan New England, according to Edward Cook's study, family political dynasties formed in country towns of moderate size but were decidedly weak in seaports such as Boston and Portsmouth. In these commercial centers the most important political offices "went overwhelmingly to the current merchant princes and to the leaders of popular political factions, many of whom were recent immigrants or newly risen to prominence."[27] Such was the case in Philadelphia as well. Moreover, the record of Anglican founding merchants in passing on political leadership to sons was not significantly different than that of Quakers.[28]

The instability of politics before 1730 in Pennsylvania may owe something to the rapid turnover of political leadership between the first and second generations — but not much. In order to argue this case, we are obliged to accept the notion that political maturity and political stability come primarily to societies that establish stable political elites who, as Baltzell has put it, "transfer the reins of political power to a younger generation."[29] I have seen no empirical proof of this supposed connection between hereditary elites and political stability and doubt that much can be adduced. In Pennsylvania, the political instability that pervaded the colony in the early years and continued sporadically through the 1720s can be attributed mostly to the initial thorny issue of how political authority would be divided in a new society and later to battles over difficult economic problems, such as beset Philadelphia during the economic slump of the 1720s. Furthermore, political stability returned to Pennsylvania with the revival of the economy in the 1730s and was presided over by a group of political leaders whose fathers, for the most part, had never served in leadership roles.[30]

Rather than promoting political instability or anarchic egalitarianism, the avoidance of political office by so many sons of founding merchants had little effect at all.[31] It did not even hasten the gradual concentration of Quaker political power in the legislative Assembly or the eventual takeover of the Council, courts, and corporation of Philadelphia by Anglican merchants. These changes came only slowly. Quakers clung to political power with surprising tenacity in the eighteenth century in spite of the fact that sons did not often replace fathers in the Council and Assembly. This was possible because some Quaker merchants who arrived in Philadelphia after 1710, such as Thomas Griffits and Robert Strettel, assumed political leadership roles and because the sons of some first-generation country Quakers, such as Israel Pemberton and John Kinsey, also did so. By the late 1730s Anglicans (bolstered by a few prominent defecting Quakers) had eclipsed Friends in the executive branch, on the bench, and in the city corporation. But this change of power within the corps of appointed officeholders followed naturally from the shift within the proprietary family itself from Quakerism to Anglicanism. In any case, the large immigration of Scotch-Irish Presbyterians in the half-century bracketing 1750 would have eventually eroded Quaker political control in Penn's colony, and the crisis that war presented to Quaker politicians in the 1750s would have independently assured their demise.

In sum we may conclude that the building of economic dynasties — and political dynasties flowing from them — proved to be unusually difficult in the seaport towns of colonial America. Commercial centers were growth centers, always characterized by the arrival of new men on the make. Commercial fortunes were precarious; money amassed in a hurry was often lost in a hurry. And for those who did succeed on the slippery slopes of mercantile endeavour, whether they were Quaker, Anglican, or otherwise, retirement to the country was often the great goal, not the governing of cities or colonies. Paradoxically, it was in the cities, where social differentiation proceeded fastest and truly impressive wealth was most often accumulated, that economic and political dynasties least often formed. It was the countryside that provided a better rooting bed for lineally descended oligarchies, for it was there that fortunes, while amassed less quickly, were more stable and where the orientation to land rather than water nurtured the tradition of political responsibility within leading families.

NOTES

1. Gary B. Nash, *Quakers and Politics: Pennsylvania, 1681-1726* (Princeton, 1968), chap. 1.

2. The wills and inventories are in the office of the Recorder of Wills, City Hall Annex, Philadelphia. The deed books are in the City Archives, City Hall Annex. Ship registration lists are printed in *PMHB*, vols. 23-28 (1899-1904). Freemanship lists are in *Minutes of the Common Council of the City of Philadelphia, 1704 to 1776* (Philadelphia, 1847).

3. A handful of long-lived merchants spanned both periods but they have been placed in the founding group if their careers were established before 1710. The population of Philadelphia grew from 2,100 in 1693 to 4,885 in 1720 to 9,515 in 1741. See Gary B. Nash and Billy G. Smith, "The Population of Eighteenth-Century Philadelphia," *PMHB*, 99 (1975):366.

4. Gary B. Nash, "City Planning and Political Tension in the Seventeenth-Century: The Case of Philadelphia," *Proceedings of the American Philosophical Society*, 112 (1968):54-73; Hannah B. Roach, "The Planting of Philadelphia: A Seventeenth-Century Real Estate Development," *PMHB*, 92 (1968):3-47, 143-94.

5. For a description of the "Barbadoes distemper" that struck Philadelphia in 1699, see Isaac Norris to Jonathan Dickinson, 2 June 1699, Isaac Norris Letterbook, 1699-1702, HSP. Merchant deaths have been traced for Quakers in William Wade Hinshaw, ed., *Encyclopedia of American Quaker Genealogy* (Ann Arbor, 1936-50), vol. 2; for Anglicans in the Register Books of Christ Church: Marriages, Christenings and Burials, 1709-1750, GSP; and for unchurched Philadelphians in "An Account of the Burialls of such as are not Friends within this town of Philadelphia," in Hinshaw, *Encyclopedia*, 2:441-49.

6. Tolles, *Meeting House*, p. 43.

7. All of the biographical and genealogical data in this essay have been gleaned from the collection of published and unpublished materials in GSP.

8. They had been preceded by Isaac Miranda, who arrived from Italy about 1712.

9. Nicholas Brown, Samuel Hassell, John Inglis, Anthony Palmer, Thomas Porter, John Reynell, John Thomas, and John Wilson. The origins of many merchants arriving in the eighteenth century are noted in the deed books.

10. The degree of mobility from artisan to merchant was greater in the founding merchant group than in the succeeding group.

11. These 24 merchants produced 31 merchant sons.

12. For even higher mortality rates in the founding cohort of another seventeenth-century colony, see David W. Jordan, "Political Stability and the Emergence of a Native Elite in Maryland," in *The Chesapeake in the Seventeenth Century: Essays on Anglo-American Society*, ed. Thad W. Tate and David L. Ammerman (New York, 1979), pp. 247-48. Susan E. Klepp ("Social Class and Infant Mortality in Philadelphia, 1720-1830," typescript) finds that nearly half the children born to colonial Philadelphians died before reaching age 15 and one-fourth died in the first year. For

a general view of high mortality rates in the city, see Billy G. Smith, "Death and Life in a Colonial Immigrant City: A Demographic Analysis of Philadelphia," *Journal of Economic History,* 37 (1977):863-89.

13. Other founding merchants with sons who retired to the country include Thomas Budd, James Claypoole, Anthony Morris, Abraham Bickley, and Andrew Robeson.

14. Under the revised plan, the 2% bonus was granted in the Northern Liberties. Nash, "City Planning," p. 61.

15. In a number of cases, founding merchants who had been First Purchasers or early purchasers of large amounts of land left only modest or middling personal estates. For example, Griffith Jones left £916, Christopher Taylor left £388, Samuel Finney left £749, and Samuel Richardson left only £289.

16. On rising land values, see Gary B. Nash, *The Urban Crucible: Social Change, Political Consciousness, and the Origins of the American Revolution* (Cambridge, Mass., 1979), pp. 122-23. A few second-generation merchants were sons of First Purchasers who had never emigrated to Pennsylvania but sent their sons to take up their land claims. The city lots of these non-emigrating First Purchasers, however, were usually located on the undeveloped Schuylkill side of Philadelphia. Entry into the landed mercantile elite was possible, of course, by marrying a daughter of a founding merchant. For example, Thomas Griffitts married the daughter of Isaac Norris, Samuel Hassell married the daughter of Samuel Bulkley, and Peter Lloyd married the daughter of Thomas Masters. I have not attempted to trace the perpetuation of family businesses through the marriage of merchant daughters.

17. Eunice S. E. Wellman, "The Gabriel Wilkinson Family," *Pennsylvania Genealogical Magazine,* 26 (1969-70):61-91.

18. The 1693 tax list is reprinted in *PMHB,* 8 (1884):85-105; the 1709 tax list is in ibid., 99 (1975):3-19.

19. Of 42 merchants who died before 1720 and whose estates were inventoried, 31 left personal wealth of less than £1,000.

20. The three sons who served in Council were Charles Read, Jr., William Logan, and John Finney. The 12 sons who served in assembly were Isaac Norris, Jr., Anthony Morris, Jr., James Morris, John Jones, William Allen, Jr., Samuel Hudson, John Cook, Thomas Tress, Jr., Joseph Shippen, William Clymer, Jonathan Robeson, and Septimus Robinson. This list of 12 includes 2 "doubtfuls": John Jones, who may not have been the son of founding merchant John Jones; and John Cooke, whose father may not have been founding merchant Arthur Cooke.

21. Baltzell, *Puritan Boston and Quaker Philadelphia: Two Protestant Ethics and the Spirit of Class Authority and Leadership* (New York, 1979).

22. This is the argument of Jordan, "Political Stability," and Bernard Bailyn, "Politics and Social Structure in Virginia," in *Seventeenth-Century America: Essays in Colonial History,* ed. James Morton Smith (Chapel Hill, N.C., 1959), pp. 90-115.

23. Jordan, "Political Stability," p. 247.

24. Bailyn, "Politics and Social Structure."

25. Thomas L. Purvis, "'High-Born, Long-Recorded Families': Social Origins of New Jersey Assemblymen, 1703 to 1776," *WMQ,* 3d ser., 37 (1980):598.

26. Alan Tully, *William Penn's Legacy: Politics and Social Structure in Provincial Pennsylvania, 1726-1755* (Baltimore, 1977), p. 97.

27. Edward M. Cook, Jr., *The Fathers of the Towns: Leadership and Community Structure in Eighteenth-Century New England* (Baltimore, 1976), pp. 98-100. The quotation is from p. 98.

28. Quakers represented 70% of the founding merchant group and produced six of the nine sons who became assemblymen and one of the two councilors who did so. The names of these fathers and sons are given in Tables 19.3 and 19.4.

29. Jordan, "Political Stability," p. 246. This is also the thesis of Baltzell's *Puritan Boston and Quaker Philadelphia*.

30. Of the 14 political leaders in Philadelphia after 1725 mentioned by Alan Tully in his study of provincial politics, only 5 had fathers who had been important officeholders. The 14 (names of those with politically prominent fathers are italicized) were: William Allen, Benjamin Franklin, *Job Goodson,* Andrew Hamilton, John Kearsley, John Kinsey, Jr., *Thomas Leech,* Evan Morgan, *James Morris, Issac Norris, Jr., Israel Pemberton,* Richard Peters, Joseph Trotter, and Edward Warner.

31. Of 29 merchant sons of founding merchants (see table 19.4), 2 were councillors and 6 served in the Assembly. Eighteen of the 29 had fathers who had served in Council or Assembly.

TABLE 19.1   *Religious Affiliation of the Philadelphia Merchants*

	Quaker	Anglican	Presbyterian	Jew	Unknown	Total
The Founding Generation, 1681-1710						
New Arrival						
1682–1689	48	3			5	56
1690–1700	19	5			4	28
1701–1710	4	6	1		7	18
TOTAL	71	14	1		16	102
The Second Generation, 1711-1740						
Sons of Founding Merchants	17	10	3		1	31
Sons of Non-Merchants in Pennsylvania	15	10			1	26
New Arrival						
1711–1725	15	9	1	1	1	27
1726–1740	6	5	1	3	3	18
Origin Unknown	6	23	1		11	41
TOTAL	59	57	6	4	17	143

TABLE 19.2   *The Personal Wealth of Philadelphia Merchants at Death*

	First Generation		Second Generation	
	No.	%	No.	%
£1–100	2	3.9	5	7.7
£101–500	23	45.1	16	24.6
£501–1,000	9	17.6	13	20.0
£1,001–2,500	12	23.5	13	20.0
£2,501–	5	9.8	18	27.7
TOTAL	51	99.9	65	100.0

TABLE 19.3   *First-Generation Philadelphia Merchants*

	Origin	Year of Arrival	Year of Death	Reli-gion	Merchant Sons
Arrived 1682–1689					
David Breitnell	Derbyshire, Eng.	1682	1732	Q	Joseph
Lionell Brittain	England	c1684	1721	A	
John Budd	Somerset, Eng.	1682	1704	Q#	John, Jr.
Thomas Budd	Somerset, Eng.	1682	1698	Q#	
Samuel Bulkley	England	1682	1704	Q	
Abraham Carpenter	Sussex, Eng.	c1683	1708	?	
x★Samuel Carpenter	Barbados	1683	1713	Q	Samuel, Jr.
★Samuel Cart	Tewkesbury, Eng.	1685	1711	Q	
William Carter	England	c1685	1738	Q	
Benjamin Chambers	Kent, Eng.	1682	1715	Q	
x★William Clark	Dublin and W. Jers.	1683	1705	Q	
x★James Claypoole	London, Eng.	1682	1687	Q	George
Thomas Coates	Leicester, Eng.	1683	1719	Q	Samuel
x Arthur Cooke	Portsmouth, R.I.	1684	1699	Q	
★Francis Cooke	England	1688	1714	Q#	
John Day	London, Eng.	1682	1696	Q	
x John Delavall	New York	1687	1693	Q	
Thomas England	?	c1688	1717	Q	
Robert Ewer	Wilts, Eng.	1684	1697	Q	
★James Fox	Plymouth, Eng.	1686	1699	?	
x William Frampton	New York	1683	1686	Q	
John Fuller	Dublin, Ire.	1686	1692	Q	
Charles Goss	?	c1689	1698	?	
★William Hudson	Yorkshire, Eng.	1683	1741	Q	
George Hutcheson	Yorkshire and W.Jers.	1683	1698	Q#	
Phillip James	England	1683	1702	Q#	
Michael Jobson	London, Eng.	c1688	1711	Q	Samuel
x★Griffith Jones	London, Eng.	1682	1712	Q#	
John Jones	Barbados	1683	1708	Q	
★William Lee	New York	1685	1716	Q	
x★Thomas Masters	Bermuda	1687	1723	Q	Thomas, Jr.

TABLE 19.3   *Continued*

	Origin	Year of Arrival	Year of Death	Reli-gion	Merchant Sons
Arrived 1682–1689					
x*Humphrey Morrey	New York	1685	1716	Q	
x*Anthony Morris	London and W. Jers.	1687	1721	Q	Anthony, Jr., Luke, James
*Charles Pickering	Cheshire, Eng.	1682	1694	Q#	
x*Clement Plumstead	London, Eng.	1683	1745	Q	William
x*Francis Rawle	Cornwall, Eng.	1686	1727	Q	Francis, Jr., William
*Charles Read	Eng. and W. Jers.	c1689	1705	Q#	Charles, Jr.
Philip Richards	New York	1684	1698	Q	Joseph
x*Samuel Richardson	Jamaica	1683	1719	Q	
Edward Roberts	Wales	c1683	1741	Q	Hugh
x*Andrew Robeson	Ireland and W. Jers.	1686	1694	Q#	
Patrick Robinson	England	1683	1701	Q#	
William Roydon	London, Eng.	c1682	1694	?	
x*William Salway	Somerset, Eng.	1683	1695	Q	
James Stanfield	Cheshire, Eng.	1683	1699	Q#	
William Stanley	England	c1685	1689	Q	
Christopher Taylor	Middlesex, Eng.	1682	1686	Q	
Joshua Tittery	England	1683	1709	Q	
x*William Trent	Leith, Scot.	1682	1724	A	William, Jr., James
Thomas Tress	?	c1686	1714	A	Thomas, Jr.
x Robert Turner	Dublin, Ire.	1683	1700	Q#	
William Warden	?	c1689	1699	?	
Thomas Wharton	Westmoreland, Eng.	c1684	1718	Q	Joseph
Zachariah Whitpaine	London, Eng.	c1683	1697	Q	John
George Wilcox	Bristol, Eng.	c1682	1694	Q#	
*Joseph Wilcox	Bristol, Eng.	c1682	?	Q#	

TABLE 19.3   *Continued*

	Origin	Year of Arrival	Year of Death	Reli-gion	Merchant Sons
Arrived 1690–1700					
William Allen	Ireland	c1700	1725	P	William, Jr., John
★Abraham Bickley	Burlington, W. Jers.	1692	1725	Q	
Richard Brewer	Jamaica	c1695	1701	Q	
★John Cadwalader	Wales	1699	1734	Q	
Richard Clymer	Bristol, Eng.	1699	1734	A	William
x★Jonathan Dickinson	Jamaica	1697	1722	Q	
x Samuel Finney	Ireland	1700	1712	A	
x★William Fishbourne	Maryland	1700	1742	Q	
x★Richard Hill	Maryland	1700	1729	Q	
Randall Janney	Cheshire, Eng.	1699	1715	Q	
Francis Jones	England	1692	1742	A	
x James Logan	Dublin, Ire.	1699	1743	Q	William
Cornelius Mahoney	Maryland	c1690	1699	?	
x★Isaac Norris	Jamaica	1691	1735	Q	Isaac,Jr., Charles, Samuel
Alexander Paxton	England	c1700	?	A	
x Joseph Pidgeon	Bristol, Eng.	1691	1713	?	Joseph, Jr.
x Samuel Preston	Maryland	1696	1743	Q	
Edward Robinson	?	c1695	1699	?	
x Charles Sanders	Bristol, Eng.	1691	1699	Q	
Abraham Scott	London, Eng.	1699	1709	Q	
x★Edward Shippen	Boston, Mass.	1693	1712	Q	Edward, Jr., Joseph
Thomas Smith	?	c1695	1699	Q	
Samuel Spencer	Barbados	c1700	1705	?	
Johann Sprogel	Saxony	1700	1713	Q	
★Lodwick Sprogel	Saxony	1700	?	Q	
Nathan Stanbury	Boston, Mass.	1697	1721	Q	
★James Steel	Sussex, Eng.	1699	?	Q	
★Pentacost Teague	Cornwall, Eng.	1693	1719	Q	
Gabriel Wilkinson	Lower Counties	1691	1733	A	

TABLE 19.3   *Continued*

	Origin	Year of Arrival	Year of Death	Reli-gion	Merchant Sons
Arrived 1701–1710					
Matthew Andrews	Antigua	c1710	1717	Q	
Andrew Dulaney	Jamaica	1705	1709	?	
John Freke	Barbados	c1710	1720	?	
John Gilbert	?	c1710	1711	Q	
John Hunt	?	c1702	1708	?	
Caleb Jacob	Cork, Ire.	1707	1724	A	
John McWilliams	?	c1710	1720	?	
Edward Mankin	?	c1710	1720	A	
John Murdock	?	c1710	1715	?	
x Anthony Palmer	Barbados	c1707	?	A	
Samuel Perez	?	c1707	1720	A	
x*George Roche	Antigua	1703	1739	A	
Edward Shippen, Jr.	Boston, Mass.	1704	1714	Q#	
Joseph Shippen	Boston, Mass.	1704	1741	Q#	Edward III, Joseph II
Henry Tregany	?	c1704	1715	A	Brian
Benjamin Vining	?	c1710	?	?	
Henry Ward	Barbados	c1701	1709	?	

KEY:
* Member of Assembly
x Member of Council
Q Quaker
Q# Quaker on arrival, but left or was disowned (mostly during Keithian schism)
A Anglican
P Presbyterian

TABLE 19.4   *Second-Generation Philadelphia Merchants*

Sons of Founding Merchants	Religion
John Allen	P
★William Allen, Jr.	P
Joseph Breitnall	Q
John Budd	A
Samuel Carpenter, Jr.	Q
George Claypoole	A
William Clymer	A
Samuel Coates	Q
Samuel Jobson	Q
xWilliam Logan	Q
Thomas Masters, Jr.	Q
★Anthony Morris, Jr.	Q
James Morris	Q
Luke Morris	Q
Charles Norris	Q
★Isaac Norris, Jr.	Q
Samuel Norris	Q
Joseph Pidgeon, Jr.	?
William Plumstead	A
Francis Rawle, Jr.	Q
William Rawle	Q
xCharles Read, Jr.	A
Joseph Richards	Q
★Hugh Roberts	Q
Edward Shippen III	P
★Joseph Shippen II	A
Brian Tregany	A
James Trent	A
William Trent, Jr.	A
★Thomas Tress, Jr.	A
Joseph Wharton	Q

Sons of Non-Merchant Pennsylvanians	Religion	Father's Occupation
Peter Baynton	A	Yeoman
James Boyden	?	Mariner
William Coleman, Jr.	Q	Carpenter
Robert Ellis	Q	Yeoman
George Fitzwater	Q	Minister
Joseph Harwood	A	Mariner
★Thomas Leech	A	Yeoman
John McComb	A	Tailor
Samuel Mickle	Q	Yeoman
John Mifflin	Q	Yeoman
George Mifflin	Q	Yeoman
John Newman	A	Saddler
Evan Owen	Q	Yeoman

TABLE 19.4   *Continued*

Sons of Non-Merchant Pennsylvanians	Religion	Father's Occupation
Benjamin Paschall	Q	Malster
*Israel Pemberton	Q	Yeoman
Joseph Pennock	Q	Cardmaker
Samuel Powel	Q	Carpenter
*Joseph Redman	A	Bricklayer
Thomas Redman	A	Bricklayer
Edward Roberts	Q	Yeoman
John Roberts	A	Yeoman
Dennis Rochford	Q	Potter
Benjamin Shoemaker	Q	Turner
Attwood Shute	A	Yeoman
John Sober	A	Surgeon
Jeremiah Warder	Q	Hatter

Arrived 1711–1725	Religion	Date of Arrival	Origin
William Bell	A	1719	Yorkshire, Eng.
Jonathan Bennett	A	c1718	Cork, Ire.
William Biddle	A	c1725	Burlington, W.N.J.
William Branson	?	1708	Berkshire, Eng.
John Bringhurst	Q	1700	London, Eng.
George Chalmers	A	c1725	Edinburgh, Scot.
Joshua Cockfield	Q	c1712	?
Thomas Denham	Q	1716	Bristol, Eng.
William Dowell	Q	c1725	London, Eng.
Thomas Flexney	Q	1718	London, Eng.
xThomas Griffits	Q	1716	Cork & Jamaica
xSamuel Hassell	A	c1716	Barbados
Thomas Hatton	Q	1725	Dublin, Ire.
Edward Horne	Q	1723	Sussex, Eng.
xThomas Lawrence	A	1720	New York
Peter Lloyd	Q	1719	Bristol, Eng.
Thomas Lloyd	Q	1719	Bristol, Eng.
Hugh Lowden	Q	c1713	Ireland
Benjamin Mayne	Q	c1711	Cork, Ire.
George McCall	A	c1714	Glascow, Scot.
Isaac Miranda	J	c1712	Italy
Richard Nixon	A	c1725	Ireland
John Stamper	Q	1722	Cumberland, Eng.
xAbraham Taylor	A	c1724	Bristol, Eng.
Joseph Turner	P	1714	England
John Wilson	Q	c1715	Jamaica
Caspar Wistar	Q	1717	Palatinate

TABLE 19.4   *Continued*

Arrived 1726–1740	Religion	Date of Arrival	Origin
John Ambler	Q	1736	York, Eng.
Nicholas Brown	?	c1738	Barbados
David Franks	J	c1739	New York
John Inglis	A	c1735	Nevis
Robert Jordan	Q	c1730	Virginia
Isaac Levy	J	1738	New York
Nathan Levy	J	1738	New York
Joshua Maddox	A	c1727	England
Reese Meredith	Q	1730	Wales
Thomas Porter	?	c1738	Barbados
John Reynell	Q	1729	Jamaica
Joseph Richardson	?	c1735	Lower Counties
Richard Siddall	A	c1735	Manchester, Eng.
xRobert Strettel	Q	1736	Dublin, Ire.
John Thomas	Q	c1726	Antigua
William Till	A	c1730	Lower Counties
xJohn White	P	c1728	Bristol, Eng.
Charles Willing	A	1728	Bristol, Eng.

Origins Unknown	Religion
Matthias Aspden	Q
William Attwood	Q
John Baker	A
Henry Bishop	?
Samuel Bond	P
Samuel Boude	A
Thomas Bourne	A
Edward Bridges	A
Giles Cambridge	A
Thomas Campbell	A
Edward Carleton	A
Thomas Chase	A
Thomas Denton	?
William Fraser	A
Nathaniel French	A
Edward Fretwell	A
Benjamin Godfrey	A
William Graham	?
William Graves	?
Arent Hassert	Q
Henry Hodge	A
Samuel Holt	A

TABLE 19.4   *Continued*

Origins Unknown	Religion
Joseph Howell	A
John Hunn	?
John Hyatt	A
Benjamin Jackson	?
John Leacock	A
Robert Lowry	A
Joseph Lynn	Q
*William Monington	Q
William Parker	?
James Pearson	A
Edward Pleadwell	Q
Thomas Polgren	A
William Ranberry	A
Robert Reynolds	A
Charles Rogers	?
Richard Sanger	?
Thomas Thompson	?
John Watt	?
Alexander Wooldrop	A

KEY:
*   Member of Assembly
x   Member of Council
Q   Quaker
Q#   Quaker on arrival, but left or was disowned (mostly during Keithian schism)
A   Anglican
P   Presbyterian
J   Jewish

JACOB M. PRICE

20 ‹ The Great Quaker Business Families of Eighteenth-Century London:

The Rise and Fall of a Sectarian Patriciate

A Problem and a Paradigm

One of the great themes of modern British social history is the rise between 1688 and 1846 of the upper middle class as the element in society preeminently shaping and transmitting national culture, ethos, and polity in the ensuing century 1846–1945. Before 1688 it was extremely difficult for a distinctive class to emerge between the traditional trading classes below and the landed classes above. The existing state of the economy greatly restricted the number of professional openings remunerative enough to lift their holders above the general rank of the trading classes, and the evolution of the state had not yet reached a stage where very many equivalent positions existed in the king's service. Even the church had disappointingly few well endowed livings. Most important of all, there was a restricted number of investments in which fortunes made in trade could safely be placed. Thus before 1688 rising individuals who accumulated wealth in precarious trades had great difficulty finding less risky occupations for their sons outside of agriculture, or safe opportunities in which to invest their money other than land, mortgages, or personal bonds. But land was hard to manage at a distance, particularly when in small parcels, and land, mortgages, and bonds could be difficult to realize in an emergency. They could also be difficult to divide as desired between several children, and the land law threatened the intestate with the rigors of primogeniture. However, the development of the national debt and the three great monied companies (the Bank of England, the East India Company, and the South Sea Company) between 1689 and 1815 opened up numerous relatively safe opportunities for the saving classes, just as the development of the economy greatly multiplied the number of families able to accumulate significant savings. The development of the state apparatus in those same years increased opportunities for army, navy, and bureaucratic careers, while the general increase in national prosperity, particularly for the property-owning classes, increased career opportunities in the liberal professions; even the income of clergymen rose with agricultural prices and rents. The ultimate definition of a professional, office-holding, and rentier *haute bourgeoisie* probably came with the emergence in the 1840s of the public schools as national institutions, thanks in great part to the railroads.

While the outlines of this development are so familiar as to be trite, the inner dynamics by which families came to realize a distinctive upper middle class way of life are rather hard to study and probably will be illuminated only to a limited degree by the mere counting of heads, or fathers' occupations. We must try to look at the process in part from within the families affected. Given the many thousands of such families at any one time, this is a frighteningly difficult task to contemplate; some sort of sampling is obviously necessary. Local studies offer one possibility, though communities small enough to be studied easily may misrepresent upper middle class experience nationally. In this essay I am going to approach the problem through another sort of sample: fourteen leading (and related) Quaker families of the eighteenth century.[1] Quakers, it may well be thought, are a rather odd sample of the upper middle class. Members of the Society of Friends, after all, could not hold office in church, state, or armed forces or engage in the legal professions; they could not attend public school or university; they even excluded themselves in most cases from certain allegedly strategic business activities such as slave trading, privateering, or supplying the armed forces. Yet the very liabilities under which Quakers labored make them a purer sample in one respect. For them we can generally eliminate political influence or patronage as factors and view their rise as a relatively uncomplicated market and cultural phenomenon. To use another terminology, we can eliminate considerations of primitive accumulation and concentrate upon bourgeois or capitalist accumulation. Quakers are also somewhat easier to study than equivalent non-Quaker families because the Society of Friends encouraged the keeping of diaries and the drawing up of annual accounts making clear one's resources and commitments. Quaker and ex-Quaker families have been more likely than others to preserve such records and to produce family histories, though these have usually been written by non-Quaker descendants.

This essay will concentrate therefore on the histories of fourteen eighteenth-century Quaker families. Eleven resided in London: the Barclays, Beaufoys, Bevans, Blands, Eliots, Gurnells, Hanburys, Harmans, Hoares, Mildreds, and Trittons; two, the Gurneys and Lloyds, were provincial but closely related to the London group; while one, the Harfords, had both a London and a Bristol branch. By 1790 all had achieved a considerable degree of material success and in fact include all known eighteenth-century Quaker families in southern England with members reportedly worth £100,000. Also by 1790 almost all had intermarried with other families in this same group and had at one time or another occupied a prominent place in Quaker sectarian governance.

We shall start with one of the most celebrated of these families whose history suggests a model for analyzing the fate of the others. Undoubtedly the best known family among Scottish Quakers of this period was the Barclays of Mathers and Urie.[2] David Barclay (1610–1686), scion of a family of minor lairds established at Mathers for three hundred years and hero of Whittier's poem, was militant protestantism personified. Enlisting as a volunteer in the armies of Gustavus Adolphus during the Thirty Years War, he rose to the rank of major and acquired part of the competence necessary to purchase the estate of Urie. On his return to Scotland in 1639, he was appointed a colonel of cavalry in Montrose's army and fought in the most difficult opening phases of the civil war. Retiring from military service, he married in 1647 a woman with aristocratic and even royal family connections that later were to prove useful to his persecuted family. After his wife's death in 1663, David Barclay underwent serious spiritual travail out of which he became a Quaker. He, his son, and his estate agent, David Falconar, helped introduce Quakerism into their part of eastern Scotland and all suffered imprisonment for their efforts.

David Barclay's son Robert (1648–1690) received an exceptionally good education at the Scots College in Paris and turned his great abilities and learning to the service of Friends. He used his diplomatic skills and family connections to get his father and other Friends out of prison and to help with that rapprochement with the governments of Charles II and James II that benefited Penn and other Quakers. He was the good friend of William Penn and helped promote the Quaker colony of East New Jersey in which he was nominal governor and substantial proprietor. Robert Barclay was however best remembered in succeeding centuries as "the Apologist," the author of the *Apology for . . . the People Called in Scorn, Quakers,* the best-known formal theological justification of the beliefs and practices of the Society of Friends.

Robert Barclay the Apologist inherited Urie from his father and passed it on to his eldest son, Robert. He had, however, a younger son, David, to whom he was able to give no more than a younger son's portion of £500. With this, and the dowry obtained from marrying his master's daughter,

David Barclay set up in business in London during Queen Anne's reign, as both a Scots factor, selling Scottish linen on commission, and a wholesale linendraper.[3] In addition to Scottish linens, he was soon handling the more important German and Irish linens, the latter of which were purchased for him by a brother in Dublin, cutting out the Irish export merchants and the London linen factors.[4] By the 1720s he was an established figure in London business, proprietor of a large house opposite Bow Church in Cheapside. So respectable was he that the first three Georges, at the beginning of their reigns, each visited his well-situated house to watch the Lord Mayor's show from his balcony.[5]

Slowly, cautiously, even nervously, David Barclay branched out into foreign trade. His cousin John Falconar was already an established Chesapeake merchant when Barclay was starting in London.[6] His son James Barclay was described as a "Dutch merchant," implying that the family firm was importing its own linens from the Low Countries and Germany.[7] By the 1720s David Barclay was not only filling orders from a few trusted Quaker acquaintances in Philadelphia but was also sending goods there on joint account with local merchants. Like other of the more cautious Quaker wholesalers and merchants of the time, he expected to be paid in cash or bills of exchange and found the Philadelphia market for his linens quite limited. (He sometimes took payment in tobacco or flour for Ireland.) One of his correspondents there explained to him that while cash and bills of exchange were very scarce in Pennsylvania, provisions were plentiful; he tried to persuade Barclay to let his goods be sold for local produce (which could be sent to the West Indies on his account and converted there into sugar, rum, or bills). David Barclay was reluctant at that time to become a general merchant owning ships and trading all over the North Atlantic complex.[8] However, with the passage of years, his reluctance broke down and by the time of his retirement in 1767 he was not only one of the greater linendrapers of London but was also a merchant owning ships and trading to New York, Pennsylvania, the Chesapeake, and the West Indies.[9] He is believed to have been worth at least £100,000 at his death, a considerable improvement over the £500 younger son's portion with which he had started some sixty years before.[10]

David Barclay's initial accumulation of trading capital was undoubtedly helped when, a few years out of his apprenticeship, he married his former master's daughter. Even more helpful to the family in the long run were to be the marriage of his eldest son, James, to Sarah Freame and his own second marriage to Priscilla Freame, Sarah's niece.[11] This marriage connected the Barclays with the first Quaker bank in London, which had evolved out of a goldsmith's business (going back at least to the 1690s) of the Quaker Thomas Gould and his son-in-law John Freame. Gould and Freame ended their partnership in the 1720s with John Freame continuing alone (at the site of the present Barclays headquarters in Lombard Street) in partnership (from 1736) with his son Joseph and his son-in-law James Barclay. When James Barclay died in 1766, neither of his sons was apparently considered suitable for a banking career. For a time the Barclays were represented in the Freame bank only through a nephew, Silvanus Bevan. However, when Joseph Freame died in 1770, his major share in the bank passed to his daughter Priscilla, widow of David Barclay, and then ultimately to Barclay's two sons by his second marriage, David the younger and John. At first they preferred devoting their efforts to their mercantile house but became more active in the bank from 1776.[12]

The energy which the elder David Barclay could spare from his business and family was devoted in good part to Quaker activities. He served in the Society's Monthly, Quarterly, and Yearly Meetings and on the Yearly Meeting's standing committee for public questions, the Meeting for Sufferings, and its subcommittee on American affairs.[13] His son, David the younger, continued his father's work on these bodies but threw himself more energetically into public affairs. The Barclays, like many Quakers but few other merchants of London, were actively pro-American from the agitation to repeal the Stamp Act through the crisis of the 1770s. David the younger was a good friend of Benjamin Franklin and with his close ally, the celebrated Quaker physician John Fothergill, he tried unsuccessfully in 1774–75 to mediate between Franklin and the government and avoid the impending break between the mother country and the colonies.[14]

The failure of these efforts and the onset of the war appear to have encouraged David Barclay the younger and his brother John to rethink their position in the world. As early as 1770, they had decided to confine themselves to their linen wholesaling and had turned over their merchant-commission business to their kinsmen Harford & Powell. During the war they were forced to reduce the activities of their Cheapside firm even further and in 1783 decided to wind it up gradually. First David (1776) and then John became partners in the former Freame bank, which since 1776 has always been known as Barclays.[15] In addition, David Barclay took advantage of the death of the brewer Henry Thrale to purchase from his widow the Anchor brewery, which eventually became Barclay, Perkins & Co. The initial partners were the Quakers David Barclay, his nephew Robert Barclay, born in Philadelphia, another nephew Silvanus Bevan, and Thrale's old manager, John Perkins. It was this transaction that Mrs. Thrale's adviser, Doctor Johnson, referred to as selling not "a parcel of boilers and vats, but the potentiality of growing rich, beyond the dreams of avarice." Mrs. Thrale got £135,000 for her boilers and vats but the purchasers' families got an assured income for generations to come. Until converted into a public joint stock company in the 1890s, the brewery (like the bank) remained tightly controlled by a few families, including the Barclays, the Bevans, and the Perkinses.[16]

David Barclay the younger lived till 1809. In his last years, he, like his father before him, was one of the most respected figures among London Quakers. His philanthropies were many and he used his great influence to help move English Quakers into a stronger stand against slavery. This was not easy for a retired West India merchant. To demonstrate the seriousness of his commitment, he freed the slaves on a Jamaica cattle ranch which he had acquired in settlement of a mercantile debt. At his own expense, he sent the ex-slaves to Philadelphia where they were entrusted for training to a local society to aid free blacks. This practical philanthropy was particularly remembered at the time of his death.[17]

David Barclay the younger had only one surviving child, a daughter Agatha who had married Richard Gurney of Norwich. His only grandson and principal heir was Hudson Gurney, the first English Quaker to be called a millionaire. After the peace of Amiens in 1802, Hudson Gurney made a tour of the continent and came back rather prejudiced against the Napoleonic regime. On the resumption of hostilities in 1803, he contributed to a fund to support volunteer companies, much to the horror of his pacifist Quaker neighbors in Norwich. When their Friendly entreaties failed to dissuade him, Hudson Gurney was expelled by the local meeting. The young man took this in his stride and eventually became both an Anglican and a member of Parliament, but his aged Quaker grandfather Barclay was deeply troubled.[18] Hudson Gurney's apostasy was to prove an ominous portent. David Barclay' great-nephews, the sons of Robert Barclay of the brewery, joined the militia about the same time and perforce left the Quaker community. The banking Barclays (descended from David's brother John) remained Quakers longer but began drifting away as the century progressed. The last banking Barclay with noticeable if rather lonely Quaker commitments, Joseph Gurney Barclay, died in 1898.[19] By then, despite their continued connection with the bank and the brewery, the Barclays appeared more and more as just another family in *Burke's Landed Gentry,* with the usual quota of canons and colonels.

We have gone into this much detail about the Barclays to try to make certain patterns clear: in business an advance from rather small wholesalers at the beginning of the eighteenth century to substantial overseas merchants by the 1760s; then, in reaction to the risks and disappointments of the American Revolution, a retreat from foreign trade into the safer businesses of banking and brewing. With this went an inward looking social pattern that manifested itself in endogamous marriages and a restricted range of extra-sectarian interests. By the early nineteenth century, under the weight of great prosperity, this pattern of social restraint broke down and conversion to Anglicanism opened new careers in politics, church, and the army as well as new interests. To what extent, we must now ask, did other prominent Quaker families share this evolution?

TABLE 20.1   *Characteristics of 14 London Quaker Business Families*

	Head of Family Worth £100,000 Before 1800	Bankers by 1780	Brewers by 1801	Inter-married with Others by 1790	Repre-sented Quakers Publicly[a]	Began to Leave Quakers	
						Before 1793	1793–1825
Barclay	X	X	X	X	X		X
Beaufoy				X	X	X	
Bevan		X	X	X	X	X	
Bland		X		X			
Eliot	X				X	X	
Gurnell				X		X	
Gurney	X	X	X	X	X	X	X
Hanbury	X	X	X	X	X	X	X
Harford							
(London branch)			X	X		?	X
(Bristol branch)	X	X					X
Harman	X			X			?
Hoare	X	X		X	X		X
Lloyd	X	X		X	X		X
Mildred		X		X	X		?
Tritton		X	X	X		X	X

KEY   [a] In presenting addresses to the king, 1740–93.

Dramatis Personae

Two families very close to the Barclays were the Bevans and the Trittons. The first Quaker Bevan was William, a small merchant of Swansea, who like the Barclays was imprisoned for his Quaker activities in the time of Charles II. His son Silvanus (1661–1725), also a merchant, was a pioneer investor in the copper refining industry in Swansea, later to be of great importance. A son of this Silvanus, also called Silvanus, served an apprenticeship in London and was admitted freeman of the apothecary's company. He opened a pharmacy in Plough Court off Lombard Street which was to prove the germ of a great firm. This Silvanus was an active Quaker and carved a posthumous bust of William Penn, whom he had known. To help in his apothecary, Silvanus Bevan brought up from Swansea a younger brother, Timothy (1704–1786), who greatly expanded the wholesale side of the business, including exports to North America and the West Indies.

Timothy Bevan married twice: first (in 1735) to Elizabeth, daughter of David Barclay the elder; second (in 1752) to a widow, Hannah Springall, daughter of Joseph Gurney of Norwich. In retrospect we can see that Timothy Bevan commenced a course of alliances that within two generations would tie most of the Quaker families we are considering into a single cousinhood. The only son of the second marriage, Joseph Gurney Bevan, a strict and celebrated Quaker, inherited the Plough Court pharmacy.[20] The eldest son of the first marriage, another Silvanus (1743–1830), tried the pharmacy but did not like it. Instead, he appears to have persuaded his Barclay uncles to find a place for him in the Freame-Barclay bank after the death of James Barclay in 1766 had temporarily left the family unrepresented. This Silvanus Bevan, banker, had a younger brother, Timothy Paul, who died relatively young leaving a widow who subsequently married John Perkins, manager of Thrale's brewery. Silvanus Bevan was the link connecting Perkins with the Barclays and obtained for himself a quarter interest in the former Thrale brewery when the great sale went through in 1781. He gave up his share in the bank in order to finance his entry into the brewery but obtained a promise of a partnership in the bank for his eldest son when of age. Thus Silvanus Bevan was able to withdraw from the world of retail and overseas trade and obtain for his eldest son a partnership in the Barclay bank and for his two younger sons partnerships in the Barclay, Perkins brewery. His descendants remained partners or directors of the brewery through the 1960s. When the bank became a public company in 1896, the first chairman of the board was Silvanus's great-grandson, Francis Augustus Bevan, whose great-grandson (Timothy Hugh Bevan) is now chairman of Barclays Bank.

To return to the eighteenth century, shortly after joining the bank, Silvanus Bevan married (1769) a Quaker girl who died within the year. His second wife, Louisa Kendall, was the daughter of a London banker, but an Anglican. As the Quakers at this time (1773) were adamant on the issue of intermarriage, this led to the disownment or expulsion of Silvanus Bevan from the Society. Thus the banking and brewing Bevans broke their ties with Quakerism rather earlier than did most of the other families with whom we are concerned. This did not mean that they could not continue to thrive commercially in a world of Quaker cousins; it did mean, however, that they entered much earlier than the others into the great world of public school and university, clerical benefices, and aristocratic marriages.[21] By contrast, the pharmaceutical side of the family, Joseph Gurney Bevan and his connections, remained, as we shall see, staunch Friends for another century.

The Trittons were distinguished among our eighteenth-century Quaker notables by the directness with which they moved toward brewing and banking without going through the intermediary steps of wholesale or foreign trade. Of Kentish yeoman background, they were early Quakers and one of them was imprisoned for his beliefs at the Restoration. In calmer times, John Tritton (d. 1739) purchased a small brewery at Ashford in 1726. His younger son Thomas was also a brewer and wine merchant at Ashford when in the early 1750s he married Anna Maria, daughter of Henton Brown (1698–1775), Quaker watchmaker and merchant turned banker of London. Brown was interested in having his Tritton son-in-law join his bank along with his other son-in-law, Thomas Collinson, but Thomas Tritton preferred to put his money into a second and larger brewery in Wandsworth, which brought the family into metropolitan Quaker society.[22]

Tritton's brother-in-law Thomas Collinson was the son of James Collinson and the nephew of Peter Collinson, the celebrated Quaker botanist. The elder Collinsons operated a family woollendrapery and mercery business with substantial exports to the American colonies. Thomas Collinson (d. 1803) was thus in his own way repeating the now familiar pattern of a retreat from wholesale and overseas trade into banking at the time of the American Revolution.[23]

Although Thomas Tritton would not join Browns & Collinson, arrangements were made for his son, John Henton Tritton, to join that bank as an apprentice. When Henton Brown died in 1775, his will made provision for the admission of his Tritton grandson as a partner in the bank when he came of age.[24] The firm then consisted of Henton Brown's son James, son-in-law Thomas Collinson, and grandson John Henton Tritton. Unfortunately, after the death of James Brown in 1781, the books of the firm were discovered to be in disorder owing to some "defalcations," and it went bankrupt in 1782.[25] By that time, however, the young John Henton Tritton was courting Mary Barclay, daughter of John Barclay. The Barclays remained loyal to Tritton and took the young bankrupt into their bank next door, first as an employee (1782), then as a partner (1783). This enabled him to marry Mary Barclay a few months later. John Henton Tritton was for decades the operating head of the Barclays' bank and devised the procedural rules it followed through much of the next century, rules designed presumably to prevent any further "defalcations." John Henton Tritton was succeeded as a partner in the bank by his sons and grandsons, and after the incorporation in 1896 descendants of his name have continued to appear among the directors of Barclays Bank down to the present day.[26]

With John Henton Tritton provided for in the Barclays' bank, his father, Thomas, felt free to leave his breweries to his younger son George, who apparently made a very good thing of them. This established among the Trittons, as among the Barclays and Bevans, separate banking and brewing branches of the family. George Tritton the brewer became an Anglican at marriage in 1790. John Henton Tritton stayed nominally a

Quaker long after that but was obviously wavering, as he sent three sons to Harrow and two to Cambridge. Two of these sons became Anglicans in 1814, and the whole family can be considered Anglican by the 1820s. One of the sons educated at Cambridge became an Anglican minister very much identified with the evangelical movement.[27] Evangelical Anglicanism was to prove a stirring and challenging contrast to the quietist and somewhat complacent Quakerism of the late eighteenth century.

Related to both the Barclays and the Bevans were the Gurneys of Norwich, the most celebrated of English Quaker families — at least if the number of entries in the *Dictionary of National Biography* is any guide.[28] John Gurney of Norwich, variously described as a cordwainer, a silk dealer, wool-stapler, yarn-merchant, and master weaver, became a Quaker in the time of Charles II and for his zeal he too suffered imprisonment. At his death in 1721, he left two sons, John and Joseph, founders respectively of the senior (St. Augustin's) and junior (Magdalen Street) branches of the family. He reportedly left £20,000, giving both these sons solid help in their business careers. John, the eldest (d. 1740), was a successful woolen merchant and was remembered as the "weavers' friend" because of his success in testifying before the House of Lords on the Calico Act.[29] His sons, John and Henry, successful linen merchants and woolen manufacturers,[30] founded the Gurney bank in Norwich in 1775, allegedly because Henry's son, Bartlett, wanted to get out of the cloth business: an extreme example of the retreat from trade into banking! After the deaths of the aforementioned John (1779) and Henry (1777), Bartlett continued the bank in partnership with cousins from the junior branch who eventually took over the bank completely on Bartlett's death in 1803.[31]

The junior or Magdalen Street branch of the family was founded by John the Prisoner's younger son Joseph (1692–1750), also a successful Norwich cloth merchant, who acquired a country residence at Keswick. The real eminence of the junior branch was established by this Joseph's eldest son, John (1716–1770), who, first in partnership with his father (d. 1750) and then with his younger brothers Samuel and Joseph (d. 1761), pioneered the trade of importing attractively priced Irish woolen yarn from Cork for the use of the expanding East Anglian cloth manufacturing industry. The firm's capital increased from £12,000 in 1741 to £70,000 in 1769, while John's own net worth increased from £4,000 in 1741 (£1,000 of his own, £1,000 from his father, and £2,000 of his wife's dowry) to £80–100,000 by the time of his death in 1770.

Joseph, this John Gurney's younger brother, married Christiana, the daughter of David Barclay the elder of Cheapside, while their widowed sister, Hannah, married Timothy Bevan. So began a pattern that was to tie the Gurneys by marriage tightly to the leading London Quaker families, particularly the Barclays. This is shown most clearly in the marriages of the children of the older brother John: Richard, the first son, married

Agatha, daughter of David Barclay the younger and was the father of the Hudson Gurney already mentioned; John, Jr., the second son, married Catherine Bell, also a granddaughter of David Barclay the elder; Joseph, the third son, married Jane Chapman, a great-granddaughter of the same David Barclay, while Rachel, the only daughter, married Robert Barclay, originally of Philadelphia but later of the brewery, another grandson of the same David Barclay. There can be no doubt that by the 1780s the Gurneys of Norwich were part of the London Quaker inner circle.[32]

Richard and Joseph Gurney, two of the three sons just mentioned of John Gurney of Keswick, were taken into the "Norwich and Norfolk Bank" in partnership with their cousin Bartlett, the official style of the firm in the 1780s being Richard, Bartlett & Joseph Gurney. The middle brother, John, remained outside the bank till shortly before Bartlett's death in 1803, devoting himself instead to the management of the family's yarn business, now styled Gurney & Bland. This also had a financial side in that the firm borrowed more money than it needed for its trade and lent out the balance on interest.[33] This John Gurney acquired a country residence at Earlham and was the father of the eleven fascinating siblings of Earlham whose spiritual travails have been chronicled at great length by Augustus Hare and later writers. As already mentioned, Hudson Gurney of Keswick had left the Society of Friends quite early in the new century as did his half brother Richard. Cousin Bartlett had left in 1785. The Earlham cousins, however, orphaned by the death of their tolerant father in 1809, struggled with the issue for a decade. When the dust finally settled around 1820, the score was Anglicans 7, Quakers 4. However, the four who remained loyal to the Society of Friends included the best-known members of the family: Elizabeth Fry, the great prison reformer; her sister, Priscilla Gurney, a saintly Quaker minister; their brother, Joseph John, Quaker minister, theologian, and Norwich banker; and Samuel, the London financier, co-founder of Overend & Gurney, the greatest firm of discount brokers in Europe. The victory of Quakerism here was not to prove permanent, for we are told that none of Elizabeth Fry's eleven children remained Quaker. Though differently timed, the spiritual evolution of the Gurneys was not in the end significantly different from that of the Barclays.[34]

Among the Quaker families with close connections with the Gurneys were the Hoares of London, a family tracing its descent from Major Edward Hoare who had served in Ireland in Cromwell's time and was rewarded for his services by substantial land grants in County Cork. His younger son Joseph, the only one of his family to become a Quaker, was a merchant of Cork and landowner in the county, a position inherited by his son Samuel. The latter, however, left Cork for London upon his marriage in 1744 to the daughter of Jonathan Gurnell, a prominent London Quaker merchant.[35] He invested the £4,000 he had received as his new wife's dowry and another £4,000 of his own in buying a one-third interest in his father-in-law's firm, Jonathan Gurnell & Co., London correspondents of the senior Gurneys of Norwich.[36]

Jonathan Gurnell (1684–1745) had left a Quaker farming background in Westmorland to try his fortune in London. By his mid-twenties, he was an established Portuguese merchant. William Penn and other leading Quakers had attended his marriage in 1711 to Grizell Wilmer of a family with the highest Quaker and earlier Puritan credentials. This marriage brought Jonathan Gurnell three sons and three daughters; one daughter, Hannah, in 1732 married Jeremiah Harman, who was to die young in 1741, leaving several minor children. The Harmans, like the Wilmers and the Hoares, were descended from military officers who had served in Ireland in Cromwell's time before the families became Quaker.

After the death of Jonathan Gurnell and two of his sons in the early 1750s, his firm was reorganized as a partnership of his remaining son, Thomas Gurnell, and his son-in-law Samuel Hoare, who were in about 1762 joined by his grandson John Harman.[37] The resulting firm of Gurnell, Hoare & Harman was undoubtedly the most prominent Quaker merchant firm trading to the continent, specializing in the trade to Portugal, Ireland, and Holland.[38] When Samuel Hoare in turn came to retire in 1774, his place in the firm was taken by his son Jonathan.[39] His other son, Samuel, Jr., who had served an apprenticeship in the merchant house of Henry and John Gurney in Norwich, preferred becoming a banker; his father gave him the wherewithal to buy a partnership in the Bland, Barnett bank. Samuel Hoare, Jr., was as great a success as a banker[40] as his brother Jonathan was a disappointment as a merchant. Taking advantage of his position in one of the most prestigious firms in the City and his great income, Jonathan Hoare moved in un-Quakerly fashion into rather fast society, ultimately becoming a close companion of the Prince of Wales, leaving the merchant firm to be run more and more by his cousin John Harman. After the deaths of Thomas Gurnell, also something of a sportsman, and Samuel Hoare, Sr., the Harmans eased Jonathan Hoare out of the firm which then became Harman & Co. Jonathan Hoare's other business ventures also proved unsuccessful and in his last years, in reduced circumstances, he was dependent in part on the charity of his brother Samuel, Jr., the banker.[41]

This drama of contrast between the successful banker brother and the unsuccessful merchant brother so striking in the Hoare family had been enacted earlier in the Bland family whose bank Samuel Hoare had joined. John Bland, Sr., who had been operating the second oldest Quaker bank in London from the 1720s, had three sons, two of whom, John, Jr., and Stamper, had by 1749 become partners in his bank, John Bland & Sons. Stamper subsequently broke with his father and founded his own bank about 1754. The third, Elias, was apparently considered unsuitable for banking and in 1744, after an apprenticeship in Philadelphia, set up in trade in London as a Pennsylvania merchant. After failing twice, he was forced to flee back to America where he retired to a farm in New Jersey. In 1761 Benjamin Barnett, an Anglican, was taken into the banking firm of John Bland & Son; some years after John Bland, Sr., died in 1765, Samuel Hoare, Jr., was added. When John Bland, Jr., died in 1788, his entire substantial fortune went to his only child, a daughter who subsequently married Charles Hanbury, of a prominent London Quaker family.[42] Thus, in the contest of life, the Barnetts and Hoares won the Bland bank and the Hanburys the Bland money; while Elias Bland had perforce to console himself with New Jersey. More seriously, the retreat from trade into banking by a John Bland or a Samuel Hoare, Jr., was not a matter simply of pride or laziness; it might be a successful strategy for family survival.

Shortly after Samuel Hoare, Jr., became a banker, he not inappropriately married a Gurney of Norwich. His son, Samuel III, who succeeded him in the bank, also married a Gurney, Louisa, one of the eleven lively siblings of Earlham. When the Gurneys of Earlham split on the religious issue after 1809, Samuel Hoare and Louisa, his wife, came out on the Anglican side.[43] The Gurnells had gone that way long before. As early as the 1740s, one of Jonathan Gurnell's sons had married a non-Quaker and been disowned by the Society. Another son, Thomas Gurnell, and his wife had been disowned in 1770 for their un-Quakerly style of life. They were, however, interred in a Quaker burial ground. The Harmans remained Friends longer, but John Harman's son, Jeremiah, a distinguished merchant, art collector, and governor of the Bank of England, received an Anglican burial when he died in 1844. Only the Green family, descendants of the marriage of Jonathan Gurnell's third daughter, Mary, to Joseph Green, a London silk merchant, remained Quakers into the twentieth century.[44]

One cannot understand the European-wide importance of the merchant firm of Gurnell, Hoare & Harman without considering their relationship to Hope & Co. of Amsterdam. The Hopes were a family of Scots Quakers settled in Rotterdam from at least 1664 as minor merchants. Henry, the eldest of the eight sons of Archibald Hope of Rotterdam (1664–1743), was unsuccessful in business and moved to Boston, Massachusetts, in the late 1720s. However, two of his younger brothers, Thomas and Adrian, moved from Rotterdam to Amsterdam a few years before and very soon became one of the more prominent and, from the time of the Seven Years War, the leading merchant house in that great commercial center. Their correspondents in London were their Quaker friends, Gurnell & Co. and successor firms. When Henry Hope of Boston decided to send his son, Henry, Jr., back to Europe for a career, he obtained a clerkship for him in the London counting house of Gurnell & Hoare where young Henry stayed from 1754 to about 1762 when he was invited by his uncles to join the Amsterdam house. He ultimately became the head of the firm and the first authentic Quaker millionaire. He showed the deftness of his skills when in his old age he extracted his family and art collection and most of the firm's money from Holland at the time of the French revolutionary invasions. The Hopes remained Quakers until 1756 when Thomas's son John became a member of the English Presbyterian Church in Amsterdam, in communion with the Dutch Reformed Church, thus qualifying himself for public office. The remainder of the family drifted gradually in the same direction in succeeding decades, though the branch that stayed in England after the Napoleonic wars became Anglican.[45]

The firms of Gurnell, Hoare & Harman and Hope & Co. differed from almost all the other Quaker merchant houses in London in their willingness to venture into the rarified and risky world of state finance and court politics. Hope & Co. were for years financial and mercantile agents of the French government and performed such tasks as procuring masts for the French navy from Russia. Through Hopes, Gurnells became the London correspondents of Jean-Joseph de La Borde, the French court banker, and, for a brief time, the buying agents of the French tobacco monopoly. When Hopes became the financial agents of the Russian government in the 1790s, their London friends, now styled Harman, Hoare & Co., were drawn into the network and helped remit British war subsidies to both Russia and Prussia.[46] When Harman & Co. failed spectacularly in 1846, they were still representatives of the Russian government, the greatest loser by their crash. Jonathan Gurnell's grandson, John Harman, had left a fortune of about £233,000 when he died in 1817; his three sons, Jeremiah (governor of the Bank of England and art collector), Edward, and Henry, managed to lose everything through unsuccessful commodity speculations and bad debts.[47] The abandonment of Quaker prudence along with other Quaker qualities obviously had some costs.

Thus far, we have been dealing with families based primarily in the southeast of England and frequently active in the textile trades. There were, however, other prominent Quaker families with roots in the west of England and Wales and more closely connected with the metallurgical industries. The association of Friends with metallurgy, as Arthur Raistrick has shown, was substantial, long-lasting, and widespread.[48] Silvanus Bevan of Swansea invested in copper refining, and John Freame, London goldsmith and founder of the Freame-Barclay bank, was the banker of the Welsh Society of the Mines Royal Copper and an investor in the London Lead Company of which he eventually became governor (1733–42). So overwhelming was the investment of Friends in the latter concern that it was commonly called the Quaker Lead Company.[49] Far more common, however, was Quaker participation in ironworks. In fact, scholars have estimated that from one-half to three-fourths of the ironworks in England and Wales in the first half of the eighteenth century were either owned or managed by Quakers.[50] The celebrated Abraham Darby, the first to smelt iron with coke, was thus only the most famous of a large tribe.

The first outstanding Quaker family in the iron trade was the Crowleys. Ambrose Crowley I (1601–1680) was a poor nailer; his son Ambrose II (1635–1720) started out as an illiterate nailer at Stourbridge in Worcestershire but through thrift and considerable business acumen became a manufacturer of nails on the putting-out system, an ironmonger, and an owner of iron refining works. His interests extended to Taff Vale in South Wales where he was a part owner of an ironworks with Major John Hanbury, a prominent figure in the South Wales iron trade who invented the rolling process used in the manufacture of tinplate. Ambrose Crowley II was an early, active, and generous Quaker.[51] Far more prominent was his son Ambrose III (1658–1713), who served an apprenticeship and settled in London as a great wholesale ironmonger with interests in manufacturing works near Newcastle-on-Tyne. His great prosperity came during the wars of 1689–1713 when he was a major supplier of ironware to the navy. Ambrose Crowley III became an Anglican, sheriff of London, and a knight. The firm which Sir Ambrose Crowley founded was continued by his son and grandsons and lasted well into the nineteenth century, prospering from all the wars of the century following his death. At its height in the second quarter of the eighteenth century, the firm, then worth over £100,000 and employing over one thousand workers, was reputed the largest iron-manufacturing concern in Europe.[52] A large part of its trade was for export, particularly to America, and despite the family apostasy the Crowleys were not above cultivating their Quaker connections in Philadelphia. However, after the death of Sir Ambrose's son John in 1729, the Crowleys no longer accepted risky export orders from abroad but insisted on dealing only with merchants domiciled in England.[53] Some large wholesalers, Quaker and otherwise, followed this policy all along; others made an equivalent retreat from the risks of the export trade only after the chastening experience of the American Revolution.[54]

As Sir Ambrose Crowley had left the Quakers by the time of his marriage in 1682, his descendants do not fit within the scope of this essay. Two of his Quaker sisters, however, married into the Lloyd family of Dolobran and Birmingham, which certainly does warrant inclusion. Charles Lloyd (1637–1698) was descended from a respectable line of country gentry seated at Dolobran in Montgomeryshire (near the Shropshire border) since at least the fifteenth century, and which had provided numerous J.P.'s to the county from the reign of Elizabeth to the Interregnum. Charles, however, became a Quaker in 1662 and suffered ten years imprisonment (some of it severe; some of it house arrest). His brother Thomas, who suffered with him, later accompanied William Penn to Pennsylvania where he became deputy governor and founded a family. Charles, too, was interested in Penn's venture and became a First Purchaser of land in Pennsylvania.[55] There was nothing commercial or industrial about the family until 1693–95 when Charles Lloyd II, the eldest son of Charles the prisoner, married

Sarah, daughter of Ambrose Crowley II, while his younger brother Sampson married her sister Mary, and their sister Elizabeth Lloyd married John
Pemberton, a prosperous Quaker ironmonger of Birmingham. Charles
Lloyd II of Dolobran (1662–1748) was seemingly propelled by his Crowley
marriage into the operation of an iron forge in which he was reasonably
successful and an iron furnace which forced him and his son Charles III
(1697–1767) into bankruptcy; the senior branch of the family eventually
had to sell Dolobran and fell out of sight.[56]

The first Charles Lloyd's younger son Sampson (1664–1724) was more
successful. After twelve years of farming, he sold his real estate and moved
to Birmingham in 1698, where he became a wholesale supplier of bar iron,
rods, and other metals to fabricators thereabouts. He frequently acted on
commission for his brother-in-law Sir Ambrose Crowley of London. When
he died in 1724, Sampson Lloyd left about £10,000 — quite a respectable
sum for the younger son of a rather straitened Quaker country gentleman.[57] However, Sampson's son, Sampson II (1699–1779), was to prove
the true inheritor of the Crowley business genius. He took the rather
modest business of his father and built it into something more substantial,
integrating backward into slitting mills, forges, and ultimately furnaces —
all quite successful — as well as investing in less profitable steel and brass
ventures.[58] In 1765 he joined with a rich Unitarian neighbor, John Taylor,
manufacturer of buttons and snuffboxes, to found the Birmingham bank
of Taylors & Lloyds with his son Sampson III and Taylor's son John, Jr.,
as equal partners. Sampson Lloyd II's iron business which had prospered
enormously during the Seven Years War was in something of the doldrums
at the peace, and he was apparently interested in the bank as an alternative
way of supporting his five sons. In the end he was able to arrange for
partnerships in both the bank and the iron company for his three eldest
sons (Sampson III, Nehemiah, and Charles) while satisfactory provision
was made for the two younger sons (John and Ambrose) in London businesses.[59] These Lloyds retained their interests in iron manufacture and trade
until early in the nineteenth century, and their interest in the bank (incorporated in 1865) continues to the present.[60]

Sampson Lloyd II was a serious and active Quaker, serving twice in
the responsible position of clerk of London Yearly Meeting.[61] His own
two marriages established links with two quite prominent Quaker families:
the Parkes of Birmingham and Wednesbury, ironmongers and mine owners; and the Champions of Bristol, merchants with metallurgical interests.
The marriages of his children, however, for the first time linked his family
with the main Quaker business families of London: son Charles in 1774
married Mary Farmer of Birmingham, related to the Freames and Barclays
of London (she reportedly brought a dowry of £30,000); daughter Mary in
1757 had married Osgood Hanbury, son of John Hanbury, great Chesa-

peake merchant of London, and daughter Rachel ten years later became the second wife of David Barclay the younger, of Cheapside.[62]

When Sampson Lloyd II died in 1779, he left seven grown children who between them were to produce 44 grandchildren and 120 great-grand-children.[63] The marriages of all this tribe could have produced a vast cousinhood linking Quaker families all over the country. That was, however, not to be. During the Napoleonic Wars, Sampson Lloyd III quarreled with the local Friends' meeting over his defense of a "friend in Birmingham, who came under . . . censure . . . for manufacturing weapons of war"; as a result Sampson III was suspended or "laid on the shelf" for the rest of his life.[64] In succeeding decades, other members of the family left the Friends for one reason or another (some becoming Anglican, others Plymouth Brethren) so that by 1860 the family could be described as no longer Quaker.[65]

Intimately associated with the Birmingham Lloyds from 1757 onwards were the Hanburys who came out of the same South Wales Quaker iron-making milieu. John Hanbury (1700–1758), distantly related to his name-sake, the inventor of the tinplate rolling process, was the son of Charles Hanbury, M.D. (1677–1735) of Panteg (Monmouthshire) whose grand-father, Richard (1610–1695), had been an early and active Monmouthshire Quaker.[66] Although nothing is known of his apprenticeship, John Hanbury appears to have commenced business as a Virginia merchant in London in the early 1720s. By 1729 he had acquired rather splendid premises in Great Tower Street which his family and firm were to occupy for three genera-tions.[67] About the same time, he married Anna Osgood, only daughter and heiress of Obadiah Osgood, a well-to-do Friend and grand-daughter of John Osgood, a very prosperous London Quaker linen-draper and mer-chant. John Hanbury emerged into prominence in the trade in the 1740s when he brought his cousin Capel Hanbury, son of a Bristol soapmaker of the same name, up to London as a partner. By 1747 their firm was the largest in the Chesapeake trade.[68]

Unlike most Quakers, the Hanburys were not afraid of venturing into politics. Their closeness to successive Lords Baltimore, to whom they were personal bankers, made them a powerful channel of influence in Maryland patronage and thus attracted to their house the business of many great planters with a thirst for office.[69] At a higher level, they made themselves discreet and valued advisers on American affairs to a variety of great figures including Lord Granville (Carteret) and the duke of Newcastle.[70] When the Ohio Company of Virginia was set up in 1748, the Hanburys were invited to become partners and London agents. The government consulted with them while formulating the strategy that led to Braddock's expedi-tion; this enabled a prominent anti-government pamphleteer to describe that campaign as a Quaker plot to get others to fight for them to protect the Hanburys' interests in the Ohio lands and to win transport and supply contracts for their firm.[71] In fact, John Hanbury was part of a syndicate that obtained contracts in 1754 and 1756 to remit funds for the payment of the army in America between 1754 and 1765. These contracts — unusual for a Quaker — produced many difficulties and John Hanbury's successors afterward avoided such entanglements.[72]

After John Hanbury's death in 1758, his firm was continued as a partnership between his son Osgood and his cousin Capel. After Capel's death in 1769, the partners became Osgood Hanbury and Capel's widow, Mary Hanbury, then (from 1774) Osgood Hanbury, his brother-in-law John Lloyd (1751–1811) of Birmingham, and Capel Hanbury's son John (1751–1800).[73] A turning point for the firm came in 1769. The year of Capel Hanbury's death marked the most serious phase of the nonimportation agreements in America against the Townshend duties, and when Osgood Hanbury's next door neighbor Richard Gosling, a West India merchant for whom Osgood was executor, also died in 1769, Osgood decided to redeploy his resources. He began a gradual withdrawal from the Chesapeake trade which went so far that he sent no ships to America in 1775 when everyone else was scrambling for tobacco.[74] Part of the resources thus freed was invested in a new West India firm styled Hanbury & Gosling which carried on the old Gosling business.[75] Another part went into banking. When the Taylors and Lloyds of Birmingham had been planning their own small bank in 1764 with a capital of only £8,000, they offered a one-third interest to Osgood Hanbury who was not interested. However, in 1769 he took the initiative in setting up a larger London bank which opened in 1770 under the style, Hanbury, Taylor, Lloyd & Bowman: his partners in this £20,000 venture were the younger Sampson Lloyd and John Taylor from Birmingham, and William Bowman, formerly a clerk at Smith & Payne's bank who was to be the manager. This bank under various styles persisted until 1864 when it merged with that other former Quaker bank, Barnett, Hoare & Co. to become Barnetts, Hoares, Hanburys & Lloyd, the London correspondents of the Lloyds' bank of Birmingham; in 1884 it was absorbed by the Birmingham concern which subsequently became based in London.[76]

Osgood Hanbury, of course, had become one of the Lloyds when he married Sampson Lloyd II's daughter Mary in 1757. The marriages of his own children in the 1780s and 1790s were to be so striking that the Hanburys could almost be described as lynchpins tying the whole Quaker *haute monde* together. Osgood Hanbury II (1765–1852) married a daughter of John Barclay of the bank; his brother Charles (1766–1825) married the daughter and sole heiress of John Bland, Jr., the banker; another brother, Sampson (1769–1835), married Agatha, daughter of Richard Gurney of Keswick and sister of Hudson Gurney, while sister Rachel became the same Richard Gurney's second wife; another sister, Mary Elizabeth, married her first cousin David Lloyd, son of Sampson Lloyd III of Birmingham. Still another sister, Anna, married an Anglican, Thomas Fowell Buxton (Sr.), but unusually was allowed to keep her Quaker connection. Of these, the

Hanbury-Barclay marriage of 1789 was the most striking and attracted both a good number of distinguished guests, including the French ambassador, and the detailed attention of part of the press.[77]

Osgood Hanbury in Quaker fashion provided for his younger sons almost as well as he did for his eldest.[78] One of them, Sampson, used his inheritances to buy an eighteenth share in the long-established Truman brewery of which he soon became managing partner with ultimately a one-third stake. With no children of his own, Sampson eventually brought into the firm his nephews Robert Hanbury (son of Osgood II) and Thomas Fowell Buxton the younger, thus creating the great brewery of Truman, Hanbury & Buxton in which the Hanbury and Buxton families retained a strong interest until the 1960s.[79]

Capel Hanbury's sons most likely did not start out with as much as Osgood's,[80] but their line achieved at least as much distinction. Two of Capel's sons, John and Capel II, both married Bells, granddaughters of David Barclay (the elder) of Cheapside,[81] while his daughter Charlotte married William Allen, a promising pharmacist with scientific interests. The eldest son, John Hanbury, left the family's old Chesapeake house in the 1780s and became a brewer; his younger brother, Capel II (1764–1835), became a cornfactor and in that trade lost his fortune around 1810.[82] Capel II's two sons, Daniel Bell and Cornelius, were, however, taken into the Plough Court pharmacy by their uncle William Allen (1770–1843). This was the old Bevan family business which Allen had taken over from Joseph Gurney Bevan when the founding family lost interest. Allen and the Hanbury brothers converted this modest concern into Allen & Hanburys, a major pharmaceutical manufacturing company to this day.[83]

Osgood Hanbury's descendants, who included Sir Thomas Fowell Buxton, the antislavery leader, and W. E. Forster, the education reformer, remained Quakers only slightly longer than the brewing Barclays. Osgood II died a nominal Friend in 1852 but long before that most of his children seem to have become Anglicans as did the children of his brother Charles. The two families produced three clergymen in the Church of England, some holding livings purchased for them by their remaining Quaker relatives. On Capel's side of the family, the sons of John (1751–1800) entered the armed forces;[84] the pharmaceutical Hanburys, however, remained loyal to the old ways until about 1870, but, with the death of Cornelius and Daniel Bell Hanbury and their sons, the very strong Quaker commitment in this Plough Court branch going back to Joseph Gurney Bevan and William Allen evaporated, and the next generation followed the by now familiar route to the Church of England.[85]

Three families that represent a Bristol-London axis present some interesting contrasts that will have to be dealt with briefly. Elizabeth, the sister of our original Capel Hanbury (d. 1769), married Mark Beaufoy (1718–1782), son of an Evesham maltster of a family with a long Quaker tradition.

Young Mark had served an apprenticeship to a Bristol distiller but a view of Hogarth's *Gin Lane* series and his own Quaker scruples convinced him that distilling was not to be his way. Instead, Mark Beaufoy studied vinegar making in Holland and established a firm in that line in south London which lasted under family control well into this century. However, all four of his children became Anglicans, three of them by elopements. The eldest, Henry (1750–1795), became an M.P. and secretary of the Board of Control for India and celebrated his emancipation by having portraits painted by Gainsborough depicting himself and his wife in anything but Quaker attire.[86] This contrast between the committed Quaker and the equally convinced worldly children suggests that the process of acculturation to the great world need not take the more common three or four generations.

The Harford family of Bristol was connected by marriage to both the Lloyds of Birmingham and some of the London Quaker families. This family was founded by Charles Harford (1631–1709), who moved to Bristol from a nearby Gloucestershire village in the 1650s. He became a Virginia merchant and an active Quaker and friend of William Penn and suffered imprisonment in the 1680s as did his wife and his son Charles.[87] This younger Charles (1662–1725) founded a branch of the family that eventually settled in London though most other branches remained near Bristol. In the latter part of the eighteenth century the London Harfords included Truman Harford, a substantial brewer, and his uncle John Harford, partner in the merchant house of Harford & Powell, trading to Pennsylvania and South Carolina on the eve of the Revolution. Harford & Powell from 1765 took over most of the commission business of their kinsmen David Barclay & Sons where Thomas Powell had been trained. In the 1760s John Harford had married Beatrice Harman while his sister Elizabeth had married Beatrice's brother John Harman, partner in Gurnell, Hoare & Harman, thus further connecting the London Harfords to an important section of the Quaker establishment there. Two of John Harford's nephews, however, entered the navy in the 1780s and thus left the Society of Friends.[88]

We have far more information about the Harfords who stayed in Bristol. The first Charles Harford's eldest son, Edward (1658–1705), was a soap boiler, but his son Edward II (1691–1779) became a Virginia merchant by the 1720s. He retired in the late 1740s and handed over his Virginia business to his son Edward III (1720–1806, usually designated "junior").[89] This Edward was one of the founding partners in 1769 of the Harford Bank in Bristol, the fourth bank in the town and the third with Quaker partners.[90] Edward Harford III prospered as a Virginia merchant and does not appear to have lost too much by the American Revolution, his personal fortune having increased from £7,050 in 1748 to £43,093 in 1780 even before he received over £19,000 from his father's estate.[91] He was, however, unable to resume his Virginia business after the war and instead devoted his time and resources to his bank and to the Bristol Brass Company in which his family had long had an investment. This firm was around 1800 the largest brass manufacturing concern in Europe.[92] When Edward Harford III died in 1806, he was worth £136–154,000.[93] He had married Sarah Scandrett who, through her mother, was heiress to one-fourth of the Birmingham Parkes' fortune (another quarter going to Sampson Lloyd). This interest passed to his son John Scandrett Harford who at his death in 1815 was worth £300,000.[94]

The senior line of the Bristol Harfords remained Quakers down to the death of Edward Harford III in 1806. However, shortly after, his grandsons became Anglicans.[95]

A third family with Bristol connections was the Mildreds about whom we know relatively little. Thomas Mildred (d. 1753) was a successful London wholesale hardware dealer (with some export trade). His son Daniel, who married Lydia Daniel of Bristol, did not continue his father's hardware business but instead, in partnership with his Bristol brother-in-law John Roberts (from a distinguished Quaker family), started the London merchant house of Mildred & Roberts trading to New York, Pennsylvania, and the Chesapeake.[96] Like other Quakers, Daniel Mildred seems to have been able to extract most but not all of his fortune from America before the Revolution and in 1778 was able to found a London bank, Mildred & Walker, later (1781) Mildred, Masterman & Walker. After his death in 1788, this was continued by his son-in-law William Masterman and—as Mastermans—lasted till it merged in 1865 with a joint-stock bank which failed the following year.[97] Except for the marriage in 1790 of his son Daniel, Jr., to Elizabeth Harman (the daughter of John Harman and Elizabeth Harford), the large family of Daniel Mildred does not appear to have intermarried much with the leading Quaker families of London. One can only speculate why. Daniel Mildred, we know, was clerk (an honored and responsible position) of the Devonshire House meeting while some of the other families here discussed preferred the allegedly more easy going Gracechurch Street meeting.[98]

That neither endogamy nor even the growth of fortunes was automatic is confirmed by the annals of the Eliots, our last family. John Eliot (I) inherited some land and mining interests in Cornwall where he was for a time a middling merchant at Falmouth. By 1719, however, he had moved to London where he prospered as a merchant and insurance underwriter, increasing his fortune from about £18,000 in 1722 to almost £100,000 at his death in 1762.[99] His grandson John Eliot III (1735–1813) also attempted to be an insurance underwriter if not a merchant, but was unable to increase his inherited net worth of £60,000 after forty years of trying.[100] John Eliot I, though nominally a Quaker, was not particularly interested in Quaker marriages for his four daughters. He suspected every young Friend who came visiting to be a hypocrite parading his Quaker virtues in the hope of

winning a wealthy bride. As a result, two of his daughters remained unmarried and two married Anglicans. John Eliot's son and grandson disapproved of this policy and by contrast became committed, active, and
endogamous Friends. In the end, the only daughter and ultimate heiress of
the grandson John Eliot III married Luke Howard, a committed Friend
and one-time partner of William Allen in the Plough Court pharmaceutical
firm which he left to found an equally long lasting drug manufacturing
firm of his own. However, almost inevitably, Howard's descendants became Anglicans in the latter part of the nineteenth century.[101]

Conclusions

At the beginning of this essay I suggested that some features of the Barclay
history might be common to most leading Quaker business families in
eighteenth-century London. We can now see more clearly certain shared
patterns. With the exception of the Crowleys, who were no longer Quaker,
all our families were, in mercantile terms, quite unimportant at the beginning of the eighteenth century. For many, the breakthrough to commercial
importance and affluence came in the war generation 1740 to 1763. Although Quakers did not engage in privateering or, with the small exception
of Hanbury's remittance contract, in supplying the armed services, Quaker
businessmen, like others, benefited from the buoyancy of the economy
through most of these years, particularly in the export trades. It was at this
time that fortunes in or near six figures are reported for such businessmen
as David Barclay the elder, John Gurney of Keswick, Samuel Hoare I,
Sampson Lloyd II, John Hanbury, and John Eliot, with younger men such
as John Harman and Edward Harford III not there yet in the 1760s but
well on the way. Many — the Barclays, Bevans, Hanburys, Harfords, and
Mildreds, in particular — were exporters to North America, and for them
this era of great opportunity came to an end with the nonimportation
agreements of the 1760s and the American war in the 1770s. Osgood Hanbury was the first to realize this and began to withdraw from the North
American trade in 1769; the Revolution forced the Barclays, Bevans, Harfords, and Mildreds to the same conclusion. In place of the dangerous
American trades, more attention was given to the safer inland metallurgical
trades, to banking, and to brewing. Instead of two Quaker banks in London as in 1738, there were seven banks forty years later.[102] While only one
of our fourteen families was interested in brewing before 1780, six were
involved by 1801.[103] If individual members of some of the families traded
overseas to areas other than North America, the fate of Harman & Co.
and others in 1846–47 showed that such trades could also be ruinously
risky.[104] Even traditional manufactures could appear less attractive in an era
of changing technologies as is suggested by the retreat from manufacture

of the Birmingham Lloyds, the Bristol Harfords, and the Norwich Gurneys in the early years of the new century.[105] In all of this we can detect intergenerational changes so that trades which appeared rewarding and not unduly risky to founders did not appear so to grandsons who lacked their grandfathers' peculiar combination of shrewdness, prudence, and flair.

We suggested at the beginning that the history of these families is a special case in the emergence of the British upper middle class. As we have seen, the Quakers were excluded by their faith from ecclesiastical, civil, and military employments, from the law, and from businesses with the windfall opportunities of privateering and defense contracting. They were perforce obliged, insofar as they were ambitious for advancement, to seek alternative employments for themselves and their funds in some risky overseas trades and in some technologically difficult fields such as metallurgy, pharmaceuticals, and watchmaking; even brewing might perhaps be considered difficult in an era of changing tastes and methods. Because they were prepared to invest money and entrepreneurship in fields which others avoided, they were able for a time, once they had solved the initial technological and financial problems, to derive above-average returns on their investments, at least until changing technologies and economies of scale altered the rules of the game.

The success of Quakers in the precarious overseas trades is something of a paradox. These trades were risky because one's assets or the assets of those to whom one sold were of necessity overseas and the duration of credit was so long, from nine months to two years.[106] Taking such risks was disturbing to the Society of Friends who regarded all the activities of their members as legitimate subjects of communal scrutiny. Friends were expected to visit and remonstrate with neighboring Friends about business as about other transgressions. In the injunctions which London Yearly Meeting sent down to local quarterly and monthly meetings, nothing was a more frequent cause for concern than the danger of overtrading. Friends were again and again urged not to let the desire for material gain lead them into engagements beyond their means, engagements that would endanger the security of both their own families and the families of those from whom they obtained credit. Foreign trade was sometimes held out as a particularly dangerous temptation.[107]

However, Quakers did venture into risky foreign trade, and in it they had some advantages to counterbalance the uncertainty inherent in long credits. The principal exports to America were light textiles and metalware, businesses in which Quakers were, we have seen, quite active. Quaker wholesale linendrapers and ironmongers might well have felt that less than the usual risk was involved in selling to an export merchant or even a merchant overseas who was a Friend because of the great emphasis which the Society put on the payment of debts. Yearly Meeting exhorted those who lived in the Truth to be both conscientious and prompt in paying their debts. Even a legally discharged bankrupt Friend was held morally bound to repay the balance of his prebankruptcy debts to the best of his ability. Some did so and were praised; others who did not were threatened with disownment as was anyone who refused to pay his just debts.[108] Friends were forbidden to sue each other in courts of law but urged to submit to arbitration all disputes whether with Friend or stranger.[109] One cannot exaggerate the importance Quakers attached to the payment of debts. Members of the most prominent families, including Elizabeth Fry's husband, Joseph, were disowned for failure to pay their debts.[110] As a result, Quakers had very high "credit ratings" both in dealings among themselves and with non-Quakers. Their dependability in paying debts removed some of the normal risks of overseas trade and helped free consciences from the self-accusation of possible overtrading.

This entire moral system was placed under great strain by the advent of the American Revolution. Richard Champion, a Bristol Quaker, wrote that as the gathering storm became more threatening, the debt owed British merchants from America was reduced from six million sterling at the end of 1774 to only two million at the end of 1775 by the exertions of correspondents and debtors in America.[111] Champion's picture may have been true for the Quaker merchants he knew who traded primarily to Pennsylvania and New York, but it was not as true for the American trade elsewhere. The reduction of debt to Britain in the Chesapeake colonies between 1774 and 1775 was probably only about one-third instead of Champion's two-thirds.[112] This, of course, left a large body of unsettled debt to plague British-American relations in the two decades after the war. Yet the remarkable thing is how little of this touched the Quakers. No postwar debt claims were filed on behalf of the Barclays, the Bevans, or the Bristol Harfords.[113] Harford & Powell of London in 1804 filed a single claim for one partially paid debt in South Carolina.[114] Although an unofficial 1790 compilation showed that Hanburys were still owed £46,340 plus interest and Mildred & Robert £68,126 plus interest,[115] both must have been able to collect a good bit of this in the 1790s for they filed claims in 1804 for only £12,802 and £7,111 (plus interest) respectively.[116] But even though Friends had better fortune than other merchants in collecting their prewar debts, they could sense that the moral climate had changed. With the future collection of debts less certain, trading to America now did transgress the Quaker injunctions against improvident risks. Hence the withdrawal from this trade by the great Friends of London after 1783. (Other trades too had their risks and Quaker houses continued to fail. But the greatest crashes of the next century seemed to involve those in our families who were no longer Quakers.)

Because of the Quaker antipathy for overtrading, Quaker success in business was rarely the work of a single brilliant individual, but more commonly the achievement of a family over several generations. Even those successes who made fortunes of about £100,000 in the generation after 1740 did not start from scratch. Most in fact started with £5–10,000 obtained by inheritance or dowry. There was no one in the London Quaker community of the eighteenth century who could be compared with the contemporary Anglicans, Sir Gilbert Heathcote or Sir Samuel Fludyer, who allegedly started with nothing and ended up with fortunes of £700,000 and £900,000 respectively.[117] Such fortunes usually involved much more politics than went with the Quaker style.

The ability of the family to accumulate over many generations was facilitated by Quaker inheritance and marriage patterns. Friends almost never practiced primogeniture. Some went to the opposite extreme and divided their estates evenly between all sons and daughters. Others left a little more to sons than to daughters and a little more still to the eldest son, yet by contemporary standards treated younger sons and daughters well.[118] This meant that one spendthrift heir could not waste a family fortune nor one ill-humored testator leave everything to strangers. If a younger son had more business ability than his elder brother, he would get the necessary stake to show what he could do.

More than any other Protestant body, the Society of Friends put an enormous emphasis upon endogamy, upon marrying one's own kind.[119] For the sons and daughters of the leading Quaker families of London this usually meant marrying into a small circle of similarly affluent Friends — though sincere Quakers put more emphasis on Friendship than on fortune. One gains the impression that most Quaker fathers, unlike John Eliot, did not want their daughters to stay spinsters and were tolerant of less affluent Quaker suitors for the hands of unmarried daughters over twenty-five. One of the elder David Barclay's daughters so situated married a farmer, and what appear to be comparable *mésalliances* were tolerated in the Gurnell, Hoare, and other families.[120]

Frequent intermarriage within a relatively restricted number of families tied almost all of our families into two extended cousinhoods: (1) a more important and closely linked alliance of the Barclay, Lloyd, Gurney, and Hanbury families (together with the more or less closely related Bell, Tritton, and Bevan families); and (2) a more peripheral and less integrated group consisting of the Gurnell, Harman, (London) Harford, and Mildred families. The Hoares by their marriages provided a link between the two groups. The frequency of inside marriages in the first group created complicated kinship patterns with the marriage of first cousins a recognized problem by the early years of the nineteenth century. However, such a cousinhood proved an efficient communications network for placing surplus sons and funds, and for finding partners and lenders for banks and breweries and other companies.

These intricate cousinhoods were created in a relatively short time. None of our fourteen families was related to another in 1730. However, starting with the Barclay-Bevan alliance in the 1730s, gradually at first and more rapidly after 1750, the bonds were tied that eventually linked together all fourteen families, some closely, others more tangentially. The cousinhood was probably at its apogee in the early years of the nineteenth century when the will of David Barclay the younger, who died in 1809, left bequests to kith and kin named Barclay, Bevan, Tritton, Gurney, Lloyd, Hanbury, Falconer, Masterman, and Bell among those whom we have mentioned, as well as to kindred with other surnames we have had to neglect. The coherence of this system was, however, soon to be broken by the drift of so many cousins out of the Society of Friends.

The experience ultimately common to almost all these families between 1770 and 1870 was departure from the Society of Friends either by disownment or apostasy. Before 1790 the most common cause for such a break was marriage outside the Society, normally leading to disownment. Exceptions were few and the Society tried to make them fewer, so that marrying out led to separation for members of the Gurnell, Bevan, Tritton, Eliot, and Beaufoy families in these years. War created in patriotism an additional and frequent cause of disownment during the years 1793–1815. Enlistment or other participation in the war effort led to conspicuous breaks in the Gurney, Barclay, Lloyd, Harford, and Hanbury families.[121]

Patriotism is only one manifestation of the assimilative pull of the dominant national culture upon a small minority never numbering more than 60,000 souls (if that many) in the seventeenth and eighteenth centuries. The attractions of the circumambient culture were felt particularly keenly by these fourteen families whose wealth enabled them to move about, both geographically and socially. Sarah Hoare, the daughter of Samuel Hoare II, saw in retrospect that when her family moved from the Quaker *barrio* of Stoke Newington to the grander ambience of Hampstead, they had in fact moved from one world to another.[122] Even more did the acquisition of country properties pull the wealthier of our families out of the inward looking Quaker milieu and almost oblige them to mix with the neighboring Anglican gentry. Strict Quakers deplored hunting and shooting as a waste of time[123] — but the acquisition of country properties almost always brought with it the acquisition of a taste for country pastimes, shooting more frequently for the first generation than riding to hounds. In retrospect, though, shooting was usually just another step out of the Quaker community. So were the attractions of fashionable education. Young men sent to public school or university almost inevitably became Anglicans before they were thirty.

Finally, there was the *Zeitgeist*. In the mid-eighteenth century, modern writers have suggested, the only real choice for most Friends was Quakerism or indifference. And most stayed Quaker, though not necessarily the best of Friends. By the early nineteenth century, new alternatives were presented by the rise of the evangelical movement. While traditional Quak-

erism was inner-directed, quietist, and inward-looking, evangelicalism was
Bible based, enthusiastically hortatory and missionary, and socially active.
In the early years of the nineteenth century, the evangelical spirit made
itself felt in the Church of England and most Protestant dissenting bodies,
increasing the isolation of traditional Quakerism. Some Friends responded
to the new *Zeitgeist* by urging Quakers to become socially active too, whether
in the antislavery movement[124] or with Elizabeth Fry in prison reform.
Such activism, however, brought Friends into even closer association with
evangelicals. Some like Elizabeth Fry's brother Joseph John Gurney sought
to move still closer by developing a more evangelical variety of Quakerism, alien to the older tradition.[125] These and analagous efforts led to serious disputes within the Society of Friends which lie outside the scope of
this essay. However, the very fact that these disputes were dividing the
Friends must have helped destroy what was left of the sense of cohesion in
many parts of the Quaker community. Some of the Lloyds of Birmingham
reacted by joining the Plymouth Brethren.[126] Far more common among
the families studied here was the move toward the evangelical wing of the
Church of England. Thus, the religious coherence of these Quaker families
was broken in the first quarter of the nineteenth century. By the end of the
century, hardly a trace of Quakerism was left among them.

With Quakerism gone, endogamy followed in due course, as did the
old restricted choice of occupations. Although legal disabilities no longer
kept Quakers out of public positions, only departure from the Society of
Friends could open up the full range of opportunities in church and state
and thus effect the final integration of these families into the national upper
middle class. The generation of the break almost inevitably produced an
army officer or clergyman of the establishment. Soon almost every family
had its quota of canons and colonels, with many adding later a sprinkling
of university dons and higher civil servants. Some were even to produce
bishops, admirals, and ambassadors. But, as readers of E. Digby Baltzell
might have predicted, politics was not much more attractive to ex-Quakers
than it had been to their Quaker predecessors. I am aware of only two
cabinet ministers produced by these families: W. E. Forster, a great-grandson of Osgood Hanbury, and Sir Samuel Hoare, foreign secretary in the
1930s, a direct descendant of the Samuel Hoare who left Cork for London
in the 1740s to join the firm of his father-in-law, Jonathan Gurnell.

What residue did the experience of several generations in the Society
of Friends leave behind in these families? The Quaker qualities of moderation, prudence, sobriety, responsibility, and dependability were not, of
course, virtues unappreciated in the marketplace. They were qualities particularly suitable for modern banking, both private and corporate. In addition to the Quaker family banks already mentioned which were founded in
London, Bristol, and Norwich before 1780, numerous others were to be
started in the early years of the nineteenth century. A good number of both

creations survived through the century to be absorbed at the end into one of the big joint-stock banks, particularly Lloyds or Barclays. But the families did not disappear. Their names can not only be found recurring with startling frequency among bank directors in this century[127] but appear as well in the latest editions of *Burke's Landed Gentry* or *Who's Who*. Excluding families who were foreign (the Hopes) or who ceased being Quaker in the seventeenth century (the Crowleys) or who only entered our story in the 1790s or later (the Allens and Howards), we have concentrated in this essay upon fourteen families. Three of them (Gurnell, Bland, and Eliot) became extinct rather early in the direct male line. Of the remaining eleven, eight can be found today in *Burke's Peerage* or *Landed Gentry* (Barclay, Bevan, Gurney, Hanbury, Harford, Hoare, Lloyd, and Tritton), while one more (Harman) turns up in *Who's Who*. This leaves a question mark about only two (Beaufoy and Mildred) of our fourteen. Though the measurement is crude, one wonders whether any other comparable bourgeois group in the eighteenth century could be found with an equivalent rate of conspicuous or status survival.

We do not want to suggest that these families are timeless units pursuing consistent family strategies over centuries. Yet the problem of family strategy, both career choice and investment choice, may well be timeless. The most interesting thing about our fourteen Quaker families is that they followed similar family strategies and experienced similar patterns of social evolution in the century between 1725 and 1825. The study of such clusters of families thus appears to be a useful way to analyze more generally the evolution of the upper middle class.

NOTES

1. For earlier studies of this general problem, see Isabel Grubb, *Quakerism and Industry Before 1800* (London, 1930); Arthur Raistrick, *Quakers in Science and Industry* (London, 1950); Paul Herman Emden, *Quakers in Commerce* (London, [1940]).

2. For the earlier Barclays, see George B. Burnet, *The Story of Quakerism in Scotland 1650-1850* (London, 1952), pp. 82-91; Charles Wright Barclay, Hubert F. Barclay, and Alice Wilson-Fox, *A History of the Barclay Family . . . from 1066 to 1924* (London, 1924-34), 3:1-97 on Col. David Barclay, and pp. 98-191 on Robert Barclay the Apologist; John E. Pomfret, *The Province of East New Jersey 1609-1702* (Princeton, 1962), passim; *PWP*, 1:274-76, 367-70, 374-76, 425-46.

3. On David Barclay of Cheapside, see Barclay, *Barclay Family*, 3:235-47. For David Barclay as a "Scots factor" in London, see Alastair J. Durie, *The Scottish Linen Industry in the Eighteenth Century* (Edinburgh, 1979) pp. 47-48. Barclay was also interested in a linen manufacturing firm in Montrose in the 1740s.

4. Information supplied by Professor Louis M. Cullen. For the Irish-English linen trade, see his *Anglo-Irish Trade 1660-1800* (Manchester, 1968).

5. When David Barclay the elder died in 1769, the *Gentleman's Magazine* (39:168) reported that he had "had the singular honour of receiving at his home in Cheapside three successive kings when at their accession they favoured the city with their royal presence." Shortly before his death in 1809, David Barclay the younger also com-

mented upon "the Royal Family's coming to my father's house to view therefrom Lord Mayor's Show (which Queen Anne, George I, and George II had done, the two latter when my father lived in the house, which was supposed to have been the most convenient one for the purpose)" (quoted in W. H. Bidwell, *Annals of an East Anglian Bank* [Norwich, 1900], pp. 28-29). Because of its location and suitable balcony, the house had from its construction after the Great Fire been used for such royal visits long before David Barclay bought it: by Charles II, William and Mary in 1689, and Anne in 1708 (see Morris Charles Jones, *Reminiscences Connected with Old Oak Panelling Now at Gungrog* [Welshpool, 1864], pp. 11-19). However, Barclay (*Barclay Family*, 3:235) found "no record" of a visit of George II, not to mention George I. It is true that the London newspapers in reporting the visit of the royal family to the City in Oct. 1727 recorded only that they watched the show from the balcony of a house in Cheapside near Bow Church (see *Historical Register*, 12 [1727]:279; *Daily Courant*, no. 8130 [31 Oct. 1727]; *Weekly Journal* [4 Nov. 1727]; *London Journal* [4 Nov. 1727]). However, Samuel Powel, Jr., of Philadelphia in a letter to David Barclay good humoredly ascribed the latter's neglect of some business to the fact that "thee was so well Employ'd about Entertaining their Majesties . . . that thee forgott all thy friends here. . . . however we had the pleasure to hear your Guests was very well pleased" (Powel to Barclay, 17 Mar. 1727/8, Samuel Powel, Jr., Letterbook, 1:14, HSP). For evidence that George I most likely also visited the Barclays in 1714, see Jones, *Reminiscences,* p. 19; Spencer Cowper, ed., *Diary of Mary Countess Cowper, Lady of the Bedchamber to the Princess of Wales 1714-1720,* 2d ed. (London, 1865), p. 11. There is considerable literature on the visit of George III to the Barclays of Cheapside in 1761. See *Gentleman's Magazine,* 78 (Dec. 1808):1068-70; J. Herbert Tritton, *Tritton: The Place and the Family* (London, 1907), pp. 287-304; Audrey Nona Gamble, *A History of the Bevan Family* (London, 1924), pp. 33-37; Bidwell, *Annals,* pp. 28-33.

6. John Falconer or Falconar was the son of David Falconar mentioned above. David Falconar and Robert Barclay the Apologist married sisters. See William F. Miller, ed., "Gleanings from the Record of the Yearly Meeting of Aberdeen, 1672 to 1786," *JFHS,* 8 (1911):41n-42n; John Falconer's will proved 2 Jan. 1729/30 in which he leaves 20 guineas to his cousin and executor, David Barclay, Prob.11/635 (P.C.C. 7 Auber), PRO.

7. *Gentleman's Magazine,* 3 (1733):268.

8. A good view of David Barclay's transatlantic business can be found in Samuel Powel, Jr.'s Letterbooks (1727-47) in the HSP, esp. 1:3, 8, 14, 18, 45, 50, 58, 61, 71, 80, 88, 106, 114, 155, 181-82 and passim. In a letter to J. Simpson, 16 May 1728 (ibid., 1:32-33), Powel recommended Barclay as "better Acquainted with our Trade than any Draper in Londo[n]." For a later view, see the Jones & Wister invoice book, 1759-62, HSP. Barclays sometimes acted as mercantile correspondents for Jones & Wister of Philadelphia, purchasing up to £2,000 worth of textiles at a time and charging a 2.5 % commission. By contrast, no commission was usually charged on goods ordered by Richard Waln, indicating that Barclays supplied these from their own warehouse stock. Richard Waln's English invoice book 1762-68, and letter book, 1766-94, HSP; see also Owen Jones, Jr., invoice book, HSP.

9. Joshua Johnson in 1771 described the Barclay firm as "undoubtedly the first house in their business [linens]; they will not open an account with anyone in our trade but Hanbury. They have 2 or 3 ships that runs from Philadelphia and New York which they load with goods, likewise ship large quantities to the West Indies which is all they do." Jacob M. Price, ed., *Joshua Johnson's Letterbook, 1771-1774: Letters from a Merchant in London to His Partners in Maryland,* London Record Society, vol. 15 (London, 1979), p. 38. There are interesting letters to D. & J. Barclay from America in the Gurney Papers, RQG 546-47, NNRO.

10. Barclay, *History of the Barclay Family*, 3:242.

11. Ibid., 3:234-35, 242-43.

12. Jacob M. Price, *Capital and Credit in British Overseas Trade: The View from the Chesapeake, 1700-1776* (Cambridge, Mass., 1980), pp. 71-74, 182; P. W. Matthews and A. W. Tuke, *History of Barclays Bank* (London, 1926), pp. 32-38. The will of James Barclay with revealing codicils on the incompetence of his sons is in Prob.11/919 (P.C.C. 210 Tyndal), PRO.

13. For communal activities of David Barclay, see Anne Thomas Gary (afterwards Pannell), *The Political and Economic Relations of English and American Quakers* (D. Phil. thesis, Oxford University, 1935), pp. 34-35, 46, 86; Joseph J. Green, ed., *Souvenir of the Address to King Edward VII, 1901: The Right of the Society of Friends to Present Addresses in Person to the Sovereign 1654-1901* (London, [1901]), pp. 45, 46, 48-51; *Political State of Great Britain*, 36 (1728):578-79.

14. In the Dickinson Collection in HSP is a note in the hand of William Lee listing the relatively few North American merchants of London considered "friendly to the Liberties of Am[eric]a" in 1775. Prominent in the list are the Quakers D. & J. Barclay, Mildred & Roberts, Harford & Powell, Richard Neave, and "Chapman, Son in Law to the late Wm Neate." See Gary, "English and American Quakers", pp. 244-49, 294-336; Barclay, *Barclay Family*, pp. 243-44; Betsey C. Corner and Christopher C. Booth, eds., *Chains of Friendship: Selected Letters of Dr. John Fothergill of London, 1735-1780* (Cambridge, Mass., 1971), pp. 27-29, 257-64, 434n, 443-44, 447, 461-63; Green, *Souvenir*, pp. 51-52.

15. Matthews and Tuke, *Barclays Bank*, pp. 38-39; Barclay, *History of the Barclay Family*, pp. 243, 249-50; D. & J. Barclay to Pemberton & Reeves, 5 Feb. 1765, in Pemberton Papers, 17:157, HSP; D. & J. Barclay to I. Pemberton, 28 June 1770, in ibid., 22:22; D. & J. Barclay to J. Pemberton, 14 Jan. 1771, in ibid., 22:92. David Barclay withdrew from the Cheapside linendrapery and mercantile firm in 1781, leaving it a partnership between his brother John and his nephew Robert Barclay, a partner from 1773. There are indications of the firm's declining activity in Robert Barclay's "Private Ledger", FLL. The winding up ledger of the Cheapside firm is in the Barclay Perkins Papers in the Greater London Record Office; see also D. & J. Barclay to I. Pemberton, 12 Feb. 1773, in Pemberton Papers, 24:114, HSP.

16. James Boswell, *Life of Johnson*, ed. G. B. Hill and L. F. Powell (Oxford, 1934-50), 4:86-87, 488-89; Barclay Perkins & Co. Ltd., *Three Centuries: the Story of our Ancient Brewery*, comp. Bernard W. Cockes and William Cook (London, 1951), pp. 3-24; Peter Mathias, *The Brewing Industry in England 1700-1830* (Cambridge, 1959), pp. 265-74, 287-94. When the brewery became a public company in 1895-96, its first board of directors included two Barclays, three Bevans, and one Perkins. From 1748 to 1846 it was usually the first or second largest brewery in London. Robert Barclay's Private Ledger in FLL shows profits of £25,000 p.a. during 1792/3-1802/3, or 18.5 % on the £135,000 investment.

17. David Barclay, *An Account of the Emancipation of the Slaves of Unity Valley Pen, in Jamaica* (London, 1801); *Gentleman's Magazine*, 53:1 (1783), pp. 267, 535; James Jenkins's "Record and Recollections," pp. 741-42, FLL; obituary from *Morning Chronicle*, no. 12,501 (5 June 1809), reprinted in Bidwell, *Annals*, pp. 395-98. His political correspondence on the eve of the American Revolution is in Gurney Papers, RQG 536, NNRO.

18. Barclay, *History of the Barclay Family*, 3:245-46; Bidwell, *Annals*, pp. 74-76.

19. Barclay, *History of the Barclay Family*, 3:266, 278. No male Barclay of the banking family had an obituary published in the Quaker *Monitor* after Ford Barclay in 1859. Joseph J. Green, ed., *Quaker Records: Being an Index to "The Annual Monitor"*, *1813-1892* (London, 1894).

20. Gamble, *Bevan Family*, pp. 15-32, 37-43; "The Quaker Family of Bevan," *JFHS*, 22 (1925):15-16; Ernest C. Cripps, *Plough Court: the Story of a Notable Phar-*

macy 1715-1927 (London, 1927), pp. 7-16. On the bust of Penn, see William I. Hull, *William Penn: A Topical Biography* (New York, 1937), pp. 300-301, 304.

21. Gamble, *Bevan Family*, pp. 41-59, 128-29, 136-37; *Burke's Landed Gentry; Who's Who* (1985); *Directory of Directors* (1980).

22. Tritton, *Tritton Family*, pp. 84-141.

23. *Gentleman's Magazine*, 73 (1803):795. On Peter Collinson and his brother, see *DNB;* Norman G. Brett-James, *Peter Collinson, F.R.S., F.S.A., an Eighteenth Century Quaker Botanist and His Circle of Friends* (London, [1924]); *JFHS.*, 23 (1926): 38, 42-44, 52.

24. Prob.11/1011 (P.C.C. 367 Alexander), PRO.

25. For the bankruptcy papers of Brown, Collinson & Tritton, see B.3/814- 5, PRO. The bank's clientele appeared to be heavily provincial, even rural, in contrast to Barclays which was much more "City" and mercantile.

26. Tritton, *Tritton Family*, pp. 173-83, 190-93, 198 passim; Matthews and Tuke, *Barclays Bank*, pp. 389-90; *Who's Who* (1985).

27. Tritton, *Tritton Family*, pp. 189-90, 193-96, 201-3, 227-28, 233-34, 249, 255, 261. George Tritton apparently made enough out of the brewery to enable his son and grandson to live as fashionable rentiers.

28. Gurneys in the *DNB* include John, "the weavers' friend" (d. 1741); Elizabeth (Fry); her brothers Daniel, Joseph John, and Samuel; her cousin Hudson; and his sister Anna.

29. *DNB*, s.v. "Gurney, John"; *Gentleman's Magazine*, 11 (1741):50; Daniel Gurney, *The Records of the House of Gournay* (London, 1848-58), pp. 504, 508, 540-44, 551-55, but see *JFHS*, 32 (1935):81-82; Augustus J. C. Hare, *The Gurneys of Earlham* (London, 1895), p. 10; Bidwell, *Annals*, p. 9; J. K. Edwards, "The Gurneys and the Norwich Clothing Trade in the Eighteenth Century," *JFHS*, 50 (1963):134. According to Edwards, the first John Gurney "as early as 1680, had provided work for above two hundred persons."

30. John and Henry Gurney are described in a newspaper advertisement of 1756 as dealers in Irish and English linens, canvas, and cottons (*JFHS*, 32 [1935]:42n). They are, however, described by modern writers as woolen man- ufacturers, e.g., Bidwell, *Annals*, pp. 13, 18; Hare, *Gurneys of Earlham*, p. 10; Edwards, "The Gurneys and Clothing Trade," p. 134.

31. Bidwell, *Annals*, pp. 18-21.

32. D. Gurney, *Records*, pp. 523, 556-57, 562-63; Edwards, "The Gurneys and Clothing Trade," pp. 134-52 (with a few slips on financial details). Bidwell (*Annals*, p. 9) quotes from the diary of Hudson to the effect that when the first John Gurney (the prisoner) died in 1721, he was worth £20,000; when his grandson, John Gurney of Keswick, died in 1770, he was worth £100,000, while in 1850 his grandson (Hudson Gurney) was worth £800,000. The "Private Account Book" of John Gurney of Keswick, however, shows that on 31 Dec. 1769 his net worth was £81,200 (Gurney Papers, RQG 300, 302, NNRO; see RQG 298, no. 1, for his stock in 1741). The style of the firm was Joseph Gurney & Son in the 1740's; John, Samuel & Joseph Gurney, 1751-63; John, Samuel & Richard Gurney, 1764-70; Richard & John Gurney in the 1770s and Gurney & Bland in the 1780s. The financial correspondents in London of John, Samuel & Joseph Gurney were the firm of their brother-in-law, Timothy Bevan & Son, pharmacists of Plough Court, but the account was transferred in 1773 to the bank of Smith, Bevan & Bening in which Timothy's son Silvanus was a partner, and in which John Gurney Jr. was trained. RQG 495-96, 505-7, NNRO; David E. Swift, *Joseph John Gurney: Banker, Reformer and Quaker* (Middletown, Conn., 1962), pp. 70-71.

33. Bidwell, *Annals*, pp. 21-25, 38-40, 59; RQG 495-96, 505-7, NNRO. The Bland in Gurney & Bland was Thomas Bland, a former employee who in 1775

married the widow of Samuel Gurney (d. 1770). Thomas Bland's descendants remained active in the direction of the Gurney bank and Barclays Bank Ltd. to the present day. See *Burke's Landed Gentry* (1966) s.v. "Bland of Copdock."

34. Hare, *Gurneys of Earlham,* 1:273, 328; 2:89 and passim; Swift, *J. J. Gurney,* pp. 16, 92; *JFHS,* 34 (1937):35-38. The careers, particularly post-1820, of the Gurneys of Earlham lie outside the scope of this essay. There are many biographies of Elizabeth Fry, the most recent of which is June Rose, *Elizabeth Fry* (London, 1980). For her brother Joseph John Gurney, see Swift, *Joseph John Gurney, Banker.* There is also a considerable literature on Overend, Gurney & Co., including Bidwell, *Annals,* pp. 77-88, 109, 241-44, 250-54; and W. T. C. King, *History of the London Discount Market* (London, 1936), pp. 238-56.

35. There is a good account of the descendants of Maj. Edward Hoare in L. G. Pine, *The New Extinct Peerage* (Baltimore, 1973), pp. 264-66. An older account dependable for Edward's descendants but not his antecedents is Edward Hoare, *Some Account of . . . the Families of Hore and Hoare* (London, 1883), esp. pp. 8, 36-43; see also *Burke's Landed Gentry.* For a more impressionistic account of the family by a direct descendant, see Samuel John Gurney Hoare, Viscount Templewood, *The Unbroken Thread* (New York, 1950).

36. MSS. 31, 31A, ledger and journal of Samuel Hoare, University College Library, Cork.

37. Joseph Joshua Green, "Biographical and Historical Notices of Jonathan Gurnell of London, Merchant, and of . . . Grizell Wilmer, His Wife, and Their Family and Descendants" (1914 typescript in BL), pp. 1-7, 11-19, 25-28. For a time John's brother Jeremiah Harman was also in the firm which appears in the directories as Harmans.

38. Green (see n. 37, above) refers to them primarily as Portuguese merchants, but Thomas Mortimer, *The Universal Director* (London, 1763), lists them as Dutch and Irish merchants. Their interests were European in scope.

39. Samuel Hoare's retirement as early as 1774 is suggested by his ledger and journal (see n. 36, above). He received no distributions of profits on business after 1774.

40. Templewood, *Unbroken Thread,* pp. 32-33; Sarah and Hannah Hoare, *Memoirs of Samuel Hoare by his Daughter Sarah and his Widow Hannah,* ed. F. R. Pryor (London, 1911), pp. 6-8; F. G. Hilton Price, *A Handbook of London Bankers,* 2d ed. (London, 1890-91), pp. 13-14; Richard S. Sayers, *Lloyds Bank in the History of English Banking* (Oxford, 1957), pp. 43-45.

41. Hoare, *Memoirs of Samuel Hoare,* p. 25; Templewood, *Unbroken Thread,* p. 56; Green, "Jonathan Gurnell," p. 57.

42. Nicholas Carlisle, *Collections for a History of the Ancient Family of Bland* (London, 1826), p. 205. The family was originally from Maidwell, Northants., and Elias Bland named his estate in New Jersey "Maidwell." John Bland, Jr., married Margaret, sister of Thomas Bland of Gurney & Bland, Norwich. Thomas's family was originally from Yorkshire. On Elias Bland, see Carl L. Romanek, "John Reynell, Quaker Merchant of Colonial Philadelphia" (Ph.D. diss., Pennsylvania State University, 1969), pp. 53, 71-73, 82, 84-85, 115, 132-33; *Gentleman's Magazine,* 17 (1747):544; 58:2 (1788):939; E. Bland to James Pemberton, 4 Aug. 1743, Pemberton Papers, 3:85ff, HSP; see also S. Powel to J. Bland, 6 Dec. 1736, Powel letterbook, 1:402, HSP, for Powel's refusal to take E. Bland as apprentice. Stamper Bland's banking partners in 1754 were John Plumstead and Richard Sargeant (S. Bland to J. Pemberton, 18 Aug. 1754, Pemberton Papers, 9:32, HSP). From 1757 the firm was known as Bland, Gray & Stephenson. After Stamper Bland's death in 1762, the directories show it as Smith, Wright & Gray. There was another Quaker John Bland active in London, c. 1763-74. He was a Virginia merchant related to the Blands of Virginia but not to these Blands.

43. Hoare, *Memoirs of Samuel Hoare*, pp. 35-39; Templewood, *Unbroken Thread*, pp. 72-73.

44. Green, "Jonathan Gurnell," pp. 26-27, 43-48, 63-64.

45. Marten G. Buist, *At Spes non Fracta: Hope & Co. 1770-1815: Merchant Bankers and Diplomats at Work* (The Hague, 1974), pp. 4-18, 49; Henry William Law and Irene Law, *The Book of the Beresford Hopes* (London, 1925), p. 15; William I. Hull, *Benjamin Furly and Quakerism in Rotterdam* (Swarthmore, Pa., 1941), pp. 247-53. Some of Hull's family data are questionable.

46. Buist, *Hope & Co.*, passim; Paul Walden Bamford, *Forests and French Sea Power 1660-1789* (Toronto, 1965), pp. 143-47. Both firms were also heavily involved with the London Scots merchant, banker, and speculator Alexander Fordyce and lost heavily at the time of his failure in 1772. Buist (*Hope & Co.*, pp. 21-22) reports that they were £50,000 in advance at the crash, as Thomas Bland reported at the time (T. Bland to R. Gurney, 15 June 1772, Gurney MSS., I:93, FLL). For the 1790s, see (besides Buist) John M. Sherwig, *Guineas and Gunpowder: British Foreign Aid in the Wars with France 1793-1815* (Cambridge, Mass., 1969), pp. 46-48, 119-20, 127n: P.R.O.30/8/142 fols. 162-92, PRO.

47. Green, "Jonathan Gurnell," pp. 8-10; D. Morier Evans, *The Commercial Crisis, 1847-1848,* 2d ed. (London, 1849), pp. 48-50; app., pp. i-iv.

48. Raistrick, *Quakers in Science and Industry,* chaps. 4-6.

49. Arthur Raistrick, *Two Centuries of Industrial Welfare: The London (Quaker) Lead Company, 1692-1905* (London, 1938), pp. 134-35, 140, 148.

50. Charles K. Hyde, *Technological Change and the British Iron Industry* (Princeton, 1977), p. 16.

51. Michael W. Flinn, *Men of Iron: The Crowleys in the Early Iron Industry* (Edinburgh, 1962), pp. 8-23.

52. Ibid., pp. 31-76, 224 and passim.

53. Ibid., pp. 144-45. The Crowleys were also substantial buyers of the pig iron which came home as ballast in the tobacco ships from Virginia.

54. See J. M. Price, *Capital and Credit*, pp. 117-18.

55. Humphrey Lloyd, *The Quaker Lloyds in the Industrial Revolution* (London, 1975), pp. 3-31. Among the Pennsylvania cousins who visited the Lloyds, c. 1708-9, were Isaac Norris and James Logan (ibid., p. 88). On Thomas Lloyd, see also *DAB;* Tolles, *Meeting House,* pp. 120-21.

56. H. Lloyd, *Quaker Lloyds,* pp. 33-61.

57. Ibid., pp. 67-95.

58. Ibid., pp. 96-150.

59. Ibid., pp. 163-69; Sayers, *Lloyds Bank,* pp. 5-10, 24-27.

60. Between 1801, when Nehemiah Lloyd died, and 1812 his brothers Sampson III and Charles gradually withdrew from the iron manufacturing business. They never attempted coke smelting. H. Lloyd, *Quaker Lloyds,* pp. 210-15.

61. Ibid., p. 181.

62. Ibid., pp. 97-99, 106-10, 144, 151, 187-93. Charles Lloyd served an apprenticeship with Barclays in Cheapside; his brother Sampson III married Rachel, daughter of Samuel Barnes, a prosperous Spitalfields silk-dyer.

63. Ibid., p. 186.

64. Jenkins "Records & Recollections," pp. 706-7, FLL.

65. H. Lloyd, *Quaker Lloyds,* p. xi.

66. Amy Audrey Locke, *The Hanbury Family* (London, 1916), 2:232, 239, 248-49, 288-89.

67. London County Council, *Survey of London,* vols. 12, 15, *All Hallows Barking* (London, 1922, 1934), 2:30 and plates.

68. Locke, *Hanbury Family,* 2:249-50, 252, 289, corrected by Prob. 11/511 (P.C.C. 251 Lane), and Prob. 11/637 (P.C.C. 135 Auber), PRO. On the lead of the Hanbury firms in 1747, see T. 1/326 fols. 133-46, PRO.

69. See Aubrey C. Land, *The Dulanys of Maryland* (Baltimore, 1955), pp. 232, 235, 279; *The Calvert Papers* (Baltimore, 1889-99), 2:201, 207, 209-10, 224-26; *Archives of Maryland,* vols. 6, 9, *Correspondence of Governor Horatio Sharpe* (Baltimore, 1888, 1890), 1:15, 66-67, 72-74, 109-11, 120, 131, 184-85, 394-95; 2:34-36, 38-43, 88-89.

70. Barclay, *Barclay Family,* 3:251-52; Corner, *Letters of Fothergill,* pp. 246-47. There are a good number of letters from John Hanbury to the duke of Newcastle in the Newcastle Papers, BL, e.g., Hanbury to Newcastle, 14 June 1754, Add. MS. 32,735, fol. 462.

71. [John Shebbeare], *A Letter to the People of England on the Present Situation and Conduct of National Affairs, Letter I* (London, 1755), pp. 33-43; Gary, "Quaker Relations," pp. 64-76; Winthrop Sargent, *History of an Expedition Against Fort Du Quesne* (Philadelphia, 1855), pp. 103-11, 161-62. There are a mass of references to John Hanbury's role in the Ohio Company in *George Mercer Papers Relating to the Ohio Company of Virginia* (Pittsburgh, 1954). I expect to investigate this whole question more fully in a later paper on the Hanburys.

72. There were two remittance contracts: one of 29 Nov. 1754 with John Thomlinson and John Hanbury covering £489,797; the other of 28 July 1756 with Thomlinson, Hanbury, Arnold Nesbitt, and Sir George Colebrooke covering £3,563,642. The final accounting can be found in A.O. 1/190/592, 593, PRO. For some of the troubles with these contracts, see also T. 1/456, fols. 333-34; T. 1/656/999, fols. 279-87, PRO.

73. See London directories and T.S. 11/689/2186, fols. 2, 49, PRO.

74. Hanbury & Lloyd to J. P. Custis, 7 May 1775, Custis Papers, Virginia Historical Society.

75. Gosling letterbook, 1769-1774, Truman, Hanbury & Buxton Papers, Greater London Record Office; London *directories.* Hanbury & Gosling disappeared after Osgood's death in 1784.

76. Sayers, *Lloyds Bank,* pp. 10-11 and passim; Lloyd, *Quaker Lloyds,* pp. 170-71, 272-74; F. G. H. Price, *London Bankers,* pp. 77, 102.

77. Barclay, *Barclay Family,* 3:251-52; Locke, *Hanbury Family,* 2:254-55; see also *JFHS,* 13 (1916):165.

78. Prob. 11/1113 (P.C.C. 79 Rockingham), PRO for O. Hanbury's will. His executors were David Barclay the younger, Richard Gurney of Keswick, and his partner John Lloyd.

79. Mathias, *Brewing Industry,* pp. 274-75, 294-95, 297-98; *Trumans the Brewers, 1666-1966: The Story of Truman Hanbury Buxton & Co. Ltd.* (London, 1966), pp. 22-27, 44-45, 53, 59. The Hanbury interest disappeared after the chairmanship of J. M. Hanbury, 1911-23, but in 1966 there were still four Buxtons on the board representing a sixth generation family association with the brewery.

80. For Capel Hanbury's will, see Prob. 11/949 (P.C.C. 210 Bogg), PRO.

81. See Georgina Charlotte Clive, Lady Chapman, "The Bell Family," typescript in FLL.

82. Locke, *Hanbury Family,* 2:290-92. His brewery was Hanbury & Smith of 48 Whitecross Street, London, mentioned in the London *directories,* c. 1783-1800.

83. William Allen came from a familiar Quaker background: his father was a silk manufacturer, his uncle a brewer. See Clement Young Sturge, ed., *Leaves from the Past: The Diary of John Allen . . . 1777* (Bristol and London, 1905), p. xiv; Cripps, *Plough Court,* pp. 25-66 and passim.

84. Locke, *Hanbury Family,* 2:257-58, 263, 277, 279, 290.

85. Ibid., 2:297-300, 304, 306; Cripps, *Plough Court,* pp. 90-92. The break appears to have come first with Cornelius Hanbury's son Cornelius II (1827-1916) after the elder Cornelius's death in 1869. However, Sir Thomas Hanbury (1832-1907), son of Daniel Bell Hanbury, was a member of the Society of Friends at his death.

86. Gwendolyn Beaufoy, *Leaves from a Beech Tree* (Oxford, 1930), pp. 65-133 and passim; Sir Lewis Namier and John Brooke, *The History of Parliament: The House of Commons, 1754-1790* (London and New York, 1964), 2:72-73. The last Beaufoy active in the vinegar works was killed in a bombing raid in 1941; the works survive today as part of British Vinegars Ltd. See Barbara Kerr, *The Dispossessed: An Aspect of Victorian Social History* (London and New York, 1974), chap. 4.

87. Alice Harford, *Annals of the Harford Family* (London, 1909), pp. 23-30. The Bristol port book for 1680 (E. 190/1141/3, PRO) shows Charles Harford importing 88,648 pounds of tobacco.

88. Harford, *Annals,* pp. 31-32, 162 (with Beatrice erroneously described as daughter of John instead of Jeremiah Harman); T. 79/20 (claims of John Harford), PRO ; Owen Jones, Jr., invoice book, and Richard Waln's English invoice book, 1762-68, HSP; Hoare, *Memoirs of Samuel Hoare,* p. 22; D. & J. Barclay to Pemberton & Reeves, 5 Feb. 1765, in Pemberton Papers, 17:157, HSP; D. & J. Barclay to Israel Pemberton Jr., 28 June 1770, in Ibid., 22:22.

89. Harford, *Annals,* pp. 33-36.

90. Charles Henry Cave, *A History of Banking in Bristol from 1750 to 1899* (Bristol, 1899), pp. 9-12. The founding partners in the first or Old Bank in Bristol included the Quaker Harford Lloyd, grandson of Charles Harford, Sr. The second or Miles's Bank included the Quakers Thomas Goldney and Richard Champion, both with Birmingham Lloyd connections.

91. J. M. Price, *Capital and Credit,* pp. 31-33.

92. Harford, *Annals,* p. 37; Joan Day, *Bristol Brass: A History of the Industry* (Newton Abbot, 1973), pp. 109-16.

93. Harford, *Annals,* p. 47 gives the figure £136,000; J. M. Price, *Capital and Credit,* p. 33, gives £156,511, citing Harford Papers, VIII/9 (estate papers, 1806), Bristol Archives Office.

94. Harford, *Annals,* pp. 39-40, 71.

95. Ibid., p. 63.

96. Thomas Mildred's account at the Bank of England (Drawing Office ledgers 140ff, Bank Record Office, Roehampton) shows dealings with export merchants to the Chesapeake such as Hyde, Forward, Hanbury, and Buchanan. See Prob. 6/129, PRO for administration (19 July 1753) granted to Daniel Mildred, only child of Thomas (and Rebecca) Mildred. For the Pennsylvania connection, see Jones & Wister invoice book, 1759-62, HSP; see also typescript "Dictionary of Quaker Biography," FLL, s.v. "Daniel Mildred (1731-1788)"; "Lydia (Daniel) Mildred (1738-1810)"; and "John Roberts."

97. London *directories;* F. G. H. Price, *London Bankers,* p. 113. Daniel Mildred's will of 8 Sept. 1786 (proved 23 Feb. 1788) refers to large sums owing in America to his former firm, Mildred & Roberts. See Prob. 11/1162 (P.C.C. 85 Calvert), PRO.

98. *Gentleman's Magazine,* 60:2 (1790):1146; Jenkins, "Records and Recollections," pp. 211, 280-81, 752, 920, 939-40, FLL.

99. Eliot Howard, *The Eliot Papers* (Gloucester, 1893-94), 1:1-6; J. M. Price, *Capital and Credit,* p. 32.

100. See note to this effect in Eliot Papers, 1017/929, 944, Greater London Record Office; see also Jenkins, "Record and Recollections," pp. 822-28, FLL. John Eliot III was a not very active "minister" of Peel Meeting.

101. Howard, *Eliot Papers*, 1:8-13, 56, 78, 93, 109-15; *Burke's Landed Gentry* (1966 ed.), s.v. "Howard of Ashmore."

102. *Kent's Directory for . . . 1779* shows: Barclay, Bevan & Bening; Bland, Barnett & Hoare; Brown, Collinson & Tritton; Hanbury, Taylor, Lloyd & Bowman; Mildred & Walker; Smith, Wright & Gray; and Staples, Baron Thomas Dimsdale, John Dimsdale & Josiah Barnard. On the last two firms, see Namier and Brooke, *House of Commons*, 2:325-26; Jenkins, "Record and Recollections," pp. 75, 211, 280-81, 410-25 and passim, FLL; F. G. H. Price, *London Bankers*, pp. 52-53.

103. Barclay, Bevan, Gurney, Hanbury, Harford (of London), and Tritton.

104. The firm of Barclay, Brothers & Co. (trading to Mauritius) in which a son and grandson of Robert Barclay I of Bury Hill were interested, failed in 1847. Barclay, *Barclay Family*, 3:277, 280-81, 286; Evans, *Commercial Crisis*, app., pp. xxv-xxvi.

105. Lloyd, *Quaker Lloyds*, pp. 210-15; Day, *Bristol Brass*, pp. 113-16.

106. See J. M. Price, *Capital and Credit*, chap. 6.

107. Society of Friends, *Extracts from the Minutes and Advices of the Yearly Meeting of Friends Held in London* (1802; reprint, London, 1822), pp. 143, 195-99, 200, 292; see also Ambrose Rigge, *A Brief and Serious Warning To Such as are Concerned in Commerce . . . Written . . . in the Year 1678* (London, 1771), pp. 1-4; Richard E. Stagg, "Friends' Queries and General Advices: A Survey of their Development in London Yearly Meeting, 1682-1860," *JFHS*, 49 (1961):209-35, esp. 231, 235; Grubb, *Quakerism and Industry*, pp. 38, 69-70, 77.

108. *Extracts from Minutes and Advices*, pp. 195-96, 199; Grubb, *Quakerism and Industry*, pp. 39, 86, 90; G. W. Edwards, "London Six Weeks Meeting," *JFHS*, 50 (1969):237; *Epistle from the Yearly Meeting, Held in London . . . 1769* (London, 1769), p. 3. The case is often cited of David Barclay of Cateaton Street (cousin of David Barclay the elder, of Cheapside), an insurance broker who failed but who, despite discharge from bankruptcy, spent the rest of his life repaying his prebankruptcy debts; see also *Gentleman's Magazine*, 53:2 (1783):717.

109. *Extracts from Minutes and Advices*, pp. 5-10.

110. "Extracts from the Journal of Joseph Fry, 1833-1857," *JFHS*, 28 (1931):47-49. Other Quaker businessmen disciplined by Friends for the nonpayment of debts included Henry Hope of Rotterdam in the 1680s and Charles Lloyd II of Dolobran in the 1730s.

111. Richard Champion, *Considerations on the Present Situation of Great Britain and the United States of America*, 2d ed. (London, 1784), p. 269n.; David Macpherson, *Annals of Commerce* (London, 1805), 3:581.

112. J. M. Price, *Capital and Credit*, p. 165, n. 13.

113. The claims presented to the binational commission in Philadelphia, c. 1797-98, are summarized in T. 79/123, PRO; the claims presented to the compensation commission in London, c. 1804, are summarized in T. 79/98, 118, PRO.

114. In 1797-98, Harford & Powell claimed 11 debts (£5,200) in South Carolina (see T. 79/123, n. 136, PRO). By 1804 this was reduced to a single claim for £1,215, allowed in full. T. 79/98, fol. 45, PRO.

115. P.R.O. 30/8/343, PRO.

116. T. 79/98, fols. 27, 124, 127; T. 79/118, fols. 93, 123, 124, 132, PRO.

117. On Sir Gilbert Heathcote (1652-1733), see *DNB*; Romney Sedgwick, *The History of Parliament: The House of Commons 1715-1754* (London and New York, 1970), 2:123; Jacob M. Price, *The Tobacco Adventure to Russia*, Transactions of the American Philosophical Society, vol. 51, no. 1 (Philadelphia, 1961), pp. 107 and passim. On Sir Samuel Fludyer (?1704-1768), see *DNB*; Namier and Brooke, *House of Commons*, 2:442-44.

118. See, for example, in PRO the wills of John Falconer, Prob. 11/635 (P.C.C. 7 Auber); Silvanus Grove (P.C.C. 24 Adderley); Capel Hanbury, Prob. 11/949 (P.C.C. 210 Bogg); Osgood Hanbury, Prob. 11/1113 (P.C.C. 79 Rockingham); Daniel Mildred, Prob. 11/1162 (P.C.C. 85 Calvert); see also Templewood, *Unbroken Thread,* p. 26.

119. *Extracts from Minutes and Advices,* pp. 62–72.

120. See the account of the Bell family cited in n. 81, above.

121. Emden, *Quakers in Commerce,* p. 100, adds Osgoods and Mastermans; see also Stagg, "Queries," p. 229; idem, "Marriages Out," *JFHS,* 43 (1951):37.

122. Hoare, *Memoirs of Samuel Hoare,* p. 22.

123. Yearly Meeting in 1795 urged that "our leisure be employed in serving our neighbour, and not in distressing the creatures of God for our amusement." *Extracts from Minutes and Advices,* pp. 20–25, no. 13.

124. The antislavery movement was, I believe, the last issue on which a noticeable number of our leading Quaker families of London acted together publicly. Among the founding members of the London Abolition Committee in 1787 were Samuel Hoare, Jr., his brother-in-law Joseph Wood, and John Lloyd, brother-in-law of Osgood Hanbury. See Roger Anstey, *The Atlantic Slave Trade and British Abolition 1760-1810* (Atlantic Highlands, N.J., 1975), pp. 231–32, 249n; see also n. 17, above, for D. Barclay's stand on this issue.

125. Stagg, "Queries," p. 225.

126. Lloyd, *Quaker Lloyds,* pp. 260–67.

127. The following families with direct patrilineal Quaker antecedents were represented on the board of Barclays Bank Ltd., 1896-1926, by two or more directors: Backhouse, Barclay, Bassett, Bevan, Birkbeck, Gurney, Mounsey, Pease, Seebohm, Tritton, and Tuke. In addition, the Buxtons, although not Quaker in the direct male line, were descended from the Quaker Hanburys and Gurneys. Matthews, *Barclays Bank,* p. 389.

Notes on Contributors

HUGH BARBOUR is Professor of Religion at Earlham College and Professor of Church History at Earlham School of Religion. His publications include *The Quakers in Puritan England* (1964); *Early Quaker Writings* (1973); "William Penn, Model of Protestant Liberalism," *Church History* (1979); and *Slavery and Theology: Writings of Seven Quaker Reformers, 1800–1870* (1985). He is currently collaborating with J. William Frost on a history of American Quakerism.

EDWIN B. BRONNER is Librarian, Professor of History, and Curator of the Quaker Collection at Haverford College. His publications include *William Penn's "Holy Experiment," The Founding of Pennsylvania, 1681–1701* (1962); *An English View of American Quakerism, The Journal of Walter Robson, 1877* (1970); *"The Other Branch": London Yearly Meeting and the Hicksites, 1827–1912* (1975); and *William Penn, 17th Century Founding Father* (1975). He is co-author of *William Penn's Published Writings: An Interpretive Bibliography, 1660–1726,* to be published in 1986 as the fifth volume of *The Papers of William Penn.*

NICHOLAS CANNY is Professor of Modern History in the National University of Ireland at University College, Galway. His publications include *The Elizabethan Conquest of Ireland: A Pattern Established, 1565–1576* (1976); *The Upstart Earl: A Study of the Social and Mental World of Richard Boyle, First Earl of Cork* (1982); and *From Reformation to Restoration: Ireland, 1534–1660* (1985). He is currently engaged upon a comparative study of British settlement in Ireland and North America, 1580–1650.

MARY MAPLES DUNN is President and Professor of History at Smith College. Her publications include *William Penn: Politics and Conscience* (1967); an edition of Alexander von Humboldt's *Political Essay on the Kingdom of New Spain* (1972); "Women of Light" in Carol Berkin and Mary Beth Norton, eds., *Women of America* (1979); and "Saints and Sisters: Congregational and Quaker Women in the Early Colonial Period," in Janet Wilson James, ed., *Women in American Religion* (1980). Since 1978 she has been co-editor of *The Papers of William Penn,* and she was the principal editor of the first volume in this series, published in 1981.

RICHARD S. DUNN is Roy F. and Jeannette P. Nichols Professor of American History at the University of Pennsylvania. His publications include *Puritans and Yankees: The Winthrop Dynasty of New England, 1630–1717* (1962); *Sugar and Slaves: The Rise of the Planter Class in the English West Indies, 1624–1713* (1972); and *The Age of Religious Wars, 1559–1715* (1979). Since 1978 he has been co-editor of *The Papers of William Penn,* and he was the principal editor of the second volume in this series, published in 1982.

MELVIN B. ENDY, JR. is Dean of the College and Professor of Religion at Hamilton College. His publications include *William Penn and Early Quakerism* (1973); and "Just War, Holy War, and Millennialism in Revolutionary America," *The William and Mary Quarterly* (1985). His two major areas of scholarly interest are colonial American religious history and the history of American religious and cultural attitudes toward war.

J. WILLIAM FROST is Jenkins Professor of Quaker History and Research at Swarthmore College, Director of the Friends Historical Library, and Editor of *The Pennsylvania Magazine of History and Biography.* His publications include *The Quaker Family in Colonial America* (1973); *The Keithian Controversy in Early Pennsylvania* (1980); and *Quaker Origins of Antislavery* (1981). He is currently collaborating with Hugh Barbour on a history of American Quakerism, and is also writing a history of religious liberty in Pennsylvania to the 1830s.

MICHAEL J. GALGANO is Professor of History and Head of the Department at James Madison University. He has published several articles on recusant and women's history, including "Negotiations for a Nun's Dowry: Restoration Letters of Mary Caryll, O.S.B. and Ann Clifton, O.S.B.," *American Benedictine Review* (1973); and "Iron-Mining in Restoration Furness: The Case of Sir Thomas Preston," *Recusant History* (1976). He is presently writing a social history of women during the Restoration era in Northwestern England.

FRANCIS JENNINGS is Director Emeritus, the D'Arcy McNickle Center for the History of the American Indian at the Newberry Library. His many publications include *The Invasion of America: Indians, Colonialism, and the Cant of Conquest (1975);* and *The Ambiguous Iroquois Empire: The Covenant Chain Confederation of Indian Tribes with English Colonies from its beginnings to the Lancaster Treaty of 1744* (1984). He is currently writing a history of the Seven Years War in America.

JAMES R. JONES is Professor of History in the School of English and American Studies at the University of East Anglia. His many publications include *The First Whigs: The Politics of the Exclusion Crisis, 1678–1683* (1961); *The Revolution of 1688 in England* (1972); *Court and Country* (1978); and *The Restored Monarchy* (1979). He is currently engaged on a study of Charles II, and a further work on the first Tories.

NED LANDSMAN is Associate Professor of History at the State University of New York at Stony Brook. His publications include " 'Of the Grand Assembly of Parliament': Thomas Rudyard's Critique of an Early Draft of The Frame of Government of Pennsylvania," in *Pennsylvania Magazine of History and Biography* (1981); and *Scotland and its First American Colony, 1685–1765* (1985). He is currently studying eighteenth-century Scottish religious revivalism.

BARRY LEVY is Assistant Professor of History at Case Western University. He is the author of "The Birth of the 'Modern Family' in Early America: Quaker and Anglican Families in the Delaware Valley, 1681–1750," in Michael Zuckerman, ed., *Friends and Neighbors: Group Life in America's First Plural Society* (1982); and " 'Tender Plants': Quaker Farmers and Children in the Delaware Valley, 1681–1735," in Stanley Katz and John Murrin, eds., *Colonial America: Essays in Politics and Social Development* (1983). He is currently completing a book on the transplanting of Quakers from Wales and Cheshire to early Pennsylvania.

GARY B. NASH is Professor of History at the University of California, Los Angeles. His many publications include *Quakers and Politics: Pennsylvania, 1681–1726* (1968); *The Urban Crucible: Social Change, Political Consciousness, and the Origins of the American Revolution* (1979); and *Race, Class and Politics: Essays on American Colonial and Revolutionary Society* (1986). His latest book, soon forthcoming, is entitled *Forging Freedom: The Black Urban Experience in Philadelphia, 1760–1820.*

JACOB M. PRICE is Professor of History at the University of Michigan. His many publications include *France and the Chesapeake: A History of the French Tobacco Monopoly, 1674–1791, and of its Relationship to the British and American Tobacco Trade* (1973); and *Capital and Credit in British Overseas Trade: The View from the Chesapeake, 1700–1776* (1980). He is broadly interested in British trade with America in the seventeenth and eighteenth centuries.

CAROLINE ROBBINS is Professor Emeritus of History at Bryn Mawr College. Her many publications include *The Eighteenth-Century Commonwealthman: Studies in the Transmission, Development and Circumstance of English Liberal Thought from the Restoration of Charles II until the War with the Thirteen Colonies* (1959); *Two English Republican Tracts* (1969); and *Absolute Liberty: A Selection from the Articles and Papers of Caroline Robbins*, ed. Barbara Taft (1982). Between 1968 and 1975, as chairman of the Committee on the Papers of William Penn, she supervised production of a microfilm edition of 2600 Penn documents, issued in 1975.

CAROLE SHAMMAS is Associate Professor of History at the University of Wisconsin–Milwaukee. Her publications include "How Self-Sufficient was Early America?," *Journal of Interdisciplinary History* (1982); "The Eighteenth-Century English Diet and Economic Change," *Explorations in Economic History* (1984); "Black Women's Work and the Evolution of Plantation Society in Virginia," *Labor History* (1985); and in collaboration with Marylynn Salmon and Michel Dahlin, *Inheritance, Family, and the Evolution of Capitalism in America* (1986). She is currently working on a book about consumer behavior in preindustrial times.

JOAN THIRSK was Reader in Economic History at the University of Oxford until 1983, and Professorial Fellow of St. Hilda's College; she is now an Honorary Fellow. She is General Editor of *The Agrarian History of England and Wales;* serving as volume editor and a contributor to vol. 4 in this series, *1500–1640* (1967); and in the same capacity for vol. 5, *1640–1750* (1984, 1985). Among her other publications is *Economic Policy and Projects: The Development of a Consumer Society in Early Modern England* (1978).

RICHARD T. VANN is Professor of History and Letters and Director of the Center for the Humanities at Wesleyan University, and Executive Editor of *History and Theory*. His publications include *The Social Development of English Quakerism, 1655–1755* (1969); and "Friends' Sufferings — Collected and Recollected," *Quaker History* (1972). In collaboration with David Eversley, he is now completing a new book, *Friends in Life and Death: The Demography of British and Irish Quakers*.

STEPHEN SAUNDERS WEBB is Professor of History at Syracuse University. Among his publications are "William Blathwayt: Imperial Fixer," *The William and Mary Quarterly* (1968, 1969); " 'Brave Men and Servants to His Royal Highness': The Household of James Stuart in the Evolution of English Imperialism," *Perspectives in American History*, vol. 8 (1974); *The Governors-General: The English Army and the Definition of the Empire, 1569–1681* (1979); and *1676: The End of American Independence* (1984). He is now working on the next segment of his multi-volume study of English military imperialism.

MARIANNE S. WOKECK is Associate Editor of *The Papers of William Penn,* and the principal editor of the third volume in this series, to be published in 1986. She has published "The Flow and Composition of German Immigration to Philadelphia, 1727–1775," in *The Pennsylvania Magazine of History and Biography* (1981); "German Immigration to Colonial Pennsylvania: Prototype of a Transatlantic Mass Migration," in Frank Trommler and Joseph McVeigh, eds., *America and The Germans: An Assessment of a Three-Hundred-Year History,* vol. 1, (1985); and is currently completing a book on German and Irish immigration to Pennsylvania, 1683–1776.

Index

A

Aberdeen, Scotland, 243, 245, 251, 252
Aberhafesp, Wales, 226
Act of Settlement, 120
Act of Uniformity, 18
Acts of Trade and Navigation, 181, 183, 185–186, 261
Affirmation Act, 313, 316–318
Agriculture
  in Cheshire, 219–232
  in England, 39, 87–96, 104–111, 118–119
  in Ireland, 38, 142–151
  in New Jersey, 249–254
  in Pennsylvania, 46–48, 233–234
  in Scotland, 244–247
  in Wales, 219–233
Ahlstrom, Sydney, 282
Ahookasoongh, Chief, 205
Albany, New York, 196, 203, 204, 205
Aldam, Thomas
  False Prophets and Teachers, 16
Allegheny River, Pennsylvania, 204, 209
Allen, William, 340, 381, 384
Allostock, Cheshire, 228, 229
Ambo Point, New Jersey, 252
American Revolution, 259, 261, 263, 269–270, 272–273, 287, 318
American Weekly Mercury, 338
Amsterdam, Netherlands, 43, 46, 148, 243, 260, 375

Anabaptists, 305, 309, 311
Anderson, Michael, 231
Anderton, William, 121
Andros, Edmund, 196
Anglican church. *See* Church of England
Antinomians, 24, 290, 297
Ap Arthur, William, 230
Appleby, Westmorland, 17
Archdale, John, 166
Aristotle, 79
Arlington, earl of. *See* Bennett, Henry
Armstrong, Sir Thomas, 56
Arundel, Sussex, 11
Ashford, Kent, 371
Atkinson, Christopher, 17
Aubrey, John, 92, 93, 166
Audlem, Cheshire, 222
Augustine, Saint, 20
Austin, Joseph, 222

B

Baber, Sir John, 56, 57
Bacon, Francis, 74
Bacon's Rebellion, 187, 196
Bailyn, Bernard, 337
Baltimore, Lord. *See* Calvert
Baltzell, E. Digby, 348–350, 389
Bandonbridge, Ireland, 148
Bangor, Wales, 226, 229
Bank of England, 364
Banks, John, 16

Baptists, 28, 281, 285, 288–290, 296–297
Barbados, 24, 165, 176, 341, 344
Barbican debates, 28–29
Barbour, Hugh, 282
Barclay, Agatha, 368, 373
Barclay, Christiana, 372
Barclay, David I, 251, 365
Barclay, David II, 365–367, 372, 381, 384
Barclay, David III, 367–368, 373, 379
Barclay, Elizabeth, 370
Barclay, James, 366, 367, 370
Barclay, John I, 251, 252
Barclay, John II, 367, 371, 380
Barclay, Mary, 371
Barclay, Robert I, 15, 72, 78, 81, 324, 328, 365
    Apology for the People Called Quakers, 243, 293, 365
    colonizer in New Jersey, 246–254
    and Quakerism, 26–29, 82, 243, 292–294, 307
Barclay, Robert II, 367, 373
Barnes, Rebecca, 125
Barnett, Benjamin, 375
Barton, Lancashire, 120
Bastwick, John, 288
Bauthumley, Jacob, 289, 290
Baxter, Richard, 7, 8, 16, 17, 39, 56, 288, 289
Baynton, Benjamin, 341
Baynton, Peter, 341, 348
Beaufoy, Henry, 382
Beaufoy, Mark, 381, 382
Bedfordshire, England, 158, 164
Belfast, Ireland, 248
Bell, Catherine, 373
Bellers, John
    Some Reasons for an European State, 74
Bellingham, Alan, 124
Bennett, Giles, 147
Bennett, Henry, earl of Arlington, 7, 17
Bennett, Jonathan, 341
Benson, Gervase, 311
Berkshire, England, 158, 346
Bermuda, 185
Besse, Joseph, 159, 166
Bethune, Maximilien de, duc de Sully, 74
Bevan, Francis Augustus, 370
Bevan, John, 231

Bevan, Joseph Gurney, 370, 381
Bevan, Silvanus, 367, 369, 370, 376
Bevan, Timothy, 370, 372
Bevan, Timothy Hugh, 370
Bevan, William, 369
The Bible, Quaker interpretation of, 17–22, 303–318
Bickley, Abraham, 343
Bickley, Elizabeth Gardiner, 343
Biddle, John, 20, 21
Biddle, William, 341
Birmingham, England, 378
Bishopsgate, London, 331
Blackwell, John, 9
Bland, Elias, 374, 375
Bland, John, 374, 375
Bland, John, Jr., 374, 375, 380
Bland, Stamper, 374
Blathwayt, William, 42, 175, 185–189
Blew Hills, New Jersey, 249, 250
Blundell, William, 121, 130, 131
Board of Trade, 75, 76. *See also* Council for Trade
Boate, Arnold and Gerard, 147, 148
    Ireland's Natural History, 143
Bolton, John, 24, 26
Book of Discipline, 325, 327–332
Book of Oaths, 309, 310
Boreman, Mary, 25
Boston, Massachusetts, 339, 349
Boult, John, 229
Boult, Thomas, 229
Bowden, Peter, 222
Bowman, Alice, 129
Bowman, William, 380
Bowness, Westmorland, 128
Boyle, Richard, earl of Cork, 145
Boyle, Roger, earl of Orrery, 150–151
Bradshaw, John, 72
Braithwaite, William C., 304
Bramber, Sussex, 61
Brandywine Creek, Pennsylvania, 206, 207, 208
Branson, William, 346
Brassey, Thomas, 48
Brecknockshire, Wales, 220
Bremer, Francis, 295
Brent, Robert, 56, 58
Brindle, Lancashire, 120
Bringhurst, John, 341, 348
Bristol, England, 10, 11, 24, 46, 48, 92, 147, 158–160, 162, 163, 243, 317, 339, 341, 346, 382

Brown, Anna Maria, 371
Brown, Henton, 371
Brown, James, 371
Browning, Charles, 232
Bryanson, William, 122
Buckeley, Joseph, 230
Buckingham, duke of. *See* Villiers,
    George
Buckinghamshire, England, 11, 46, 94,
    158, 166
Bucks County, Pennsylvania, 46, 201,
    326, 341, 344
Budd, Thomas, 339, 340
Bunyan, John, 28, 289
    Pilgrim's Progress, 60–61
Burlington, New Jersey, 325, 326, 328
Burns, George, 303
Burnyeat, John, 72
Burrough, Edward, 16, 17, 292–293,
    310
    A Description of Mankind, 292
    A Standard Lifted Up, 292
Butler, Jon, 332
Butlers of Ormond, Ireland, 139
Buxton, Thomas Fowell, Jr., 381
Buxton, Thomas Fowell, Sr., 380
Byllynge, Edward, 42, 74

C
Cadwalader, John, 339
Calamy, Edmund, 56
Callowhill, Hannah. *See* Penn, Hannah
Calveley, Lady, 219
Calvert, Caecilius, second lord
    Baltimore, 151, 178, 179, 183,
    187, 188, 190
Calvert, Charles, third lord Baltimore,
    45, 50, 202
Calvinists, 285, 288, 289
Cambridge Platonists, 313
Cambridgeshire, England, 46, 92, 158,
    220,
Canasatego, Chief, 203, 209
Cappoquin, Ireland, 139
Carlisle, England, 17, 125, 126
Carlisle, earl of. *See* Howard, Charles
Carolina, 166–167, 181, 206
Carpenter, Samuel, Jr. 340, 343, 344
Carteret, Sir George, 74
Catholics, 26, 174, 295, 304, 306,
    309–310, 313
    in northern England, 117–132
    and William Penn, 57–60, 62, 64, 65

Cavalier Parliament, 117
Cedar Brook, New Jersey, 249, 250,
    252
Chalmers, George, 341
Chambers, Benjamin, 340
Champion, Richard, 378, 386
Chapman, Jane, 373
Charles I, king of England, 178, 190
Charles II, king of England, 26, 56–57,
    65, 222
    and Catholics, 120–121, 313
    Irish policy, 141, 148
    and Pennsylvania charter, 37, 41, 51,
        173, 175–176, 178, 182–186,
        188–191, 198, 325
    and Quakers, 117, 126, 304
    and William Penn, 5–6, 58–63
Charter of Liberties, Pennsylvania, 330
Charter of Privileges, Pennsylvania,
    72, 330
Charter of Property, Pennsylvania, 330
Cheltenham, Pennsylvania, 344
Chesapeake Bay, 42, 45, 196, 202, 204
Cheshire, England, 46, 48, 94, 158,
    215–235
Chester, England, 219, 231
Chester, Pennsylvania, 166, 203, 231,
    234, 325, 327
Chester County, Pennsylvania, 46,
    207, 218, 344
Chesterfield, New Jersey, 326
Chichester, Pennsylvania, 218
Chigwell, Essex, 87
Child, Josiah, 74
Chippenham, Cambridge, 92
Cholmoldely, Robert Viscount, 228
Church of England, 174, 226, 281, 288,
    290, 293, 296–297, 328
    and Pennsylvania Charter, 184, 189
    persecution of Quakers and
        Catholics, 59–66, 117, 304–309,
        313
    and Scots, 248, 250–252
    and William Penn, 26, 60
Clancarty, earl of. *See* MacCarty,
    Callaghan
Clapham, Jonathan, 17, 19, 23, 29
    A Full Discovery of the Quakers, 18
    A Guide to the True Religion, 18
Clarendon, earl of. *See* Hyde, Edward
Claridge, Richard, 315, 316
Clark, Alice, 99–101, 103, 106, 111,
    113

Clark, Benjamin, 43
Clarke, Elizabeth, 127
Clarkson, Laurence, 289–290
Claymont, Delaware, 326
Claypoole, James, 338, 339, 345, 349
Claypoole, Joseph, 345
Claypoole, Nathaniel, 345
Clayworth, Devon, 220, 225
Clone, Jonas, 148
Clonmel, Ireland, 139
Clymer, Richard, 339, 346
Coale, Josiah, 23, 72
Coates, Samuel, 343, 348
Coates, Thomas, 340, 343
Coleman, Edward, 56, 58
Collinges, John, 20
Collinson, James, 371
Collinson, Peter, 371
Collinson, Thomas, 371
Commons, House of, 173, 176,
        179–181, 186, 313, 317
Compton, Henry, bishop of London,
        184, 189
Conestoga Indians, 206, 210
Conestoga, Pennsylvania, 200, 203,
        204, 206
Congregationalists, 281, 285, 288, 290,
        296
Conoy Indians, 206, 210
Conventicle Acts, 18
Cook, Edward, 349
Cooke, Arthur, 339
Cooper, Anthony Ashley, earl of
        Shaftsbury, 59–62, 173, 183–184,
        198
Coppe, Abiezer, 289, 290
Coppin, Richard, 289
Cork County, Ireland, 11, 38, 148,
        159, 373
Cork, earl of. *See* Boyle, Richard
Cornwall, England, 339, 383
Council for Trade and Plantations,
        174–77, 179–84. *See also* Board
        of Trade
Council of the North, 57
Covenant Chain with Indians, l96, 197,
        206
Coventry, Sir William, 58, 59
Cranage, Thomas, 120
Crawe, Margaret, 122
Crisp, Stephen, 28
Cromwell, Oliver, 18, 23, 73, 89, 141,
        143, 191, 197, 304, 312, 315,
        373, 374

Crook, John, 307, 311, 312
Crook, Westmorland, 127
Crosswicks, New Jersey, 326
Crowley, Ambrose I, 377, 378
Crowley, Ambrose II, 377
Crowley, Ambrose III, 377
Crowley, John, 377
Crowley, Mary, 378
Crowley, Sarah, 378
Cruce, Emeric, 74
Culcheth, Lancashire, 124
Culpeper, lord Thomas, 176
Cumberland, England, 88–90, 94, 118,
        121, 128, 291, 317
Cumberland, Richard, 80

D
Danby, earl of. *See* Osborne, Thomas
Daniel, Lydia, 383
Danson, Thomas, 19–21
        Synopsis, 21
Darby, Abraham, 376
Darby, John, 20
Darby, Pennsylvania, 218
Darien Company, 253
Davenant, Charles
        Discourses on the Publick Revenues, 75
David, Catherine, 229
David, Lewis, 48
David, Morgan, 229
Davies, Margaret Gay, 94
Davies, Richard, 48
Day, John, 340
De Bethune, Maximilien. *See* Bethune
De Labadie, Jean, 23
De La Borde, Jean-Joseph, 376
De la Noy, Peter, 75
De Witt, Jan, 74
Declaration of Breda, 304
Declarations of Indulgence, 26, 59, 64,
        65
Defoe, Daniel, 118, 218, 219, 244, 246
Delaval, John, 339
Delaware Indians, 197–210
Delaware River, 43, 45, 49, 175, 177,
        196, 202–203, 209, 263–264, 330
Delaware Valley, 165, 196, 203, 216,
        234, 254, 259, 324–325, 328, 332
Delaware County, Pennsylvania, 195
Delaware (colony), 165, 175, 177, 204,
        241, 325, 326
Dell, William, 288–290
Demos, John, 216

Denison, John, 230
Deptford, Kent, 4, 72
Derby, Derbyshire, 121
Derbyshire, England, 94
Dicconson, Hugh, 121
Discipline. See *Book of Discipline*
Dixon, Jeremiah, 202
Doglelley, Wales, 226
Dolobran, Wales, 377
Dongan, Thomas, earl of Limerick, 203, 204
Doolittle, Thomas, 19
Dover, Kent, 117
Dowell, William, 341
Downing, Emanuel, 151
Drake, Thomas E., 333
Drummond, James, earl of Perth, 243
Drummond, John, viscount Melfort, 243
Dublin, Ireland, 11, 38, 42, 139, 159, 243, 324, 326
Dundas, James, 253
Dunn, Richard S., 337
Durham, bishop of, 181
Dutton, Mary, 230

E

East India Company, 364
East New Jersey, 74, 174, 241, 243, 249–254, 326, 328, 343
Easton, Pennsylvania, 210
E.B.'s, *A Trip to Wales,* 218
Eccleston, Theodore, 311, 312
Edgemount, Pennsylvania, 218
Edinburgh, Scotland, 245, 246
Eliot, John I, 383, 384, 387
Eliot, John III, 383
Elizabeth I, queen of England, 305
Elizabeth, Princess Palatine, 10
Elizabethtown, New Jersey, 253
Ellis, John, 229
Ellis, Robert, 341
Ellis, Thomas, 233–235, 341
    A Song of Rejoicing, 233, 235
Ellwood, Thomas, 28, 39
Endy, Melvin B., Jr., 28
England
    agriculture and economic conditions in, 87–96, 117–119
    Catholics in, 59–60, 117–132
    Civil War and Interregnum in, 131, 164, 281–284, 287, 290, 296, 304, 330

    northwestern, 117–132, 218–235
    religious toleration in, 59–60, 62–67, 117–132, 294, 312
    Restoration era in, 18, 56, 148–150, 288, 293, 313, 323
    women's role in, 99–113, 117–132
    See also Charles II; Church of England; James II
Esk River, Scotland, 244
Essex, England, 46, 87, 88, 130, 227
Eusebius, 309
Euxton, Lancashire, 121
Evan, Lewis William, 229
Evan, Owen, 230
Exclusion Parliament, 177, 180, 181, 186
Exeter, Devonshire, 24
Eyre, Mary, 121
Eyre, Rowland, 121

F

Falconar, David, 365
Falconar, John, 366
Faldo, John, 25, 27, 28, 29
Familists, 27, 282, 283, 284, 285, 288
Family of Love, 290
Farmer, Mary, 378
Farnworth, Richard, 16, 304
Farrington, William, 121
Fell, George, 102
Fell, Margaret. *See* Fox, Margaret Askew Fell
Fell, Sarah, 102, 107, 129
Fell, Thomas, 101, 102
Fenwick, John, 166, 325
Fiennes, Celia, 118
Fifth Monarchy Men, 305
Finney, Charles, 344
Finney, Joseph, 344
Finney, Samuel, 339, 344
Firmin, Thomas, 21
Fishbourne, William, 339, 343, 348
Fisher, Samuel, 19, 292, 307, 308, 311
Fleming, Daniel, 124–126
Fletcher, Andrew, 76
Fletcher, Robert, 122
Flexney, Thomas, 341
Fludyer, Sir Samuel, 387
Ford, Bridget, 9
Ford, Philip, 9, 37–41, 43, 46, 48, 50–51
Forster, W.E., 381, 389
Fothergill, John, 367

Fothergill, Samuel, 345
Fox, George, 11, 17, 101–102, 125,
    128, 234, 243, 330
  and Quaker Meetings, 314, 323–324
  religious beliefs of, 19, 20, 24–26,
    127, 288, 291–293, 304, 307,
    311–312, 323
  and William Penn, 9, 45, 72–73
Fox, John
  Book of Martyrs, 309
Fox, Margaret Askew Fell, 11,
    101–102, 107, 128
Frampton, William, 339, 343
France, 5, 46, 65, 77, 90, 165, 206, 313
Frankford, Pennsylvania, 344
Frankfort Company, 259
Franklin, Benjamin, 340, 367
Franks, David, 341
Freame, John, 366, 376
Freame, Joseph, 367
Freame, Priscilla, 366, 367
Freame, Sarah, 366
Free Society of Traders, 218
The Friendly Association, 207, 210
Fry, Elizabeth, 373, 386, 389
Fry, Joseph, 386
Furly, Benjamin, 260
Furness, Lancashire, 101–102, 122

G
Galloway, Scotland, 248
Germantown, Pennsylvania, 259, 260,
    261
Germany, 8, 10, 11, 41, 46, 165, 210,
    259–273
Gerrard, James, 230
Gerrard, Mrs. James, 230
Gilpin, John, 16
Gist, Christopher, 208
Glamorganshire, Wales, 231
Glasgow, Scotland, 246
Glassbury, Wales, 226
Glenn, Thomas Allen, 232
Gloucestershire, England, 93
Gnostics, 23
Goodaire, Thomas, 16
Goodwin, John, 288
Gookin, Daniel, 151
Gordon, Patrick, 200, 204
Gordon, Sir Robert, 243
Gosling, Richard, 380
Gough, Richard, 222, 231
  History of Myddle, 231

Gould, Thomas, 366
Green, Joseph, 375
Green, Myles, 120
Greven, Philip, 130, 131
Grevill, Samuel, 28
Griffits, Thomas, 341, 347, 350
Guildford, Surrey, 61
Gurnell, Hannah, 374
Gurnell, Jonathan, 373–376, 389
Gurnell, Mary, 375
Gurnell, Thomas, 374, 375
Gurney, Agatha, 380
Gurney, Bartlett, 372, 373
Gurney, Hannah, 372
Gurney, Henry, 372, 374
Gurney, Hudson, 368, 373, 380
Gurney, John, 372–374, 384
Gurney, Joseph, 370, 372, 373
Gurney, Joseph John, 373, 389
Gurney, Louisa, 375
Gurney, Priscilla, 373
Gurney, Rachel, 373
Gurney, Richard, 368, 372, 373, 380
Gurney, Samuel, 372
Gustavus Adolphus, king of Sweden,
    365

H
The Hague, Netherlands, 64
Halifax, marquis of. *See* Savile, George
Hall, David, 283, 285, 286
Haller, William, 282, 283, 295
Hallywell, Henry, 27, 28, 29
Hamilton, Andrew, 348
Hammond, Henry, 22
Hampshire, England, 164
Hampstead, London, 388
Hanbury, Anna, 380
Hanbury, Capel, 379–381
Hanbury, Capel II, 381
Hanbury, Charles, 375, 379–381
Hanbury, Charlotte, 381
Hanbury, Cornelius, 381
Hanbury, Daniel Bell, 381
Hanbury, Elizabeth, 381
Hanbury, John, 377–381, 384
Hanbury, Mary, 380
Hanbury, Mary Elizabeth, 380
Hanbury, Osgood I, 380, 381, 384, 389
Hanbury, Osgood II, 380, 381
Hanbury, Rachel, 380
Hanbury, Richard, 379
Hanbury, Robert, 381

Hanbury, Sampson, 380, 381
Hare, Augustus, 373
Harford, Charles, 382
Harford, Edward I, 382
Harford, Edward II, 382
Harford, Edward III, 382–384
Harford, Elizabeth, 382, 383
Harford, John, 382
Harford, John Scandrett, 383
Harford, Truman, 382
Harman, Beatrice, 382
Harman, Elizabeth, 383
Harman, Edward, 376
Harman, Henry, 376
Harman, Jeremiah, 374–376
Harman, John, 374, 376, 382–384
Harris, John, 48
Harwich, Essex, 11
Hassell, Samuel, 345
Haughton, Cheshire, 230
Haverford, Pennsylvania, 218
Hease, James, 230
Heathcote, Sir Gilbert, 387
Heaton, Henry, 121
Heckewelder, John, 207
Hedworth, Henry, 21–23, 25
Henretta, James, 216
Henry IV, king of France, 74
Herefordshire, England, 158
Herford, Germany, 23
Hertfordshire, England, 87, 93, 94, 158
Hetherington, Thomas, 122
Heyes, Anne, 124
Heyes, John, 124
Hicks, Thomas, 28, 29
    *Dialogue between a Christian and a
        Quaker,* 28
Higginson, Robert, 228
Higginson, William, 228
High Wycombe, Buckinghamshire, 166
Hill, Christopher, 295
Hill, Richard, 339, 343
Hinshaw, William Wade, 158
Hoare, Jonathan, 374
Hoare, Joseph, 373
Hoare, Edward, 373
Hoare, Samuel, 373, 374, 384, 389
Hoare, Samuel, Jr., 374, 375, 388
Hoare, Samuel III, 375
Hoare, Sarah, 388
Hogwill, Francis, 307
Holland. *See* Netherlands
Holme, Dorothy, 128

Holme, John, 128
Holme, Reginald, 128
Holme, Thomas, 218
Hookes, Ellis, 310
Hope, Adrian, 375
Hope, Archibald, 375
Hope, Henry, 375
Hope, Henry, Jr., 375
Hope, Isaac, 261, 263
Hope, John, 376
Hope, Thomas, 375
Hope, Zachary, 261, 263
Hoskins, W.G., 227
Howard, Charles, earl of Carlisle, 175
Howard, Luke, 384
Howell, David W., 220
Howgill, Francis, 16
Hubberthorne, Richard, 16, 18–19
    Truth and Innocencie, 18
Hudson, William, 340, 343
Hull, John, 150
Hull, Sir William, 145
Hunt, John, 269
Huntingdonshire, England, 158, 164
Hutcheson, George, 339
Hutchinson, Anne, 24, 287
Hutton in the Forest, Cumberland, 126
Hyde, Edward, earl of Clarendon,
    57–59
Hyde, Laurence, earl of Rochester, 58,
    59

I

Illick, Joseph, 163
Imokilly, barony of, 142, 148
Independents, 296, 297
Indians
    Brandywine, 207–208
    Conestoga, 206, 210
    Conoy, 206, 210
    Delaware, 197–210
    Iroquois, 196–206
    "Jersey", 209–210
    Minisink, 209
    Onondaga, 203, 205, 209
    Piscataway, 206
    Seneca, 206
    Shawnee, 206, 209–210
    Susquehannock, 196–197, 200,
        204–205
    Tulpehocken, 208–209
    Tuscarora, 206
Inglis, John, 341

Irchenfield, Herefordshire, 93
Ireland
    agriculture in, 38, 142–151
    English settlers in, 141–149, 210
    landholdings of the Penns in, 5,
        37–39, 41, 72, 139, 141–143,
        150, 241
    Quakers in, 150, 158–162, 168
Iroquois Indians, 196–206

J
Jamaica, 175, 176, 179, 191, 339–341,
    368
James I, king of England, 305
James II, king of England, 11, 55–67,
    71, 118, 173–179, 190–191
James, Philip, 340
Jensen, Reynier, 328
Jesuits, 60, 64, 121
Johnson, Sir William, 210
Johnstone, James, 250
Jones, Francis, 222
Jones, Griffith, 338, 340, 344
Jones, Humphry, 226
Jones, Joseph, of Pennsylvania, 344
Jones, Joseph, of Wales, 226
Jones, Rees, 229
Jones, Rufus, M., 282, 292, 330
Jones, Sir William, 180, 185–187
Jordan, David, 337
Josselin, Ralph, 88

K
Kalm, Pehr, 119
Kearsley, John, 348
Keith, George, 28, 167, 247, 251, 252,
    254, 326, 328
Keith, Sir William, 208
Keithian Schism, 328, 332
Kendal, Westmorland, 102, 126, 128
Kendall, Louisa, 370
Kenebie, Anne, 125
Kent, England, 39, 40, 227
Kerry County, Ireland, 147
Kidderminster, Worcestershire, 16
Kilmorey, Lady, 219
Kincardineshire, Scotland, 243
King, Gregory, 39, 222, 224, 225
Kinsale, Ireland, 148
Kinsey, John, 348, 350
Kirkby, Agnes, 121
Kirkby, Roger, 121
Krefeld, Germany, 259
Kriegsheim, Germany, 259

L
Lamb, John, 309, 316, 317
    Friendly Advice, 309
Lancashire, England, 46, 94, 95, 101,
    102, 117–124, 128, 222, 243, 317
Lancaster, Lancashire, 24, 102
Lancaster, Pennsylvania, 203
Landack, Wales, 230
Lanercost, Lancashire, 122
Larkham, George, 16
Latitudinarians, 26, 313. *See also*
    Church of England
Lawrence, Thomas, 341
Lawrie, Gawen, 249
Lebanon Valley, Pennsylvania, 208
Leeward Islands, 185
Lehnmann, Philip Theodore, 9
Lemon, James, 216
Levinz, Sir Cresswell, 180
Levy, Isaac, 341
Levy, Nathan, 341
Lewis, George, 226
Leyton, Essex, 88
Lichfield, Staffordshire, 224, 225
Limerick, earl of. *See* Dongan, Thomas
Limerick, Pennsylvania, 344
Lincolnshire, England, 46
Lismore, Ireland, 139
Liverpool, Lancashire, 121, 125
Llanvaire, Wales, 230
Lloyd, Ambrose, 378
Lloyd, Charles I, 377, 378
Lloyd, Charles II, 377, 378
Lloyd, Charles III, 378
Lloyd, David, of England, 380
Lloyd, David, of Pennsylvania, 218,
    329
Lloyd, Elizabeth, 378
Lloyd, John, 378, 380
Lloyd, Mary, 378, 380
Lloyd, Nehemiah, 378
Lloyd, Peter, 341, 347
Lloyd, Rachel, 379
Lloyd, Sampson I, 378, 383
Lloyd, Sampson II, 378–380, 384
Lloyd, Sampson III, 378–380
Lloyd, Thomas, 218, 226, 341, 343,
    347, 377
Lloyd, William, 224
Loe, Thomas, 23, 72
Logan, James, 12, 166, 196, 206–210,
    254, 339, 340, 344, 348
Logan, William, 340

London, 4, 9, 11, 40, 46, 87, 92,
    158–163, 261–265, 272, 317,
    323–333
Long, Samuel, 175
Lords, House of, 313, 317
Louis XIV, king of France, 60, 65, 313
Loveday, John, 244
Lowe, Roger, 124
Lower, Margaret, 129
Lower, Mary Fell, 129
Lowther, Sir John, 90
Lytham, Lancashire, 122

M

MacCarty, Callaghan, earl of
    Clancarty, 148
Macclesfield, Cheshire, 219
Macky, John, 246
Macroom, Ireland, 148
Maddocks, William, 19
Magdalen College, Oxford, 66
Manicheans, 23
Manton, Thomas, 57
Marietta, Jack, 166
Markham, William, 200
Marple, Pennsylvania, 218
Mary II, queen of England, 64, 65
Maryland, 45, 167, 178–181, 185, 189,
    195–196, 202–203
Mason, Charles, 202
Massachusetts, 24, 37, 184–186, 217,
    287
Masse, Edward, 230
Masters, Thomas, 340
Masters, Thomas, Jr., 340
Matthew, Saint, 306, 307, 310, 314, 316
Mayne, Benjamin, 341
McCall, George, 341, 348
McNeill, John T., 281
Meesham, Alice, 229
Meifod, Wales, 226
Melfort, Viscount. *See* Drummond,
    John
Mennonites, 260, 304, 311
Merchants
    in London, 363–390
    in Philadelphia, 50, 337–362
Meredith, Reese, 341
Merion, Pennsylvania, 341
Merionethshire, Wales, 219–222,
    226–227, 229, 232
Middlekauf, Robert, 286
Middlesex, England, 158

Mifflin, John and George, 341, 348
Mildred, Daniel, 383
Mildred, Daniel, Jr., 383
Mildred, Thomas, 383
Milford Haven, Wales, 4
Miller, Perry, 282, 283, 286
Minisink Indians, 209
Mississippi River, 206
Mobberley, Cheshire, 232
Mohawk Valley, New York, 202
Molesworth, Robert, 76
Monmouth County, New Jersey, 250
Monmouth's Rebellion, 63
Montaigne, Michel, 76–77
Montgomeryshire, Wales, 219, 225,
    232, 233, 245
Montrose, James Graham, 365
More, Henry, 290, 294
Morgan, Edmund, 296
Morgan, Evan, 348
Morgan, Mathew, 226
Morland, Elizabeth, 129
Morrey, Humphrey, 340, 349
Morrey, Richard, 344
Morris, Anthony, 340
Morris, William, 39
Morse, John, 26
Mortimer, Russell, 161
Mucklow, William, 24–26
    The Spirit of the Hat, 25
Muggleton, Ludowick, 7, 23
Munster province, Ireland, 139–150
Myddle, Shropshire, 220, 222, 231
Myers, Albert Cook, 159

N

Nantes, Edict of, 65
Nantwich, Cheshire, 219
Navigation Acts. *See* Acts of Trade
Nayler, James, 17, 23, 24, 292, 293
Nemacolin (an Indian), 208
Neshaminy, Pennsylvania, 326
Netherlands, 8, 10, 11, 18, 21, 41, 43,
    46, 147–148, 165, 259, 262, 268
New Ark, Delaware, 326
New Castle, Delaware, 92, 325
New England, 42, 46, 167, 196, 217,
    324, 331
New France, 203–204
New Jersey, 42, 163, 166, 178, 186,
    196, 325, 331
    East New Jersey, 74, 174, 241, 243,
    249–254, 326, 328, 343

West New Jersey, 42, 46, 74, 174, 195, 204, 241, 324, 326, 330, 343
New Sweden, 204
New York, 75, 165, 167, 195, 202–206
Newce, Captain, 151
Newgate prison, London, 6, 21
Nicholas, Henry, 290
Nightengale, Gilbert, 120
Nixon, Richard (Pennsylvania colonist), 341
Nixon, Richard (U.S. president), 168
Norfolk, England, 46, 89, 158, 164
Norris, Isaac, 339, 341, 344
Norris, Isaac, Jr., 340
North Carolina, 166
North, Sir Francis, 176–180, 184–189
Northamptonshire, England, 42, 94
Northern Liberties, Philadelphia, 341, 344, 345
Norwich, Norfolk, 158, 368, 370, 372
Nuby, Ann, 127
Nutimus, Chief, 201, 202, 209
Nuttall, Geoffrey, 282, 283, 287

O
Oates, Titus, 60, 124
Oaths, Quaker opposition to, 65, 125, 303–318
Occasional Conformity Acts, 314
Ohio, 204, 206, 208–209
Onondaga Indians, 203, 205, 209
Ormond, Ireland, 139
Ormskirk, Lancashire, 120, 124–125
Orrery, earl of. *See* Boyle, Roger
Osborne, Thomas, earl of Danby, 58–61, 173
Osgood, Anna, 379
Osgood, John, 379
Osgood, Obadiah, 379
Overton, Lancashire, 230
Owen, Griffith, 218
Owen, John, 289
Owen, Leonard, 225, 232
Oxford Parliament, 63, 184, 186
Oxford University, 5, 11, 59, 66, 178
Oxford, Oxfordshire, 89
Oxfordshire, England, 158, 164

P
The Papers of William Penn, 189
Parliament, 176, 311–317; *See also* Commons, House of *and* Lords, House of

Pascal, Blaise, 76–80
Pensees, 76
Paschall, Thomas, 342
Paul, Saint, 20, 306, 308, 310–315
Paul, Timothy, 370
Pemberton, Israel, 341, 350
Pemberton, James, 269
Pemberton, John, 378
Penington, Isaac, 16, 21–24, 292, 293, 307
Penn, Gulielma, 4, 10–11, 21, 39–40, 52, 71
Penn, Hannah, 4, 10–11
Penn, John, 208
Penn, Springett, 71
Penn, Thomas, 3, 4, 209, 210
Penn, William
  books and pamphlets by, 41
    The Advice of William Penn to his Children, 77, 79
    A Brief Account, 43
    A Brief and Plain Scheme, 75, 81
    The Christian Quaker, 22, 28
    England's Great Interest, 61
    An Essay towards the Peace of Europe, 73, 81
    Frame of Government, 80
    Good Advice to the Church of England, 64
    The Guide Mistaken, 18
    Innocency with Her open Face, 20, 21
    The Invalidity of John Faldo's Vindication, 27
    Judas and the Jews, 27
    The New Witnesses Proved Old Heretics, 23
    No Cross No Crown, 15, 18, 21–22, 29
    One Project for the Good of England, 62
    Persuasive to Moderation, 64
    A Prefatory Observation, 24
    Quakerism a New Nick-name, 27
    The Rise and Progress of the People Called Quakers, 72, 73
    Sandy Foundation Shaken, 19–20, 22
    A Seasonable Caveat, 59
    Serious Apology, 22, 28–29
    Some Account of Pennsylvania, 43
    Some Fruits of Solitude, 29, 76–77, 79–81
    Some Proposals for a Second Settlement, 81

*The Spirit of Alexander the
    Coppersmith,* 26
Spirit of Truth Vindicated, 22, 28
Truth Exalted, 18
Urim and Thummim, 28
Wisdom Justified of Her Children, 27
and Charles II, 5–6, 56–59, 173–191,
    325
and the English government, 41,
    55–59, 61–67, 173–191
family of, 3–4, 6–7, 10, 52, 71
financial problems of, 9, 37–41,
    48–51, 67
and the Germans, 10–11, 259–260
and the Indians, 49, 81, 195–210
and the Irish, 139–143, 150–151,
    339–340
and James II, 11, 55–67, 174–178,
    185–186, 190
landholder
    in England, 12, 37–50
    in Ireland, 37–39, 41, 72,139,
        142–143, 150, 241
    in Pennsylvania, 12, 37, 41–52,
        157–159, 162, 241, 243, 337,344
moralist, 5, 7, 8, 22, 27, 60–65, 73,
    76–79, 307, 309, 312
papers of, 3, 7, 9, 10
and the Pennsylvania charter, 8, 11,
    41, 43, 63, 74, 173–191, 230, 325
and the Pennsylvania colonists, 9, 37,
    50, 71, 74–76, 81, 157, 173–191,
    234, 243, 337–338
promoter of Pennsylvania, 37,
    42–48, 74, 77, 162, 241, 247,
    259–260, 337–338, 344–345
and Quakerism, 5–6, 12, 15–29, 93,
    37, 41, 55, 58, 63, 67, 71–72,
    81–82, 150, 157, 241–243, 259,
    309–313, 316, 325, 337
and the Scots, 47, 241, 247
theological writer, 15–29, 41, 59, 76,
    79–81, 293, 307, 312
trials and imprisonment of, 6–7, 15,
    20, 51
and the Welsh, 29, 241, 344–345
youth of, 3–5, 7, 87–88
Penn, William, Sr.
    finances of, 41, 51
    property in Ireland, 5, 38, 141–143,
        150
    relations with son, 4, 6–7, 15, 55
    service as admiral, 4, 41, 174,
        190–191

Penn-Mead trial, 6, 8, 21, 29, 305
Pennsbury, Pennsylvania, 12, 50
Pennsylvania
    Assembly in, 196, 210
    charter of, 8, 11, 37, 41–43, 51, 63,
        74, 173–191, 198, 230, 325, 330
    emigration to, 37, 41, 51, 157–168,
        215, 217–219, 227, 232–235, 241,
        243, 259–273, 337–338, 344, 347,
        377
    First Purchasers in, 37–38, 43–48, 51,
        159, 162, 195, 247, 344
    maps of, 43–45, 47, 218
    promotional literature, 37–38, 43–45,
        74, 162
    settlement of, 37, 49–51, 165–167,
        233–234, 243, 259–261, 337–340
Pennsylvania Gazette, 338
Pennyman, John, 24, 25
Pennyman, Mary, 24, 25
Pepys, Samuel, 118
Perkins, John, 367, 370
Perrot, John, 24, 25, 27
Perth Amboy, New Jersey, 252–253
Perth, earl of. *See* Drummond, James
Peter the Great, czar of Russia, 72
Petre, Edward, 56, 58, 64, 67
Pettit, Norman, 295
Petty, Sir William, 58, 143, 149, 166
Philadelphia, Pennsylvania, 45, 67,
    323–333, 337–353
Philadelphia County, Pennsylvania, 46
Phillip, Phillip John, 230
Phoenixville, Pennsylvania, 196
Pidgeon, Joseph, 339
Piscataway Indians, 206
Plantations committee. *See* Council for
    Trade
Plato, 79
Plumstead, Clement, 343, 348
Popish Plot, 59–61, 119, 173, 175, 186
Portsmouth, New Hampshire, 349
Potomac Valley, 204, 205
Powell, Samuel, 342
Powell, Samuel, Jr., 342
Powell, Thomas, 382
Pownal Fee, Cheshire, 232
Presbyterians, 57, 249–252, 285, 288,
    290, 296–297
Preston, Lancashire, 121, 230
Preston, Samuel, 343
Privy Council, 20, 182, 185, 187–189,
    249

Proctor, John, 120
Puritanism, 16, 37, 88, 126, 281–297

Q

The Quaker Ballad, 28
Quaker Meetings
    in Bristol, England, 161
    in Burlington, New Jersey, 325
    in Chester, Pennsylvania, 166, 327
    in Dublin, Ireland, 326
    in Kendal, Westmorland, 128
    in London, England, 25, 311, 314,
        316, 323–333, 385
    Meeting for Sufferings, 310, 311,
        313–317
    in Philadelphia, Pennsylvania, 159,
        166, 207, 323–333
    Women's Meetings, 25, 102, 326, 332
Quakers
    and the Bible, 303–318
    in Cheshire, 217–232
    emigration to Pennsylvania,
        157–168, 215, 217, 227, 232–234
    family life of, 127–131, 158, 162,
        215–219, 231–235
    in Ireland, 150, 158–162
    merchants in London, 363–390
    merchants in Philadelphia, 50,
        337–362
    in New Jersey, 46
    opposition to oaths, 65, 125, 303–318
    organizational structural of, 25, 72,
        323–333
    persecution of, 18–29, 42, 55, 60, 63,
        82, 117–118, 122, 125–126, 150
    and Puritanism, 16, 281–297
    and rival sects, 16–29, 37
    in Scotland, 46
    social attitudes of, 5–6, 25, 125–130
    and spiritualism, 16, 127, 281–297
    in Wales, 217–233
Quarles, John, 148
Quarry, Robert, 253
Quebec Act, 210

R

Radnor, Pennsylvania, 218
Radnorshire, Wales, 219–222, 227, 232
Raistrick, Arthur, 376
Ranger, Terence, 149
Ranters, 24, 128, 281–285, 288–290
Raritan River, New Jersey, 250
Rawle, Francis, 340, 349

Reading, Pennsylvania, 208
Reay, Barry, 232
Redford, William, 252
Redman, John, 342
Redman, Joseph, 342
Redman, Thomas, 342
Reeve, John, 23
Reid, John, 249
    The Scots Gardener, 252
Revolution of 1688, 66, 313
Reynell, John, 341, 347, 348
Rhine district of Germany, 43,
        259–260, 273
Rhode Island, 189, 304
Rich, Robert, 24
Richardson, Elizabeth, 343
Richardson, Joseph, 344
Richardson, Joshua, 231
Richardson, Richard, 309, 311
Richardson, Samuel, 340, 349
Rickmansworth, Hertfordshire, 39–40
Roberts, John, 383
Robinson, Anne, 125
Roche, George, 348
Rochefoucauld, duc Francois de la,
        77–79
    Moral Reflections and Maxims, 76
Roman Catholics. *See* Catholics
Romford, Essex, 87
Ross, George, 216, 234
Rotterdam, Netherlands, 43, 260–270,
        272, 375
Roxburgh, Scotland, 252
Rudyard, Thomas, 8, 43
Rules of Discipline. See Book of Discipline
Rutman, Darrett, 295

S

Sabine, George, 285˙
St. Albans, Hertfordshire, 307
St. Mary Redcliffe, Bristol, 7
St. Pierre, Charles, 74
Salem, New Jersey, 325
Saltmarsh, John, 289, 290
Sandbach, Cheshire, 229
Sassoonan, Chief, 208
Saunders, Charles, 339
Savile, George, marquis of Halifax
    Maxims, 76
Scandrett, Sarah, 383
Scarborough Castle, Yorkshire, 323
Schackamaxon, Pennsylvania, 198
Schlatter, Richard, 283

Schuylkill River, Pennsylvania, 196,
    204, 208, 326
Scollitchy, Chief, 205
Scotland, 43, 46, 75–76, 93–94, 118,
    150, 173, 181, 187, 241–254,
    287, 317
Scull, Ireland, 145
Secetarius, Chief, 208
Seekers, 282–285, 288, 290
Seller, John, 43, 45
Seneca Indians, 206
Seven Years War, 207, 261, 266
Severn river, England, 147
Shaftesbury, earl of. *See* Cooper,
    Anthony Ashley
Shakerlcy, Sir Geoffrey, 219
Shamokin, Pennsylvania, 209
Sharpless, Isaac, 163
Shawnee Indians, 206, 209–210
Sheldon, Gilbert, 57
Shenandoah Valley, Virginia, 206
Shippen, Edward I, 339, 343
Shippen, Edward II, 340
Shoemaker, Benjamin, 263, 342
Shoemaker, Isaac, 342
Shoemaker, Samuel, 263
Shrewsbury, New Jersey, 326
Shropshire, England, 220, 222, 231
Sidney, Algernon, 11, 61
Simcock, John, 48, 218
Simpson, Alan, 282, 287
Skelwith Bridge, Lancashire, 128
Skidmore, Joseph, 316
Smith, Nathaniel, 24–25
Smith, William, 307
Society for the Propagation of the
    Gospel, 328
Society of Friends. *See* Quakers
Socinians, 19–23
Socrates, 28
Solemn League and Covenant, 309
Somerset, England, 92
Sommelsdijk, lord of, 10
Sonmans, Arent, 247, 252
South Sea Company, 364
Southport, Lancashire, 121
Southwark, Surrey, 160
Sowle, Jane, 77
Spencer, Robert, earl of Sunderland,
    58–59, 173–174
Spiritualists, 283–285, 290–294,
    296–297
Spitalfields, London, 19–20

Springall, Hannah, 370
Springett, Gulielma. *See* Penn,
    Gulielma
Springett, Sir William, 10, 71
Sprogel, Christian, 345
Sprogel, John, 345
Spufford, Margaret, 92, 220
Stafford, Lord, 186
Staffordshire, England, 121, 126, 129,
    158
Stamper, John, 341, 348
Stansbury, Nathan, 339
Stedman, Alexander, 263
Stedman, Charles, 263
Stedman, John, 261, 263
Steel, James, 339
Stillingfleet, Edward, 20
Stoke Newington, London, 388
Stoke-on-Trent, Staffordshire, 225
Stokes, Jane, 24
Story, Thomas, 26–27
Stourbridge, Worcestershire, 377
Stout, William, 222
Strettel, Robert, 341, 347, 350
Suffolk, England, 46
Sully. *See* Bethune, Maximilien de
Sunderland. *See* Spencer, Robert
Surrey, England, 158
Susquehanna River, Pennsylvania, 43,
    45, 196, 202–210
Susquehanna Valley, 74, 196, 202,
    204–206
Susquehannock Indians, 196–197, 200,
    204–205
Sussex, England, 12, 27, 39–40, 46,
    158, 218, 227, 339
Swansea, Wales, 369, 376
Swarthmoor, Lancashire, 101–102, 107
Switzerland, 210

T
Tamenend, Chief, 201, 208
Tammany. *See* Tamenend
Taponemus, New Jersey, 250–252
Taylor, Abraham, 341
Taylor, Christopher, 339, 344
Taylor, John, 378, 380
Taylor, John, Jr., 378
Taylor family, 210
Teague, Pentecost, 332, 339
Temple, Sir William, 74, 76
Tennent, William, 254
Terling, Essex, 220, 223

Tertullian, 23
Test Act, 57, 64, 185
Thirty Years War, 365
Thomas, George, 209
Thomas, John, 229
Thornton, John, 43, 45
Thrale, Henry, 367
Tinicum Island, Pennsylvania, 344
Tohickon Creek, Pennsylvania, 201, 203, 209
Toleration Act of 1689, 66, 293, 294, 312
Tolles, Frederick, B., 82, 163, 282, 291, 333
Toppin, Isabel, 126
Tories, 63–64
Tower of London, 7, 15
Towyn, Wales, 228
Tregany, Henry, 344
Trent, Council of, 129
Tritton, John, 371
Tritton, John Henton, 371
Tritton, George, 371
Tritton, Thomas, 371
Truman brewery, 381
Tully, Alan, 349
Tulpehocken Indians, 208–209
Turnbull, William, 89
Turner, Francis, 63
Turner, Henry, 148
Turner, Robert, 338, 339, 343
Tuscarora Indians, 206

U
Ulster, Ireland, 141, 150, 243
Ulverston, Lancashire, 102
Underhill, Thomas
  Hell Broke Loose, 16
Unitarians, 19–21, 288
Upland. *See* Chester, Pennsylvania

V
Vann, Richard T., 46
Vaughan, William, 229
Verney family, 94
Vickris, Richard, 48
Villiers, George, duke of Buckingham, 8, 17, 59
Vincent, Thomas, 19–21, 23
  The Foundation of God, 20
Virginia, 75, 148, 167, 175–176, 185, 187, 196
Voltaire, 198

Letters Concerning the English Nation, 216
Von Hoorn, Countess Anna Maria, 10
Von Hugel, Friedrich, 284
Von Schurman, Anna Maria, 10

W
Wales, 43, 46, 48, 76, 94, 158, 163, 215–235, 241, 243
Walking Purchase, 209
Waller, Sir Hardress, 146
Wallis, Peter, 38, 150
Walpole, Robert, 317, 318
Walzer, Michael, 295
Wanstead, Essex, 87
Wandsworth, Surrey, 371
Warder, Jeremiah, 341
Warder, John, 341
Warminghurst, Sussex, 11–12, 39–40, 51
Warwickshire, England, 94
Waterford, Ireland, 11
Watkins, Morgan, 307, 311
Watson, John, 125
Waugh, Dorothy, 125
Webster, John, 289
Welsh, in Pennsylvania, 201, 215–218, 232–235, 326
  See also Wales
Werden, Lancashire, 121
Werden, Sir John, 174, 177, 185
Wereneter, Cheshire, 230
West Indies, 5, 42, 148, 266
West New Jersey, 42, 46, 74, 174, 195, 204, 241, 324, 326, 330, 343
West, Benjamin, 198
Westminster, London, 76, 88, 94, 287, 312
Westmorland, England, 88, 94, 102, 118, 124–125, 129, 158, 291, 317, 374
Wharton, Joseph, 340
Wharton, Thomas, 340, 345
Whigs, 11, 57, 59–63, 66, 175, 313
Whisham, Joseph, 229
Whisham, Marie, 229
White, John, 341
Whitehead, George, 17–21, 23, 28, 292–293, 307, 313
Whitelegge, James, 230
Whitelocke, Sir Bulstrode
  Memorials, 78
Whittier, John Greenleaf, 365

Wigan, Lancashire, 121
Wilkinson, Gabriel, 340, 345
Wilkinson, John, 26, 27
Wilkinson-Story separation, 25, 126
William III, king of England, 64–65, 313
Williams, Roger, 287, 296
Willing, Charles, 341, 348
Willson, Izabell, 127
Wilmer, Grizell, 374
Wilson, John, 122, 230
Wiltshire, England, 46, 48, 92, 218
Windermere, Westmorland, 126
Winstanley, Gerrard, 285, 288, 290
Wistar, Caspar, 341, 346, 348
Women
  and Catholicism, 117–132
  employment of, 99–115
  family life of, 119–123, 127–131, 223–235
  and Quakerism, 101–102, 117–132
  religious life of, 101–102, 119, 125–128
Woolman, John, 168
Worcester, Worcestershire, 117
Worcestershire, England, 158
Wramplingham, Norfolk, 17
Wrightington, Lancashire, 121
Wrightstown, Pennsylvania, 201
Wynne, Thomas, 48

Y
York, duke of. *See* James II
Yorkshire, England, 42, 48, 91, 95, 158, 163, 291, 317
Youghal, Ireland, 148

Z
Ziff, Larzer, 295

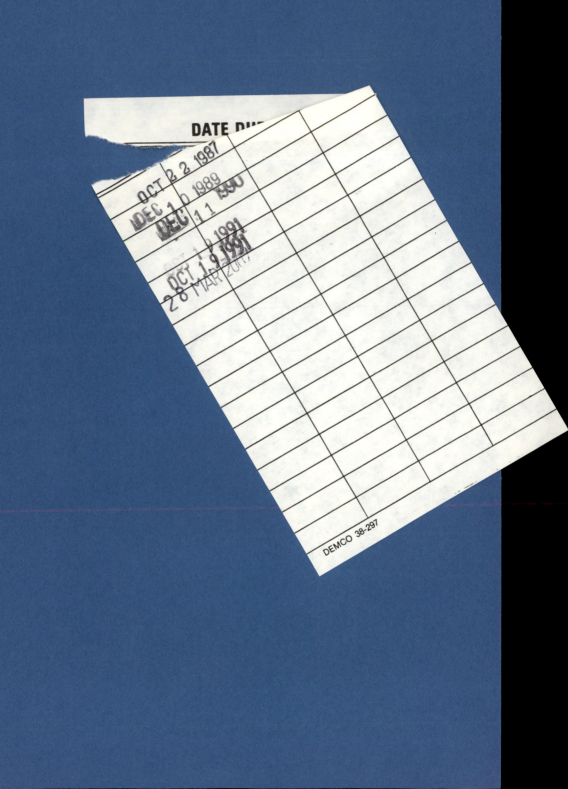